INTERNATIONAL RESOURCES
AND NATIONAL POLICY

INTERNATIONAL RESOURCES
AND NATIONAL POLICY

Olin T. Mouzon

UNIVERSITY OF NORTH CAROLINA

HARPER & BROTHERS, PUBLISHERS, NEW YORK

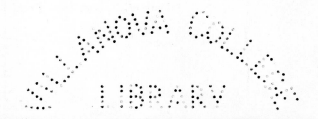

OTM/kbm

Contents

v

Preface

The emphasis of this book is stated in the title *International Resources and National Policy*. The overall plan of the units, parts, chapters, and sections is to present a minimum of facts bearing on problems requiring national policy decisions. Policy is then discussed, followed by conclusions and recommendations.

Unit One gives the general objectives and policy of the United States and the nature of resources. Policy is brought up to 1953, to the beginning of the first Eisenhower administration.

Unit Two contains a detailed analysis of the strength and production potentials of the United States under the three-fold analysis of natural resources, capital resources, and human resources. The core of Unit Two and of the book is Parts I, II, and III on natural resources—spatial, agricultural, and energy and material.

Unit Three considers the question: How can the elements of strength and production potential of the United States best be employed strategically to achieve security? The final chapter of this Unit reviews the additional commitments and foreign policies during the four-year period 1953–56 of the first Eisenhower administration, and suggests improvements in these policies to strengthen our strategy of security.

This book is the result of materials and methods developed in the study of international resources. It is written to be used as a text for students and as a guide to policy making for all those concerned with resource problems.

The writer has used a dynamic functional analysis of resources for over twenty years, but experimental instructional techniques employed during the post-World War II years have indicated that students' interest is at a peak when the students are confronted with a current national problem that requires a solution. Visual presentation of the facts bearing on the problem has further stimulated this interest. The method of problem study and visual presentation of facts employed in this book will prove helpful when *International Resources and National Policy* is used as a text. Problems studied herein should be supplemented by assigning to each student current applications of these, or newer, problems to be threshed out in classroom presentation where students meet for cabinet-level discussions and decision making. The subject matter covered is sufficiently flexible to be adapted to the requirements of several different areas of specialization and for two- and one-semester courses. For example, a one-semester course might draw together Units One and Three with a brief study of objectives, policy, and the strategy of security to be followed by a thorough analysis of natural resource problems based on Parts I, II, and III of Unit Two.

The second major use of this book has achieved importance from the fact that during the last decade an endless series of resource problems has required national policy decisions. Industry and government officials have been acutely aware of most of these problems, which have grown out of the tremendous increase in production and resultant pressure on resources during and after World War II. A sustained series of government, industry, and special committee reports has been made presenting the problems, developing the facts, drawing conclusions, and recommending action. *International Resources and National Policy* reviews many of these problems and policy decisions, with special emphasis during the first Eisenhower administration, and thus should be of interest and serve as a guide to policy making for all those concerned with resource problems.

A third, and most important, purpose of this book is to call attention to the need for and to recommend a strategy of security for the United States based on production potential, international resource interdependence, and the objectives and policies of other nations.

This book was written over a period of four years. Wherever possible the terminal date for data and policy decision is January 1, 1957, or later. Many sources, both continuations and background material, have been used. These are listed in the Bibliography in order, first, to indicate the author's indebtedness and, second, to enable students of resource problems to keep abreast in the dynamic area of resource appraisal.

The writer wishes to express his sincere appreciation to the members of the staff of Harper & Brothers who assisted in the preparation and publication of this book.

O. T. M.

August, 1958

Unit One

Introduction

CHAPTER 1

Objectives, Policy, and Resources

OBJECTIVES AND POLICIES

We the people of the United States set forth as our objectives to form a more perfect Union, establish justice, insure domestic tranquillity, provide for the common defense, promote the general welfare, and secure the blessings of liberty to ourselves and our posterity. These objectives are our cherished aims and ends of action which we need to understand and keep constantly before us.

In order to achieve these objectives it is necessary that courses of action be adopted and followed by the government of the United States, and in our dynamic world these courses of action must remain flexible in order to meet new situations at home and abroad. These courses of action adopted and followed by government are policy. Our policy should be definite, but the dictionary use of the word "settled" in describing policy should be avoided because it has given rise to and reflects standard acceptance of policy as a static concept. In this sense, then, policy is understood to be a course of action adopted and followed by government to attain aims and ends of action—objectives—which as contrasted with policy should be both settled and definite.

As we analyze our cherished settled and definite objectives, two fundamental aims and ends of action toward which our policy must be directed stand out—freedom and security.

1. Freedom

Freedom for which our forefathers struggled, and which sets our economic system apart from alien philosophies, has often been forgotten as our principal accomplishment and enduring goal. This first objective was brought into focus by President Roosevelt in his annual message to Congress on January 6, 1941, when he stated:

In the future days, which we seek to make secure, we look forward to a world founded upon four essential human freedoms.

The first is freedom of speech and expression—everywhere in the world.

The second is freedom of every person to worship God in his own way—everywhere in the world.

The third is freedom from want . . . —everywhere in the world.

The fourth is freedom from fear . . . —anywhere in the world.

The recurring last three words of the Four Freedoms, *in the world,* set forth an international objective which was then, as even now, only a hope and a dream. Support to this objective in the form of a policy was forthcoming on August 14, 1941, when President Roosevelt and Prime Minister Churchill met together and in joint declaration in the Atlantic Charter made known certain common principles of the national policies of their respective countries on which they based their hopes for a better future for the world. These common principles included fullest collaboration among all nations with the object of securing economic advancement, and the hope of establishing a peace which would afford all nations the means of dwelling in safety within their own boundaries, and which would afford the assurance that all the men in all the lands might live *in freedom* from fear and want.

Hope ran high on June 26, 1945, when the peoples of the United Nations determined through the United Nations Organization to employ international machinery for the promotion of the economic and social advancement of all peoples and to unite our *strength* to maintain international peace and *security* in order to promote social progress and better standards of life in *larger freedom.*

Thus *freedom* rings as the major objective of the people of the United States, and we have taken the lead to advocate it as an international policy which we hope might be adopted as an objective and achieved by all men in all lands.

2. Security

Security stands out as a major objective of the United States. In the Preamble to the Constitution this goal is seen in the insurance of domestic tranquillity, the provision of common defense, and the promotion of the general welfare. In present-day terms these objectives may be stated as a twofold function of security: (1) the maintenance of peace through police and military readiness and action against internal and external forces; and (2) the promotion of economic progress, by which is meant rising planes of living that individuals would like to enjoy.

There has been and certainly always should be a consideration of the threats to peace and what constitutes an adequate defense against these threats. However, it has generally been accepted that this field of security is a function of government with policies to be made in the light of changing conditions.

In the area of economic and social security an economist might restate the objectives as the improvement in, and stabilization of, our plane of living. This is the welfare portion of security, with progress and stability as goals. Contrary to our acceptance of government as a unifying force of strength necessary to achieve peace, the people of the United States have desired a minimum of government control and a maximum of freedom in economic and social action. The why of this is the knowledge that a free economy underlies individual freedom and that under a free economy great gains of economic progress have been and can be made. However, the fact remains that the insecurity of personal income due to cyclical fluctuations and changing purchasing power has been character-istic of our economy.

Thus our basic economic problem has been stated as "How can we raise our plane of living by making economic progress and at the same time attain a reasonable degree of security?" Unfortunately the attainment of individual security has, in many instances, required the sacrifice of indi-vidual freedom. Therefore the problem needs to be amplified by the in-clusion of the words "a maximum amount of individual freedom within the limits of a free economy in a political democracy."

Further, the presentation of the problem in its original form is usually preceded by a statement that, since war and defense are separate prob-lems of security and noneconomic in character, they will not be included within the scope of the study. However, this is a means of oversimplifi-cation because external threats to our security have required that a larger amount of our national effort be engaged in production for defense. As typically stated above, the basic economic problem is broad enough to include threats to peace and needs no modification if it is understood that security covers both threats to peace and economic security. Never-theless, the solution to the problem becomes much more difficult because these external threats limit increases and may lead to decreases in our plane of living.

This interdependence of economic progress, individual and national security, and freedom can be illustrated by a few additional comments which are worthy of elaboration. The people of the United States have been quick to realize that when the security of the nation was threatened, individual freedom was threatened and thus have accepted individual and collective responsibility for national security. Whereas this is a continuing trend, it is observable that there is less acceptance of the idea that individual economic security is a responsibility of the individual. More and more areas of individual economic security are being taken over by, and considered to be functions of, government. Thus the area of our free economy is being narrowed and this is being accompanied by the loss of individual freedom. The rate of attrition is greatly accelerated by inroads on freedom necessitated by requirements for national security.

Just as our objective of freedom has gained international acceptance by many nations, a similar study beginning with the Atlantic Charter will reveal that national and individual economic security have been endorsed as international objectives. These were clearly stated in the preamble of the United Nations charter, under which the signatory nations pledged "to unite our strength to maintain international peace and security" and "to employ international machinery for the promotion of the economic and social advancement of all peoples." The real genius of the United Nations lay in the possibilities of international economic and social action through the organization and its related agencies; and substantial gains in economic security have already been achieved through collective action on the part of these agencies. Even though it was not anticipated that the military Security Council would have to solve international disputes between major powers by military action, the United Nations have acted collectively in defense of their security to thwart Soviet Russia and her satellites' aggression. As a result of these international actions on the part of the United Nations, individual, national, and international security has been strengthened.

The present policy of the United States is to strengthen our own security by coöperating with other free nations to protect each one against aggression. This is the policy of collective security. The responsibilities of the United States under the policy of collective international security are so great that serious doubts have been expressed as to the extension of our commitments. The fear is that freedom is being lost in defense of freedom. The other extreme is the loss of freedom through inadequate security measures.

It becomes clearer day by day that economic and military security cannot be separated under a program of collective security. Thus we can restate our basic problem. How can we raise our plane of living by making economic progress and at the same time attain a maximum degree of security and a maximum amount of individual and national freedom in a political democracy?

3. Strength

In order to further the United States' objective of freedom and security, we have adopted the policy that the world's only hope of peace lies in the *strength* of the free world. Over a decade ago Mr. Wendell Willkie made great contributions to the understanding of the necessity of national strength when he went about the nation declaring: "Only the productive can be strong and only the strong can be free." The whole background of the 1930's, with its deëmphasis on production under the notion that we were a mature economy faced only with problems of distribution, was a period characterized by economic and social confusion and weakness and a lack of knowledge and understanding of, and even a desire to learn about, what was going on in the rest of the world. During this same time strong, evil men were taking advantage of weak situations in Germany, Japan, and Italy to build up situations of strength. As peaceful people we imputed this same peace objective to others, or were lulled through ignorance or other reasons into a false sense of security. Not until the tragedy of Pearl Harbor, twenty-seven months after the outbreak of war in Europe, did we become fully aware of the threat to our security.

Free men rallied in defense of freedom to build up our economic and military strength into the world's greatest productive and military striking power, which led to the defeat of our enemies. After victory in Europe and Japan, in spite of the warning of many people and recommended policies to the contrary, in twelve short months our military force was permitted to fade away. The flesh of a strong body was gone and a skeleton remained. From a maximum position of strength at Potsdam the clarion sound of trumpets began to be replaced by a lullaby of false security in Europe.

We waged a war and once again almost completely accepted the dangerous notion that there is something final about a military decision— that it is the happy ending of something, rather than the beginning. At best a military decision can only establish geographical boundaries and the possibility of changing political control, and thus set the stage for the creation of new policies under worse economic and social conditions than existed prior to the war.

In Europe we were so determined to deprive Germany of the capacity

for again waging aggressive war that our initial policy was to agricultural-
ize Germany with little apparent understanding of the interdependence
of Germany, and the Ruhr in particular, with the rest of western Europe.
Thus we were creating a situation of weakness. At the same time the
United States was confused with respect to Russian intentions. We did
not distinguish between policy and objectives. The primary objective
of Soviet Russia has been the communization of the world, the overthrow of democratic government with the resultant enslavement of all
men everywhere—the very antithesis of the United States' primary objective of freedom.

Barbara Ward, in establishing the fact of Soviet hostility, indicates the
degree of our confusion in pointing out that such men as Wendell Willkie
and President Roosevelt felt for a time that it might be easier to rebuild
the world in alliance with the "progressive" Soviet Union than with the
tradition-bound backward-looking Britain of Mr. Winston Churchill.

A few backward looks are often very helpful to keep from flying
blindly into the future. Just as during World War II we specialized in
military objectives, ignoring in large measure Mr. Churchill's advice on
political objectives, at the end of the war with Germany and Japan we
seemed to be unaware that the destruction of the war caused a "vacuum
of power" in Europe and Asia. Indeed, as we have seen, we proposed to
weaken Europe further; and, in addition, we withdrew our supporting
strength in Europe and Asia.

Into these areas of weakness aggressive, not "progressive," Soviet
Russia poured her strength in accordance with her long-standing objectives. We slowly began to realize that the Soviet's limited coöperation
was an instrument of policy to further her objectives. Mr. Churchill,
while reminding us that in the early days of the Soviet-Western alliance
in 1941 the Soviet Union was a hostile and distrustful ally, nevertheless
admits that even he was hopefully optimistic for better things in the
future. However, he has stated that the gulf which was opening between
the Asiatic Communist Russia and the Western democracies was already
brutally obvious to the war cabinet before Hitler was destroyed. His
warnings at Fulton, Missouri, in April, 1946, and suggestions of a power
alliance were received by many as the advice of an elder statesman who
was out of touch with the times. Once again, the United States was re-
fusing to look at the facts and to change her policy to meet current conditions.

Beginning in 1945 Poland, Bulgaria, Rumania, Hungary, Albania, and
Czechoslovakia disappeared behind the Iron Curtain. Russian actions in

daily contacts with United States officials and at United Nations tables, which were contributing to our slow realization of Soviet objectives, were dramatized to the American public with the Berlin blockade of 1948. The fall of China to the Communists in Asia with its tremendous implications was barely noticed at first by the people of the United States because of the national election in 1948. However, the fact of Soviet hostility was firmly established with the sudden attack on the Republic of Korea on June 25, 1950, when the tactics of Communist imperialism shifted from subversion and pressure to open aggression.

In March, 1947, with announcement of the Truman Doctrine, the United States adopted a new policy for the containment of Soviet Russia. This was followed by the European Recovery Program, which was introduced by Secretary of State George Marshall on June 5, 1947. This policy was to join with our allies in building *the strength* of the free world as a bulwark against Soviet aggression.

In October, 1948, Mr. Churchill only wondered that it took the British and American people, in spite of lessons of the past, so long to realize the fearful challenge to their life and freedom which had opened upon them from the East. Speaking at a Conservative Party Convention on the topic "Peace Rests upon Strength," Mr. Churchill stated, "It is my belief—and I say it with deep sorrow—that at the present time the only sure foundation of peace and prevention of actual war rests upon *strength*." Similarly Barbara Ward develops her *Policy for the West* thesis that: "The only hope lies in creating in the free world conditions of such *strength* and *stability* that even the Soviet leaders cannot misunderstand or underestimate them."

Secretary of State Dean Acheson declared that the United States policy was to build up *positions of strength*. Thus, our motto for Armed Forces Day, May 17, 1952, was *Unity, Strength, Freedom*. We clearly state in "Our Foreign Policy 1952" that: *"The policy of the United States is to strengthen our own security by coöperating with other free nations to protect each one against aggression."*

Thus a fundamental question must be asked and answered: If strength is a requisite of *security* and *freedom*, what is the basis of *strength?*

The Department of Social Sciences of the United States Military Academy believes that the attainment of all our national objectives involves the artful and scientific employment of all our *national resources*. These resources—both tangible and intangible—are seen to be numerous and to include economic, political, social-psychological, and military factors. A moment's thought will reveal that these are closely related, mutually supporting, and largely indivisible. All elements of our national *strength* are derived from military, political, moral, and economic factors.

The Department of State sees the threat to our security as military, political, economic, and psychological; and the Council of Economic Advisers enumerated the segments of our strength as economic, military, political, moral, and psychological. Thus there seems to be remarkable agreement among the executive office, the military, and the diplomatic branches of our government as to the elements of national strength: *economic, military, political,* and *moral-psychological* factors.

In view of this remarkable agreement, it is quite possible that these elements of strength might even prove to be a generally acceptable basis of analysis. The point of great dispute will arise, however, on the method of evaluation and implementation of the elements of strength as we attempt to solve our redefined basic problem. How can we raise our plane of living by making economic progress and at the same time attain a maximum degree of security and a maximum amount of individual and national freedom in a political democracy?

RESOURCES

We have seen that the elements of strength—economic, military, political, and moral-psychological—have been called our *national resources,* and that they are closely related, mutually supporting, and largely indivisible. Our purpose for the study of these resources is to evaluate them and to determine how they can be used most strategically in the attainment of maximum freedom, security, strength, and economic progress. By economic progress, it will be recalled, we mean rising planes of living —i.e., increased want satisfaction through increased consumption.

In order to achieve this consumption, goods must be produced. In a simple type of economy the production-consumption function may be achieved within a family unit, but in our more complex economic organization the want satisfaction must be accomplished through the exchange of "bundles of utilities." This transfer takes place by the consumer's translating his wants into an effective demand by giving up purchasing power in the form of money for the bundles of utilities (goods, services, psychic income). How much effective demand a consumer has is a function of his income, which is derived through his creation of utilities in the production process. Thus there are at least three fundamental divisions of economics —production, exchange, and consumption.

The objective of the production process is the creation of utilities, and production is accomplished through the use of land (natural resources), man-made facilities (capital resources), and manpower (human resources). These resources as factors of production are more familiar tools of analysis than our elements of strength. A moment's reflection, however, will reveal that all of the elements of strength can be attributed to one or more of these agents. Therefore, we will attempt to evaluate our national productive potential with a study of each of these resource factors of production. While doing so we will remember that these factors, like our elements of strength, are mutually supporting and largely indivisible.

The primary purpose of this analysis is to study the United States' national resource production potential and policies relating thereto. This approach seems justified in view of the lack of emphasis that has been given to this division of economics and the increasing number of national policy decisions that are being made in this area.

In summary let us recall Mr. Wendell Willkie's statement: "Only the productive can be strong and only the strong can be free."

Strength and Production Potentials

CHAPTER 2

Spatial Resources

Natural resources include all the non-man-made aspects of our environment on the surface of the earth, in the ground, and in the air. In addition to all the natural materials, these include the spatial or area aspects. Modern economists use this concept of natural resources to describe land as a factor of production, whereas earlier economists thought of land as soil.

As the study of natural resources is begun, several important characteristics are observable from the outset: (1) There are limiting factors to be overcome in the use of natural resources. (2) Increased demand for natural resources and materials has led to technological developments which have in part overcome these limitations and resistances and thus increased the supply of natural resources. (3) The types of natural resources are not uniformly distributed, and the maldistribution has led to interdependence. (4) This interdependence has not been solved through technological developments. Rather has it been increased by creating a demand for specialized products, which in many instances are rarer and less uniformly distributed. And finally, (5) The dynamic forces at work in creating shifts in the demand for and supply of natural resources necessitate a continuous study of natural resources and reformulation of policies relating thereto.

Natural resources as a contributing factor to strength and production have many uses. Perhaps the simplest classification for the purposes of analysis is the study of spatial resources, agricultural resources, and energy and material resources. These will be the subjects of Parts I, II, and III of Unit Two.

The study of spatial or area resources as a contributing element of strength and security should take into consideration: (1) location of a country; (2) size, shape, and depth of a country; (3) topography of a country; and (4) locational relationship of a country's noncontiguous areas and commitments. Spatial resources are equally important as economic and military factors as contributing elements of strength and security. Indeed, as has already been noted, these two functions are largely inseparable.

LOCATION

The most important spatial aspect is location. Strategic military position is in large measure dependent on distances from other power centers; and international trade is in part conditioned by spatial aspects of location.

The conclusions that are drawn in the study of location are often conditioned by the type of map that is used.[1] The most significant fact about the position of North America in the world to be observed from a Miller projection centered on the Western Hemisphere is that our continent lies halfway between the European and Asiatic power centers and is separated from them by oceanic distances.[2] In addition the forty-eight United States may be seen to be the most isolated of those nations that have been great powers during the twentieth century. Thus for a long time the military deemed the United States virtually immune to invasion except in the "improbable event" that one (or both) of its neighbors, Canada or Mexico, were to become the base of operations of an enemy from overseas. Canada and Mexico have not been considered potential threats because of the enormous disproportion in strength between either of them and the United States.[3]

[1] For a clear discussion of the relative merits of different types of maps, see Nicholas John Spykman, *The Geography of the Peace*, Harcourt, Brace and Company, 1944, pp. 8–18.

[2] *Ibid.*, p. 18.

[3] Army Service Forces, *Geographical Foundations of National Power*, Section 1, Headquarters, Army Services Manual M 103–2, Government Printing Office, 1944, p. 88.

This feeling of geographic separation and military security contributed to the sense of isolation which prevailed in the United States prior to World War II. A direct result was a minimum expenditure for military security and the maintenance of a small standing army. The idea was that our spatial protection would provide time for the expansion of this professional army core in the "improbable event" that it should be needed. A much more important result was the neglect of our international relationships, both political and economic.

A student of spatial relationships might have concluded from observing this same cylindrical map (Figure 2.1) that the United States was encircled by the land masses of the Old World. However, this can be shown much more vividly by using a map drawn on an azimuthal equidistant projection. Figure 2.2 is such a map centered on St. Louis. By looking at a similar map centered on Moscow (Figure 2.3) this condition of encirclement will also be seen to prevail. Focusing attention on one spot in the use of this type of map has the obvious advantage of enabling the student to acquire a better understanding of the relation of other land masses to the area under consideration. Nevertheless, in this initial exercise the word "encirclement" has purposely been used to bring about an awareness of this condition in any spot upon which we focus attention, and in order to show that no one country has a monopoly in the use of this mapping tool and terminology for insisting on additional expenditures for military security. It is true that these geographical spatial relationships are often the cause of wars, but it is also true that "Wars are born in the minds of men."

The primary purpose for the use of the above exercise was to show how the use of different tools might have counterbalanced some of the United States' pre-World War II isolation attitudes. Indeed, as will be shown in Chapter 14 on geoecopolitics, this very technique was being used to further the German and Japanese expansion movement before World War II as a threat to our security, just as it has been used by Soviet Russia. As we began to have a better general understanding of these spatial relationships, our sense of military security through isolation faded away rapidly with the widening range and increasing speed of naval action, with the rise in air power, and perhaps most importantly through the employment of nuclear energy and missile propulsion. All but the most skeptical seem to be convinced that militarily the United States is of the world as well as a part of the world.

Location has also been a dominant factor affecting international trade. The study of agricultural resources and energy and material resources

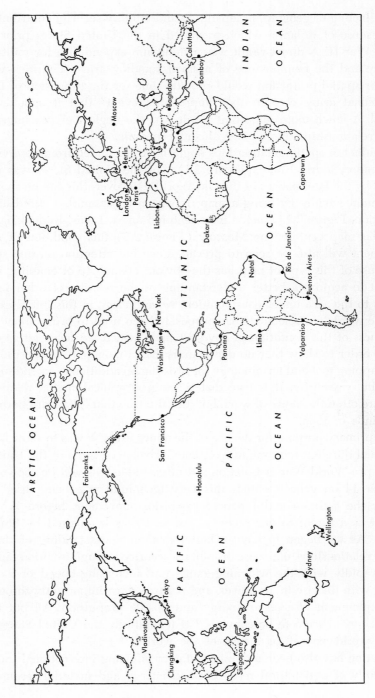

Figure 2.1. Miller Projection World Map.

will indicate the importance of location in the international trade in these resources. For the present the simple facts should be noted that the United States is the best customer of Canada, of Mexico, and of most Caribbean and South American countries. A large part of this latter trade, however, is not based as much upon nearness as it is on economic reciprocity due to specialization in production. Also it should be noted that

Figure 2.2.   World Map Centered on St. Louis.

the United States occupies an advantageous position athwart the trade routes of the Atlantic and Pacific and that the greatest volume of international trade is carried in the bottoms of ships that sail the North Atlantic.

The United States trade with the Pacific and Asiatic countries is primarily based upon specialized production. Proximity as a factor would favor less United States trade and more inter-Asiatic trade.

The conclusion can be drawn that the geographic location of a state is of basic importance. It in part defines potential enemies and allies and is a determinant of economic relations through international trade. In addition, it will be seen that climatic factors which are natural aspects of location are one of the principal contributing factors to the development

Figure 2.3.   World Map Centered on Moscow.

of agricultural resources, which in part determine the domestic and international economic structure of an area.

SIZE, SHAPE, AND DEPTH

While the size of the land area of a state is not an absolute prerequisite to strength and production potential, it is generally a desirable attribute in combination with compactness of shape and great depth.

In extent of area the United States is far below Soviet Russia, only three-fourths as large as China, and not much larger than Brazil.

A large area may be of economic advantage in that it offers greater potential for the discovery of energy and mineral resources and, when properly located, for the production of diversified agricultural resources. On the other hand, distances in a large area may take the form of resistance or space handicaps which must be overcome by the development of transportation and communication facilities. Thus little is to be gained by comparing miles of transportation and communication of two countries such as the United States and Germany. However, a railway system of 54,487 miles in Russia as compared with 227,244 miles in the United States indicates that we have overcome our smaller space handicap much more effectively.

In yet another way space may prove to be a handicap: if it proves to be barren of natural production potentialities or unusable for human habitation.

Very little of the United States area could be so classified. The whole continental United States is considered "coreland," by which is meant the territory on which the predominant people have established themselves. While this introduces only that area suitable for human habitation, it is interesting to note that during World War II the War Department considered our "coreland" very nearly equal in area to the coreland of Russia or China and enormously larger than that of any of the other great powers.[4] Therefore, the tentative conclusion might be that for economic purposes the wasted-space handicap as related to size is much greater in Russia and China than in the United States.

The shape of the United States is compact and almost rectangular except for the salients of New England, Florida, and southern Texas and for the V-shaped indentation in the northern boundary with Canada between the three lower Great Lakes.

Shape is important in relation to the technique of warfare and it also has a bearing on economic and political unity. Compactness minimizes the length of the borders to be defended and provides maximum ease and security to meet external thrusts over short interior lines. However, compactness increases the vulnerability of the country, especially to air attack. Compactness needs to be accompanied by large size. Germany in 1939 had an efficient shape and size for a peacetime economy, but its compactness was a disadvantage as soon as Allied air power could be brought into action.

On the other hand, excessive elongation of the land and dispersion not only increase vulnerability but may also be an obstacle to internal national unity when they encourage the development of sectionalism. Thus policies, domestic and international, are often formulated out of sec-

[4] *Ibid.*, p. 90.

tional interests with a disregard for national interests. Size and not shape has led to sectionalism in the United States. As size has been an important contributing factor to specialization of production, sectional interests have often been overriding in the development of national policies. Those areas that have engaged in foreign trade have been international policy minded, while other areas, such as the Midwest, have been more domestic minded and hence isolationist in attitudes.

A common language, our fundamental objectives of freedom and security, and our political democracy and federal union have been the advantages and methodology with which we have dealt effectively with problems of great size and sectionalism which otherwise might have led to disunity.

Depth is derived from size and in part from shape. Depth is of principal importance as related to military security as it adds to the defensibility of any objective from attack by land, sea, or air. Large size and compact shape give the United States the advantage of great depth.

Depth as a strategic factor has not received as much attention in the United States as in other areas, for the military have believed that we were not vulnerable to attack by land. But the military strategy of trading space for time is well understood. In addition to time gained, the enemy can be led far into the interior through a campaign of continuing retreat in order to lengthen his lines of supply and communication, which may then be attacked. Germany in World War II, like Napoleon, lost the Russian campaign in large part because of this lengthening of the supply lines, and the successful defense of Moscow and Stalingrad became the turning points. China, as well as Russia, has this advantage of depth.

In the warfare of today, however, the location of production facilities in conjunction with depth is one of the most important elements which must be studied. Russia was thoroughly aware of this in her strategic expansion of industrial facilities during the 1930's behind the Ural Mountains. In addition, the development of air power and missile power, and atomic weapons has in part offset the advantage of depth in industrialized countries. To retain the advantage, production facilities must be decentralized. These, then, are important problems to be analyzed in our study of man-made facilities (capital resources).

Our military strategists would conclude that space and its ally, time, are weapons hard to conquer. Depth is favorable or unfavorable only in relation to other factors, but it remains a factor which usually only a quick, decisive, and destructive military thrust can overcome. Missiles with nuclear war heads are the weapons that can annihilate time and space.

TOPOGRAPHY

Topography, together with size, location, and other natural resources, is considered by Spykman to be one of the most important factors in the determination of the position of a state in international relations.[5] The importance of topography as directly related to other aspects of domestic production potentialities, especially agricultural, is much easier to understand.

The Western Hemisphere, as has been observed, is a great land mass surrounded by three oceans, the Atlantic, the Pacific, and the Arctic. The most outstanding topographical feature of North America is the location of the chain of Rocky Mountains. The Rocky Mountains have cut off the Pacific coast from easy communication by land with the major portion of the United States. The Pacific coast has only a few harbors and an economy that is only in a small degree supplementary to the economy of the Far East. Thus partly because of the location of the Rocky Mountains, the development of the United States has been oriented eastward to the Atlantic coast.

Not until the opening of the Panama Canal was the Pacific coast brought into close contact with the Atlantic region. In addition, this cut through Central America had the effect of giving all of the United States more direct access to the Pacific Ocean. The port of New York was then nearer to the Asiatic ports north of Shanghai than the port of Liverpool is by way of Suez. Thus the topographical barrier of the Rocky Mountains was in part offset by the building of the Panama Canal, and the whole of the United States has access to Europe and Asia across the oceans.

The Atlantic will probably remain the more important oceanic region not only because American culture originated as a transatlantic projection of western European civilization but because, for many years, its opposite coast will be economically and politically more significant than the more distant shores of the Pacific.

Although the Atlantic is the smaller of the two oceans, it has a much longer United States coastline and a much greater drainage basin. As will be seen, the real center of power in the United States lies in close

[5] Spykman, *op. cit.*, p. 22.

proximity to the Atlantic coastline, and it is toward the Atlantic that most of the economic life of the United States flows.

Thus topography has been a conditioning factor in the determination of policy decisions which have been oriented with first priority to western Europe. We must now consider how our policies have been and need to be modified in terms of our commitments with specific reference to locational relationships of our noncontiguous areas.

LOCATIONAL RELATIONSHIPS TO NONCONTIGUOUS AREAS AND TO COMMITMENTS

The present continental limits of the United States were achieved in 1853. The elimination of France in 1803 and of Spain in 1822–23 left only Great Britain as a great power in the Western Hemisphere with Canada to our north. However, in 1823 the United States assumed an obligation outside of our continental limits when President Monroe extended the protection of the United States to all of the Western Hemisphere. This commitment was undertaken after Monroe had consulted with Madison and Jefferson, who approved it only after Canning, the British Foreign Secretary, had assured the American Minister, Richard Rush, that Britain and the British Navy would support the United States. As Walter Lippmann states most emphatically: "Unfortunately, however, for the education of the American people in the realities of foreign policy—that commitments must be balanced by adequate power —the understanding with Britain, which preceded Monroe's Message, was never avowed. To this day most Americans have never heard of it."[6]

In 1861 Napoleon III defied the Monroe Doctrine, sent an invading army into Mexico, and established an empire on our southern frontier with Maximilian enthroned as emperor. This was made possible by the lack of a clear and binding agreement with Britain, and because the United States was rent by civil war. It is quite possible that we might have had to fight an international war in Mexico as soon as our own Civil War was over if Maximilian had not been unfortunate in Mexico and Napoleon had not become involved in trouble at home.[7]

Thus, the feeling of geographic separation and military security contributed to the sense of isolation which prevailed in the United States prior to World War II, but as early as 1823 our commitments for defense extended to the entire Western Hemisphere.

[6] Walter Lippmann, *U.S. Foreign Policy*, Little, Brown and Company, 1943, p. 18.

[7] *Ibid.*, p. 21.

For seventy-five years Monroe's concert with Great Britain provided adequate force to cover the foreign commitments of the United States, which were confined to the Western Hemisphere. Lippmann suggests that the Anglo-American concert worked so well and so long and exacted no payment in return that in our times men have refused to recognize, because events did not compel them to do so, that the effective substance of an alliance with Britain was the cardinal element in United States foreign relations.[8]

Our foreign commitments were extended further with the purchase of Alaska, the annexation of the Hawaiian Islands, and the acquisition of Guam and the Philippines. This committed the United States to the defense of a territory 7000 nautical miles west of California but only 700 miles off the coast of China and only 250 miles from Formosa. A circle with Manila as its center with a radius of 1500 miles enclosed the industrial region of Japan, all of Korea, practically all of China, French Indochina, Burma and Malaya, and the Netherlands Indies.

By 1900 the direct United States commitment included the protection of the entire Western Hemisphere and extended across the Pacific almost to the China coast. James Truslow Adams described the period following the Spanish American War: "Atlases had been in much request during the war, and great numbers of citizens whose interests before had scarcely gone beyond their 'Main Street' found themselves thinking in terms of both Europe and the Far East. Minds were opened and victory brought a sense of power. For the next twenty years, until we shut ourselves up again, it seemed as though we were destined to play the role in international affairs which all expected that we should."[9]

After 1900 our extended commitments into the Pacific and Asia required the United States to have new extensions of military force and political agreements. This need was increased by a rising German imperialism and the building of a German navy as a threat to British sea power in the Atlantic. Monroe's concert covered only the Atlantic and it assumed that Britain's command of the sea was invincible. If the United States did have a definite policy to stay in the Pacific, then a basic error was made in that our political and military strength was not built up to cover our new commitments and in view of a change in the balance of military strength in the Atlantic. It has been stated that from the day Admiral Dewey sailed into Manila Bay until the day when General

[8] *Ibid.*, p. 67.
[9] James Truslow Adams, *The March of Democracy from Civil War to World Power*, Charles Scribner's Sons, 1933, p. 259.

Wainwright surrendered Corregidor the United States never made a sustained and prudent, or remotely adequate, effort to bring its obligations and its power into balance.[10]

Actually, it appears that President Theodore Roosevelt had the elements of a sound foreign policy because he improved our position by constructing the Panama Canal, by enlarging the navy, and by developing friends and virtual allies against the rising imperialism of Germany and later on against the rising imperialism of Japan. Unfortunately, this policy was not made plain to the nation.

Presidents Taft and Wilson, who followed Roosevelt, were idealists who rejected the premises of politics of power, partly as a result of mental attitudes formed during the period of illusory isolation from 1823 to 1898 and partly because in them was combined the idealism which prompts Americans to make extensive commitments and the pacifism which causes Americans to shrink from the measures of force required to support the commitments.

As a result, with the beginning of World War I in Europe in 1914, the United States had no foreign policy which enabled the nation to determine its interest in the conflict. The reason for entering the war in 1917 was to preserve the security of the United States from an aggressive German empire which in the event of a victory would have made Britain, France, and Italy its vassals and Japan its ally. While this fact was understood by many, it never was made clear to the general public. At the end of the war the public and their elected representatives did not understand what British and French power meant to the security of the vital interests and commitments of the United States all over the world. Entry into the League of Nations was looked upon as an additional commitment to defend Europe. So it was that the United States withdrew within her shell of isolation.

For twenty years after the end of World War I United States foreign relations were conducted as if the nation had no conception of its commitments. Lippmann points out that in 1922 we reduced our naval strength to a ratio which gave Japan superiority in the western Pacific and agreed not to improve the fortifications of Corregidor, Cavite, and Guam, which were under the guns of the Japanese fleet. At this same time, the United States renewed its commitment to oppose Japanese imperialism in Asia and to encourage Chinese resistance to it. Hence at the very time we reduced our power, we renewed and even enlarged

[10] Lippmann, *op. cit.*, p. 28.

our commitments. In addition, we turned upon our natural allies, Britain and France, and treated them as rivals whose armaments it was a diplomatic triumph to reduce.[11]

The events of the 1930's made it obvious that Germany, Japan, and Italy were on the march and that they would dominate the world if they were not successfully resisted. In July, 1939, two months before the outbreak of World War II, the Senate Committee on Foreign Relations made two decisions which afford a perfect example of the total incompetence guiding the nation's foreign policy. The Committee advised the State Department to declare economic war against Japan by abrogating the commercial treaty. This was done and Japan was put on notice that the United States was her avowed enemy. The Committee's second decision was to refuse to lift the arms embargo which prohibited Britain and France from buying arms in the United States to resist Germany, Japan's ally since 1936. Thus, the Senate Committee invited war in the Pacific and refused to fortify our long-standing defenses in the Atlantic. "At this juncture we found ourselves opposed to our future enemies but with our exposed possessions undefended, without allies, isolated from our friends, and yet committed over the length of the Western Hemisphere and across the vast expanse of the Pacific. At the zenith of our commitments, we were at the nadir of our precautions."[12]

Between 1937 and 1941 a series of disputes divided the nation over the repeal of the arms embargo, over the transaction of overage destroyers and bases, over conscription, over lend-lease, and over the repeal of the Neutrality Act. It is possible that none of these costly controversies would have taken place if President Franklin D. Roosevelt had been able to present them to a nation which realized the vast extent of its commitments and had acquired the habit of covering its commitments.

The isolationists devoted their efforts to opposing alliances which were needed to validate our commitments. They argued that only by doing nothing to save our friends and later allies from defeat could we stay out of the war. This they believed to be the best policy because they were confident that the continental United States could not be invaded, and they chose to ignore the long-established transoceanic commitments of the United States.

The interventionists based their case on the fact that the United States

[11] *Ibid.*, pp. 40–41.
[12] *Ibid.*, p. 42.

without allies could not sustain its commitments against the combined power of the totalitarian alliance. It was not until only the British Isles and General Chiang Kai-shek were left as allies that President Franklin D. Roosevelt publicly presented the case for intervention, which was considered then to be his policy rather than a national policy.[13] After Pearl Harbor this was no longer true.

At the end of World War II, the abiding illusions of more than a century of inexperience in the realities of foreign policy continued to plague the United States. During the postwar years from 1946 to 1953 we showed that we had learned the lesson of the necessity of collective security. However, we continued on an expanded scale to make worldwide commitments without providing sufficient strength to back them up. The post-World War II disarmament was a repetition in part of the post-World War I disarmament. But the loss of our position of strength immediately after World War II was more serious because there was a better understanding of our international responsibilities and our commitments were greater. Figure 2.4 shows the extent of the United States commitments as of 1952; it indicates the areas we are committed to defend by treaties and by other agreements, the countries receiving military supplies, ECA and Point 4 assistance; and it presents limited evidence of the extent to which these commitments and pacts were covered by military strength. The best indication that the strength was not adequate to cover the commitments of all types was the large percentage of United States military strength that was tied down in Korea without achievement of victory in that one limited area. Of course the argument can also be made that we did not have the type of military force required in the area and by political policy, or that the military were not permitted to use the type of force we had.

Figure 2.4 presents clearly the location relationships of the United States to the nation's noncontiguous areas and commitments at the beginning of 1952. We have seen that the spatial resources of a nation must include this study and that adequate strength must be present to back up these commitments. This strength consists not only of the elements of our national strength but of that provided by those nations with which we have alliances. The development of policies to this end must be studied in more detail under the topic of the strategy of security. This will be done in the final chapter, "Strategy of Security," which will review the additional commitments and foreign policies during the

[13] *Ibid.*, p. 46.

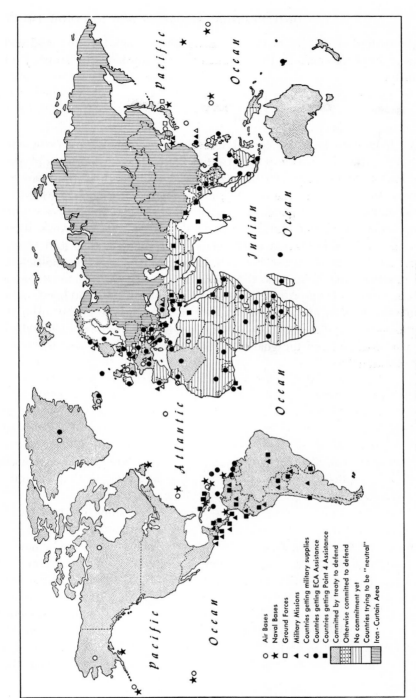

Figure 2.4. United States Commitments, 1952.

Air Bases
Naval Bases
Ground Forces
Military Missions
Countries getting military supplies
Countries getting ECA Assistance
Countries getting Point 4 Assistance
Committed by treaty to defend
Otherwise committed to defend
No commitment yet
Countries trying to be "neutral"
Iron - Curtain Area

four-year period 1953–56 of the first Eisenhower administration, and will suggest improvements in these policies to strengthen our strategy of security.

SUMMARY

We have seen how the spatial resources are contributing factors to the strength and security of the United States by considering (1) the location of the country; (2) the size, shape, and depth of the country; (3) the topography of the country; and (4) the locational relationship of the nation's noncontiguous areas and commitments. Technological developments are racing ahead with such speed in this space age that only the impossible takes a little longer. This suggests that the United States must prepare for and keep ahead of all developments, and adjust our practices and policies to the realities of our time. Senate Majority Leader Lyndon Johnson asked at the beginning of 1958: "What should be our goal?" His answer was: "If, out in space, there is the ultimate position—from which total control of the earth may be exercised—then our national goal and the goal of all free men must be to win and hold that position."

Natural Resources—Agricultural

CHAPTER 3

Agricultural Production

In analyzing natural resources as contributing factors to strength and production, we have adopted the classification of spatial resources, agricultural resources, and energy and material resources. By agriculture is meant the efforts of man to make use of and to improve the natural genetic or growth processes of plant and animal life in order that these processes may yield the vegetable and animal products needed or wanted by man. Thus, agriculture includes field cropping, animal husbandry, tree culture, forestry, and fishing.

The plan of this Part II on agricultural resources is first to consider in this chapter on agricultural production some of the facts that bear on agriculture in general under two categories—controlling forces and land use, and agricultural production with particular reference to food and fibers. In Chapter 4 a detailed study by specific commodities will be made of the United States interests in international agricultural trade and related problems and policy. Finally, Chapter 5 returns to a consideration of general United States agricultural problems and policy.

CONTROLLING FORCES AND LAND USE

1. Controlling Forces

Agricultural production is controlled by and is a function of nature, man, capital, technology, and institutional factors. For purposes of emphasis, technology and institutions are listed separately from the other factors. Actually, technology is expressed in its tangible form in capital and in its intangible form through the ability of man. Thus, technology is applied through man's know-how of the use of capital in the form of the plow. Similarly, institutions are a result and function of, and are expressed in, all three factors.

Perhaps the most important fact to be learned about agriculture is its relation to and dependence on nature. Nature sets the outer limits on agricultural production. Land area is the absolute physical controlling factor. Additional natural controls are topography, soils, and climate. Obviously, topography—mountains, valleys, and plains—affects the type of agriculture; but in addition, it affects drainage, air currents, and winds. The physical structure and chemical and bacterial characteristics of soils are important to agricultural production. Climate is a dominant controlling force through sunshine, temperature, precipitation, wind, humidity, pressure change, and fog.

Land area of the ten leading countries is shown in the world identification map, Figure 3.1. The United States ranks fifth, behind the U.S.S.R., Canada, Brazil, and Australia.

Topographical features by principal classes are indicated in Figure 3.2. The estimate has been made that about 41 percent of the earth's land surface falls in the plains area, 33 percent in the plateaus and tableland area, 14 percent in the hill lands, and 12 percent in the mountains. About 5 percent of the mountain area, 25 percent of the hills, 75 percent of the plateaus, and 95 percent of the plains area have a topography suitable for crop production. However, as has been seen, topography is only one of the natural limiting factors, and when climate and soils are also considered, it has been estimated by the United States Department of Agriculture that only 25 percent of the earth's surface can be used for all agricultural purposes. The significance of the plains area can be noted by observing on individual crop maps the large areas falling in the Great Plains of the United States. This should be compared with the crop production in the great plains of Canada, the Pampas of Argentina, the North European and Russian plains, the Po Valley plain of Italy, and the Australian plains area in New South Wales, Victoria, and Queensland.

Soil groups are given in Figure 3.3. Particular soil types are essential for the production of grain, vegetables, meat, and many of the basic agricultural raw materials of industry. Even though soil may have a high natural fertility, it is productive only if temperature and moisture conditions are suitable for the growth of crops. Productivity, even in

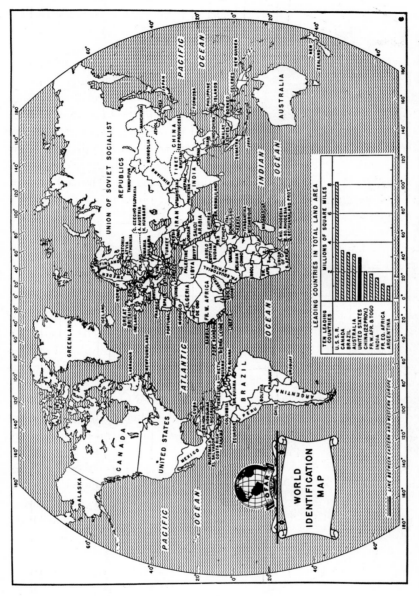

Figure 3.1. World Identification Map and Land Area. (U.S. Department of Agriculture, Office of Foreign Agricultural Relations)

33

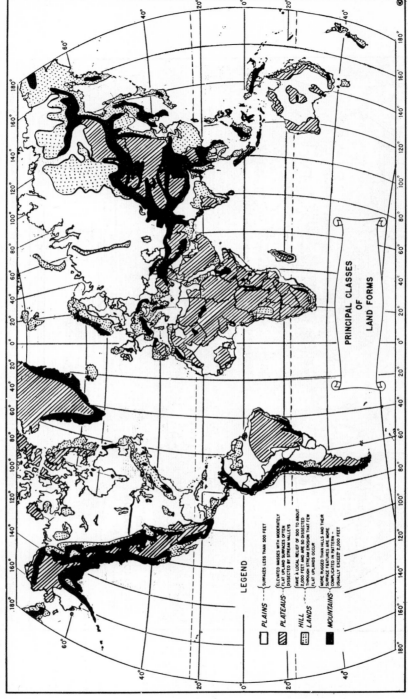

LEGEND

PLAINS {SURFACES LESS THAN 500 FEET}

PLATEAUS {ELEVATED MASSES WITH MODERATELY FLAT UPLAND SURFACES OFTEN DISSECTED BY STREAM VALLEYS}

HILL LANDS {HAVE A LOCAL RELIEF OF 500 TO ABOUT 2,000 FEET AND ARE SO DISSECTED THROUGH STREAM EROSION THAT FEW FLAT UPLANDS OCCUR}

MOUNTAINS {MORE RUGGED THAN HILLS AND THEIR SURFACE FEATURES ARE MORE COMPLICATED IN PATTERN — USUALLY EXCEED 2,000 FEET}

PRINCIPAL CLASSES OF LAND FORMS

Figure 3.2. (U.S. Department of Agriculture, Office of Foreign Agricultural Relations)

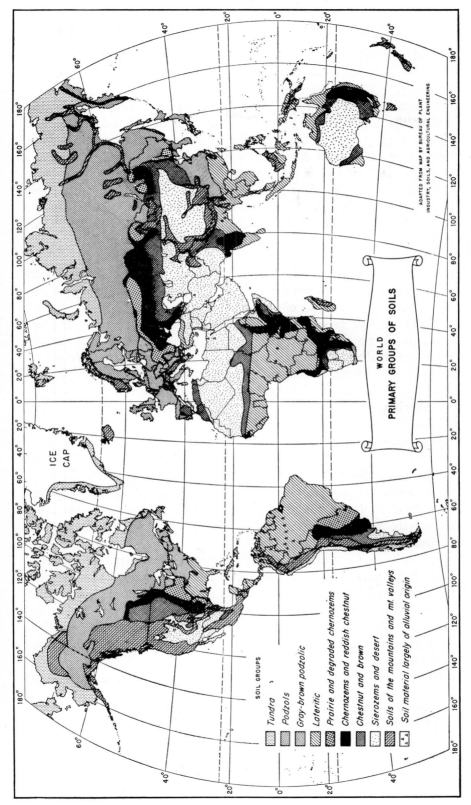

SOIL GROUPS

Tundra

Podzols

Gray-brown podzolic

Lateritic

Prairie and degraded chernozems

Chernozems and reddish chestnut

Chestnut and brown

Sierozems and desert

Soils of the mountains and mt. valleys

Soil material largely of alluvial origin

WORLD

PRIMARY GROUPS OF SOILS

ICE CAP

ADAPTED FROM MAP BY BUREAU OF PLANT
INDUSTRY, SOILS, AND AGRICULTURAL ENGINEERING

Figure 3.3. (U.S. Department of Agriculture, Office of Foreign Agricultural Relations)

suitable climatic areas, depends on the balance of plant nutrients and the physical condition of the soil—its structure, consistency, and plasticity.

Climate sets the broad outlines and limits of agricultural production. This is the contention of geographers, who point out that the type of climate largely controls the type of natural vegetation and animal life. Thus, they conclude that climatic regions are to a considerable extent also flora regions and fauna regions.[1]

Figure 3.4 gives the four great temperature zones of the earth. From the equator outward in either direction to about latitude 30° there is a warm-to-hot tropical zone. In both Northern and Southern hemispheres, a hot-to-cool subtropical zone lies approximately between latitudes 30° and 40°. Between latitudes 40° and 65° there is a hot-to-cold cyclonic zone. Above latitude 65° there is a cool-to-cold polar zone. Within each of the four zones there are from two to four subdivisions, each possessing its own general type of climate.[2]

There are four types of climate in the tropical zone: rainy tropical, monsoon (wet-and-dry) tropical, semiarid tropical, and arid tropical. In the subtropical zone there are three types of climate: Mediterranean subtropical on the western margins of the continents, humid subtropical on the eastern margins, and dry subtropical in the interior regions. These are the climates of the lower southern portion of the United States. Most of the United States lies within the cyclonic zone (the four-season, changeable-weather zone), which has three types of climate: the temperate marine on the western continental margins, the dry continental in the interior regions, and the humid continental over the rest. The polar zones have two types: the polar icecap on the continental land masses and the subpolar climate on the maritime areas. These major climate zones are subdivided into climatic regions, which, together with characteristic agricultural production, are shown in Figure 3.5.

Not only are these climatic regions important as controlling factors of agricultural production, but geographers have contended these regions have exercised a general differentiation on all economic production and patterns of economic development. The climatic regional approach to the study of agricultural production has been used as an accepted procedure for a long time by geographers because of the emphasis of climate as a controlling factor.

Thus the conclusion can be drawn that nature sets the outer limits

---

[1] George T. Renner, Loyal Durand, Jr., C. Langdon White, and Weldon B. Gibson, *World Economic Geography*, Thomas Y. Crowell Company, 1951.

[2] *Ibid.*, p. 40.

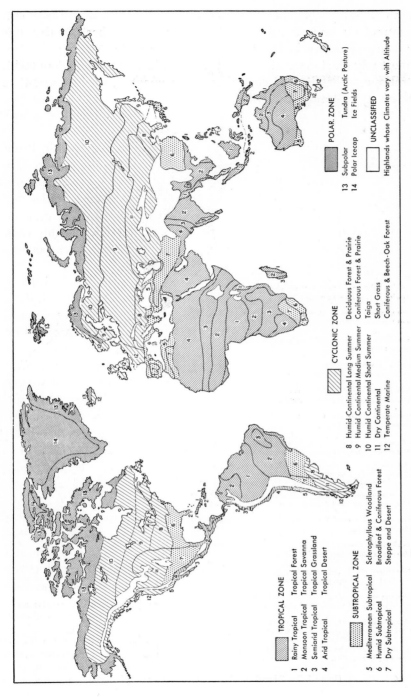

Figure 3.4.   Temperature Zones and Climate. (Renner's Semi-Hemispheric Projection, Copyright, 1945)

TROPICAL ZONE

1 Rainy Tropical   Tropical Forest
2 Monsoon Tropical   Tropical Savanna
3 Semiarid Tropical   Tropical Grassland
4 Arid Tropical   Tropical Desert

SUBTROPICAL ZONE

5 Mediterranean Subtropical   Sclerophyllous Woodland
6 Humid Subtropical   Broadleaf & Coniferous Forest
7 Dry Subtropical   Steppe and Desert

CYCLONIC ZONE

8 Humid Continental Long Summer   Deciduous Forest & Prairie
9 Humid Continental Medium Summer   Coniferous Forest & Prairie
10 Humid Continental Short Summer   Taiga
11 Dry Continental   Short Grass
12 Temperate Marine   Coniferous & Beech-Oak Forest

POLAR ZONE

13 Subpolar   Tundra (Arctic Pasture)
14 Polar Icecap   Ice Fields

UNCLASSIFIED

Highlands whose Climates vary with Altitude

on agricultural production and that climate is the most important limiting natural element. But an additional point of emphasis is that this dominance of nature limits man's control over agricultural production. He must rely on stores and forces of nature which are not subject to his control and so has limited control over the quantity, quality, and time cycle of agricultural production.

Tropic forest climate: hot all the year; enough rainfall to cause forests, less tall and more like thicket at edges.

Tropic grassland climate: short, rainy season; grass and scrub.
Tropic savanna climate: longer rainy season; grass and scattered trees.

Desert climate: scanty pasture in places for a short season.
Sandy and stony desert.

Temperate grassland climate: winter cool or cold; summer hot; rain scanty. More rain; better grass; some farming in better spots.

Tundra climate: very cold in winter; cool, short summer; moss, lichens, shrubs, grass; caribou, reindeer and musk ox pasture; no trees, no farms.

High plateau climate: cold; summer too frosty for trees; a little barley in warm nooks; pasture for sheep, goat, llama, yak.

Northern coniferous forest: long, cold winter; short summer; forest, spruce and other conifers; furs, game, fish, wood; frosts stop farmer.

Cool, moist west coast: oceanic climate; rainy winter; showery summer; good grass, potatoes, oats; dampness bothers farmer. Too cool for grain.

Small grain, potato, grass climate: long, cold, snowy winter; cool, moist summer; forests, conifer and deciduous; grass, potatoes, rye, oats, barley.

Spring wheat, continental climate: very cold winter, little snow; too dry for forests; natural grassland; summer warm, moist.

Corn and winter wheat: winter frost, rain, snow; summer hot; mostly natural forest; corn; winter wheat, better at north and west.

Mediterranean climate: cool, rainy winter, some frost; summer dry; suits wheat, grape, olive, oranges in sheltered nooks.

Cotton, rice and corn: winter warm, rainy, cold waves and frost; natural forest; suits cotton, rice, corn, and many other crops.

Florida climate: long, hot, rainy summer, short winter; frost in most parts; oranges, corn, many crops. (Note altitude in South America.)

Tropical Upland: elevation makes climate cooler than lowlands near by; all have rainy season; coffee, corn, millet, sorghums.

Polar ice cap: snow does not melt, piles up, becomes glacier; many mountains have small areas not shown.

High mountains: all types of climate from that at base to ice cap if high enough.

Irrigated land: only the largest could be shown. There are hundreds of patches of it.

Figure 3.5. Climatic Regions and Agricultural Production.

The dominance of nature as a limiting factor in agricultural production, especially as reflected in food production, has been emphasized by many writers as being of vital importance because food is necessary for life and is thus a limiting factor in all production. The relation between food and life and population growth will be discussed in Chapter 13. This emphasis on the limits of nature tends to ignore the function of man

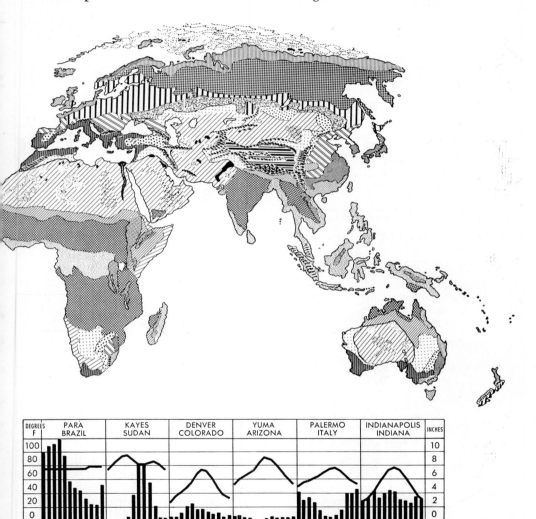

Figure 3.5—(Continued)

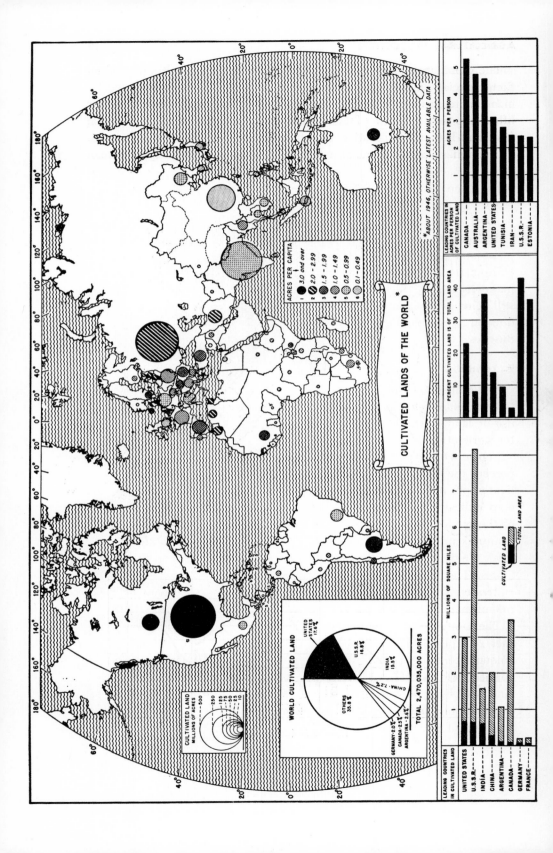

CULTIVATED LANDS OF THE WORLD*

*ABOUT 1946, OTHERWISE LATEST AVAILABLE DATA

ACRES PER CAPITA
1 3.0 and over
2 2.0 - 2.99
3 1.5 - 1.99
4 1.0 - 1.49
5 0.5 - 0.99
6 0.1 - 0.49

CULTIVATED LAND
MILLIONS OF ACRES
500
250
175
100
25
10

WORLD CULTIVATED LAND
UNITED STATES 17.6%
U.S.S.R. 16.8%
INDIA 13.5%
CHINA 7.2%
GERMANY 2.0%
CANADA 2.5%
ARGENTINA 2.6%
OTHERS 35.8%
TOTAL 2,470,035,000 ACRES

LEADING COUNTRIES IN CULTIVATED LAND
UNITED STATES
U.S.S.R.
INDIA
CHINA
ARGENTINA
CANADA
GERMANY
FRANCE

MILLIONS OF SQUARE MILES
1 2 3 4 5 6 7 8
CULTIVATED LAND
TOTAL LAND AREA

PERCENT CULTIVATED LAND IS OF TOTAL LAND AREA
10 20 30 40

LEADING COUNTRIES IN
ACRES PER PERSON
OF CULTIVATED LAND
CANADA
AUSTRALIA
ARGENTINA
UNITED STATES
TUNISIA
IRAN
U.S.S.R.
ESTONIA

ACRES PER PERSON
1 2 3 4 5

and capital, together with their applied technology and institutional factors in agricultural production.

In man's attempt to satisfy his needs and wants for food and all other products of nature, he is constantly faced with the problem of overcoming the resistances of nature. To solve it, technology in the form of intangible know-how and its scientific expression and tangible capital —tools, machinery, equipment, structures, transportation facilities, etc. —has been used to broaden the resource base—land use—and to increase production. In agricultural land use and production, an increased understanding of means of modifying the limits of topography, soil, and climate, improved methods of land use and knowledge of plant and animal life, increased availability and efficiency of capital equipment, and increased use of inanimate energy have in large measure made it possible to overcome nature as a limiting factor. But nature still remains dominant in limiting man's control over agricultural production as compared with the control that can be exercised in other industries.

2. Land Use

The limits to the physical supply of land have ceased to have meaning but the manner of land use remains of critical importance. The major use of land in the United States is shown in Table 1. Total land used for agriculture represents 82.6 percent of the total land area.

Figure 3.6 shows the cultivated lands of the world by countries, the percent the cultivated land is of the total land area, and the acres cultivated per person in the leading countries. The size of the circles on the map indicates the amount of cultivated land, and the surface shadings of the circles show the cultivated land per capita. The fifteen leading countries in cultivated land have more than 75 percent of the world's total, ranging from 1.4 percent in Australia to 17.6 percent in the United States. The data on cultivated acres per person and the percent the cultivated land is of the total land area offer striking evidence of the role of man and capital in modifying natural limits of land use.

The United States, with 17.6 percent of the world's cultivated land, uses 24.3 percent of the land in the United States for cropland, which amounts to more than three acres per capita. China with 7.2 percent of the world's cultivated land cultivates about 14 percent of her total land, which approximates less than one-half acre per capita. Part of the explanation is that the United States has employed the use of capital in the form of machinery powered by inanimate energy to cultivate large

TABLE 1. Major Land Use in the United States

Land Use	Acreage (million acres)	Percent of Total
In farms:		
Cropland:		
Cropland cultivated	368	19.3
Cropland pastured	70	3.7
Other cropland	25	1.3
Total available for crops	463	24.3
Wild hay	15	0.8
TOTAL	478	25.1
Pasture:		
Permanent pasture	416	21.8
Woodland pastured	134	7.0
TOTAL	550	28.8
Woodland not pastured	85	4.5
Other land	45	2.4
Total land in farms	1,158	60.8
Not in farms:		
Grazing land	415	21.8
Total land used for agriculture	1,573	82.6
Forest and other land	332	17.4
GRAND TOTAL LAND AREA	1,905	100.0
Total land not in farms	747	39.2

SOURCE: United States Department of Agriculture.

areas of land and has developed transportation and marketing facilities to supply the urban areas with food and agricultural raw materials. On the other hand, China, with a population of approximately 583 million as compared with 170 million in the United States, has not been able to use capital on the farm or to develop an exchange economy. Zimmermann points out that Chinese agriculture exhausts itself by trying to provide the energy to work the fields and that lack of mobility in China leads to incredible crowding on the cream of the land and accounts for the sedentary character of China and its division into thousands of local self-sufficient hsiens.[3]

The conclusion can be drawn that manpower and capital have modified the limits of nature on land use and that technology and cultural institutions are the important contributing factors.

AGRICULTURAL PRODUCTION

Perhaps more important than land used for agriculture is agricultural production. Agriculture has felt the impact of the Industrial Revolution

[3] Erich W. Zimmermann, *World Resources and Industries,* Harper & Brothers, 1951, p. 89.

on production in two principal ways: through the mechanization of agriculture and through the increased employment of scientific procedures. These have resulted in increased productivity per man and per acre. Mechanization tends to supplement and replace manpower and thus increase productivity per man, whereas the application of science tends to increase per acre productivity. The United States has felt the impact of both types of these increases in productivity.

Figure 3.7 presents basic background information on acreage, population, and mechanization from 1900 to 1952. The coming of the machine is indicated by the steep rise in the number of tractors and trucks and the steady drop in the number of horses and mules used on farms. The

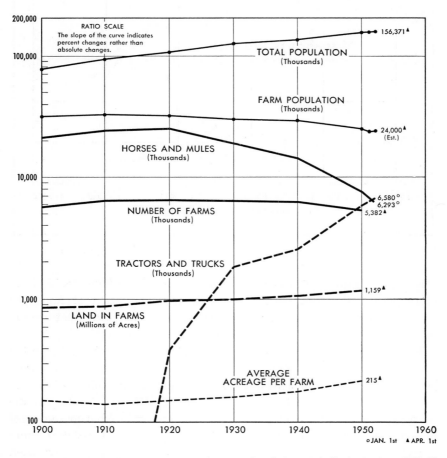

Figure 3.7. United States Agriculture, Acreage, Population, and Mechanization, 1900–52. (Bureau of the Census; Bureau of Agricultural Economics)

curves crossed in 1951–52. The average farm is larger and farm population has declined.

Per man output is presented in Figure 3.8, which gives data on farm output and labor input as a percentage of 1947–49 from 1910 through 1956 and shows the rapid increase in output per man-hour of labor on farms. Output per man-hour rose to the greatest in history and in 1956 was almost twice that of 1940. The period 1910 through 1956 was one of

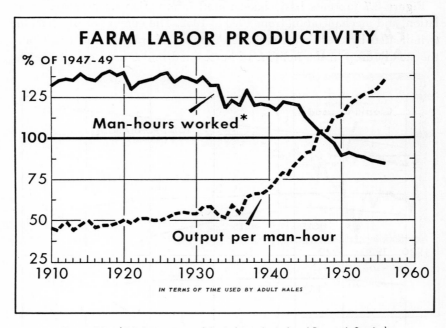

Figure 3.8.   (U.S. Department of Agriculture, Agricultural Research Service)

very rapid progress in farm mechanization and sharp increase in yields of crops and livestock because of widespread adoption of improved farming practices. These changes have brought about a great rise in total farm output, with fewer man-hours spent at farm work.

Farm production per acre and per animal unit for the 1919–56 period as a percentage of 1947–49 is presented in Figure 3.9. The upward trend in crop production per acre has been a major factor which made possible the large increase in farm output during World War II and the postwar years. Higher yields have resulted primarily from greater uses of fertilizer in recent years, use of higher-yielding seed varieties, more spraying and dusting for insect control, and from favorable weather. Total cropland has changed very little since World War I. In livestock production, both a greater number of breeding units and more production per unit have increased output of meat animals and animal products.

While, as indicated above, total cropland has changed little, that portion used for the production of food has increased significantly. This is seen in Figure 3.10, which gives crop acres harvested 1910 through 1956 by major uses. Replacement of animal power by mechanical power since 1935 has released 46 million acres from the production of food for

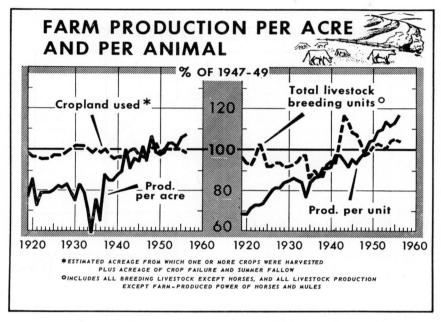

Figure 3.9. (U.S. Department of Agriculture, Agricultural Research Service)

horses and mules so that it could be used for food for humans. Since World War I almost 82 million acres have been released. Further declines in horses and mules are expected in the future, but with the numbers so drastically reduced this source of cropland is rapidly vanishing.

The increased farm output for human use—production of food livestock, and crop production for food, fiber, and tobacco—and decreased output for horse and mule feed is shown for the period 1918–22 through 1952 in Figure 3.11 as expressed in constant 1935–39 dollars. Obviously all the changes in production which have been made physically possible by mechanization and science have been made economically feasible by favorable cost-price relationships. Figure 3.11 also presents the conclusion reached by forty-eight State Productive Capacity committees that agricultural production in the United States could increase one-fifth within about five years, given favorable cost-price relationships as well as availability and use of greatly increased quantities of fertilizer, machinery, and other production goods. The increase, it was estimated, would have to come primarily from increased crop and livestock through greater adoption of known improved production practices.

In August, 1956, the United States Department of Agriculture pub-

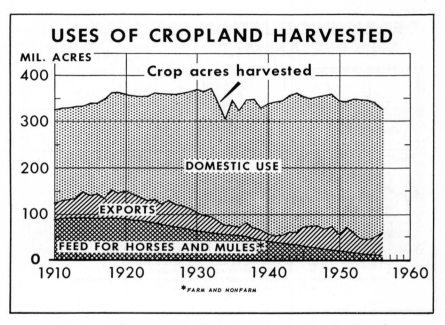

Figure 3.10.   (U.S. Department of Agriculture, Agricultural Research Service)

lished a report on "Farm Output" the chief purpose of which was to describe and analyze the size of the production job ahead for United States farmers. The estimates of future production needs were based on projections of potential demands for agricultural products in 1960 and 1975 under specific assumption regarding growth in our economy and the upward trend in our population indicated by the Bureau of the Census reports of August, 1953, which are used in Chapter 13. The volume of farm output needed in 1975 was estimated to be about one-third larger than the output in 1951–53. Annual increases required in farm output between the two dates may be about 50 percent greater than those which occurred during the long-run period 1910–12 to 1951–

53, and about 20 percent greater than the post-World War II annual increase from 1944–46 to 1951–53.

The 1956 report on "Farm Output" concluded that important problems or questions will revolve around *how* rather than *whether* the production requirements can be met in the years ahead. The conclusion was drawn that the future requirements for crop and pasture could be attained through a combination of factors, including (1) shifting of

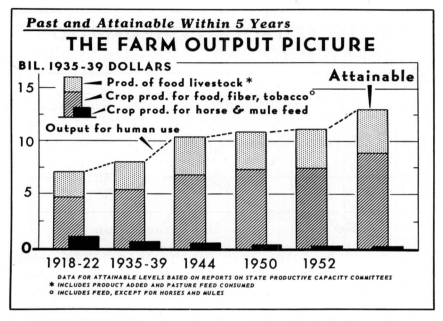

Figure 3.11. (U.S. Department of Agriculture, Bureau of Agricultural Economics)

acreages among crops, (2) adding to cropland and pastureland area, and (3) increasing production per acre. More efficient conversion of feeds through livestock is a part of the challenge of providing the additional requirements for meats and livestock products. To accomplish the required farm output the *how* involves (1) production research to furnish farmers with the technological know-how necessary in meeting production needs; (2) the development of techniques that will continue to enable farms to meet production requirements with decreasing costs per unit in terms of labor, land, and capital resources; and (3) the provision of economic guides as to the most profitable adjustments for farmers in meeting changing market requirements.

1. Food

Increased domestic production and consumption of food from 1910 through 1952 is shown on Figure 3.12. The United States Department of Agriculture suggests that the two solid lines indicate in *overall terms* how nearly self-sufficient the United States has been with respect to food. This *overall* analysis of self-sufficiency can be misleading because it hides

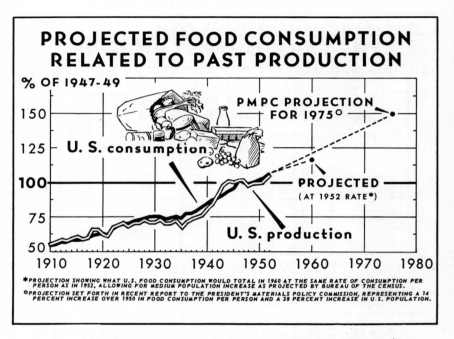

Figure 3.12.   (U.S. Department of Agriculture, Bureau of Agricultural Economics)

within the aggregate individual exports and imports of commodities and grades of particular commodities.

The Office of Foreign Agricultural Relations of the United States Department of Agriculture presents additional comparisons of production and consumption of food on a world basis in Figure 3.13 by showing production as a percentage of consumption. In commenting on this figure, the Office of Foreign Agricultural Relations suggests that some of the sparsely settled countries, such as Canada, Argentina, and Australia, produce much more food than is consumed domestically, while, on the other hand, a few highly industrialized countries produce only a small part of their food supply and are largely dependent upon the trading countries with surpluses for much of their food requirements. (The United States Department of Agriculture should have pointed out that most of western Europe and Japan lie within this category.) In addition, there are many nations that, in normal years, produce in the aggregate about as much food as they consume, but they may also be large importers and exporters of food products. For example, the United States and Brazil are two of the largest exporters and importers of food

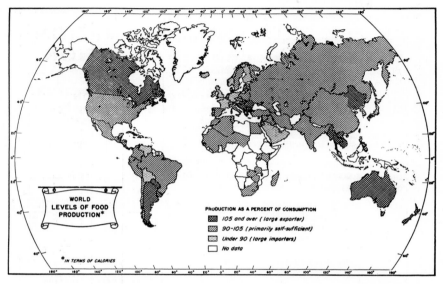

Figure 3.13. (U.S. Department of Agriculture, Office of Foreign Agricultural Relations)

products, and through their world trade in food products they are able to maintain a higher standard of living. The Office of Foreign Agricultural Relations should also have pointed out the surplus-rice-producing areas of densely populated southeast Asia and their interrelationship with Japan. However, these and other flows of international trade will be discussed later.

Significant comparisons of food production must be related to the needs of particular people. Food consumption, as shown in Figures 3.12 and 3.13, is a function of the amount available from production and is determined partly by consumers' ability to pay. Where food is cheap in terms of human effort or where industrial activity is high, food consumption is relatively high (2800 calories or above). Food consumption is also a function of the amount of work to be done, the heat provided by clothing and housing, the climate, the stature of people, and customs.

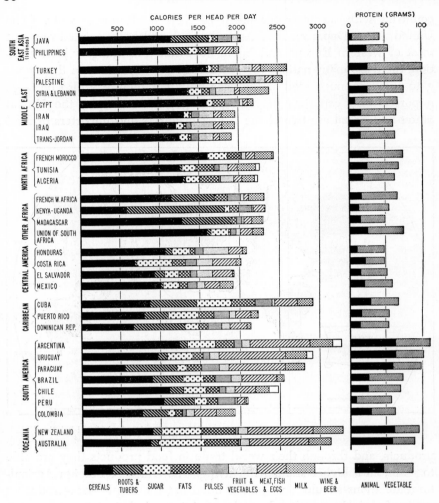

Figure 3.14. Prewar Food Supplies in Seventy Countries, per Head per Day at the Retail Level. (Data from *World Food Survey*, Food and Agriculture Organization of the United Nations, 1946)

The Food and Agriculture Organization of the United Nations undertook and published in 1946 a "World Food Survey" to compare actual food consumption with the needs of the different peoples of the world.

The FAO report covered the years just before World War II and included seventy countries, whose people made up about 90 percent of the earth's population. The food supplies (production plus imports minus exports) available were estimated and are summarized in Figure 3.14 in terms of calories per head of population daily by nine different food groups.

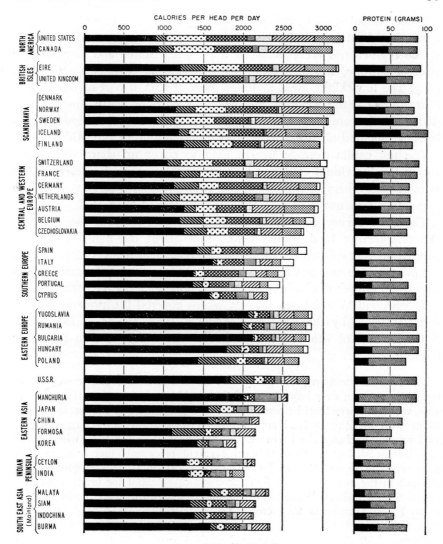

Figure 3.14—(Continued)

The tremendous variation in the dietary patterns of the seventy countries is obvious. The FAO study calculated that:

"In areas containing over half the world's population, food supplies at the retail level (not actual intake) were sufficient to furnish an average of less than 2250 calories per caput daily.

"Food supplies furnishing an average of more than 2750 calories per caput daily were available in areas containing somewhat less than a third of the world's population.

"The remaining areas, containing about one-sixth of the world's population, had food supplies that were between these high and low levels."

The high-calorie areas included the United States and Canada and most of Europe, Russia, Oceania, and Argentina, Uruguay, and Paraguay. The low-calorie areas included most of Asia, a part of the Middle East, all of Central America, and probably parts of South America and Africa which were not covered by the survey. The areas of greatest deficiency included all these areas with the exception of the Middle East.

The per capita average figures tend to cover up sharp differences within the individual countries as some people received more than the average and others less. Even in the United States a large part of the population was not well nourished before World War II.

The FAO survey concluded, after taking into account the different factors affecting food requirements, that about one-half the world's population was subsisting before World War II at a level of food consumption which was not high enough to maintain normal health, allow for normal growth of children, or furnish enough energy for normal work.

The Second World Food Survey, which covered the postwar period, was completed by the FAO in November, 1952. Norris E. Dodd, Director-General of the FAO, summarized the report in the following fashion:

The new information gives no ground for complacency. The average food supply per person over large areas of the world, five years after the war was over, was still lower than before the war. The proportion of the world's population with inadequate food supplies has grown appreciably larger. World food production has indeed expanded since the end of the war, when it fell to a low point, but much of this achievement represents merely a recovery from wartime devastation and dislocation. Clear signs of any far-reaching changes in the entire scale of food production, essential for improvement of nutrition on a wide scale are lacking. Annual increases in food production are barely keeping pace with the increasing population.

Figure 3.16 should be compared with Figure 3.15 to show the per capita food consumption in each nation during 1950–51 with revised consumption figures for the prewar period. Table 2, which was computed by the FAO from detailed information, compares the recent postwar with the prewar distribution of population according to national average supplies of calories and animal protein. This table covers about 80 percent of the world's population and the remainder of the population lives in areas where food supplies are deficient.

The prewar figures are in general agreement with the findings of the first World Food Survey. As indicated in Mr. Dodd's summary, the unsatisfactory prewar conditions, despite some gains in the early postwar years, had grown worse. In most of the Far East, where almost one-half of the world's population lives, the decline in food availability was about 10 percent. Like reductions occurred in North Africa and in a number of the Near Eastern countries. In most countries in western and northern Europe, average calorie supplies were back to prewar levels, but in parts of southern, eastern, and central Europe, the serious war-time declines had not been overcome. On the other hand, the high pre-

TABLE 2. Distribution of Population According to National Average Supplies of Calories and Animal Protein

Calorie Supplies and Animal Protein	Percent of Total Population[a]	
	Prewar	Recent Postwar
Calorie Levels		
Over 2700	30.6	27.8
2700–2200	30.8	12.7
Under 2200	38.6	59.5
Animal Protein Levels		
Over 30 grams	22.1	17.2
30–15 grams	18.9	24.8
Under 15 grams	59.0	58.0

[a] Comprising approximately 80 percent of the world's population.
SOURCE: *Second World Food Survey*, FAO, 1952, p. 11.

war calorie levels in North America and Oceania were continuously maintained and in most of Latin America, especially in the River Plate countries, there was a steady and substantial improvement. Therefore, not only had there been a substantial fall in the average calorie supply for the world, but the gaps between the better- and worse-fed nations had widened.

The unavailability of adequate food supplies to over half the people of the world is the fundamental agricultural problem. Looked at from an overall standpoint, the existence of this situation becomes much more difficult to understand when one learns that one of the most serious agricultural problems in the United States is "overproduction," so called. As previously indicated in Mr. Dodd's summary remarks, the Second World Food Survey showed no clear signs of any far-reaching changes in the entire scale of food production essential for the improvement of nutrition.

The Second World Food Survey presents detailed data for the area, yield, and production of the world's major food crops by regions for

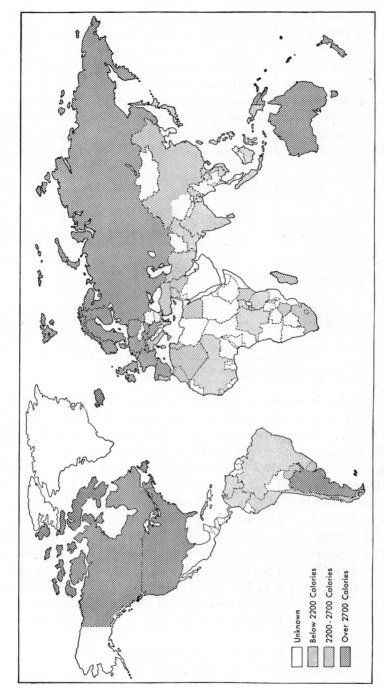

Figure 3.15. Per Capita Food Consumption, Prewar. (Data from *The State of Food and Agriculture: Review and Outlook, 1952*, FAO, p. 20)

Unknown

Below 2200 Calories

2200 - 2700 Calories

Over 2700 Calories

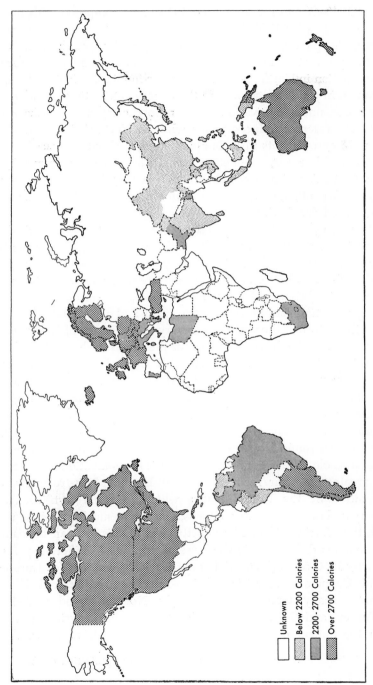

Figure 3.16. Per Capita Food Consumption, Postwar. (Data from *The State of Food and Agriculture: Review and Outlook, 1950,* FAO, p. 21)

Unknown

Below 2200 Calories

2200 - 2700 Calories

Over 2700 Calories

the years 1946–47 and for the period 1949–51 as compared with prewar years. The figures for 1946–47 show the results of the war: a serious decline in grain, potato, and sugar production in Europe, the greatly reduced rice production in the Far East, and the tremendous increase in grain production in North America and sugar in middle Central America. The changes in yields per acre were the major contributing factors rather than the area under cultivation. In Europe shortages of fertilizer and depleted soil reserves reduced yields while in North America mechanization and improvements in techniques brought about increased yields. The pattern of livestock production was similar to that for crops. However, in South America livestock production was increased greatly as wheat from Argentina, which normally would have gone into export markets, was used for feed.

The first two years, 1946–47, following the end of the war marked the low point in the world food position, and it was during these years that the United States accepted as its primary responsibility export of food, especially wheat and rice, to the deficient areas of western Europe and Japan. Since 1946–47 the situation for the world has improved, but agricultural production has been "uneven, fitful and inadequate."[4]

A concise picture of the postwar recovery and progress of food production per capita in the different regions of the world is shown in Table 3. Only in Oceania, Africa, and North and Central America had food production kept pace with the increased population. The decreases in South America were due to declines in production in Argentina, where government policy favored increased industrialization at the expense of agriculture. The pattern of postwar recovery for most countries within each region was found by the FAO study to be the same as that for the region as a whole. The major exception to this generalization was Europe.

The greatest postwar recovery was in Europe. This recovery was greatly aided by the United States, which provided fertilizer, farm machinery and other agricultural needs, and the means to purchase these through the Marshall Plan. The effectiveness of this aid can be seen in the tremendous differences in the rates of progress in different parts of Europe. By 1950–51 in the OEEC countries (Organization for European Economic Cooperation: Austria, Belgium-Luxembourg, Denmark, France, Western Germany, Greece, Ireland, Italy, Norway, Sweden, Switzerland, Turkey, and the United Kingdom) as a whole, agricultural production for human consumption was 11 percent above prewar. The

[4] *Second World Food Survey,* Food and Agriculture Organization of the United Nations, 1952, p. 4.

division of Austria and Germany into different zones of occupation delayed recovery. Production in Western Germany has risen rapidly in
recent years, but in Austria agricultural output in 1950–51 was more
than 10 percent below and livestock production 20 percent below pre-

TABLE 3.   Indices of Total and per Caput Production of Food Crops[a]

Region	Average 1946 and 1947		Average 1949 to 1951	
	Total	Per Caput	Total	Per Caput
	Prewar = 100			
Europe	71	68	96	90
North and Central America	143	124	150	124
South America	106	87	93	72
Far East	93	85	99	87
Near East	103	91	115	95
Africa	110	96	125	105
Oceania	104	94	116	103
World (excl. U.S.S.R.)	100	91	111	97

[a] Eight principal crops (wheat, rye, barley, oats, maize, rice, sugar [raw], and potatoes) converted to wheat
equivalent (calorie based). Although the above table does not take into consideration crops like millets and
sorghum, pulses, sweet potatoes and other starchy roots, of importance in certain areas of the Far East,
Africa, and Latin America, nevertheless about 80 percent of the world's food supply in terms of calories
comes either directly or indirectly through animal products, from the crops included. It, therefore, gives a
useful indication of the trends in food production, region by region, in convenient summary form.
    SOURCE: *Second World Food Survey*, FAO, 1952, p. 4.

war levels. Food production in eastern Europe after the war was much
lower than in western Europe, and recovery in most countries in eastern
Europe was at a slower rate than in those of western Europe.[5]

In the underdeveloped areas progress after 1946–47 was very slow. In
the Far East average production of rice in 1949 and 1950 was 2.5 percent below prewar while the increase in population was 10 percent.
This is a problem of tremendous concern since rice normally constitutes
70 percent of the food supply in terms of calories. The situation is made
worse since much of this increase in production was brought about by
expanding the area in rice at the expense of the area planted to industrial crops. The situation was similar for coarse grains such as millets
and sorghum, and for pulses. Appreciable increases were made in the
production of starchy roots, such as sweet potatoes and yams. Japan had
a record postwar output of sweet potatoes. This was a reflection of a
difficult food situation as farmers frequently turn to these crops as a
means of alleviating a food shortage since they can be produced quickly
and in abundance at a low cost.

The postwar shortage of food, raw materials, and foreign exchange
stimulated programs for the development of the African territories.

    [5] *Ibid.*, p. 5.

Faced with the loss of other sources of supply, the United Kingdom directed its policies toward Africa. However, development programs had more effect on exports such as fats, coffee, and cotton, and high prices probably caused concentration in these commodities at the expense of subsistence production. Africans producing cash crops benefited to some extent by increased cash incomes, but except where they were protected by price stabilization and other marketing arrangements, the profits largely accrued to the merchants.[6]

In Latin America, except in Argentina, where production was greatly below prewar, agricultural output was increased by expanding the area under cultivation. With the exception of Argentina, food production appears to have expanded faster than population. However, for the region as a whole the food supply is still inadequate. High prices for a number of important minerals and other raw materials and for the export crops coffee, cocoa, and sugar have sporadically expanded foreign earnings and intensified demand for machinery and consumer goods. One of the principal postwar problems of the region has been waves of prosperity, followed by depletion of exchange reserves and repeated imposition of exchange controls to achieve equilibrium in the balance of payments. Meanwhile, over the years the food export surplus of Latin America steadily dwindles.[7]

In the food surplus regions of the world the high levels of food production developed during and right after the war have continued in all areas except Argentina. Table 4 shows how production in the United States,

TABLE 4.   Indices of Agricultural Production in the United States,
Canada, and Australia

Countries	Average of 1946–47 and 1947–48	Average of 1949–50 and 1950–51
	Prewar = 100	
United States	128	131
Canada	119	130
Australia	99	112

SOURCE: FAO, *Yearbook of Food and Agricultural Statistics, Production, 1950* and *1951*.

Canada, and Australia stood out in contrast to the slow development in other areas. The FAO Second World Food Survey concluded that North America responded with great resilience to the expanding food needs of its own increasing population and that:

[6] *Ibid.*, p. 6.
[7] *Ibid.*, p. 7.

It has also pursued a policy of maintaining food reserves for exports to other parts of the world where underproduction has been a feature of the post war years. The far-sightedness of this policy, in the face of fears of unsaleable surpluses sometimes expressed in various quarters, has been fully justified by events. It is not difficult to imagine how catastrophic the plight of the world might have been in the absence of these food reserves. At the same time, the remarkable succession of abundant harvests in this region, even though partly due to favorable weather, is eloquent testimony of the efficacy of mechanization, soil conservation, research, and the application of scientific practices in raising the entire scale of food production.

A summary for each country's food production comparing 1949–50 with 1934–38 and for the postwar changes between 1946–47 and 1949–50 is given in Figures 3.17 and 3.18. The evidence presented by the Second World Food Survey and by these figures does not show encouraging results in the postwar recovery of global production and consumption of food. The question today is the same one that was before the governments of forty-four nations when they met in Hot Springs, Virginia, in May, 1943, at the organizational conference of the FAO to find an answer to the age-old riddle of surplus and starvation. "Can the real needs of human beings for food ever be brought into balance with the real capacity of modern agriculture to produce?" The situation was summarized in April, 1953, by Gove Hambidge, FAO's North American Regional Representative. The statement might be entitled "We Are Two Worlds":

What we can be sure of is this: The world has long been divided into two parts.

We have a half-world of plenty, inhabited by the people of countries like the United States, Canada, Australia, New Zealand, and most of Western Europe.

We have a half-world of hunger and want, inhabited by the people of most of Asia and the Middle East, practically all of Africa, and large parts of Latin America.

We know too that since the war world food production has increased by 9 per cent, while the number of people has grown by 13 per cent. So there is less food for each person than there was before the war; and there was not enough then, by quite a long way.

The lag since the war has been in the half-world of want, which makes a bad situation worse. The tide of hunger has been creeping up on tens of millions of human beings.

In the half-world of plenty, where you and I live, production has continued to keep ahead of population growth, so that on the average we are now even better off than we were before. And we did not do too badly then.[8]

[8] *Memo*, North American edition, Food and Agriculture Organization, Vol. 1, No. 2, April, 1953, p. 1.

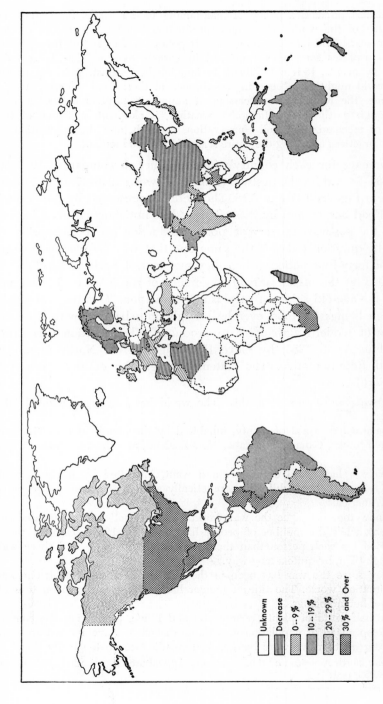

Figure 3.17. Increase in Food Production Above Prewar. Average 1949–50 compared with 1934–38. (Data from *The State of Food and Agriculture: Review and Outlook, 1952*, FAO, p. 12)

Unknown

Decrease

0 -- 9%

10 -- 19%

20 -- 29%

30% and Over

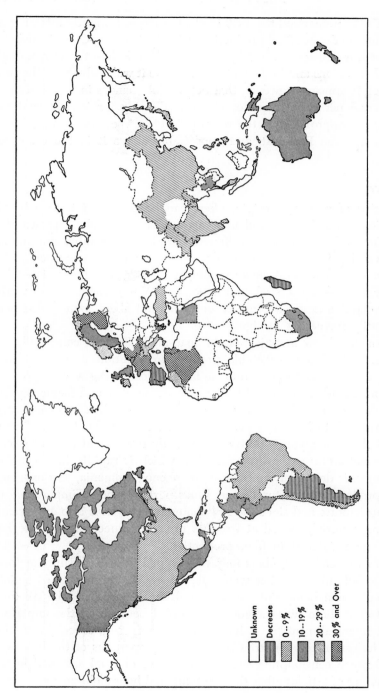

Figure 3.18. Postwar Increase in Food Production. Average 1949–50 compared with 1946–47. (Data from *The State of Food and Agriculture: Review and Outlook,* 1952, FAO, p. 14)

Unknown

Decrease

0–9%

10–19%

20–29%

30% and Over

The FAO summarized the 1956 food situation in a slightly more favorable light: "Per caput food production in Latin America, Oceania and the Far East was still some 5 to 10 percent less than before the war, though in all other regions and in the world as a whole it was well above the prewar level. It appears, however, that because of changes in the pattern of trade actual per caput supplies of food, allowing for imports and exports, are at approximately the pre-war level in Western Europe, Latin America and the Far East, and appreciably above it in the other regions."

2. Fibers

In terms of source of origin, fibers can be divided into two broad categories—natural fibers and man-made fibers. Natural fibers are produced from a large variety of different material of vegetable and animal origin. Of these the FAO has determined the following nine fibers to be of major economic significance: cotton, wool, silk, flax, hemp, jute, and the hard fibers—abacá, sisal, and henequen. While nine-tenths of world fiber production is still accounted for by natural fibers, man-made fibers are steadily increasing in significance.

The range of raw materials of the man-made fibers is continually increasing. Animal and vegetable proteins in addition to minerals are used in the production of man-made fibers. Most of the world's production of man-made fibers consists of rayon staple fiber and filament yarn. Rayon data on a global basis include acetate, which a few years ago was permitted to have a separate nomenclature in the United States. The cellulose for rayon is derived principally from wood pulp and to a lesser extent from cotton linters. Nylon, which is rapidly increasing in importance, is derived from benzene or phenol, ammonia, and oxygen.

The production of natural fibers ranks next to food in importance to world agriculture and since the raw material of rayon is also an agricultural raw material, looked at from its broadest aspects agriculture has the dominant interest in fiber production.

In terms of end uses, fibers may be grouped into (1) mainly apparel and household fibers: cotton, wool, silk, flax, rayon and nylon; (2) mainly industrial fibers: hemp, jute, abacá, sisal, and henequen. The dividing line between these two categories is blurred because all the important apparel fibers also are used for industrial purposes; especially is this true in industrialized countries where large proportions of the total cotton and rayon consumption and a minor share of wool are used in the manufacture of articles other than clothing and household goods. In spite of the arbitrariness of this classification, the FAO has found this to be a convenient working tool for analyzing broad trends in world production and consumption of fibers. The FAO has made most significant contributions in the study of the world's fibers in its first three and continuing reports.[9] According to the FAO's studies "apparel and household" fibers account for about 80 percent of the physical volume of world fiber production, and if the data were on a value basis, the share of the apparel and household group would be considerably larger because it includes the more expensive fibers.

Not only is fiber production vital to the agricultural economy, but textiles made from fibers generally rank second after food in consumers' expenditures. In the case of fibers, however, it is not possible, as it is with food, to draw up a general pattern of requirements and to balance against these present and potential production. However, important data have been developed by the FAO on per capita consumption.

Table 5 gives world per capita consumption of cotton, rayon-acetate, and wool for 1938 and 1952–54. World per capita consumption of the three fibers in 1954 was almost 19 percent greater than the pre-World War II 1938 average. The United States has been the leading consuming country and in 1954 used 33.3 pounds per capita as compared with 26.2 pounds in 1938; however, the 1954 consumption represented a decline from 37.8 pounds in 1953.

A similar decline took place in Canadian per capita use of these fibers, the 1954 figure of 23.0 pounds being 4.6 pounds or 17 percent below that for 1953; this decline put Canada in a tie with New Zealand for fourth place in the world picture, marking an interruption in Canada's steady growth in per capita fiber consumption from 19.4 pounds in 1938 to 27.6 pounds in 1953. In second place was the United Kingdom, whose per capita use increased by 15 percent to the 1954 figure of 26.5 pounds. In third place was Australia with a per capita fiber usage of 25.6 pounds.

In two sections of the world besides North America there have been notable increases in per capita fiber consumption. The level for Africa rose from 2.9 pounds in 1938 to 4.5 pounds in 1954. And in eastern Europe the per capita use was up from 9.0 pounds in 1938 (U.S.S.R. average only) to 12.3 pounds in 1954, an increase of 37 percent. However, the eastern European figure was still below the per capita use in geographically comparable areas; for example, in western Europe the per

[9] See *World Fiber Survey*, Food and Agriculture Organization, 1947; *World Fibers Review*, FAO Commodity Series, No. 9, Food and Agriculture Organization, 1948; *Fibers, World Fiber Review*, FAO Commodity Series Bulletin, No. 14, Food and Agriculture Organization, August, 1949.

TABLE 5. Pounds per Capita Consumption of Cotton, Wool, and Rayon (incl. Acetate)

Continent and Country	Cotton 1938	1952	1953	1954	Wool 1938	1952	1953	1954	Rayon 1938	1952	1953	1954	Total Cotton, Wool, and Rayon 1938	1952	1953	1954
Western Europe:																
Austria	9.2	6.4	4.8	6.2	2.9	1.8	2.4	2.4	0.9	5.9	4.8	5.5	13.0	14.1	12.1	14.1
Belgium-Luxembourg	10.3	9.7	7.3	8.4	4.0	4.0	3.3	2.9	1.1	2.6	3.5	4.2	15.4	16.3	14.1	15.4
Denmark	10.1	9.9	10.6	10.3	3.7	4.6	5.3	5.1	1.3	2.4	2.9	3.1	15.2	16.9	18.9	18.5
Finland	9.9	11.9	8.8	9.7	3.1	4.2	3.7	4.6		3.5	3.5	4.2	13.0	19.6	16.1	18.5
France	10.6	11.0	9.9	11.7	4.4	3.5	4.0	4.0	1.3	2.6	3.3	3.3	16.3	17.2	17.2	18.7
German F.R.[a]	7.5	8.1	9.5	10.8	3.1	3.1	3.1	3.7	7.0	5.9	6.2	6.4	17.6	17.2	18.9	20.9
Greece	6.4	6.6	7.3	7.7	2.2	2.2	3.1	2.2	0.1	0.9	1.1	1.5	8.6	9.7	11.4	11.4
Iceland		7.3	9.5	9.5		2.4	3.5	3.7		2.4	5.5	5.9		12.3	18.7	19.1
Irish Republic	5.1	3.7	5.5	4.8	3.7	2.9	4.8	4.0	0.9	1.5	2.4	2.4	9.7	8.1	12.8	11.0
Italy	4.6	6.8	6.8	7.3	0.4	2.2	2.0	1.5	3.3	2.0	2.2	2.9	8.4	10.8	11.0	11.7
Netherlands	12.3	8.6	11.7	12.8	3.7	3.3	4.2	4.8	1.5	3.1	4.0	4.6	17.6	15.2	19.4	22.3
Norway	9.5	9.5	10.3	11.0	4.0	5.1	5.5	5.3	0.4	3.3	3.5	4.8	13.9	18.0	19.8	21.1
Portugal	5.1	7.3	6.6	6.2	1.5	1.1	1.3	1.1	0.1	1.3	1.5	1.8	6.6	9.7	9.2	9.0
Spain	3.1	4.8	5.5	5.1	0.9	1.3	1.3	1.3	0.1	2.4	2.4	3.1	4.0	8.4	9.2	9.2
Sweden	12.1	10.6	10.7	12.5	4.2	3.5	5.5	4.6	2.0	3.5	4.6	5.1	18.3	17.8	21.8	22.3
Switzerland	11.4	14.7	10.8	14.5	3.5	4.0	5.5	5.3	1.5	2.0	1.3	2.0	16.5	20.7	17.6	21.8
United Kingdom	16.9	13.0	10.3	14.1	7.0	4.6	6.4	5.7	2.2	3.7	6.2	6.6	26.2	21.1	23.0	26.5
Yugoslavia	5.5	3.7	3.1	2.9	1.8	1.1	0.9	0.9		0.9	0.7	1.1	7.3	5.9	4.6	5.1
Average	8.4	8.8	8.4	9.7	2.9	3.1	3.5	3.3	2.4	3.1	3.7	4.2	13.6	14.7	15.8	17.2
Eastern Europe and U.S.S.R.[b]	7.5	6.4	8.9	8.6	1.3	0.9	1.1	1.3	0.2	2.0	2.2	2.4	9.0	9.2	11.7	12.3
North America:																
Canada	14.1	15.4	16.5	13.2	3.7	3.5	4.6	3.5	1.5	6.2	6.4	6.2	19.4	25.2	27.6	23.0
United States	21.6	26.9	27.2	24.3	2.2	3.3	3.3	2.6	2.4	7.0	7.3	6.4	26.2	37.5	37.8	33.3
Average	20.9	25.8	26.1	23.2	2.4	3.3	3.5	2.6	2.2	7.0	7.0	6.4	25.5	36.2	36.7	32.3
Central and South America:																
Argentina	10.1	14.5	10.1	10.8	3.3	3.5	2.9	3.5	0.4	1.4	0.9	1.3	13.9	19.4	13.9	15.6
Bolivia		2.2	1.5	1.3		2.2	2.2	2.2		0.4	0.3	0.7		4.8	4.0	4.2
Brazil	7.7	7.0	6.8	7.5	0.4	0.7	0.4	0.7	0.2	0.9	1.3	1.3	8.4	8.6	8.4	9.5
British West Indies	4.4	3.3	4.0	3.3	0.2	0.2	0.2	0.2	0.7	1.8	2.0	2.4	5.3	5.3	6.2	5.9
Chile	6.2	5.7	7.3	8.4	1.8	3.1	2.9	2.9	0.7	1.5	1.3	1.8	8.6	10.3	11.4	13.0
Colombia	4.2	4.8	5.3	5.5	0.4	0.7	0.4	0.7	0.2	0.9	1.3	1.3	4.8	6.4	7.0	7.5
Costa Rica		4.2	5.7	5.9		0.2	0.4	0.4		2.0	1.8	1.5		6.4	7.9	7.9
Cuba	6.4	6.2	4.6	3.3	0.4	0.1	0.1	0.1	0.7	4.0	1.9	5.0	7.5	10.3	6.6	8.4
Ecuador	4.0	3.5	3.3	2.3	0.2	0.1	0.1	0.1		0.4	0.3	1.3	4.2	4.0	3.7	3.7
El Salvador	4.2	3.7	4.8	4.4		0.1	0.1	0.1		0.4	0.8	1.0	4.2	4.2	5.7	5.5
Guatemala	4.0	3.7	3.3	3.1		0.1	0.2	0.2		0.2	0.2		4.0	4.0	3.7	3.3
Mexico	6.4	5.3	5.5	5.3	0.2	0.2	0.7	0.4	0.7	1.5	1.1	1.6	7.3	7.0	7.3	7.3
Nicaragua		5.1	5.1	5.7		0.4	0.7	0.9		0.7	0.6	0.4		6.2	6.4	7.0
Peru	2.6	3.3	3.3	4.0	1.3	0.9	0.9	1.3	0.1	0.4	0.4		4.0	4.6	4.6	5.3
Uruguay	5.1	5.5	5.7	8.6	1.1	4.6	3.1	4.6	0.9	2.9	3.7	1.3	7.0	13.0	12.5	14.5
Venezuela	3.3	4.2	6.2	6.2	0.2	0.4	0.7	0.7		2.9	2.1	1.5	3.5	7.5	9.0	8.4
Average[f]	6.2	6.4	5.9	6.4	0.9	0.9	0.9	0.9	0.4	1.1	1.3	1.5	7.5	8.6	8.1	8.4

TABLE 5. Pounds per Capita Consumption of Cotton, Wool, and Rayon (incl. Acetate) (Continued)

	Cotton				Wool				Rayon				Total			
	1938	1948	1953	1954	1938	1948	1953	1954	1938	1948	1953	1954	1938	1948	1953	1954
Asia:																
Burma	3.3	2.6	3.5	4.0	—	0.1	0.1	0.2	—	0.1	0.3	0.2	3.3	2.6	4.0	3.5
Ceylon	2.2	4.6	2.9	4.0	0.1	0.1	1.5	1.1	0.1	0.1	1.1	0.9	2.9	4.6	4.0	4.0
China, including Manchuria	3.1	3.5	2.9	3.5	…	0.1	…	…	0.1	0.1	…	…	3.7	3.5	3.5	3.7
Cyprus	5.9	8.4	5.9	9.0	1.3	0.9	1.3	1.8	0.1	1.3	0.2	0.2	…	8.4	9.0	9.0
India[b]	4.4	2.0	2.2	4.6	0.1	0.2	0.1	0.2	0.1	0.1	0.2	0.4	4.2	2.0	4.6	4.6
Indochina	1.3	3.3	2.2	1.8	0.2	0.2	0.2	0.2	0.2	0.1	0.2	0.2	2.2	3.3	2.0	1.8
Iran	3.7	3.5	4.0	2.9	2.9	2.2	2.2	2.9	0.2	2.2	1.8	4.0	4.8	3.5	2.9	3.5
Iraq	7.9	7.5	3.5	8.6	0.2	0.9	1.3	2.0	0.4	1.3	1.8	3.1	8.1	7.5	8.6	9.9
Israel	9.5	6.6	6.8	9.7	0.9	1.5	1.1	4.6	0.9	0.4	3.3	4.8	7.0	6.6	9.7	12.3
Japan	1.5	12.3	8.4	14.5	…	0.4	0.4	1.3	1.3	0.1	4.7	4.3	20.2	12.3	14.5	15.4
Jordan	2.9	…	1.1	3.1	…	…	0.1	0.4	…	…	2.0	3.1	…	…	3.1	3.5
Korea	9.0	2.6	2.2	2.6	…	…	3.5	1.8	…	…	0.9	2.0	5.7	2.6	2.6	3.5
Lebanon[d]	4.4	13.6	8.1	12.1	…	2.2	2.2	0.2	…	0.2	0.1	0.2	…	13.6	12.1	15.4
Malaya	4.3	6.4	3.1	4.2	1.1	1.1	1.3	4.6	1.3	1.1	1.3	5.3	5.3	6.4	4.2	6.6
Pakistan[e]	7.0	3.7	5.7	2.0	2.2	2.0	2.2	0.2	2.0	0.2	0.2	0.2	…	3.7	2.0	6.3
Syria[d]	…	10.1	5.7	11.4	…	…	6.2	8.1	…	…	12.1	8.4	12.1	10.1	11.4	13.4
Turkey	7.0	8.4	6.4	8.8	…	2.0	0.2	8.1	…	…	…	9.2	8.1	8.4	8.8	9.2
Average[f]	4.2	4.4	3.7	4.6	0.2	0.2	0.4	0.7	0.2	0.2	0.4	0.4	4.8	4.4	4.6	4.9
Africa:																
Algeria	2.6	4.6	3.3	4.0	0.4	0.7	0.7	0.9	0.2	0.7	0.9	0.9	4.4	4.6	4.2	4.2
Angola	2.9	…	3.2	3.1	0.1	0.1	0.1	0.1	…	…	…	0.7	…	…	2.6	3.1
Anglo-Egyptian Sudan[c]	3.3	4.0	3.3	4.0	0.4	0.4	0.4	0.7	…	0.2	0.4	0.7	3.3	4.0	5.9	4.0
Belgian Congo[c]	2.4	2.9	2.4	3.3	0.1	0.2	0.2	0.4	—	0.1	0.1	0.4	1.8	2.9	2.6	3.3
British East Africa	2.6	3.1	2.2	3.3	0.1	0.2	0.2	0.7	0.4	0.2	0.4	0.9	1.5	3.1	2.4	3.3
Egypt	6.2	7.7	6.4	7.3	1.8	1.8	1.8	0.9	0.7	1.8	0.9	0.9	6.2	7.7	7.7	7.3
French Morocco	3.5	6.4	4.0	6.2	0.1	0.1	0.1	0.9	…	0.4	0.9	0.2	5.9	6.4	6.6	6.2
French Cameroons	2.4	…	1.5	2.2	0.1	0.1	0.1	0.2	…	0.7	0.2	0.5	…	…	2.2	2.9
Madagascar and Reunion	3.5	2.6	2.0	3.3	0.1	0.1	…	…	…	…	…	1.3	3.5	2.6	3.3	4.0
Mauritius	4.2	…	2.9	6.4	0.2	…	…	…	…	…	…	…	…	…	6.4	5.7
North Rhodesia and Nyasaland	3.3	1.8	3.1	…	0.9	0.2	0.2	0.7	…	…	0.2	0.7	…	1.8	{4.0}	…
Southern Rhodesia	} 3.1	6.6	} 5.7	4.6	0.9	0.2	0.7	0.7	…	0.9	0.7	0.7	6.8	6.6	4.0	4.6
Spanish Morocco	1.5	5.7	1.8	2.6	1.8	1.5	0.4	0.4	0.2	0.2	0.4	0.4	5.9	5.7	2.6	2.6
Tunisia	3.3	6.8	3.1	5.3	0.7	1.8	1.5	4.2	0.7	0.7	1.8	3.1	6.2	…	5.3	5.3
Union of South Africa	5.6	6.8	5.1	11.9	1.5	1.8	1.8	…	…	…	…	…	…	6.8	9.9	11.9
Average[f]	3.3	3.7	3.1	4.0	0.3	0.3	0.3	0.9	0.2	0.2	0.4	0.2	2.9	3.7	4.0	4.5
Oceania:																
Australia	13.2	27.6	13.0	25.6	7.5	7.5	4.4	4.8	…	…	3.7	4.8	19.8	27.6	13.0	25.6
New Zealand	10.8	23.0	14.5	23.0	10.1	9.2	7.5	2.9	…	…	1.8	2.9	11.9	23.0	14.5	23.0
Average[f]	10.3	21.3	11.5	20.7	6.4	6.6	6.6	3.7	…	…	2.6	3.7	14.5	21.3	11.5	20.7
World Average	6.8	8.8	6.6	9.3	0.9	0.9	0.9	1.8	1.0	0.9	2.6	1.8	8.1	8.8	9.3	9.6

(. . .) not available.   (—) nil or negligible.   [a] 1938 figures are for Syria and Lebanon combined.   [b] 1938 figure for India and Pakistan combined.   [c] Includes Ruanda-Urundi.   [d] 1938 figures are for Syria and Lebanon combined.   [e] 1938 figure for India and Pakistan combined.   [f] Including countries not listed separately by FAO or omitted by IWS on the grounds that no estimates have been made of wool consumption.

Note.—Due to rounding, the figures for the separate items may not add up to the totals shown. Many estimates for 1953 have been revised; all 1954 figures are provisional.
Source: *Textile Organon*, November, 1956.

capita use of cotton, wool, and rayon increased steadily to the 1954 figure of 17.2 pounds. This was a general increase shared by the majority of the western European nations itemized.

Examination of the table shows that only ten of the nations of the world consume more than 20 pounds of textile fibers per head, eighteen countries consume 10 to 19.9 pounds each, and the remaining forty-two nations have an annual per capita consumption of less than 10 pounds. While an important reason for this disparity is the geographical location of certain nations, a comparison of data for adjoining or comparable areas points up the great variance in living standards involved. The overall figures reflect the fact which all studies show—that fiber consumption is a function of income rather than need.

Most of the vegetable fibers are produced between 35° North and 25° South latitude. This generalization is true in the case of all cotton culture except that of the U.S.S.R., northern China, and Argentina. It applies to jute and abacá, which are grown only in tropical areas, and to sisal, which is cultivated principally in Tanganyika, Kenya, Indonesia, Portuguese Africa, and the West Indies. The exceptions to the general latitude rule are flax and hemp, which are mainly European crops.

Vegetable fiber production tends to be concentrated in specific geographic areas partly because of exacting climatic and soil requirements. Except where modified by irrigation, the area of potential cotton cultivation is determined by requirements of a 200-day frost-free growing season, with adequate rains, and dry weather during harvesting. Similarly the growth of almost all the world's jute in the Ganges is partially explained in that jute requires very fertile, sandy loams, warm weather, and abundant moisture for growth. Abacá needs fairly rich well-drained soils and a continuously warm, moist, tropical climate. However, the geographic concentration of these and other vegetable fibers is furthered by the necessity of abundant and comparatively low-paid workers for the cultivation, harvesting, and separation of leaf and stalk. Many of these fibers still have processing problems of equal complexity to that which prevailed in cotton before the invention of the cotton gin.

In the case of the animal fibers, cheap labor is the limiting factor in the concentration of silk production in Japan. Wool production, however, is largely concentrated in sparsely populated countries with an abundance of land.

Location of the production of man-made fibers is concentrated in consuming areas, and the manufacturing requires large capital investment. The plants are located in the major industrialized countries with available capital, advanced technology, adequate power and chemicals. Individual site locations are determined by additional considerations of labor availability, etc. In the case of rayon and acetate manufacture, the principal raw material, high-alpha-content cellulose, is becoming less of a natural limiting problem as the range of raw materials is widened. With the increased production of nylon and other nonagricultural raw material man-made fibers, it is possible that natural factors will become even less significant in limiting areas of production.

World production of fibers for 1934–38, 1947–48, and 1948–49 are given in Table 6. These data substantiate previous remarks made on the im-

TABLE 6. World Production of Fibers, Prewar, 1947–48, and 1948–49[a]

Fiber or Fiber Group	Quantities			Index			Distribution	
	1934–38	1947–48	1948–49[b]	1947–48	1948–49[b]	1948–49[b]	1934–38	1948–49[b]
	Thousand metric tons			1934–38 = 100		1947–48 = 100	Percent	
1. Cotton	6,651	5,513	6,281	83	94	114	56	57
2. Wool (clean)	943	928	948	98	101	102	8	9
3. Raw silk	54	13	13	24	24	100	1	—
4. Flax	790	350	450	44	57	129	7	4
5. Hemp	454	267	345	59	76	129	4	3
6. Jute	1,875	1,568	1,391	84	74	89	15	13
7. Hard fibers[c]	522	456	483	87	92	106	4	4
8. Rayon filament yarn	446	595	706	133	158	119	3	6
9. Rayon staple fiber	186	308	417	166	224	135	2	4
10. Nylon[d]	—	20	30	—	—	150	—	—
Total	11,921	10,018	11,064	84	93	110	100	100
Natural fibers (1–7)	11,289	9,095	9,911	81	88	109	95	90
Man-made fibers (8–10)	632	923	1,153	146	182	125	5	10
Mainly apparel and household (1–4 and 8–10)	9,070	7,727	8,845	85	97	114	77	80
Mainly industrial (5–7)	2,851	2,291	2,219	80	80	97	23	20

[a] Data for cotton, wool, and jute relate to production seasons; those for silk, flax, hemp, hard fibers, rayon, and nylon to calendar years.
[b] Preliminary figures.
[c] Abacá, sisal, and henequen.
[d] Approximate estimates.
SOURCE: *World Fiber Review, 1949*, Commodity Series Bulletin, No. 14, FAO, p. 3.

portance of natural fibers and the apparel and household uses of fibers. They also show the continued importance of cotton, jute, and wool and the doubling of significance of rayon. Figure 3.19 and the supporting data in Table 7 are not strictly comparable with Table 6, but they give the most recent information on the major textile fibers. The increases in production are clearly indicated, as is the expansion of the man-made fibers from 14 percent of the six fiber total in 1949 to 21 percent in 1955. Of the total world production of rayon and acetate in 1955 of 5,017,000,-000 pounds, the United States' share was 1,260,700,000 and that of Europe was 2,682,100,000. Japan was second to the United States with

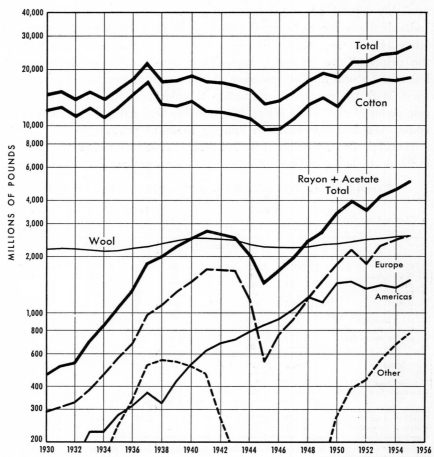

Figure 3.19.   World Production of Four Textile Fibers. (Data from *Textile Organon*, June, 1956, p. 85)

732,100,000 pounds, and Western Germany produced 486,500,000 pounds.

Changes in production of fibers by continents are indicated in Table 8. Sixty percent of all fibers is produced in North America and Asia. Record cotton production and continued high level of rayon output in the United States raised fiber production in North America in 1948–49 to 129 percent of prewar and to 35 percent of the world total as compared with 25 percent during 1934–38. In Asia, however, output of fibers in 1948–49 was only 64 percent of 1934–38 owing to small cotton crops, a poor jute crop in Pakistan, a reduced abacá output in the Philippines, and slow rates of recovery from the drastically curtailed wartime production

TABLE 7. World Production of Six Textile Fibers[a]

Year	Millions of Pounds									Percent of Total[b]				
	Man-Made Fibers					Cotton	Wool	Silk	Six Fiber Total	Man-Made	Cotton	Wool	Silk	Total
	Rayon+Acetate			All Other	Total									
	Yarn	Staple	Total											
1946	1,112	581	1,693	NA	NA	9,675	2,088	38	13,494	13	72	15	—	100
1947	1,308	671	1,979	NA	NA	11,160	2,100	41	15,280	13	73	14	—	100
1948	1,549	901	2,450	NA	NA	13,105	2,160	44	17,759	14	74	12	—	100
1949	1,638	1,064	2,702	NA	NA	14,310	2,219	47	19,278	14	74	12	—	100
1950	1,926	1,567	3,493	149	3,642	12,840	2,302	42	18,826	20	68	12	—	100
1951	2,119	1,891	4,010	220	4,230	16,445	2,339	47	23,061	19	71	10	—	100
1952	1,835	1,735	3,570	269	3,839	16,520	2,540	55	22,954	17	72	11	—	100
1953	2,081	2,062	4,143	332	4,475	17,990	2,554	54	25,073	18	72	10	—	100
1954	2,037	2,451	4,488	414	4,902	17,725	2,607	54	25,288	20	70	10	—	100
1955	2,296	2,721	5,017	562	5,579	18,600	2,730	59	26,968	21	69	10	—	100

NA means not available.

[a] The man-made fiber and silk data are on a calendar year basis, while the cotton and wool figures are shown seasonally.

[b] The man-made fiber percentages of total for 1946–49 are figured on the rayon+acetate data only.

Cotton: Data are from the New York Cotton Exchange Service.

Wool: Data are from the Commonwealth Economic Committee (London), clean basis.

Silk: Data for 1946 and 1947 are our estimates, 1948 from the Food and Agriculture Organization of the United Nations, and 1949 forward from the International Silk Association (France) except that the 1955 data are partly estimated by us.

SOURCE: *Textile Organon*, June, 1956, p. 84.

TABLE 8.World Fiber Production by Continents, Prewar, 1947–48, and 1948–49[a]

Continent	Index: 1934–48 = 100		Percentage of World Total		
	1947–48	1948–49 (Prelim.)	1934–38	1947–48	1948–49 (Prelim.)
Natural Fibers[b]					
Europe	76	94	4	4	5
U.S.S.R.	61	64	14	10	10
North America	93	116	25	29	33
Latin America	105	118	9	11	11
Asia	72	65	38	34	28
Africa	85	108	7	8	9
Oceania	106	112	3	4	4
World	81	88	100	100	100
Synthetic Fibers[c]					
Europe	123	155	52	44	44
U.S.S.R.	87	425	1	1	3
North America	345	396	21	51	48
Latin America	656	750	1	2	2
Asia	10	21	25	2	3
Africa	—	—	—	—	—
Oceania	—	—	—	—	—
World	146	182	100	100	100
Total Fibers					
Europe	95	119	7	8	9
U.S.S.R.	61	66	13	9	9
North America	105	129	25	31	35
Latin America	107	120	8	10	10
Asia	70	64	37	31	25
Africa	85	108	7	7	8
Oceania	106	112	3	4	4
World	84	93	100	100	100

[a] Data for cotton, wool, and jute relate to production seasons; those for other fibers to calendar years.
[b] Cotton, wool (clean), silk, flax, hemp, jute, abacá, sisal, henequen.
[c] Rayon filament and staple fiber, nylon.
SOURCE: *World Fiber Review, 1949,* Commodity Series Bulletin, No. 14, FAO, p. 5.

of hard fibers in Indonesia and of rayon manufacture and sericulture in Japan. Europe produces an extremely small share of natural fibers— 5 percent—in relation to its importance as a consumer. This deficiency is made up in part through the production of man-made fibers, of which Europe produced 44 percent of the world total in 1948–49 and about 50 percent in 1955. The production of natural fibers in the U.S.S.R. was only 64 percent of prewar owing to a decline in cotton production and the reduced size of the postwar flax and hemp crops. Oceania, though the leading producer of apparel wool, continued in 1948–49 to produce the smallest share of the world natural fiber output by volume.

The significance of the United States in the world fiber economy is shown in Table 9. In the production of natural fibers the United States' share of the world total increased from 25 percent during 1934–38 to 29 percent in 1947–48 and 33 percent in 1948–49. During the same years, the United States' percentage of consumption changed from 19 to 29 to 25. This indicates a total increase in the United States' share of production and consumption and shows that the United States is a net exporter of natural fibers. In the case of the synthetic fibers, the United States' share of the world's total in both production and consumption increased in almost the exact order of magnitude of 2½ times from the prewar to the postwar periods, i.e., from approximately 20 to 50 percent.

The data in Table 9 are quite helpful in summarizing the United States' position in the world fiber picture with respect to the individual fibers. However, such a summary table is not adequate to present even the minimum facts that bear on the problems of production and consumption of these fibers. But it does show that the United States was during the prewar period and has continued to be the predominant producer and consumer and exporter of cotton. It shows that the United States consumption of wool doubled while the balance of the world demand remained the same. The United States consumes approximately 30 percent of the wool. United States imports of wool increased 350 percent. On the other hand, United States consumption of silk in 1948, while four times as great as in 1947, was still only 13 percent of what it was during the prewar period.

One of the most significant facts presented in Table 9 is that the production of rayon staple fiber increased 64 percent in all countries outside the United States while the increase within the United States was tremendous, from 100 prewar base to 2033 during 1948. This increase is most noteworthy in that, since staple fiber is mixed with and substituted for natural fibers, it is indicative of a technological trend of interfiber competition.

There are numerous problems in connection with production potentialities that require study and policy determination on an individual commodity basis. The discussion which follows in the section on "The United States and International Agricultural Trade" will provide an opportunity to give supplementary detailed information on cotton and wool, the two major natural fibers produced in the United States. For the moment we should note that the production of domestic wool has been decreasing and imports have been increasing. For the other major fiber the Department of Agriculture Joint Committee on Agricultural Productive Capacity concluded that a sustained United States

TABLE 9. The United States in the World Fiber Economy

Period	Index: 1934–38 = 100			U.S. as % of World	Period	Index: 1934–38 = 100			U.S. as % of World
	U.S.	All Others	World			U.S.	All Others	World	
	Cotton: Production					Rayon filament: Production			
1934–38	100	100	100	41	1934–38	100	100	100	27
1947–48	94	75	83	47	1947	282	79	133	57
1948–49[a]	118	78	94	52	1948[a]	323	98	158	55
	Cotton: Consumption					Rayon staple: Production			
1934–38	100	100	100	22	1934–38	100	100	100	3
1947–48	146	84	98	32	1947	1,733	113	166	34
1948–49[a]	121	85	93	29	1948[a]	2,033	164	224	31
	Cotton: Exports					All rayon: Consumption			
1934–38	100	100	100	42	1934–38	100	100	100	21
1947–48	43	93	72	25	1947	338	91	143	50
1948–49[a]	90	82	85	44	1948[a]	392	120	178	48
	Wool: Consumption					Jute: Consumption[b]			
1934–38	100	100	100	17	1934–38	100	100	100	15
1947	203	97	115	30	1947–48	126	69	77	24
1948[a]	201	102	119	28	1948–49[a]	111	73	78	21
	Wool: Imports					Jute: Imports[b]			
1934–38	100	100	100	11	1934–38	100	100	100	18
1947	308	112	135	26	1947–48	112	61	70	28
1948[a]	355	101	130	31	1948–49[a]	111	65	73	27
	Silk: Consumption					Hard fibers: Consumption[c]			
1934–38	100	100	100	50	1934–38	100	100	100	29
1947	3	30	17	7	1947	127	65	83	45
1948[a]	13	48	30	27	1948[a]	103	78	85	35
	Silk: Imports					Hard fibers: Imports[c]			
1934–38	100	100	100	66	1934–38	100	100	100	30
1947	4	21	10	25	1947	127	51	74	51
1948[a]	9	29	15	33	1948[a]	115	64	79	44

United States as Percentage of World Total

	Production	Consumption	Exports	Imports
	Percent			
Natural fibers[d]				
1934–38	25	19	25	10
1947–48	29	29	14	18
1948–49[a]	33	25	28	17
Synthetic fibers[e]				
1934–38	20	21	—	16
1947–48	50	51	13	19
1948–49[a]	47	50	8	16

[a] Preliminary.
[b] Including jute manufactures.
[c] Abacá, sisal, and henequen.
[d] Cotton, wool, silk, jute, abacá, sisal, henequen.
[e] Rayon filament and staple, nylon.
SOURCE: *World Fiber Review, 1949*, Commodity Series Bulletin, No. 14, FAO, p. 10.

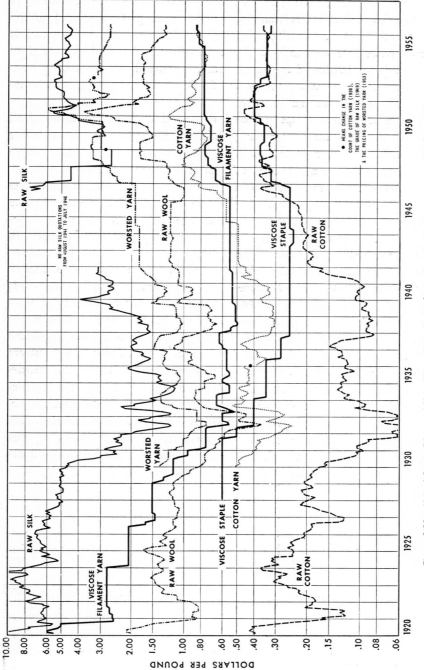

DOLLARS PER POUND

10.00
8.00
6.00
5.00
4.00
3.00
2.00
1.50
1.00
.80
.60
.50
.40
.30
.20
.15
.10
.08
.06

1920   1925   1930   1935   1940   1945   1950   1955

RAW SILK

VISCOSE FILAMENT YARN

WORSTED YARN

RAW WOOL

VISCOSE STAPLE

COTTON YARN

RAW COTTON

NO RAW SILK QUOTATIONS FROM AUGUST 1941 TO JULY 1946

● MEANS CHANGE IN THE
COUNT OF COTTON YARN (1938),
THE GRADE OF RAW SILK (1949),
& THE PRICING OF WORSTED YARN (1953)

Figure 3.20.   United States Fiber and Yarn Prices, Ratio Scale. (Data from *Textile Organon*, July, 1956, p. 104)

production of 17 million bales of cotton was possible with the use of 14 percent fewer man-hours than were used on a crop of about 15.3 million bales in 1951. A sustained production of this size would make possible considerable increases in both domestic consumption and exports. Production potentialities of cotton emphasize the need of encouraging cost-reducing practices and other ways of effectively competing with man-made fibers and foreign growths.[10]

The most important fact in considering production potentialities of all fibers is the increasing interchangeability of fibers as raw materials for the textile and other industries. Man has now reached the state where he can technically and economically produce fiber raw materials in accordance with the end use to which he wishes to put the fiber. As this development has gone forward in the man-made fibers, it has given these fibers a quality-wise competitive advantage. In addition, continual decreases in the viscose and acetate staple fiber prices and increases in raw cotton prices have put these commodities in the same price class. (See Figure 3.20.) The price of viscose staple became lower than that of raw cotton in 1946, and the price of viscose filament yarn has been less than that of cotton yarn since 1944. Further, the relative stability of man-made fiber prices is in sharp contrast to the fluctuation in prices of the natural fibers. This increasing interchangeability of fibers is an important factor not only in appraising the production potentialities of agriculture but also in indicating a source of fiber raw materials for the textile-processing industries where the dividing lines between the textile-processing industries classified on the basis of raw material used are becoming blurred. Cotton, wool, and silk are blended with rayon, nylon, and other new fibers on machinery formerly used for processing one specific type of raw material. At the same time, finished textile products are becoming increasingly specialized and diversified.

[10] *Agriculture's Capacity to Produce*, United States Department of Agriculture, Government Printing Office, June, 1952, p. 36.

CHAPTER 4

International Trade in Agricultural Products

THE SIGNIFICANCE OF INTERNATIONAL TRADE IN AGRICULTURAL PRODUCTS

For the most part, people throughout the world produce at home the foods they consume. This is to be expected because populations have grown in those areas in which the food supply would support them, and their dietary habits have been adjusted to the types of foods that are locally available. Therefore, food does not play as important a role in international trade as one might expect. However, where food does enter international trade, it is of critical importance to the importing countries and in many instances is a major source of revenue to the exporting country, e.g., sugar from Cuba and Java and coffee from Brazil.

International trade in foodstuffs consists principally of grains, meat, animal and vegetable fats and oils, sugar, and specialty commodities such as coffee, cocoa, bananas, fruit, vegetables, and wines. The grain trade is clearly divided into the intra-Asiatic trade in rice and wheat exported from the United States, Canada, Argentina, Australia, and other thinly populated areas to crowded western Europe and the United Kingdom. The meat trade, though not clear, increasingly is from the thinly populated lands of the Southern Hemisphere to the densely populated areas of western Europe and the United Kingdom. International trade in sugar consists more and more of the shipment of cane sugar from tropical or semitropical islands to industrial centers. Similar trade trends are observable in vegetable fats and oils.

International trade in fibers is of much greater importance than that in food. It is estimated that only about 6 percent of the world's food production crosses continental frontiers. In sharp contrast is the high ratio of world exports of fibers to world production. About one-half of the world's output of cotton and wool is normally exported from producing countries. Prewar raw silk exports represented 72 percent of world output and about 52 percent of all raw jute, and the bulk of world hard fiber production was shipped from countries of origin to foreign markets.[1]

The fact that fiber production is highly specialized and regionally localized has already been noted. The high degree of geographical concentration of the production of major fibers is shown in Table 10. It is clearly observable how a few countries export a very large percentage of

TABLE 10.   Shipments of Fibers from the Chief Exporting Countries as
Percentages of World Exports, 1934–38 Averages

Fiber	Chief Exporting Countries	Percentage of World Exports
Cotton	United States, India, Egypt, Brazil	84
Wool	Australia, Argentina, New Zealand, South Africa	80
Silk	Japan	77
Flax	U.S.S.R., Belgium	54
Jute	India	98
Abacá	Philippine Republic	95
Sisal	British East Africa	50
Henequen	Mexico	92

SOURCE: *World Fiber Survey*, FAO, 1947, p. 6.

the world's fibers. This is substantial proof of the interdependence of the world for natural fibers.

In addition, the dependence of individual countries on fibers is very great because of the importance of the fiber crops in the economies of the major export countries. Cotton, the major textile fiber, provides the principal source of cash income for millions of farmers in the different producing areas of the world. Average receipts from cotton and cottonseed in the United States during 1934–38 amounted to 40 percent of total cash receipts of farmers in the ten principal cotton states. Cotton exports represented 74 percent of the value of all Egyptian exports

[1] *World Fiber Survey*, Food and Agriculture Organization, 1947, p. 5.

during the prewar period and thus were essential to the Egyptian economy. Cotton exports are also of considerable importance to the agricultural prosperity of Brazil and of a large number of smaller cotton-producing countries. These percentages of cotton and other fiber exports to total exports by countries are shown in Table 11. Australia's income from exports of wool is greater than that for any other commodity. In South Africa and Uruguay, wool is the most important agricultural ex-

TABLE 11. Fiber Exports as Percentages of Total Exports,
by Countries, 1936–38

Country	Fiber Exports as Percentage of Total Exports
Western Hemisphere	
Brazil (cotton)	19
Peru (cotton)	23
United States (cotton)	11
Uruguay (wool)	46
Africa	
Egypt (cotton)	74
Kenya (sisal)	15
Nyasaland (cotton)	13
Sudan (cotton)	63
Tanganyika (cotton and sisal)	52
Union of South Africa (wool)	10
Asia	
China (cotton and silk)	13
India (cotton and jute)[a]	42
Japan (silk)	14
Philippines (abacá)	14
Australasia	
Australia (wool)	35
New Zealand (wool)	24

[a] Includes jute manufacturers.
SOURCE: *World Fiber Survey*, FAO, 1947, p. 6.

port, and in New Zealand wool is next in importance to butter and meat.[2]

Thus the significance of fibers in international trade has been established. Further summary evidence can be seen from the fact that during the pre-World War II period international trade in fibers accounted for more than 50 percent of all agricultural raw material exports and for about 25 percent of exports of all agricultural products.[3]

The volume of world trade in all agricultural products for the years 1949–50, 1950–51, and 1951–52 as a percentage of 1934–38 is given in

[2] *Ibid.*, pp. 5–6.
[3] *Ibid.*, p. 5.

TABLE 12. Index Numbers of Volume of Trade in Agricultural Products, 1949–52[a]
(1934–38 = 100)

Region	Exports			Imports		
	1949–50	1950–51	1951–52	1949–50	1950–51	1951–52
Agricultural Products[b]						
Europe[c]	56	68	65	90	91	89
North America	171	183	200	126	143	139
Latin America	94	96	84	152	181	159
Far East	68	82	84	74	89	101
Near East	111	129	107	216	234	241
Africa	122	127	125	125	131	145
Oceania	132	128	110	140	166	191
World[d]	97	105	102	96	103	103
Food						
Europe[c]	55	70	71	88	89	89
North America	268	282	335	92	100	98
Latin America	84	83	74	144	174	158
Far East	37	42	44	78	79	96
Near East	121	103	86	247	291	291
Africa	110	112	101	109	113	128
Oceania	116	118	95	143	163	140
World[d]	90	96	91	91	95	91
Aromatic Crops						
Europe[c]	58	50	54	86	83	91
North America	116	117	128	154	138	144
Latin America	125	105	110	140	130	146
Far East	94	88	100	68	81	86
Near East	217	156	160	161	146	155
Africa	147	158	166	130	145	147
Oceania	90	100	74	119	131	142
World[d]	115	124	112	110	124	112
Natural Fibers and Rubber						
Europe[c]	56	64	53	93	96	88
North America	92	105	91	146	199	184
Latin America	88	125	81	191	236	173
Far East	97	130	129	68	102	108
Near East	96	135	108	350	351	454
Africa	124	129	137	419	423	484
Oceania	148	138	124	173	238	365
World[d]	100	119	104	98	115	108

[a] In basic data for trade indices the same commodities are included as for production indices as far as international trade existed, and they have been weighted by corresponding or applicable uniform price weights.

[b] Trade data relate to calendar years, with the exception of wheat, rye, barley, maize, and oats where the data for trade season July–June beginning in the year stated have been used.

[c] European exports and imports include trade between eastern Europe and western Europe but exclude trade between the eastern European countries and the U.S.S.R. and between themselves for the most part. For some major commodities estimates have been made of intra-eastern European trade. This may slightly bias the European index. Unreported China trade 1949–51, partially estimated in the same way, may also affect the Far Eastern index. All other regions present a full trade coverage.

[d] Most of the inter trade between non-reporting countries is excluded (see footnote c).

SOURCE: *The State of Food and Agriculture: Review and Outlook, 1952*, FAO, p. 16.

Table 12 for all agricultural products and separately for food,[4] aromatic crops,[5] and natural fibers and rubber.[6]

The most striking feature of international trade in all agricultural products in the ten-year period after World War II was perhaps its relative stagnation. This was in marked contrast to international trade as a whole, which developed fairly rapidly during this period, exceeding the prewar level by some 25 percent as early as 1950 and 55 percent in 1954 (Table 13). Trade in food and feeding stuffs regained its prewar level only in 1951 and after that did not move up or down from the prewar level by more than 1 or 2 percent. After a peak in 1950 at the time of the Korean boom, world trade in natural fibers and rubber settled down at a level

TABLE 13. Volume of World Trade in Agricultural Products, 1946–54

Item	1946	1947	1948	1949	1950	1951	1952	1953	1954[a] Provisional
				1934–38 average = 100					
Food and feeding stuffs	73	80	87	93	90	103	98	102	100
Natural fibers and rubber	87	90	93	96	116	105	103	105	102
Beverages and tobacco	95	95	98	110	103	110	107	115	109
All agricultural products	80	85	90	96	100	105	101	104	102
Forest products	65	84	83	85	103	118	107	112	. . .
All items (agricultural and nonagricultural)[a]		100	103	111	125	140	138	148	155

[a] U.N. Index of world exports adjusted to 1937–38 base.   . . . Not available.
SOURCE: *The State of Food and Agriculture, 1955,* FAO.

some 3–5 percent higher than before the war. The beverages and tobacco group showed a rising trend, though much less steep than that for world trade generally. For agricultural products as a whole the level of world trade varied between 100 and 105 percent of the 1934–38 level in each year after 1950.

This lack of growth, particularly in the food and feeding stuffs sector, largely reflects the strong move toward a greater degree of self-sufficiency in agricultural products, whether for security, balance of payments, or other reasons. In the case of natural fibers and rubber it reflects also the increasing use of substitute materials. This means that trade in agricultural products was becoming a gradually decreasing part of world trade. Moreover, since the stagnant condition of trade contrasts with the steady expansion of agricultural production, it follows that production for export

[4] Food comprises wheat, rye, barley, oats, maize, millet and sorghum, rice, dry beans, dry peas, broad beans, chick peas, lentils, unspecified pulses, sugar, potatoes, sweet potatoes, vegetable oils, animal and marine fats and oils, and meat.

[5] Aromatic crops comprise cocoa, coffee, tea, and tobacco.

[6] Fibers and rubber comprise cotton, wool, jute, hard fibers, hemp, flax, and rubber.

is becoming a smaller sector of agricultural production as a whole. And therefore, producers of surplus agricultural commodities will find it more difficult to dispose of their products in the world market. The proportion of the world's agricultural output moving into international trade was of the order of 20 percent before the war and in 1955 was nearer 15 percent.

THE UNITED STATES AND INTERNATIONAL
AGRICULTURAL TRADE

The United States is the world's largest exporter of agricultural commodities and ranks in second place, next to the United Kingdom, as an importer. Imports of agricultural commodities in the Korean boom year of 1951 amounted to $5.16 billion, or approximately 50 percent of the total imports for that year. About one-half of these imports in 1951 of agricultural commodities may be classified as *complementary* to indicate that they are not similar to commodities produced commercially in the United States. Approximately 95 percent of the complementary imports consisted of rubber, coffee, cocoa beans, tea, spices, bananas, raw silk, and carpet wool. The other half of the 1951 agricultural imports consisted of commodities also produced in the United States. These are classified as *supplementary*. Agricultural exports from United States production in 1951 reached $4.04 billion or approximately 27 percent of total exports. Grains, cotton, and tobacco are the major export items.

The value of all United States exports and imports is given in Figure 4.1. The level of United States exports is normally limited by the amount of imports the United States accepts in payment. However, there have been major exceptions to this generalization. Exports rose to more than $4 billion over imports in World War I, when the excess was financed by liquidation of foreign-held dollar investments and by loans. In World War II the export surplus rose to more than $10 billion, fell off considerably at the end of the war, and then increased during the postwar reconstruction period. The recent export surplus was for the most part financed through United States foreign aid grants and loans under the lend-lease, UNRRA, Army Civilian Supply, British loan, and ECA programs.

United States foreign trade has grown tremendously in both value and volume above the pre-World War II level. United States exports in 1952 constituted 20 percent and imports 15 percent of the trade of the free world. Figure 4.1 shows clearly that since World War II the United

States has exported far more and imported more than before the war. The rest of the free world has become more dependent on the United States for necessary imports and for markets for its exports.

The United States' interest in world trade is tremendous. From 7 to 9 percent of the total United States production in movable goods is normally exported. This proportion reached a peak of 12 percent in 1947. Exports of foods and feedstuff rose from 12 percent of the total before World War II to 16 percent of the total in 1951. In 1951 United States

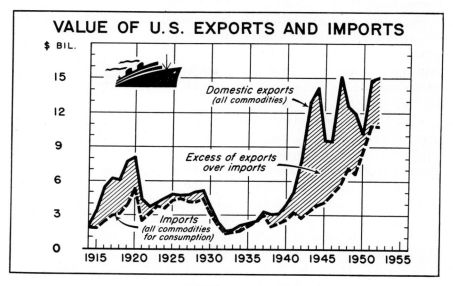

Figure 4.1. (U.S. Department of Agriculture)

agricultural exports of $4 billion were nearly one-eighth of total cash farm receipts and averaged about $1100 per commercial farm. During 1949–51 annual exports of the two leading field crops, cotton and wheat, were almost $1 billion each and averaged about one-third of the crop. A serious decline in agricultural exports would therefore necessitate far-reaching readjustments. Total exports of manufactures in 1951 amounted to over $10 billion and covered a wide range of manufactured goods, including industrial equipment, farm machinery, and manufacturing equipment. Exports of manufactures exceed 10 percent of production in quite a few major industries.

Imports are also vital to the United States economy. Almost 54 percent of United States imports in 1951 consisted of crude and semimanufactured materials. The significance of these imports other than those from agricultural sources will be considered later. For the present it will be helpful to note that many of the materials, such as crude rubber, tin, and industrial diamonds are not produced in this country. Others such as wool, lead, zinc, and copper are not produced in sufficient quantity to meet domestic requirements. The use of substitutes would mean decreased efficiency and increased cost.

Imports of crude and manufactured foodstuffs amounted to $3.1 billion in 1951; most important of these were coffee, cane sugar, and cocoa beans. Imports of finished manufactures, excluding manufactured foodstuffs, amounted to $1.3 billion. These consisted of a diversified collection of articles, only one of which—wool manufactures, including yarn— amounted to as much as $100 million. These imports provided consumers with a more varied pattern of consumption, and without them the United States' standard of living would have been lower and the cost of living higher.

Thus United States exports and imports increased tremendously. Europe, as well as other regions, has become more dependent on the United States for essential supplies because the world-wide expansion of industrial production and the increase of world population have not been accompanied by an equal expansion in the production of foodstuffs and raw materials in the non-dollar countries. Similarly, the United States has come to depend on the free world for larger markets for its agricultural and industrial products. In addition, the United States has come to depend on the free world for larger supplies of raw material and consumer goods. However, during the post-World War II period United States exports increased faster than imports and the dollar earnings of other countries and their receipts from investments have been insufficient to pay for their imports from the United States. From 1946 to 1952 the deficit of the rest of the world with the United States was $34 billion. About $4 billion of the deficit was met by the use of gold and dollar reserves and over $30 billion was met by United States aid. During 1952 increasing attention was being given to the elimination of the so-called "dollar shortage" through "trade not aid." The United States' great share in world trade was threatened because of the inability of other countries to earn enough dollars to pay for their imports. Enough introductory data have already been presented to show how detrimental this inability can be. Now let us examine in more detail the importance of international trade to agriculture.[7]

[7] The preceding paragraphs on the importance of international trade in general and the nature of the "dollar shortage" problem were in large part drawn from *A Trade and Tariff Policy in the National Interest,* Public Advisory Board for Mutual Security, February, 1953.

The volume of exports of United States agricultural products followed an upward trend after the Civil War and reached an all-time peak in 1918–19 but declined until 1940–41 when it was at the lowest point since 1869. It expanded during World War II to a peak in 1951–52 which was only 13 percent below the all-time record. The value of agricultural exports generally paralleled the volume except during the two world wars and the postwar periods, when value as a result of higher prices expanded faster than volume. The $4043 million in 1951–52 was a fiscal year record. Figure 4.2 shows these trends. It also shows the low volume and

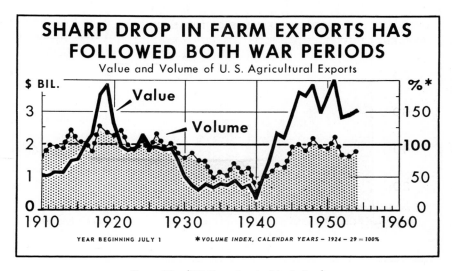

Figure 4.2.   (U.S. Department of Agriculture)

value of agricultural exports during the depression of the thirties and after the imposition of the Smoot-Hawley Tariff of 1930. Nations cannot buy from us when we refuse to buy from them. Because of agricultural producers' share and interest in exports, they have understood that international trade is a two-way street and have advocated low tariffs.

Agriculture's share of the value of total United States exports has declined fairly steadily. Before 1890 agricultural exports consisted of about 80 percent of the total. By 1910 these exports had dropped to 50 percent and they were only 9 percent of the total in 1940. Under the impact of the war and United States aid programs they increased to 35 percent in 1945 and since then have averaged between 25 and 30 percent. This long-run downward trend, which is shown in Figure 4.3, is an indication of the increased industrialization of the United States and of the rising share of industry in the export trade. The increased interest on the part of industry in exports has given rise during the post-World War II period to industrial support for the removal of restrictions to trade.

United States interdependence in agricultural products with the many areas of the world may be studied by reference to the series of Figures 4.4–4.9. Figure 4.4 presents the destination and origin of United States exports and imports. The most significant trends that can be observed are the tremendous increase in the share of our agricultural exports that western Europe, excluding the U.K., took during 1946–51 over the prewar

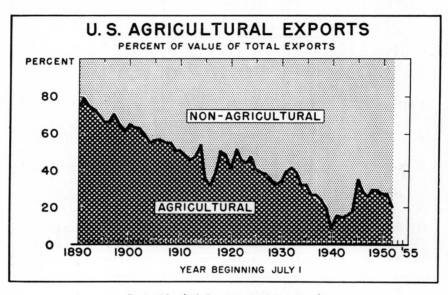

Figure 4.3. (U.S. Department of Agriculture)

period and the declining share that went to the U.K. Asia and Oceania also increased their imports of our agricultural exports. United States exports to western Europe and the U.K. in 1950 and 1951 were over 50 percent of our total exports, but they represented substantially less than the prewar percentage and that of early postwar years. The reduced shipments to continental Europe after 1948 were a result of European recovery and less U.S. aid. The smaller postwar share to the U.K. was a result of the dollar shortage and other U.K. financial and economic problems. Postwar exports of cotton to Japan and grain to India increased the share of agricultural exports going to Asia and Oceania. United States import figures reflect our dependence on Asia and Oceania and the Western Hemisphere both before and after the war. Almost 90 percent of our agricultural imports originated in these regions.

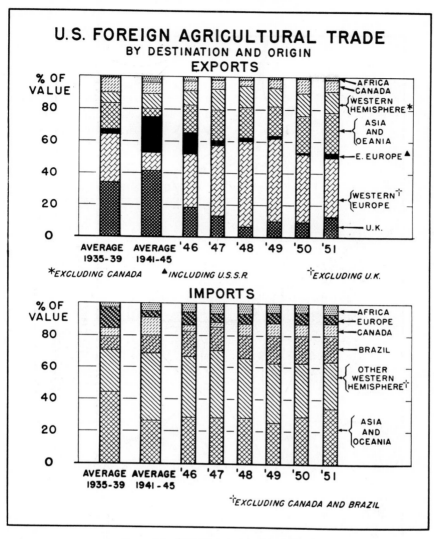

Figure 4.4. (U.S. Department of Agriculture)

Figures 4.5 and 4.6 offer a means of comparing the prewar and postwar flows of United States agricultural imports. During the prewar period 1935–39 the United States imported $1199 million of agricultural products annually. About $475 million of these imports originated in the Far East and about $420 million in Latin America. Only $150 million came from Europe. Canada, Africa, and India each accounted for smaller values. The total value of agricultural imports in 1951 was $5164 million or

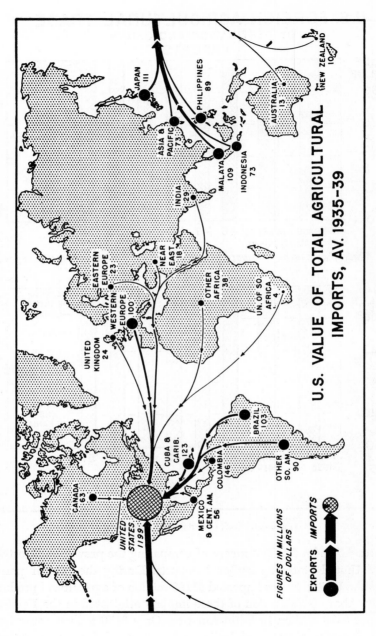

Figure 4.5. (U.S. Department of Agriculture)

U.S. VALUE OF TOTAL AGRICULTURAL
IMPORTS, AV. 1935–39

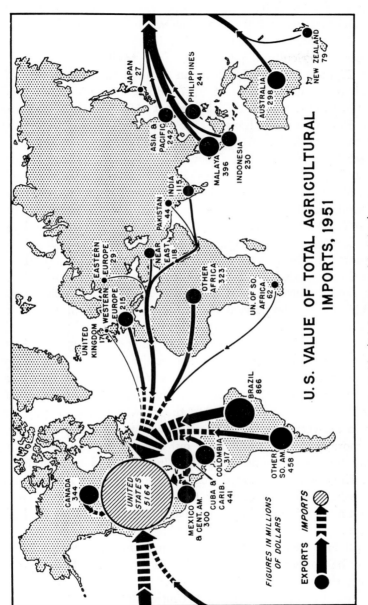

U.S. VALUE OF TOTAL AGRICULTURAL IMPORTS, 1951

Figure 4.6.   (U.S. Department of Agriculture)

approximately four and one-third times the $1199 million prewar figure. The value of agricultural imports from Latin America increased 470 percent and there was a 220 percent increase in the value of those coming from the Far East. The Near East and India also became more important as sources of agricultural imports.

From Figures 4.7 and 4.8 one can observe that the United States exported an annual average of $747 million of agricultural products during the prewar period 1935–39. About $500 million of this amount went to Europe, which through time has been the largest market for United States agricultural exports. The United Kingdom was our most important European market, followed by France, Germany, and the Netherlands. As Europe supplied us with only $150 million of agricultural imports, other sources of dollars had to be found to pay for the excess of agricultural purchases over sales to this country. During the prewar period 1935–39 a little more than $100 million of our agricultural exports went to the Far East, and Japan received $74 million of this total.

In contrast to the prewar period, in 1951 total United States exports of agricultural products of $4040 million were more than five times the prewar figure. Our eastward shipments to Europe, Africa, and the Middle East were 400 percent above the prewar amount and westward shipments to the Far East were up 440 percent. United States agricultural exports to Latin America increased 880 percent. Europe continued to be our largest market with a value of more than $2000 million of agricultural imports. As our agricultural imports from Europe were only about $261 million in 1951, Europe had to find $1739 million each year as compared with $350 million during the prewar period to pay for the difference between our agricultural exports to and imports from her. Of the more than $2000 million of our agricultural exports to Europe, Germany took $501 million and the United Kingdom imported $366 million. Thus Germany jumped from third to first place in our European market, whereas before the war the United Kingdom was our most important market followed by France and Germany and the Netherlands in Europe.

These data for United States agricultural import and export trade in 1951 may be compared with the total 1954 flow of this trade by country and value through study of Figure 4.9.

In contrast to $5.16 billion in 1951, United States imports of all agricultural commodities during the fiscal year 1955–56 amounted to $4.8 billion or only 33 percent of the total value of all commodities imported. Supplementary agricultural imports in 1955–56 were only about 39 percent of agricultural imports.

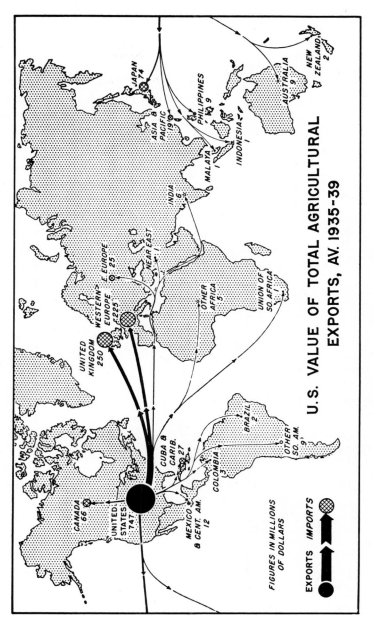

FIGURES IN MILLIONS
OF DOLLARS

EXPORTS IMPORTS

U.S. VALUE OF TOTAL AGRICULTURAL
EXPORTS, AV. 1935-39

Figure 4.7.   (U.S. Department of Agriculture)

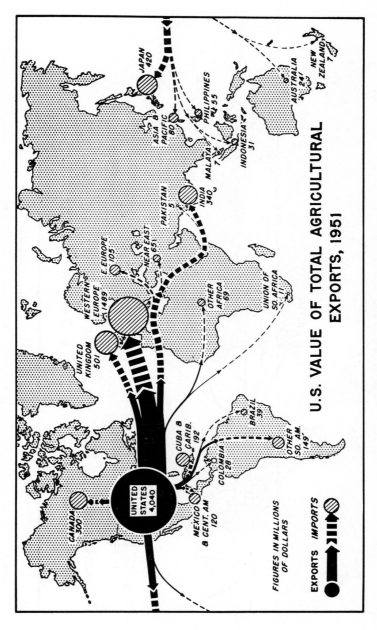

U.S. VALUE OF TOTAL AGRICULTURAL
EXPORTS, 1951

Figure 4.8. (U.S. Department of Agriculture)

90

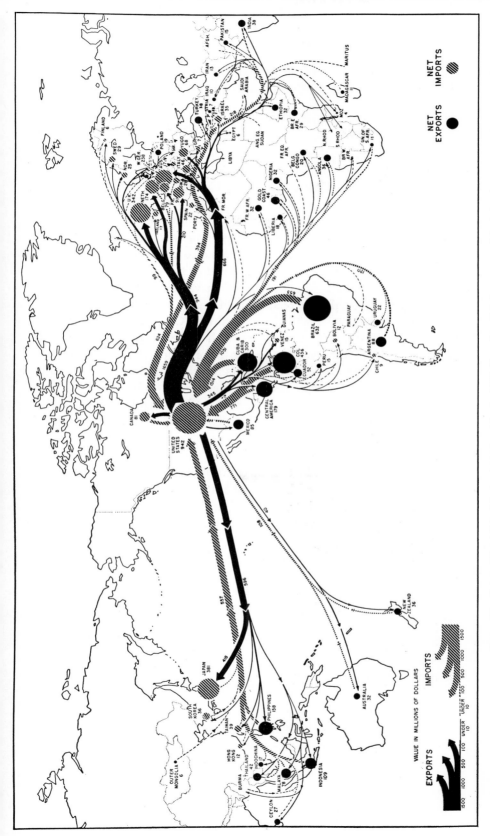

Figure 4.9.   Value of Total United States Agricultural Trade, 1954. (Data from U.S. Department of Agriculture)

United States exports of all agricultural products for the fiscal year 1955–56 amounted to $3.49 billion as compared to $4.04 billion in 1951.

The export market picture in 1955 as seen from Figure 4.10 was quite different from that of 1951. Japan was the best customer for United States farm products during these four years. She was second to the United Kingdom in 1951 and to West Germany in 1949 and 1950. In 1955 Japan was followed by the United Kingdom, Canada, the Netherlands, and West Germany.

United States agricultural exports to Japan totaled about $400 million a year for the five years. Dollar earnings from special procurement and troop spending associated with the maintenance of United States security forces in Japan helped to support this level of trade. Shipments of farm products to the United Kingdom gained in value after a sharp cutback in 1952 due principally to relaxation of many import controls which discriminated against United States products. Canada exports many of the same products as the United States; however, because of our geographic position south of Canada, we have an expanding market for fruits, nuts and vegetables. Shipments of these products to Canada constitute nearly half of their United States farm imports and half of total United States exports of fruits, nuts, and vegetables to the world. United States exports of grain to the Netherlands increased because a large part of this was feed for the intensive livestock operations. Agricultural exports to West Germany in 1955 were second lowest since the war, principally because of reduction in cotton purchases. Larger shipments in earlier years were helped by United States aid. West Germany, alone among the top five markets, received large amounts of commodities donated to private welfare agencies for assistance of eastern European refugees.

Thus the interdependence of the United States in agricultural products with the many areas of the world has increased since the prewar period. Agriculture and the United States interest in the world market as an importer and exporter of agricultural products is greater now than ever before.

On the import side, the United States has a vital stake because of her dependence on certain agricultural imports that cannot be produced commercially in this country and; in addition, the United States and agriculture are concerned with those agricultural imports that supplement domestic supplies. The United States has an interest as a consumer and the agricultural producer is worried about the competition. On the export side, foreign markets contribute substantially to the income of the agri-

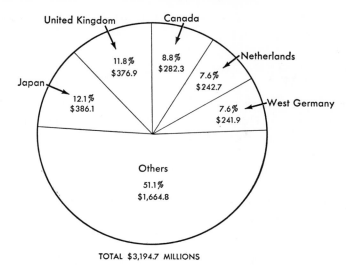

TOTAL $3,194.7 MILLIONS

Figure 4.10. United States Farm Exports by Countries, 1955. (Data from U.S. Department of Agriculture)

cultural producer. Let us consider these problems in some detail in the order enumerated.

1. Import Interests

Imports of agricultural products are compared with total United States imports in Figure 4.11. Agricultural imports have followed about the same

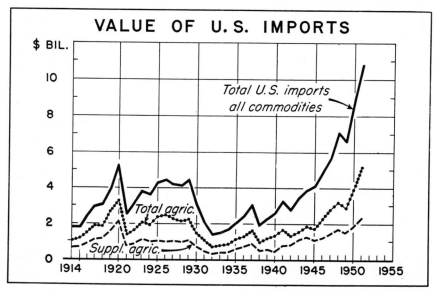

Figure 4.11. (U.S. Department of Agriculture)

pattern as total imports over the years 1914–51. The latter reached peak levels in three periods of high business activity and relatively high national income after the two world wars and during the 1920's. The big increase of agricultural imports during the 1920's was due to imports of silk and rubber. On the average, about 50 percent of agricultural imports has been complementary products which are not produced commercially in the United States. This shows the United States' dependence on outside sources. Since agricultural imports were 50 percent of total United States imports in 1951, the share of complementary agricultural imports represented 25 percent of total United States imports.

A. Complementary Products—Rubber and Coffee

As previously indicated, 95 percent of these agricultural imports which we could not produce commercially at home consisted of rubber, coffee, raw silk, cocoa beans, carpet wool, bananas, tea, and spices. Rubber and coffee have been quantitatively the most important of these necessary imports.[8]

Rubber

It took the tragedy of Pearl Harbor to bring home to the United States the vital role that rubber played in the economy of the United States and her 100 percent dependence on outside sources. Table 14 presents world natural and synthetic rubber production by countries from 1935 through 1956. Before World War II, the Far East was the source of 98 percent of all natural rubber. When Japan captured Malaya, the Netherlands East Indies, Siam, and Indochina, these vital sources of supply were lost, and the United States was forced to build plants which could produce materials to substitute for natural rubber.

After World War II a major policy decision had to be made by the United States in terms of continued operation of the synthetic rubber plants and the extent to which natural rubber would be relied upon in the future. This was a problem that required very careful and thoughtful study because both national and international interest were concerned.

The national policy on synthetic rubber plants was established with the Rubber Act of 1948, which stated:

It is the policy of the United States that there shall be maintained at all times in the interest of the national security and common defense, in addition

[8] See *Farm Products in Foreign Trade,* United States Department of Agriculture, 1953, Table 22, pp. 25–27, for the value of principal agricultural imports into the United States, 1939–50, by classification, complementary and supplementary.

TABLE 14. World Rubber Production
(in thousands of long tons)

	Natural												Synthetic			
Year	Ceylon	India	Indochina	Indonesia	Malaya	Sarawak	Other Asia	Africa	Brazil	Other Latin Amer.	Oceania	World Total	Canada	Germany	United States	World Total
1935–39 av.	59	14	50	351	392	21	46	11	14	5	1	964	—	75	1	8
1940–44 av.	99	17	69	309	280	17	35	33	22	14	2	897	8	85	206	298
1945	98	16	12	10	9	—	2	54	24	23	2	250	46	N.A.	820	866
1946	94	16	20	175	404	9	33	47	24	16	1	838	51	16[a]	740	807
1947	89	16	38	278	646	37	80	39	26	9	1	1,260	42	8[a]	509	559
1948	95	15	44	432	698	40	128	42	20	9	1	1,525	40	3[a]	488	532
1949	90	16	43	433	672	39	125	45	21	6	1	1,490	47	—	394	440
1950	114	16	48	696	694	56	152	55	19	8	2	1,860	58	1[a]	476	535
1951	105	17	52	814	605	42	144	73	21	9	3	1,885	62	5[a]	845	908
1952	97	20	63	750	584	32	134	74	26	9	2	1,790	74	6[a]	799	878
1953	99	21	75	695	574	24	125	77	26	9	4	1,728	81	7[a]	848	936
1954	94	21	78	739	584	23	147	85	22	6	4	1,803	87		623	716
1955	94	22	93	734	639	39	163	98	22	6	4	1,913	104	11[a]	970	1,085
1956	95.4	23.4	87	686.7	627.4	40.7	166.5	102	23	6	3.9	1,873	120.7	11[a]	1,079.6	1,211

[a] Western Germany only.
SOURCE: Rubber Study Group, *Commodity Year Book*, 1956 and 1957.

to stock piles of natural rubber which are to be acquired, rotated and retained pursuant to the Strategic and Critical Materials Stockpiling Act (Public Law 520, 79th Cong., approved July 23, 1946), a technologically advanced and rapidly expandible rubber-producing industry in the United
States of sufficient productive capacity to assure the availability in times of
national emergency of adequate supplies of synthetic rubber to meet the essential civilian, military, and naval needs of the country. It is further declared to be the policy of the Congress that the security of the United States
can and will best be served by the development within the United States
of a free, competitive, synthetic rubber industry. In order to strengthen national security through a sound industry it is essential that Government ownership of production facilities, Government production of synthetic rubber, regulations requiring mandatory use of synthetic rubber, and patent pooling be
ended and terminated whenever consistent with national security, as provided
in this act.

To carry out this policy, the act authorized the President to exercise
controls over rubber materials and their use in rubber products. Furthermore, the President was empowered to continue the operation of government-owned rubber-producing facilities until the Congress enacted additional legislation permitting the development of a synthetic rubber
industry in private hands under conditions consistent with the national
security. Machinery for disposing of the synthetic rubber plants was
authorized by the first session of the 83rd Congress in 1953.

The Rubber Act of 1948 authorized the issuance of regulations to insure
the consumption in the United States of (1) general-purpose synthetic
rubber in a specified percentage of the combined total estimated annual
consumption of natural rubber and general-purpose synthetic rubber, and
(2) special-purpose synthetic rubbers in specified percentages of the
combined total estimated annual consumption of natural rubber, general-
purpose synthetic rubber, and special-purpose synthetic rubbers consumed within the United States. These percentages were to be established to assure the production and consumption of the various types of
synthetic rubbers in quantities necessary to carry out the policy of the
act and the stockpiling provisions of Public Law 520, 79th Congress. The
act also provided that the minimum percentages established should result
in the consumption of at least the following total annual tonnages of
synthetic rubbers: (1) 200,000 long tons of general-purpose synthetic
rubber, and (2) 21,667 long tons of special-purpose synthetic rubbers, of
which at least 15,000 long tons shall be of a type suitable for use in
pneumatic inner tubes.

The act also provided that any mandatory consumption in excess of
the amount required to carry out both the policy of the act and opera-

tions under Public Law 520 should not be more than is deemed to be necessary in the interest of national security and the common defense.[9]

Thus the Rubber Act of 1948 established a policy in the national interest which also took into consideration our international obligations to the natural-rubber-producing countries whose economic and political stability is so dependent on rubber and is so vital to the security of the United States.

Before World War II the International Rubber Regulation Agreement of 1934 was in effect. The agreement was participated in by France, the United Kingdom, India, the Netherlands, and Siam and thus covered virtually the whole world of production. It was revised and renewed in 1938, continued in 1943 by the United Kingdom, India, and the Netherlands, and came to an end in 1944. The scheme operated through export quotas, and a considerable measure of price stability was achieved. This control scheme was strenuously opposed by United States buyers of natural rubber. By 1944 the producers of natural rubber were no longer in a position to dominate the world market for rubber because of the new synthetic capacity in the United States, so they were quite willing to work with the United States in the formulation of postwar international policy. As a result, in 1945 a Rubber Study Group was established by the Netherlands, the United Kingdom, and the United States. France later joined the group in 1947. The group has met periodically and has provided a forum for government representatives to discuss problems relating to the production or consumption of rubber, or to international trade in rubber. The secretariat of the group has regularly published statistical information, and at its meetings the Rubber Study Group has discussed the statistical position of rubber and its implications and has issued its estimates of the world supply-and-demand position for the year.

Table 15 gives the rubber production and consumption for the United States and the world as forecast by the International Rubber Study Group.

Restrictions on rubber consumption were in effect in the United States in 1951, but nevertheless it can be seen that in 1951 and 1952 natural rubber consumption was about 37 percent of our total consumption. United States restrictions were that at least 510,000 tons of synthetic rubber (450,000 GR-S and 60,000 butyl) must be consumed. Natural rubber was still obtained from the same prewar sources and was preferred and required for many uses. Therefore natural rubber continued to be a

[9] *Rubber*, First Annual Report by the Secretary of Commerce, United States Department of Commerce, 1949, pp. 3–4.

"strategic and critical material." "Strategic and Critical Materials are those raw or semi-processed materials that are required for essential uses in a war emergency, and whose procurement in adequate quantities, quality or time is sufficiently uncertain for any reason to require prior provision for their supply." Table 15 shows that the estimated world excess production over consumption of all rubber in 1952 of 280,000 tons was much smaller than that in the previous year. For natural rubber, it was 244,000 tons as against 386,000 tons. Looked at from the United States national point of view, this might appear to have been unfavorable, but from the international point of view, it was deemed favorable. How-

TABLE 15.   Rubber: Production and Consumption—United States and World Total

Year and Area	Production			Consumption		
	Natural	Synthetic	Total	Natural	Synthetic	Total
	Thousand Metric Tons					
1951						
United States	—	859	859	462	771	1,233
World	1,910	923	2,833	1,524	828	2,352
1952						
United States	—	838	838	472	803	1,275
World	1,717	925	2,642	1,473	889	2,362

SOURCE: *The State of Food and Agriculture: Review and Outlook, 1952*, FAO, October, 1952, p. 115.

ever, there were underlying situations that were unfavorable. The United States stockpiling program was nearing completion and purchasing was on a decreasing scale, and the prevailing downward trend in prices was not conducive to imports and holding of stocks in importing countries. The average spot crude rubber prices per pound in New York were 17.6 cents in 1949, 41.3 cents in 1950, 60.9 cents in 1951, and 38.6 cents in 1952. In view of these uncertainties in the rubber situation, the International Rubber Study Group resolved to establish a Working Party "to consider whether measures designed to prevent burdensome surpluses or serious shortages of rubber are necessary and practicable; to prepare drafts of any agreements required to implement such measures; and to report back to the Study Group as soon as possible."[10]

The average New York spot price for crude rubber continued downward in 1953 to 24.1 cents per pound and to 23.4 cents per pound in 1954; it rose to 39.0 cents in 1955; in 1956 it fell to less than 30 cents and rose again; but it dropped again in 1957 as tire companies turned to synthetics because of the price advantage of 23 cents and the automobile demand for original equipment slowed down.

[10] *The State of Food and Agriculture: Review and Outlook, 1952*, Food and Agriculture Organization of the United Nations, October, 1952, p. 116.

TABLE 16. World Consumption of Natural and Synthetic Rubber
(in thousands of long tons)

Year	Natural								Synthetic						World Grand Total
	Australia	Brazil	Canada	France	Germany	United Kingdom	United States	World Total	Canada	France	Germany	United Kingdom	United States	World Total	
1935–39 av.	13.9	2.1ᵃ	28.2	58.2	76.4	107.7	527.8	1,025	—	—	4.3	—	.4	5	1,030
1940–44 av.	17.0	7.7	34.2	12.3	16.2	104.1	452.4	824	5.7	4.3	65.6	9.0	152.8	252	1,076
1945	8.5	7.6	5.9	3.6	1.0ᵇ	27.3	105.4	263	35.9	17.4	22.5ᵇ	63.8	693.6	865	1,128
1946	15.6	13.5	9.6	29.8	1.7ᵇ	96.6	277.6	565	29.6	28.7	11.9ᵇ	30.1	761.7	913	1,478
1947	23.0	14.1	32.3	61.2	8.1ᵇ	153.6	562.7	1,110	29.2	12.6	7.9ᵇ	2.8	559.7	625	1,735
1948	26.3	15.6	41.6	86.5	45.6ᵇ	193.7	627.3	1,423	20.6	7.4	4.4ᵇ	2.6	442.1	480	1,903
1949	27.7	19.1	38.3	91.2	65.9ᵇ	184.3	574.5	1,438	18.1	8.3	2.2ᵇ	2.4	414.4	450	1,888
1950	34.2	23.4	46.1	102.6	78.6ᵇ	219.7	720.3	1,705	22.6	7.4	3.4ᵇ	2.8	538.3	580	2,285
1951	35.9	26.2	44.4	119.3	91.5ᵇ	234.2	454.0	1,498	26.4	8.6	5.2ᵇ	3.9	758.9	813	2,311
1952	28.5	27.7	33.5	121.6	93.5ᵇ	197.3	453.8	1,455	33.6	11.3	9.8ᵇ	4.9	807.0	885	2,340
1953	33.0	31.8	37.5	114.8	106.2ᵇ	219.6	553.5	1,630	35.9	12.9	11.5ᵇ	4.9	784.8	873	2,503
1954	43.2	37.8	41.6	127.0	130.0ᵇ	238.9	596.3	1,765	30.1	14.4	17.0ᵇ	8.7	636.7	740	2,505
1955	46.0	40.0	44.3	135.0	140.0ᵇ	246.4	632.2	1,830	40.2	20.0	25.0ᵇ	20.5	890.4	1,055	2,885
1956	46.0	38.0	43.1	133.0	140.0ᵇ	192.8	563.1	1,885	48.4	26.5	34.0ᵇ	39.5	877.3	1,135	3,020

ᵃ Average 1935 and 1936. ᵇ Western Germany only.
SOURCE: Rubber Study Group, *Commodity Year Book*, 1956. (See 1957 issue for minor revisions in 1955 figures.)

At a meeting of the International Rubber Study Group in Colombo, Ceylon, in May, 1954, an attempt was made to stabilize world prices for rubber. A report was presented which stated that the "price relationship of synthetic rubber to natural rubber is of vital importance to the producers of natural rubber, especially in countries which were mainly dependent on the proceeds of their natural rubber exports for their economic welfare and development." The Study Group, however, did not reach agreement as to the means by which prices should be stabilized, nor as to the necessity of an international rubber agreement at that time. The Study Group met again in June, 1957, to consider the problem of the stabilization of rubber prices.

The *immediate* problem of the post-Korea period was an excess of synthetic and natural rubber production over rubber consumption and a continued instability of natural rubber prices.

Actual world consumption by countries of natural and synthetic rubber from 1935 to 1956 is given in Table 16, which shows a general trend of increased United States total consumption of rubber. This was true of natural rubber, which was above pre-World War II levels. However, the role of the United States in the world market in 1956 was diminishing as domestic consumption of natural rubber had declined from about half the world total prior to World War II. Of major significance was the tremendous increase in domestic use of synthetic rubber, which continued to move ahead of natural rubber after 1950.

The *long-run* 1950–75 problem as foreseen by The President's Materials Policy Commission was just the opposite in terms of production and consumption.

The consumption of rubber in the United States and the rest of the free world for 1950 and estimated 1975 is given in Table 17. Consumption of

TABLE 17.   Free World Rubber Consumption, 1950 and Projected 1975
(thousands of long tons)

	United States		Other Free Countries		Total Free World	
	1950	1975	1950	1975	1950	1975
Natural rubber	738	a	785	a	1,523	2,300
Synthetic rubber	582	a	40	a	624	2,700
Total new rubber	1,320	2,500	825	2,500	2,147	5,000
Reclaimed rubber	300	800	125	400	421	1,200
Total consumption	1,620	3,300	950	2,900	2,568	6,200

a Not separately projected.

SOURCE: *Resources for Freedom*, Vol. II, *The Outlook for Key Commodities*, The President's Materials Policy Commission, Government Printing Office, 1952, p. 102.

rubber in the United States was expected to double approximately in the United States between 1950 and 1975. An even greater rate of increase is expected for other free countries, so that total free world consumption may possibly be around two and a half times 1950 consumption.

To accomplish the production to achieve this estimate the Materials Policy Commission made the following recommendations:

The competition of synthetic rubber is expected to bring the long-run world price of natural rubber down to the real cost of producing synthetic rubber—that is, to perhaps 20 cents a pound in terms of 1950 dollars.

The physical basis for a very substantial increase in the production of natural rubber is provided both by the development of a new highly productive tree stock, and by the possibility of increasing acreage. However, at the price likely to be set by the competition of synthetic rubber, and with the uncertainties generated both by the security interests of rubber-consuming countries in stimulating their own synthetic production and by the possibility of unsettled political conditions in southeast Asia, natural rubber production is not likely, in the long run, to keep pace with the growth in total demand.

In the near future total supplies of rubber are likely to be ample, but eventually there can be expected a growth of demand that will require construction of new capacity for synthetic rubber production as well as the expansion of natural rubber production.

It appears evident that fundamental market forces, if permitted to operate, would bring about a marked expansion in the production of both natural and synthetic rubber during the next 25 years. To the extent that natural rubber production fails to keep pace with growing world demands for new rubber, and that the price of natural rubber is significantly above the real costs of synthetic rubber, the production of synthetic rubber can appropriately be expanded to make up the difference. This would tend to hold the world rubber price close to the real cost of producing synthetic rubber.

The market forces can operate only indirectly on synthetic production, however, so long as synthetic rubber continues to be produced principally by the United States Government, and this factor must also strongly influence natural rubber producers. Government production of synthetic rubber may operate in two ways to inhibit natural rubber countries from expanding production:

1. To the extent that it leads to an administratively determined and somewhat lower price for synthetic rubber, it would reduce profit potentials on natural rubber.
2. It confronts natural rubber producers with the possibility of administrative price actions possibly more severe than normal market conditions would provoke.

In much the same manner, private industry in this country would hesitate to build synthetic rubber plants that might have to meet such competition from Government plants.

If then synthetic rubber production is to expand adequately and with sufficient rapidity, and without injury to the economies of the natural rubber producing countries, it should be allowed to take place through normal market forces. The synthetic rubber production expansion that would take place under such circumstances would be consistent with national security, provided the appropriate stockpiling policies are also followed. The Commission, therefore, concurs in the declared United States Government policy "that the security interests of the United States can and will best be served by the development within the United States of a free competitive synthetic-rubber industry." To this end, it appears desirable that efforts be continued toward an early disposal of Government plants and removal of Government regulations.[11]

In the spring of 1955 the United States government sold its twenty-four synthetic rubber plants to private industry. Following this, though not as a result, there was a rapid rise in United States synthetic rubber production during the latter half of 1955 and the early part of 1956. This was perhaps a result of the sharp rise in the price of natural rubber and indications of an increased consumption of rubber. President Eisenhower reported to Congress on April 30, 1956, that several companies had successfully produced a synthetic rubber with compositions and properties similar to those of natural rubber and that it might be possible to produce types of rubber domestically to take the place of natural rubber in large truck, bus, and airplane tires, in which synthetic rubber previously had not proved satisfactory.

One would like to conclude that the sale of the United States government synthetic rubber plants to private industry and the favorable 1956 outlook for synthetic rubber would solve the long-run rubber problem. Up to that time synthetic rubber had been supplementary to, rather than competitive with, natural rubber. Natural rubber might have to face this competition in the future and this might further the conditions of economic and political instability in the producing areas which had prevailed during the post-World War II period.

The Rubber Study Group must study continuously the international problem, and the United States government must continuously review its policy in the light of its international and domestic interests.

Coffee

Coffee would place high on the personal "critical materials" list of millions of United States customers. The coffee problem has been one of production and price instability.

World exportable production of coffee from 1935 through 1956 is given by countries in Table 18. During the pre-World War II period, world

[11] *Ibid.*, p. 99.

Table 18. World Exportable[a] Production of Coffee
(in thousand bags of 132,276 pounds)

Crop Years	Brazil	Colombia	Costa Rica	El Salvador	Guatemala	Haiti	Mexico	Venezuela	Total America	Africa	Asia	Oceania	World Total
1935–39 av.	21,740	4,202	330	1,011	922	438	609	740	31,402	2,315	1,647	53	35,017
40–44 av.	13,261	4,936	358	928	848	371	516	532	22,398	2,465	126	25	25,032
1945	12,200	5,051	205	748	812	400	550	500	21,016	2,993	233	30	24,908
1946	13,965	5,500	306	972	792	411	491	541	23,704	2,882	450	30	27,066
1947	13,572	5,240	410	980	827	375	511	530	23,177	3,876	345	30	27,428
1948	15,740	5,600	275	1,225	980	485	725	500	26,310	3,970	310	50	30,640
1949	14,950	5,200	347	1,150	900	447	700	270	24,923	4,097	239	52	29,311
1950	15,692	4,750	275	1,000	811	319	900	338	25,214	4,569	—(502)—		30,285
1951	14,371	5,175	305	1,100	1,000	395	905	325	24,759	4,587	—(450)—		29,796
1952	15,200	5,705	478	1,232	939	411	1,245	746	27,295	5,357	—(625)—		33,277
1953	14,300	6,348	331	927	951	578	1,215	439	26,549	6,540	—(1,251)—		34,340
1954	14,200	5,665	508	1,190	892	328	1,400	557	26,419	6,680	—(664)—		33,763
1955	21,300	6,100	364	1,105	917	535	1,240	300	33,952	8,379	—(1,207)—		43,538
1956	12,700	6,700	552	1,265	1,012	433	1,550	600	26,945	8,250	—(1,340)—		36,535

[a] Data prior to 1941 are for total production.

Source: Pan-American Coffee Bureau; Foreign Agriculture Service; Commodity Year Book, 1956 and 1957.

coffee production greatly exceeded coffee consumption. From Figure 4.12 it can be observed that prewar world coffee production (1935–40) averaged 41.6 million bags, visible stocks 28.5 million, and availability

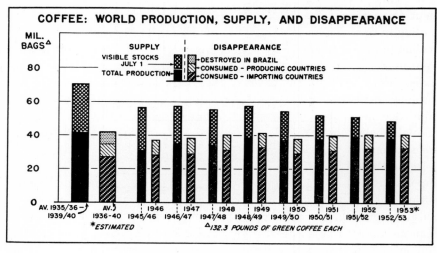

Figure 4.12.   (U.S. Department of Agriculture)

about 70.1 million. World prewar average consumption was 34.7 million bags, but disappearance was 41.8 million because Brazil destroyed 7.1 million bags of coffee annually in an attempt to raise prices and regulate marketing and production under control schemes. Some of the best coffee land in Brazil passed out of production as growers put their plantations to more remunerative uses or abandoned them.

After the outbreak of the Second World War, when European markets were cut off from the world's coffee trade, the Latin-American producing countries met with serious difficulties in marketing their output. To assure them a stable market, the United States in November, 1940, entered into an agreement with fourteen producers. Under this Inter-American Coffee Agreement, export quotas to the United States and to foreign markets were set and revised yearly by the Inter-American Coffee Board. After the agreement expired, on September 30, 1948, there was some international coöperation through the Pan-American Coffee Bureau and through a Special Commission on Coffee under the Inter-American Economic and Social Council.

Since World War II the coffee situation has changed drastically from the prewar surplus of production as world consumption has exceeded production and coffee stocks have been drawn on to meet the difference. The world coffee economy seems to have been characterized by three long-term cycles of about twenty years' duration which occurred after 1890. While consumption grew gradually, production had a cyclical movement characterized first by an expansion brought about by high prices, leading to the emergence of surpluses and a fall in prices, followed by a decline in prices, followed by a decline in production lasting until stocks were used up and prices began to rise. The last cycle appears to have ended during 1948–49. The postwar 1946–49 period was characterized by sustained demand, not supported by an equivalent rise in production, a rapid decline in stocks, and a rise in prices. Production was still substantially below prewar and on a per capita basis in the major consuming areas, about 23 percent lower.

In the United States, which absorbed almost 70 percent of total world imports in 1946, rising national income, changes in consumption habits during the war years, and relatively low prices continued to stimulate consumption. United States coffee imports increased about 60 percent from an annual prewar average of 13.9 million bags to a peak of 22.1 million bags in 1949. As seen from Figure 4.13, the leading sources of

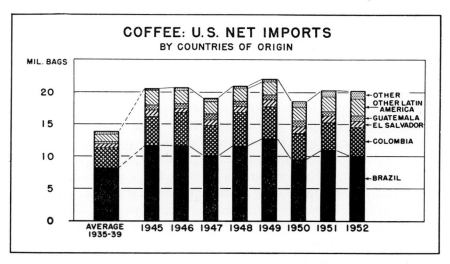

Figure 4.13. (U.S. Department of Agriculture)

United States coffee imports are Brazil, Colombia, El Salvador, Guatemala, and Mexico. Approximately 95 percent of United States imports came from Latin America. Although price control had been terminated in 1946, large carry-over stocks prevented a marked price rise until 1949, when the last Brazilian government stocks were liquidated, and in that year United States imports reached an all-time peak.

The exhaustion of stocks, coupled with rising European imports, was followed by an unprecedentedly rapid rise in prices. In 1950 the average wholesale price in New York rose by more than 50 percent (Santos No. 4) as compared with the previous year. If the 1934–38 average is taken as 100, the price of Santos No. 4 reached 524. Although United States consumption and imports were reduced in 1950 as a result of the high prices, various factors combined to prevent a substantial reaction. Indeed, in 1953 a new price advance set in, when a freeze in Brazil reduced yields and destroyed millions of young trees, and gained momentum in 1954. Retail prices in the United States rose during the summer of 1954 to almost 400 percent above the 1934–38 average and wholesale prices to 800 percent.

The result was inevitable. Consumption in the United States, which had been sustained by an unprecedented growth in per capita income, fell precipitately in 1954 and imports declined by 19 percent as compared with the previous year and by 23 percent in comparison with 1949. In Europe, where the percentage rise in retail prices was much smaller, since import duties had always constituted a significant proportion of the consumer prices, imports and consumption continued to expand. But even in Europe high prices have had very adverse effects on consumption. In contrast to practically all other commodities, the per capita consumption of which had recovered or surpassed prewar levels, net western European imports of coffee in 1954 were still 4 percent below the 1934–38 average, and per capita supplies were 13 percent lower.

More important from a long-term standpoint were the production effects. Stable prices encouraged planting, both in Latin America and in Africa. In Brazil, a major proportion of the price increase was withheld from producers by techniques of multiple exchange rates; yet coffee planting became extremely profitable even there. Vast areas of new lands were cleared, and considerable replanting with higher-yielding varieties took place in old coffee areas of declining productivity.

United States consumers were not happy about the increases in price which coffee producers claimed were justified because of higher costs. Unquestionably, part of the high price of coffee was due to a closer balance between supply and consumption.

In June, 1954, the Brazilian government announced a minimum export price for coffee at a record level of 87 cents a pound to go into effect on

July 1 and run for a year. Leading planters, including some members of the Brazilian Coffee Institute's executive board, believed the government's minimum, based on dollar exchange quotations and backed by the assurance that the government would buy coffee before allowing it to be exported at less than the minimum, would prove disastrous. They argued that green coffee prices could not be expected to stay above 87 cents through the year and that the result would be that the government would be forced to accumulate coffee stocks only to be resold later below the minimum price, with the national treasury absorbing the loss.

The coffee experts stressed the fact that during the 1954–55 year— barring another frost disaster—coffee prices would be under pressure. Many predicted an open break in prices in February and March of 1955. They believed that government minimum price in dollars would only complicate what they expected to be a difficult transition period even in the best of circumstances.

The predictions of price declines proved correct. Coffee prices, which began to increase in 1953, hit a retail peak of $1.45 a pound. In August, 1954, the trend was reversed with a drop at retail of about 10 cents a pound. An additional drop of 5 cents in October was cut by a temporary rise of 3 cents a pound in November. However, a 3-cent-a-pound cut was announced in January, 1955, a 12- to 16-cent reduction followed in February, a decline of 5 cents was made in March and of another 5 cents in May.

World coffee production for 1955 was the largest in history and greatly in excess of consumption. In addition most producing countries had carry-overs from the previous crop year. Under these circumstances coffee roasters anticipated further declines on price and thus allowed their inventories to fall too low. They had to replenish their stock with rush orders and bid up the price of coffee.

Low stocks in consuming countries and lower prices stimulated demand throughout 1955 and 1956. United States imports, which had fallen severely during the great price rise in 1954, were 15 percent larger although still 7 percent below 1953. United States per capita consumption also began to recover from the adverse effects of the price rise, but in 1955 it was still 16 percent below the average consumption of the immediate postwar years. Imports into France, Western Germany, and other European countries continued to rise; however, notwithstanding the great increases in incomes, per capita consumption remained below 1934–38.

In all these instances of price increases in the 1950–55 period, the

United States public wanted to know: Why? The first increases were investigated by Congressional committees. Price increases throughout the first quarter of 1954 were in large part due to increased hoardings by consumers and purchases by speculators. In addition, the Interim Coordinating Committee for International Commodity Arrangements reported, "Prices of Brazilian coffee, supported by minimum export prices and other measures, for a time exceeded those of coffee from other sources, such as Colombia." Asked about the price increases in 1955, Horacio Cintra Leite, the Brazilian Coffee Institute's representative in the United States, replied that the then current increase in the price of coffee was due to supply-and-demand factors: "Brazil has imposed no minimum export price and has not established an export quota."

The United States public has seen as its coffee problem rising coffee prices. Clearer answers than those which have been supplied in the past are deserved. When coffee prices are falling the United States public is happy. Actually these fluctuating coffee prices should be of United States concern and of national interest.

Coffee is of great importance to a number of countries, accounting in 1953 for 95 percent of the value of exports in Colombia, 86 percent in Salvador, 77 percent in Guatemala, 67 percent in Brazil, and 65 percent in Haiti. The economic and political stability of these countries depends on coffee. United States policy recognized this problem when we participated in the Inter-American Coffee Agreement.

The Colombian government called on the United Nations in September, 1954:

. . . to set up an international study group like the existing study groups dealing with other primary commodities in international trade, namely cotton, rubber, tin, and wool. The only international body studying the coffee problem is a Commission of the Inter-American Economic and Social Council of the Organization of American States. The members of this commission are of course the Latin American producing countries and the United States, the great consumer country of this hemisphere; but the producers of other hemispheres, particularly Africa, and the European consumer markets, are not represented.

After this matter was raised by the government of Colombia, the problems of trade in coffee were discussed at a conference, held at the end of November, 1954, in Rio de Janeiro, of the ministers of finance and economy of the members of the Organization of American States. The conference decided:

(1) that the Special Committee of the Inter-American Economic and Social Council should make, through a special committee appointed from among its

members, a detailed study of the world coffee situation and the prospects for the future.

(2) if this study should show the possibility of adopting measures of international cooperation capable of appreciably reducing the range of fluctuations in the price of coffee and keeping them within limits satisfactory for producers and consumers, the special committee shall prepare draft texts suitable for attaining that objective, to be submitted for consideration to the member countries affected by the problems.

In view of this decision the Interim Coordinating Committee for International Commodity Arrangements deferred calling an international study group for coffee.

Early in 1957 a document entitled "Proposals for an International Coffee Agreement" prepared by the Secretariat of the Inter-American Economic and Social Council was submitted to the Sub-Committee of the Special Committee on Coffee of the Council. At its meeting on February 13, 1957, the Sub-Committee decided not to proceed further with the proposals for the time being but to ask its Secretariat to draft a plan for the establishment, as an interim measure, of a World Coffee Council to be composed of representatives of producing countries.

At a Mexico City conference in October, 1957, seven Latin-American coffee-producing nations (Brazil, Colombia, Costa Rica, El Salvador, Guatemala, Mexico, and Nicaragua) signed an agreement to limit coffee shipments and to spread their shipments throughout the year rather than dumping their crop right after harvest. The African and Asian producers were opposed to an agreement of this type as they had been increasing coffee exports substantially during the previous five years. However, the African and Asian coffee-producing nations joined with the Latin-American producers in January, 1958, to form an International Coffee Organization. The purpose of the organization is to exchange technical and statistical information and to promote the sale of coffee throughout the world. No regulatory measures were adopted, but the organization provides a framework for such measures if they are decided to be advisable by the members.

As a result of the recovery of consumption and, above all, unforeseeable production developments in 1955–56, coffee prices were more firm than had been anticipated. World production for 1956–57 was estimated to be lower than in 1955–56. There was a real fear that the existing prices, which were very remunerative to producers, might continue to stimulate new planting. Should the experience of the three previous coffee cycles be repeated, the FAO concluded that during the next five to seven years production might rise very substantially, while consumption expansion would be much more gradual even at prices substantially lower than those of 1955. "Governments of some producing countries forecast great producing increases in the next few years. It is possible, therefore, that the world coffee economy will again be confronted with very difficult conditions in the future, unless effective international co-operation can be developed."

United States policy should be to coöperate fully in the studies to achieve greater coffee price stability in order to maximize economic and political stability in the coffee-growing areas.

B. Supplementary Products—Sugar and Wool

The second aspect of the significance of agricultural imports is their competitive relation to agricultural commodities that are produced domestically. One overall comparison usually made, because of the competitive relationship, is that of United States exports of agricultural products to supplementary agricultural imports. Figure 4.14 shows that

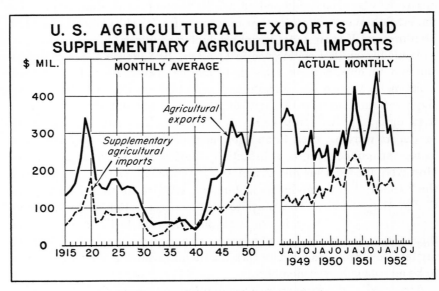

Figure 4.14.   (U.S. Department of Agriculture)

agricultural exports normally exceed supplementary imports. The latter were greater only in 1937 when the United States experienced a drought and in 1940 and 1941 when domestic demand first felt the impact of war. Aggregate comparisons such as this, however, tend to cover up individual commodity competitive problems, which can be studied only on a commodity basis. Sugar and wool are two important supplementary agricultural products which the United States imports.

Sugar

Sugar is one of the most important basic world foods. A pure carbohydrate, it is an excellent source of energy.

PRODUCTION AND INTERNATIONAL TRADE. Commercial sugar is produced almost entirely from sugar cane and the sugar beet. Sugar cane is a perennial which grows in tropical and semitropical climates where sufficient moisture or irrigation is available. It is produced in only two states in the United States: Florida and Louisiana. The sugar beet is cultivated in almost every country in the Temperate Zone and in nineteen states of the Union from Ohio to the Pacific. The growing of sugar beets has been more restricted to areas where subsidies or protection are available. Table 19 presents production of sugar from 1935 through 1956 by types and by countries. About 80 percent of all sugar is consumed in the countries where it is produced. Consequently 20 percent enters into international trade. Post-World War II sugar production is given by types and by countries in Figure 4.15. Where sugar beet production was possible, individual countries have provided various measures to encourage production to maximize self-sufficiency. B. C. Swerling delineates world trade in the following fashion:

The areas participating in transoceanic or international trade in sugar fall fairly easily into the following categories: (1) those areas in which it is an important if not the principal export crop—Cuba, Java, Peru, Dominican Republic, Mauritius, Fiji Islands, British West Indies and British Guiana, Puerto Rico, Hawaii, the Philippines, French West Indies (Guadeloupe and Martinique), and Formosa (formerly Japanese Taiwan); (2) those which sell abroad their surplus above domestic needs—Australia, South Africa, Poland, Czechoslovakia, and to a lesser extent Brazil, Hungary, Belgium and Germany; (3) normally self-sufficient areas—the French, Portuguese, and Japanese empires; Italy; British India (since 1937); the USSR; and Argentina; (4) those which supplement by imports an inadequate domestic production —United States, United Kingdom, Canada, Switzerland, China, and to a lesser extent Turkey, Egypt, Sweden, and Eire; and (5) a declining list of smaller countries dependent entirely on imports—Chile, Greece, Finland, New Zealand and Uruguay, among others.[12]

PROBLEMS AND POLICY. The major sugar trade problem has been the sale of sugar by the surplus producers into a limited market. Cuba and

[12] B. C. Swerling, *International Control of Sugar, 1918–1941*, Stanford University, Food Research Institute, Commodity Policy Studies No. 7, 1949, pp. 21–22.

TABLE 19. World Production of Sugar (Centrifugal Sugar—Raw Value)
(in thousands of short tons)

Crop Year	Brazil Cane	United States Beet	United States Cane	Cuba Cane	Puerto Rico Cane	Hawaii Cane	Philippines Cane	Indonesia Cane	European Beet[a]	India Cane	U.S.S.R. Beet	World Total Beet	World Total Cane	World Total All
1935–39 av.	830	1,517	474	3,183	982	980	1,058	1,207	7,278	1,303[b]	2,761	11,773	16,763	28,536
1940–44 av.	958	1,451	429	3,686	961	880	320	953	6,615	1,410[b]	1,350	9,690	16,301	25,991
1945	1,399	1,266	475	4,476	916	680	115	22	3,822	5,094[b]	1,200	6,575	19,657	26,232
1946	1,633	1,523	425	6,448	1,095	872	132	25	5,584	5,503[b]	775	8,172	23,035	31,188
1947	1,496	1,835	376	6,675	1,108	835	398	100	5,077	1,416	1,700	8,879	19,207	27,914
1948	1,647	1,370	477	5,763	1,277	956	730	265	7,569	1,348	2,183	11,405	20,225	31,630
1949	1,480	1,570	521	6,127	1,286	961	685	306	7,542	1,310	2,205	11,641	20,584	32,225
1950	1,737	2,012	564	6,349	1,228	996	935	386	9,856	1,469	2,400	14,705	21,477	36,182
1951	1,860	1,549	419	7,964	1,360	1,020	1,076	472	9,562	1,901	2,700	14,318	24,014	38,332
1952	2,151	1,505	605	5,687	1,182	1,099	1,134	637	8,314	1,686	2,500	12,834	23,366	36,200
1953	2,328	1,816	630	5,391	1,204	1,077	1,435	683	11,457	1,320	2,700	16,523	23,931	40,454
1954	2,479	2,043	555	4,994	1,166	1,127	1,371	787	10,501	2,000	2,500	15,597	24,945	40,542
1955	2,470	1,800	600	5,000	1,175	1,120	1,208	937	10,514	2,100	3,000	15,963	25,163	41,126
1956	2,684	1,925	510	5,700	1,200	1,200	1,205	900	10,483	2,475	4,400	17,685	26,772	44,457

[a] Excluding U.S.S.R. [b] Mostly "Gur" (low grade sugar)—"white" production.
SOURCE: Department of Agriculture; *Commodity Year Book*, 1956. (See 1957 issue for minor revisions in years prior to 1956.)

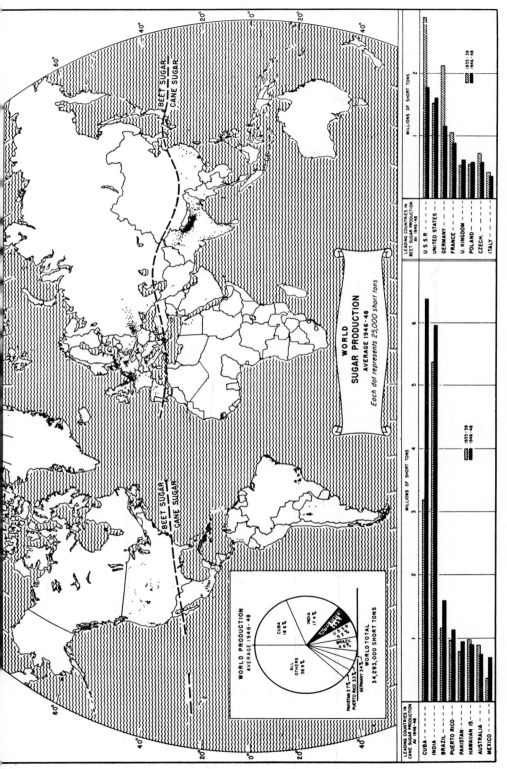

Figure 4.15. (U.S. Department of Agriculture, Office of Foreign Agricultural Relations)

Java have been the principal producers of sugar for export, and this surplus problem, which led to revolution in Cuba and unremunerative production of sugar, gave rise before World War II to two major international agreements: the International Sugar Agreements of 1931 and 1937. The latter agreement was participated in by twenty-two countries. It was based on recognition of the national interest of the principal consuming areas and resulted in the dividing of the free market in order to assure the survival of Cuba and Java, the most efficient producers. The control provisions of this agreement were not operative after 1944, but by a series of annual protocols certain portions of the agreement were maintained. The International Sugar Council, which was originally established to administer the agreement, in the postwar period collected statistics, kept the international sugar position under review, and provided an opportunity for intergovernmental discussions regarding the desirability of a new agreement. There were many special arrangements concerning trade in sugar that had to be considered in the formulation of the agreement. In particular, the United States together with its suppliers and the United Kingdom together with other Commonwealth countries constitute two groups, the major part of whose trade in sugar is separated by special arrangements from the so-called "free" market—a term covering all other international trade in sugar, including transactions of the two groups with countries outside the group.

The general pattern of international trade in sugar in 1950 is shown in Table 20. The direction of trade does not vary significantly from year to year because a very large portion takes place within preferential trading systems.

The United States is the world's largest sugar market. Domestic consumption averaged 6,635,000 tons during 1935–39, rose to a peak of 8,279,000 tons in 1950, was 7,735,000 tons in 1951, and then began to rise again in 1956. Beginning with the tariff on sugar in 1789 and continuing through the sugar quota acts of 1934, 1937, and 1948, federal legislation has protected the sugar economy of the United States.

At present, domestic production and imports of sugar are controlled by a system of quotas set each year by the Secretary of Agriculture in accordance with the Sugar Act of 1948, as amended. The quota for 1956 was set at 8,392,000 tons. There is also a tariff of one-half cent a pound for sugar from Cuba and five-eights cent a pound for other foreign countries. The Philippines began to pay duties in 1954. In addition to the duty, there is a tax on all sugar imported or processed in the United States. The revenue from this tax is used in a program of payments to

TABLE 20. International Trade in Sugar—1950
(thousands of metric tons; mainly raw values)

Importing Country	Exporting Countries											Total Exports Shown[c]	Actual or Estimated Gross Imports[c]
	Australia	Belgium	Cuba	Dominican Republic[a]	France	Hawaii Philippines Puerto Rico	Mauritius[b]	Netherlands	Peru	United Kingdom	United States		
Algeria	—	1.4	—	—	105.8	—	—	—	—	—	—	107.2	114.1[d]
Austria	—	0.9	36.8	—	—	9.9	—	1.4	—	—	—	49.0	116.5[d]
Belgium	—	—	62.0	—	—	—	—	—	9.6	0.8	—	72.5	36.3
Canada	69.3	—	4.1	4.3	—	—	51.8	—	—	—	0.1	129.6	580.4
Ceylon	—	—	—	11.0	—	—	116.9	—	8.3	19.3	0.1	155.5	123.1
Chile	—	5.6	59.5	—	—	—	—	—	116.4	—	1.1	177.0	203.8
Finland	—	4.2	3.4	—	—	—	—	10.0	—	—	—	19.0	110.9[d]
France	—	0.2	86.1	—	—	—	—	41.8	—	21.1	—	153.2	370.0
Germany	—	42.8	155.2	—	31.6	181.7	—	79.4	—	27.5	—	518.2	616.1
Greece	—	—	43.2	—	—	—	—	—	—	2.0	0.1	45.5	89.4
India	—	—	—	—	—	—	—	0.6	—	35.8	0.1	36.4	3.3
Iran	—	—	—	—	—	—	—	—	—	141.6	—	141.7	177.6
Iraq	—	12.6	—	—	—	—	—	16.9	—	63.8	—	93.3	90.0
Ireland	—	—	48.3	3.5	—	—	—	—	—	1.0	—	52.8	66.5
Italy	—	0.3	14.8	—	—	—	—	—	—	2.0	0.1	17.2	28.5
Japan	—	14.1	122.9	—	—	—	—	0.5	—	—	8.2	145.7	380.1[d]
Morocco, French	—	18.2	106.2	—	48.7	—	—	7.5	—	—	—	180.6	201.4
Netherlands	—	3.7	346.6	1.8	—	—	—	—	12.2	0.8	—	365.1	311.1
New Zealand	75.8	—	—	—	—	—	—	—	—	—	—	75.8	124.5[d]
Norway	—	0.2	29.1	—	—	—	—	—	—	—	0.3	29.6	91.3
Pakistan	—	—	33.1	—	—	—	—	—	—	22.1	—	55.2	110.0
Portugal	—	10.6	19.0	—	—	—	—	—	—	0.2	—	29.8	107.5
Sweden	—	—	10.5	—	—	—	—	1.1	—	—	—	11.6	126.6
Switzerland	—	5.4	90.1	0.9	30.3	—	—	32.1	—	135.1	—	293.9	324.4
Tunisia	—	11.5	5.4	—	31.1	—	—	—	—	—	—	48.0	51.3
United Kingdom	228.9	—	893.5	405.1	—	—	193.9	—	—	—	—	1,721.4	2,150.0
United States	—	5.4	2,873.1	11.3	—	2,423.3[e]	—	—	15.0	—	—	5,322.7	5,239.1
Uruguay	—	—	13.4	0.7	—	—	—	—	46.9	6.8	—	72.5	84.9
Venezuela	—	—	6.6	—	—	—	—	—	20.2	—	4.9	32.4	37.7[d]
Other countries	7.0	57.4	197.9	6.9	30.5	—	72.3	20.0	48.2	368.9	11.8	820.9	—
Total	381.0	194.5	5,260.8	445.5	278.0	2,614.9	434.9	211.3	276.8	848.8	26.8	f	—

a Year ended 31 August 1950.
b Exports from 1950–51 crop.
c Differences between last two columns result principally from omission of exports of French, Portuguese, and some British oversea territories, and of eastern Europe, Taiwan, and Denmark.
d Any refined or semi-refined sugar included at actual physical weight.
e Entries against quotas for United States market.
f Total of exports shown is 10,973,300 metric tons, but this figure includes duplication of over one million tons of refined sugar exported by the United Kingdom, the Netherlands, Belgium, and the United States from raw sugar which originated largely in the other exporting countries shown. The net total of about 9.8 million metric tons is estimated to be over 80 percent of the total world trade in sugar.

Source: Secretariat of the International Sugar Council.

domestic mainland and insular producers. To be eligible for such payments, producers must meet certain requirements with respect to the
quantity of sugar produced, wages paid, and avoidance of the use of
child labor. The rate of the payment is graduated downward as the size
of the producing enterprise increases. The tariff and the tax do not affect
the volume of sugar imported, which is determined by quotas. The
general conclusion can be drawn that the present quota system has
worked reasonably well to provide price stability for a notably unstable
commodity.[13]

The sources of the United States sugar supply for two pre-World War II
periods and for 1948–51 are given in Table 21.

TABLE 21.   Sources of United States Sugar Supply, Selected Periods
(average percent)

Area	1932–33	1935–39	1948–51
Domestic areas:			
Mainland beet	21.2	21.6	21.6
Mainland cane	3.8	6.6	6.5
Hawaii	16.1	14.1	11.6
Puerto Rico	13.7	13.3	13.4
Virgin Islands	.1	.1	.1
Total domestic	54.9	55.7	53.2
Foreign areas:			
Philippines	18.0	14.3	6.4
Cuba	26.7	29.2	39.8
Full-duty areas	.4	.8	.6
Total foreign	45.1	44.3	46.8
All areas	100.0	100.0	100.0

SOURCE: International Federation of Agricultural Producers, *Sugar*, commodity memorandum, August,
1952.

Mainland producers of sugar strive continuously for a larger share of
the total United States quota and thus lobby against offshore producers.
Yet at the same time mainland beet producers and can producers work
against one another for a larger share of the mainland quota. While the
total share allocated to mainland producers was only 28 percent, any
increase in this allocation requires taking into account our national interests in international producers. Particular emphasis must be placed
on the possibility of increasing allocations to foreign areas which produce
cane sugar under favorable cost conditions. Sugar production is of great
importance in the economy of these areas and of United States territories.
Economics and political stability of these areas is of vital interest to the
United States. In addition, increased imports from these areas means

[13] *A Trade and Tariff Policy in the National Interest*, p. 26.

increased United States exports. Cuban interests have placed special emphasis on the fact that the volume of goods Cuba can buy from the United States is controlled by sales of sugar to the United States. They have emphasized that Cuba is one of the best customers of the United States and that about four-fifths of all Cuba's visible imports have been bought from this country. United States exports to Cuba in 1947 amounted to almost half a billion dollars.[14] Cuba deserves, as in the past,

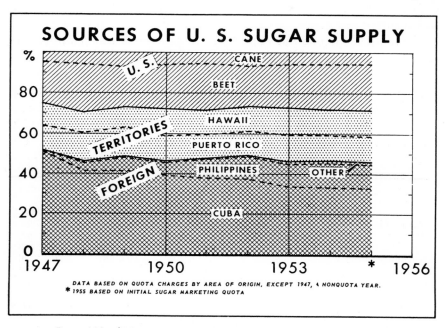

Figure 4.16.   (U.S. Department of Agriculture, Agricultural Marketing Service)

to receive special consideration as a source of our sugar supply. She has continually been a residual area on which we have drawn in emergencies. The last major one was World War II, when beet production, which had been protected through the years, dropped from 1,897,000 tons in 1940–41 to 1,000,000 in 1943. Recognition of Cuba's special importance to the United States has been an established United States policy and the quantitative results of this policy can be observed from Table 21, which shows that Cuba's share of the United States sugar supply increased from 26.7 percent in 1932–33 to 39.8 percent during 1948–51. However, from Figure 4.16, which gives sources of United States sugar supply for 1947 to 1956, one can see that Cuba's share began to decline in 1952 until it was only

[14] *Sugar Facts and Figures*, United States Cuban Sugar Council, 1948.

about 33 percent in 1955. Cuba has restricted production each year since 1952 in response to declining prices and mounting stocks.

An amendment to the Sugar Act of 1948, passed by the Congress and approved by the President in May, 1956, provided important changes in the formula for prorating the sugar marketing quota among the suppliers of sugar for the United States market.

The amendment again gave the domestic producing areas a share of the expanding United States market for sugar. Prewar sugar legislation had incorporated such a provision, but the domestic areas in postwar legislation had forgone this entitlement to give Cuba an opportunity to return gradually to a normal production level and ease the impact of postwar adjustment on her economy. Previously, the quantity of sugar which could be marketed in the United States by the domestic producing areas was fixed at a total of 4,444,000 tons, raw value, allocated as shown in Table 22. The Philippines, with a statutory quota equivalent to 980,000 tons, raw value, was also limited in the quantity of sugar it could sell in

TABLE 22.   Sugar Quota and Proration—1957

Area and Country	Actual Quota Under Amended Act (tons)	Proration Under Act Prior to Amendment (tons)	Percent Change
Domestic beet sugar	1,953,952	1,800,000	+8.6
Mainland cane sugar	601,250	500,000	+20.2
Hawaii	1,090,496	1,052,000	+3.7
Puerto Rico	1,140,253	1,080,000	+5.6
Virgin Islands	15,549	12,000	+29.5
Total domestic area	4,801,500	4,444,000	+8.0
Republic of Philippines	980,000	980,000	0
Cuba	3,001,295	3,432,960	−12.6
All other	217,205	143,040	+15.2
Total	9,000,000	9,000,000	

SOURCE: Department of Agriculture.

the United States market. Ninety-six percent of the difference between the announced quota and 5,424,000 tons (sum of fixed domestic and Philippines quotas) was given to Cuba and 4 percent to other foreign countries. Deficits in filling quotas were prorated 96 percent to Cuba and 4 percent to certain foreign countries other than the Philippines.

Under the amended act, domestic areas will have added to their base quotas 55 percent of all requirements above 8,350,000 tons, raw value, the announced quota at the beginning of 1956. Thus the quota of 9,000,-000 tons for 1957 provided for domestic area quotas 357,500 tons higher than they would have been under the unamended act [.55 (9,000,000 − 8,350,000)]. The amended act provides that the first 165,000 tons of this amount will be apportioned 51.5 percent to the domestic beet area and 48.5 percent to the mainland cane area; the next 20,000 tons goes to Puerto Rico; and the next 3000 tons to the Virgin Islands. Any quantity remaining after this first 188,000 tons has been apportioned is prorated on the basis of the quotas in effect after this total has been distributed. Apportioning the remaining 169,500 tons (357,500 − 188,000) by the percentages shown above fills out the total quotas for domestic areas based on a United States sugar marketing quota of 9,000,000 tons. These figures are shown in Table 22.

Important changes were also made in the formula for apportioning that part of the quota filled by foreign countries. Beginning in 1957, Cuba was allotted 96 percent and other countries 4 percent of the difference between 8,350,000 tons, raw value, and 5,424,000 (sum of fixed domestic quotas of 4,444,000 tons and the Philippines' quota of 980,000 tons). In addition, Cuba was assigned 29.59 percent of quotas exceeding 8,350,000 tons, and other countries were given 15.41 percent of such quotas. Cuba's quota then was .96 (8,350,000 − 5,424,000) + 29.59 (9,000,000 − 8,350,000) or 3,001,295.

Proration of the 9,000,000-ton marketing quota for 1957 under the amended act and what the proration would have been under the act of 1948 prior to this amendment are shown in Table 22.

The amendment also made important changes in prorating quota deficits. The act prior to the latest amendment provided that a deficit in any of the domestic areas or in Cuba was to be prorated among the other domestic areas and Cuba on the basis of quotas then in effect. A deficit in the Philippine quota was prorated 96 percent to Cuba and 4 percent to other foreign countries. Deficits in foreign countries other than Cuba and the Philippines were given to Cuba to fill. Finally, the Secretary of Agriculture was authorized to use his discretion in apportioning deficits resulting when an area could not fill its proration of another area's deficit.

But under the amended act a deficit in any domestic area which results when the area fails to market its share of the amount of sugar by which the quota exceeds 8,350,000 tons is first prorated to other domestic areas on the basis of quotas in effect at the time the deficit is declared. Whenever an area is unable to fill the higher quota resulting from this proration, this deficit is prorated among the other domestic areas. It is only when the domestic quotas cannot be filled by the domestic areas that a domestic deficit will be allotted to Cuba.

Renewed recognition of the international aspects of sugar and the problems of surplus producers exporting into the "free market" came

January 1, 1954, when a new International Sugar Agreement formulated by the International Sugar Council went into effect. Outside of the "free market" sugar trade is under special arrangements. These include: the United States; the Commonwealth Sugar Agreement; and movements of sugar between the Belgo-Luxembourg Economic Union (including the Belgian Congo), France and the countries which France represents internationally, the Federal Republic of Germany, and the Kingdom of the Netherlands (including Surinam).

The basic objective of the agreement was to stabilize the "free market" in sugar at an equitable price range for both producers and consumers, which was considered to be 3.25 to 4.35 cents per pound. The agreement does not contain export quotas in the restrictive sense; instead it provides certain basic quotas which are to be varied upward or downward in response to the needs of the market. If prices rise above a certain level, this is taken as an indication that supplies are insufficient, and the quotas in effect at that time are increased. Increases in quotas will continue to be made, in fact, until a reversal in the price trend indicates that a shortage no longer exists. This arrangement is intended to insure that the agreement cannot be used to restrict supplies so as to increase returns to producers above levels agreed upon by both importers and exporters. In addition, consumers are safeguarded by the fact that the participating exporting countries must hold certain minimum stocks, which act as protection to consuming countries. An amendment to the International Sugar Agreement went into force January 1, 1957. Revised quotas were established for the "free market" at levels between 3.15 and 4 cents a pound. All quotas are suspended when the price is above 4 cents.

The United States Senate ratified the agreement, but only after extensive hearings during which assurance was given that the United States was not obligated in any way. Thus United States policy is to recognize the sugar problem of surplus-producing countries. United States national sugar policy is expressed in the Sugar Act of 1948. No international sugar action would be undertaken that would interfere with our national policy.

Wool

Wool, the second important supplementary agricultural product which the United States imports, is also imported in the form of carpet wool, a complementary agricultural product that is not produced in the United States.

PRODUCTION, CONSUMPTION, AND INTERNATIONAL TRADE. We have already seen that wool production is largely concentrated in sparsely

TABLE 23. World Production of Wool
(in millions of pounds, greasy basis)

Year	Argentina	Australia	China	Europe Excl. U.S.S.R.	French North Africa[a]	India[b]	New Zealand	Spain	Turkey	Union of So. Africa	United Kingdom	United States	Uruguay	U.S.S.R.	World Total
1935–39 av.	389	1,018	81	529	88	82	308	71	60	246	108	425	121	244	3,800
1940–44 av.	500	1,129	83	484	76	80	344	81	69	250	94	440	137	279	4,122
1945	505	936	75	407	75	75	365	82	70	210	84	378	175	250	3,800
1946	515	977	75	398	52	55	367	79	69	210	88	342	176	287	3,820
1947	475	973	75	398	50	55	362	77	71	205	72	309	150	286	3,710
1948	419	1,031	75	433	48	53	367	88	76	219	83	278	144	305	3,770
1949	415	1,110	75	448	54	46	390	82	71	218	88	249	163	315	3,890
1950	430	1,118	75	465	64	51	390	90	67	228	89	271	185	350	4,022
1951	420	1,080	75	476	70	52	407	90	73	240	93	270	188	380	4,054
1952	407	1,281	75	495	75	51	418	93	78	257	102	290	190	400	4,372
1953	397	1,246	75	505	73	51	426	94	82	265	105	302	203	400	4,423
1954	364	1,294	75	520	74	51	455	95	80	280	108	308	198	390	4,496
1955	348	1,331	N.A.	520	74	51	475	95	79	295	106	304	200	410	4,560
1956	386	1,500	105	515	74	74	470	84	77	301	108	275	185	520	4,870

[a] Algeria, Tunisia, and French Morocco. [b] Pakistan excluded beginning 1946.
SOURCE: Department of Agriculture; Commodity Year Book, 1956. (See 1957 issue for minor revisions in years prior to 1956.)

populated countries with an abundance of land. Table 23 presents the world production of wool by countries from 1935 to 1957. We have also already noted from Table 10 that 80 percent of the world's exports of wool during 1934–38 came from four countries: Australia, Argentina, New Zealand, and South Africa.

Figure 4.17 gives world wool production and consumption for 1934 through 1956. From Table 23 and Figure 4.17 it is observable that total world production of wool has not varied substantially over the period of

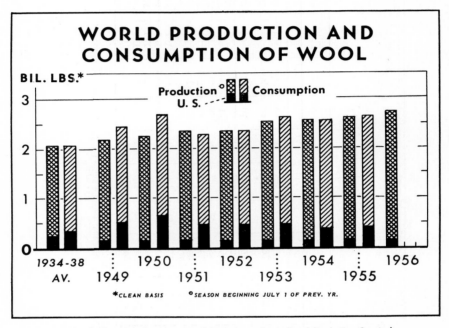

Figure 4.17. (U.S. Department of Agriculture, Agricultural Marketing Service)

years covered. World consumption, however, declined substantially during World War II as Europe's normal imports were stopped, and this led to a tremendous accumulation of stocks which reached a peak in 1945. From 1945 through 1950 world production of apparel wool was slightly lower because of a smaller United States output and of drought in Australia, South Africa, and Argentina. Consumption during 1945–50 rose much higher than the 1934–39 and 1940–45 averages because of the backlog of demand. Stocks were reduced, and production and consumption were approximately in balance during the post-World War II period.

The shifting patterns of international trade in wool between 1935–39 and 1954 are indicated in Figures 4.18 and 4.19. World exports of raw wool in 1935–39 averaged almost 2.2 billion pounds. The five most im-

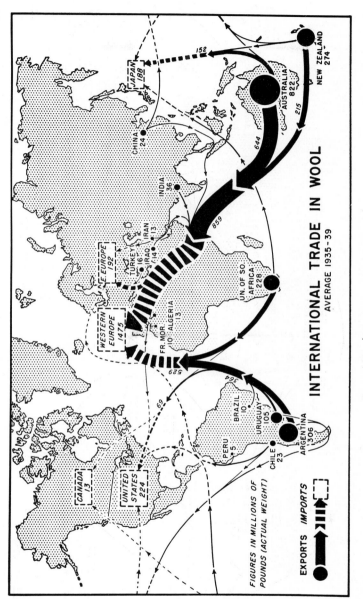

INTERNATIONAL TRADE IN WOOL
AVERAGE 1935-39

FIGURES IN MILLIONS OF
POUNDS (ACTUAL WEIGHT)

EXPORTS ● ➤➤➤ IMPORTS

Figure 4.18. (U.S. Department of Agriculture)

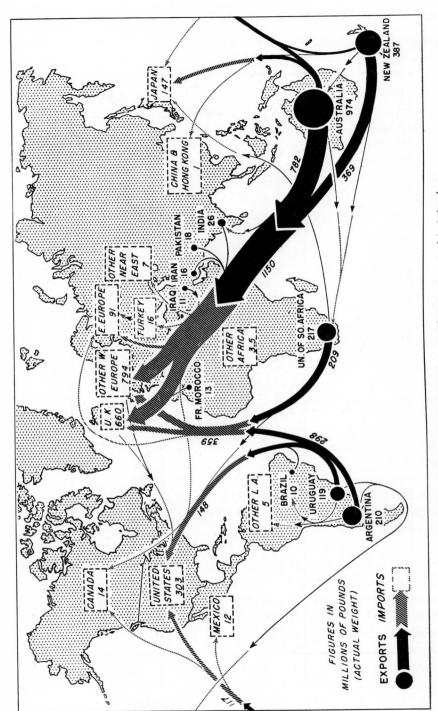

Figure 4.19. International Trade in Wool, 1954. (U.S. Department of Agriculture)

portant exporting countries—Australia, Argentina, New Zealand, South Africa, and Uruguay—exported 1.7 billion pounds. Australia, the world's largest exporter, furnished an annual average of 822 million pounds or about 38 percent of the world's exports. Europe imported slightly more than 75 percent of the world's total exports, and the United States, Japan, and Russia took most of the balance.

World War II greatly changed the pattern of international trade in wool. We have already seen from Table 9 that the United States imports increased three and one-half times between 1934–38 and 1949 while there

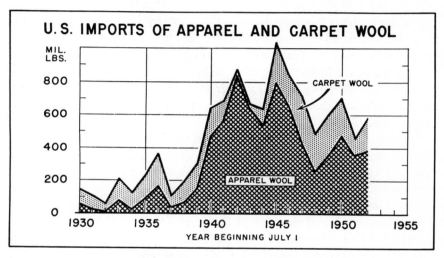

Figure 4.20.   (U.S. Department of Agriculture)

was practically no change in the imports of all other countries. The United States' share of world imports jumped from 11 to 31 percent. In 1951 the United States imported 555 million pounds, compared with 225 million pounds annually during 1935–39. Figure 4.19 shows that United States imports were down to 303 million pounds in 1954. Western Europe imported 1.45 billion pounds of wool in 1954, which was about the same as the 1.47 billion in the prewar years. The United Kingdom, France, Belgium, Germany, and Italy were the main European importing countries. In 1951 the United States was the chief wool deficit country as a result of increased consumption of wool and a much smaller production than in prewar years.

As indicated by Figure 4.20, which gives imports of apparel and carpet wool, United States imports of apparel wool rose rapidly beginning in 1939 to the peaks of the war years. Consumption of apparel wool increased from an annual average of 281 million pounds during 1935–39 to a peak of 610 million pounds in 1946 and declined to 339 million pounds in 1949 and 266 million pounds in 1954. Domestic production of wool declined to the lowest level in seventy years—249 million pounds—in 1949 and can be compared with an annual average production of 425 million pounds during 1935–39. Therefore imports of apparel wool are necessary. Practically all carpet wool consumed must be imported as the United States produces predominantly medium and fine wools.

Further proof of this dependence and changes during the post-Korean War period is illustrated in the two charts shown in Figure 4.21, which give United States wool production, net imports, and consumption. It is clear that the trend of consumption of both apparel and carpet wool was downward during the immediate postwar years. This trend in consumption was reflected in lower imports and was in part the result of the competition of synthetic fibers. However, consumption of wool turned up again in 1955 and there was some indication that wool was gaining favor once again.

The United States imports its duty-paid wool (mostly fine wools) from the five major exporters, New Zealand, Uruguay, South Africa, Argentina, and Australia (Figure 4.22). Before World War II United States imports were relatively small and were obtained from secondary sources. During 1940–45 continental Europe and Japan could not obtain Southern Hemisphere wool and the United States was the world-leading market. In 1942, imports of fine wool, principally from Australia, were high as military requirements shot up. In 1946 imports reached a peak which coincided with the peak demand as civilians rushed into the market. Imports, as noted, have since declined because of lower consumption.

United States production was marked by a continual decline of over 45 percent between 1942 and 1950. This was in contrast to the rising imports which we have just discussed as necessitated by an increased domestic consumption as well as the decline in production. The decline in the production of wool in the United States took place because other agricultural products were more profitable. Figure 4.21 shows that during the post-Korean period production increased slightly and leveled off at between 270 and 280 million pounds.

PROBLEMS AND POLICY.   One of the problems that must be considered is whether some adjustment is required in our wool import and agricultural policy. There is no duty on carpet wool as only insignificant quantities are produced in this country. The duty on the finer grades (ap-

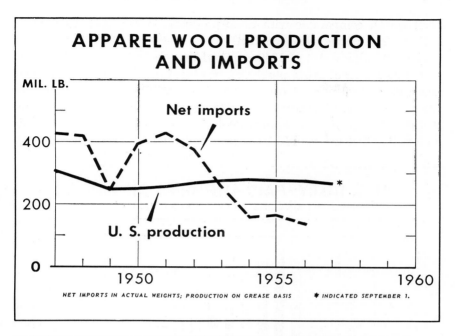

APPAREL WOOL PRODUCTION AND IMPORTS

MIL. LB.

Net imports

U. S. production

400

200

0

1950   1955   1960

*

NET IMPORTS IN ACTUAL WEIGHTS; PRODUCTION ON GREASE BASIS   * INDICATED SEPTEMBER 1.

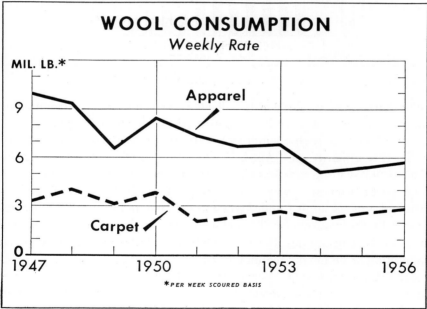

WOOL CONSUMPTION
Weekly Rate

MIL. LB.*

Apparel

9

6

3

Carpet

0

1947   1950   1953   1956

*PER WEEK SCOURED BASIS

Figure 4.21.   (U.S. Department of Agriculture, Agricultural Marketing Service)

parel wool), comparable with those produced in the United States, is 25½ cents a pound clean content.

The Agricultural Act of 1949 required that the price of wool be supported by means of loans, purchases, or other operations at the level between 60 and 90 percent of parity which the Secretary of Agriculture determines to be necessary in order to encourage an annual production of 360 million pounds of shorn wool, as it was established as an agricultural policy that we would like to have this quantity produced domesti-

Figure 4.22. (U.S. Department of Agriculture)

cally. Since wool production has declined well below this amount, this means in effect that price support is mandatory at 90 percent of parity. Wool prices were high enough so that no support prices were necessary under this authority until April, 1952. As the world wool price, plus the United States tariff, was less than the support level after April, 1952, a large part of domestic production went (and will go as long as this situation and policies apply) under government loan and was likely to be acquired by the government. To achieve the price objective without losses from support operations, the Secretary of Agriculture recommended the imposition of an import fee under Section 22 of the Agricultural Adjustment Act. During the first part of 1953 the Tariff Commission had under investigation the recommendation to impose import fees on wool and wool tops so that the cost of imported apparel wool, including the tariff and fee, would reflect at least 90 percent of the parity price and so as not to interfere with the domestic wool price-support program.

Without such a fee imported wool is purchased by the domestic manufacturers at the world price plus the United States tariff. As the tariff is a large part of the price of wool to manufacturers, it becomes a major factor in the competition between wool and the synthetic fibers such as rayon, acetate, orlon, Dacron, Dynel, Vicara, and Acrilan. The use of wool tends to be reduced below the level that would result from free choice by buyers at prices that would prevail in the absence of the wool tariff. Imposition of additional import fees to permit the achievement of the objectives of the domestic wool program would further handicap the woolen manufacturers and the consumers and cause additional shifts to synthetics. If the consumption and production of woolen goods are not to be penalized, raw wool should be imported without additional fees and without a tariff.[15]

Such a policy as recommended above is also beneficial to the exporters of wool to this country. We have already seen that Australia's exports of wool are 35 percent of total exports and thus her overseas income from wool is greater than that from any other commodity. In South Africa with 10 percent of exports and Uruguay with 46 percent, wool is the most important exportable agricultural product; and in New Zealand with 24 percent of total exports, wool ranks next in importance as an export commodity to butter and meat. Since wool exports are such a large percentage of total exports of these countries, United States policy that increases wool exports of these countries works to their benefit and to our international interests.

On the other hand, it is probably desirable for security reasons to maintain a flexible minimum level of domestic wool production. The most desirable practice is that the most efficient producers achieve this objective under competitive conditions. However, if this is determined not to be possible, then a policy should be adopted to subsidize domestic wool producers by direct payments to achieve the production goal, and let wool imports come in without tariffs or fees so that wool manufacturers and consumers may benefit from lower prices and textile manufacturers and consumers may exercise their choice between wool and synthetics by bidding for these commodities in a competitive international free market.

In July, 1953, on the advice of the Secretary of Agriculture, President Eisenhower requested the Tariff Commission to make an investigation under Section 22 of the Agricultural Adjustment Act to determine the effect of imports of certain varieties of wool on the operation of the domestic price-support program for wool. At the same time, he requested

[15] *A Trade and Tariff Policy in the National Interest*, p. 26.

the Secretary of Agriculture to make a comprehensive study of domestic factors which have contributed to the decline in sheep numbers and wool production. The study was undertaken, as he stipulated, "with a view toward development of a sound and prosperous domestic wool industry consistent with an expanding international trade."

On the basis of this study, which was carefully analyzed and discussed by the interested agencies of the executive branch of the government, it was determined that domestic wool growers required continued price or income assistance. The recommendation was made that this be accomplished by government assistance to growers under an incentive payment plan during periods when wool prices are below the desired support level. It was believed that the enactment of such an incentive payment program by Congress would eliminate the necessity for an increase in import fees or other limitations on wool imports, and further, that the new program would appreciably contribute to the achievement of a sound and prosperous domestic wool industry. This resulted in an announcement by the U.S. Department of Agriculture on October 11, 1954, of a shorn wool incentive price for the 1955 marketing year. Incentive prices were established under the provisions of the National Wool Act of 1954, which was passed March 1, 1954, and is described as a "bill to provide for the development of a sound and profitable domestic wool industry under our national policy of expanding world trade, to encourage increased domestic production of wool for our national security, and for other purposes." The bill authorizes the Secretary of Agriculture through the Commodity Credit Corporation to enter into agreements for the purpose of developing advertising and sales promotion programs for wool, mohair, sheep or goats, or the products thereof. Wool production, under the act, was stipulated at 300 million pounds of shorn wool annually. The method of support is also at the discretion of the Secretary of Agriculture and may be by incentive payments, loans, purchases, or other operations. Price supports of the Agricultural Adjustment Act of 1949 were repealed by the National Wool Act.

Under the payments program which went into effect with the 1956 season, growers sold their wool in the open market at prices reflecting world supply-and-demand conditions. After the close of the season they were eligible for government payments which brought the average return per pound up to the support or incentive level.

The incentive level for shorn wool for the 1956 marketing year beginning April 1, 1956, was 62 cents per pound, grease basis, to the producer. The level was equivalent to approximately 106 percent of the August 15, 1955, parity price for wool. The incentive price was established under the provisions of the National Wool Act of 1954, which directs the Secretary of Agriculture to support the price of shorn wool at such a level, not to exceed 110 percent of parity, as he determines to be necessary to encourage the annual production of approximately 300 million pounds of shorn wool. The incentive payment of 62 cents was still in effect for 1958.

The interdependence of the United States in agricultural products with the many areas of the world has been examined in some detail on the import side with respect to (a) complementary agricultural imports and (b) supplementary agricultural imports. Rubber and coffee were the complementary products singled out for study and sugar and wool were the supplementary commodities. Now attention must be focused on the second major interest of the United States in international agricultural trade: exports.

2. Export Interests

The United States agricultural producer has, as has been seen, a vital stake in exports because of the importance of export markets. As the United States is the world's greatest exporter of agricultural products, it hardly seems necessary to reëmphasize this fact, but there is a need for further study on an individual commodity basis. By way of introduction, the composition of United States agricultural exports is shown by value in Figure 4.23. Wheat, cotton, and tobacco have been the big three of the United States exports. From our illustration, it may be seen that the most significant shift is that grains have become relatively more important than cotton. In 1951 grains represented 38 percent and cotton 28 percent, as compared with 15 percent for grains and 41 percent for cotton during the prewar period. In 1956 exports of wheat alone were larger than those of cotton and linters, and livestock products had surpassed cotton.

The importance of foreign markets to United States farmers is clearly demonstrated in Figure 4.24 by the large proportion of flue-cured tobacco, wheat, rice, soybeans, lard, and cotton. In 1955 more than one-third of the United States crops of flue-cured tobacco, wheat, and rice was exported. In 1925 American tobacco farmers sold for export 67 percent of their tobacco. In 1940 this figure was 20 percent. The portion of the United States wheat exported has varied from less than 1 percent in 1935 to more than 48 percent in 1951. Percentage of the milled rice crop exported has ranged from 5 percent in 1925 to more than half of the total crop in 1951. In general, the share of production for export was

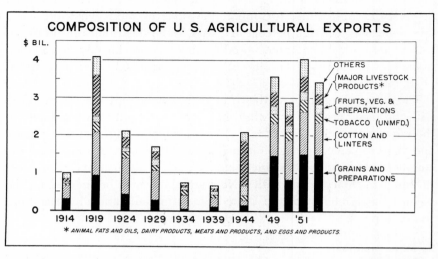

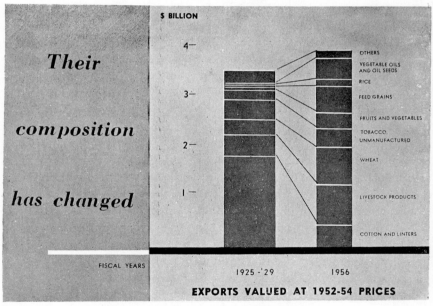

Figure 4.23. (U.S. Department of Agriculture)

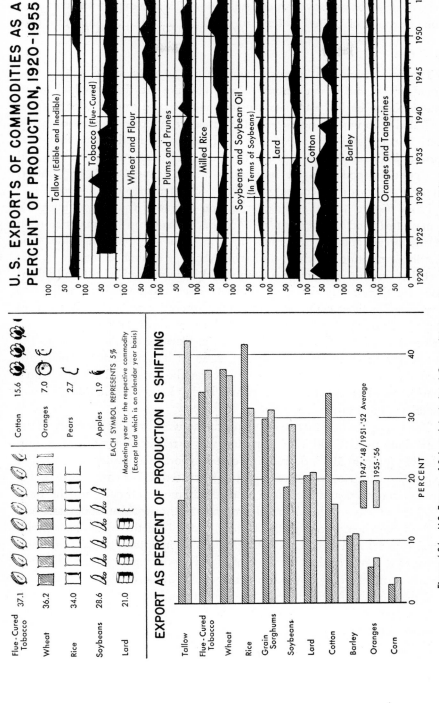

Figure 4.24.   U.S. Exports of Selected Agricultural Commodities as a Percentage of Production. (U.S. Department of Agriculture)

greater in the earlier years for cotton, flue-cured tobacco, and lard; less for wheat, soybeans, soybean oil, and tallow. This change in the composition of exports of United States farm products has been an important one.

A. Grains

The most important postwar agricultural exports are classified into bread grains and coarse grains. Wheat and rye are the principal bread grains. Corn, barley, and oats are the major coarse grains. Rice is often included with wheat and rye and the three are referred to as food grains. Corn, barley, and oats are largely feed grains. As feed grains they perform a dual role in that they are the basis of work done by animals and of secondary foods derived from animals, such as meat, milk, and butter. In some instances the coarse grains are consumed directly as food.

From Figure 4.25 the observation can be made that throughout the years wheat and wheat flour and corn have made up the major portion of the bread and coarse grains entering into international trade. The dominant position of wheat and wheat flour is explained largely by the fact that consumers throughout the world have wanted wheat and wheat flour for their many desirable characteristics and have been willing to pay more for these commodities than for any other grain. Rye has always stayed at home; about 95 percent of the rye crop is normally produced in continental Europe and Soviet Russia. Corn is dominant among the coarse grains entering international trade as it is used much more for feed than other grains and because it can be produced more cheaply than its possible substitutes. Oats and barley have been limited international trade items.

The United States' increasing share of the world's grains exports in the immediate post-World War II period was a result of our aid programs. The big jump in 1955, despite increased export availability in the major exporting countries, was due in part to increased dollar earnings by many foreign countries and increased feed requirements abroad; but the principal cause was surplus disposal programs authorized by Congress.

Because wheat is one of the United States' "big three" of the agricultural exports and because of its importance in international trade and because it is one of the "big two" of world foods, the facts and problems of wheat need to be studied in some detail. Some of these wheat facts and problems will now be reviewed and then, because rice is the other of the "big two" world foods, a few facts will be presented to show the position of rice in international trade.

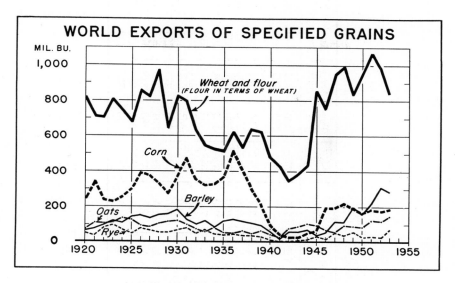

U.S. IS WORLD'S BIGGEST EXPORTER OF GRAINS.

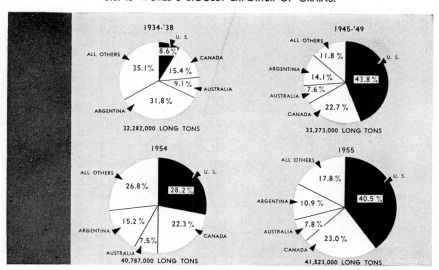

Figure 4.25. World Exports of Specified Grains. (U.S. Department of Agriculture)

TABLE 24. World Production of Wheat
(in millions of bushels)

Crop Year	United States	Canada	Spain	Italy	Germany	France	Rumania	China	India[b]	Turkey	Argentina	Australia	World Total[a]
1935–39 av.	759	312	158	278	151	287	112	750	379	136	222	170	6,085
1940–44 av.	926	423	103	246	154	240	80	782	385	136	235	113	5,735
1945	1,108	318	73	168	N.A.	184	N.A.	854	394	80	144	142	5,120
1946	1,153	414	133	238	N.A.	250	N.A.	888	337	175	206	117	5,704
1947	1,367	342	103	205	N.A.	150	N.A.	920	297	130	245	220	5,780
1948	1,314	386	110	250	74c	300	N.A.	900	326	145	191	191	6,395
1949	1,141	371	110	275	91c	297	N.A.	760	358	95	189	218	6,185
1950	1,019	462	125	285	96c	283	N.A.	775	383	150	213	184	6,320
1951	981	553	175	260	113c	265	N.A.	800	385	205	77	160	6,465
1952	1,299	688	170	295	120c	310	N.A.	800	330	239	279	195	7,295
1953	1,169	614	125	333	116c	330	N.A.	N.A.	381	294	228	198	7,390
1954	988	309	180	266	106c	388	N.A.	N.A.	431	180	283	167	6,945
1955	938	494	150	338	124c	385	N.A.	N.A.	435	260	240	210	7,300
1956	997	512	155	312	117c	240	N.A.	N.A.	439	240	220	180	7,510

a Estimated. b Includes Pakistan. c Western Germany.
SOURCE: Department of Agriculture; *Commodity Year Book*, 1956. (See 1957 issue for revisions in years prior to 1956.)

Wheat

Wheat is the "staff of life" of the Western world.

PRODUCTION, CONSUMPTION, AND INTERNATIONAL TRADE.   Wheat is grown over widespread areas of the world (see Table 24); however, the surplus-producing countries have been limited to the United States, Canada, Argentina, and Australia. Eastern European countries also have had wheat for export but at the present time reliable statistical information is not available. Wheat production in Europe, exclusive of Russia, can be seen from Figure 4.26 to have been in most years greater

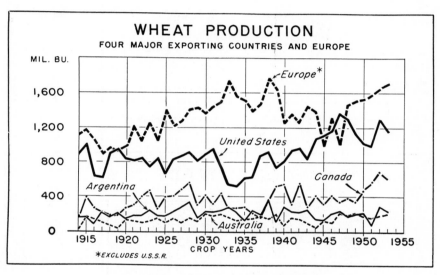

Figure 4.26.   (U.S. Department of Agriculture)

than that in any one of the four major exporting countries. Most of the wheat from the four major exporting countries has gone into the European market, and the decline in world trade in wheat during the twenties and in the thirties in particular, as seen in Figure 4.25, was a result of the upward trend in European production in an attempt to increase self-sufficiency. The effect of World War II on European production is very noticeable in Figure 4.26, as is the expansion that occurred in United States production to meet European and world needs. Similarly the postwar effects are observed in increased European production and a decline in United States production.

The shifts in world trade in wheat between 1935–39 and 1950–51 and 1954–55 are clearly indicated in Figures 4.27, 4.28, and 4.29. In the pre-

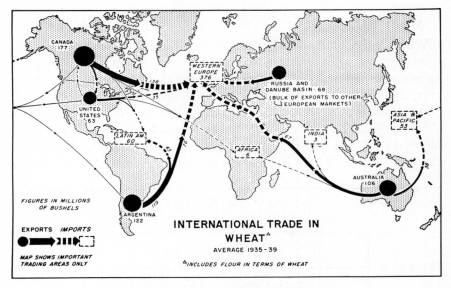

Figure 4.27. (U.S. Department of Agriculture)

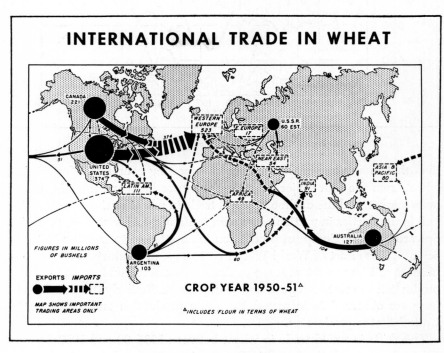

Figure 4.28. (U.S. Department of Agriculture)

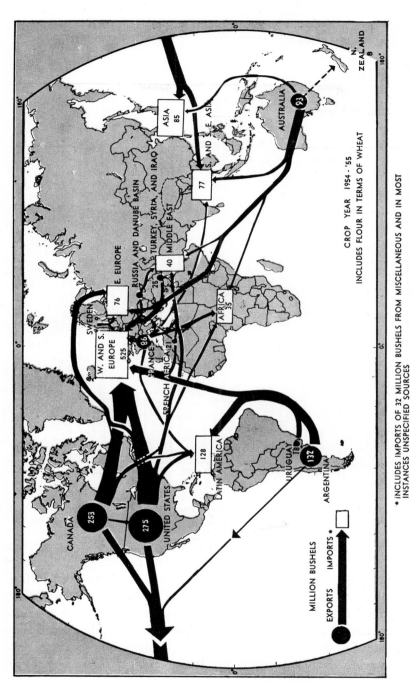

CROP YEAR 1954 - '55
INCLUDES FLOUR IN TERMS OF WHEAT

* INCLUDES IMPORTS OF 32 MILLION BUSHELS FROM MISCELLANEOUS AND IN MOST
  INSTANCES UNSPECIFIED SOURCES

Figure 4.29. International Trade in Wheat, 1954–55. (U.S. Department of Agriculture)

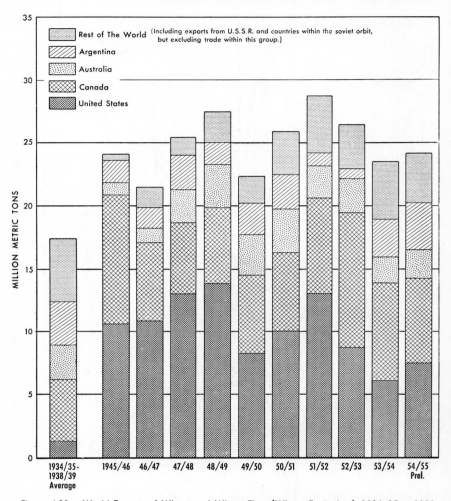

Figure 4.30.   World Exports of Wheat and Wheat Flour (Wheat Equivalent), 1934–35 to 1938–39 Average and 1945–46 to 1954–55 (July–June). (*State of Food and Agriculture, 1955,* FAO)

World War II period it can be seen, as noted above, that the western European countries were the leading importers. Sizable quantities were imported by deficit-producing countries in the Latin-American and Caribbean area and in Asia. During 1950–51 and 1954–55, as in the 1935–39 period, the deficit-producing countries of western Europe were the principal importers of wheat, with a total of about 525 million bushels as compared with the prewar total of 376 million bushels. Shipments to Asia, Latin America, and Africa were also larger. Most significant, however, was the shift in the relative importance of the export countries between

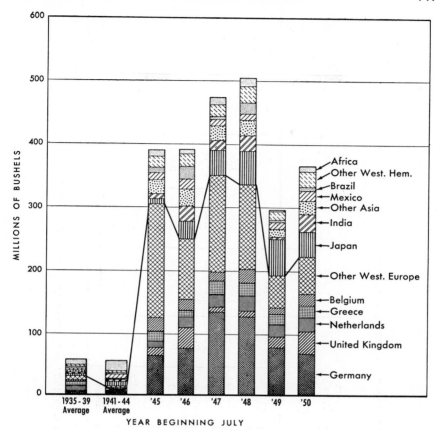

Figure 4.31. United States Exports of Wheat Including Flour to Specified Countries. (U.S. Department of Agriculture)

the prewar and postwar periods. The United States was the world's largest exporter of wheat in 1950–51 and in 1954–55. Our exports of 374 million bushels in 1950–51 were almost six times greater than during 1935–39. Shipments from Canada and Australia in 1950–51 were also up from the prewar period, but those from Argentina and Russia showed a substantial reduction. In 1954–55 Argentina was ahead of her prewar position, but Australia had fallen. Before World War II exporters in order of rank were Canada, Argentina, Australia, and the United States as a poor fourth with 63 million bushels. This shifting importance of the exporting countries of wheat and wheat flour and the tremendous increases in exports over the prewar period can be more easily seen from Figure 4.30. The dominant role that the United States played in supplying the hungry

TABLE 25.   Salient Statistics of Wheat in the United States

Year	Acreage Harvested (1,000 acres)	Average Yield Per Acre (in bushels)	Production (1,000 bushels)	Farm Price (cents per bushel)	Kansas City Price[a]	Farm Value (1,000 dollars)	Foreign Trade Including Flour[d] (million bushels) Domestic Exports[b]	Imports[c]	Net Exports	Per Capita[e] Consumption of Wheat in Lbs.
1935–39 av.	57,293	13.2	758,629	81.4	96	617,524	63.0	23.6	39.4	225
1940–44 av.	54,017	17.1	925,984	109.9	124	1,031,365	43.5	46.8	3.3[f]	218
1945	65,167	17.0	1,107,623	150.0	160	1,660,891	318.7	13.6	305.1	227
1946	67,105	17.2	1,152,118	191.0	209	2,201,036	366.1	2.0	364.1	211
1947	74,519	18.2	1,358,911	229.0	252	3,109,445	479.8	.1	479.7	193
1948	72,418	17.9	1,294,911	199.0	219	2,577,191	505.3	4.6	500.7	191
1949	75,910	14.5	1,098,415	188.0	216	2,061,897	308.2	11.8	296.3	190
1950	61,610	16.5	1,019,389	200.0	228	2,042,392	374.0	20.0	354.0	190
1951	61,492	16.0	980,810	211.0	243	2,073,645	479.6	37.4	442.2	192
1952	70,926	18.3	1,298,957	209.0	232	2,714,404	323.7	27.9	295.8	186
1953	67,661	17.3	1,169,484	204.0	227	2,385,167	183.2	8.4	174.8	179
1954	54,279	18.1	984,846	212.0	235	2,084,743	226.2	5.2	221.0	175
1955	47,285	19.8	934,700	198.0	223	1,854,189	294.0	10.0	284.0	172
1956	49,817	20.0	997,200	198.0		1,969,806				170

a No. 2 hard winter weighted average. b Includes flour milled from imported wheat. c Includes wheat imported for milling in bond and export. d Year beginning July.
e Civilian only, 1941 to date. f Net imports.
Source: Department of Agriculture; Commodity Year Book, 1956. (See 1957 issue for minor revisions in years prior to 1956.)

wheat consumers of the world from 1944 through 1952 is clearly indicated.

United States leadership in the export of wheat can be more closely
examined by reference to Figure 4.31. A study of this figure in conjunction with Table 25 ("Salient Statistics of Wheat in the United States")
and Figure 4.32 ("Wheat Distribution") will reveal significant information on the wheat economy of the United States. Just as was the case in

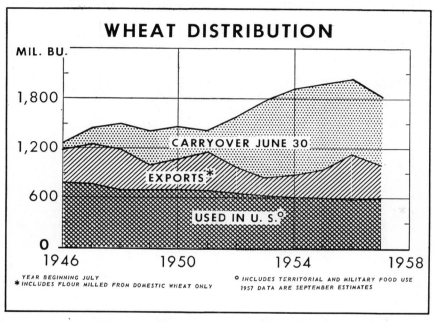

Figure 4.32.   (U.S. Department of Agriculture, Agricultural Marketing Service)

World War I, wheat production was expanded during World War II to
help food win the war and write the peace. Peak United States wheat
production in 1947 was almost 1.8 times the average production during
1935–39 and peak domestic exports in 1948 were over eight times greater
than the prewar quantity. United States exports were shipped primarily
to aid the postwar recovery of western Europe; however, it is clearly discernible that United States policy was to supply wheat to the Asiatic
countries as well. Shipments to Japan alone, to offset the loss of rice imports, were greater during one postwar period than our total average
wheat exports during 1935–39. As the United States policy became effective and western Europe increased wheat production, United States exports to that area began to fall sharply after 1948.

The prospects in 1957 for future United States exports of wheat were for a general leveling off and possible decline depending upon economic trends and policy decisions. One reason for this trend was that, as observed from Figure 4.33, international trade in wheat and flour had become more or less stabilized between 950 and 1000 million bushels grain equivalent annually. Through the years, the bulk of the exports has been supplied by "the Big Four": United States, Canada, Argentina, and Australia. Although each of these countries undoubtedly will continue to be

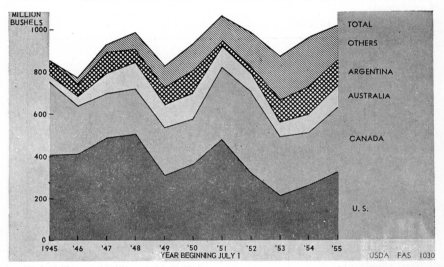

Figure 4.33. World Wheat Exports. Four countries now account for ⅘ of world's wheat exports. (U.S. Department of Agriculture)

included among the world's leading exporters for many years, several other countries are definitely demonstrating their intentions of participating on an increasing scale to help supply the world's import requirements. This is especially true of France, Turkey, Sweden, Uruguay, French North Africa, and Syria, from each of which substantial quantities of wheat and flour may be expected to be available for export during good crop years. The United States' share of the total was about 34 percent in 1955–56 and 28 percent in 1954–55.

Since the total domestic use of wheat had become stabilized to about the 1935–39 average after a sharp decline from the wartime peaks (Figure 4.32) any future decline in exports necessitated a drastic revision in United States wheat production and policy, and such a decline was of major importance to United States wheat producers. The significance of wheat exports to the wheat farmers can be dramatically illustrated by showing that during the post-World War II years wheat exports averaged one-third of domestic wheat production, which was equivalent to the production of one out of every three farmers.

PROBLEMS AND POLICY. We will consider problems and policy under two related categories—domestic and international.

Domestic wheat problems and policies requiring action during the middle 1950's were centered around production adjustments, international trade, surplus disposal, and related price considerations. In order to appreciate some of the problems involved in United States wheat production and exports, it is necessary to have some basic understanding of the United States agricultural policy.

During World War I and World War II agricultural production was expanded rapidly and increased exports contributed greatly to the military, economic, and political stability of our allies. Between the two wars and in the early thirties in particular, agricultural prices dropped sharply and production was maintained at approximately the same aggregate level. Agricultural policy in the United States, as established under the Agricultural Adjustment Act of 1938, was designed to stabilize farm prices and income. At the time of the passage of the act the main problem was one of preventing disastrous price drops due to "overproduction." Therefore it has often been said that the act of 1938 had two objectives: the first, to prevent price drops due to overproduction and the second, to prevent overproduction itself. This is not correct, however, because agricultural production policy and practice have been aimed at the maintenance of a volume of agricultural production sufficient to insure adequate supplies for domestic consumption, and in the case of certain commodities, for export. The concept of "adequate" has been one of sufficiency and not too much. Price policy, although designed by the act to accomplish stabilization, has more often been practiced to achieve agricultural price supports and higher agricultural prices. The basic agricultural policy in its present form had its origin in the Agricultural Adjustment Act of 1938. There are two fundamental and interrelated parts of the act—production adjustments and price policies.

The production adjustment features of the act provided for: (1) acreage allotments for individual basic crops and payments to coöperators based on the amount of acreage in the allotment; (2) marketing quotas to be used if, in a special referendum called for the purpose, producers approved their use by a two-thirds majority; and (3) marketing agreements permitting farmers and processors to organize for the control over the marketing of agricultural produce and exempting such action from antitrust laws. Other features of the act provided for: (1) soil conservation payments to farmers following specified soil conservation practices; (2) production payments, based on parity, to help make up the difference between actual market prices and the price-support standard adopted; and (3) continuation of the authority of the Secretary of Agriculture, originally granted in 1935, to use up to 30 percent of the receipts from import duties and tariffs to divert surplus agricultural produce into foreign or domestic channels and to develop new uses for agricultural commodities.

Price support operations became the backbone of the farm program under the act of 1938. In addition to the Commodity Credit Corporation's authority to support prices of any agricultural commodity, the agency was required (1) to support prices of certain agricultural commodities and (2) to support these commodities at not less than certain specified percentages of parity.

The parity price of an agricultural commodity, generally speaking, is the price which will give the commodity the same purchasing power as it had during a given base period in terms of (1) prices of commodities farmers buy, (2) interest on mortgage indebtedness, (3) taxes on farm real estate, and (4) for most commodities, wage rates for hired farm labor. Thus the parity price of an individual farm commodity is a standard for measuring the purchasing power of that commodity in relation to prices of goods and services during a definite base period.

During World War II production adjustment, as a means used primarily to restrict output, was deëmphasized in favor of production "goals," price supports, and production subsidies to expand output. Increases in output were achieved by guaranteeing farmers that they would not be penalized by low prices if they expanded production. This was accomplished through the so-called Stegal Amendment, which required the Secretary of Agriculture to support the price of any agricultural commodity for which an increase in production had been requested at not less than specified percentages of parity for the war period and two years thereafter. Support was provided beyond the immediate war period to permit orderly readjustment. The fear was that surpluses would occur during the postwar period, as was the case after World War I, and serious price declines would follow.

The Agricultural Act of 1949, and as amended by the Agricultural Act of 1954 and by the National Wool Act of 1954, made it mandatory for the Secretary of Agriculture to support prices of twelve commodities at specified percentages or ranges of parity. The twelve commodities were:

corn	rice	honey	mohair
wheat	peanuts	tung nuts	milk
cotton	tobacco	wool	butterfat

Price support is provided principally by non-recourse government loans and to a limited extent by purchases. Prices of wool and mohair are supported by incentive payments.

Control over supplies of agricultural products is authorized under specified conditions by use of acreage allotments and marketing quotas. Marketing quotas can be used only for the first six of the above commodities (basic) subject to a favorable vote by two-thirds of the producers. When producers disapprove marketing quotas, price support is prohibited for tobacco and is reduced to 50 percent of parity and limited to coöperators for other basic commodities. Acreage allotments may be used for any commodity under specified supply conditions; however, they have actually been used mainly to supplement marketing quotas by specifying the acreage from which products can be marketed without penalty or loss of price support benefits. As a counterpart to these devices for holding down production and supplies, voluntary production goals are announced to encourage needed production increases.

In the particular case of wheat, legislation provides for acreage allotments each year except in time of national emergency and for marketing quotas when supplies get out of line with demand.[16]

Acreage allotment for the nation is "proclaimed" by the Secretary of Agriculture for the next crop not later than July 15 each year. The size of the allotment must be large enough to produce a supply equal to 130

[16] Acreage allotments for wheat were in effect six times from 1938 to 1954 as follows:

Crop	Acres
1938	62,000,000
1939	55,000,000
1940	62,000,000
1941	62,000,000
1942	55,000,000
1950	72,776,000

Acreage allotments were proclaimed for the 1943 and 1951 crops but were terminated under the emergency powers of the Agricultural Adjustment Act after winter wheat was planted. Acreage allotments for the crops of 1944–49, inclusive, and for 1952 and 1953 were dispensed with under the emergency powers of the Adjustment Act. Prior to 1954, marketing quotas were in effect only for the 1941 and 1942 crops of wheat.

percent of a normal year's domestic consumption and exports. However, legislation established in 1953 provided that the national acreage allotment could not be less than 62 million acres. The national acreage allotment is apportioned to states and counties on the basis of the acreage seeded to wheat during the preceding ten years, with adjustments for abnormal weather and trends during the ten-year period. County acreage is apportioned to individual farms on the basis of tillable acres, crop-rotation practices, type of soil, and topography. Producers are not penalized for failure to comply with acreage allotments when marketing quotas are not in effect, except that the producer who is not a coöperator is entitled to only such support as the Secretary, in his discretion, may make available to such non-coöperators.

Marketing quotas are required in accordance with the determination of legal formulas which must be followed by the Secretary of Agriculture. He must proclaim quotas when (1) the *total supply* (carry-over on June 30 plus production and imports) of wheat for the next marketing year will be more than 20 percent larger than the *normal supply* (the domestic consumption for the current marketing year added to estimated exports for the next marketing year plus 15 percent of the total as a carry-over reserve) or (2) the total supply for the current marketing year is not less than the normal supply, and the average farm price for three successive months of the current marketing year has not exceeded 66 percent of the parity price.

When the Secretary of Agriculture determines that wheat marketing quotas are required he must "proclaim" this fact, for example, not later than July 1, 1953, for the marketing year that began on July 1, 1954.

After the Secretary of Agriculture proclaims that quotas are required, he must conduct a referendum, by secret ballot, of farmers who will be subject to the quota to determine whether such farmers favor or oppose the quota program. If more than one-third of the farmers voting in the referendum oppose the quota program, the Secretary is required, prior to the effective date of the quotas, by proclamation to suspend the operation of the marketing quota program.

If producers disapprove marketing quotas for wheat the 1949 and the 1954 Agricultural Acts provided that the level of price support of coöperators shall be 50 percent of the parity price.

Individual marketing quotas are based on acres—not bushels. Generally speaking, the marketing quota for an individual farm is the quantity of wheat produced on the farm acreage allotment.

If the farm acreage allotment is exceeded, the "farm marketing excess" must be determined. This is computed, in terms of bushels, on the basis of the normal production of the excess acreage. The "farm marketing excess" may be marketed by the producer, but the producer was subject to a penalty per bushel equal to 50 percent of the basic loan rate under the 1949 act and 45 percent of parity price of May 1 under the 1954 act. The basic loan rate on the 1953 crop was $2.21 per bushel.

The Secretary of Agriculture proclaimed wheat quotas on July 1, 1953, when the total supply for 1953–54 was indicated at a record 1717 million bushels, which exceeded the normal supply of 1156 million bushels by 48 percent. A later crop report in August, 1953, increased the expected 1953 crop to 1203 million bushels. This crop together with a carry-over of 559 million bushels and an estimated import of 5 million bushels raised the total indicated supply to 1767 million bushels, 53 percent above normal. Since the indicated 1953–54 wheat supply stood at an all-time high, the minimum acreage of 62 million was called for.

On August 14, 1953, wheat farmers voted over 87 percent in favor of marketing quotas for 1954. Price support at 90 percent of parity was available for those who stayed within their acreage allotment. Marketing penalties equal to 54 percent of the wheat parity as of May 1, 1954, applied on any wheat produced on acres in excess of the farm's allotment. The parity price on July 15, 1953, was $2.44.

Marketing quotas were in effect again in 1955, in 1956, and in 1957. By a majority of 77½ percent the wheat farmers voted for controls in 1956 in return for a support price of $1.81 a bushel. The final support price was $2.00. The acreage for 1956 was reduced to a national allotment of 55 million acres. In 1953, the last year in which farmers grew wheat without quotas, support price was $2.21 a bushel, and almost 79 million acres were planted. Thus, in three years, the average wheat grower received an acreage cut of 30 percent and a decrease of 40 cents a bushel in federal price support. For 1957 the goal was to cut 12 to 15 million acres out of the 55-million-acre allotment under the Soil Bank program so that planted acreage would be 40 to 43 million acres. Wheat growers voted 87.4 percent in favor of controls and a minimum support price of $2.00 per bushel.

Figure 4.34, which gives wheat prices and loan rates, definitely indicates that support prices for wheat were not necessary during 1946–47 and 1947–48. Surplus, as indicated by the carry-over in Figure 4.32, did not occur and prices were high because demand was exceptionally strong, owing principally to the very large wheat exports. The leveling off of domestic consumption and exports and the continued high production sustained and encouraged by the support price and inadequate production adjustments gave rise to the dramatic increases in carry-over shown in Figure 4.32.

The basic problem facing the United States wheat producers in 1956 was the rapid build-up of wheat stocks in spite of the quotas which had been in effect in 1954 and 1955. Carry-over stocks increased from 256 million bushels following the 1951–52 crop year to 1020 million on July 1, 1955, after the 1954–55 crop year.

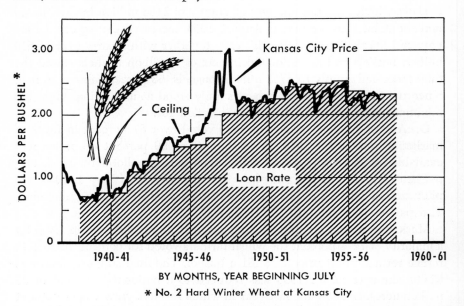

Figure 4.34. Wheat Prices and Loan Rates. (U.S. Department of Agriculture, Agricultural Marketing Service)

The billion-bushel wheat carry-over might be reduced if domestic consumption of wheat as feed or food and exports could be increased. Will decreases in price bring about an increase in domestic consumption? There may be some increase in the amount of wheat fed to livestock where corn is relatively high priced. But in most areas corn will continue to be a much cheaper feed. Wheat use per capita for flour as food has been declining in the United States steadily since 1910. It is generally conceded that the demand for wheat as flour baked into bread is inelastic. There was in 1956 about 3 cent's worth of wheat in an 18-cent loaf of bread. So even a 50 percent decrease in the price of wheat would have very little effect on the cost of bread. Evidence points to a leveling off or further decreases in exports of wheat rather than an increase.

Secretary of Agriculture Benson indicated in July, 1955, that if average wheat yields prevailed for the 1955–56 crop year the billion-bushel stock might be reduced by 50 million bushels by July 1, 1956. However, carry-over stocks increased to 1,034,000 on July 1, 1956. Nevertheless this was the first year since 1952–53 in which the carry-over of wheat did not increase substantially. He estimated that it would take ten years of rigid controls to reduce carry-over to a level of 500 million bushels. This would still be much more than the pre-World War II carry-over.

Lower wheat prices and/or rigid controls will reduce wheat production and eventually reduce the carry-over, but they will not solve the wheat growers' problem of what to do with the diverted acreage. The wheat-belt farmers' crops are limited by soil and climate. Sorghum is about the only other cash crop, but it also has a surplus problem. In the corn belt, where wheat is also grown, soil and climate give the farmer a wider variety of crops, but many of them were in surplus supply in 1955–56. Corn was under limited controls. Soybeans are considered the second most profitable crop, but they were also in surplus supply. Thus the wheat carry-over is part of a general farm surplus problem.

The supply of wheat for the 1956–57 marketing year was estimated at 2015 million bushels, a new all-time record. If exports total 415 million bushels and domestic disappearance continued at about 600 million bushels, the carry-over July 1, 1957, would be about a billion bushels compared with 1034 million on July 1, 1956.

The reduction in carry-over in 1956–57 to 905 million bushels reflects the effects of the largest exports in our history. These were estimated at 547 million bushels, which was about 201 million bushels above those in 1955–56. This increase in exports was in part due to the United States government's major export program under P.L. 480 (83rd Congress), Agricultural Trade Development and Assistance Act of 1954. This act authorized sales for foreign currencies, barter transactions, grants for emergency foreign relief, and donations to private charities for the needy overseas.

The quantity of exports depended upon a number of factors, including the availability of shipping and the completion of a number of negotiations under P.L. 480. Most important was the emphatic point made by the FAO: "Almost the whole United States' wheat and flour exports now move under direct subsidy, or under one or other of the special export programs."

The wheat outlook for 1957–58 was for a big reduction of production because of a possible 13 million decrease in acres withdrawn under the

Acreage Reserve Program of the Soil Bank as provided for under the 1956 act. It was estimated that domestic disappearance in 1957–58 would not be greatly different from current levels of about 600 million bushels. According to the United States Department of Agriculture, exports were dependent upon a number of factors, including production in both importing and other exporting countries, foreign developments which might stimulate stockpiling in certain importing countries, and whether some form of government aid to exports is continued after June 30, 1957, when P.L. 480 terminated. If exports were at the 1955–56 level of 345 million bushels, total disappearance would amount to about 945 million bushels. And a crop of only about 740 million bushels would make it possible to reduce the carry-over by July 1, 1958, by about 200 million bushels.

The longer-time outlook was that the minimum acreage allotment established by law at 55 million acres, with average yields, does not permit a reduction in carry-over under ordinary conditions since it involves exports of around 250 million bushels, considered by the United States Department of Agriculture "a high level to maintain year after year." The Acreage Reserve Program, however, offered an opportunity to reduce the carry-over. In the two years after the 1957 crop that the Acreage Reserve Program had to run, an additional substantial cut in the carry-over was expected. However, Frederick V. Waugh, Director of the Agricultural Economics Division of the United States Department of Agriculture, pointed out that "changes in world developments could make it desirable to have relatively large wheat supplies on hand, under which circumstances we might want to reappraise the need for continued stock reductions."

On the international wheat problem and policy front, wheat-exporting countries have long been concerned about the uncertainty of markets, and wheat importers have struggled with the problem of uncertainty of long-run supplies. Both exporters and importers have suffered from price fluctuations and uncertainties. As a result, negotiations toward an international wheat agreement date back to 1931. A formal International Wheat Agreement was signed in London in 1933, but it broke down after one year. A series of wheat crop failures during 1933–36 in North America raised prices and reduced by two-thirds the stocks in the main exporting countries. A world-wide bumper crop in 1938 caused the Wheat Advisory Committee, created under the 1933 agreement, to begin negotiations for a new agreement, which were interrupted by World War II.

A successor to the International Wheat Advisory Committee, the International Wheat Council, was formed at an International Wheat Meeting, held in Washington in July, 1941. A Memorandum of Agreement was signed April 22, 1942, putting into effect *ad interim* some of the provisions of the preliminary draft of a new wheat agreement. By terms of the agreement, signatory nations had to indicate formal acceptance by July, 1948. Ratification by a sufficient number of countries was not obtained, and the new agreement never went into effect.

A new International Wheat Agreement was negotiated in Washington on March 23, 1949, by thirty-seven importing nations—this number increased to forty-two—and by the exporting nations of the United States, Canada, Australia, and France. These included all principal traders in wheat except Argentina and the U.S.S.R. The agreement became effective September 1, 1949, for a four-year period. The International Wheat Agreement was aimed at assuring markets for wheat to exporting countries and supplies of wheat to importing countries at equitable prices. Under its terms the United States, Canada, Australia, and France guaranteed to sell specified quotas of wheat if offered the *maximum price* set; and the importing nations, in turn, agreed to buy their quotas during each of the four years if the wheat were offered at the *minimum price*.

The International Wheat Agreement, which otherwise would have expired on July 31, 1953, was revised and renewed to be in effect for a three-year period ending July 31, 1956.

Under the agreement exporting countries could ship each year a maximum of about 421 million bushels of wheat to forty-five importing countries. This was a little less than half the then current annual world trade in wheat. The United States, Canada, Australia, and France were obligated to sell their respective quotas of 209,588,085; 163,230,880; 48,000,-000; and 367,000 bushels at only the maximum price of $2.05 per bushel, basis bulk wheat in store at Fort William-Port Arthur, Canada, in terms of United States currency. This maximum price amounted to about $1.70 to United States growers. Importing nations were obligated to buy their specified quotas of wheat at the minimum price of $1.55 per bushel. All the important wheat importers were included in the renewed agreement except the United Kingdom. Between the floor and the ceiling price, wheat was free to move at prices agreed upon between the buyer and seller.

During almost the entire period of the initial four-year agreement, world wheat prices were above the maximum specified price and United States prices were above the world prices. Therefore importers purchased United States wheat and since United States prices for wheat were above the maximum, a subsidy to United States exporters was required covering the difference between the United States market price and the agreement price. From August 1, 1949, through July 30, 1953, sales under the agreement totaled above 917 million bushels, including wheat and wheat flour in wheat equivalent.

Under the last year of the original agreement the maximum price was $1.80 a bushel. Up to January, 1953, subsidies had cost the United States about $400 million. This occurred in part because world wheat prices remained high owing to the cold war and the Korean hostilities.

In the area of international policy it is argued that the agreement has aided United States policy by strengthening the economies of our western European allies by relieving them of the necessity of becoming self-sufficient in wheat and enabling them to concentrate on crops they can grow most efficiently. Assurance of supplies of wheat at reasonable prices through the International Wheat Agreement played an important part in the decision of western Europeans to limit their wheat production to an acreage of from three to four million below that planted just before World War II. This is a valid point, but it also must be remembered that United States foreign aid programs that helped certain countries to buy our wheat also were an important, though temporary, factor. In addition, before World War II, western Europe imported large quantities of grain, especially wheat, from the U.S.S.R., Poland, and the Danube Basin. As a result of the Wheat Agreement and other United States aid, free countries of western Europe have not been dependent on Russian-controlled grain and thus have not been subject, because of their need for grain, to Soviet pressures to gain control.

The basic argument for the Wheat Agreement in the area of domestic policy is that it gave the United States markets that she would not have had without some form of export subsidy. The increased western European market is offered as proof of this contention. It has also been pointed out that during the first year of the original agreement Canadian wheat sold outside the IWA for export averaged 36 cents a bushel less than United States wheat sold outside of IWA for export. Under these price conditions, if it had not been for the agreement or some arrangement like it, it would have been difficult to sell United States wheat in many markets abroad. Within the agreement we were able to compete with Canada and other IWA exporters at an agreed-upon price by means of export payments to commercial shippers. The agreement guaranteed and offered a means of bridging the gap between United States domestic prices and higher world prices through these export subsidies and, in addition, offered a certain specified minimum export quota.

A simplified two-price system, one domestic and another lower export price with an export subsidy to cover the difference, might enable the United States to sell wheat abroad; but it is contended that this would lack the advantages of international coöperation.

An alternative to no Wheat Agreement and no export subsidy would be to cut down acreage and produce only for the domestic market. In answer to this the United States Department of Agriculture contended: "But we have areas of cropland, particularly in the Great Plains and the Pacific Northwest, that can be used better for wheat than for anything else. Farmers on this land now have labor, machinery, and storage facilities for wheat production. A major shift to any other type of agriculture would be both difficult and expensive."[17]

It can also be argued with force that it is expensive to subsidize exports and it is expensive to subsidize domestic production under the price support system. A more reasonable approach might be to lower the domestic price support so that United States domestic prices would be more in line with international wheat prices.

In spite of the many cogent arguments given for the agreement, the Commission on Foreign Economic Policy came to the following conclusion and recommendation:

The International Wheat Agreement has contributed little to the solution of wheat problems of the United States and the world at large. Its chief significance has been to accord official sanction, on the part of the participating nations, to United States export subsidization of the United States quota when non-quota export prices were at or above the agreed maximum. At heavy expense to the United States Treasury, this has contributed to the persistence of excessive domestic support prices, which have given undue stimulus to wheat production here and abroad, and has tended to obstruct, rather than to facilitate, normal readjustments in United States agriculture, and to lead to abnormal accumulation of stocks of wheat. In the current season, when export prices are below the agreed maximum, the importing countries are relieved of their obligation to purchase wheat unless the prices drop below the agreed minimum level. Furthermore, the most important importing country is no longer a party to the agreement. Under these circumstances the significance of the agreement in relation to our wheat export problem is relatively slight. . . .

The International Wheat Council may constitute a useful body for international consultations on current wheat problems, although this value is limited by the absence of certain nations that are important as importing or exporting countries. The Commission recommends that during the life of the 1953 International Wheat Agreement its operation be kept under critical review,

[17] *How Is the Wheat Agreement Working?* Agricultural Information Bulletin No. 74, United States Department of Agriculture, January, 1952.

that efforts be made to make the organization contribute its maximum to
solving pressing problems, and that its termination in 1956 be given consideration.[18]

A new International Wheat Agreement was negotiated for a three-year
period in April, 1956. The United Kingdom remained outside the agreement, but new participants were Argentina and Sweden. The price range
was reduced by 5 cents to $1.50–$2.00 per bushel for Northern Manitoba
No. 1, in store Fort William-Port Arthur, Canada.

Rice

Rice is the other of the "big two" world foods.

Asia produces annually more than nine-tenths of the world's rice. The
world's largest surplus for export is produced in Burma and Thailand.
Prior to World War II (1936–40) French Indochina (Cambodia, Laos,
Viet Nam) vied with Thailand as the second largest exporter, but that
area failed to recover the prewar production rate and during the postwar
period exported little rice. Most of the leading rice-importing countries of
the Far East also are important producers of rice. This is particularly true
of China, India, and Japan.

In the rice-growing areas during World War II from 1942 to 1945,
physical destruction and economic dislocation were widespread, and
when military operations were ended, civil unrest and actual warfare
prevailed over large areas including three of the four prewar exporting
countries. Political units were broken up and new trade barriers erected.
Drainage and irrigation were disrupted and the movement of labor, capital, and goods needed to restore them was retarded. Consequently, in
1945 world production of rice was down about 17 percent from prewar.

The year 1952 marked a turning point. Recovery in production was
slow until 1951, and the amount remained below the prewar level. In
most of the rice-producing countries of Asia, the 1952 harvest was larger
than the 1935–39 average. Production was still smaller in China, Burma,
and Indochina. Rice supplies of principal Far East exporting and importing countries for the prewar period and 1952 are given in Figure 4.35.
Between the end of World War II and 1952, demand for rice was fostered by social changes, international aid, and the increased incomes of
those who benefited by the Korean boom. In addition, population had
grown so rapidly that in 1951 the Far East had 100 million more people
to feed than in 1938. Thus per capita supply of rice was greatly reduced

[18] *Commission on Foreign Economic Policy,* Report to the President and the Congress, January, 1954, Government Printing Office, 1954, pp. 29–32.

in the Asiatic countries. To meet the rice shortages the countries tried to provide more rice, to supplement the rice with other foodstuffs, and to share the existing rice supplies. The latter was facilitated through domestic rationing and drastic changes in international trade.

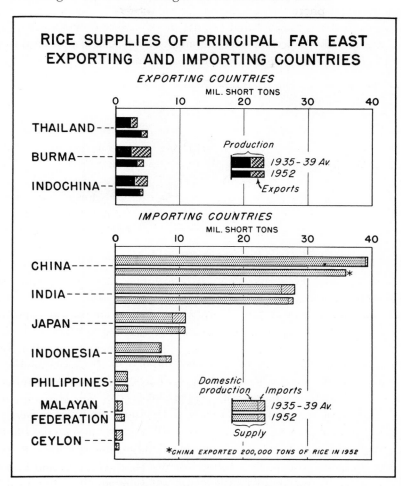

Figure 4.35.   (U.S. Department of Agriculture)

The world's rice trade channels changed during World War II. A comparison of international trade in rice between the years 1936–40 and 1952 is given in Figures 4.36 and 4.37. Only 8 percent of the annual average world production of rice during the period 1936–40 moved in international commerce. About 94 percent of the rice that was shipped from the surplus-rice-producing countries of Asia went to other countries on that continent. Outside of Asia, Europe was the most important market, particularly France, Germany, the Netherlands, and the United Kingdom. Whereas before the war Asia exported rice to all world areas, in postwar years it has been importing increasing quantities, especially from the Western Hemisphere.

Most dramatic is the fact that exports in 1952 were only about 60 percent of the 1936–40 period. Rice shipments from Korea and Taiwan to Japan before World War II accounted for as much as 20 percent of the

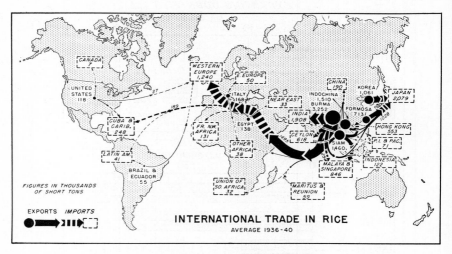

Figure 4.36. (U.S. Department of Agriculture)

world trade in rice, but in 1952 the net imports of these two countries exceeded exports. Rice exports of Asia in 1952 comprised only 70 percent of the world trade compared with 93 percent in 1936–40. Japan in 1952 was the largest rice importer, followed by India, Indonesia, Malaya, Ceylon, Cuba, and Hong Kong. Asia was still the primary source for imports, but most significant were the considerable quantities taken from the United States, Egypt, Brazil, Italy, Australia, and the Belgian Congo.

From a relatively small exporter of rice in 1936–40, the United States increased its exports nearly eight times to 1952 and after World War II rose to third place, behind Thailand and Burma. In 1935–39 rice exports accounted for only 15 percent of domestic production, but by 1951, 57 percent of United States rice production was exported.

The drastic efforts to meet the postwar rice shortages began to pay off, and by the end of 1952 the results were beginning to be noticeable. Larger crops were reaped in every continent and, as previously noted,

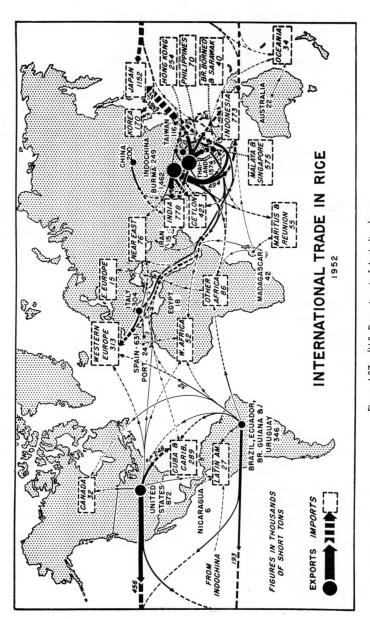

Figure 4.37. (U.S. Department of Agriculture)

Asia at last exceeded her prewar output. This increase continued even more sharply in 1953. As the Asian crop expansion had taken place mainly in the importing countries, the reaction on international trade in the following years was marked. India's imports fell by about three-quarters and Indonesia's by well over one-half. Rice shipments began to be determined by decisions of importers rather than by quantities made available for export.

United States exports of rice reached a peak level in 1952, when exports were 16 percent of the world total. After that year, however, United States rice exports declined steadily to 10 percent of the world total in 1955. At the same time, rice exports increased from Burma and Thailand, owing chiefly to government-to-government contracts and to disposal of low-quality rice at relatively low prices. Export gains had also occurred in Communist China, Pakistan, Italy, Spain, Iran, Madagascar, Portugal, Australia, and an increased number of smaller exporters. Nevertheless, as shown in Figure 4.38, the United States was still the third largest rice exporter. The new peak for 1956, indicated in Figure 4.39, gave evidence that this position might prevail.

Cuba traditionally has been the principal foreign market for United States rice (Figure 4.38). In 1951 Japan became a major market and the shipments to Korea were stepped up. Our usual markets are countries taking lesser amounts, including Canada, Bolivia, Liberia, Saudi Arabia, and countries in Europe and Oceania. However, destinations for a large part of the United States rice exports vary from year to year.

Because of our very heavy shipments to Japan in 1953, United States rice exports did not immediately reflect 1952 as a turning point in international rice trade. With the drastic decline in exports in 1954 the United States was in the initial stages of a surplus problem, as shown by the tremendous increase in carry-over (Figure 4.39). The price of rice, one of the "basic crops" under the Agricultural Adjustment Act, fell below the loan rate in 1954, and rice began to go into storage under the Commodity Credit Corporation. Before this continued strong demand for rice had kept rice prices above the loan rate in every year except two since the program went into effect in 1941. Those two years were 1951 and 1952, when *price* reflected a turning point but government purchase for export kept rice out of the surplus problem.

Surpluses had accumulated in all the export countries by 1954, and by 1955–56 rice-producing countries were beginning to find it increasingly difficult to locate export markets. Burma, for example, was making barter deals with Iron Curtain countries to dispose of its surplus rice output.

U.S. IS THIRD LARGEST RICE EXPORTER.

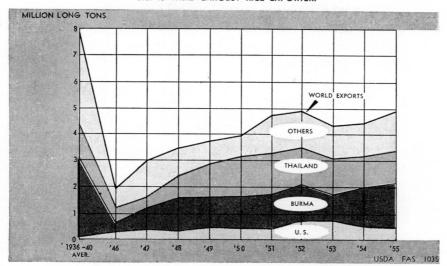

CUBA AND JAPAN ARE GOOD CUSTOMERS FOR U.S. RICE.

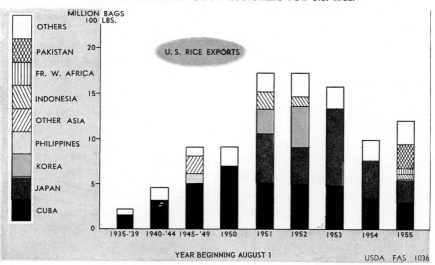

Figure 4.38.   Rice World Trade. (U.S. Department of Agriculture)

One reason, as we have noted, for the diminution of foreign markets was the profound change in the production of rice. For example, non-Asiatic countries doubled their production between World War II and 1956, although 90 percent of the world supply was still grown in Asia. Production of rice was going up everywhere except in North America. The 1955–56 world crop was 424,444 million pounds as compared with 400,000 million pounds in 1954–55, and 234,000 million pounds average

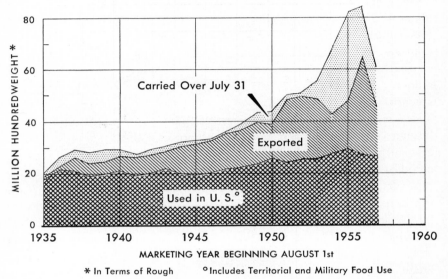

Figure 4.39.   Rice Distribution. (U.S. Department of Agriculture, Agricultural Marketing Service)

between 1945–46 to 1949–50. The preliminary estimated 1956–57 crop was 431,776 million pounds.

Another disturbing factor in the rice export market was that for eight years after World War II rice was scarce and a marked increase in price occurred. This resulted in a shift in consumption to cheaper and more abundant substitute cereals. In the Far East the shift was made only because of this scarcity and not because of any change in diet preference. On the basis of import unit values between rice and other cereals imported into Asia between 1937 and 1953, the average prices for imported rice rose twice as much as those paid for other cereal imports. Simultaneously, the relative share of rice in all Asian cereal imports fell sharply. In 1937, rice made up 88 percent of the total cereal imports, compared with 31 percent in 1953, when rice was scarce and prices were relatively high.

A further disturbing factor in the rice export market in 1956 was the heavy exporting of rice by Red China while Chinese were going hungry.

The rice outlook in 1957 centered around exports which were uncertain for the years ahead. Approximately half of the rice exports in 1955–56 were the result of government transactions made under Public Law 480 and Section 402 of the Mutual Security Act of 1954 as amended. For the immediate, the record United States carry-over on August 1, 1956, of about 34.6 million cwt., together with an estimated 1956 crop of about 43.3 million cwt., and imports of about 0.3 million, indicated that total supplies would be 81.2 million cwt., the highest on record. However, domestic disappearance in 1956–57 of 25.7 million cwt. plus greatly increased exports of 38 million cwt. might reduce the carry-over to 17 million cwt. on August 1, 1957, or half of the previous year's total. The Department of Agriculture drew the conclusion: "The prospective increase in United States exports (mostly under the P.L. 480 program for foreign currency) is possible because surpluses, which accumulated in other exporting countries during 1954–55, have now largely been eliminated by reducing prices." Since the P.L. 480 program was due to expire June 30, 1957, there was added reason to conclude that, even though the rice surplus problem was being alleviated with a disposal program and by the Soil Bank, rice exports were "uncertain for the years ahead."

Cuba will continue to be a dependable foreign outlet for United States rice, but changing conditions in Asia will be of vital concern to United States rice producers.

B. Cotton

Cotton is the *Big One* in the world fiber economy, and the United States has been the *Big One* producer, consumer, and exporter.

PRODUCTION, CONSUMPTION, AND INTERNATIONAL TRADE. In contrast to the widespread cultivation of wheat, cotton is produced principally in the nine countries shown in Table 26. Through the years the United States has been the dominant area of production and has accounted for over 40 percent of the world's supplies. The trend of United States and foreign production of cotton is shown in Figure 4.40. As United States cotton production was curtailed in the 1930's (restrictions were off in 1937), foreign production rose steadily to a peak of 20 million bales in 1937–38. Early in World War II, however, a decline set in which carried foreign production down to 12 million bales in 1945–46. It recovered rapidly after the war, however, and again reached 20 million bales in 1951–52 and increased to new records in 1955–56. United States produc-

TABLE 26. World Production of Commercial Cotton
(in thousands of bales[a])

Season	United States[a]	Foreign Countries										World Total
		Argentina	Brazil	China[b]	Egypt	India	Mexico	Pakistan	U.S.S.R.	Others	Total	
1935–39 av.	12,873	289	1,931	1,742	1,874	4,984	291	c	3,430	2,276	16,817	29,630
1940–44 av.	11,709	398	2,171	819	1,228	4,292	403	c	2,400	2,069	13,905	25,614
1945–46	8,972	285	1,389	660	1,059	3,160	405	c	2,000	1,960	10,918	19,890
1946–47	8,582	314	1,310	775	1,227	3,360	433	c	2,240	1,911	11,570	20,152
1947–48	11,689	412	1,167	900	1,295	2,220	451	778	2,400	2,698	11,563	23,252
1948–49	14,671	450	1,487	865	1,814	1,652	540	758	2,600	3,130	12,636	27,307
1949–50	16,008	578	1,344	700	1,757	2,092	897	970	2,700	2,771	13,809	29,817
1950–51	9,897	509	1,725	1,315	1,713	2,451	1,138	1,264	3,500	3,235	16,850	26,747
1951–52	15,215	550	1,931	2,070	1,618	2,898	1,275	1,102	4,000	3,604	19,048	34,263
1952–53	15,216	578	1,600	1,800	2,005	2,688	1,228	1,410	4,000	3,894	19,203	34,419
1953–54	16,433	643	1,465	2,000	1,428	3,466	1,193	1,085	5,500	4,271	21,051	37,484
1954–55	13,707	490	1,720	1,800	1,561	4,152	1,743	1,083	5,800	4,868	23,217	36,924
1955–56	14,590	500	1,895	1,856	1,766	3,940	2,035	1,277	5,800	5,090	24,159	38,749
1956–57	13,210	625	1,500	2,200	1,452	4,084	1,710	1,320	5,800	5,262	23,953	37,163

[a] American cotton, running bales; foreign cottons, equivalent 478 lb. bales. [b] Including Manchuria. [c] Included in India.
Source: New York Cotton Exchange; Commodity Year Book, 1956; 1957 for 1956–57 data.

tion fell to very low levels at the end of World War II but increased to a peak of 16 million bales in 1949–50 and, except in 1950–51, increased to a record of 16.4 million bales in 1953–54 and was reduced gradually to 13.2 million bales in 1955–56.

Cotton consumption in foreign countries has increased nearly 60 percent in post-World War II years from 18 million bales in 1946–47 to 28.5 million bales in 1954–55 (Figure 4.50, p. 179). The net-exporting countries had the greatest proportionate increase and through stepped-up production supplied most or all of their larger need. This trend has

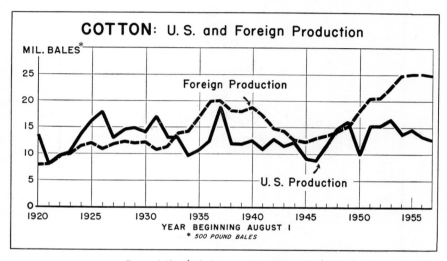

Figure 4.40. (U.S. Department of Agriculture)

tended to reduce textile export outlets of other countries and has limited the potential expansion of United States cotton exports to countries that produce textiles for export. United States consumption of cotton increased gradually in the middle 1930's to about 7.7 million bales in 1939, rose rapidly to a peak of almost 11 million bales in 1941–42, and remained at between 9 and 10 million bales during World War II. These trends are clearly discernible from Figure 4.48 (p. 174), together with the postwar dip in 1949 and the rise to the postwar peak of over 10.3 million bales during the Korean boom year of 1950. Domestic mill consumption of cotton per person trended downward thereafter, but population growth over the five years prior to 1957 kept the total at an average of around 9 million bales a year.

The flow of international trade in cotton for the pre-World War II period and two postwar periods are given in Figures 4.41–4.43. These

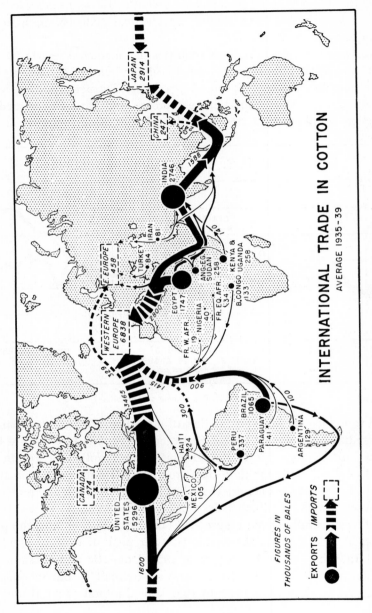

INTERNATIONAL TRADE IN COTTON
AVERAGE 1935-39

Figure 4.41. (U.S. Department of Agriculture)

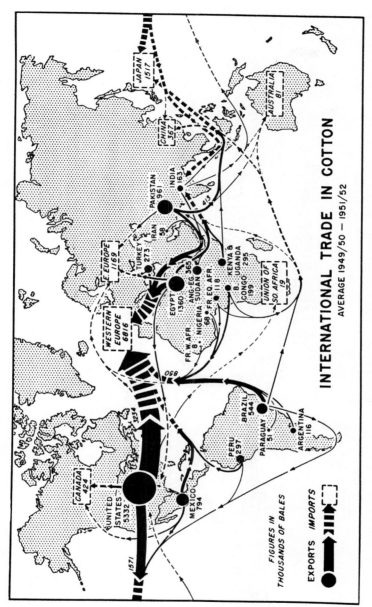

INTERNATIONAL TRADE IN COTTON

AVERAGE 1949/50 — 1951/52

Figure 4.42. (U.S. Department of Agriculture)

167

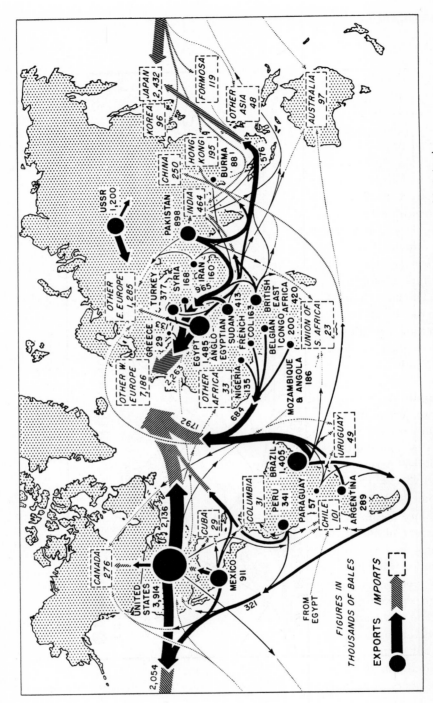

Figure 4.43.   International Trade in Cotton, 1953–54. (Data from U.S. Department of Agriculture)

168

figures indicate the extent of changes in the international trade in cotton and present data which show clearly those cotton producing and exporting countries with which the United States is competing for a share of the world cotton market. Before World War II the total volume of the world's cotton export trade was about 13,000,000 bales a year. The United States exported about 5,300,000 bales annually during 1935–39, and the other principal exporters of American-type cotton were Brazil and India. Egypt's exports were long-staple cotton. International cotton trade had recovered from its wartime low by 1949–50 to 1951–52, when the European Recovery Program gave it new impetus. Mexico, Turkey, and Pakistan gained importance as postwar exporters of cotton, but Brazil's trade had declined almost 50 percent. With the partition of the Indian subcontinent, Pakistan succeeded to British India's prewar cotton export trade, and the Republic of India, the world's second largest manufacturer, found itself a net importer.

The flow chart for 1953–54 (Figure 4.43) shows a drastic deterioration of the United States' export position to 3,914,000 bales. Brazil had increased her exports over two and one-half times the 1949–52 total to more than outdistance her pre-World War II exports.

World exports of cotton, as noted above and seen from Figure 4.44, were around the 13-million-bale level before World War II, declined rapidly during the war and were almost at the prewar level during the years just prior to 1957. What concerned the United States was that her share of this stable level of trade had dwindled rapidly. The United States' share in the world cotton trade, which stood at 42 percent in the 1935–39 period, rose to 48 percent in 1949–50 but declined to 19 percent in 1955–56. This was an actual decline in the two latter postwar periods from 6.0 to 2.3 million bales.

Since cotton in the pre-World War II period was in first place with 41 percent of the United States agricultural exports, and since cotton exports have constituted such a large percentage of our total cotton production, the loss of foreign markets was of vital concern to us and raised the question: Who stopped buying from us, and what were the foreign sources of production competition?

The first part of the question is answered to some extent by the two illustrations in Figure 4.45 which present a clear picture of the destination of our cotton exports and the trends. The United States exports to the United Kingdom, which had averaged 3.8 million bales annually in the five years preceding 1916–17, began a long decline thereafter owing to the United Kingdom's loss of her export market for cotton textiles. The drastic downward trend of United States cotton exports to Japan and the major European countries, which began in the early 1930's and continued to World War II, was due in part to a drive toward self-sufficiency through the increased production and use of rayon in these countries and in part to the use of foreign-held dollar exchange for war preparations. In the post-World War II years payment problems of many importing countries had a retarding effect on trade but were partially offset by United States foreign aid programs. Western Europe continued

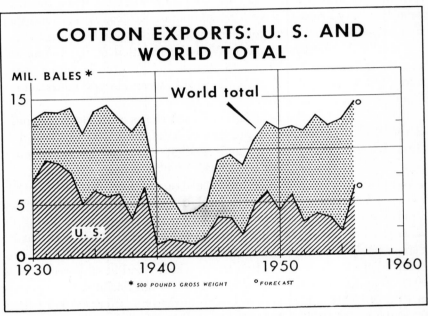

Figure 4.44.   (U.S. Department of Agriculture, Agricultural Marketing Service)

to be the destination of the greater part of United States cotton exports, although to a lesser extent than before World War II. In Asia the Republic of India, which became the world's second largest cotton manufacturer, was a net importer since the partition of the subcontinent and in 1953–54 took 153,000 bales of United States cotton, but this figure declined by 62 percent to 59,000 bales in 1954–55. Japan, however, with the postwar restoration of its cotton mills and partial recovery of its textile export trade, regained its prewar position as the leading cotton customer of the United States.

The second part of the question, as to the relation between foreign production competition and United States exports, is partially answered by Figure 4.46, which reveals significant comparisons. United States ex-

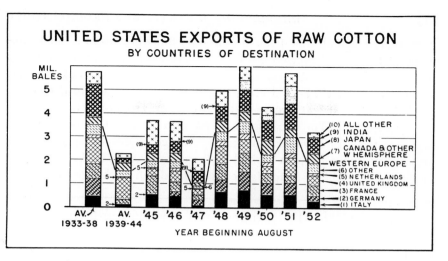

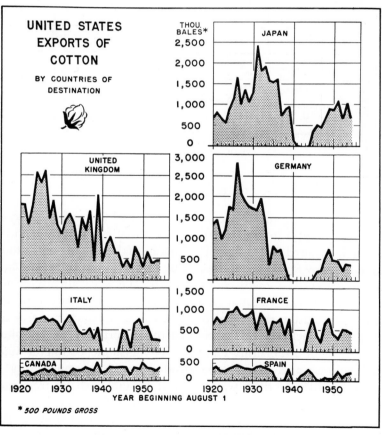

Figure 4.45.   (U.S. Department of Agriculture)

ports reached an all-time peak of almost 11 million bales in 1926. Thereafter the trend was reversed and continued downward through the 1930's while foreign production rose rapidly. Interruptions in the five war years, 1940–41 through 1944–45, decreased United States exports to the lowest levels in almost seventy years and also discouraged production in most foreign countries. The increase in post-World War II United States exports up until 1951 was facilitated by United States foreign aid programs. The sharp drop in United States exports after 1951 was due to increasing availability of foreign cotton, the dollar exchange position of

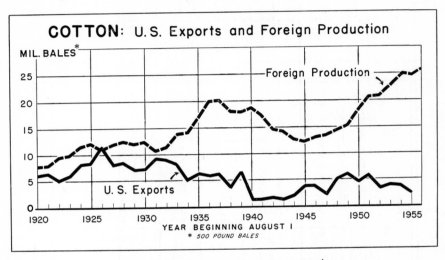

Figure 4.46. (U.S. Department of Agriculture)

importing countries, and the reduction in United States foreign aid programs. The increase in foreign production was stimulated by high cotton prices under United States supports. This special emphasis on cotton production in many foreign countries, using improved varieties and cultural methods, increased foreign cotton exports. We have already seen that Mexico, Turkey, and Pakistan gained importance as postwar exporters of cotton, that Pakistan succeeded to British India's export trade, and that Brazil's share declined. Russia entered the export picture, but she also made a deal to swap arms for Egypt's long-staple cotton in 1956, so Egypt's cotton was destined to be diverted from her normal export markets. During 1955–56 there was a shift of 1.3 million bales from imports of United States cotton to imports from other free world sources.

The summary United States cotton position is presented in Figures 4.47 and 4.48 which give cotton production, carry-over, consumption, exports, and price. With huge surplus stocks of cotton on hand in the United States in the early 1940's, due principally to the loss of foreign markets, production was restricted by crop controls until July, 1943, at an annual level of roughly 12 million bales a year. With subnormal crops in

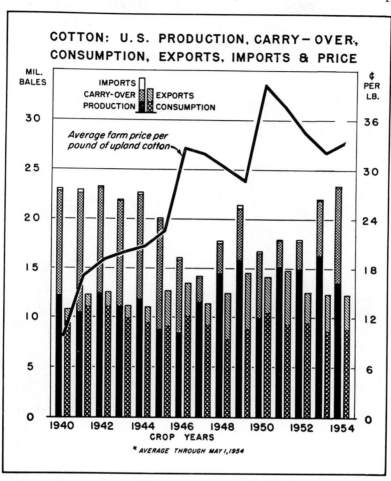

Figure 4.47. (U.S. Department of Agriculture)

1945 and 1946, coupled with a large consumption and increased exports, the surplus disappeared and prices rose sharply. Acreage was controlled again in 1950, and a poor short crop resulting from poor growing conditions coincided with the expansion of business activity stimulated by the invasion of South Korea. Cotton prices rose to the highest levels in more than eighty years.

Figure 4.48 shows clearly why cotton stocks accumulated in the late 1920's and early 1930's when United States cotton production was larger than United States mill consumption plus exports. From 1947 to 1954 cotton production was larger than disappearance each year except 1950, when marketing quotas and acreage allotments were in effect. The net effect of this gap between production and disappearance on carry-over is clearly seen in Figure 4.47.

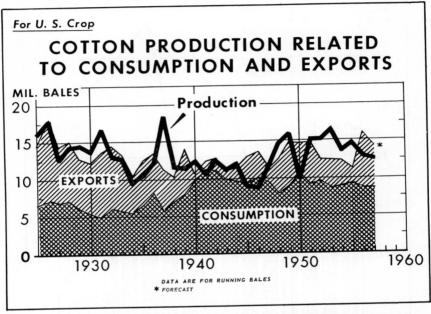

Figure 4.48.   (U.S. Department of Agriculture, Agricultural Marketing Service)

UNITED STATES COTTON PROBLEMS AND POLICY.   The major cotton problem is that the United States productive capacity for cotton has been more than adequate to meet the requirements of both domestic and foreign consumers.

The domestic cotton price support scheme was one of the factors that encouraged foreign cotton production before World War II and helped price United States cotton out of the world market, and thus was and is likely to continue to be a contributing factor to our loss of foreign markets, and a retarding influence on domestic consumption. Figure 4.49 indicates how the cotton loan rate has shored up cotton prices. During most of the ten-year period after World War II, cotton prices received by farmers have been higher than the Commodity Credit Corporation loan rate. Prices were close to or below loan rates in large parts of the 1948–49 and the 1949–50 seasons.

From mid-February, 1950, through mid-November, 1952, prices received by farmers were well above the loan rate. However, from November, 1952, to 1954, they were very close to the loan rate and in January and February, 1953, they were below the loan rate.

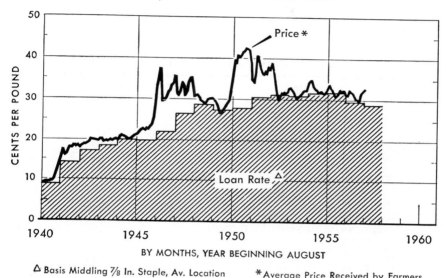

Figure 4.49.   Cotton Prices and Loan Rates. (U.S. Department of Agriculture, Agricultural Marketing Service)

Against this background, the United States cotton program and policies will be examined. As indicated from Table 27, the supply of cotton in the United States was estimated in October, 1953, to be 21,000,000 bales for the 1953–54 marketing season. This was 15 percent larger than in 1952–53. Normal supply—domestic consumption, 9,500,000 bales, plus estimated exports, 3,200,000 bales, plus reserve for carry-over of 30 percent, 3,810,000 bales—was indicated to be 16,500,000 bales. Thus total supply over normal supply was estimated to be 4,200,000 bales or 25.5 percent.

The Agricultural Adjustment Act of 1938 as amended required the Secretary of Agriculture to proclaim quotas if the normal supply exceeds total supply. National marketing quotas of 10 million bales of American upland cotton and 30 thousand bales of extra-long-staple cotton were proclaimed by the Secretary of Agriculture on October 9, 1953. Before these marketing quotas could become effective they had to be approved by two-thirds of the cotton farmers voting in a national referendum. The quotas were overwhelmingly approved on December 15, 1953.

What the farmers really voted for was a marketing quota on the 1954 crop to implement an acreage allotment of 17,910,000 on the 1954 crop which had already been proclaimed by Secretary of Agriculture Ezra T. Benson, in accordance with the law.

The national acreage allotment was based on plantings in the years 1947 through 1952, with the exception of 1949. The allotment to states

TABLE 27.   Cotton—Total Supply and Normal Supply

Item	Bales
Total supply	
Carry-over August 1, 1953	5,156,082
Production (October crop report)	15,381,000
Imports	175,000
Total	20,712,082
Normal supply	
Domestic consumption	9,500,000
Exports	3,200,000
Subtotal	12,700,000
Reserve for carry-over (30 percent)	3,810,000
Total	16,510,000
Excess, total supply over normal supply	
Bales	4,202,082
Percent	25.5

and to counties was on virtually the same basis as the national allotment. Local county committees then allocated to each individual farm a fixed acreage based on the average plantings for 1951 through 1953. Thus each individual farmer knew what his fixed acreage for 1954 would be before he voted for marketing quotas on December 15, 1953. Since acreage planted to cotton in Arizona and California increased substantially in the base years over previous years, the Southeastern cotton growers were not satisfied with their share of the allotment. As a result of this dissatisfaction, the Congress passed legislation authorizing a minimum of 21,000,000 acres to be planted to cotton.

This increase of approximately 3,000,000 acres normally would mean an increase of about 1,300,000 bales in yield to add to the 10,000,000 bales that the Department of Agriculture was seeking for the 1954 crop. In this legislation we have an excellent illustration of political action that works to defeat the objectives of the cotton program. The net result is sustained production in high-cost areas and increased production of cotton, which means increased quantities of cotton placed under government loan with the CCC.

The agricultural program supporting cotton prices at 90 percent of parity expired with the 1954 crop. The approval of cotton quotas by the farmers meant that cotton prices would be supported at the minimum of 90 percent of parity for the 1954 crop. Thus the problem remained of increased quantities of cotton supported at a high price level.

The basic problem remained of establishing a domestic cotton program in order to produce and to sell cotton that could compete at favorable prices with foreign cotton in the world market and with substitute synthetic fibers in the domestic and foreign market.

The Agricultural Act of 1949 provided that after the 1954 cotton crop flexible price support would be in effect as follows:

The level of support shall not be less than the following percentage of the parity price: | If the actual supply percentage in relation to normal supply as of the beginning of the year is

The level of support shall not be less than the following percentage of the parity price:	Over	Not Over
90	—	108
89	108	110
88	110	112
87	112	114
86	114	116
85	116	118
84	118	120
83	120	122
82	122	124
81	124	125
80	125	126
79	126	127
78	127	128
77	128	129
76	129	130
75	130	

The purpose of this program was to enable downward adjustments of price in years of oversupply and to reduce production and thus improve the competitive position of cotton.

On August 28, 1954, the Agricultural Act of 1954 was signed by President Eisenhower. The flexible price support feature of the act of 1949 was incorporated in the new act. However, the 1954 act provided that in 1955 the support level for upland cotton would range from 82.5 percent to 90 percent of parity, and that after 1955 the flexible price support scale would range from 75 to 90 percent of the parity price.

The Agricultural Act of 1954 tackled the problem of carry-over by specifying a "set-aside" for upland cotton of 3 to 4 million bales. Cotton placed in the set-aside by the Secretary of Agriculture may be disposed of for foreign relief purposes, sold for foreign currency to develop new and expanded markets, transferred to the national stockpile, used for research, experimental, or educational purposes, used for disaster relief in the United States, or sold for 105 percent of the parity price for "unrestricted use" to meet a need for increased supplies. The quantity placed in the set-aside is included in the supply when computing marketing quotas but excluded from the supply when computing the level of price supports.

Marketing quotas were in effect for the 1955 cotton crop and again in 1956. The marketing quota for the 1956 crop was the same as for the 1955 crop of upland cotton, 10 million bales. The 1956 marketing quotas were the minimum which could be set under the Agricultural Adjustment Act of 1938, as amended, as were the quotas for 1954 and 1955. The national acreage allotment for 1956 was 17,391,301 acres for upland cotton, as compared with 18,113,208 acres for the 1955 crop. The acreage allotment for 1956 was smaller than for 1955 because of higher yields during the base period 1950–54 used to determine the allotments.

The cotton outlook as of January, 1956, was summarized by the United States Department of Agriculture as follows:

The cotton situation for the 1955–56 marketing year is one of very large supply and increasing stocks. The 1955 crop is larger than expected disappearance and the carryover at the end of the 1955–56 season probably will be about 14 million bales, or approximately 3 million bales larger than the carryover at the start of the season. This will be a million bales larger than the previous record of 13 million bales in 1939. The carryover has increased each year since the post World War II low of 2.3 million bales in 1951.

The supply of cotton in 1955–56 is estimated at a record of about 25.9 million bales, 2.4 million above that of a year earlier and 1.3 million above the previous record of 24.6 million bales in 1939–40. Acreage in cultivation on July 1, 1955, was about 14 per cent below that of a year earlier but the estimated yield per harvested acre of 431 pounds was up about 90 pounds. As a result the 1955 crop of about 14.6 million running bales was about 7 per cent larger than the 1954 crop. Yields per acre have set new records in each of the last 3 years.

Disappearance in 1955–56 is expected to be less than 12.0 million bales. This compares with 12.3 and 12.4 million in the two preceding seasons. Although domestic mill consumption will probably increase from the 8.8 million bales of 1954–55. exports probably will be considerably smaller than the 3.4 million bales of that season.

The conclusion is drawn that the carry-over was getting larger and larger and that the loss in foreign markets continued.

In a comprehensive report on the future of cotton, the National Cotton Council in October, 1955, made a concise study of the United States export market.[19] The Council presented Figure 4.50, "Foreign Cotton Pro-

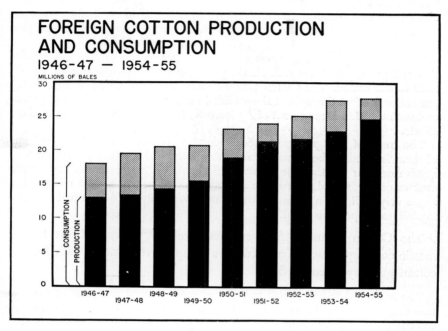

Figure 4.50. (M. K. Horne, Jr., *et al., Price and the Future of U.S. Cotton,* National Cotton Council of America, 1955; data from International Cotton Advisory Committee Estimates as of October 5, 1955)

duction and Consumption," as a key to the analysis of the export market. In this figure consumption is represented by the top of each bar; production by the black portion of each. The shaded part of each bar represents the excess of foreign consumption over foreign production. The United States has a vital interest in keeping this spread as wide as possible, because over the long run there is no practical way that our average exports can be substantially different from this average spread. The average spread narrowed after the late 1940's, not because the consumption did not increase, but because production increased faster.

[19] M. K. Horne, Jr., Frank A. McCord, and George Townsend, *Price and the Future of U.S. Cotton,* National Cotton Council of America, 1955.

During the years 1951–52, 1952–53, 1953–54, and 1954–55 the vital spread between foreign consumption and production of cotton averaged less than 3.4 million bales a year. The Council saw the 1955–56 season squeezing "very hard on even last year's margin of 3.0 million." The report continued:

We just have to look straight at this. Our industry cannot survive with an export market of only three million bales, more or less; but here you see the picture. . . . If we want our export market to average more than three million bales or so, there are only two ways to make it do so: Either we must make the foreign consumption go up faster, or we must keep the foreign production trend from going up so fast. We might do some of both.

The consumption line depends on the increases in the world-wide population and per capita income. It also depends on the aggressiveness of our efforts to sell cotton. The Cotton Council's new program aimed at stimulating promotional effort throughout the world, in cooperation with industry groups and with the U.S. Department of Agriculture, is becoming a vital part of these efforts.

The trend of foreign cotton production depends on many things, and one of them is price. Nobody can be sure *how much* price cut could obtain *how much* result, or whether the result would come in one season to any significant extent or would all require a longer period of years. But nobody can argue very well that a price cut would not eventually become a real restraining influence upon this trend.[20]

The Cotton Council's final summary relating price policies to domestic cotton production and cotton's competitive position with foreign cotton and rayon concluded:

The real need is for a price policy reasonably geared to a cost of production that is pointed downward—and on downward—indefinitely into the future. If there is good ground for hope that the costs of growing U.S. cotton can be reduced farther and faster than the cost of producing rayon or foreign cotton during the next five or ten years, then we have the basis for a long-range price policy that might help our cotton become the most aggressive competitor in the world of fibers. We now see, from the rate of progress during recent years, that there is indeed good ground for just that hope.

On the demand side and on the supply side, we have found real limitations on the immediate advantages of a price reduction—limitations on what it would gain us and limitations on what we could afford. But on both the demand and the supply sides, we have found great reasons why we should start immediately on a long-range downward course for the price of cotton —reasons why it would benefit us and reasons why we can afford it. If we cannot afford it, we cannot survive in cotton. We have an opportunity to adjust our planning now to price adjustments that would come gradually in the future—spread out over time in such a way that farmers could offset them

[20] *Ibid.*, p. 20.

with improvements in efficiency and would actually be stimulated by them toward greater efficiency. Quick and unforeseeable price adjustments are the deadly enemy of farm efficiency. Gradual and foreseeable adjustments would encourage efficiency, and those who could not or would not respond to that encouragement would be on notice that there is no possible place for them in this dynamic fiber competition unless they are willing to see their low incomes go even lower.[21]

The United States cotton program and policy for 1957 was explained in the September 17, 1956, issue of *Time* magazine as follows:

THE COTTON SURPLUS[22]

New Hope for a Permanent Cure

Old King Cotton has been sick for years, and getting progressively worse. But now, for the first time since the Korean war, there are hopeful signs of recovery. In the 1956–57 marketing year the staggering cotton surplus, currently at an alltime record 14.1 million bales [Figure 4.51], is expected to

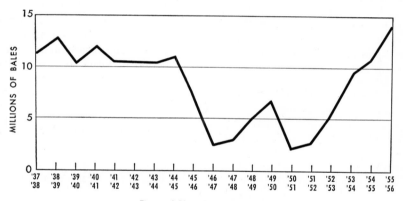

Figure 4.51.   Cotton Surplus.

level off or perhaps even decline a bit. More important, the Government is trying new medicines on cotton, all aimed at effecting a permanent cure in the years to come.

Last week the U.S. Export-Import Bank lent Japan $60 million to be used for importing more raw cotton from the U.S. The loan was one part of a broad program designed to boost both overseas and domestic consumption while holding down production. The goal for 1956–57 is a 20%–25% increase over total cotton sales in 1955–56 by doubling exports to 4,500,000 bales while keeping domestic consumption at last year's 9,200,000-bale level or even increasing it. With flexible price supports between 75% and 90% of parity, Agriculture Secretary Ezra Taft Benson hopes that minimum acreage allotments (17.4 million acres in 1957) and marketing quotas (11 million

[21] *Ibid.*, p. 55.
[22] Courtesy *Time;* copyright Time Inc., 1956.

bales) will hold next year's crop to 13 million bales, or about this year's level. Furthermore, under the new soil-bank program Benson hopes that farmers will increase the number of acres taken out of production well beyond last year's 1,064,000-acre total. Though some cottonmen fear that only the poorest acreage will be allowed to lie fallow, and that farmers will produce as much as ever by working their remaining acres harder, most applaud the program.

. . . .

The biggest battle will be fought in the world market, where the U.S. has been taking its worst beating. The U.S. hopes to dispose of much of the surplus by stepping up grants and loans to underdeveloped nations, selling the rest. Though the U.S. is flatly against "dumping," i.e., selling at any price, it has moved into world markets with a big program to dispose of some 7,000,-000 bales of high-grade Government-owned cotton abroad at competitive world prices by subsidizing U.S. exporters, has already sold 3,000,000 bales. On the total, the U.S. stands to lose as much as $220 million (it paid 32¢ per lb. for the cotton, can sell it for, at most, 25¢ to 26¢ per lb.).

Heavy exports of cotton at world prices may reduce U.S. raw-cotton supplies, but they will also boost foreign production of cheap finished textiles—to the detriment of competing U.S. manufacturers, who still pay U.S. prices. The Government's answer is still another program: textile exporters will get a 6.58¢-per-lb. subsidy on cotton products made for export, will thus be able to cut prices to compete in world markets.

While many cottonmen cry for higher tariffs or strict import quotas, the Administration is determined not to give in. Textilemen want protection, demand restrictions on Japan, which is "flooding" domestic markets with cheap finished cotton goods, forcing the closing of some U.S. mills. Actually, Japanese exports to the U.S. are barely 2½% of the U.S. cotton-goods market. Moreover, Japan is also one of cotton's best customers, bought $120 million worth of raw cotton last year from the U.S. To still the protests, the U.S. has worked out agreements for voluntary curbs, e.g., Japan has pledged to limit exports to the U.S. of cotton cloth, blouses.

. . . .

Overall, the hope is to cut the current 14.1 million bale surplus to a manageable 4,000,000 bales by 1959. But few cotton economists are that hopeful or think that any Government program alone can offer a final solution. The real answer is for Old King Cotton to grow up to the new U.S. industrial revolution. With mechanized farming methods, the U.S. currently produces more cotton on 17 million acres than it did on 36 million acres in 1930. Yet efficient growers cannot take advantage of their progress because cotton has been grown under an uneconomically high, Government-supported price system favoring the small marginal farmer. Cotton economists are convinced that the marginal farmer must get out of cotton to make way for the big mechanized producer, who can farm vast tracts of land on the Texas plains, California's well-irrigated valleys or Mississippi's rich delta lands—and do it at such a low cost that he can compete, without government subsidies, with both synthetic fibers and foreign cotton.

Textilemakers themselves must also build up new markets. Cotton consumption has held steady at some 9,000,000 bales annually for the past decade, while consumption of almost everything else has greatly increased. Says Dr. McDonald K. Horne Jr., chief economist of the National Cotton Council: "We need very much to invest new money in research, to do some long-range planning. The auto industry gives power steering, while we wear old shirts and look like the devil. We haven't met the test."

The export program spelled out by *Time* was part of a major United States cotton export policy initiated in early 1956 "intended to re-establish the traditional share of United States cotton in the world markets."

Early in 1955 cotton buyers in foreign importing countries appeared to be convinced that the high level of foreign production and the record accumulation of cotton stocks in the United States would necessitate an early downward adjustment in prices. Foreign importers and mills curtailed their purchases below the level of current mill needs in order to reduce their stocks of cotton. However, increases in mill consumption in some countries, especially Japan, China, and Western Germany, caused their total imports of cotton to increase considerably with little increase in stocks. Inventories of cotton yarns and textiles were also reduced in most foreign countries by maintaining mill output below the offtake. World prices soon declined below the United States support level, and shippers in foreign countries offered cotton for export during the 1955–56 market year at prices as much as 8 cents a pound lower than those asked for United States cotton.

The increasing discounts in prices of foreign cotton beginning early in 1955 and the steady decline in export sales of United States cotton prompted an increasing demand in the United States for government action to initiate a program for cotton export sales at competitive world prices. Anticipation of such action caused foreign importers and mill owners to intensify their efforts to reduce stocks to a minimum. For the same reason, exporters in foreign countries continued to reduce their prices and intensify their efforts to liquidate all surplus stocks before the United States price was reduced.

These developments in the world cotton situation in 1955–56 emphasized the need for adjustments in export prices of United States cotton to avoid almost total loss of cotton export trade. This led to the program for competitive pricing of United States cotton for export which was begun on a limited basis in January, 1956, and enlarged in April.

Exports of cotton from the United States totaling 2,320,000 bales in 1955–56 were, with the exception of 1947–48, the lowest for any peacetime year since 1871–72. This low level of United States exports was attributed to the inability of United States cotton to compete on export markets with comparable foreign qualities being sold at prices well below the United States support level. Anticipation by foreign buyers of a decline in United States export prices in 1956–57 was also a factor influencing reduced United States exports in 1955–56. The drop of 1.3 million bales in United States exports in 1955–56 from the level of the previous year was more than offset by an increase of 1.9 million in exports from other countries.

In contrast to 1955–56, the total United States cotton exports for 1956–57 were expected to be about 6.5 million bales and probably would be the largest since 1933–34, when exports totaled 7.5 million bales. The principal reasons for this sharp rebound in United States cotton exports were the competitive pricing of United States cotton for export sale, low stocks in nearly all foreign countries, rising consumption abroad, and a desire on the part of foreign mills and importers to rebuild inventories of cotton and cotton goods as a hedge against prospective inflation derived from the disturbances in the Middle East and eastern Europe.

To what extent the major drop in cotton prices would discourage production could not be readily determined. But it could provide a disincentive for the cotton-producing countries of Central and South America and the man-made fiber producers in Europe and thus enlarge the United States cotton export market.

Most important, however, were the implications in the international area of the United States government subsidy method of reëstablishing the United States' traditional share of cotton in the world market. By January, 1957, both Mexico and Peru had registered protests against the United States' dumping of cotton on the export market. The disturbance of foreign cotton economies by the United States government could have disastrous consequences. A more appropriate method of reëstablishing the United States' historical position in the cotton export market would be to practice true competitive pricing as suggested by the National Cotton Council. This could not bring forth a diplomatic protest, although it could cause disruptions in foreign cotton economies which had shared the protection of the United States domestic production and price umbrella.

INTERNATIONAL COTTON COÖPERATION. At the international cotton policy level a desire for coöperation resulted in the formation of an International Cotton Advisory Committee in 1939. Meetings of the Committee were held in 1940 and 1941, after which activities were suspended. In 1945, however, meetings were resumed. At its May, 1952, session the

International Cotton Advisory Committee received from its Standing Committee a survey of arrangements that might be made to bring greater stability to international trade in cotton. This study provided a basis for a detailed examination of the problems involved in concluding an international cotton agreement designed not only to remove excessive price fluctuations but also to assure sources of supplies for importing in times of scarcity and markets for exporting countries in times of surplus.

The discussions of this study brought out so many problems of pricing, currency considerations, national measures, and the relation of cotton to textile trade that the Standing Committee was asked to undertake further studies and to submit a report on the question of an international cotton agreement for the consideration of the International Cotton Advisory Committee. The Standing Committee submitted a report to the meeting of the ICAC which was held in June, 1954, at São Paulo. After examination of the report, it was concluded by the governments generally that the world situation at that time did not warrant further efforts to reach an international cotton agreement.

John H. Davis, Assistant Secretary of Agriculture, presented the United States policy position to the ICAC at the São Paulo meeting. "With respect to an international cotton agreement, we believe that any further steps leading towards the negotiation of an agreement are not warranted at this time. . . . In our opinion, the great need at the present is for an effective program on a worldwide basis to increase purchasing power and to expand the use of cotton products."

Mr. Davis suggested that research was needed to help produce better products at lower prices and that promotion was needed to make these improvements known to prospective buyers.

"The major role in such efforts, we believe, must be performed at the national level, and the greater part of the work will doubtless have to be done by industry itself. However, governments can make a positive contribution at the national level and at the international level through disseminating facts and basic information. The exchange of ideas at the international level such as the ICAC meetings, we think, is definitely useful. . . . Proper cooperation and teamwork on the part of producers, the various segments of industry, and government can be helpful in attaining this objective of expanding cotton consumption."

C. Tobacco

The third of the United States' big three agricultural exports is tobacco.

PRODUCTION, CONSUMPTION AND INTERNATIONAL TRADE. There are many varieties of tobacco, each having its particular purpose. Each type of tobacco grows best under its own particular conditions of soil composition and climate. Production of tobacco is classified by use or by the method in which the tobacco is treated or cured. The principal types are (1) flue-cured or bright tobacco, (2) burley tobacco, (3) fire-cured tobacco, and (4) cigar-leaf types.

The most important United States product is flue-cured tobacco, which accounts for more than 60 percent of the entire tobacco crop. It is the most important type exported from the United States. Even in 1952, when exports of flue-cured were 27 percent less than they were in 1951, they accounted for 81 percent of total exports. During the prewar period 1935–39 exports of flue-cured accounted for 42.5 percent of domestic production. During 1952 this percentage was 30, as compared with 41 in 1951. In 1955 the percentage was 34.5. In 1956, 37 cents of each $1 income from flue-cured tobacco came from exports. Production of flue-cured is concentrated in Virginia, North and South Carolina, Florida, Georgia, and Alabama. United States salient statistics for flue-cured tobacco are given in Table 28.

Since flue-cured is primarily used in the production of Virginia cigarettes, made entirely from flue-cured tobacco, and blended cigarettes, containing predominantly flue-cured tobacco, world production and consumption of flue-cured has depended on the extent of consumer preference for Virginia and blended cigarettes.

The world-wide trend of increased demand for cigarettes stimulated the consumption of both flue-cured and oriental tobaccos during and after World War I. The Virginia cigarette dominated tobacco consumption in the United States, in the United Kingdom, and in China. Therefore, these two latter countries became the most important foreign outlets for American flue-cured leaf during the interwar period. In central Europe, Turkish cigarettes, made from oriental tobaccos, came to be almost exclusively used.

After World War II the world-wide trend of increased consumption was not only accelerated but accompanied by a shift in consumer preference in a number of central and northern European areas from oriental cigarettes to blended cigarettes. The shift to blended cigarettes was especially pronounced in Western Germany. The shifts were due in large measure to the introduction of the blended cigarette into these areas by United States military and civilian personnel.

This increased demand abroad for blended cigarettes has resulted in increased foreign consumption and production of flue-cured tobacco. World production of tobacco by flue-cured and all other types is given

TABLE 28. United States Salient Statistics for Flue-Cured[a] Tobacco

Crop Year	Acreage Harvested (1,000 acres)	Yield Per Acre (100 pounds)	Production	July 1 Stocks	Total Supply	Disappearance			Farm Price (cents per pound)	Crop Value (million dollars)
						Total	Exports	Domestic		
					(in millions of pounds)					
1935–39 av.	982	8.8	864	881	1,745	732.2	367.8	364.4	20.5	172
1940–44 av.	822	9.9	820	1,406	2,226	876.4	309.1	567.3	33.1	279
1945	1,079	10.9	1,173	1,126	2,299	1,152.4	485.1	667.3	43.6	511
1946	1,189	11.4	1,352	1,147	2,499	1,212.5	553.4	659.1	48.3	653
1947	1,161	11.4	1,317	1,287	2,604	1,054.1	359.3	694.8	41.2	543
1948	884	12.3	1,090	1,550	2,640	1,101.6	382.1	719.5	49.6	541
1949	935	11.9	1,115	1,538	2,653	1,168.2	438.9	729.3	47.2	526
1950	958	13.1	1,257	1,485	2,742	1,184.2	427.7	756.5	54.7	688
1951	1,110	13.1	1,453	1,557	3,010	1,278.7	502.0	776.8	52.4	761
1952	1,111	12.3	1,365	1,731	3,096	1,244.0	416.0	828.0	50.3	687
1953	1,022	12.5	1,272	1,852	3,124	1,209.0	431.0	778.0	52.8	672
1954	1,042	12.6	1,314	1,915	3,229	1,173.0	429.0	744.0	52.7	692
1955	992	15.2	1,481	2,056	3,537	1,260.0	510.0	750.0	52.8	782
1956	876	16.1	1,410	2,258	3,668	1,205.0	480.0	725.0	51.2	722

[a] Types 11–14.
SOURCE: Department of Agriculture; *Commodity Year Book*, 1956; 1957 for 1956 data.

in Figure 4.52. World production of tobacco reached a record high of 8.1 billion pounds in 1955. This continued an upward trend and was 13 percent greater than the 1947–51 level and 25 percent above the 1935–1939 average. The United States production of leaf tobacco in 1955 was almost 55 percent more than the prewar 1935–39 average; the U.S. remained the largest producer, supplying over 27 percent of world production. Output in China, Japan, Brazil, Turkey, Italy, and Canada also exceeded prewar. Production of flue-cured tobacco in 1955 accounted for about 34 percent of world production as compared with an average 19 percent in 1935–39. During 1955 the United States supplied about 55 percent of the world flue-cured production; China, Japan, India, Canada, and Italy supplied most of the remainder.

Figure 4.52 does not show the extent of the tremendous expansion of flue-cured tobacco production in China from an average of 186 million pounds during 1934–38 to 580 million pounds during 1955 and a planned production goal of 860 million pounds for 1957. It does show the large increase in postwar production of flue-cured over prewar in Canada, the Central African Federation, India, and Japan, in addition to the United States. The United States' share in world production of flue-cured declined from 70 percent in the prewar period to the previously indicated 55 percent in 1955. The increase in the proportion of world production of flue-cured in foreign areas is most significant in view of the fact that United States production is more than 50 percent greater than it was in prewar years. These production figures are important as they are related to United States exports of tobacco. Increased production of flue-cured in Japan and Canada was required for increased consumption in those areas; in contrast, almost the entire Central African Federation production is exported. Increased production of tobacco in China is to enable China to pay for the goods it needs for greater industrial development. "Tobacco admirably fills this bill in several important respects: (1) light cigarette tobaccos are needed in other areas of the Soviet bloc—particularly Eastern Europe—from which steel and other basic industrial products may be purchased; (2) the returns and foreign exchange earnings per acre devoted to tobacco are high and the value per pound of tobacco is also high, making the transportation problem less difficult than for more bulky products; (3) tobacco production utilizes much of Communist China's most plentiful commodity—labor—and at the same time utilizes comparatively little of its overworked land."

Free world exports of all types of unmanufactured tobacco as given

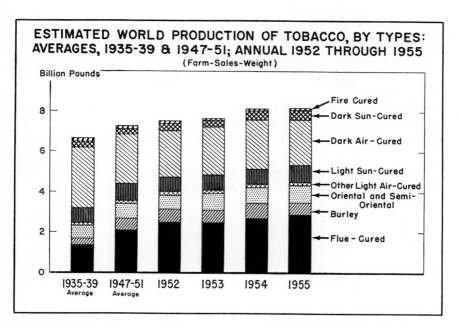

**ESTIMATED WORLD PRODUCTION OF TOBACCO, BY TYPES:
AVERAGES, 1935-39 & 1947-51; ANNUAL 1952 THROUGH 1955**
(Farm-Sales-Weight)

Billion Pounds

- Fire Cured
- Dark Sun-Cured
- Dark Air-Cured
- Light Sun-Cured
- Other Light Air-Cured
- Oriental and Semi-Oriental
- Burley
- Flue-Cured

1935-39 Average 1947-51 Average 1952 1953 1954 1955

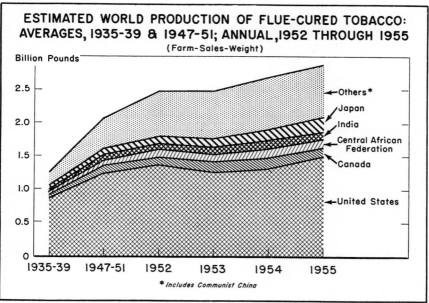

**ESTIMATED WORLD PRODUCTION OF FLUE-CURED TOBACCO:
AVERAGES, 1935-39 & 1947-51; ANNUAL, 1952 THROUGH 1955**
(Farm-Sales-Weight)

Billion Pounds

- Others*
- Japan
- India
- Central African Federation
- Canada
- United States

1935-39   1947-51   1952   1953   1954   1955

Includes Communist China

Figure 4.52. World Production of Flue-Cured and All Other Types of Tobacco. (U.S. Department of Agriculture, *World Tobacco Analysis*)

in Figure 4.53 indicate a sustained growth trend which reached a peak of 1389 million pounds in 1955, which was 34 percent above the 1935–39 average. The United States has retained first place among the world's tobacco-exporting countries with 39 percent of the total as compared with 41 percent during the 1935–39 period. Flue-cured tobacco accounts for about one-half of the total amount of leaf tobacco exported. As can be seen from Figure 4.54, the United States dominates the flue-cured export market. The other important free world exporters of flue-cured

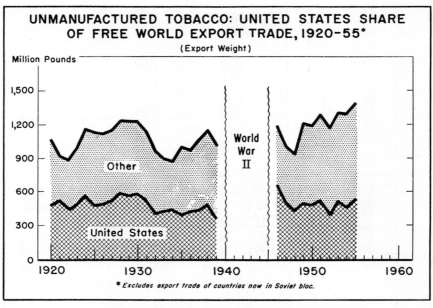

Figure 4.53.   (U.S. Department of Agriculture, World Tobacco Analysis)

tobacco are the Central African Federation, India, and Canada. Of particular importance are the increased exports of India and the Central African Federation. The 1955 exports of the latter (destined to other British Commonwealth countries) were almost four times as large as the 1935–39 average.

World imports of flue-cured tobacco are not given separately, but world imports of all types of leaf tobacco are presented in Figure 4.55 along with world exports of tobacco. The United Kingdom in the 1930's supplanted Germany as the most important leaf tobacco importer, and now takes about one-fourth of all leaf tobacco moving in world trade— mostly flue-cured for cigarette manufacture. Despite considerable domestic leaf production, Germany remains the second largest importer. It is a major market for oriental tobaccos, United States flue-cured cigarette leaf, and Indonesian and Brazilian cigar leaf. The United States is the third largest importer of tobacco, largely oriental leaf from Greece and Turkey used in small percentages as a flavor ingredient in cigarettes. Cigar leaf imports into the United States—mainly Cuban filler—are also fairly substantial.

United States exports of tobacco (mostly flue-cured) are given in Figure 4.56 by countries of destination. During 1952 total United States ex-

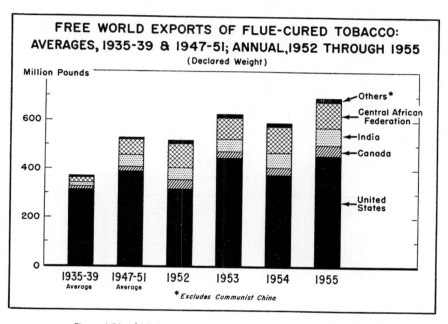

Figure 4.54. (U.S. Department of Agriculture, World Tobacco Analysis)

ports of tobacco declined 24 percent from the 1951 figure, reflecting for the most part a drop of about 75 percent in shipments to the United Kingdom. As a result, in contrast to the United Kingdom's traditional position as the principal buyer for United States tobacco, she dropped to third place as an outlet and accounted for only 14 percent of total United States exports. Exports to Belgium and Luxembourg also declined substantially, but those to the Netherlands and Germany increased by 48 percent and 67 percent, respectively. In 1952 Germany was the largest importer of our leaf tobacco. The years following 1952 show the United Kingdom returning to first place but still below the 1951 total. Exports to Germany were declining.

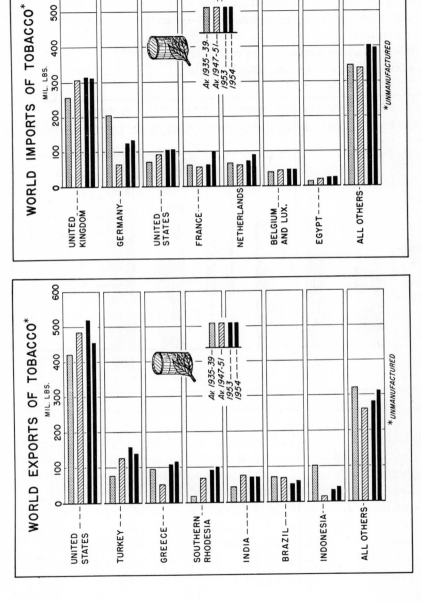

Figure 4.55. World Exports and Imports of Tobacco. (U.S. Department of Agriculture)

The above export data for flue-cured tobacco and import-export data for all types of tobacco reflect important trends. World flue-cured exports have been decreasing to the Far East, increasing to Europe. The decline in exports to the Far East reflects increasing production in India and the fact that China has not been an important outlet for flue-cured since 1940. The rise in exports to Europe reflects increased consumer preference for blended cigarettes, particularly in the Netherlands, Belgium, Denmark, Norway, Sweden, and Western Germany.

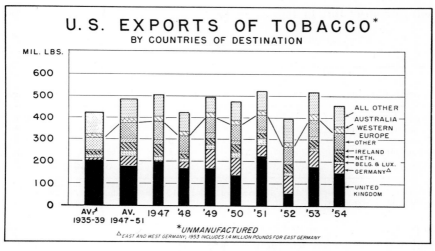

Figure 4.56.   (U.S. Department of Agriculture)

Joseph W. Hines made a study in 1951 of the effect of the trends in flue-cured tobacco export. Some of his findings and conclusions follow.

During 1935–39, as shown in Table 29, over 60 percent of the United States exports of flue-cured tobacco went to the United Kingdom as compared with 39.7 percent during 1949–50. During the postwar 1949–50 period, our market was still concentrated, but in the two countries of the United Kingdom and Western Germany, which together took 53.5 percent of our exports. Other countries began to take larger quantities of United States flue-cured during the postwar period: Ireland, New Zealand, the Netherlands, Belgium, Denmark, and Switzerland.[23]

Figure 4.56 indicates for all types of tobacco these same trends, except that in 1952 the extent of concentration was diminishing. Most significant in all of these data is the declining importance of the United King-

[23] Joseph W. Hines, "Trends in Flue-Cured Tobacco Export Trade," *The Southern Economic Journal,* January, 1952, p. 384.

dom and the increasing importance of Western Germany as exports markets. The factors accounting for these significant and opposite trends deserve further comment.

The two principal factors in the decline of exports to the United Kingdom were the dollar position of the United Kingdom and the nationalistic policies of the British government. United States grants-in-aid under the British loan and the Economic Cooperation Administration and other agencies were helpful in sustaining the level of flue-cured exports; the British attempted to reduce the consumption of tobacco to prewar levels and to restrict further the use of their scarce dollars by increasing the

TABLE 29.   United States Flue-Cured Tobacco Exports
(thousands of pounds)

Importing Nation	Average, 1935–39		1949–50	
	Amount	Percent	Amount	Percent
United Kingdom	203,053	63.7	153,625	39.7
Western Germany	4,012[a]	1.3	53,587	13.8
China	38,025	11.9	6,969	1.8
Other countries	73,775	23.1	172,937	44.7
Total:	318,865	100.0	387,118	100.0

[a] All Germany.
SOURCE: *Annual Report on Tobacco Statistics*, Production and Marketing Administration, United States Department of Agriculture, 1950.

import duty on tobacco from $7.16 per pound to $11.72 per pound. In addition, the United Kingdom pursued a policy of using flue-cured tobacco from empire sources. This policy was carried out through mixing ratios, the exchange control mechanism, and restrictive arrangements.

As a result of these policies the percentage of United States flue-cured to total leaf use of the British declined from 73 percent in 1938 to 57 percent in 1950 and continued to decline. In addition, British purchases of empire flue-cured from Canada, India, and Southern Rhodesia were more than three times as great in 1950 as in the 1934–38 period. Production of flue-cured in Southern Rhodesia, the most important flue-cured exporter of the empire areas, increased from 20 million pounds in the 1930's to over 100 million pounds in 1950. The largest relative gain in world exports of tobacco was made by Southern Rhodesia with a 370 percent increase in 1952 over the prewar 1935–39 average and a gain of more than 34 percent over 1951.[24] (We have already seen that in 1955 exports of the Central African Federation—Southern Rhodesia, Northern

[24] *Ibid.*, p. 386.

Rhodesia, and Nyasaland—were almost four times as large as the 1935–39 average.)

Increased exports of United States flue-cured tobacco to Western Germany resulted from the phenomenal popularity of American blended cigarettes after their introduction into Germany by United States military forces. Before World War II, about 90 percent of German cigarette consumption consisted of oriental cigarettes. Surveys indicated in 1950 that from 85 to 90 percent of German consumers preferred blended to oriental cigarettes.[25]

Flue-cured exports to Western Germany were financed in part by ECA funds. Continual pressures were exerted on the Bonn government to re-establish trade channels with Greece and Turkey based on the importation of oriental tobaccos. Developments in 1950 and 1951 indicated that the German government was attempting to discourage imports of United States tobacco. As a result of these pressures a United States mission was sent to Western Germany in 1951 and agreement was reached at Bonn which provided for additional purchases of United States tobacco through use of ECA funds. A further projected program was worked out in Washington for the 1951–52 marketing year in which the German delegation indicated that Western Germany would be willing to purchase $40 million worth of tobacco (approximately the amount purchased in 1949–50 marketing year—see Table 29—53,587,000 pounds flue-cured imports) provided adequate aid and coöperation were received from the United States. The aid envisaged was an additional ECA grant and the coöperation anticipated was increased use of private barter transactions on the part of United States exporters and German importers.[26]

The conclusion was drawn in 1952, therefore, that the high postwar German consumer demand for flue-cured tobacco provided a basis for the maintenance and expansion of flue-cured exports to Western Germany. The future volume of flue-cured exports to Western Germany, however, appeared probably to depend on the strength of pressures from the United States as compared with pressures exerted by groups interested in increased German imports of oriental tobaccos.[27]

Figure 4.57, which compares the calendar year averages 1947–51 and 1952–54, shows that Western Europe's imports of all unmanufactured tobacco during the latter three years increased 52 million pounds over the

[25] *Ibid.*, p. 387.
[26] *Ibid.*, pp. 388–389.
[27] *Ibid.*, p. 390.

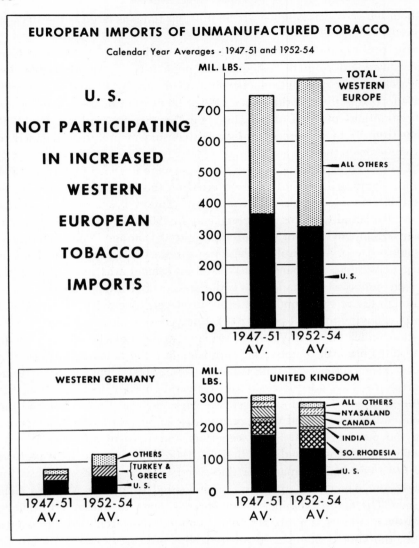

Figure 4.57.   (U.S. Department of Agriculture)

earlier postwar years, but its imports from the United States fell 48 million. The United Kingdom, chief factor in the fall, cut its United States purchases by 43 million pounds but increased purchases elsewhere by 19 million, mainly in the Commonwealth. While United States exports to Western Germany were greater, our share in the larger West German market was less. The United States Department of Agriculture drew the conclusion that the United States was not participating in increased western European tobacco imports.

The postwar picture (Figure 4.58) for flue-cured tobacco shows that the United States faced increased competition from foreign production and exports. Postwar flue-cured tobacco abroad increased rapidly. United States prewar output was twice that of foreign output, and in 1954 United States production was only slightly greater. While production abroad increased, foreign exports grew while United States exports held

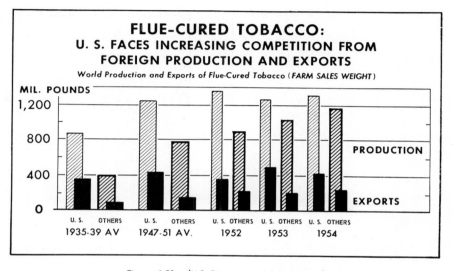

Figure 4.58. (U.S. Department of Agriculture)

about steady. Prewar foreign exports of flue-cured were less than one-fifth of those of the world total compared with more than one-third in 1954.

These trends in flue-cured exports must now be related to the total picture of United States flue-cured tobacco as presented in Figure 4.59 and through additional analysis of United States tobacco policy.

TOBACCO PROBLEMS AND POLICY. The United States agricultural programs for tobacco are somewhat more rigid than those for other commodities. A national marketing quota must be proclaimed by December 1 for each marketing year for each kind of tobacco for which a national marketing quota was proclaimed for the immediately preceding year. Price support is required at 90 percent of parity, if marketing quotas are in effect. If marketing quotas are not approved by a two-thirds vote, no price supports are available for tobacco as compared with 50 percent of parity support for other basic crops. Marketings by the producer in excess of the farm marketing quotas are subject to a penalty of 40 percent of the preceding season's average price. Thus one basic difference between tobacco price supports and other basic crops is that price support is required at 90 percent of parity if marketing quotas are in effect.

Flue-cured tobacco quotas have been in effect continuously since 1935 and kept production in balance with disappearance and a minimum accumulation of stocks up to 1954, as indicated in Figure 4.59. This together

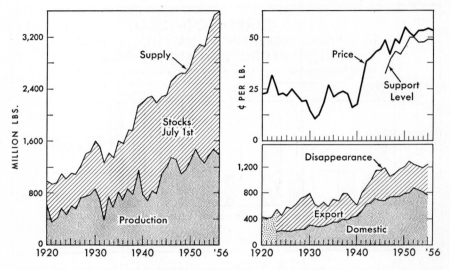

Figure 4.59. Flue-Cured Tobacco. (Data from U.S. Department of Agriculture, Bureau of Agricultural Economics and Agricultural Marketing Service)

with a rising domestic demand led to an increase in the price of flue-cured from 20.5 cents a pound in 1935–39 to 33.1 cents per pound during 1940–44 to 54.7 cents per pound in 1950. Prices in 1951, 1952, 1953, 1954, and 1955 were slightly lower, at 52.4 cents, 50.3 cents, 52.8 cents, 52.7 cents, and 51.5 cents respectively. During the postwar years only in one year, 1952, were prices below the support level.

Probably the greatest cause of domestic dissatisfaction with the Agricultural Adjustment program has been the accumulation of great stores of surplus commodities by the government while prices to consumers have risen and remain high. Through their system of rigid controls, flue-cured tobacco farmers did not until 1956 permit the accumulation of surplus stocks even though in one year (1947) a 27.52 percent reduction in acreage was required. Cigarette smokers have not felt the effect of the increase in tobacco prices because it has not been reflected in higher cigarette prices.

Since neither one of the principal causes of dissatisfaction had existed in the case of tobacco, and because the cost of the tobacco program had been small, the Eisenhower administration recommended its continuation after 1954 without change. There are many factors other than the three mentioned above which should be considered, but the major factor ignored is the effect of high tobacco prices on export markets for flue-cured.

An analysis of the flue-cured tobacco situation made in March, 1954, indicated the following favorable and unfavorable conditions:

Favorable:
1. Extension of the Reciprocal Trade Act for one year in 1953.
2. Approval for the use of foreign aid funds for exports.
3. An increase in flue-cured exports from 362 million pounds in 1952 to 498 million pounds in 1953, or 38%.
Unfavorable:
1. Increased foreign production in flue-cured and other cigarette type tobacco.
2. A drop in the domestic consumption of cigarettes for the first time since 1930's.
3. Increased consumption of oriental type leaf in Western Europe.[28]

A glance at the favorable factors would indicate that the increased exports might be the only one of the three of permanent significance. However, an analysis of this increase indicated that most of it was accounted for by heavy shipments of tobacco, which had been deferred from 1952 to the first half of 1953. United States exports of unmanufactured tobacco in 1954 were 453.6 million pounds as compared with 518.7 million pounds in 1953, but they were back up to 538.6 million pounds in 1955. Dr. Joseph Weybrew, in reporting the results of a survey of foreign markets for flue-cured tobacco, indicated that most serious complaints against United States flue-cured were the nonuniformity of sorting and high price.[29]

Thus it appears that high prices for United States flue-cured tobacco were restraining the purchase of our tobacco by importers and encouraging the production of flue-cured tobacco in other areas.

The *Charlotte Observer* (North Carolina) was not very concerned over the loss of British markets for American tobacco. Commenting on the removal of three Tarheel auctioneers to Southern Rhodesia, whose

[28] *Raleigh News and Observer,* March 3, 1954, pp. 1 and 3.
[29] *Ibid.*

tobacco is taking the place of American tobacco in Britain, and the decrease in British purchases of tobacco in this country, the Charlotte daily observed:

"Sometimes, however, such things turn out to be blessings in disguise. With their market reduced, the farmers might have to turn to other crops and to cattle. It could result in a better balanced agriculture, but the transition period is likely to be painful."

The *Durham Morning Herald* (North Carolina) did not share the complacency of the Charlotte paper. The Durham paper summarized the 1954 position of the tobacco program as follows:

WHERE THE TOBACCO PROGRAM NEEDS STRENGTHENING

In the course of his comment that "no single solution is appropriate for all commodities" in his speech at the 117th annual meeting of the Darlington County Agricultural Society Tuesday, Secretary of Agriculture Benson observed that "for some farm products, such as tobacco, the present program seems to be working well. . . ."

In some respects the tobacco program is working well. The support price program is administered by a growers' cooperative organization, the Stabilization Corporation. This corporation borrows money from the Commodity Credit Corporation to finance its purchases of flue-cured tobacco at support prices (90 per cent of parity) when such tobacco does not receive a bid equal to the support price. Its consistent record has been that it not only pays back with interest the money it borrows, but it has also been able to sell the tobacco it has taken in at a profit, which is distributed among its members after its expenses and government obligations have been paid.

Currently there is considerable demand for tobacco stocks held by the Stabilization Corporation, and there is indication that the creditable record will be maintained. Thus the tobacco program works out in this respect as a government-supported farm program should; it helps the farmer and at the same time does not prove a burden to the general taxpayer.

On the other hand, there is room for improvement in the tobacco program. An expanded market is needed if production is not to be further diminished and total farm income from tobacco reduced. The investment required to produce a crop of tobacco is such that a certain level of production must be maintained to make it economically profitable for the grower. A satisfactory tobacco program must enable the farmer to produce at this level and at the same time yield him a total income which will provide a living for himself and his family above expenses of production.

Diminishing foreign markets for American tobacco mean continued reduction in acreage allotments. To hold present markets and to expand them are the principal needs now of the tobacco program.

However, during the years 1955 and 1956 the flue-cured tobacco situation began to push to the surface some fundamental problems resulting from shifts in the demand for flue-cured. These arose from (1) continuing changes in the foreign market and (2) developing changes in the domestic market. Both of these involved shifts in the demand for flue-cured from mild to strong types of leaf. In addition, domestic consumption was off as a result of the "cancer scare," which related lung cancer to cigarette consumption. However, even though more cigarettes were being used, less flue-cured tobacco was being used. This latter was a result of the increased use of filter tips, which, because of the filter and the fact that the cigarettes are thinner, require 10 percent less tobacco. The cancer scare led to an increase in filter tips sold from 1 percent of the total cigarettes in 1951 to 20 percent in 1955 and 30 percent in 1956. Another factor causing less consumption of flue-cured tobacco was "homogenization." In this process, the tobacco leaves are "reconstituted." The leaf, including stems and other scraps, is ground up and put back together to form a sheet of tobacco. It is estimated that 20 percent less tobacco could be required by using this process.

These changes were reflected in the overall outlook for flue-cured tobacco for 1957 (see Figure 4.59). In 1955–56 total supply stocks plus production increased more than 10 percent above those for 1954–55. The total supply for the crop year 1956–57 beginning July 1, 1956, exceeded that for 1955–56 and was the largest on record. There was a 10 percent decrease in production of flue-cured during 1955–56, but a 10 percent increase in stocks from July 1, 1955, to 1956, which more than offset the decrease in production and led to the record total supply. The 1956–57 total supply was 2.9 times prospective annual disappearance compared with the average ratio of 2.5 for the five years prior to 1955–56. Carry-over on July 1, 1957, was estimated to be about 4 percent higher than the record high of 2258 million pounds of July 1, 1956.

On the consumption side (or disappearance) exports of flue-cured in 1955–56 were large—29 percent above 1954–55 and a new high. This big increase was due partially to Title 1 of Public Law 480, which enables certain commodities, including tobacco, to be traded for foreign currencies. Exports for 1956–57 were estimated to be about 10 percent less than in 1955–56. It was clearly apparent at the beginning of 1957 that the flue-cured export problem was still present in the form of an increasing amount of foreign competition in the export trade. Proof of this could be found in the fact that flue-cured production of the four principal surplus producers in 1956 was 24 percent above 1955 production. The United States Department of Agriculture drew the conclusion at the beginning of 1957 that the long-term competitive export outlook for United States tobacco was not encouraging.

Domestic use of flue-cured tobacco began to decline in 1953 to 778 million pounds from a peak of 828 million in 1952 and continued to decline to 744 million in 1954 and 729 million in 1955. This was about a 2 percent decline in the crop year 1955–56 from the previous years, in spite of the fact that about a 2 percent larger number of cigarettes was produced. Apparently more cigarettes were being produced per pound of tobacco leaf. The Department of Agriculture saw the 1957 outlook as one in which more cigarettes would be produced but it was doubtful if a larger quantity of flue-cured tobacco would be used. The principal contributing causes we have seen to be the increased use of filter tips, which required less tobacco, and the substitution of "homogenized" or reconstructed leaf.

Thus the flue-cured tobacco growers were faced in 1957 with growing stocks of flue-cured tobacco. To meet this situation partially, the Department of Agriculture announced a 20 percent cut in acreage allotments for 1957.

A related, and equally if not more important, problem was that the types of flue-cured being produced and held in stock were not the types that were in demand. The shift to filter tips changed the demand from mild tobacco to aromatic, heavy-bodied, darker tobaccos so the flavor would come through the filter. These were the tobaccos that we had been exporting in quantity. Thus the increase in demand for this type of tobacco raised the price in the world market and hence made our export problem more difficult. Our export markets do not like our mild tobacco because they say its nicotine content is too low and it lacks flavor.

The flue-cured tobacco control program from its beginning relied on acreage control rather than quantitative allotments and thus growers set out to maximize production. Then Granville wilt and Blackshank, tobacco diseases, entered the flue-cured areas. Domestic demand was for mild, low-nicotine tobacco that could be used for blending. These three factors led to the development of varieties that would produce the milder grades in demand, resist wilt and Blackshank, and maximize the yield per acre. The new varieties, plus over-fertilization and planting too close together, produced a pale, slick type of tobacco that was mild with a low nicotine content. The estimate was made that from 25 to 50 percent of the 1955–56 flue-cured crop production was in this light leaf variety with further increases anticipated for 1957. In addition, the Tobacco Stabilization Corporation was holding increasing stocks of these varieties unwanted by both the domestic and foreign market.

Thus at the beginning of 1957 the United States Department of Agriculture found itself supporting a program of producing unwanted types of flue-cured tobacco and facing the problem of increasing stocks. To meet the problem of the unwanted varieties the Department of Agriculture announced in late December, 1956, that price supports for varieties "139," "140," and "244" of the 1957 crop, irrespective of grade, would be at one-half the rate for comparable grades of other varieties. These were the varieties developed to meet the pre-filter tip demand for disease-resistant, mild, bright lemon tobacco low in nicotine content. The Department specifically stated that this change was due to the shift in consumer demand to filter tips and to the fact that export markets were lacking for tobaccos with low flavor and aroma. The announcement was made in order to enable farmers to shift to varieties demanded by tobacco manufacturers.

At the same time the above announcement was made, the Agriculture Department also said if the Congress decided to modify tobacco legislation it would suggest that the Department be permitted to establish marketing quotas for individual farms on a poundage basis. Such a suggestion would include the request that the high 1956 and 1957 acre yields be excluded in establishing poundage allotments.

At the beginning of 1957, then, the United States Department of Agriculture was moving toward a qualitative and quantitative program of production adjustments for flue-cured tobacco facilitated by flexible price supports.

CHAPTER 5

Agricultural Problems and Policy

In this study of agricultural resources as contributing factors to strength and production potentials emphasis has been placed on (1) "Controlling Forces and Land Use," (2) "Agricultural Production," and (3) "International Trade in Agricultural Products." In the last instance special consideration has been given to facts, problems, and policy of the important United States import and export commodities.

President Eisenhower's message to the Congress of January 11, 1954, was introduced with the statement: "The agricultural problem today is as serious and complex as any with which the Congress will deal in this session." The purpose of this final section on "Agricultural Problems and Policy" is to stress and point up only those problems which are of international significance. The complexity of "the agricultural problem," which President Eisenhower has emphasized, is far beyond the scope of these summary remarks.

INADEQUATE FOOD SUPPLIES

In the section on production of food, the lack of availability of adequate food supplies to over half the people of the world was considered to be "the fundamental agricultural problem." *This is not the United States agricultural problem* to which President Eisenhower was referring, but it is the international agricultural problem which the United States must lend coöperative help in solving. The battle for men's minds will be more difficult to win as long as these men are hungry. But as will be developed in Chapter 13 on human resources, food supplies are so closely related to population growth that their increased availability alone will not solve the problem of making economic progress in these underfed areas.

The United States has addressed itself to the problem of inadequate food supplies through the numerous aid programs to export food to deficiency areas. More fundamentally, through support of the Food and Agricultural Organization the basic problem of increasing agricultural productivity in these areas has been attacked.

EXCESS AGRICULTURAL SUPPLIES

The United States farm problem is not a single farm problem. Indeed, in the section on the Condition of Agriculture of the *Economic Report of the President,* the Congress was advised in the opening sentence that

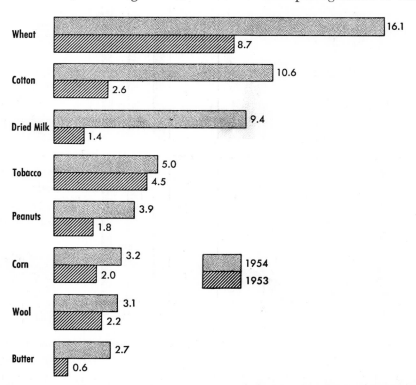

Figure 5.1. Farm Products in Government Inventory and Pledged for Loans, February 28, 1954 and 1953, Showing Months of Supply. (Data from U.S. Department of Agriculture and *The New York Times*)

agriculture was beset in 1954 "with more problems than any other major part of our economy." The first point made was that agriculture would "continue to be confronted in 1954 with problems growing out of excess supplies of some major farm products—notably wheat, cotton, and corn." Figure 5.1 which gives farm products in government inventory and

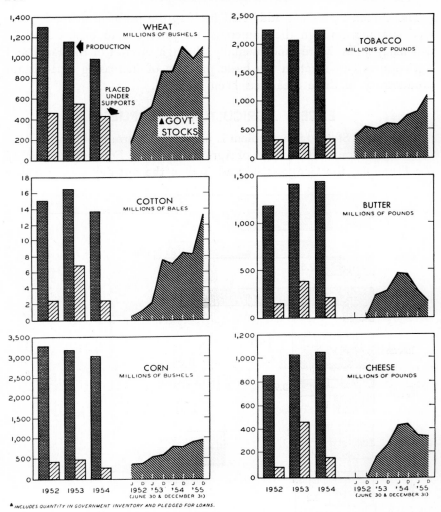

Figure 5.2. Farm Output and Government Stocks, Six Commodities, 1952–55. (Data from U.S. Department of Agriculture)

pledged for loans, indicates that the excess supplies were not confined to these three major products. Figure 5.2 supplements this chart and gives farm output and government stocks. The summary report of 1957 on the three products emphasized by the President may be seen in Figure 5.3. The existence of surplus agricultural products is in sharp contrast to an inadequacy of food supplies in over half the world.

Farm surpluses may be defined as supplies of food and agricultural commodities for which no effective demand exists at current price levels.

One of the long-standing and most successful objectives of United States farm policy has been increased productivity; and one of the recurring problems has been surplus commodities. With these facts in mind, one can fairly safely say that present surpluses are the result of the great increase in the capacity to produce which occurred during the first three or four years of World War II. At that time productive capacity was increased about 40 percent to meet war needs.

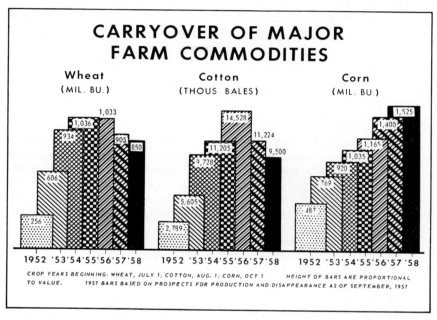

Figure 5.3. (U.S. Department of Agriculture, Agricultural Marketing Service)

Once productive capacity of agriculture is increased, it is not readily cut back. United States policy of rigid price supports, without firm production control, has thus enhanced the inability to make downward production adjustment. In addition, high and rigid price supports have priced both wheat and cotton out of important domestic and foreign markets. Thus as seen from the stocks and the results, the problem is one of unbalanced farm production, resulting in specific surpluses. One of the most serious complicating factors, as has been noted from the study of the individual commodities, is the continuing loss of some of those foreign markets on which United States agriculture has depended for a large part of its prosperity. In the post-World War II years, high levels of specific exports have been aided and abetted by various foreign aid programs and export subsidies. Surpluses have increased as exports have declined owing to decrease in foreign aid programs, increased foreign production, the desire for foreign buyers to spend these scarce dollars elsewhere and to purchase from other sources at world prices, which have been lower than United States prices.

Surpluses will continue to build up as long as the above circumstances prevail. The problem then is one of preventing further accumulation of stocks of these specific agricultural commodities and of disposal of existing stocks. However, the necessity of disposal of existing stocks must be modified by the desirability of maintaining buffer stocks to minimize price fluctuations and to serve as emergency reserves.

In mid-1954, when the United States, in an attempt to maintain exports, was still using an export subsidy for wheat and was cutting the foreign price and maintaining the price support program, one of the popular weekly news magazines put the case in this fashion:

Price war has broken out in wheat, as major suppliers try to move heavy stocks. Importing countries, in no hurry to buy, watch from the side lines.

Canada and the U.S. are major battlers for world wheat markets. First one, then the other, takes the lead in cutting export prices. Shaving of Canadian price in February was immediately matched by the U.S. On June 4, U.S. price was marked down 10 cents to $1.70 a bushel. Canadians followed suit on June 7.

Further price slashing probably lies ahead.

Worried Australians and Argentines, also big wheat exporters, can't be left behind if they want to try to keep their shares of the world market.

Lower export prices do not mean that you, as a consumer, will pay less for your bread and flour. *Domestic wheat prices* ride serenely above the price-support level ($2.20 a bushel). Only foreign buyers get bargain rates on U.S. wheat. The export subsidy now has climbed to 55 cents a bushel at Eastern U.S. ports.

Wheat-price war simply means that you, as a taxpayer, must foot the bill for a larger and larger export subsidy to move wheat into world markets.

Taxpayers' dollars pour out to maintain the price-support program. High prices result in surplus production. Then—to try to get rid of the surplus—a whopping loss is taken to subsidize lower prices for export wheat. Clear?[1]

If one remains fully aware of the fact that surpluses did exist before government programs were in effect, the conclusion seems justified that government agricultural policy and expenditures create existing specific surpluses, and then additional government expenditures are made to subsidize United States exporters and foreign importers of United States agricultural commodities.

Many proposals have been made for the disposal of the surplus com-

[1] *U.S. News and World Report,* June 18, 1954, p. 121.

modities. With so many underfed and underclothed people, the most obvious solution would be a gigantic giveaway program. Such a temporary solution must be immediately rejected in so far as it would have a depressing effect on the prices of foreign-produced commodities. What is needed is a permanent solution to prevent additional accumulations of stocks. President Eisenhower's proposals to Congress on January 11, 1954, for a revised farm program, which included flexible farm price supports, listed as the first of its seven major features: "1. The new program should first be given an opportunity to start operating without the handicap of such large surpluses. This is to be done by setting aside certain quantities of our surplus commodities, eliminating them from price support computations."

Following up the above, the *Economic Report of the President* transmitted to the Congress in January, 1954, "recommended that Congress authorize the setting up of $2.5 billion worth of CCC stocks, with the objective of insulating them from regular domestic and foreign markets. This measure, however, can succeed only if further major additions to carry-overs cease after 1954. To the extent that foreign disposal is undertaken, it should be carried out so as to augment, rather than displace, the normal volumes of world trade in surplus commodities. The magnitude of our surplus problem could lead to practices harmful to the economies of other friendly nations—a result that must be scrupulously avoided in the interest of the entire free world economy."

The Agricultural Act of May, 1956, directed the Commodity Credit Corporation to dispose of all stocks as rapidly as possible and provided for the appointment of a Surplus Disposal Administrator. A clear and concise graphic and verbal explanation of the United States government programs developed to dispose of these surpluses and to help farm exports is given in Figure 5.4. There was evidence that by 1957 in some instances "foreign disposal" had resulted in "practices harmful to the economies of other friendly nations." The surplus problem as defined included not only the disposal of existing stocks but the prevention of further accumulation of stocks. The correct approach to the latter should be through production adjustments under competitive conditions where possible, and through expanding markets.

PRICE AND INCOME INSTABILITY AND THE ALLOCATION OF RESOURCES

Probably the most basic United States agricultural problem is price and income instability, and resource allocation.

About 2/5 of farm exports are under programs

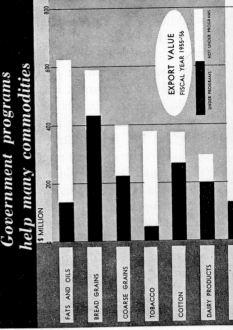

$ BILLION

FISCAL YEAR
ENDING JUNE 30

1954

1955

1956

0   1   2   3   4

■ GOVERNMENT PROGRAMS
□ OTHER

GOVERNMENT PROGRAMS INCLUDE SALES FOR FOREIGN CURRENCIES,
BARTER SALES, ECONOMIC AID GRANTS, WELFARE AND
RELIEF DONATIONS AND LOANS

USDA FAS 997

There are four kinds of programs

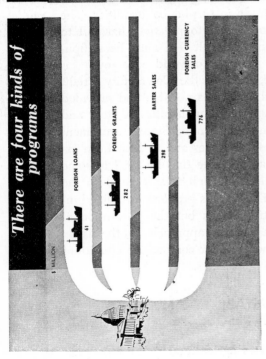

$ MILLION

FOREIGN LOANS
61

FOREIGN GRANTS
282

BARTER SALES
298

FOREIGN CURRENCY
SALES
776

USDA FAS 998

Government programs help many commodities

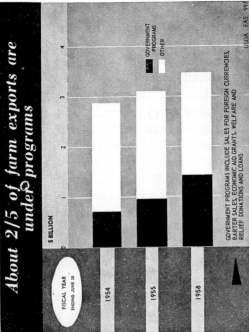

$ MILLION

FATS AND OILS

BREAD GRAINS

COARSE GRAINS

TOBACCO

COTTON

DAIRY PRODUCTS

OTHER

0   200   400   600   800

EXPORT VALUE
FISCAL YEAR 1955-56

■ UNDER PROGRAMS   □ NOT UNDER PROGRAMS

Agricultural commodities under U.S. government export programs accounted for about 25 percent of exports in 1954 before the newer programs were under way. Subsequently, program exports rose to 30 percent of the total in 1955 and to 41 percent in 1956. Sales outside of programs have remained fairly steady. The increase in program activity has been in sales for foreign currency under P.L. 480 and P.L. 665, and barter arrangements under P.L. 480. Direct foreign aid grants and loans have declined in importance. In the years immediately following World War II, when many countries tottered on the brink of economic collapse, by far the largest share of foreign assistance took the form of outright grants. The newer U.S. export programs are based on the ability of foreign countries to pay for their purchases, although these payments may have to be made in their own currency. Last year U.S. government programs accounted for these shares of major export groups: cotton, 72 percent; dairy products, 55 percent; bread grains, 72 percent; coarse grains, 58 percent; fats and oils, 22 percent; and tobacco, 14 percent.

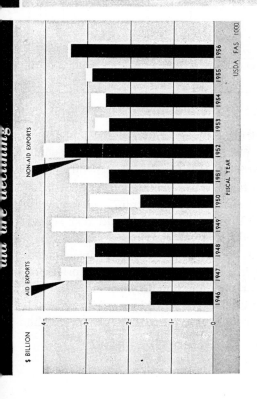

Export prices often often less than domestic prices

EXPORT SALE VALUE PER $1 OF DOMESTIC VALUE

Commodity	Export Value	Price Gap
GRAIN SORGHUMS	91¢	9¢
ORANGES, FRESH	88¢	12¢
COTTON	80¢	20¢
RICE	79¢	21¢
WHEAT	74¢	26¢
GRAPEFRUIT SECTIONS	71¢	29¢
CHEDDAR CHEESE	67¢	33¢
BUTTER	64¢	36¢
NON-FAT DRY MILK	59¢	41¢

EXPORT VALUE — THE PRICE GAP

SEE TABLE 13   USDA   FAS   1001

CCC commercial export sales nearly $1 billion

COMMITMENTS FISCAL YEAR 1956

Commodity	Million $
UPLAND COTTON	435
WHEAT	330
FEED GRAINS	125
RICE	32
BUTTER	12
SOY BEANS	10
COTTONSEED OIL	10
DRY BEANS	9
NON-FAT DRY MILK SOLIDS	8
LINSEED OIL	7
FLAXSEED	6
CHEDDAR CHEESE	2
OTHERS	6

TOTAL $992 MILLION

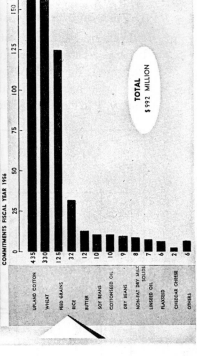

AID EXPORTS   NON-AID EXPORTS

$ BILLION — FISCAL YEAR — 1946 1947 1948 1949 1950 1951 1952 1953 1954 1955 1956

USDA   FAS   1000

Present government export programs are designed essentially to assure that neither lack of financing nor high domestic prices shall hinder exports. For many commodities an appreciable price gap exists between domestic and export sale prices. This gap ranges from 9 percent of the domestic price for grain sorghums to 41 percent of the price for nonfat dry milk solids. These figures give an indication of the extent to which export prices must be reduced before U.S. products become competitive with those of other exporting countries. To close or narrow this gap, CCC sells surplus commodities to exporters at competitive prices, or export subsidies are paid to them. Last year CCC decided to sell exporters nearly $1 billion worth (dollar return) of surplus products at competitive prices, an amount equivalent to 28 percent of total agricultural exports. Principal items were cotton, wheat, and feed grains; most of the cotton was for export after August 1, 1956, under CCC's new program. Selling cotton at competitive prices was the most recent important step taken to solve a difficult U.S. marketing situation.

Figure 5.4.   Government Programs Help Farm Exports. (U.S. Department of Agriculture)

1. Price and Income Instability

Price and income instability, while not peculiar to agriculture, is a basic characteristic of agriculture. It is beyond the scope of this summary to present its extent. However, Figure 5.5 clearly shows that in agriculture price has varied much more and production much less than in industry. Particular attention should be given to the early 1930's, when the

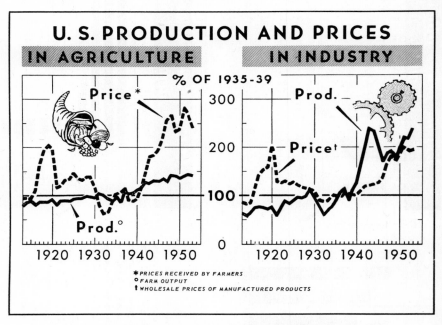

Figure 5.5.   (U.S. Department of Agriculture, Bureau of Agricultural Economics)

basic principles of the present agricultural program were developed. Between 1929 and 1932 agricultural prices declined from 138 to 61 while production actually increased from 97 to 101. On the other hand, industrial prices declined only from 113 to 87, while production was cut from 110 to 58. Thus agriculture took a sharp beating in purchasing power. During and immediately after both World War I and World War II and during the Korean War farm product prices rose more rapidly than wholesale prices of manufactured goods. The weakening in demand following each war was reflected in rather sharp declines in prices of agricultural products, with little or no reduction in output.

Figure 5.6 is another excellent visual aid which gives prices received and paid by farmers, and prices received as a percentage of parity. The latter is given in the lower part of the chart and clearly indicates the tremendous fluctuations of the purchasing power of farmers.

Farm prices and income have been discussed in relation to parity in at least three different ways. First of all, as has been seen, the idea was that the purchasing power of a given commodity should be maintained at a percentage relationship to a base period. Second, total farm pur-

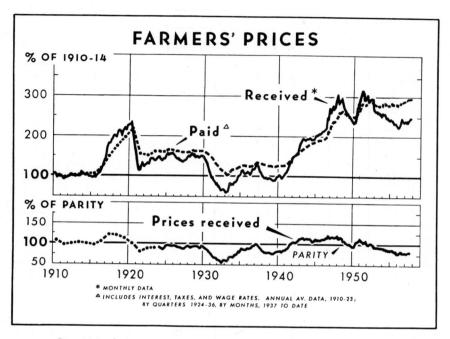

Figure 5.6. (U.S. Department of Agriculture, Agricultural Marketing Service)

chasing power should be maintained at a percentage relationship to a base period. The fluctuations in the latter have been discussed in the previous paragraph. More recently, and particularly since World War II, continual reference has been made to the difference in incomes between the farm and the nonfarm population. Frequent references have been made to the desirability of parity in income between the farm and the nonfarm population. A recent reference was President Eisenhower's suggestion in his January, 1954, proposals to Congress as a fundamental consideration that "5. A farm program first of all should assist agriculture to earn its proportionate share of the national income."

This third reference to parity of incomes is an entirely different concept from the first two. Because of the more recent pronouncements that farm income should be equal to nonfarm income, Table 30 is presented to give these differences in per capita net income. Per capita farm income in 1955 was $881, of which $275 came from nonfarm sources. Per capita nonfarm income was $1935 or over twice as high. Farm income

TABLE 30. Average per Capita Net Income

Year	Farm Population						Nonfarm Population			Total Population from All Sources
	From Agriculture			From Nonfarm Sources	From All Sources		From Agriculture	From Nonfarm Sources	From All Sources	
	Excluding Government Payments	Government Payments	Total		Amount	Percent of Nonfarm Average				
1910	$147	$ 0	$147	—	—	—	$12	—	—	$ 360
1911	121	0	121	—	—	—	12	—	—	345
1912	154	0	154	—	—	—	13	—	—	367
1913	132	0	132	—	—	—	13	—	—	386
1914	145	0	145	—	—	—	13	—	—	368
1915	148	0	148	—	—	—	14	—	—	384
1916	157	0	157	—	—	—	16	—	—	443
1917	278	0	278	—	—	—	22	—	—	529
1918	305	0	305	—	—	—	23	—	—	567
1919	322	0	322	—	—	—	25	—	—	643
1920	282	0	282	—	—	—	22	—	—	711
1921	129	0	129	—	—	—	17	—	—	546
1922	158	0	158	—	—	—	18	—	—	554
1923	187	0	187	—	—	—	19	—	—	640
1924	182	0	182	—	—	—	19	—	—	624
1925	243	0	243	—	—	—	17	—	—	659
1926	220	0	220	—	—	—	17	—	—	689
1927	215	0	215	—	—	—	17	—	—	665
1928	224	0	224	—	—	—	17	—	—	676
1929	230	0	230	—	—	—	16	—	—	715
1930	166	0	166	—	—	—	14	—	—	613
1931	129	0	129	—	—	—	10	—	—	484
1932	80	0	80	—	—	—	8	—	—	345
1933	90	3	93	—	—	—	9	—	—	323
1934	94	12	106	$ 59	$165	35.3%	9	$ 459	$ 468	391
1935	167	15	182	62	244	47.2	10	507	517	448
1936	148	8	156	72	228	38.5	10	582	592	502
1937	207	9	216	80	296	46.1	10	632	642	558
1938	153	12	165	74	239	40.6	9	580	589	506
1939	147	21	168	81	249	39.8	10	616	626	537
1940	153	21	174	88	262	38.2	10	675	685	588
1941	230	16	246	103	349	42.4	13	810	823	715
1942	360	19	379	130	509	49.2	16	1,018	1,034	920
1943	476	21	497	157	654	52.7	17	1,223	1,240	1,126
1944	497	27	524	172	696	52.4	17	1,311	1,328	1,211
1945	528	26	554	166	720	54.9	17	1,295	1,312	1,205
1946	605	26	631	162	793	61.3	20	1,274	1,294	1,200
1947	631	10	641	181	822	59.0	21	1,372	1,393	1,286
1948	752	9	761	197	958	62.8	21	1,505	1,526	1,425
1949	558	6	564	201	765	51.0	20	1,480	1,500	1,372
1950	607	10	617	211	828	52.6	19	1,556	1,575	1,451
1951	735	10	745	232	977	56.0	20	1,725	1,745	1,625
1952	692	10	702	251	953	52.0	20	1,813	1,833	1,697
1953	657	8	665	265	930	49.6	18	1,857	1,875	1,741
1954	640	10	650	260	911	49.8	18	1,810	1,828	1,704
1955	597	9	606	275	881	45.5	17	1,917	1,935	1,793

SOURCE: Department of Agriculture.

in 1955 should be compared with a per capita farm income in 1934 of $165, of which $59 came from nonfarm sources. In this same year, per capita nonfarm income was $468, or almost three times as great as farm income. Thus during this twenty-year period of the farm program, the farm population improved relative to the nonfarm population so that per capita income of the latter was twice as great in 1955, while in 1934 it was almost three times as great as the per capita income of the farm population. Nevertheless the size of the income differential is clearly indicated. Any farm program that has as an objective the elimination of this differential has a difficult if not impossible task.

Without considering in detail the causes of these price and income problems, a brief enumeration of a few of the underlying reasons is fundamental to the understanding of the problem.

First, as has been seen, the most important fact about agriculture is its relation to and dependence on nature. Nature limits man's control over agricultural production. This in combination with the vagaries of nature leads to tremendous instability of output.

Second, the inelasticity of demand for many agricultural goods leads to an increased severity of price drops when bumper crops are produced. On the other hand, a short crop results in rapid price increases.

Third, market prices often mislead farmers in production decisions, especially where the gestation period is long, as is the case with perennial crops and animals. High market prices induce an expansion of output which will not be produced for a period of months or years. Since this expansion has been undertaken without a knowledge of what the future demand will be, the result is often a serious decline in prices. On the other hand, a sudden increase in demand for agricultural products with long gestation periods leads to rapid rises in the prices of these products. Thus the gestation period is a contributing factor to price instability.

2. Resource Allocation

Resource allocation, which is one of the principal functions of price, is not effectively accomplished in agriculture. As a result price and income instability and income inequalities are increased. The problem is one of allocation of resources within agriculture and between agriculture and industry.

The case has often been made that there is low mobility in shifts within agriculture and between agriculture and industry. In some instances this has been due to the fact that farmers have not been fully informed; in other instances institutional factors involving the production and marketing of farm commodities have been the cause; and in still others farming as a way of life has diminished shifts from agriculture into industry. However, the nature of agricultural costs is fundamental to the problem.

Labor is the most important resource used in agriculture. D. Gale Johnson has concluded that the contribution of labor to gross farm output is roughly twice that of land and is equal to all inputs purchased from non-agriculture.[2] Thus the proportions are 2, 1, 2. Labor is normally thought of as a variable cost. Fixed costs, such as rent and property taxes, are considered to be the principal factors limiting mobility. In those many instances where farm labor is part of the farm family, labor becomes a fixed cost. High fixed costs contribute to high sustained productivity even in the face of falling prices.

The conclusion is drawn, therefore, that farm policy should be developed to overcome the immobility due to high fixed costs, and most importantly to increase the mobility of labor within agriculture and between agriculture and industry. Our present farm programs through the allocation of production based on past acreage have tended to freeze production in existing areas. However, Johnson further concludes that: "The effect of any interferences or restrictions on the use of land could be more than offset by actions that would improve the use of labor. It is true—I believe all too true—that the agricultural programs have not been designed to facilitate the movement from agriculture to non-agriculture."[3] Fortunately other changes in our economy, such as continuous full employment, plus improved means of communication and transportation, have created both an important degree of regional readjustment in agriculture and a downward adjustment in farm employment.

3. Conclusion

The most important summary conclusion with respect to price and income instability and resource allocation is that agriculture has an exceedingly strong interest in the overall growth and stability of the economy. This is true because of the necessity of a sustained high level of demand for agricultural products and for labor in nonagricultural employment. Since agriculture prices and incomes fall rapidly during a recession and depression, and nonfarm labor tends to move back to the farm, it is

[2] D. Gale Johnson, "Competition in Agriculture: Fact or Fiction," *American Economic Review*, May, 1954, p. 111.

[3] *Ibid.*, pp. 111–112.

during such periods that agriculture needs effective protection. The international significance of the most basic United States agricultural problem of price and income instability and resource allocation is that it has led to restrictive agricultural programs which are inconsistent with our international trade policies.

INTERNATIONAL TRADE AND AGRICULTURAL POLICY

The significance of international trade in agricultural products to the United States has been established. Our agricultural policies have been seen to price United States products out of world markets and encourage production in other areas by forcing up world prices. In addition, export subsidies and import quotas and tariffs have tended to interfere with the free flow of international trade. There is ample evidence to prove that the agricultural policies we have followed have not only interfered with the free flow of trade but also caused the United States to adopt restrictive international trade policies at a time when we were advocating liberalization of trade and the free world was demanding trade not aid.

There is no real assurance that if the United States adopts a policy of freer trade other countries will follow, but the conclusion can safely be drawn that if this is not done other countries will adopt increasingly restrictive policies which will diminish the volume of world trade and agricultural trade.

Further, the prediction has been made that: "Our trade policy and the economic assistance that we are providing indicate the only alternative course of action open to most nations presently following a policy of state trading. A world in which most of the international trade—as well as national trade—is conducted directly by the state is not one in which private enterprise finds a friendly atmosphere. Thus a strong possibility exists that more is at stake in the nature of our trade policy than the organization of international trade; our emphasis on private enterprise might well have to be shifted."[4]

There is ample justification to conclude then that the United States foreign trade policy should pursue an objective of liberalization and that our agricultural policy needs revising. If possible, consistent courses of action should be followed. How can this be accomplished?

1. D. Gale Johnson in his excellent study on the inconsistent United States international trade and agricultural policies concludes that: "Advocates of a liberal international trade policy have overemphasized the

[4] D. Gale Johnson, *Trade and Agriculture*, John Wiley and Sons, 1950, p. 6.

increased efficiency in the utilization of land, labor and capital which results from multilateral trade; and have failed to tackle the problem of
unstable agricultural prices of internationally traded raw materials."[5]

2. Our study has shown that stability of agricultural prices and income
is of tremendous importance to agriculture and that United States agricultural policy has been designed to achieve this objective. On the other
hand, too little emphasis has been given to the problem of more efficient
allocation of agricultural resources within agriculture and between agriculture and industry. Indeed, United States agricultural policies have
worked against the most efficient allocation.

3. Thus agricultural policy must be modified to achieve more efficient
utilization of resources, and international trade policy must place more
emphasis on measures to achieve the stability of international agricultural
prices.

The Commission on Foreign Economic Policy drew the following conclusions with respect to the "Conflict Between Farm Policies and the
Enlargement of World Trade."

In the opinion of the Commission, it is necessary to harmonize our agricultural and foreign economic policies without sacrificing the sound objectives of
either.

The inherent conflict is not between foreign trade policy and farm policy
as such, but rather between foreign trade policy and the means by which an
important phase of our farm policy is being implemented. To put the matter
boldly, it is necessary to emphasize that inflexible *price-support* programs
which hold domestic prices above world prices become *price-fixing* programs
and result in accumulations of surpluses that would otherwise have moved
into consumption here or abroad. To maintain such *price-fixing* programs it
may become necessary for the United States to apply trade restrictions of
various kinds, including import quotas, to keep down foreign importations. To
move high-priced surpluses into export markets it may seem necessary to use
export subsidies or dumping procedures that, if practiced with respect to imports into this country, would involve the application of our antidumping and
countervailing-duty laws. Price-fixing, particularly with reference to commodities moving in international trade, is inherently incompatible with a pattern of
private trade, free enterprise, and nondiscriminatory commerce among nations. . . .

The great strides made by farmers in increasing the productivity and efficiency of our agriculture during the past decade give ample evidence of the
great vitality and flexibility of the agricultural sectors of our economy. Good
prices based upon a broadened demand for farm products at home and
abroad constituted an important factor in this upsurge of farm productivity
and general farm progress. Flexibility in agriculture itself, and in agricultural

[5] *Ibid.*, p. 10.

policy, would appear to be essential in the present situation if farmers are to be in the best position to adapt their farming operations to the changing needs of domestic and foreign markets. This flexibility, especially with respect to foreign markets, can be largely lost if a system of fixed prices is allowed to become permanently imbedded in our farm policy as it relates to possible export markets.

If to a scheme of fixed prices in agriculture are added the inevitable implementing devices of production quotas, import controls, and export subsidies, the ability of agriculture to play a continuing dynamic role in expanding international trade will be largely lost. This would be a serious loss, not only to agriculture, but to our entire economy and to the productivity of the free world. Furthermore, the repercussions from the standpoint of the trading policies of our friends and allies of the free world would be to the detriment of all concerned. . . .

The Commission believes that a dynamic foreign economic policy as it relates to agriculture cannot be built out of a maze of restrictive devices such as inflexible price-support programs which result in fixed prices, open or concealed export subsidies, import quotas at home and abroad, excessive use of tariffs here and abroad, exchange restrictions, and state trading. If we are to have a foreign economic policy which will make its best contribution to the strengthening of our long-term development of foreign markets for farmers, we must move as rapidly as feasible toward the elimination of such devices as a part of, or supplement to, our own agricultural policy.[6]

President Eisenhower in his proposals to Congress in January, 1954, recommended a farm program the key element of which he described as "a gradual adjustment to new circumstances and conditions." In addition to the previously described insulation of surpluses, the announced objectives were further expansions of markets at home and abroad; the establishment of modernized parity effective January 1, 1956; and the establishment after 1954 of a flexible price support scheme with the expiration of the rigid price supports provided for under the amendment to the 1949 Agricultural Act. These latter supports were described as "attuned to war needs and demonstrably unworkable in peacetime."

The flexible price support scheme was the most important objective of President Eisenhower's proposal. The manner in which prices were to be supported and income stabilized was described as follows:

Under the provisions of the Agricultural Acts of 1948 and 1949 the Government will:

1. Support the prices of basic crops of those farmers who cooperate with acreage allotments and marketing quotas when such are in effect;

2. Announce the price support level for various crops before those crops are planted, insofar as practicable;

[6] Commission on Foreign Economic Policy, *Report* to the President and the Congress, Government Printing Office, January, 1954, pp. 29–32.

3. Support price levels at up to 90 per cent of parity. For some products a schedule of price floors will also be provided as authorized by the 1949 Act, ranging from 75 per cent to 90 per cent of parity, according to the relationship of total to normal supply; and

4. Vary the price support level one percentage point for every two percentage points of variation in the total supply. If the supply is short, higher support levels will encourage production. If the supply is over-abundant, a lowered price will stimulate consumption. Thus, not only will a floor be placed under all basic crop prices, but variations in price and supply will tend to offset each other, and thus stabilize the income of the farmer.

President Eisenhower concluded that the program would "provide added incentive to make wise use of all our agricultural resources, and promises the Nation's agriculture a more stable and reliable financial return than any alternative plan." The explanation was fairly clear with respect to stability of income, but much more will be required to secure the necessary facilitation in the allocation of resources.

President Eisenhower's recommendations were incorporated in the Agricultural Act of 1954.

Item one on the Eisenhower farm program for 1955 and 1956 was to give the flexible price support program a chance to operate. However, in April, 1956, Congress passed a farm bill the second section of which restored rigid price supports by directing the federal government to support the prices of wheat, cotton, corn, and peanuts at 90 percent of parity. The bill also called for the support of oats, barley, grain, sorghum, and rye at 85 per cent of parity. In the election year of 1956 Congress was aware that farmers' income was down; and an increase in the level at which the government would support prices was considered to be the fastest method to increase farm income. It was estimated that the higher price supports under the bill would increase farm income $1 billion a year. The administration had consistently argued that rigid price supports were the reason for the stockpile of surplus farm products and that this surplus had forced farm prices down. Immediately after the bill was passed Secretary of Agriculture Benson declared that it was "unacceptable to me." President Eisenhower vetoed the bill in spite of political advice to the contrary.

The first section of the vetoed farm bill was noncontroversial and called for a Soil Bank program to curb surpluses by paying farmers to withdraw acres from production. This section was subsequently rewritten and became Public Law 540, Agricultural Act of 1956, "The Soil Bank Act." The "Bank" had two depositories, or reserves—the acreage reserve and the conservation reserve.

The acreage reserve program provided that for 1956, 1957, 1958, and 1959 the producers of crops of wheat, cotton, corn grown in the commercial corn-producing area, peanuts, rice, flue-cured tobacco, burley tobacco, Maryland tobacco, fire-cured tobacco, and other specified tobaccos should be paid for reducing their acreages of each commodity below the farm acreage allotments or their base acreage. The aim of this program was to get some of the most productive acres out of production. The *New York Times* explained the program in the following fashion:

A wheat farmer with an acreage allotment of 100 acres would agree to withdraw 20 of them. He would guarantee not to plant these withdrawn acres in other crops, or to graze them. (This is to prevent other surpluses— of feed grains and cattle and hogs—from developing.)

At harvest time he would get from the Government a certificate representing the net income from these diverted acres, plus a little bonus as an incentive to cooperate. The net income would be his normal bushel yield multiplied by the support price per bushel, less his normal expenses in working those acres.

The farmer can cash his certificate for money, or he can take the value in kind—bushels of the same crop from Government surplus stocks. It will be to his advantage to take surplus and sell it if the market price is higher than the support price. Otherwise he will probably take cash—unless it will be more profitable to use the wheat as feed for cattle.

Thus the twofold objective of the acreage reserve plan was to prevent the accumulation of further surpluses and to reduce the stockpiles held in government storage. The net effect of the program was to pay farmers for *not producing* basic crops.

The conservation reserve plan was designed to withdraw from production marginal lands placed under production during World War II under the incentive of high price supports. To accomplish this, payments were to be made to those farmers who would put these lands into trees, soil conservation grasses, and water storage. This plan seemed simply to supplement the provisions of the basic Soil Conservation Act of 1938.

Thus the Eisenhower-Benson farm policy was to follow a program with a plan, the key element of which was flexible price support as a partial means of facilitating production adjustments. In addition attempts were being made to reduce the stockpiles of farm commodities. It was hoped that these elements working together, given the chance and the time to operate, would raise per capita farm income. Many of the alternative proposals had no plan but did have the object of raising farm income. In most instances the latter proposals were politically motivated.

Total income of the farm population in 1957, which included farm wages of $1.8 billion and $6.3 billion of income from nonfarm sources in addition to the adjusted net income of farm operators, was $20.2 billion. This was 1 percent above 1956. With the farm population dropping off sharply in 1957, per capita income rose 10 percent to $993. This was a new record high, 2 percent above the previous peak reached in 1951. Per capita income of the nonfarm population increased only 1 percent from $2018 in 1956 to $2045 in 1957.

Thus there was evidence that the Eisenhower-Benson program was beginning to work in a limited degree by moving people off the farm and raising farm per capita income. This was a fact that both Republicans and Democrats seemed to be unaware of at the beginning of the political year 1958 as Congressional leaders of both parties demanded the resignation of Secretary of Agriculture Benson. However, what was needed was a complete rethinking and reworking of the total farm program. One statement, "Toward a Realistic Farm Program," was prepared by the Committee for Economic Development in December, 1957. The implementation of a "realistic program" seems far from a policy reality even though there is a growing enlightened public opinion that such is required. Congress passed a bill to "freeze" farm price supports and acreage allotments in 1958. President Eisenhower described this as a "one hundred and eighty degree turn in the wrong direction" and vetoed the bill.

CHAPTER 6

Mineral Characteristics and Energy Resources

Energy, the capacity to do work, and the materials for harnessing and applying energy are the subject of Part III. These natural resources are the basis of industrialization. The continued availability of these resources and those of agriculture are thus absolutely essential to the productive strength and the foundation for growth and security of the United States.

Energy sources and energy that will be studied are coal, petroleum, natural gas, atomic energy, and electric power. The discussion of natural resources required to harness and apply this energy will be limited primarily to minerals. Minerals are classified by the Bureau of Mines into mineral fuels, metals, and nonmetals. The mineral fuels have been the basic source of our inanimate energy supply, and the metallic minerals have been the basic materials of modern industrialization. We will look briefly at certain general characteristics of mineral resources and minerals that give rise to special problems, then study separately and in detail energy and materials, and finally consider collectively some of the United States problems and policies in this area.

I. Mineral Characteristics

1. Localized Occurrence

As compared with agricultural resources, most mineral resources are highly localized in occurrence. This leads to possible dominance of production control by individual firms and to uniform price patterns which are said to be the result of prices administered to the public—"administered prices." In addition, since minerals are not evenly distributed among countries, the control of the minerals is localized in those nations where they occur. The localized occurrence of the combination of iron and coal, the basis of heavy industry, is found very infrequently. The control of these localized fund mineral resources has been the basis of power of the modern fuel-power-metal civilization. In addition, the world-wide dispersion of many localized minerals has led to the necessity of international trade in minerals. Technological developments have increased the need for special-purpose minerals and have therefore increased this international interdependence. Thus localized occurrence of mineral resources has resulted in the dominance of a few nations as world powers; and technological developments have not lessened this dominance, but they have tremendously increased the interdependence of nations.

2. Exhaustibility

Most minerals differ from other natural resources in that they are funds, which when used long enough become exhausted. This is in sharp contrast to the flow resources of agriculture, which when used properly tend to be renewable. The exhaustible nature of minerals creates several problems.

From the standpoint of the individual firm, adequate reserves against depletion must be set up. From the standpoint of nations, the exhaustion of mineral reserves becomes of critical importance because of the effect upon the total strength to produce and resultant position among the world powers. Great Britain's declining position as a world power during and after World War II was in part a direct result of the decline in her coal production.

The exhaustible nature of minerals creates a problem of increasing costs. High fixed costs are combined with rising variable costs. Since mines have no alternative use they may often be operated at a loss as long as variable costs can be covered and only a small portion of fixed costs paid. This is of course not an abnormal condition in competitive enterprise. But because mines have no abandonment value, and because they are very often the principal source of income to a community, both economic and social pressures are at work to keep them open over a long period of time, even when it is not economically profitable to do so. Political pressures often become dominant in these decisions, and the combination of forces may result in government aid of some type.

A final and critical problem created by the exhaustibility of mineral resources is the development of the most efficient uses of the minerals, the use of scrap as secondary sources, the development of substitute commodities where feasible, and the use of more efficient methods of recovery and development of known reserves. In addition, continuous programs must be carried on for exploration and development of new sources of supply.

3. Discovery Problems

Most mineral deposits are hidden from view. Many major metal discoveries have been made by following surface exposures in mountain regions; but the conclusion has been drawn that few of these exposures remain undiscovered in the United States. Usually the most obvious reserves are found first, and subsequent discoveries are more difficult and costly. Adequate incentives for discovery are thus necessary. In the United States the legal right of ownership of mineral reserves on one's property has been fundamental as an incentive to discovery. However, as discovery has become more costly in the United States, additional incentives have been provided through indirect means of restrictive tariffs and quotas and direct subsidies of government purchase and high depletion allowances. Recently the United States government offered $10,000 for the discovery of a valuable deposit of uranium.

The cost of discovery and development of foreign reserves is much higher than that of domestic reserves. The risks are greater and consequently United States companies have undertaken this discovery and development only when they thought the returns would justify the investment. In most instances, costs have been so high that only very large corporations have been able to undertake the commitments. Further, many underdeveloped countries have been forced to seek outside capital because of the investment cost of discovery and development. Although this reciprocal dependence would appear to be mutually beneficial, serious problems are involved. For example, initially United States and other companies are often more powerful than the governments of those areas in which investment is made; later, as the governments become more powerful and more autonomous, they begin to demand and to secure greater rights and revenues from their mineral enterprises. These greater risks of foreign investment in minerals have led to demands by United States concerns for investment guarantees.

4. Demand

An elementary fact about the demand for minerals is that requirements arise from the mechanization of modern society and are more a function of technology and industrialization than population. Between 1900 and 1950, United States population doubled. National output during this same time increased five times. Total consumption of agricultural products of all kinds increased only two and one-half times and thus was closely related to population growth. However, United States consumption of minerals in 1950 was six times 1900 totals.

In 1950 we were taking from the earth

> two and one-half times more bituminous coal;
> three times more copper;
> three and one-half times more iron ore;
> four times more zinc;
> twenty-six times more natural gas;
> thirty times more crude oil;

than in the year 1900. The quantity of most metals and mineral fuels used in the United States since the first World War exceeds the total used throughout the entire world in all of history preceding 1914.[1]

The close correlation between world mineral and industrial output may be seen from Figure 6.1. This clearly indicates the fundamental importance of minerals for industrial production. Put another way, the tremendous advance of world industry has brought about a ninefold increase in mineral production for the period shown.

Figure 6.2, which gives mineral production by types in the United States, shows how production declined sharply during the depression of the 1930's and then increased during World War II and during the postwar period. Mineral fuel, principally petroleum, has been the leader in the increase. Higher demand of transportation has been the major causative force. One contributing factor to the differential rate of growth of production between fuels and metals is that fuels are consumed in their initial use, while metals can be reclaimed as scrap and thus a

---

[1] *Resources for Freedom*, Summary of Vol. I of a report to the President by the President's Materials Policy Commission, Government Printing Office, June, 1952, p. 7.

secondary reserve can be built up. An important effect of this is that during a depression mineral production is reduced sharply as more scrap is used. However, during war years mineral production is accelerated because so much of metal production is used up. Thus the end use to which metals are put is of critical importance in evaluating the role of scrap as a secondary reserve.

The rapid rise in production of minerals as a result of increasing demand poses the fundamental question as to the adequacy of mineral

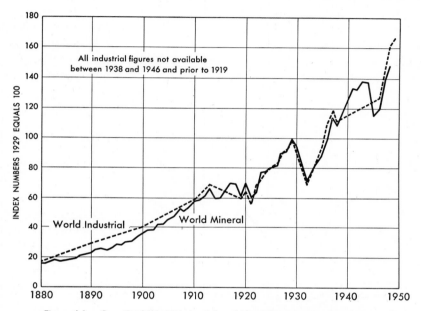

Figure 6.1.   Growth of World Industrial and Mineral Production, 1880–1949.

supplies for the future. The answer cannot be discovered because of the impossibility of predicting future world demand for minerals. Adequacy of mineral supplies measured by current rates of production is almost a meaningless concept unless used properly. One thing is certain, however: with goals of economic progress throughout the world, the demand for minerals will increase at an accelerated rate.

5. Reserves

The other major element of uncertainty in the adequacy of mineral supplies is the extent of reserves. Study of this problem requires an appraisal of known reserves, the outlook for future expansion, and technological developments which will affect production. Discovery problems

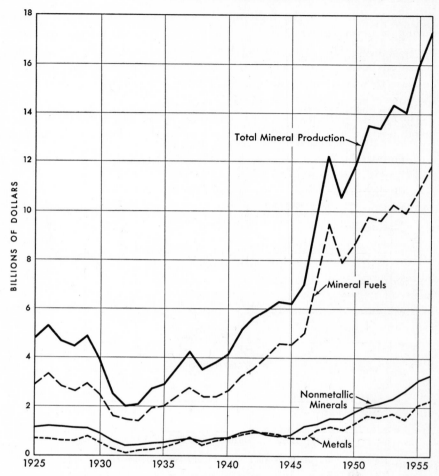

Figure 6.2. Value of Mineral Production in Continental United States, 1925–56, by Mineral Groups. Data for 1925–46 are not strictly comparable with those for subsequent years, since for the earlier years the value of heavy clay products has not been replaced by the value of raw clays used in such products. The 1953 figures for nonmetallic minerals, metals, and total mineral production are revised figures. The 1954 total mineral production figure has been adjusted to eliminate duplication in the value of clays and stone. (Data from U.S. Bureau of Mines)

have already been discussed. Not only are estimates of mineral reserves difficult to make, but mineral terminology used is so varied that what is difficult is compounded by confusion. Known mineral reserves must be thought of as those that are known to exist and that can be recovered with the application of present technology. In addition, economic feasibility must be taken into consideration. When technology and economic considerations are taken together, reserves become commercially feasible and are then thought of as available resources and ore. These may also be referred to as actual, proved and indicated reserves, resources and ore. In addition, references are made to potential and ultimate reserves, sub ore, sub resources, "neutral stuff," and assorted other nomenclature.

When considering the extent of knowledge about world mineral reserves, the fact should be kept continuously in mind that even in the United States geological investigations have not been intensively carried out. The Minerals Subcommittee of the Senate Committee on Interior and Insular Affairs reported in July, 1954, that less than 1 per cent of the area of this nation has been included in geological investigations, only 12.7 percent has been geologically mapped, and 31.1 percent has been topographically mapped by the United States Geological Survey.

However, within the limit of all the above considerations, an attempt was made by Elmer W. Pehrson of the Bureau of Mines of the United States Department of the Interior to bring together the present judgments of experts concerning world reserves and to consider these data in the light of current rates of use and other factors that will condition the mineral economy of the future.

The results of this effort in a summary of world reserves of thirteen important industrial minerals and a comparison of these reserves with the then current rate of production are given in Figure 6.3. The reserve figures represent the judgment of various experts on the quantity of known reserves amenable to commercial recovery under technological and economic conditions present and those likely to exist in the foreseeable future. Estimates of potential reserves of iron ore and petroleum are also given; similar data for other commodities shown were not available.

After taking into consideration estimates of known reserves and the outlook for discovery, the above study summarized the world outlook for mineral reserves as follows:

Conclusions about the adequacy of mineral resources differ whether the appraisal is made for the world as a whole or for an individual country. No curtailment of current rates of use due to resource limitation is imminent for the world as a whole. Known reserves of some minerals, however, particularly the ores of certain of the nonferrous metals, are small. Although this situation doubtless will be modified to some extent by discovery, total resources appear to be inadequate to support large and widespread expansion of consumption in the underdeveloped areas. Such expansion, however, is not likely to occur suddenly. Moreover, as mineral shortages arise, science and invention, motivated by economic considerations, will provide acceptable substitutes or adapt presently unused resources to industrial requirements. Thus it appears

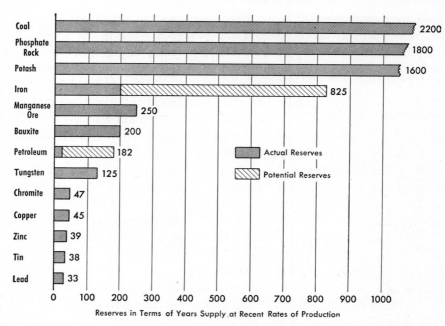

Figure 6.3.   World Position in Reserves of Major Industrial Minerals as Estimated in 1949.

that drastic consequences resulting from exhaustion of mineral resources need not be feared. Temporary shortages can result from failure to anticipate expanding requirements in time to permit construction of necessary production facilities, or from destruction of the incentives necessary to maintain vigorous mining enterprise. On the whole, however, it may be concluded that if relatively free and unhampered access to world mineral resources can be maintained, and resort to military action to preserve national security becomes unnecessary, the mineral resources of the world are adequate.[2]

However, the assumptions behind the above conclusions are totally unrealistic. Nations will probably continue to use their mineral reserves to their own advantage and to consider mineral deficiency as the most fundamental detriment to economic progress and national security.

The United States is and will continue to be in competition with other nations for a limited non-renewable supply of mineral reserves. The resulting summary problems and policy issues will be discussed in the final chapter of this Part after separate and detailed discussion of energy and material resources.

[2] William Van Royen and Oliver Bowles, *The Mineral Resources of the World,* Prentice-Hall, Inc., 1952, pp. 5–6.

II. Energy Resources

Energy is the capacity to do work. Obviously, the availability of energy and the efficiency with which it is used is fundamental to productivity and economic progress. Fairgrieve tells us, ". . . It may be said that in its widest sense on its material side history is the story of man's increasing ability to control energy."[3] Zimmermann elaborates: "One could almost concentrate the whole history of economic development into this simple transition: man power to animal power to machine power."[4]

Man's interest in energy has centered around its conversion through the process of photosynthesis into his food supply and its use to supplement his own energy in the productive process. Thus as more and more energy has been made available through the use of inanimate energy and stored-up funds of energy, man has been able (1) as we have seen, to increase the production of food and other agricultural products and (2) to generate net products—capital—for further production which renders possible the development of an advanced industrialized society.

Almost all of the energy that man uses is of atomic origin. In the past the nuclear (atomic) energy has been stellar, chiefly solar, in origin and has been derived from current receipts (flow) and stored-up supplies (fund). The most significant advance in economic productivity was achieved when the shift was made from the exclusive reliance on flows of energy to the utilization of the funds of fossil fuels—coal, petroleum, and natural gas. This shift, accompanied by the harnessing of these fuels by the heavy metals, we have called the Industrial Revolution. Students of energy and material have told us that this phase of history was rapidly drawing to a close, and that we were entering upon a stage which would be characterized by continuous energy sources, principally water power converted into electricity and direct solar power harnessed by light metals. Yet even as this stage was dawning a new era has exploded.

Now nuclear (atomic) energy funds are used directly by man—induced chain reactions in certain fissionable materials. The point is that technology is developing with such dramatic rapidity that there are no

[3] James Fairgrieve, *Geography and World Power*, E. P. Dutton and Company, 2nd ed., 1921, p. 3.

[4] Erich W. Zimmermann, *World Resources and Industries*, Harper & Brothers, rev. ed., 1951, p. 58.

distinct phases of energy history. Further energy resources and potentials must be appraised with extreme caution, but with the certainty that the combination of sources or energy mix will be the important basis for future appraisal.

In the study of energy resources, first a general comparison of the United States with the rest of the world will be made; this will be followed by a study of specific energy sources and energy.

UNITED STATES ENERGY POSITION

The President's Materials Policy Commission was very clear in the conclusion that ". . . A supply of energy sufficient to meet the total demand of the United States can be achieved only if the Nation looks at its energy resources as a whole; only if it exploits fully the shifting interrelationships among various sources of energy; only if it takes the fullest economic and technical advantages of the flexibilities in end-use, in distribution, in drawing on each energy source for its best and most efficient contribution. Moreover, the energy position of this Nation must be judged and acted upon in the light of energy needs and resources of other free nations."[5]

The Commission doubtless did not expect the "energy needs" of other nations to be determined, but considerable light can be thrown on the problem by looking at total energy consumption and per capita energy consumption in different regions of the world. Figure 6.4 presents this information for the year 1947. The most obvious fact discernible is the great disparity in the quantities of energy used in various parts of the world.

With only 7 percent of the world's population the United States consumed 45 percent of the world's total energy. On a per capita basis the comparison is even more striking. In 1947 per capita consumption in the United States was equivalent to about 250 million BTU, whereas the consumption per person for all foreign nations was only 20 million. Canada, which used 206 million BTU per person, was the only nation close to the United States.

The use of energy in the underdeveloped areas of the world is very low by United States standards. The "Other Eastern Hemisphere" area, which includes Asia, Oceania, and most of Africa, used only 10 percent of the world's inanimate energy even though it contains 60 percent of

[5] *Resources for Freedom*, Vol. III, *The Outlook for Energy Sources*, Government Printing Office, June, 1952, p. 1.

the world's populations. On a per capita basis the people of this extensive area used only one-fourth of the energy consumed in the United States.[6]

More recent studies indicate that per capita energy consumption is gaining throughout the world. In 1953, the world (outside China, Korea, and the U.S.S.R.) was using some 50 percent more energy (measured in coal equivalents) than in 1937. Consumption rose almost 40 percent in Canada, 48 percent in Australia, 67 percent in the United States, and 31 percent in Italy. South America consumed 157 percent more energy in

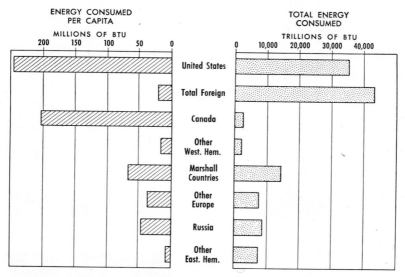

Figure 6.4. World-Wide Consumption of Energy in 1947.

1953 than in 1937. The great disparities in energy consumption continued in 1953. The United States share of the world's total was 48 percent.[7]

In addition to differential rates of energy use, another significant difference between the use of inanimate energy in the United States and in foreign areas is that most foreign areas are relying primarily on coal, but petroleum and natural gas do the significant amount of work in the United States.

Hedlund's study showed that, outside the United States, coal supplies 68 percent of energy requirements. This was four times the 17 percent

[6] The writer is indebted to C. J. Hedlund of the Standard Oil Company (N.J.) for these world-wide energy data.

[7] World Facts and Figures, United Nations Department of Public Information, October, 1955, pp. 24–25. This source has a table giving "Per Capita Energy Consumption" by countries for 1937, 1952, and 1953.

supplied by petroleum and natural gas. In the United States in 1953 coal supplied only about 35 percent of the energy, whereas petroleum and natural gas provided about 62 percent of the total. About 40 percent of the total was petroleum.

With the great increase in energy requirements throughout the world, with the United States committed to a policy of economic progress at home and abroad, and with the knowledge that energy is the powering force of progress, the question which must be asked and to which the Materials Policy Commission gave us the answer for the United States is: Are the physical energy resources of the world sufficient for the gigantic task?

Taking the world as a whole and considering all sources of energy then currently in use, the study of the Standard Oil Company (N.J.) came up with the answer: Yes, more than ample. The summary results of this study are presented in Figure 6.5. In order that the magnitude of the

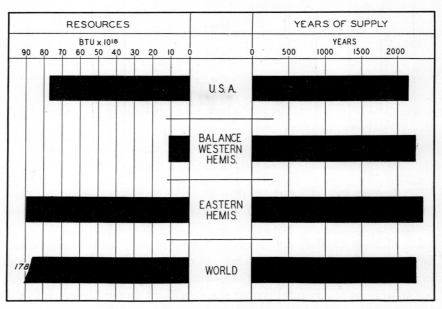

Figure 6.5. World Energy Resources—Ultimate Recovery. (Data from Standard Oil Company of New Jersey)

reserves (ultimate resource recovery) can be understood, they are compared to the number of years of supply at 1947 rates of consumption, shown at the right of the chart. At that rate of consumption, the world should recover enough energy ultimately from coal, crude oil, oil shale, tar sands, and natural gas to last approximately two thousand years. The known energy supplies are evenly distributed between the Eastern and Western Hemisphere.

In each of the areas shown—the United States, the balance of the Western Hemisphere, and the Eastern Hemisphere—the ratio of 1947 consumption to indigenous reserves is about the same figure of something greater than two thousand years. This seems unusual in view of the great differences between the rate of consumption in the United States and the rest of the world. One possible explanation is that in other areas much less is known about total reserves than in the United States. As the demand increases in areas outside of the United States, just as has been and will be the case here, new developments and new discoveries will be made.

It is important to emphasize that this estimate was of energy then currently in use. Already new and revolutionary discoveries have been made. Uses in the field of solar heat and atomic fission are being pushed rapidly ahead. As effective demand develops, new and important discoveries will be made. But blind reliance on technology is not the answer.

Energy sources are and can be made partially interchangeable, but this allocation of resources must be accomplished in terms of the composition of the reserves and their end uses. Of the total quantity of recoverable reserves in the Standard Oil (N.J.) study, 93 percent is in the form of coal; petroleum represents only about 3 percent, natural gas about 1 percent, and tar sands and shale oil about 3 percent. Thus there is approximately thirty times more coal than petroleum in the world energy reserves. The data previously given indicate that the differential rates of energy consumed by types in the United States and in foreign areas do not correspond to the energy mix of the reserves.

The logical expectation is that the types of energy used would be determined by the reserves available. But this does not follow, as energy has particular end uses that determine the type employed. For example, oil and gasoline are of greatest advantage when used in mobile units; petroleum is required where transportation is a necessity as a space-conquering device, such as is the case in the United States. Similarly coal is vital when processed into coke for the iron and steel industry. Thus the problem is the most efficient use of the energy reserves. Further, when the most desirable type of energy is not available, the task is one of securing the type demanded from some other area, or changing the form of the type available to correspond to the characteristics desired.

Although the Standard Oil (N.J.) study asserted that the energy re-

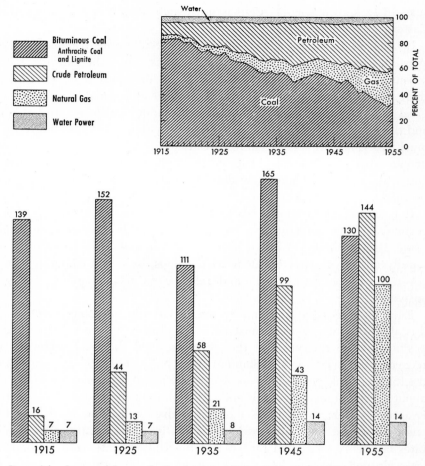

Figure 6.6. Sources of Energy, Continental United States, 1915–55. (In billions of therms.) (Data from U.S. Bureau of Mines)

serves of the world as a whole are more than ample to meet the require-ments, the President's Materials Policy Commission qualified this answer for the United States with "only if" the nation: (1) looks at its energy resources as a whole, (2) exploits fully the shifting interrelationships among various sources of energy, (3) takes the fullest economic and technical advantage of the flexibilities in end use in drawing on each energy resource, and (4) judges and acts upon the energy needs and resources of other free nations.

Energy use in the United States increased from approximately 169 bil-lion therms in 1915 to about 388 billion therms in 1955. Figure 6.6 shows the energy sources generally used by the economy—coal, petroleum, natural gas, and water power. Data on atomic energy were unavailable, and other sources such as the wind and tides, which are little used, are excluded. This chart is an excellent introduction to the study which follows of specified energy sources.

The lower half of the chart shows that quantitatively coal was less important in 1955 than in 1915. During this same time petroleum and natural gas have grown enormously. The top half of the chart shows the absolute figures as percentages of the total. Noteworthy is the small and constant percentage of water power use. So drastic are the changes in coal, natural gas, and petroleum that the reader's attention hardly needs to be called to them. Coal—the power behind the nation—declined from 82 percent in 1915 to about 32 percent of the total in 1955. Crude petroleum accounted for 37 percent of the total in 1955 in contrast to about 10 percent in 1915. Natural gas increased from about 3 percent to 26 percent of the total.

Thus in a short span of forty years the energy mix of the United States underwent dynamic changes. Coal's proportion of the total declined by about 60 percent, while the percentage of petroleum almost quadrupled and natural gas increased ninefold. These dramatic changes point up the necessity of a detailed examination of specific energy sources, at the same time that they paint a most vivid picture of the quantitative and percentage relationship of United States energy sources. The specific energy sources and energy to be studied are: coal, petroleum, natural gas, atomic energy, and electric power.

COAL

Coal remains the "power behind the nation" in spite of the fact that petroleum has advanced to the principal energy source in the United States. Coal as an energy source, in combination with iron ore, has been the basis of modern industrialization. No modern nation has made sustained economic progress without continuous availability of coal. The world powers, the United States, Germany, Russia, and Great Britain, are the leading producers of coal (see Figure 6.7). Together in 1951 they produced 70 percent of the world total. The United States alone produced 27 percent of the world total. It is significant that United States production was 38 percent of the total in 1947. This represents a positive decline, as shown by Table 31, from a peak of 624 million tons to 523 million tons during the Korean boom year of 1951. United States production continued to fall, to a low level of 380 million tons in 1954 or 19 percent of the world total. All other countries had increased production. Was 1954 the lower turning point for the United States coal industry?

The two largest consumers of coal in the United States are the coke industry and the electric power utilities. These two industries increased their use of coal substantially over the pre-World War II rates. Railroads, even though their consumption has been sharply reduced, remain large users of coal, along with steel rolling mills and cement mills. Coal can be

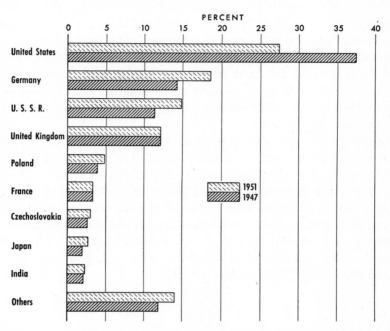

Figure 6.7.   Percentage Distribution of World Coal Production. (Data from National Coal Association)

used when necessary in the production of synthetic gasoline and oil, and it is a basic raw material of the chemical industry. Though coal is widely distributed through the United States, the Appalachian coal region has been the source of power of the nation's industrial strength.

Great Britain's early rise and long-time dominance as a world power was due to her easily accessible supplies of coal. Indeed the comment has been made that Great Britain's power has been chiefly due to two factors, "industrial production and sea power; it would be oversimplification to say, then, that each of these factors depends upon the other— and that both depend upon coal."[8] As already noted, Great Britain's

[8] Van Royen and Bowles, *op. cit.*, p. 18.

$$\text{TABLE 31. World Production of Coal}^a$$
(in millions of metric tons)

Year	Australia	Belgium	Canada	Czechoslovakia	France	Germany	India	Japan	Netherlands	Poland	Union of South Africa	United Kingdom	United States	U.S.S.R.[b]	World Total[b]
1935–39 av.	16	29	14	31	47	404	26	45	14	40	16	234	409	119	1,487
1940–44 av.	19	23	16	46	40	444	29	61	12	83	20	209	555	130	1,821
1945	19	16	15	26	35	149	30	24	5	27	24	186	574	146	1,356
1946	20	23	16	34	50	226	30	23	9	48	24	193	539	161	1,471
1947	21	24	14	39	47	236	31	30	11	64	24	201	624	175	1,654
1948	22	27	17	41	45	257	31	36	11	75	24	213	596	209	1,715
1949	22	28	17	44	53	304	32	40	12	79	25	219	436	236	1,656
1950	24	27	17	46	53	330	33	40	12	83	26	220	508	264	1,813
1951	26	30	17	45	55	362	35	45	13	88	27	226	523	281	1,920
1952	28	30	16	52	57	374	37	45	13	91	28	230	460	301	1,926
1953	27	30	14	53	55	391	37	48	13	95	28	228	443	323	1,959
1954	30	29	13	58	56	400	37	44	12	98	29	228	380	347	1,952
1955	30	30	12	64	55	428	39	42	12	101	32	225	449	391	2,139
1956	30	30	14	58	57	430	40	45	12	90	34	226	525	405	2,400

[a] Bituminous, anthracite, and lignite. [b] Estimate.
SOURCE: Bureau of Mines; United Nations; *Commodity Year Book*, 1956; 1957 for 1955 and 1956 data.

declining coal production has been a contributing factor to her decline in power.

Germany's industrial might has been powered by the coal of the Ruhr. Even after World War I when the iron ore of Lorraine was given to France, Germany was able to rebuild her economy. Her production of coal was just about equal to that of the United States during 1935–39. Indeed the Ruhr coal is the power behind western Europe. In view of this fact, the United States early post-World War II policy to "agriculturize Germany" should be characterized as stupid and/or a deliberate attempt to destroy the strength of western Europe. The decision to reverse this policy and to insist upon and aid European recovery required increased production of Ruhr coal. West Germany's increased industrial strength and "European Recovery" have followed greater production of Ruhr coal.

Finally and most significantly, Russia's industrialization and emergence as a world power have been gained by coal from the Donets, Kuznets, Ural, Moscow, and Karaganda basins.

Sustained economic progress and positions of national power require continuous availability of coal reserves. The United States has nothing to fear in this respect. The United States has an estimated coal reserve of almost 1.9 trillion tons. This is enough to last into the unpredictable future and is the energy resource that pushes our years of supply far past the 2000-year mark in Figure 6.5.

The United States coal reserves are compared with those of other areas of the world in Table 32. The figures in the table are estimates and are comparable in only a general way because they were calculated on a number of different bases. The data (illustrated in Figure 6.8) show that coal reserves are distributed unevenly throughout the world. Although each continent includes coal that is minable at least locally, about 97 percent of the coal reserves are believed to be in the Northern Hemisphere. The largest reserves are in the United States, Russia, and China, which have about 78 percent of the total. Over 34 percent of the world's coal reserves is in the United States. The reader will note that these reserves are so-called "remaining reserves."

The National Coal Association presents in Table 33 an estimate of United States coal reserves as compared with other domestic mineral fuels. These data can be helpful if they are carefully studied. All the reserves are designated "proved reserves." The first column is headed "Bituminous Coal" with a footnote by Pennsylvania to the effect that anthracite coal in that state is included. Yet when this column is com-

TABLE 32. World Coal Reserves

	Remaining Reserves (in million net tons)	Percent of Continent Total	Percent of World Total
North America:			
United States	1,895,758	90.2	34.4
Alaska	107,154	5.1	2.0
Canada[a]	98,609	4.7	1.8
Total	2,101,521	100.0	38.2
Asia:			
U.S.S.R.[b]	1,320,000	52.2	24.0
China	1,112,760	44.0	20.2
India	71,472	2.8	1.3
Japan	18,360	0.7	.3
Others[c]	8,319	0.3	.2
Total	2,530,913	100.0	46.0
Europe:			
Germany	369,901	51.0	6.7
United Kingdom	189,420	26.1	3.4
Poland	88,019	12.1	1.6
Czechoslovakia	20,845	2.9	.4
France	12,483	1.5	.2
Portugal	11,259	1.7	.2
Others[d]	33,998	4.7	.6
Total	725,925	100.0	13.1
Africa:			
Union of South Africa	74,815	97.2	1.4
Others[e]	2,123	2.8	[f]
Total	76,938	100.0	1.4
Australasia:			
Australia	58,410	99.0	1.1
Others[g]	600	1.0	[b]
Total	59,010	100.0	1.1
South and Central America:			
Colombia[h]	11,000	72.8	.2
Chile	2,327	15.4	
Others[i]	1,783	11.8	
Total	15,110	100.0	.2
World Total	5,509,417		100.0

[a] Includes only reserves of coal considered minable in 1946 estimate of the Canadian Geological Survey. [b] Total for European U.S.S.R. included with Asiatic U.S.S.R. [c] Includes Korea, Federation of Malaya, Manchuria, and Turkey. [d] Includes Austria, Belgium, Bulgaria, Denmark, Eire, Greece, Hungary, Italy, the Netherlands, Norway, Rumania, Sweden, and Yugoslavia. [e] Includes Algeria, Belgian Congo, French Morocco, Madagascar, Nigeria, and Tanganyika. [f] Negligible. [g] Includes New Zealand and New Caledonia. [h] Q. D. Singewald, "Mineral Resources of Colombia (other than petroleum)," *U.S. Geological Survey Bulletin* 964-B, 1950, p. 94. [i] Includes Peru, Honduras, and Brazil. Estimate of reserves in Brazil by MacKenzie Gordon, Geologist, U.S. Geological Survey, personal communication.

SOURCE: Frederick Brown, *Statistical Yearbook of the World Power Conference*, No. 4, Central Office, World Power Conference, London, 1948; No. 5, Central Office, World Power Conference, London, 1950; with the exception of the United States, Alaska, Colombia, and Brazil; National Coal Association.

pared with the next to last column in Table 34, it is clear that the data are identical and thus what is contained in column 1 of Table 33 is a compilation of the "remaining reserves" of *all types* of coal in the United States. Thus the bituminous case is overstated in this mislabeling. Secondly, and most important, the case of all coal is exaggerated because what should be compared with the other mineral fuel reserves is the "recoverable reserve" figures for coal given in Table 34, which are 50

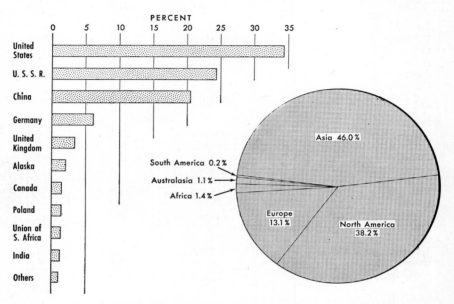

Figure 6.8.   Coal Reserves of the World. (Data from U.S. Geological Survey)

percent of remaining reserves (proved reserves). Thirdly, "proved reserves" of petroleum are, as will be seen, continuously being added to by new discoveries. The National Coal Association wants to make and prove the point: "America's reserves of natural gas and petroleum are sharply limited. The one reliable source, in terms of available reserves, is bituminous coal." One key word in the resource concept is "available." Only "recoverable reserves" are *available*. The Association wants to establish an additional point: "More than one-third of the world's *known reserves* of coal is to be found in the United States, the biggest coal producer on the face of the globe. Moreover, these reserves of coal amount to more than 90 percent of the nation's reserves of mineral fuels, a fact that enhances coal's importance to the national economy and to national security." Actually, according to the estimates, the amount of

TABLE 33. Estimated Proved Reserves of Coal, Petroleum, and Natural Gas

(coal, thousands of short tons; petroleum and natural gas liquids, thousand barrels; natural gas, million cubic feet)

	Bituminous Coal Jan. 1, 1953	Crude Petroleum Jan. 1, 1954	Natural Gas Jan. 1, 1954	Natural Gas Liquids Jan. 1, 1954	Bituminous Coal Equivalent (thousand tons)			
					Crude Petroleum	Natural Gas	Natural Gas Liquids	Total
Alabama	65,848,000	17,160	—	—	3,799	—	—	3,799
Arkansas	1,528,000	358,231	1,211,266	49,585	79,307	49,699	7,591	136,597
California	—	3,919,379	9,159,347	324,866	867,695	375,814	49,735	1,293,244
Colorado	99,440,000	319,254	1,864,275	10,689	70,678	76,492	1,636	148,806
Georgia	76,000	—	—	—	—	—	—	—
Illinois	137,009,000	624,803	231,251	17,043	138,323	9,488	2,609	150,420
Indiana	35,215,000	62,128	35,830	145	13,754	1,470	22	15,246
Iowa	28,464,000	—	—	—	—	—	—	—
Kansas	20,762,000	913,341	15,787,602	177,728	202,201	647,776	27,209	877,186
Kentucky	118,973,000	81,655	1,301,533	7,776	18,077	53,403	1,190	72,670
Louisiana	—	2,759,655	34,458,912	813,214	610,949	1,413,873	124,497	2,149,319
Maryland	1,196,000	—	—	—	—	—	—	—
Michigan	220,000	60,721	275,519	641	13,443	11,305	98	24,846
Mississippi	—	350,101	2,569,181	54,734	77,507	105,415	8,379	191,301
Missouri	78,828,000	—	—	—	—	—	—	—
Montana	221,779,000	208,985	764,000	2,908	46,266	31,347	445	78,058
Nebraska	—	25,621	182,100	3,034	5,672	7,472	464	13,608
New Mexico	61,509,000	814,902	17,522,210	320,657	180,408	718,948	49,090	948,446
New York	—	49,083	71,004	—	10,866	2,913	—	13,779
North Carolina	110,000	—	—	—	—	—	—	—
North Dakota	350,756,000	128,271	—	—	28,397	—	—	28,397
Ohio	82,972,000	31,826	755,982	1,359	7,046	31,018	208	38,272
Oklahoma	54,619,000	1,752,228	12,228,373	304,232	387,919	501,739	46,576	936,234
Pennsylvania	72,376,000ᵃ	111,083	751,844	2,768	24,592	30,849	424	55,865
South Dakota	2,031,000	—	—	—	—	—	—	—
Tennessee	24,985,000	—	—	—	—	—	—	—
Texas	30,876,000	14,998,620	106,529,626	3,267,242	3,320,483	4,370,984	500,190	8,191,657
Utah	92,904,000	37,937	1,113,058	53	8,399	45,670	8	54,077
Virginia	10,833,000	—	—	—	—	—	—	—
Washington	63,588,000	—	—	—	—	—	—	—
West Virginia	105,762,000	36,612	1,653,942	28,213	8,105	67,862	4,319	80,286
Wyoming	120,788,000	1,279,110	2,739,631	50,559	283,177	112,409	7,740	403,326
Other States	16,352,000	4,122	240,636	476	913	9,873	73	10,859
U.S.	1,899,739,000	28,944,828	211,447,132	5,437,922	6,407,976	8,675,822	832,505	15,916,303

ᵃ Includes anthracite.

SOURCE: U.S. Bureau of Mines; American Gas Association; American Petroleum Institute; National Coal Association.

TABLE 34. Coal Reserves of the United States, by States[a]
(millions of tons)

	Estimated Original Reserves					Reserves Depleted to 1/1/53			Recoverable Reserves, Jan. 1, 1953, Assuming 50 Percent Recovery
	Bituminous	Sub-bituminous	Lignite	Anthracite and Semi-anthracite	Total	Production	Production Plus Loss in Mining, Assuming Past Losses Equal Production	Remaining Reserves, Jan. 1, 1953	
Alabama	67,570	—	—	—	67,570	861	1,722	65,848	32,924
Arkansas	1,396	—	90	230	1,716	94	188	1,528	764
Colorado	90,258	9,437	—	713	100,408	484	968	99,440	49,719
Georgia	100	—	—	—	100	12	24	76	38
Illinois	137,321	—	—	—	137,321	156	312	137,009	68,504
Indiana	37,293	—	—	—	37,293	1,039	2,078	35,215	17,607
Iowa	29,160	—	—	—	29,160	348	696	28,464	14,232
Kansas	20,774	—	—	—	20,774	6	12	20,762	10,381
Kentucky	123,327	—	—	—	123,327	2,177	4,354	118,973	59,487
Maryland	1,200	—	—	—	1,200	2	4	1,196	598
Michigan	297	—	—	—	297	46	77	220	110
Missouri	79,362	—	—	—	79,362	267	534	78,828	39,414
Montana	2,363	132,151	87,533	—	222,047	164	328	221,719	110,860
New Mexico	10,948	50,801	—	6	61,755	123	246	61,509	30,754
North Carolina	112	—	—	—	112	1	2	110	55
North Dakota	—	—	350,910	—	350,910	77	154	350,756	175,378
Ohio	86,584	—	—	—	86,584	1,806	3,612	82,972	41,486
Oklahoma	54,951	—	—	—	54,951	166	332	54,619	27,309
Pennsylvania	75,093	—	—	22,805	97,898	12,761	25,522	72,376	36,189
South Dakota	—	—	2,033	—	2,033	1	2	2,031	1,015
Tennessee	25,665	—	—	—	25,665	340	680	24,985	12,493
Texas	8,000	—	23,000	—	31,000	62	124	30,876	15,438
Utah	88,184	5,156	—	—	93,340	218	436	92,904	46,452
Virginia	11,696	—	—	355	12,051	609	1,218	10,833	5,417
Washington	11,413	52,442	—	23	63,878	145	290	63,588	31,794
West Virginia	116,618	—	—	—	116,618	5,428	10,856	105,762	52,881
Wyoming	13,235	108,319	—	—	121,554	383	766	120,788	60,395
Other States	820	15,500	50	—	16,370	9	18	16,352	8,176
Total	1,093,740	373,806	463,616	24,132	1,995,294	27,785	55,555	1,899,739	949,870

[a] Footnotes in detail appear in source material, Coal Resources of the United States, Geological Survey Circular 293, 1953.
SOURCE: National Coal Association.

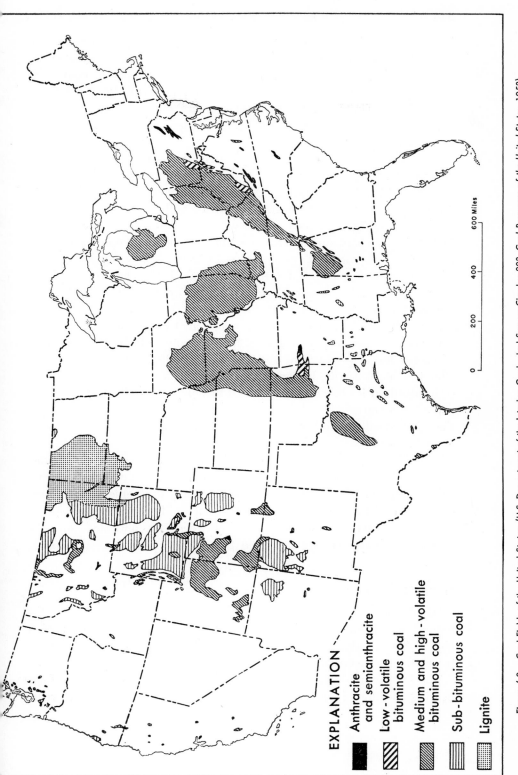

EXPLANATION

■ Anthracite and semianthracite

▨ Low-volatile bituminous coal

▨ Medium and high-volatile bituminous coal

▦ Sub-bituminous coal

▨ Lignite

0   200   400   600 Miles

Figure 6.9.   Coal Fields of the United States. (U.S. Department of the Interior, Geological Survey Circular 293, Coal Resources of the United States, 1953)

"recoverable reserves" of coal of all types is more than 90 percent of the total of "proved reserves" of the other mineral fuels and "recoverable reserves" of coal. In addition, less than 3 percent of known recoverable reserves of coal have been mined to date. The conclusion is certainly justified that United States coal reserves are more than adequate for future needs and they constitute the principal domestic fuel reserve used at the present time.

The approximation has been made that about one out of every ten acres of land in the continental United States is underlaid with coal. This, like all ratios and averages, tells part but not all of the story. The necessary question in this instance is where and what type is the coal? Table 34 and Figure 6.9 give the answer. About 30 percent of the coal is in the Appalachian and interior regions; the remainder is west of the Mississippi. Almost all Eastern coal is bituminous. Seventy-five percent of the Western coal is sub-bituminous and lignite, and most of the bituminous coal is not suitable for coking. Only about 1 percent of the United States coal is anthracite, located in Pennsylvania.

Even though bituminous coal is mined in twenty-eight states, eight states account for over 90 percent of the production. These states in order of magnitude of production are West Virginia, Pennsylvania, Kentucky, Illinois, Ohio, Virginia, Indiana, and Alabama. Thus the mineral problem of localization is characteristic of coal in only a generalized or regional way. But because of the difficulties and resultant high cost of transportation, industrialization has tended to concentrate at the most readily available sources of coal.

Instead of concentration of ownership and control, which has characterized minerals, the widespread distribution of coal reserves has resulted in the development of many mines, many companies, and intense competition. The number of bituminous coal and lignite mines producing 1000 tons a year or more has ranged between 7000 and 8000; and the largest company has only produced from 6 to 8 percent of the annual total.

1. Coal Problems

"Coal is a sick industry." This evaluation of the "power behind the nation" has been one of the most often repeated descriptions of a United States industry. If the statement is true, then it is a problem of tremendous concern to the United States.

The information revealed in Figure 6.10 is most pertinent to the facts bearing on the problem. Most significant is that within the span of years

1922–39 the bituminous and lignite mining industry did not make money. These years covered the prosperous twenties and the depression and recovery of the thirties. A comparison of the lower half of the chart with the upper half reveals that this deficit condition occurred at a time when the gap between capacity and production was greatest. When produc-

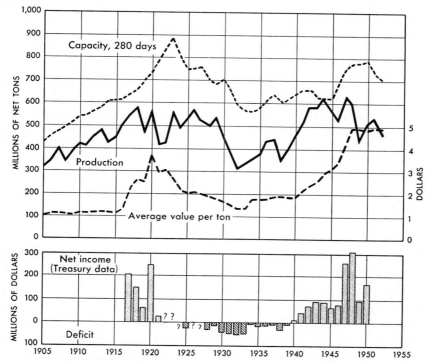

Figure 6.10. Trends of Bituminous Coal and Lignite Production, Realization, Mine Capacity, and Net Income or Deficit in the United States, 1905–52. (Data from U.S. Bureau of Mines)

tion increased and reached toward capacity during and after World War II, net income soared.

Many studies have been made of the United States bituminous coal industry. Because of the precise summarization of the sixty-year economic history of the industry preceding the Korean War, the results of an analysis of the National Coal Association are helpful. There follows an outline of the detailed summary of the three periods: pre-World War I (1890–1918), World War I to World War II (1918–39), and World War II to Korean War (1940–49).

1. Mechanical improvements have been made. Man hours required to produce a ton of coal have declined for nearly half a century.

2. The decline has not been enough to offset increasing labor costs since 1917, although intervening ups and downs have taken place.

3. While the use of capital equipment has been extended, technical progress since World War I has slowed down. As indicated by data for the more important and typical machine, output per machine has not greatly increased. It was, of course, easier to make technological progress in the earlier period because it largely represented shift from hand operations to machine operations. As time passed, further technological progress required radical improvements in machinery, which are more difficult to accomplish.

4. Labor costs per ton have increased because labor saving has not been enough to offset rising wages.

5. Prices have risen in order to cover the increased costs of labor.

6. Profits have been meager, irregular, and not general throughout the industry. This has clearly been an influence retarding capital improvements. The profits of World War I brought about many mechanical improvements in the 1920's. Continued losses for more than a decade before World War II seriously retarded progress in extending and improving mechanization. The lack of profits had three effects:

(a) Earnings were insufficient for reinvestment in plant and equipment.

(b) No attraction existed for new risk capital investment through capital stock flotations and the like.

(c) Impaired credit in many cases made it difficult to borrow for capital improvements.[9]

Just prior to the Korean War, when coal production declined 30 percent from a post-World War II peak in 1947 to a low in 1949, the coal industry was beginning to worry about the economic position of the industry. This situation was alleviated temporarily during the first part of the war, but returned in an aggravated form at the close of the war. Obviously no simple presentation can be made of facts that bear on the problem, but a pointing up of some of the more important issues may shed some light on the position of this basic industry. To simplify presentation the line of thought previously mentioned of the gap between capacity and production will be pursued.

A. Capacity

Part of the United States coal industry's problem is over-capacity. The availability of the coal under such large areas of land, accompanied by the application of the Anglo-Saxon mineral law, brought about the rapid expansion of the industry. In addition to the 8000 (plus or minus) mines which produce 1000 or more tons a year, there should be added 3000 to 4000 small mines. In 1947, 8700 bituminous coal mines of the first cate-

[9] Donald R. G. Cowan, *More Capital Equipment, Coal's Foremost Economic Need,* National Coal Association, July, 1948, p. 18.

gory produced an all-time record total of 630.6 million tons in 234 working days. Capacity at 280 days for that year was 755 million tons. Capacity rose to 790 million tons in 1950, while production fell to 516.3 million tons.

The facts are clear from Figure 6.10 that from 1905 capacity rose from 417 million tons to an all-time peak of 885 million tons in 1923. Peak production was reached in 1918. Thereafter the gap between capacity and production continued until World War II. In addition to the factors of availability and incentives, the rapid rise in coal capacity was facilitated by railroads which made available transportation for coal because of the importance of coal as a source of revenue to them, and by railroads and iron and steel industries which purchase coal mines—captive mines—to supply their own energy needs.

After 1923 capacity was decreased, but there were many facts which worked against a more rapid adjustment that would have helped close the gap between capacity and production. The nature of mining is such that, once a mine is opened, the practice is to keep it in operation because of the rapid deterioration that sets in when it is closed, and because mines have no abandonment value since they cannot be put to alternative use. These are characteristics of mining which work with full force in coal mining together with the facts that labor is such a large part of the cost of mining coal and coal is the principal source of revenue in mining communities. Thus both economic and social pressures are at work to keep mines open over a long period of time when it is not economically profitable to do so.

Other economic factors which have maintained capacity are the nature of mine ownership and competition within the industry. Almost 20 percent of United States coal is produced by "captive mines," i.e., those in which coal is produced for a parent company, principally the steel companies. The operation of these mines is determined by the position of the parent companies. The other 12,000-plus mines are highly competitive. This is a characteristic which is not typical of mining in general. The large number of mines and mining companies has worked against rational adjustments of capacity to production which are often achieved in other segments of industry where ownership is more concentrated.

Thus there have been fundamental characteristics of the bituminous coal mining industry which have expanded capacity, worked against downward capacity adjustment, and led to intense competition. These have been contributing factors to the sustained financial losses of the industry.

B. Consumption

Production of coal is determined directly by consumption. Coal companies do not stockpile because coal moves directly into railroad cars, barges, and trucks, and stockpiles would entail additional handling costs. So coal is left in the ground until needed. Consumer stockpiles tend to even out over the years. However, they are normally not large—thirty–forty days prewar and fifty–sixty days postwar; and during the early 1950's John L. Lewis manipulated labor to keep these stockpiles down in order to improve labor's bargaining position. Consequently the production line of Figure 6.10 is a direct function of consumption.

The absolute decline in production of coal before and after World War II and its relative decline in importance as an energy source are a direct result of factors which affect the consumption of coal. Although improved coal fuel efficiency has been a contributing factor to the loss of markets, coal's primary problem has arisen from increased competition from petroleum and natural gas. In an expanding energy economy coal has not even kept its market. Petroleum and natural gas have been the evil demons that have helped make coal sick while other segments of United States industry were healthy and growing into robust giants (see Figure 6.6).

Consumption of United States bituminous coal by users is given in Table 35. Two significant trends have changed the pattern of coal consumption: (1) Petroleum and natural gas have cut into coal's old major markets of the railroads and domestic and industrial space heating. (2) The rapidly expanding electric power utilities and the steel industry, through its use of coke, have increased their consumption of coal over the pre-World War II years.

Coal's loss of the railroad market has been due to the shift to Diesel- and electric-powered locomotives. The loss of the space heating market was to petroleum and natural gas. Greater convenience of use, transportation, and cleanliness have sold petroleum and natural gas to the public. In addition, heating equipment for these fuels was far ahead in design to meet the needs of the modern home. These are long-run unfavorable trends for coal that continue into the present.

Thus consumption and production of coal have lagged behind and helped create the gap between capacity and production.

World War II demands for coal brought about increased production, which temporarily closed the gap and enabled the coal industry to show net profits. But more fundamentally, the productive achievements of the

TABLE 35. United States Consumption of Bituminous Coal
(in millions of short tons)

Year	Colliery Fuel	Electric Power Utilities	Bunker, Foreign Trade	Rail-roads (Class I)	Coke Plants		Steel and Rolling Mills	Coal-Gas Retorts	Cement Mills	Other Indus-trials	Retail Dealer De-liveries	Total of Classes Shown
					Bee-hive	Ovens						
1935–39 av.	2.9	37.8	1.6	80.9	2.6	57.7	11.3	1.8	4.7	107.5	77.7	381.6
1940–44 av.	2.6	64.6	1.6	112.0	10.3	86.3	10.7	1.6	5.9	130.3	107.5	529.3
1945	2.4	71.6	1.8	125.1	8.1	87.2	10.1	a	4.2	129.6	121.8	559.6
1946	2.0	68.7	1.4	110.2	7.2	76.1	8.6	a	7.0	120.6	100.6	500.4
1947	2.5	86.0	1.7	109.3	10.5	94.3	10.0	a	7.9	124.5	99.2	543.4
1948	a	95.6	1.1	94.8	10.3	97.0	10.0	a	8.6	112.7	89.7	519.9
1949	a	80.6	.9	68.1	5.4	85.9	7.5	a	8.0	99.0	90.3	445.5
1950	a	88.3	.7	61.0	9.1	94.8	7.7	a	7.9	98.2	86.6	454.2
1951	a	101.9	.9	54.0	11.4	102.0	8.0	b	8.5	105.6	76.5	468.9
1952	a	103.3	.7	38.0	6.9	90.7	6.8	a	8.1	95.9	68.4	418.8
1953	a	112.3	.6	27.7	8.2	104.6	6.2	a	8.4	97.4	61.3	426.8
1954	a	115.2	.4	17.4	1.0	84.4	4.9	a	8.1	79.0	52.6	363.1
1955	a	140.5	.4	15.5	2.8	104.6	5.2	a	8.7	91.9	53.8	423.3
1956	a	155.0	.5	12.3	4.0	101.9	5.1	a	9.3	95.7	49.1	432.9

a Included in "Other Industrials."
SOURCE: Bureau of Mines; Commodity Year Book, 1956 and 1957.

war gave positive proof of the industrial potentials of the United States. On the positive and favorable side this set in motion a tremendous growth of the steel industry and accelerated the growth of the electric power industry. Both increased their consumption of coal. Coal in the form of coke is a commodity for which there is no substitute in the production of steel, and this is reflected in the increased consumption of coke during World War II and the Korean War. The growth in consumption of coal by the electric power industry has been sustained and accelerated. Part of this continued growth is related to the steel mills' power policies, which are shifting toward purchased electric power. Therefore decreased consumption of coal for fuel purposes by steel mills has simply been offset by a shift in the consumption of the coal by power companies.

C. Short- and Long-Run Problems

With the exception of World War II and immediate postwar years, the coal industry was concerned for years with the problems of inadequate net revenue and loss of markets to petroleum and natural gas. The prospects in the early 1950's were that for the next few years the coal industry was likely to sustain further losses of markets, but industry analysts believed that with economic progress in the United States the next decade would see a much improved coal position, unless unforeseen developments in energy revolutionized the whole fuel industry. These analysts saw the present problem as "to keep the industry from wasting away during the lean period immediately ahead."

The President's Materials Policy Commission laid the foundation for the optimistic long-run view with the conclusion that: "While coal's percentage share of the 1975 energy total is likely less than now, actual volume of coal at that date may be 60 percent above present (1950) levels. Sometime after that date—whenever the costs relationship shifts and domestic oil and gas production become too high in cost or too low in volume—coal is expected gradually to take over the energy burden in the United States. Reserves are more than ample."[10]

The Commission saw that more than a preventive "wasting away" program was required, as indicated by the further conclusion: "The extent and timing of coal's upturn will depend importantly on technological developments—better mining and processing methods, cheaper transportation methods, more efficient utilization. Advances in manufacture

[10] *Resources for Freedom*, Vol. III, *The Outlook for Energy Sources*, p. 24.

of gas or liquid fuels from coal, as well as chemicals, could increase consumption." [11]

In spite of the long-run optimism, coal's short-run problem was the same long-run one of the past, except that in 1953 and 1954 anthracite was in the sickbed along with bituminous coal. The answer to the previously posed question, "Was 1954 the lower turning point for the United States coal industry?" may be partially answered in section 3, "Trends and New Developments," which follows the next section on policy.

2. Policy—Public and Private

Conditions that have existed in the coal industry have strongly influenced labor public policy through the NIRA, the Wagner Act, the Taft-Hartley Act, and coal industry policy through the NIRA and the Bituminous Coal acts. To a lesser extent the coal problem has led to restrictive public policy against competing industries such as petroleum and natural gas. Both public and private policy have in recent years encouraged research.

Under the National Industrial Recovery Act of 1933 minimum coal prices were set by regional code authorities. Government authority granted industry the right to set prices. Intercompany and interregional rivalry led to the sale of coal under minimum prices, and code enforcement collapsed before the NIRA was declared unconstitutional in 1935. Section 7a of the NIRA gave labor the right to bargain collectively.

Coal operators and the union sponsored and obtained the passage of the Bituminous Coal Conservation Act of 1935 to replace the NIRA. The Supreme Court declared this act unconstitutional before it became operative on the grounds that regulation of labor was an intrastate problem.

In 1937 the Bituminous Coal Act was passed. It omitted the labor provisions of the 1935 act. This new act provided that minimum and maximum coal prices could be fixed by a Bituminous Coal Commission. Noncoöperating producers were taxed 19½ percent of the mine price of coal. The coal fields were divided into districts and the districts were grouped into ten price areas.

Individual district boards, made up of operators plus one representative of the union, were supposed to initiate the price-fixing process. However, in 1937 the Commission set prices without following this procedure, and a period of litigation ensued until October, 1940, when the prices pre-

[11] *Ibid.*

scribed by the Commission went into effect. The defense boom soon swept coal prices above the minimum, and when the Bituminous Coal Act expired in 1943, it was not renewed. The OPA (Office of Price Administration) set maximum prices for coal in 1942.

The short period of operation of the acts does not permit careful analysis of what the long-run effects would have been on the industry. Since there were no controls on production and entry of new firms, there is ample reason to believe that unwarranted increased production would have resulted from higher prices. The most significant result of the acts was government recognition of the problems of the industry and the establishment of a policy with industry approval of government regulation.

Beginning in 1949 there were renewed discussions of the need for government legislation to assist the coal industry. No proposals of price and production controls were actively sponsored as of 1958. But the general criticism of such plans is the same as those made of the agricultural programs. Specifically, however, any proposal for higher coal prices would hardly be a solution to the problem of recapturing lost markets from competitive energy sources.

In the areas of restrictive policy, both operator and industry groups have lobbied against programs that would lead to the development of other competitive energy sources. Examples of such policy programs are the attempt to prevent the use of the big and little inch pipelines for transportation of petroleum or natural gas after World War II and very vigorous action to put preventive tariffs and import quotas on petroleum supplies. This latter is a policy issue which will be discussed in the subsequent section on petroleum. Although policies of prevention and protection have many strong supporters, particularly in the area of tariffs and quotas where foreign competition is involved, such policies are difficult to defend in pursuance of an overall objective of economic progress. Economic progress is not to be achieved by checking and penalizing the growth of other energy sources.

A much sounder policy approach is that of sponsoring research to achieve better mining and processing methods, cheaper transportation and more effective marketing methods, and more efficient utilization. Most important are investigations to promote advances in the manufacture of gas, liquid fuels, and chemicals from coal.

The small size of the coal companies and their low rates of return on capital have prevented the active sponsoring of research programs. Attempts have been made by the industry and government to correct for this situation. The coal industry is promoting joint research, the government is sponsoring research, and the coal and petroleum industries have combined programs. In addition railroads and the electric power industry are coöperating in the research program.

To overcome the handicap of small-scale enterprise the coal industry organized at the end of World War II a coöperative research agency, Bituminous Coal Research, Inc. It is supported by more than 300 coal, railroad, and equipment companies. One of the major research projects is the design of a coal-fired gas turbine locomotive—a direct attack to recapture this market from Diesel fuel. Railroads operating in the coal regions are actively interested in the project. Nine railroads joined with four larger coal operators to form the Locomotive Development Committee of Bituminous Coal Research, Inc., and since early 1952 the American Locomotive Company has been coöperating under contract to develop the turbine for commercial application and to design a chassis for locomotive use.

The Mining Development Committee of BCR is attempting to find ways and means to produce coal cheaper and faster with minimum manpower through practical continuous mining. Other research projects are sponsored by BCR to develop more efficient utilization of bituminous coal by householders, electric utilities, and industrial plants.

The United States Bureau of Mines has had a coal research program for twenty years. One of the major objectives has been the development of synthetic fuels from coal, lignite, and oil shale. At the end of World War II, upon the recommendation of the Fuels and Lubricants Division of the Army Service Forces a surplus ordnance plant at Louisiana, Missouri, was turned over to the Bureau of Mines for research purposes. At this plant extensive research is being carried on to lower production costs of synthetic oils and gasoline from coal by the hydrogenation and Fischer-Tropsch processes. In addition, near Gorgas, Alabama, the Bureau of Mines and the Alabama Power Company have been conducting tests on gasifying coal in the ground. The purpose is to burn the unmined coal so as to produce a usable gas which can then be burned for power, used to make chemicals derived from gas, or perhaps even synthesized into liquid fuels.

Early in 1953 the Eisenhower administration canceled the Bureau of Mines program, but restored it later in that year. The administration discovered that this was an economy move of doubtful merit. Government-sponsored research applied to coal does not entail regulation of the industry and would appear to be a worth-while policy to continue in this area where the industry needs help.

A final research program that needs to be encouraged as a policy is that in which large companies—Standard Oil (N.J.) and Pittsburgh Consolidation Coal Company, Gulf Oil and Koppers—join together to improve coal-to-oil synthesis. Individual oil companies have been actively at work in this endeavor, which is already technically and economically feasible.

These research programs indicate that industry and government are working together to solve short- and long-run energy problems of the United States coal industry. This is the progressive and active type of solution that has made the United States productive and will abet economic progress in the future. Government regulation and restrictive measures would appear to be doubtful policies. Where private industry and public objectives are so closely allied there is adequate reason for optimism that the objectives will be achieved. However, an ever present problem is that policies will be adopted to correct short-run problems which will work against the achievement of long-run objectives.

3. Trends and New Developments

On January 2, 1957, the *New York Times* in a lead article in the special annual business number stated in the opening sentence: "Those prevalent descriptions of coal as a 'hard hit' industry can be filed and forgotten." What were the grounds for this optimism, which certainly should be appraised against the past history of the coal industry and a thorough appreciation that the future of coal is tied with the growth and stability of the total United States economy? The basis of optimism was to be found in the areas of production, transportation, processing and utilization, and markets—domestic and foreign.

Production of coal is accomplished by three methods of mining: underground, surface mining—variously called strip or open pit—and auger mining. Over 75 percent of coal is produced from underground mines and almost all the remainder is extracted with surface operations. Dramatic changes in the use of machines have been taking place in production methods. In underground mines 90 percent of coal is mechanically cut and almost 85 percent is mechanically loaded. But what coal production has been needing is a continuous miner to catch up with other industries which have been using flow operations for fifty or more years. There is now available for use in underground mines a continuous mining machine that combines in one operation the cutting, drilling, blasting, and loading of coal. Although the total coal produced with the continuous miner is still limited, use of the machine is increasing. Surface mining was aided by all the mass earth-moving equipment that was developed after World War II. The opportunities for auger mining are limited, but where the operation is possible, labor productivity is approximately 50 percent above the average at open-pit mines, and three and one-half times the underground average.

The real optimism in production was to be found in increased labor productivity, which had been achieved through use of machines and improved labor conditions. In the ten-year period 1946–56, output per man-day in bituminous mines had almost doubled to more than ten tons. This can be compared with other major coal-producing countries by reference to Figure 6.11.

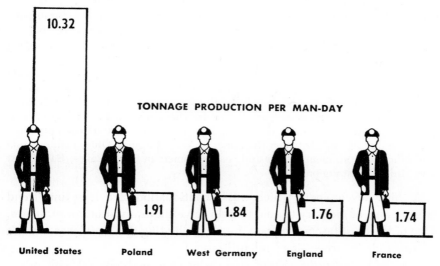

Figure 6.11. Coal Production per Man-Day, 1956. (National Coal Association)

Increased operating efficiency was improving the profit position of the coal companies. Estimates are that productivity can be increased 50 percent over the 1956 figure by 1980.

Transportation has always been the big cost factor to the coal users. Recently coal car shortages and higher rail transportation costs have plagued the industry. These factors have caused an increasing amount of coal to be shipped long distances by barge over rivers and inland waterways. The percentage of coal hauled by truck has grown since 1946. In the period after World War I, 97 percent of all bituminous coal left the mines by rail. By the end of World War II, the rails hauled 84.4 percent, and in 1955 this figure had declined to 77 percent. Rising transportation costs were of great concern to the coal industry in its fight for competitive markets with substitute fuels.

Two new developments were taking place to alleviate the transportation problem:

First, many electric utility companies were building their new plants near the mouth of coal mines, or so close that short conveyor belt systems were the only transportation required. The electric energy produced from burning the coal in the coal fields was being transmitted to points of consumption in industrialized areas.

Second:

A spectacular development in the transportation of coal began in 1956 with construction of a coal pipeline from Cadiz, Ohio, to Cleveland, a distance of 110 miles. This was the first long-distance pipeline in the world for transporting coal. The pipeline when completed will carry 1,200,000 tons of coal per year, at an estimated saving of $1 million per year over conventional shipping methods.

Specially-prepared coal will be crushed and mixed with water to form a slurry. This slurry will be pumped through the pipeline 10¾ inches in diameter at three-to-four miles per hour, the same speed as oil. At the delivery end the coal will be taken from the water, heated and dried for use. This pipeline construction raised the possibility that a network of coal pipelines may one day be built between the mines in West Virginia, Ohio, Pennsylvania and other coal-producing states and coal customers in Great Lakes, East Coast and Middle West regions.[12]

A third development which was a continuation of a long-time trend was a move of industry to coal to help solve the transportation problems. One of the most fascinating new forces facilitating this trend was a result of research in processing and utilization.

Processing and utilization of coal under new methods and with promising possibilities were under way in 1956 with the start of construction at Cresap, West Virginia, of a coal-processing plant. After almost ten years of research the Pittsburgh Consolidation Coal Company launched a plan to produce, from coal, liquids to be refined into chemicals and leave as a residue a boiler char that will be burned for power in an electric generating station located a short distance away. In addition, the plan calls for the production of synthetic fuels from coal when the economies justify this operation. This dramatic beginning of the coal industry of the future is illustrated in Figure 6.12.

The relation of this coal-processing plant to transportation is quite interesting. First coal will be delivered directly by belt from the mine

[12] *Bituminous Coal Trends,* National Coal Association, 1956, p. 85.

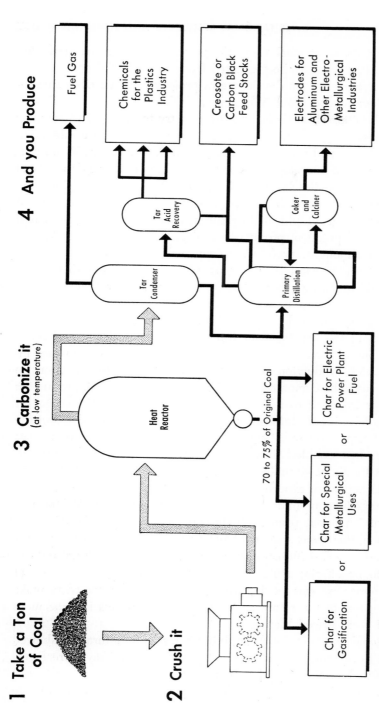

1 Take a Ton of Coal

2 Crush it

3 Carbonize it (at low temperature)

4 And you Produce

Heat Reactor

70 to 75% of Original Coal

Char for Electric Power Plant Fuel

Char for Special Metallurgical Uses

or

Char for Gasification

or

Tar Condenser

Tar Acid Recovery

Primary Distillation

Coker and Calciner

Fuel Gas

Chemicals for the Plastics Industry

Creosote or Carbon Black Feed Stocks

Electrodes for Aluminum and Other Electro-Metallurgical Industries

Figure 6.12. A New Approach to Coal's Greater Usefulness. This diagram illustrates the conversion of coal and the resulting products to be obtained by means of low-temperature fluidized coal carbonization. Pilot plants for the final testing and perfection of this process were operated at Library, Pa., by the Pittsburgh Consolidation Coal Company. The commercial application of this process is projected for the near future at Cresap, W. Va. The goal of the process is to cut the cost and improve the usefulness of coal as a boiler fuel; vastly increase the yield of coal chemicals; and make it easier to produce synthetic fuels from coal when the economics so justify. (Data from National Coal Association)

slope into a 450,000-ton stockpile at the power station. On the marketing end, the electric power to be generated from the char will go to supply three large new aluminum developments projected on the Ohio River— Kaiser at Ravenswood, West Virginia, and Olin-Mathieson, and Revere at Hannibal, Ohio. This was a move of industry to coal. A further most intriguing possibility was the reversal of this trend through a combination of coal pipelining and processing. Mr. Joseph Pursglove, Jr., Vice-President, Research and Development for the Pittsburgh Consolidation Coal Company, drew the conclusion: "The future combination of pipelining coal and then processing it hundreds of miles from the mines could greatly alter the geographical distribution of our energy supplies and the geographical points of production of coal chemicals. It is an idea to provoke much thought for future commercial possibilities."

The Pitt-Consol research led the company to the conclusion that single-purpose coal-processing plants were uneconomical, but that "multiple purpose plants attached to whole trains of other chemical processing plants can be economically attractive at this time."

Markets hold the key to coal's future—both domestically and internationally. The dominant growth factor domestically is in increasing industrial activity. Production of bituminous coal was 509 million tons in 1956. This was to be compared with 474 million tons in 1955. Production for 1957 was expected to reach 532 million tons. The outlook was for additional quantities of coal to be used in the coke-steel industry; but the real area of expansion was for use by electric utilities. The trend was that utilities had doubled their coal consumption since 1949 and had increased it by about 40 million tons since 1954. They used 157 million tons in 1956 and were expected to require 170 million tons in 1957. An annual average increase of 6 percent in utility coal use from 1956 through 1960 and of 7 percent from 1960 through 1965 was predicted.

In addition, there was some evidence that rising oil prices were shifting the trend for other industrial use of oil to coal, although natural gas appeared to be offering stiffer competition. Coal's total percentage of domestic energy use was moving up in 1956 and was expected to make substantial gains in the future as these competitive fuels became more scarce and were priced higher.

International markets for both bituminous and anthracite showed trends and developments that require separate study. They were favorable for both bituminous and anthracite coal.

Market trends of bituminous coal for the post-World War II decade are given in Figure 6.13. The National Coal Association concluded at the

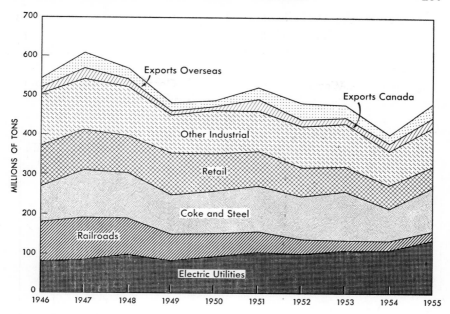

Figure 6.13. Bituminous Coal Markets, 1946–55. (Data from U.S. Bureau of Mines)

beginning of 1957: "The changing patterns of consumption in coal's various markets have fostered a growing belief, both within and outside of the industry, based on recovery beginning in the fourth quarter of 1954, that the coal industry is now on the threshold of a new era of expansion. This feeling is based on the assumption that a balance has been achieved between coal's declining and expanding markets."

4. International Trade in Coal

Before World War II the United States coal industry was not directly concerned about international trade in coal, but she should have been because of the vital issues involved. Nations with coal deficiencies are dependent on coal imports. On the other hand, not only was Great Britain's economy powered by coal, but her industrial might was strengthened and supported by her coal exports. International interdependence on coal was strongest in Europe and Japan. The drive for coal to achieve productivity and power was a motivating factor in economic, political, and military aims.

Figure 6.14 gives coal exports and imports by the major countries for the years 1929, 1937, and 1949. The data clearly indicate the importance of Great Britain, Germany, and Poland as exporters of coal, and of

France, Italy, the Netherlands, and Belgium as importers of coal in Europe. In Asia, China is shown as the exporter and Japan as the importer. In North America the United States is the exporter and Canada the importer.

Before World War II Great Britain's and Germany's strength was in their export position and France was vulnerable in her coal import po-

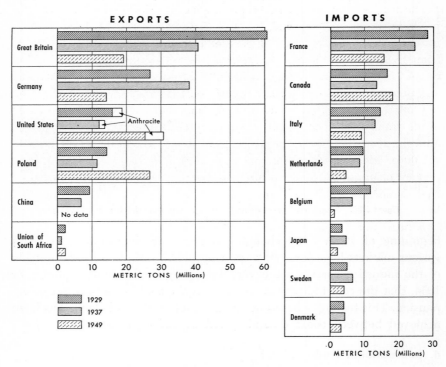

Figure 6.14.   Coal Exports and Imports by Countries.

sition. Japan's drive into Manchuria and China was to overcome her weak import position and to strengthen her import might. The United States was an exporter of coal principally to Canada. Our expressed import-export policy was an import duty of 10 cents per hundred pounds on solid fuels (including all sizes, grades, and classifications). The tax is not imposed, however, if, during the preceding calendar year, exports of solid fuels from the United States to a particular country have exceeded imports into the United States from that country. Canada has imposed restrictive tariffs on imported coal almost continuously since 1879. The duty in 1950 was 50 cents a ton on bituminous coal from the United

States; anthracite is admitted duty free. Coal from the United Kingdom entered Canada duty free under the British preference system.

Since World War II, western Europe and Japan have been short of coal and dependent on the United States and the Soviet bloc as the principal sources of supply. Canada has become increasingly dependent upon imports of coal.

The economy of western Europe (including the United Kingdom) is predominantly based on coal. In 1950, 75 percent of the total energy supply was derived from coal, 14 percent from petroleum, and 11 percent from hydroelectric power. Europe has been unable to meet rapid increases in demand for energy in recent years and has had to import coal and petroleum for a greater and greater portion of its requirements. With few oil reserves available, western Europe must supply her liquid fuel needs from imported petroleum and synthetic fuels. Coal costs at the mine head in 1950 varied from $8.00 per ton in the United Kingdom to $10.00 or more on the Continent and were expected to increase by 50 percent or more in relation to the average price level. With high costs of coal in Europe and low production costs of oil in the Middle East, the Materials Policy Commission estimated that by 1975 one-third of western Europe's energy requirements would come from petroleum.

One of the most forward steps in the solution of the coal and steel problem of western continental Europe was taken in July, 1952, with the establishment of the European Coal and Steel Community (the "Schuman Plan"). The European Coal and Steel Community is an unprecedented supranational organization with jurisdiction over the production and distribution of coal, iron, scrap, and steel within its six member countries—France, Belgium, Luxembourg, Italy, the Netherlands, and Western Germany. See Figure 15.3 in Chapter 15, "Strategy of Security." Under the plan a common market has been created for coal, iron ore, and scrap iron and steel. In the achievement of this goal, the member countries agreed to eliminate all import and export duties and other restrictions on the movement of coal and steel among the six countries. The "Schuman Plan" has been described as a "hope and a menace." Those who termed the Community a "menace" feared that it would turn out to be a super-cartel. The "hope" lies in a strong European international heavy industry which will be a stepping stone toward a federated western Europe.

The real need for the Community lies within the interdependence among the participating countries for coal and iron ore. Luxembourg produces no coal but is an important producer of steel, which requires coal. Belgium and the Netherlands lack the iron ore for their steel industries. Italy needs both raw materials and must depend on imports. France and Germany are dependent on each other; France needs coal (especially coking coal) which Germany has, while Germany needs iron ore which France has. No country in the Community can produce the necessary steel without sizable imports of one or both raw materials. This interdependence of the basic heavy industry is the most convincing argument for the economic unification of western Europe.

The United States gave full support to the Schuman Plan from the beginning. The United States loaned the Community $100 million in 1953, at which time President Eisenhower said: "This Community seems to me to be the most hopeful and constructive development so far toward the economic and political integration of Europe. As such, this European initiative meets the often expressed hopes of the Congress of the United States. . . ." A recent objective study made the following among five recommendations: "1. The United States should continue to support fully the European Coal and Steel Community. The Community points the way to the resurgence of the economic and political strength of Western Europe that is so vitally needed to shore up the defences of the free world. The Community has turned its back on the restriction and monopoly of the past, and seeks to emulate the competitive energy that animates the vast common market of the United States. The Community also seeks to encourage efficiency in production and service to consumers through cooperation." [13]

Great Britain refrained from joining the Coal and Steel Community because of her first allegiance to the British Commonwealth. British coal exports dominated the world coal market until about 1910. By 1913, the peak production year, the industry was producing 287,000,000 tons and exporting 94,000,000 tons of coal. While coal exports from the United Kingdom were higher in 1952 than in 1951, when they were 1,603,000 tons, they were still only a fraction of the 62,000,000 tons exported in 1929 and 41,000,000 tons in 1937. Part of the exports were going to the Community in 1952 and 1953. During mid-1954 there was continued shortage of coal in Great Britain. The United States press indicated that Princess Margaret had made a trip into a mine to point up the problem. The shortage was sustained and Great Britain shifted from a net exporter of coal in 1954 to a net importer of coal in 1955. The British govern-

[13] "The European Coal and Steel Community," *Studies in Business and Economics,* December, 1955, Bureau of Business and Economic Research, University of Maryland, p. 2.

ment's fuel and power policy has three broad objectives: "To obtain more coal; to use coal better; to supplement supplies of coal with other sources of energy—atomic energy as soon as possible, natural gas if it can be found and oil forthwith."

The United States increased her total exports of coal from about 14,000,000 tons in 1937 to a peak of 56,800,000 during the Korean War boom year of 1951, after which they fell off sharply to 31,000,000 tons in 1954 and then rocketed to 51,600,000 tons in 1955. This flow of exports is shown in Figure 6.15. The United States followed a post-World War II

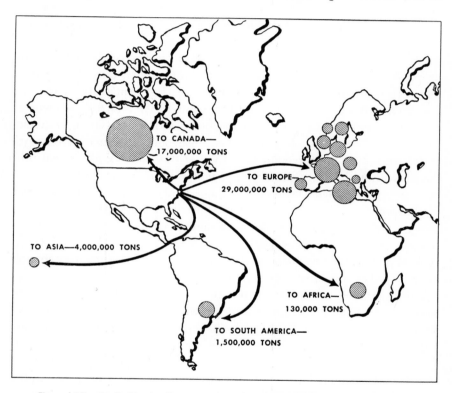

Figure 6.15.   Coal to Foreign Countries in 1955. (Data from U.S. Bureau of the Census)

policy of supplying coal to Europe under various government programs to aid European recovery. The exports to Europe ranged from a peak of 37,000,000 in 1947 to a low of less than 800,000 tons in 1950, and then in one year jumped to almost 28,000,000 tons in 1951, only to fall to 8,300,000 tons in 1953 and then to rise to the 29,000,000 shown in the flow chart for 1955. This feast to famine export business was brought about by the initial need for large exports of coal to the economically crippled nations of Europe; then, as the European economy recovered, coal imports from the United States were curtailed. The National Coal Association was optimistic enough in 1956 to conclude: "In recent years, however, the stability of the European industrial system, which is primarily based on coal, has shown a strength and vigor which would seem to indicate a more stable and continuous U.S. export market."

Just how stable and continuous the western European market would be was a function of the import requirements of the European Coal and Steel Community. Initially, exchanges of coal between countries in the Community from January to November, 1953, increased by 20.4 percent (about 3 million tons) compared with the corresponding period of 1952. As a result, imports of United States coal, a costly dollar item, dropped by 61 percent from 15.5 million to 6 million tons. This was in line with the latter part of the policy of the High Authority that: "The objective of the Community is not the maintenance and development of coal production at any price, but the best possible utilization of its resources with the view of making coal an economic source of energy." However, one of the threefold objectives of this policy is that "coal produced within the Community must under normal circumstances successfully compete with the imported coal." Taken together, this has two implications for United States coal exported to the Community: First, imports will be admitted to the Community when necessary and therefore, because of their marginal nature, will be especially sensitive to cyclical changes in economic activity; second, United States imports will be admitted on a nonrestrictive competitive basis.

The Community was certain to depend on imports to fill the gap between consumption and production of coal in future periods of high demand, as occurred in 1955 and 1956. One definite possibility of lowering the cost of United States coal delivered to France was the agreement signed in 1956 between France and Germany to build the Moselle Canal, which would link Lorraine steel mills by cheap water transport to North Sea ports. This water transport will reduce the $4-a-ton premium that Lorraine steel makers were paying for United States coal. The prospects of rising energy needs in western Europe and a sustained gap between consumption and production of coal were clearly predicted in the Organization for European Economic Cooperation's study of "Europe's Growing Needs of Energy, How Can They Be Met?" As shown in Figure 6.16 the estimate was that by 1975 western Europe would require imports of 50,000,000 tons of United States coal annually.

Japan relied on imports of coal from the Asiatic mainland to meet her pre-World War II requirements. About 4,000,000 tons were imported in 1937. After the war Japan turned to the United States for her coal requirements. The postwar policy of the United States was to supply Japan's import needs, and in 1951 Japan imported about 2,000,000 tons of coking coal and 300,000 tons of anthracite. Japan's imports from the United States were about 3,000,000 tons from 1952 through 1955. Imports from the United States of that order of magnitude are likely to continue as long as Japan cannot secure supplies from the Asiatic mainland. India has also been a source of Japanese coal imports.

Canada's energy economy is dependent on coal imports. Canada has large coal reserves in Alberta and Nova Scotia, but they are far from her industry, which is concentrated in the Toronto-Ottawa-Montreal triangle. Thus because of higher transportation costs, Canada's coal can be supplied at a lower cost from the United States. Canada's coal consumption in 1950 was about 40,-200,000 tons. Of this, 15,400,000 were produced domestically and 24,-800,000 tons were imported. Canada's coal imports were increasing;

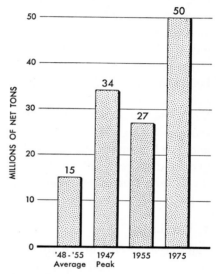

Figure 6.16. U.S. Coal for Western Europe. (Data from National Coal Association)

those from the United States increased from 11,600,000 tons in 1939 out of total imports of 13,900,000 to nearly 25,000,000 tons in 1951 during the Korean War boom. This latter figure constituted almost all of Canada's coal imports. After 1951 United States exports of coal to Canada fell to a low of 16,000,000 tons in 1954. The 17,000,000 tons shown in the flow chart for 1955 increased to 19,000,000 tons in 1956, and the same quantity was indicated for 1957. The Materials Policy Committee estimated that by 1975 about two-thirds of Canada's coal would come from the United States—more than 50,000,000 tons a year.

The long-run estimates of exports of 50,000,000 tons of United States coal to western Europe and 50,000,000 tons to Canada were indeed hopeful prospects for the United States coal industry. Convinced of the long-range stability of this export market, leading coal producers for export, major railroads hauling to tidewater, and the miners' union organized in 1956, American Coal Shipping, Inc., to "promote the export coal trade on the broadest possible basis."

Prospects of 1957 exports of both bituminous and anthracite coal were excellent. A total bituminous export of 74,000,000 tons was indicated. Exports of anthracite, including those to Canada, reached about 4,900,000 tons in 1956 and were expected to continue as a firm bulwark to sales. Overseas shipments in 1956—mainly to the Netherlands, France, Italy, Belgium, and Luxembourg—totaled about 2,500,000 tons, more than three times those in 1955. The *New York Times* summarized the export outlook for coal: "Talk of overseas shipments brings smiles to the faces of industry leaders."

Thus in contrast to her passive interest in international coal trade before World War II, the United States now has an active interest. Great Britain's decline as a world power is partially explained by her diminishing coal exports. The United States has increased exports to western Europe to aid its recovery and has supported the European Coal and Steel Community. She is exporting coal to Japan to replace Asiatic mainland sources. Interdependence with Canada is stronger because of the latter's increasing reliance on coal imports from us to support her industry.

5. Conclusion

Reserves of coal in the United States are more than adequate to meet future domestic and export requirements. While short-run problems of coal are the same as the long-run ones of the past, problems of inadequate returns and loss of markets through increasing pressure from competitive fuels, indications are that in the long run coal will gradually "take over the heavier part of the energy burden in the United States." Industry and government research is actively working toward the accomplishment of this objective. The coal industry's principal worry, but not the United States', is that other new energy sources now on the industrial horizon will rise and shine as sources of power.

PETROLEUM

Petroleum is vital to victory in war and a growing power source of peace. The importance of petroleum to the security of the United States was clearly established during World War II, when more than 50 percent of all the shipments of supplies to our military forces was petroleum products. Petroleum at the beginning of 1955 furnished approximately 37 percent of the total inanimate energy used in the United States as compared with 33 percent in 1938. In foreign areas, excluding Russia, the increase was from 13 percent in 1938 to approximately 23 percent in 1951. Estimates indicated that in 1955 the increase in the world demand for petroleum since the end of World War II was approximately equal to the total growth in demand prior to that time.

The United States petroleum industry includes all the functions from discovery and production of crude through refining and marketing of the finished products. The discovery and production of crude is engaged in by many hundreds of individuals and companies who are referred to as independents. They have discovered about 75 percent of the petroleum in the United States. Comparatively, only a few of the independents own refineries and they are predominantly a domestic interest group. There are about twenty large integrated companies referred to as majors. Up to 1954 only ten of the majors imported petroleum in addition to producing and purchasing domestic crude, and six of these companies had undertaken tremendous foreign investments. Five of these companies are American owned—Gulf Oil, Socony Mobil, Standard Oil (Calif.), Standard Oil (N.J.), Texas Company—and the sixth is the Royal Dutch-Shell group.

These six companies, together with the British Oil Company (formerly Anglo-Iranian) through concessions and other agreements with foreign governments, produce most of the oil in foreign areas, excluding Russia and Russian-controlled production. The seven companies produced 87.5 percent of the foreign crude oil in the free world in 1952. The six companies which operate in the United States accounted for 31.6 percent of United States crude oil produced in 1952. The international investments are principally in the major export areas of the Caribbean and Middle East. They were made by the United States concerns, primarily to supply foreign markets and also to insure continued domestic availability of crude petroleum. During this same period of time, imports of oil into the United States could be controlled by the American "Big Five."

1. Petroleum Production and Reserves

World petroleum production from 1935 through 1956 is shown in Table 36. The United States' share of world production was approximately 45 percent in 1956 as compared with 61 percent before World War II. Total world production of petroleum in 1956 was three times the prewar level. Significant increases were made by almost all of the countries.

TABLE 36. World Production of Crude Petroleum, by Specified Countries
(in millions of barrels, 42 gallons each)

Year	Argentina	Colombia	Iran (Persia)	Iraq	Kuwait	Mexico	Indonesia	Rumania	U.S.S.R.	Saudi Arabia	United States	Venezuela	World Totals
1935–39 av.	16.3	20.5	70.9	30.6	—	41.9	54.7	54.3	196.7	.9	1,171.0	176.8	1,911.9
1940–44 av.	23.6	19.2	73.2	21.3	—	38.9	42.1	38.2	232.0	5.3	1,465.1	199.3	2,262.5
1945	22.8	22.4	130.5	35.1	—	43.5	7.6	34.8	149.0	21.3	1,713.7	323.1	2,594.7
1946	20.6	22.1	146.8	35.7	5.9	49.2	2.1	31.4	157.7	59.9	1,733.9	388.5	2,745.4
1947	21.8	24.8	155.0	35.8	16.2	56.3	8.0	28.6	187.5	89.9	1,857.0	434.9	3,022.1
1948	23.7	23.8	190.3	26.1	46.5	58.5	31.8	34.0	218.0	142.9	2,020.1	490.0	3,433.2
1949	22.6	29.7	204.7	31.0	90.0	60.9	43.2	33.7	237.7	174.0	1,841.9	482.3	3,404.1
1950	23.4	34.1	242.5	49.7	125.7	72.4	48.4	32.0	266.2	199.5	1,973.6	546.8	3,803.0
1951	24.5	38.4	127.6	65.1	204.9	77.3	55.5	31.0	285.0	278.0	2,247.7	622.2	4,286.0
1952	24.8	38.7	10.1	141.1	273.4	77.3	62.5	45.0	322.4	301.9	2,289.8	660.3	4,509.9
1953	28.5	40.2	9.4	210.3	314.6	72.4	75.1	52.0	363.0	308.3	2,357.1	644.2	4,770.8
1954	29.7	40.5	22.4	228.4	347.3	83.7	79.4	55.0	411.0	347.8	2,315.0	691.8	4,990.8
1955	31.0	41.0	120.0	251.0	398.0	91.0	87.0	79.0	510.0	352.0	2,485.0	787.0	5,634.0
1956	35.0	47.0	105.0	234.0	399.0	90.0	93.0	80.0	540.0	360.0	2,617.0	898.0	5,750.0

SOURCE: Bureau of Mines; *Commodity Year Book*, 1956; 1957 for 1955 and 1956 data.

Venezuela and Canada registered large gains. Notable exceptions to the increases were Iran and Rumania. In Iran, output was higher through 1950, but nationalization of British oil properties in 1951 resulted in almost complete cessation of production. Not until 1955 did Iran recover its prewar production. Most noteworthy are the tremendous increases in the Middle East in Iraq, Kuwait, and Saudi Arabia.

The flow and distribution of the changes in production in the post-World War II period are shown in Figure 6.17. This chart clearly shows

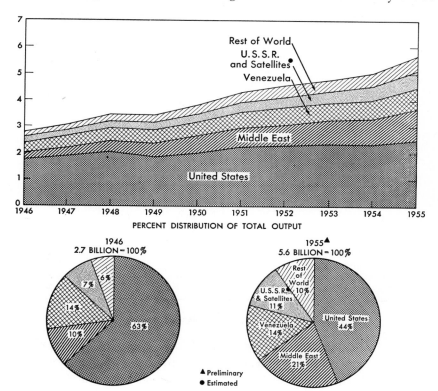

Figure 6.17. World Petroleum Production, Crude Oil, 1946–55. (Data from U.S. Bureau of Mines)

the rising importance of the Middle East in world production as her share more than doubled in the ten-year period from 10 to 21 percent. Even though Venezuela's production doubled, the percentage was the same. The United States production of crude oil was up 43 percent, yet our share of world production declined from 63 percent to 44 percent.

The three major areas of the United States, Venezuela, and the Middle East accounted for 79 percent of the 1955 world oil production. Five countries within these areas—United States, Venezuela, Iraq, Saudi Arabia, and Kuwait—produced 77 percent of the petroleum in 1955. If Canada and Iran are added, the seven-country 1956 percentage was 82.5. The percentage distribution of world crude production as shown in Table 37 for 1954, 1955, 1956 indicates the growing importance of the Middle East and the Eastern Hemisphere. The United States' share in production was only 42.6 percent of the total as compared with 46.4

TABLE 37. Percentage Distribution of World Crude Production

Principal Countries	Second Quarter[a] 1956	1955	1954
U.S.A.	42.6	44.7	46.4
Venezuela	15.9	14.2	13.8
U.S.S.R.	9.3	9.3	8.4
Kuwait	7.4	7.2	7.0
Saudi Arabia	6.3	6.4	6.9
Iraq	4.5	4.6	4.6
Iran	3.4	2.1	0.4
Canada	2.4	2.3	1.9
Mexico	1.6	1.6	1.7
Indonesia	1.5	1.5	1.6
Principal Areas			
North America	46.6	48.6	50.0
Middle East	22.92	21.6	20.4
South America	15.9	16.4	16.3
Europe and Africa (incl. U.S.S.R.)	11.1	11.4	11.1
Asia and Australasia	2.4	2.5	2.5
Eastern Hemisphere	37.5	34.9	33.7
Western Hemisphere	62.5	65.1	66.2

[a] Data for all of 1956 are affected by Suez arises.
SOURCE: *World Petroleum*, July, 1956. See January, 1957, for 1956 data.

percent in 1954 and 61 percent before World War II. Concentration of production by countries and areas was still the characteristic feature. Petroleum is thus characterized by concentration of production by area and by companies.

The real measure of strength of the petroleum industry is in its crude productive capacity. The maintenance of crude productivity is a function of petroleum reserves. Petroleum reserves are stated as "proved reserves." To these are added each year new proved reserves, which result from new developments in existing fields, and new discoveries. The growth in world crude petroleum production has been made possible by the expansion of proved reserves.

Proved crude oil reserves by areas and countries as of January 1, 1955, and January 1, 1956, are given in Table 38. New reserves added during

TABLE 38. Estimated World Crude Oil Reserves, 1956
(thousands of barrels)

Region and Country	January 1, 1956[a]	Percent of World Total	January 1, 1955[a]	Percent of World Total
North America				
Canada	2,207,614	1.17	2,850,000	1.80
Cuba	3,000	0.00	3,000	0.00
Mexico	1,900,000	1.00	1,750,000	1.11
United States[b]	30,012,170	15.86	29,560,746	18.69
Total North America	34,122,784	18.03	34,163,746	21.60
South America				
Argentina	400,000	0.21	410,000	0.26
Bolivia	50,000	0.03	45,000	0.03
Brazil	27,000	0.01	60,000	0.04
Chile	25,000	0.01	55,000	0.03
Colombia	580,000	0.31	570,000	0.36
Ecuador	25,000	0.01	28,000	0.02
Peru	225,000	0.12	225,000	0.14
Trinidad	280,000	0.15	280,000	0.18
Venezuela	12,000,000	6.34	10,930,000	6.91
Total South America	13,612,000	7.19	12,603,000	7.97
Western Europe				
France	120,000	0.06	100,000	0.06
West Germany	495,000	0.26	435,000	0.27
Italy	110,000	0.06	90,000	0.06
Netherlands	95,000	0.05	90,000	0.06
United Kingdom	5,000	0.00	4,200	0.00
Total Western Europe	825,000	0.43	719,200	0.45
Eastern Europe				
Austria	400,000	0.21	300,000	0.19
Rumania	600,000	0.32	400,000	0.25
Russia	10,000,000	5.28	9,500,000	6.01
Yugoslavia	36,000	0.02	30,000	0.02
Other Eastern Europe[c]	208,000	0.11	122,000	0.08
Total Eastern Europe	11,244,000	5.94	10,352,000	6.55
Africa				
Algeria	5,000	0.00	5,000	0.00
Egypt	150,000	0.08	92,000	0.06
French Morocco	14,000	0.01	15,000	0.01
Total Africa	169,000	0.09	112,000	0.07
Middle East				
Bahrein Island	205,000	0.11	215,000	0.14
Iran	27,000,000	14.27	15,000,000	9.49
Iraq	20,000,000	10.57	14,250,000	9.01
Israel	1,000	0.00	—	0.00
Kuwait	40,000,000	21.13	30,000,000	18.97
Qatar	1,500,000	0.79	1,500,000	0.95
Saudi Arabia	37,000,000	19.55	36,000,000	22.76
Neutral Zone	500,000	0.26	429,000	0.27
Turkey	65,000	0.04	65,000	0.04
Total Middle East	126,271,000	66.72	97,459,000	61.63
Far East				
Australia	1,000	0.00	1,000	0.00
British Borneo	500,000	0.26	525,000	0.33
Burma	45,000	0.03	45,000	0.03
China	25,000	0.01	25,000	0.02
India	60,000	0.03	50,000	0.03
Indonesia	2,300,000	1.22	1,900,000	1.20
Japan	22,000	0.01	52,000	0.03
New Guinea	50,000	0.03	115,000	0.07
Pakistan	22,000	0.01	20,000	0.02
Total Far East	3,025,000	1.60	2,733,000	1.73
Total world reserves	189,268,784	100.00	158,141,946	100.00

[a] Estimated by *The Oil and Gas Journal* except for United States.

[b] United States estimates of proved crude oil reserves by American Petroleum Institute; do not include reserves of natural-gas liquids.

[c] Includes Albania, Czechoslovakia, Hungary, and Poland.

SOURCE: *Petroleum Facts and Figures,* American Petroleum Institute.

this one year by exploration and development amounted to about 31 billion barrels. United States crude oil reserves increased from 29.6 billion barrels as of January 1, 1955, to 30 billion barrels at the beginning of 1956. As shown by Table 38, the United States' share of the world's reserves was 15.8 percent as of January 1, 1956, and the Western Hemisphere held 25.2 percent. The Middle East reserves were 66.7 percent of the world total, and all the rest of the world contained only 8.1 percent. This represents a dramatic change in the world's proved petroleum reserve in the ten-year postwar period ending January 1, 1956. The United States' share of the *free world's* proved reserves declined from 32.2 percent to 15.4 percent (Table 39) even though the quantity

TABLE 39.   Estimated Free World Crude Oil Reserves, December 31, 1946 and 1955

| Area | 12/31/46 | 12/31/55 | 12/31/46 | 12/31/55 |
	Billion Barrels		Percent of Total	
United States	20.9	30.0	32.2	15.4
Canada	0.2	2.8	0.3	1.4
Venezuela	7.5	12.8	11.5	6.6
Middle East	33.0	140.0	50.8	71.8
Other countries	3.4	9.4	5.2	4.8
Total	65.0	195.0	100.0	100.0

SOURCE: Chase Manhattan Bank.

increased 50 percent. The Middle East percentage increased from 50.8 to 71.8 as a result of a more than fourfold multiplication of reserves. Middle East reserves on January 1, 1957, were estimated in excess of 150 billion barrels, up from 140.0 at the beginning of 1956. Thus the Middle East has grown in importance in petroleum proved reserves as well as in crude production.

For many years United States crude production has been at a rate of about 7 to 8 percent of proved reserves. This is one of the reasons that has given rise to the fear that the United States would exhaust the domestic petroleum reserves. On the other hand, the continuation of this percentage might be considered favorable as it indicates that as crude production has increased, proved reserves have increased. This sustained expansion of United States proved reserves must be continued and adequate incentives must be provided for it.

The 7 to 8 percent ratio is a continual reminder that at current rates of crude production proved petroleum reserves will be exhausted in twelve to fourteen years unless new reserves are added. In addition, the existence of this ratio through time should not be considered favorable, because such a conclusion ignores the fact that United States present and future consumption of petroleum is the correct measure of requirements.

2. Petroleum Consumption and Production

Evidence previously given has indicated the tremendous increase in the rise and importance of petroleum in the United States. The Materials Policy Commission reported, as shown in Table 40, that domestic con-

TABLE 40. Consumption of Petroleum Products in the
United States, 1929 and 1950

Item	1929	1950
Total domestic consumption (millions of barrels)		
Annual	940	2,375
Daily	2.6	6.5
Use (percentage of total)		
Transportation		
Highway	36	36
Railroad	9	5
Water	10	6
Air	a	2
Total transportation	55	49
Residential and commercial	6	19
Industry and agriculture		
Manufacturing and mining	15	14
Generation of electricity	1	3
Manufacture of gas	2	2
Agriculture	3	4
Total industry and agriculture	21	23
Miscellaneous[b]	12	3
Nonfuel uses	6	6
Grand total	100	100

[a] 0.05 percent.
[b] Not allocable. The decline in this category from 1929 to 1950 undoubtedly reflects more complete statistical information for 1950.
SOURCES: 1929—Adapted from Bureau of Mines *Report of Investigations*, 4805, W. H. Lyon and D. S. Colby. 1950—Bureau of Mines, *Annual Petroleum Statement*, No. P 347; *Mineral Market Report*, MMS 2003; *Resources for Freedom*, Vol. III.

sumption of petroleum products increased from 940 million barrels in 1929 to 2375 million barrels in 1950. This is equivalent to an increase from 2,600,000 to 6,500,000 barrels a day. Petroleum products are principally used for transportation purposes—highway, railroad, water, and air. The rapid development of automobile, bus, and truck transportation has brought about enormous use of petroleum products; and, as has been noted, because of the superior advantages as a liquid fuel, petroleum has displaced coal as a source of energy for rail and water transportation. In addition, the advantages of liquid fuel in residential and commercial heating have increased the use of petroleum. The growth and importance of these latter uses are shown by an increase in the share of total consumption from 6 percent in 1929 to 19 percent in 1950. Transportation, however, continues to dominate the petroleum market even though its share of the total declined from 55 percent in 1929 to 49 percent in 1950.

The 6,500,000 barrels a day of petroleum used in 1950 were shared in the following amounts and percentages by the major petroleum products:

	Barrels	*Percent*
Gasoline	2,700,000	42
Kerosene	300,000	5
Distillate and fuel oil	1,100,000	17
Residual fuel oil	1,500,000	23
Lubricants	100,000	2
All other products	800,000	11
Total	6,500,000	100

Consumption of petroleum in the United States was less than production before World War II, as indicated in Table 41. This situation was

TABLE 41.   Production and Consumption of Petroleum in the
United States, Selected Years, 1925 to 1950
(millions of barrels)

Year	Production, Crude Oil and Natural Gas Liquids	Consumption		
		Gasoline	Other Products	Total
1925	792	224	503	727
1929	1,063	376	564	940
1940	1,412	589	738	1,327
1950	2,156	994	1,381	2,375

SOURCE: Bureau of Mines.

reversed in 1947, and in 1950, even though production had risen to 2156 million barrels, this amount was not sufficient to meet domestic consumption of petroleum products of 2375 million barrels.

These production data do not show production potentialities, as production control regulatory policies result in shut-in or idle productive capacity. Figure 6.18 indicates that at the beginning of 1950 estimated maximum efficient crude productive capacity in the United States was about 1,000,000 barrels a day in excess of crude oil production. Figure

6.19 compares United States consumption of petroleum with actual production and shut-in capacity for the years 1938, 1946, and 1952. The data in the figure show that in 1952 the United States still had a shut-in productive capacity of 1,000,000 barrels a day. Actual production was 6,868,000 barrels a day and consumption was 7,281,000. Obviously, this deficit was being made up from imports, although potential productive

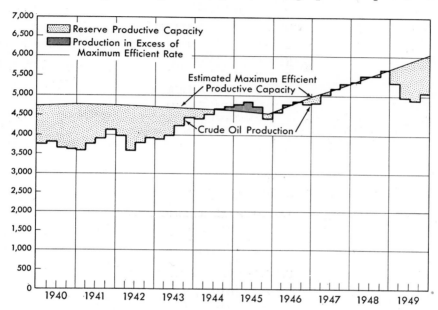

Figure 6.18. U.S. Crude Oil Production and Estimated Productive Capacity (Thousand Barrels Daily). Estimated maximum efficient productive capacity: 1940–45 as reported by Petroleum Administration for War; 1946–49 based on line connecting fourth quarter 1945 maximum efficient rate estimated by the Petroleum Administration with the actual production of 5,688,000 barrels daily in December, 1948, which was considered to be at or near the maximum efficient rate, and the estimated availability for 1949. (Data from *U.S. Crude Petroleum Reserve Productive Capacity,* National Petroleum Council, January 26, 1950, p. 6)

capacity was available to cover the difference between domestic consumption and production.

Figure 6.19 also presents graphically, with supporting data, production and consumption of petroleum for the world. As shown in the chart, petroleum consumption exceeded production in the area of the Western Hemisphere north of the United States, the Far East and the Pacific, and Europe and Africa. Petroleum production substantially exceeds consumption in the area of the Western Hemisphere south of the United States and in the Middle East.

In the deficiency areas, north of the United States, 1952 production

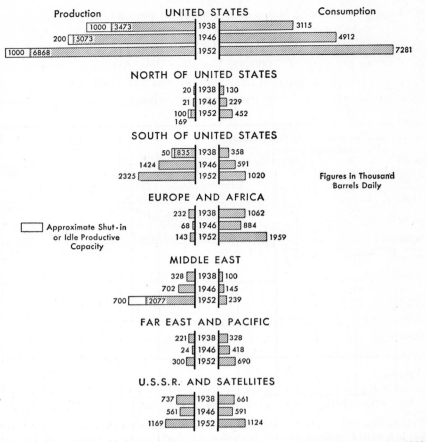

Figure 6.19. World Petroleum Production and Consumption, and Shut-In Capacity, for 1938, 1946, and 1952, Covering All Petroleum Liquids Produced and Consumed Within Each Area. (Data from Independent Petroleum Association of America and Standard Oil Co., N. J.)

(Canadian) amounted to 37 percent of area consumption (primarily in Canada). Production in this area has been increasing rapidly since World War II. Productive capacity in 1952 was indicated to be in excess of production by about 100,000 barrels a day. In the Far East and the Pacific, petroleum production in 1952 was equivalent to 43 percent of consumption within the area. Europe and Africa are clearly shown to be the greatest deficit regions. In 1952, petroleum consumption in Europe and Africa was 1,959,000 barrels a day while local production amounted to 143,000 per day, or only 7 percent of total use.

In the surplus areas, south of the United States in the Western Hemisphere, petroleum production in 1952 was 2,325,000 barrels a day while consumption was only 1,020,000 barrels a day. This excess production was supplied primarily by Venezuela and thus most of the countries south of the United States must import petroleum. The tremendous significance of the Middle East as an export area is clearly indicated as production in 1952 averaged 2,077,000 barrels a day. In addition, there was a shut-in productive capacity of about 700,000 barrels in Iran. This total Middle East productive capacity of 2,777,000 barrels a day in 1952 was over eleven times the consumption of 239,000 barrels a day.

Both production and consumption of petroleum in the U.S.S.R. and satellite countries were less in 1946 than in 1938. In 1938 the excess production was in the areas which are now the satellites. In 1946 when consumption was more than production, the U.S.S.R. was importing petroleum from the United States. For the U.S.S.R. and satellites 1951 was the last year production (943,000 barrels a day) was less than consumption (1,000,400 barrels a day) in these areas. In 1952 some Russian oil began to enter western markets. Production in 1952 was 1,169,000 barrels a day and consumption was estimated at 1,124,000 barrels a day. Most noteworthy, however, is that United States production of petroleum in 1952 was 6,868,000 barrels a day and domestic demand was 7,281,000 barrels a day. Thus, even though the territory of Russia and satellite countries is vastly greater than the United States, both our domestic production and consumption of petroleum were of an order of magnitude of six to seven times greater than within the Russian orbit.

World production and consumption of petroleum in 1955 as given in Figure 6.20 show some significant changes from 1952. The Soviet and satellites had a substantial increase in production without a corresponding increase in consumption and thus a resultant excess of production over consumption of 225,000 barrels a day. United States consumption had increased to 8,256,000 barrels a day and production was up to 6,752,-000 a day, but the United States deficit was 1,504,000 barrels a day. Western Europe's consumption increased to 2,364,100 barrels a day in 1955. Most remarkable was the increased production of petroleum in the Middle East from 2,077,000 barrels a day in 1952 to 3,279,600 barrels a day in 1955—up almost 60 percent.

Future petroleum consumption and production potentialities were considered by the Materials Policy Commission, which reported that the consumption of petroleum products in the United States could be expected to grow vigorously, although at a percentage rate considerably below that of the past twenty-five years. Total domestic demand for petroleum products in 1975 was projected by the Commission at more

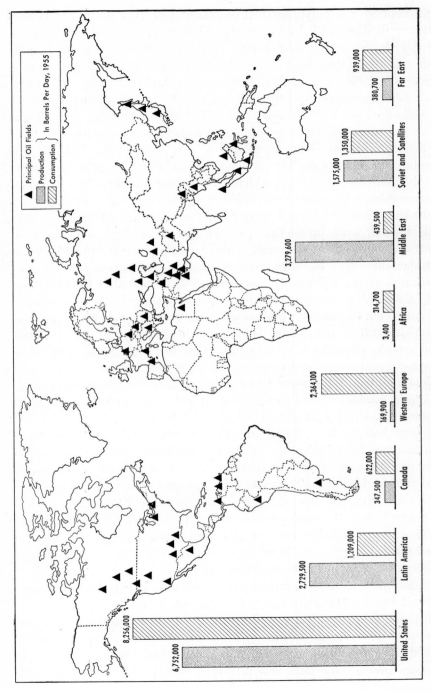

Figure 6.20. World Production and Consumption, 1955.

than double the 1950 amount, as indicated by Table 42, which gives the 1975 estimates by products as compared with 1950 consumption.

Outside the United States, the rest of the free world used in 1950 only

TABLE 42. United States Domestic Demand for Petroleum Products,
1950 and Projected 1975
(millions of barrels)

Product	1950		Projected 1975	
	Annual	Daily	Annual	Daily
Motor fuel[a]	994	2.7	2,085	5.7
Kerosene and distillate fuel	513	1.4	1,180	3.2
Residual fuel oil	554	1.5	1,110	3.1
Lubricants	39	.1	75	.2
Other products and losses	275	.8	550	1.5
Total	2,375	6.5	5,000	13.7

[a] 1950, gasoline only; 1975, gasoline, highway Diesel and LPG, and aviation fuel.
SOURCE: *Resources for Freedom*, Vol. III.

a little more than half as much petroleum as did the United States. Several studies have concluded, however, that petroleum consumption can be expected to increase much more rapidly outside the United States than domestically as other countries develop their transportation facilities and coal becomes less available and more costly. The estimates of the Materials Policy Commission for 1975 as compared with petroleum consumption in 1950 and 1929 are given in Table 43. Total free world use of petroleum outside the United States in 1975 is indicated to be almost as great as that of domestic use to give a total world consumption of 26,800,000 barrels per day.

TABLE 43. Free World Demand for Crude Oil and Products
(thousands of barrels per day)

Region	1929	1950	Projected 1975	Percent Increase 1950–75
United States	2,580	6,510	13,700	110
Other North America	210	590	2,300	290
South America	170	600	2,300	283
Total Western Hemisphere	2,960	7,700	18,300	138
Europe	460	1,200	4,000	233
Africa, Asia, and Oceania	300	1,100	4,500	309
Total Eastern Hemisphere	760	2,300	8,500	270
Free world excluding United States	1,140	3,490	13,100	275
Total free world	3,720	10,000	26,800	168

SOURCE: 1929 and 1950, Bureau of Mines estimates. 1975 for U.S.—vol. II, Projection of 1975 Materials Demand; *Resources for Freedom*, Vol. III.

The Materials Policy Commission concluded that adequate supplies should be available to meet this tremendous growth in consumption. The Commission suggested that the future balance sheet of world petroleum supplies might look something like the hypothetical pattern in Table

TABLE 44. Hypothetical Pattern of Free World Oil Supplies and Demand in 1975 Compared with 1950

(thousands of barrels per day)

Region	Production 1950	Production 1975	Apparent Consumption 1950	Apparent Consumption 1975	Net Imports— Net Exports+ 1950	Net Imports— Net Exports+ 1975
United States	5,910	11,200ᵃ	6,450	13,700	−540	−2,500
Other Western Hemisphere	2,040	5,900	1,190	4,600	+850	+1,300
Total Western Hemisphere	7,950	17,100	7,640	18,300	+310	−1,200
Europe	60	300ᵃ	1,200	4,000	−1,140	−3,700
Middle East and other Eastern Hemisphere	2,040	9,400	1,100	4,500	+940	+4,900
Total Eastern Hemisphere	2,100	9,700	2,300	8,500	−200	+1,200
Free world excluding United States	4,140	15,600	3,490	13,100	+650	+2,500
Total free world	10,050	26,800	9,940	26,800	+110	—

ᵃ Crude oil, natural gas liquids, shale oil, and other synthetics.
SOURCE: *Resources for Freedom*, Vol. III.

44, in which projections are compared with actual 1950 figures. The Commission concluded that:

This picture is merely one possible shape that the future pattern may take, but it does emphasize the prospective developments that set the background for the future oil problems of the free world. Those developments are a tremendously increased level of consumption and correspondingly increased dependence on production in the Middle East and in the Western Hemisphere outside the United States.

It is quite possible that production in the United States by 1975 may differ considerably from the 11.2 million barrels per day suggested in [Table 44]. If it should be much below, free world dependence on the Middle East and possibly on Western Hemisphere production outside the United States would be correspondingly greater. In view of the wartime essentiality of oil, and the hazards to the Middle East in particular and to world oil supplies and transport in general, the future pattern poses a serious problem of free world security and offers a strong challenge to public policy to encourage the growth of production capacity in the United States and the rest of the Western Hemisphere.[14]

[14] *Resources for Freedom*, Vol. III, *The Outlook for Energy Sources*, pp. 9–10.

3. Problems and Policy

Present and future petroleum problems and policy must be considered in relation to past problems and policy, and in the light of additional facts that bear on these issues.

Outstanding facts are that consumption of petroleum in the United States was less than production before World War II, that this situation was reversed in 1947, and that evidence points to a continuation and possible growth of this excess of domestic consumption of petroleum over production.

A. Conservation

As has been noted in the discussion of mineral characteristics, the legal right to ownership of mineral reserves on one's property has been fundamental as an incentive to discovery. However, the rule of capture, which was applied in the case of oil, had additional effects, as the petroleum under the land of many owners became the property of the person first able to produce the oil from wells drilled on his property. Adopted in the erroneous belief that oil and gas were in constant unpredictable movement, and therefore not susceptible to regulation by law, the rule of capture gave the right to the landowner to do as he pleased, and thereby destroyed another kind of property right. This rule of capture led to the drilling of many wells and the production of oil in order to get possession of it and without consideration of the damage to the producing pool. In addition, there was very little relationship between production and market demand. With large discoveries, such as the East Texas field, the price of crude fell to as little as ten cents a barrel in the early 1930's. Thus the rule of capture resulted in wasteful inefficient practices in the production of oil. In addition, refiners had little incentive to use efficient methods in the production of petroleum products.

This is the background of the conservation problem. To cope with this problem, several of the states began in the thirties to limit production of oil per well (proration), and attempted to regulate the spacing of wells and to have each oil reservoir operated as a unit (unit pool operation). State authorities have since extended regulation to include limitations on the oil-gas ratio to prevent excessive impairment of the gas pressure and to reduce the waste of natural gas. Regulations have also been used to preserve the driving force of underground water pressure.

State governments were slow to act in respect to oil and gas conservation, even though the state of Oklahoma had passed a constructive conservation law as early as 1915. In the late 1920's there were extensive investigations on the part of committees of Congress, the American Bar Association, and oil associations and producers. The remedies suggested covered many and varied approaches to the problem. The Federal Conservation Board, created in 1924, rendered the last of five reports in 1932 and pointed to the advisability of having the states assume responsibility for the conservation of petroleum in spite of the fact that some thought conditions had reached a point where regulation by the federal government was necessary. Secretary of the Interior Ray Wilbur suggested in 1929 the formation of a compact of states to bring about petroleum conservation. The Oil States Advisory Committee, sometimes known as the "Governors' Committee," organized in 1931, recommended the passage of effective conservation statutes and the formation of an Interstate Oil and Gas Compact Commission. The Cole Committee, after its very thorough investigation of the oil and gas industry, recommended the formation of a compact among the states in its preliminary report to Congress in January, 1935.

From all the thought and study that was given, three general conclusions emerged: (1) Waste prevention could be effectively accomplished only by regulation under proper law; (2) state rather than federal regulation was a course consistent with the rights and obligations of the several states expressed in the Federal Constitution; (3) a compact among the oil-producing states would be a means of effectively carrying a sound conservation program to the national level.

As a result of the need for interstate coöperation in conservation, the Interstate Oil Compact Commission was formed and sanctioned by Congress in 1935. In 1954 the Compact had twenty-two member states and six associate members. The purpose of the Compact has been to assist the various states in the formulation of sound oil and gas conservation programs. All the member states have enacted conservation laws. Many of the states have adopted almost all of the provisions of the suggested conservation act prepared by the Interstate Oil Compact Commission.

The typical oil conservation statute prohibits the waste of oil and gas and defines "waste" to mean not only physical waste but also: (1) the inefficient, excessive, or improper use or unnecessary dissipation of reservoir energy, (2) the locating, spacing, drilling, operating, or producing of any oil or gas well or wells in a manner which causes, or tends to cause, reduction in the quantity of oil or gas ultimately recoverable from a reservoir under prudent and proper operations, and (3) the production of oil and gas in excess of transportation or storage facilities, or in excess of reasonable market demands. The statute empowers an administrative agency of the state to determine at regular intervals the quantity that will be required to meet the demand for oil produced in the state. The quantity so determined must then be allocated among all the pools in the state on an equitable basis, the quantity allocated to a particular pool being its "allowable" production. When there is demand for all the oil that can be produced (as was the case during and for a few years after World War II) the administrative agency determines for each pool its "maximum efficient rate of production"—i.e., the maximum quantity that can be produced without unnecessary injury to the reservoir—and that amount becomes the allowable production for the pool. By whichever method determined, the allowable production for a pool must be prorated among all the wells in the pool in such manner that each producer will be allowed to produce his fair and equitable share of the allowable production.

The Connally Act, enacted by the Congress in 1935, has served to support state limitations on production of oil by prohibiting shipment in interstate commerce of petroleum produced in excess of quotas set by state agencies.

The first achievement of state regulation of petroleum production was the adjustment of output to market demand, which has led to greater market stability. There is little doubt that this is one of the reasons that oil producers, who are rugged individualists, do not consider conservation statutes control of business. As a result of regulation, study, and cooperation, however, there is no question about the fact that much has been accomplished in the maximum efficient recovery and conservation of petroleum. An estimate has been made that 50 percent more oil was recovered between 1932 and 1952 than would have been recovered in the absence of state regulation.

There is one major area in conservation of petroleum production which needs strengthening and that is in achieving a unified program of operations for each oil reservoir best fitted to the particular characteristics of the reservoir. Engineers have solved the technical problems of unit pool operation. The principal obstacle to a unified operation is the inevitable holdout, the leaseholder or royalty owner who thinks he can do better without unit operation, even though the pool as a whole will do much better with unit operation. In some states unit pool operation can be made compulsory when the specified majority of the acreage agree. However, few common sources of supply have been placed under unit operations, except where special conditions make unit operations imperative as in condensate reservoirs or in secondary recovery.

The advantages of unit pool operation have been clearly established. The petroleum industry knows how to operate a pool and has achieved the benefits of such operation where ownership is common in the United States and in overseas areas. The problems involved in multiple ownership can and should be worked out by industry and state legislative and control agencies so that each leaseholder will receive his fair share of the petroleum and maximum recovery can be achieved.

The problems involved in conservation in the more efficient use of petroleum products have also been solved in so far as technology is involved. Refining has been developed to such an extent that with the use of a modern catalytic cracker almost 100 percent of the crude oil can be converted into petroleum products in the proportion in which they are demanded. Improved gasoline mileage must be co-engineered with automobiles. However, the additional possibilities of improving mileage are rather limited unless the public will accept smaller cars or less powerful engines. This appears to be a remote contingency. The President's Materials Policy Commission presented an estimate that a high compression ratio and a fully automatic transmission or suitable overdrive might double automotive efficiency from the usual fifteen or twenty miles per gallon to thirty or forty without any loss in performance characteristics. This accomplishment has already been approximated under good open road conditions and by drivers who are economy minded and trained. However, most of our driving is not under such conditions. Drastic increases in gasoline prices and/or an emergency might bring about great conservation in use.

The conclusion can be drawn that conservation has developed out of a pre-World War II background when domestic production was in excess of consumption for reasons of market stabilization and waste elimination, and has been continued into the present for similar reasons. Most important, however, is that conservation measures have been effectively carried on since World War II to eliminate the discrepancy between domestic consumption and production. The problem is to develop conservation measures to the maximum extent so as to help narrow this gap.

B. Productive Capacity

The real measure of the strength of the petroleum industry is its crude productive capacity at the maximum efficiency rate. The principal problem is the maintenance of a high level of crude productivity with an adequate reserve for normal and emergency requirements. The ideal way to narrow the "gap" is through increased domestic production at the MER with adequate reserves. Basic to this achievement is the discovery and development of new crude reserves.

Economic incentives are in large measure determinant in the discovery and development of crude petroleum. The right of private ownership has been the most powerful driving force to enable the petroleum industry to make false prophets of those who have forecast the imminent exhaustion of petroleum supplies. At the beginning of 1958 petroleum proved reserves were at a record level. The petroleum industry has always contended that given adequate incentives petroleum would be found and produced. The record of performance justifies these claims.

The discovery of new oil is a function of exploration and drilling. The ultimate economic incentive for exploration and drilling is the income received from producing oil less the costs. Income is a function of price times quantity. Although many studies have been made, there is no present evidence that precise measurements can be made of the interaction of income and costs on exploration and drilling.

On the income side, however, there is ample evidence that the state conservation and regulatory agencies perform two important functions: conservation and price stabilization. In so doing, they restrict production to market demand (total domestic and export demand minus imports). Thus the agencies, through regulation of quantities produced and prices received, have a most important effect on total income received by producers of crude. Since United States Gulf prices of crude have an important effect on world prices, the state agencies through stabilized world prices have stimulated exploration, discovery, and development of crude petroleum productive capacity in both domestic and foreign areas. The problem is that, when production is adjusted to "market demand," in almost all instances production is restricted and current total income is less. The most important factor contributing to restriction of production in the post-World War II period has been the rising volume of petroleum imports. This problem is of such magnitude and significance that it will be developed separately as the final petroleum problem.

On the cost side of discovery, development, and production of crude, the petroleum industry is faced with the problem of increased costs. Higher prices for crude form one means of providing the incentive to overcome these additional costs. However, through fiscal policy the United States government has established tax provisions for depletion allowances and expensing which are most powerful means of offsetting these costs and most powerful incentives for the discovery and development of crude productive capacity. The oil producer is allowed depletion of 27½ percent of gross annual income but not to exceed 50 percent of the net income. This deduction is usually made entirely independent of capital investment, and over the life of the property it is possible for the tax-free recovery to reach a total greatly in excess of the investment. Tax provisions on "expensing" provide for deducting as current expenses all intangible "drilling and development costs," which include the bulk of outlays for exploration and development. This policy appears sound as a most significant aid to the petroleum industry.

C. Security and Reserve Capacity

A crude reserve capacity representing the difference between the MER and actual production is required by the petroleum industry in order to provide sufficient flexibility for normal operations. As a result of conservation and regulatory measures, a reserve capacity of 1,000,000 barrels a day was available before World War II that was the reservoir of strength out of which victory was achieved. Similarly, the reserve capacity of 1950, which was declared a sign of "ill health" and a result of imports, was helpful in meeting the increased demands of 1951 and 1952. The Petroleum Administration for Defense set up a program for a reserve productive capacity as a cushion against an emergency, and in October, 1952, a reserve of 1,000,000 barrels per day was a fundamental part of the security program. This reserve should not be a set figure but should be a function of anticipated emergency requirements and normal requirements. It will then be available when manpower and steel are short—but most importantly, when time is short.

How is this reserve capacity to be achieved? How can a producer of crude be expected to be satisfied with curtailed production and a reduction of current income to provide for a future emergency? At the beginning of 1955 the availability of adequate emergency reserve was not a problem, as crude capacity was 8,442,000 barrels per day and capacity of natural gas liquids was 778,000 barrels—a total of 9,220,000 barrels per day. Estimated demand was only 7,350,000.

An additional security reserve problem is that of refining capacity. Refineries offer prime targets for sabotage and aerial bombardment. Here again 1955 offered no immediate problem as there was an excess of refinery capacity. Indeed, a leading investment house listed as the first petroleum problem in 1955 an excess of refining capacity of 15 percent. The same analysis listed as the third most important problem the increasing crude producing capacity of the domestic industry. This excess was estimated at 25 percent. But these were short-run industry problems.

The long-run industry problems requiring national policy were the provision of a reserve of stand-by capacity which would be available in a national emergency, and additional increases of capacity and output that could be provided within a short period of time. The President's Materials Policy Commission concluded that, as the years go by, the normal reserves on which the oil industry bases peacetime production may prove less and less adequate for security purposes. The ratio of output to reserves, although satisfactory in ordinary years, may lack sufficient flexibility to permit a large and sustained increase in withdrawals during an emergency. Two alternative solutions to the problem have been suggested: (1) making extra efforts to find additional reserves and then "sterilizing" them to be tapped only in the event of a national emergency; (2) expanding the industry's working reserves and then maintaining them at abnormally high levels relative to production.

The first solution would require that the United States government build up large military emergency reserves. This might be done on the federal lands of the continental shelf. But exploration and development and the maintenance of wells are expensive under known conditions. In addition, the "sterilized reserve" approach might involve additional heavy costs to provide stand-by refining and transportation facilities so that the reserves could in fact be used if needed.

The second proposed solution is the expansion of proved working reserves so that of crude production would be lowered from the normal rate of 7 to 8 percent of proved reserves to about 5 percent. The President's Materials Policy Commission concluded that in view of recent experience this might be accomplished without altering seriously the normal economics of the industry. However, this recommendation enlarges the practical problem previously presented as to how domestic producers can be satisfied with shut-in production to provide for a future emergency.

The Materials Policy Commission expressed the opinion that:

The most attractive opportunity for approaching the security problem in this way is provided by the Continental Shelf. If private industry were permitted and encouraged to develop these large underwater oil resources and to overcome the technical difficulties involved, but in such a way as to keep the withdrawals at a rate that could be stepped up with reasonable speed in time of emergency, the Nation's security position in oil would be greatly strengthened. This could be accomplished by leasing arrangements (either by the Federal Government or if a portion of the rights are awarded to adjacent States, then by State governments) that would specify spacing of wells and rates of withdrawal, coupled with royalty charges sufficiently low to provide adequate incentive.

The Commission concluded:

The main challenge to industry and Government alike is to find ways of achieving a sufficiently rapid expansion of reserves to make possible a ratio between output and reserves compatible with both rising national production and a healthy oil industry. Any reasonable measure for encouraging similar results in the other oil-producing nations of the Western Hemisphere would contribute much to the security of the free world.

D. Petroleum Imports

The petroleum problem that has been most consistently in the news since the end of World War II is the matter of petroleum imports. From 1923 until 1947 the United States was a net exporter of petroleum supplies. Imports of petroleum have consisted of crude petroleum; residual fuel oil, the heavy black oil left in the bottom of the still after the lighter products have been distilled from crude; and a small quantity of other refined petroleum products. The Western Hemisphere, principally Venezuela, furnished the United States with all imports up until 1947, when crude oil and some refined products began to be imported from the Eastern Hemisphere.

Most United States exports have been refined products to Europe, which is the principal deficiency area in the Eastern Hemisphere. Before World War II Europe's deficiency was met by these exports from the United States and by supplies from the Caribbean and some exports from the Middle East. Some United States exports went to Japan and China, but most of the oil in the Far East was supplied by the Netherlands East Indies. Since World War II these interregional movements have undergone a tremendous change. United States exports to Europe have in large part been replaced by exports from the Middle East, which also has supplied most of the oil for the Far East. The Carribbean continued to supply part of the European deficiency and has been the principal source of United States increased imports. Figure 6.21 gives a comparison of world petroleum trade for 1938 and 1952.

United States imports of crude petroleum and residual fuel increased steadily between 1933 and 1952 with the exception of the war years 1942–44. Total petroleum imports, principally crude and residual fuel oil, averaged 147,000 barrels a day for the period 1933–39. Imports in barrels a day increased from 377,000 in 1946 to 958,000 in 1952, 1,048,-000 in 1953, 1,050,000 in 1954, and 1,248,000 in 1955. The total 1955 imports of crude and residual fuel oil of 1,198,000 barrels a day (Figure 6.24, p. 313) consisted of 272,000 from the Eastern Hemisphere and 926,-000 from the Western Hemisphere. Residual imports were 416,000, almost all from the Western Hemisphere. Venezuela was still the principal Western Hemisphere source of supply of crude and residual fuel oil.

Various estimates have been made of the future import requirements of the United States. The Independent Petroleum Association of America, representing domestic independent oil producers, contended in 1952 that it would be possible to produce all the petroleum that would be required in the United States by 1955. The President's Materials Policy Commission concluded that, regardless of the level of domestic production, imports of petroleum by 1975 probably will be greater than at present and suggested that net imports by 1975 might be 2,500,000 barrels a day, as compared with 540,000 barrels a day in 1950. This was based on peacetime needs. In spite of these differences, it is generally conceded that there will be an increasing gap between domestic production of petroleum and demand. The deficit must be made up by the production of petroleum products from sources other than crude and by imports. Imports are currently the most readily available source.

The effect of this increased volume of imports upon the domestic industry and the security of the United States has been the subject of many discussions and legislative and executive hearings. It gives rise to a basic problem: the establishment and implementation of a petroleum import policy that will maintain a strong domestic industry integrated with international sources of supply, which are necessary to supplement our strength in peacetime and may be absolutely essential in time of war.

Perhaps the reason so much interest centers around petroleum imports is that the basic problem breaks down into many separate problems each of which has numerous implications. Some of these individual problems that require study are the effect of petroleum imports on: production cutbacks, conservation, rate of new discoveries, the coal industry, and national security and international relations.

Imports of petroleum have a direct and immediate effect on crude production because state conservation and regulatory agencies restrict production to market demand (total domestic and export demand minus imports). Thus the producer sees imports as a subtraction from the amount of allowable production. What the independent producers would like is to produce at the MER and import just enough petroleum to sup-

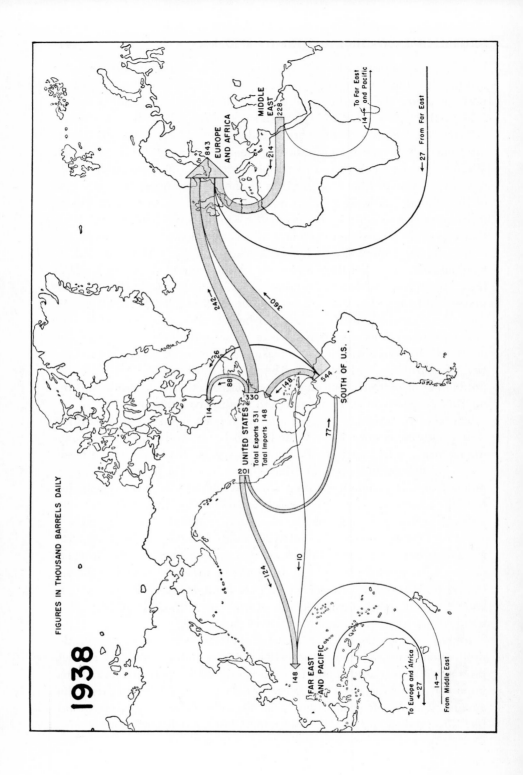

FIGURES IN THOUSAND BARRELS DAILY

1938

EUROPE AND AFRICA 843

MIDDLE EAST 228

To Far East and Pacific 14←

From Far East 27→

214↑

242→

360↓

66↙

88

114↓

330

148↗

544

SOUTH OF U.S.

77↗

UNITED STATES
Total Exports 531
Total Imports 148

201

20↓

124→

10↓

148↓

FAR EAST AND PACIFIC

To Europe and Africa 27→

From Middle East 14→

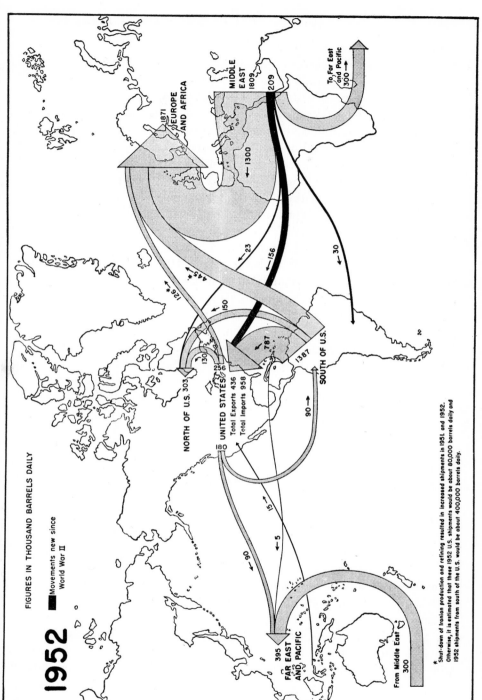

Figure 6.21. World Petroleum Trade, Excluding Russian-Controlled Areas, for 1938 and 1952. (Data from Independent Petroleum Association of America)

plement this amount to satisfy total domestic and export demand. From previous analysis it is clear that this objective would have to be modified to provide for the required reserved productive capacity within the MER. Thus the maximum allowable that national policy would permit would be at the MER minus reserves. Petroleum would be imported to the extent necessary to supplement domestic production so that total domestic and export demand would be met. Under this policy imports become the residual figure in place of production. This simplified suggestion treats a barrel of petroleum supplies as a barrel of crude. The independent producers would approve of this method, but the majors would be quick to point out that separate consideration must be given to crude oil and residual fuel oil.

One argument advanced for imports is that they conserve domestic reserves. At first this seems to be a truism. However, enough has already been said to prove that what is needed is an active productive domestic industry. The industry will accept a policy that imports should "supplement" domestic production but rejects a policy that imports should "supplant" domestic production. Another significant conservation issue is involved in the intra-industry arguments for federal legislation to limit petroleum imports. This is the issue that there is too much danger to state regulation of conservation in this approach. The fear is that if the federal government enters the field of limiting imports in order that imports and domestic production shall not exceed demand, it is only one more step to say that limitation of supply to "market demand" cannot be effectively brought about by federal action unless the federal government at the same time has control over domestic production.

One of the arguments advanced for the limitation of petroleum imports is that they are likely to retard new discoveries and development of petroleum by reducing the incentives of the independents. Since the independents have found about 75 percent of domestic reserves, this is a problem that deserves careful consideration, requiring separate analysis for crude and residual fuel oil. The basic problem is that imports should be maintained at a rate that will supplement and not interfere with the development of adequate crude productive capacity. In many instances crude oil imports supplement domestic production because of the physical characteristics of crude and geographical location. From previous study, the conclusion was drawn that the impact of imports will come primarily through adjustments of production and resultant changes in total income rather than through price. Further, the indirect impact of imports on incentives to develop crude productive capacity is tremendously reduced by much more important direct incentives of stabilized prices and tax incentives.

Residual fuel is a by-product of refinery operations. The value of residual fuel is lower than the price paid for crude oil and hence refiners minimize residual production in order to maximize return from the lighter and more valuable products. Residual is sold in markets that are competitive with coal and its price is determined by this competitive relationship. Hence, both coal and oil industries must be considered in the matter of residual imports. This presents the fourth separate petroleum import problem—the impact on the coal industry. In the discussion of the coal industry the problem of petroleum imports was shown to be an area in which the coal industry had taken vigorous action to place preventive tariffs and import quotas on petroleum supplies.

The principal markets for residual fuel are for ship bunkering, steam locomotives, steam power generating installations, and industrial plants. Many purchasers in the two latter categories have facilities that enable them to switch from one fuel to another. Residual fuel has accounted for 80 to 90 percent of the refined products imported into the United States. About 10 percent of this has been bonded tax free for ships' bunkers. In this use residual is not very competitive with coal because vessels have progressively shifted to the more convenient and efficient residual and Diesel fuel and all the new ships burn oil only. Residual fuel and coal have both been losing their market to Diesel fuel for use in the more efficient Diesel locomotive engine. In electric power generation residual has been losing the market to coal. The competition between coal and residual fuel has been keen in the area of industrial use and space heating, but coal use in this field is still greater than it was during the years 1937–40. It should be further noted that New England requires an adequate supply of residual fuel, which is effectively used in that area because of savings in transportation costs compared with coal due to the all-water shipment of fuel oil. No significant increases in supplies of domestic residuals can be expected during the next few years and there is a rising demand for residual outside the United States accompanied by declining yields. In the analysis of the 1952 Venezuelan Agreement, the State Department definitely concluded: "The United States production of residual falls far short of meeting the demand and the deficit must be met by imports." Thus imports of residual fuel supplement domestic production. However, there is no question about the fact that residual fuel is competitive with coal. But the way to economic progress and productive strength is not through restriction of competition.

The fifth import problem is the effect on national security and international relations, specifically stated as part of the basic problem: the establishment and implementation of a petroleum import policy that will maintain a strong domestic industry integrated with international sources of supply, which are necessary to supplement our strength in peacetime and may be absolutely essential in time of war.

Standard Oil Company (N.J.) argues as follows:

Oil supplies outside the United States, developed by Americans, were highly important in both World Wars I and II.

In World War I the availability of large quantities of Mexican crude oils made it possible for the United States to meet the enormous demand for fuel oil for the Allied navies and merchant ships.

In World War II Venezuela was an important supplier of oil for industry and for the Allied armed forces. In later stages of the conflict, oil from the Middle East was a large part of the fuel used for operations in the Pacific. It is estimated that at the height of the war more than a third of the combined oil requirements of the United States and its Allies for military and shipping needs were being met with oil produced outside the United States. Without Caribbean and Middle East sources to draw on, the military requirements of the United States and its Allies for oil could not have been met.

Today, defense production and the requirements of military establishments within our own borders call for strong domestic fuel industries, with reserve capacity for use in case of emergency. But access to oil sources abroad is also essential. The development of such sources depends to considerable degree on keeping markets open to them, and by far the largest single market is the United States. If American defense were limited to fuel sources within our own borders, our ability to conduct military operations on a broad scale, and to keep aggressors at a distance from our shores, would be handicapped severely.[15]

The Independent Petroleum Association of America argues the point briefly and concisely on its letterhead: "There Is No Security in Foreign Oil for the Defense of Our Own Borders."

Ample evidence has been presented to show that petroleum imports will be required in peace as well as war. The truth of the matter is that the future does not present such black and white alternatives but requires continuous defensive efforts to prevent a major war. The military have recommended an expanding oil development in the following priority: first, the continental United States; second, the Western Hemisphere;

[15] *Facts About Oil Imports*, Standard Oil Company (N.J.), April 15, 1953, p. 9.

and third, other world areas. To implement this policy with respect to imports, a recommended petroleum policy would recognize that the economic development and military security of the Western Hemisphere require that petroleum productive capacity must be available throughout the hemisphere, and that these sources should be given first priority for United States imports. The Western Hemisphere is rapidly becoming a balanced area of petroleum production and consumption. In the event of a major war all the petroleum productive capacity of the Western Hemisphere would be required and rationing for civilian use would be necessary. Oil for war is a hemispheric problem. Therefore, in order to meet economic and military requirements outside the hemisphere, petroleum productive capacity in the Middle East and other areas of the free world should be developed to minimize the use of Western Hemisphere sources and transportation facilities and to maximize non-hemispheric productive capacity. This latter poses the additional problem of threats to the Western Hemisphere industry of imports from the Middle East. However, the degree of security involved in this policy is greater than that for some other commodities, because these resources and productive facilities represent the investments of United States nationals who place national policy first and have a mutual interest in domestic and foreign operations. If we expect other oil-producing regions to supply our emergency requirements market outlets must be provided.

The problem of market outlets is much broader than that of military security as it is an integral part of our national policy to strengthen our national economy and our international interests. In addition, trade is a two-way street; our purchases of imports provide dollars for the purchase of United States exports. Venezuela is an excellent illustration. Venezuela is not only the United States' principal source of oil imports but, as will be seen, also the number one supplier of iron ore imports. In 1952 Venezuela exported $334 million worth of petroleum to the United States. At the same time Venezuela purchased $500 million worth of goods from the United States. These purchases were so varied that every state in the Union exported some kind of product to Venezuela. Thus Venezuela is a primary source of our basic resources and a major purchaser of our exports. The result is a strengthening of both United States and Venezuelan economies. Restrictions on petroleum imports must take into account all these factors. In addition, restrictions invite retaliatory actions.

This writer's conclusion with respect to petroleum imports was included in the report to the President on *A Trade and Tariff Policy in the National Interest,* in February, 1953, by the Public Advisory Board for Mutual Security: "The economy of the United States and the defense of the free world require an adequate supply of petroleum from domestic production and from imports. There is no reason for believing that imports at present interfere with exploration, development, and the growth of proved reserves, on the scale necessary for future defense requirements from domestic sources."

4. A National Petroleum Policy—Government and Industry

A. Government Policy

The Independent Petroleum Association of America was organized in 1929 "for reason that imports of oil at that time were threatening destruction of the domestic petroleum industry." The Association states that "The problem then was solved by an act of Congress in establishing in 1932 an excise tax on the importation of oil. This provides the first policy guide because it constitutes the expressed policy of Congress."

The 1932 excise tax of 21 cents a barrel on crude was an important deterrent to imports of crude when the price of crude was less than $1.00 per barrel. As the price of crude had risen to $2.53 per barrel ($2.78 in 1956) and the tax was reduced under the October, 1952, Supplementary Agreement with Venezuela to $10\frac{1}{2}$ cents per barrel on crude testing 25 degrees API or more and to $5\frac{1}{4}$ cents on crude testing less than 25 degrees API, the tax ceased to have any significance as a deterrent to imports.

The industry has testified that even at 21 cents a barrel the tax was no deterrent to imports at existing prices although some suggestions have been made that it was restrictive. However, most important to the independents is the fact that the existence of a tax is an expressed policy of the United States that domestic petroleum production is to be given protective priority. This expression of protection to the domestic industry was clearly written into the Trade Agreements Extension Act of 1951 through the provision for "peril point" findings and the inclusion of the "escape clause" in subsequent agreements. (The so-called peril point is that point beyond which tariff concessions cannot be made without threatening injury to a domestic industry.)

In the hearings on the Supplementary Agreement with Venezuela, during which discussion was confined principally to crude and residual fuel oil, three of the Tariff Commissioners found that the peril point was a tax of 10½ cents a barrel on crude oil, topped crude, gas oil (including Diesel oil), finished fuel oil, and residual fuel, while the other three Commissioners found that the then existing tax of 10½ cents a barrel and 21 cents a barrel on imports in excess of a quota of 5 percent of the crude petroleum processed in domestic refineries during the preceding calendar year represented the peril point. The peril point findings were based on potential rather than present threats to the industry, although there was no evidence given that the tax would offer a protection against such threats. The findings of all six of the Commissioners were overruled, and the President sent a message to Congress justifying the Supplementary Agreement that went into effect on October 1, 1952.

Hence, the expressed policy through the import-excise tax is that the domestic industry must be protected, that the Tariff Commission is looking into the future for threats, and, in addition, that lighter products should be taxed at higher rates. Other government officials have for years made numerous studies in an attempt to recommend an import policy as a part of a national petroleum policy.

The writer made an intensive study in 1952 of the federal government's petroleum policy and concluded that there was no integrated national petroleum policy. The above import problem was part of the picture. Other parts which have been presented previously are the recognition of the rights of states in the conservation and regulation of crude production and the passage of the Connally Act forbidding the interstate transmission of petroleum which was in violation of quantities authorized by state agencies. Tax allowances of depletion and "expensing" are another significant expression of policy. One of the first official acts of the Eisenhower administration was to modify the Supreme Court decision that the federal government had "paramount rights" to the submerged lands beyond the low-tide mark. Congress gave the coastal states title to the mineral resources of submerged lands to the limit of their historic boundaries—three miles from shore in most instances, 10½ miles in the case of Texas.

There is no clear picture of the government's policy in the world oil field. Instances of lack of coördination are numerous. The classic example is the Middle East, where there was a clear-cut recognition beginning during World War II of the role that Middle East oil would play in the energy economy of the world and the security of the United States. The United States even considered buying directly into the Saudi Arabian concession. Yet, as will be seen in a subsequent discussion of the Middle East, the United States government has advocated policies in direct conflict to the development of this oil interest. In other instances, such as during the Iranian oil crisis, one executive arm of the government (the State Department) was asking the coöperation of a group of international oil companies to help solve the problem (which they did) and at the same time another executive arm (the Attorney General's office) filed an antitrust suit against the oil companies. In another instance the international oil companies had been exempted from antitrust action to participate in an agreement against which the government later filed an antitrust action. The fifteen international petroleum companies were hoping this latter would not be the case with the Middle East Emergency Committee, which was exempted by the Attorney General temporarily from antitrust action while they pooled their resources, rerouted tanker fleets, and exchanged markets to help solve the European oil crisis resulting from the shutting off of Middle East oil by the closure of the Suez Canal and destruction of the Iraq pipeline.

B. Industry Policy

The National Petroleum Council, representing the independents and the majors, at the request of the Secretary of the Interior formulated *A National Oil Policy for the United States,* published in 1949. This recommended policy stated the "Aims of a National Oil Policy," developed the "Fundamental Principles" to a sound policy, and spelled out in detail "The Elements of a National Policy" under five headings: "Domestic Oil," "Natural Gas," "Foreign Oil," "Imports," and "National Security."

"Domestic Oil" recommendations include the following:

1. The key industry function of oil exploration and discovery presents extraordinary difficulties and risks. It is best promoted by competitive effort and by the incentive of commensurate reward.

2. Conservation of our petroleum resources will best be furthered by facilitating continued industry efforts to reduce waste and promote maximum recovery of oil through optimum-rate production, unit operation, secondary recovery, and other methods.

3. The economic and efficient development of synthetic fuels to supplement natural petroleum as needed can best be achieved by private industry.

4. The provisions in tax laws which have long recognized the requirements of petroleum operations are essential to the continued development of our oil resources and, in furtherance of the public interest, should be maintained.

5. The petroleum resources of the lands beneath the marginal seas extending to the outer edge of the continental shelf can best be explored and developed under state, rather than federal, control.

"Foreign Oil" recommendations include the following:

1. The participation of United States nationals in the development of world oil resources is in the interest of all nations and essential to our national security.

2. An effective oil policy should encourage access by our nationals to world oil resources on equal terms with other nationals, and stable agreements between foreign governments and private industry on a basis which will promote development by free enterprise methods.

3. The federal government should encourage foreign oil development by American nationals by efforts directed through diplomatic channels to reduce political risks involved in such foreign operations and by permitting United States citizens to operate abroad in conformity with the laws and customs of other countries.

"Imports" call for a policy that will encourage domestic exploration and development and will make available a maximum supply of domestic oil to meet the needs of the nation "produced under sound conservation practices, together with other pertinent factors." This "provides the means to determine if imports are necessary and the extent to which imports are desirable to *supplement* our oil supplies." It is further recommended that the implementation of the policy "should be *flexible* so that adjustments can be made from time to time."

This policy has been interpreted by some of the independents to mean that no imports will be made if the product can be produced in the United States. However, other international interests have suggested that the "other pertinent factors" phrase includes the necessity of an integrated international petroleum program that will supplement our domestic industry.

"National Security" recommendations are as follows:

1. The maintenance of a vigorous oil industry in time of peace is the best way to assure the reserves and facilities needed in time of war.

2. The government should accumulate such inventories of petroleum products in peacetime as would be needed by the armed services in the early stages of a conflict.

3. Procedures for government-industry consultation should be maintained on a permanent basis so that plans to meet emergencies can be adjusted continually to changing conditions.

C. Government-Industry Coöperation

The petroleum industry has violently opposed all types of government regulation; but where a choice has had to be made, the industry has insisted on state action. Before World War II the industry chose to take action without consultation with, and without interference from, the federal government; at the same time, the industry felt free to call on the federal government for aid—e.g., in the protection of expropriated Mexican oil properties. However, during World War II, the writer can testify from personal experience that the coöperation between the petroleum industry and the federal government was one of the most vital factors in the successful prosecution of the war. This coöperation was achieved in part through the Petroleum Administration for War and the Petroleum Industry War Council and more importantly through direct participation of members of the industry in the war effort. The same type of coöperation has been continued between agencies of government and industry with varying degrees of success since the end of World War II. Two excellent examples of industry advisory committees are the Military Petroleum Advisory Board and the National Petroleum Council. The NPC was set up at the request of government and operates only at government direction. (For example, in January, 1957, Hugh A Stewart, Director of the Interior Department Office of Oil and Gas, said he would ask the National Petroleum Council to take a look at the nation's crude oil reserves for "best appraisal of where we stand with respect to our petroleum reserves and our near-future petroleum situation, perhaps over a five year period.")

In the study made by the writer in 1952 as a member of the staff in preparing *A Trade and Tariff Policy in the National Interest*, the recommendations were made:

1. That the tariffs on petroleum be abolished and in the case of crude oil guides for productive capacity and imports might be the maintenance of a reserve productive capacity at a recommended percentage of estimated demand and/or the maintenance of total crude productive capacity in some flexible relationship to estimated demand. Another measure might be that imports be kept within a long-range flexible percentage of demand.

2. That the implementation of the national petroleum policy to safeguard the domestic petroleum productive capacity and to encourage imports necessary to supplement and strengthen the productive capacity be made the responsibility of the Petroleum Administration for Defense, which should ask for the coöperation of the National Petroleum Council through the established lines of liaison. Thus on the basis of the policy guides which these agencies have formulated, the solution of the proper level of imports and their sources should be achieved by decisions reached through the enlightened leadership of the petroleum industry in coöperation with government agencies responsible for the supply of petroleum for military security purposes. Enforcement should be voluntary action, and compulsory measures when necessary.

3. That the National Security Council serve as a coördinating agency for government national policy and action on international petroleum matters.

Government policy adopted between 1953 and 1957 included voluntary restrictions of petroleum imports, continued industry-government coöperation, and recommendation 3 above.

On July 30, 1954, the President established an Advisory Committee on Energy Supplies and Resources Policy. The Director of the Office of Defense Mobilization was designated as chairman and the heads of the following agencies served as members: Department of State, Treasury, Defense, Justice, the Interior, Commerce, and Labor.

The White House directive respecting the committee's assignment included the following specific statements:

"At the direction of the President the committee will undertake a study to evaluate all factors pertaining to the continued development of energy supplies and resources and fuels in the United States, with the aim of strengthening the national defense, providing orderly industrial growth, and assuring supplies for our expanding national economy and for any future emergency."

On February 26, 1955, the committee reported:

An expanding domestic oil industry, plus a healthy oil industry in friendly countries which help to supply the United States market, constitute basically important elements in the kind of industrial strength which contributes most to a strong national defense. Other energy industries, especially coal, must also maintain a level of operation which will make possible rapid expansion in output should that become necessary. In this complex picture both domestic production and imports have important parts to play; neither should be sacrificed to the other.

Since World War II importation of crude oil and residual fuel oil into the United States has increased substantially, with the result that today these oils supply a significant part of the U.S. market for fuels.

The committee believes that if the imports of crude and residual oils should exceed significantly the respective proportions that these imports of oils bore to the production of domestic crude oil in 1954, the domestic fuels situation could be so impaired as to endanger the orderly industrial growth which assures the military and civilian supplies and reserves that are necessary to the national defense. There would be an inadequate incentive for exploration and the discovery of new sources of supply.

In view of the foregoing, the committee concludes that in the interest of national defense imports should be kept in the balance recommended above. It is highly desirable that this be done by voluntary, individual action of those who are importing or those who become importers of crude or residual oil. The committee believes that every effort should be made and will be made to avoid the necessity of governmental intervention.

The committee recommends, however, that if in the future the imports of crude oil and residual fuel oils exceed significantly the respective proportions that such imported oils bore to domestic production of crude oil in 1954, appropriate action should be taken.

The committee recommends further that the desirable proportionate relationships between imports and domestic production be reviewed from time to time in the light of industrial expansion and changing economic and national defense requirements.

In arriving at these conclusions and recommendations, the committee has taken into consideration the importance to the economies of friendly countries of their oil exports to the United States as well as the supplies both in peace and war.

The extension of the Reciprocal Trade Act in 1955 was accomplished after a bitter fight for federal legislation on oil imports, and only after an amendment which granted the President the authority to take whatever action he deemed necessary to adjust imports of commodities should they threaten to impair the national defense industries. Although the amendment does not mention oil imports, it was said that assurances had been given that its provisions would be used to limit oil imports to 1954 levels in relation to United States production as recommended by the President's Commission.

After the passage of the Reciprocal Trade bill by the Senate, former Secretary of the Interior Douglas McKay told the National Petroleum Council that the industry must limit imports "by voluntary, individual action" to the 1954 level as had been recommended by the President's Commission, or that government action would become necessary. Previously, the National Petroleum Council had adopted a report to the effect that "fair and equitable relationships should obtain at all times between total imports of crude oil and its products and total demand for oil in the United States."

On May 25, 1955, Standard Oil Company (N.J.) announced a "voluntary" program of limiting petroleum imports. Crude oil imports in 1955 were to be held at 1954 levels. Imports of refined petroleum products (mainly residual fuel) for April through December, 1955, were scheduled at a rate 4½ percent higher than in the same period of 1954. The 4½ percent rise corresponded to an increase of 4½ percent in United States production of crude oil.

The Independent Petroleum Association of America continued its battle for limitation of petroleum imports. In 1956 the Association presented Figure 6.22 to show the rising volume of total imports (crude oil and refined products) and the extent to which total imports were in excess during 1954, 1955, and 1956 of the 1954 ratio. Imports had increased steadily and were scheduled to average about 1,530,000 barrels daily during the second half of 1956. The excess of the 1954 relationship of imports to production averaged 120,000 barrels daily in 1955 and about 200,000 barrels daily during the first half of 1956. The announced programs of the importing companies indicated an average excess of about 370,000 barrels a day for the second half of 1956. Indications were that about 300,000 barrels of this would be crude.

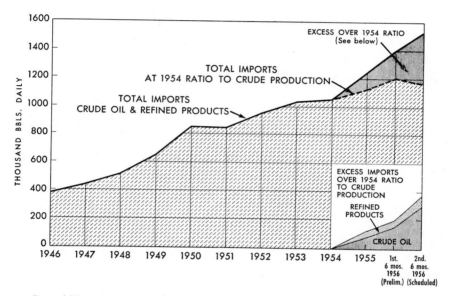

Figure 6.22. U.S. Oil Imports. (Data from Independent Petroleum Association of America)

The directors of the IPAA gave the officers of the Association a mandate in April, 1956, to accomplish effective restriction of oil imports to establish "proper relationships between imports and domestic production." In addition the Association met with the officers and authorized spokesmen of eighteen state and regional associations in Washington in July, 1956, and in joint action these groups recognized that Dr. Arthur S. Flemming, director of ODM, had made sincere but unsuccessful efforts "to bring about voluntary import limitations in compliance with Government policy and the intent of Congress." In addition these groups petitioned the Office of Defense Mobilization to:

"1. Recognize that petroleum imports have been in such quantities as to impair the national security and threaten to continue to do so to an increasing extent, and

"2. Recommend immediately to the President that he take formal action, under the authority provided in Section 7 of the Trade Agreements Extension Act of 1955 so as to limit imports to their 1954 relationship to production as intended by the Congress."

In explaining this action to the Association members the IPAA president Robert L. Wood concluded:

"Further postponement of a solution can only hasten the liquidation of the domestic petroleum industry.

"If our industry is essential to the defense of the Nation, and obviously it is, *I do not believe Government has any alternative except prompt and effective import limitations."

Dr. Flemming of the ODM acknowledged the petition and indicated that he would act on it initially by holding public hearings in the fall of 1956.

The government's 1956 position was expressed in a conservative fashion in a major address on "Petroleum Imports" to the Interstate Oil Compact Commission by Herbert Hoover, Jr., Under Secretary of the State Department. Mr. Hoover drew in this address the identical conclusions that our study has already indicated. As for action on imports he reviewed the alternative courses considered by the President's Committee on Energy Supplies and Resources Policy.

The first was to increase our duties or taxes on oil imports. This was rejected because it would have restrained imports from high-cost areas which were important to our national defense and imposed special hardships on close neighbors in the Western Hemisphere. To avoid this would have required discriminatory policies which would have violated a policy embodied in almost all of our commercial treaties.

The second alternative course was to impose quota limitations on oil imports. This was not accepted for the reasons mentioned above. But in addition Mr. Hoover explained:

From the practical standpoint, quotas are extraordinarily difficult to administer. They can—and usually do—become a source of continuing international frictions, misunderstandings and pressures. It would have been necessary to set up some administrative agency to determine how much oil should be imported, and from what countries it might come. Each of these countries would then have to determine what amounts might be imported by each country. Country, and company quotas in turn, would have to be based on historical averages. This would have the effect of denying access to countries and importers who might not already have been included in the historical base period. Such a method would have placed shackles on an industry whose dynamic qualities should be fostered rather than hampered. Sources of production would tend to be frozen, and progress and flexibility to meet changing circumstances would be defeated.

Within the United States, quotas would inevitably lead to governmental price fixing, and ultimately to further controls and regimentation. It would be an open invitation to controversies between the producing countries as to quotas to be assigned, conflicts between domestic producing and consuming interests, and a rigidity covering the entire industry at a time when flexibility is required to meet rapidly changing conditions. I do not believe that any of you in the petroleum industry wants to be placed in this sort of straight [strait] jacket.

The third alternative course, and the one which was adopted by the President's Advisory Committee, was and is that of individual, voluntary restraint by the petroleum-importing companies. As we have seen, the Committee believed that every effort should be made to avoid the necessity of government intervention.

Mr. Hoover pointed out that there was a need for flexibility in application of the formula itself which had already been recognized in the letters implementing the Committee's recommendations Dr. Flemming had sent to the importing companies under the dates of October 29, 1955, and May 11, 1956. These had to do with adjustments for specific geographic needs (e.g., the west coast), sources of supply (e.g., Canada and Venezuela), and the nature of crude and of pipeline facilities. Along this line Mr. Hoover concluded: "To lump together figures for the United States as a whole, as has been done on some occasions, tends to create a distortion of the true facts." Figure 6.22 does "lump together figures for the United States as a whole."

Mr. Hoover expressed the opinion that "By providing flexibility in the application of the import formula and by relying on individual, voluntary coöperation of the importing companies, rather than on rigid formulas, I believe that we have thus far experienced a large measure of success in handling the problems that were so urgent at the time the President appointed the Committee in July 1954." The statement appears to be in direct conflict to the conclusions of the president of the IPAA.

The director of the Office of Defense Mobilization has the responsibility, under the Trade Agreements Extension Act of 1955, to advise the President if he has reason to believe that any article is being imported into the United States in such quantities as to impair the national security. In such an event, the President would determine what steps would be taken.

Dr. Flemming's letter of May 11, 1956, indicated that the Committee on Energy Supplies and Resources Policy considered it desirable to re-examine by September 1, 1956, the import formula in the light of industrial expansion and changing economic and national defense requirements. Following this reëxamination the Committee was to review the petroleum import situation and, if it had reason to believe that import programs were threatening to impair the national security, was to recommend the scheduling of a public hearing not later than October 1, 1956, under the provisions of Section 7 of the Trade Agreements Extension Act of 1955.

On October 29, 1956, Dr. Flemming reported to the Independent Petroleum Association of America:

I am not in a position to determine at this time whether or not a certification that imports into this country threaten to impair the national security should be made to the President on the basis of the recent hearings held in Washington under the Trade Agreements Extension Act of 1955.

I can outline, however, the steps I have taken and intend to take:

No evidence has been presented which would change the conclusion reached by the Presidential Advisory Committee on Energy Supplies and Resources in its report of October 17th to the effect that the import programs for the third and fourth quarters of 1956 would constitute, if continued into 1957, a threat to our national security. I have decided, therefore, as Director of Defense Mobilization, to accept that conclusion.

As soon as the projected import schedules for the four quarters of 1957 have been received from all oil importers, they will be analyzed to determine their relationship to the objective set by the Advisory Committee in its February 1955 report. This analysis will include a careful review of proposed imports from Canada and Venezuela into Districts I–IV, as well as a review of proposed imports from all sources into District V in order to determine whether present exemptions should be continued. . . .

After the analysis has been completed, I will ask the members of the Presidential Advisory Committee to advise me on the kind of specific recommendations that should be made to oil importers relative to their import plans for the four quarters of 1957, if the Committee's over-all objective is to be achieved. It is clear that such recommendations will be necessary because government alone is in a position to analyze the total picture.

Each oil importer will be asked to give us a clear indication of whether or not he plans voluntarily to follow government's recommendations. We will ask the oil importers to provide us with this information not later than Nov. 26th.

Not later than December 1, I will decide whether or not I have reason to believe that the plans of the importers for the four quarters of 1957 constitute a threat to our national security. If I find they do, I will, of course, under the provisions of Section 7 of the Trade Agreements Extension Act, certify that finding to the President.

If on the other hand, the importers indicate their intention to follow government's recommendations, the Office of Defense Mobilization will keep the matter under continuous surveillance in order to act promptly, under the provisions of the Trade Agreements Act, if the factual situation should change in such a manner as to call for such action.

I desire to underline the fact that this Administration, because of its conviction that there is a definite relationship between the level of imports of crude oil and our national security, is going to stay with this problem until a solution is arrived at which is consistent with our national security requirements.

Dr. Flemming did not deliver his December 1, 1956, decision because during the month of November the Middle East crisis broke in all its fury with the Anglo-French-Israeli invasion of Egypt, the blockage of the Suez Canal, the damage to the Iraq pipeline and the resultant curtailment of the flow of Middle East Oil. The problem by December 1, 1956, had become the provision of emergency supplies of oil to Europe.

The Independent Petroleum Association of America was quick to release the pre-Suez crisis import plans of the majors and to make the following comment:

Planned imports of crude oil show that when interruption of oil transportation from the Middle East is overcome, domestic producing industry will be in tightest squeeze yet. World flow of oil now is affected by Middle East conditions, but importing companies' plans for future are clearly indicated in their 1957 schedules as submitted to the Office of Defense Mobilization last month.

77 per cent increase over 1954 imports is reflected in importing companies' plans for 1957, and total also would amount to 31 per cent rise over the first six months of 1956. The planned 1957 imports of crude oil average 1,160,000 barrels daily, up 270,000 barrels from the first half of 1956 and about 500,-000 barrels daily over the 1954 level. Planned 1957 imports of non-Canadian and non-Venezuelan crude oil into Districts I–IV show an increase of 11 per cent over the first six months of 1956 as compared with the reduction of 1 per cent recommended Oct. 17, 1956, by the Advisory Cabinet committee. Planned imports of Venezuelan crude into Districts I–IV show an increase of 33 per cent for 1957 over the first half of 1956. Planned imports into District V during 1957 average 255,000 barrels daily, 102,000 barrels daily or 67 per cent above the first half of 1956. Two-thirds of this planned increase of 102,000 barrels daily are from Eastern Hemisphere sources, in direct conflict with the Cabinet committee's recommendation that emphasis be placed on imports from Western Hemisphere sources.

Some importers will exceed recommendations directly and substantially. Others give the appearance of compliance by shifting imports between restricted and non-restricted countries of origin or U.S. districts. This provides little or no net gain in terms of national security or adherence to basic import policy. Planned crude oil imports for 1957 are in conflict with all of the recommendations in the October 17 report of the Cabinet committee.

IPAA submitted statement to ODM pointing out that importing company

plans for next year seriously violate government import policies and constitute
a threat to national security. The association stresses the fact that the imports problem has not been solved by Middle East situation, that, on the
contrary, the sudden interruption of Middle East shipments serves to point
up critical need for a permanent solution that would provide domestic industry a fair share of market and incentive to find and develop additional oil
reserves in this country.

Government and industry cooperation and the national petroleum
policy were sorely tested by the Suez-Middle East crisis. Every phase
of the oil industry was affected.

The dependence of western Europe on Middle East oil has already
been established and we saw that in 1955 western Europe used almost
2,400,000 barrels a day with a domestic production of less than 200,000
barrels. The Materials Policy Commission estimated that Europe's consumption would be 4,000,000 barrels a day in 1975 and that 3,700,000
barrels a day imports would be required. In the first half of 1956 the
Organization for European Economic Cooperation (the seventeen Marshall Plan countries) had, just prior to the Middle East crisis, called the
world's attention to *Europe's Growing Needs of Energy: How They Can
Be Met*. This report as summarized below by *U.S. News and World Report* on October 5, 1956, after Egypt's seizure of the Suez but prior to the
shutting off of oil supplies, shows how conservative the Materials Policy
Commission was and points up the interdependence of western Europe
and the Middle East.

European prosperity is increasingly dependent on oil—mainly Middle East
oil. The Suez trouble provides a somber background for startling predictions
on future oil needs of Western Europe, just made by experts of the 17-nation
Organization for European Economic Co-operation. Here are some high lights:

Oil has to meet more and more of Europe's fuel requirements. *Coal* production in Europe is leveling off. *Atomic power* will be a minor factor for years.
Demand for fuel and power is to continue rising sharply.

Oil consumption in Western Europe climbed from 37 million tons in 1947
to 100 million in 1955. By 1960, a little more than three years off, a further
50 per cent rise is expected. And, in 1975, consumption will be three and a
half times what it was in 1955. The experts believe these estimates are conservative.

Oil production in West Europe is to double the 1955 volume by 1960 and
to quadruple that volume by 1975. But output still will be small compared
to needs.

Oil imports, therefore, must shoulder most of the impact of increased needs.
Net imports will go from 84 million tons in 1955 to 147 million in 1960 and
on up to 334 million in 1975. Currently, more than 90 per cent of crude oil
shipped into Western Europe comes from the Middle East.

Moving such huge quantities of oil means not only that the Suez must be kept open but that it must be widened and deepened; new pipelines will be necessary both in the Middle East and in Europe; many large tankers must be added to the world's fleet; harbors must be prepared to handle big tankers; new refinery capacity will have to be built in Europe; distribution facilities and inland storage will have to be expanded. *Capital cost* of all this will be enormous.

Paying for oil imports of such size is another terrific headache. Western Europe's oil bill last year ran about 2 billion dollars. The 1960 bill is thought likely to be in the 3-billion range. The 1975 cost may be 8 billion!

The OEEC report shows how mutually dependent Europe and the Middle East really are. Europe must have the oil. The Middle East must have the cash.

The United States policy was to strengthen Europe, and requisite to this was a sustained supply of oil.

On the supplying end of the oil, the United States should have had a clear-cut oil policy because of the interdependence of Europe and the Middle East, and because of the dominant ownership of Middle East oil by United States oil companies (see Figure 6.23). Similarly, there was a most emphatic reason for a clear-cut coöperative United States government-industry policy.

The Middle East oil crisis developed rapidly after July, 1956, when President Nasser of Egypt seized the Suez Canal shortly after the United States refused a once offered loan for a high Aswan dam. In August, 1956, the Middle East Emergency Committee was created with the approval of the government by fifteen United States oil companies to develop plans in the event the Canal was closed. In September, 1956, officials of United States crude-producing states and the United States government said that United States reserve oil-producing capacity was 2,250,000 barrels a day. (Other estimates were 2,000,000.) State officials said the reserves included: Texas, 1,067,000; New Mexico, 50,000; Louisiana, 300,000; and Oklahoma, 125,000. In October President Eisenhower asked for and the Office of Defense Mobilization and the National Petroleum Council began studies looking toward fifty new super tankers with capacities up to 60,000 tons each.

In October and November, Israel, Britain, and France launched an attack on Egypt. The Suez Canal was blocked with sunken ships and bridges. The Iraq Petroleum Company's pipeline to the Mediterranean and pump stations were blown up in Syria (see Figure 6.23). Saudi Arabia refused to let her crude oil be delivered to the British or French. About 2,000,000 barrels per day of Middle East crude oil transportation was shut off.

In November a cease-fire was arranged at the request of the United

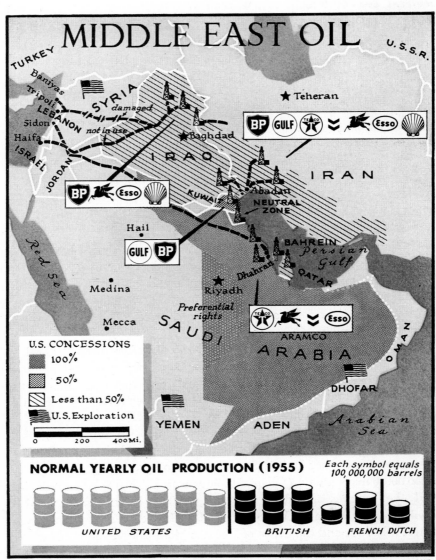

TIME Map by J. Donovan. Copyright Time Inc., 1957.

Figure 6.23. "Middle East Oil. Though Britain has populated the Middle East with British political advisers to Arab rulers, and for a time seemed to be running the whole show, in economic fact the region has in recent years been dominated by U.S. companies, who stay out of local politics. They produce about twice as much of the Middle East's oil as the British, and own nearly 60 percent of the area's known reserves. Tiny, treeless Kuwait, the richest producing state in the rich Middle East is, for example, a sheikdom under British protection and equipped with a British political agent, but its British producing company is half-owned by Gulf Oil (U.S.). Americans also team up with British, Dutch and French interests in Iraq. But Saudi Arabia's Aramco is entirely an American concession—a syndicate formed by Standard Oil of California, the Texas Co. and Jersey Standard Oil (Esso), plus a smaller share to Socony Mobil Oil." (*Time*, January 28, 1957)

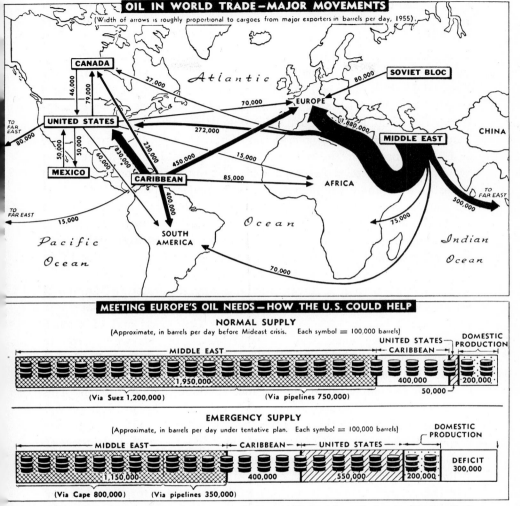

Figure 6.24. World Oil Picture—and the Problem of Western Europe's Supply. (*The New York Times*, November 25, 1956)

States through the United Nations and U.N. forces entered Egypt. The Middle East Emergency Committee revised its plans, and the individual oil companies reallocated and rerouted their petroleum supplies. The Committee and the United States government worked out the plan of supply presented in Figure 6.24; but the United States government refrained from authorizing the plan's implementation pending Great Britain's and France's agreement to withdraw from Egypt.

In December Britain and France agreed to withdraw from Egypt and on December 11, 1956, the United States government formally "invited" the fifteen oil companies to initiate the emergency oil lift to Europe. Dr. Arthur S. Flemming, director of the ODM, made public the agreement with the participating companies and the approval of Attorney General Herbert Brownell temporarily exempting the firms from anti-trust action. Administrative officials urged the Attorney General to approve the plan "lest the Suez crisis alienate the Western allies" as a result of the "rising tide of criticism of the United States, particularly in Europe," based on "the belief that we are withholding assistance which would prevent the oil shortages; and because of the crippling of European industry, widening unemployment, and the 'major importance' of orderly oil movements to the United States Armed Forces." Senator Joseph C. O'Mahoney (D., Wyo.) charged that the agreement created an "international cartel" that would manage the country's oil policy. Dr. Flemming replied: "We are not going to permit the companies to do anything that would be contrary to public policy."

The "plan of action" as it was called officially, illustrated in Figure 6.24 was based on the "lifting" of about 850,000 barrels of oil daily—in excess of the normal pickup—from United States Gulf ports and to a small extent from Venezuela. About 500,000 barrels of this were to go to Europe and the rest to United States and Canadian east coast cities, to replace the normal shipments of oil from Middle East producing areas.

Also in December, 1956, oil product rationing and restriction plans were completed in Europe, and even with the MEEC plans, Europe was from 20 to 25 percent short. In the United States, the ODM suspended action on limiting imports in view of the falling imports and increased demands for United States crude.

By the end of January, 1957, crude oil production in the United States had been stepped up by about 500,000 barrels a day to a new peak of 7,450,000. Drawing rather heavily on crude oil stocks, the shipments of petroleum and products to Europe directly and indirectly from the Gulf coast averaged about 500,000 barrels a day in the last two months of 1956. But this included refined products. On February 9, 1957, *Business Week* reported: "The fact that U.S. oil deliveries to Europe are running well under the daily goal of 500,000 barrels of crude oil we set is a sorry comedown of the optimistic statements made a few weeks ago."

World Petroleum described the Middle East oil crisis in January, 1957, as follows:

The world oil industry is going through one of its great dramas today as it meets the oil transportation shortage growing out of the Middle Eastern crisis. Following preliminary meetings, it appears that the United States government and the American petroleum industry have laid plans which indicate the free world can get along adequately, but with Europe on short rations, even with the Suez Canal and the Iraq Petroleum Co. pipelines shut down.

All plans at this time have been made on the basis that the situation will not get worse and that the Trans-Arabian pipeline will continue to operate. One school of thought holds that the free world could meet even that kind of disaster without utter catastrophe.

There were many *short-run* problems and effects arising out of the Middle East oil crisis and there were sure to be important *long-run* effects.

The *short-run* problems began when the Texas Railroad Commission, which controls 45 percent of the United States oil production, refused to increase the allowables appreciably. The background of this problem was that the independent oil men had been seeking an increase in the price of crude, and they believed that this was justified because since 1947 costs had increased 50 percent, while crude oil prices had increased only 21 percent. This they had hoped to secure in 1956, but rising stocks offset this possibility. They also wanted increased market demand through reduced imports, which would have enabled them to increase production and obtain more income at the same price. When the increased market demand came as a result of the western European demands, the independents prevailed upon the Texas Railroad Commission not to increase the production allowables on the grounds that stocks should be drawn down as an economic waste-prevention-conservation measure. The net result was that, since the major exporters were having difficulty purchasing the crude, the price was increased by 12 percent, to $3.25 per barrel. This action was described: "By taking advantage of an international emergency to ram through a price boost, the industry runs the risk of earning a Shylock reputation in the eyes of the world." This description shows how action by the independents, even though opposed by the majors, brought criticism upon "the industry." Another important implication was the possible misuse of state regulatory authority.

The independents, even though they had wanted larger allowables before the Middle East oil crisis by reducing imports, insisted that the emergency increases requested would result in surpluses as soon as the temporary European shortage was alleviated. The independents argued that the way to solve the European deficiency was for the majors to divert the petroleum imports from Venezuela to Europe instead of using them to supply their east coast refineries. This the majors were unwilling to do until and unless domestic production was made available fast enough to make up the differences necessary to supply the United States markets.

Another short-run problem arose when the United States government requested that refiners voluntarily cut down on the amount of crude oil they were using, to free it for European markets, and to adjust their refinery yield from gasoline and higher fractions to produce fuel oil for export. This the majors were reluctant to do, and they were partially supported by the independents, who suggested that Europe should import refined products, especially gasoline, so as to reduce the United States stocks. But the European countries did not want gasoline because the high cost of this and other refined products would reduce their dollar balances and force additional shutdowns in the European refineries.

These and other short-run problems brought about temporary effects, some of which could be of lasting duration. For example, even *Business Week* made this editorial comment: "It seems obvious that the way to tackle an emergency situation—such as the task of supplying oil to Europe over the critical next few months—is not to ask the oil industry voluntarily to do something that is against the companies' own business interests. In effect, that is asking commercial companies to volunteer to be noncommercial. The wiser course of action would be for the Administration to use what emergency powers it has—or to acquire from Congress such powers as it needs—to issue the necessary orders to the oil industry to get more crude oil flowing to Europe."

The fact was that once again public criticism would be levied against the industry, and that many investigations would be initiated. But this was nothing new; the industry was accustomed to being a "whipping boy" even when it was doing a good job in performing a most difficult operation. It could argue (at least the majors could) that industry policy and implementation of the supply of energy to western Europe over a long-run period and the Suez emergency had been more consistent than the United States government policy.

The Middle East oil crisis was sure to have *long-run* and permanent effects on the petroleum industry in the areas of transportation, sources of supply, and government-industry policy.

Pipeline revisions and additions were a possibility in the United States, in Europe, and in the Middle East. In the United States there was a definite probability that the Little Inch line, which was constructed during World War II to carry petroleum and changed to natural gas after the war, would be converted to an oil products system from the Gulf coast to the east coast. In addition, crude oil producers in West Texas felt the need for additional crude-carrying capacity to tidewater on the Gulf coast.

In Europe there was reconsideration of a proposed pipeline from the French Mediterranean coast through Europe to the North Sea. This would free many tankers carrying oil from pipeline terminals to western Europe.

In the Middle East several new pipelines were being planned. Two big-inch lines through Turkey, one from Kuwait and one from Iraq, were under consideration as a result of unstable conditions in Syria and Lebanon. A pipeline from the Gulf of Aqaba through Israel to the Mediterranean was proposed. Such a pipeline would be in Israel's interest.

Tanker programs were initiated and being developed during the emergency that would be of tremendous importance. President Eisenhower addressed a letter to the director of the ODM asking for studies looking toward more tankers in which he pointed out that the authority existed to order vessels built for the government. Dr. Flemming of the ODM asked the members of the NPC to rush a report on tankers planned or being built through 1965—United States and world-wide. There was the possibility that a "crash" super tanker program would be undertaken to enable shipment around the African cape rather than through the Suez Canal at reduced costs. The independents were very critical of the tanker programs, but Dr. Flemming was quick to point out to them a paragraph which was included in President Eisenhower's letter to him: "The study should proceed, of course, on the assumption that plans which are developed are to be consistent with the requests that you have made to oil importers to voluntarily keep imports of crude oil into this country at a level where they do not exceed significantly the proportion that imports bore to the production of domestic crude oil in 1954."

Search for new sources of petroleum reserves were sure to be sought after with added incentive and with renewed emphasis on strategic considerations. Exploratory work might be undertaken in Africa. Immediate long-run impacts were expanded plans in Canada and Venezuela. The strategic importance of Western Hemisphere sources would be a dramatic and lasting impression of the Middle East oil crisis. United States officials were urging a stronger reserve-producing capacity in the United States, Canada, and elsewhere in the hemisphere. Three times this reserve had proved its value, before World War II, before the Korean War boom, and before the Middle East crisis.

The independents were encouraged by a *long-run* policy effect stressed by Dr. Arthur S. Flemming, who, as Defense Mobilizer, was the key governmental official: "We certainly are not going to take any step to undermine the U.S. domestic industry. If anyone needed evidence of the wisdom of a national policy to keep this country strong in oil, he has it now. If anyone needed evidence of the need for a high domestic mobilization base, and for adequate incentive for exploration, it's on the record."

To the above statement should be added: *If anyone needed evidence of a sound long-range government-industry coöperative international oil policy, he has it now.*

In April, 1957, Gordon Gray, who succeeded Dr. Flemming as director of ODM, certified to President Eisenhower that he had "reason to believe that crude oil is being imported in such quantities as to threaten to impair national security." This certification was based on reports from importers that crude imports in the last six months of 1957 would average 1,261,000 barrels daily—an excess of 510,000 barrels over the 1954 ratio of imports to domestic production. The authority for the certification was Section 7 of the 1955 Trade Agreements Extension Act, which required the ODM director to notify the President when imports of any commodity threaten to endanger the national security. If the President concurs, he has authority to take whatever steps he deems necessary to control such imports. President Eisenhower agreed publicly that such a danger might exist and announced the White House would make its own investigation. He also asked Gordon Gray to try again to win voluntary coöperation from importers.

In conclusion, the policy pattern developing is one of government-industry coöperation, voluntary action, the avoidance of federal government regulation at all costs, and a preference for states' rights and regulation where necessary.

NATURAL GAS

Natural gas developed as a by-product of the search for and production of crude petroleum. The development of an almost nation-wide transmission system has brought about tremendous expansion of the industry. The natural gas industry is divided into three parts: production and gathering, interstate transmission by pipeline, and distribution to consumers by local distribution companies. In the United States natural gas is produced by about 8100 companies—eight of these are large oil companies which produce 28 percent of the total. About half of the total production is sold to industrial users in the gas fields. Most of the remainder is sold to over 100 transmission companies, which move the gas through about 500,000 miles of pipelines for sale to local public utilities, which distributed and sold the gas to about 24 million customers in 1955.

Figure 6.6 shows that between 1914 and 1956 the petroleum and natural gas industry had grown tremendously, and that natural gas's share as a source of United States energy had increased from 3 to 26 percent of the total.

1. Production

Public utilities distribute natural gas and manufactured gas to consumers. The growing giant of a gas industry moved ahead with Paul Bunyan strides during the post-World War II period ending in 1955. At that latter date about 95 percent of all the gas sales in the United States was natural gas. Thus for the present, the United States is primarily concerned with natural gas. In this study, our attention is focused on primary natural energy sources. However, for comparative purposes, world gas production is given in Table 45. From this table the dominant position of the United States is clearly discernible. Production of natural gas is concentrated in the United States and Venezuela. Increased production of natural gas between 1935–39 and 1957 was more than five fold in the United States and slightly more than nine times in Venezuela. Most remarkable is that natural gas production in the United States increased 82 percent from 1950 to 1956. On the other hand, production of manufactured gas in the United States declined continuously from the World War II period, 1940–44.

Natural gas is produced in twenty-eight states, but about 87 percent comes from seven states—Mississippi, Louisiana, Arkansas, Texas, Oklahoma, Kansas, and New Mexico. In 1954 marketed production was 8743 billion cubic feet. Texas supplied 4551 billion cubic feet, or over 50 percent of the total, and Louisiana produced 1399 billion cubic feet, over 16 percent of the total. Total supply available is made up of this marketed production of 8743 billion cubic feet from wells plus withdrawals from underground storage, which amounted to 330 billion cubic feet in 1954. Thus total available supply in 1954 was 9073 billion cubic feet. Underground storage is used as a reservoir to which natural gas is brought from

TABLE 45. World Gas Production
(in millions of cubic meters[a])

Year	Natural Gas			Manufactured Gas								
	Canada	United States[h]	Venezuela	Australia[b]	Austria	Belgium	Canada	France	Japan[c]	Netherlands[d]	United Kingdom	United States
1935–39 av.	872	35,552[f]	3,013[e]	570	303	719[e]	429[f]	1,692[f]	991	1,140	9,916[g]	10,868[g]
1940–44 av.	1,245	49,711	3,816	741	390	658	540	1,754	1,369	1,160	10,829	13,431
1945	1,371	61,044	7,257	889	103	443	664	1,920	426	401	12,120	15,022
1946	1,356	62,160	9,381	905	230	800	686	2,448	320	960	13,368	15,684
1947	1,491	71,220	11,402	946	240	897	696	2,448	493	1,184	13,776	17,160
1948	1,659	81,972	11,760	1,028	338	1,698	725	2,520	744	1,404	14,388	16,716
1949	1,712	88,008	14,066	1,040	364	1,632	733	2,448	913	1,449	14,676	15,948
1950	1,921	105,132	11,160	988	357	1,446	766	2,424	1,070	1,596	15,360	15,948
1951	2,250	123,948	14,400	1,073	305	1,728	797	2,436	1,397	1,680	15,948	14,892
1952	2,508	134,604	17,520	1,144	298	1,776	745	2,484	1,617	1,752	16,140	13,836
1953	2,856	145,260	21,720	1,169	292	1,764	733	2,484	1,908	1,752	15,984	12,636
1954	3,480	158,232	23,400	1,196	330	1,944	745	2,592	2,124	1,884	16,620	12,516
1955	4,100	176,700	27,400	1,226	346	2,076	550	2,496	2,352	2,004	17,016	12,816
1956	4,100	191,760	29,500	1,264	420	2,240	525	2,610	2,772	2,136	17,124	11,916

[a] 1 cubic meter is equal to 35.31445 cubic feet. [b] Twelve months ending June 30 of year stated. [c] Gas works only. [d] Gas delivered. [e] Average for 1936 to 1939. [f] Average for 1937 to 1939. [g] Average for 1938 only. [h] Gas sold by public utilities, representing 52–59% of total production.
Sources: United Nations; Commodity Year Book, 1956 and 1957.

its original location for the primary purpose of storage during the summer months to be drawn upon during peak loads in winter.

2. Consumption

Distribution of the total supply of natural gas billions of cubic feet in 1954 was as follows: consumption, 8403; exports, 29; stored, 432; lost, 255; total 9119. Consumption of natural gas in billions of cubic feet by end-use in the United States is given in Table 46 for 1954 as compared with 1945, 1953, and 1955.

TABLE 46. Consumption of Natural Gas in the United States
(billions of cubic feet)

	1945	1953	1954	1955
Residential	607	1,686	1,894	2,140
Commercial	230	531	585	665
Industrial	3,063	5,763	6,176	6,317
Field	(917)	(1,471)	(1,457)	(1,617)
Carbon black	(432)	(301)	(247)	(240)
Petroleum refineries	(339)	(589)	(563)	( )
Portland cement plants	(38)	(115)	( )	( )
Other industrial	(1,337)	(3,317)	(3,909)	(4,460)
Total consumption	3,900	7,979	8,655	9,122
Electric public utility power plants[a]	326	1,034	1,165	1,225

[a] Figures include gas other than natural gas (impossible to segregate), therefore shown separately from other consumption.

SOURCE: Bureau of Mines; *Commodity Year Book*, 1956.

From Table 46 the growth of consumption by users is clear. Residential use is the most rapidly growing market. As previously mentioned, the increase in natural gas has come largely through discoveries resulting from the search for oil and the rapid development of gathering and transportation facilities to carry the gas to markets. Markets have been developed near the source of production where gas prices have been far below those of competitive fuels for the energy contained, while in the more remote markets consumption has been stimulated both by the superiority of natural gas in specialized uses and by favorable prices.

Estimates indicate that natural gas markets will continue to grow. The American Gas Association predicted that in 1957 sales would be made to 25.7 million customers. The President's Materials Policy Commission concluded: "There is no doubt that a potential market exists for all the natural gas that can be produced, transported, and distributed in the United States, so long as it is offered at prices more favorable than for other fuels for the energy contained. The future position of natural gas in the energy economy, therefore, depends on how much more of that fuel is discovered and how efficiently the Nation recovers and uses that which is found."

3. Reserves

Proved "economically recoverable reserves" of natural gas in the United States at the close of 1950 were 186 trillion cubic feet, or about twenty-six times the 1950 net production of 7.1 trillion cubic feet. The American Gas Association reported that at the beginning of 1956 the total proved recoverable reserves were at a new high level of 223.7 trillion cubic feet. This was a gain of 12 trillion cubic feet over the record figure of 211.7 in 1955. During 1955, 5.7 trillion cubic feet of new natural gas reserves were discovered, and 16.3 trillion cubic feet were added to recoverable reserves by further exploration and drilling in existing fields. Hence, what counts is proved reserves plus new discoveries and new developments minus production. Production in 1955 was 10 trillion cubic feet. Part of production is added to underground storage of natural gas. Almost 87.6 billion cubic feet was added to reserves in underground storage during 1955.

The Materials Policy Commission reported in 1950 that the only well-known projection of the "economically recoverable" reserves expected to be discovered in the future indicated that 510 trillion cubic feet, including reserves already proved, might remain to be produced in the future. The *Commodity Year Book* for 1955 stated that "Some geologists estimate that there are more than 600 trillion cubic feet of natural gas in this country alone."

Thus as was the case in petroleum, the conclusion can be drawn that it is not just proved reserves in the ground that count, but new additions to reserves and production potentialities as compared with anticipated future demand. In addition, new discoveries and production of natural gas must be studied as a joint problem with petroleum.

4. Natural Gas Problems and Policy

The most significant problems that the industry faces are (a) reserves, production, and demand; (b) conservation at the field; (c) encouraging the highest economic uses; (d) eventual substitution for natural gas; and (e) federal government control of prices.

A. Reserves, Production, and Demand

The following statement from the Materials Policy Commission will serve to introduce and summarize this problem:

Natural gas' meteoric rise among fuels is continuing and its place in energy supply is still undergoing dynamic adjustment. More than five times as much natural gas was marketed in 1950 as in 1925. If the supply were available, use of natural gas by 1975 could readily be two and one half to three times as high as in 1950, even at somewhat higher prices.

The hard fact with which public policy must reckon is that probably before the century is out, conceivably sooner, United States supplies of natural gas will decline. The United States cannot now supplement domestic supplies with large imports, although modest imports from western Canada to the Pacific Northwest seem assured, and it may later become economical to pipe gas from Mexico. A synthetic equivalent of natural gas, derived from abundant solid fuel reserves, is not yet here, but future economic and technical developments may alter this outlook.

In contrast to petroleum, therefore, there is no such present limiting factor on the price of natural gas as large and expanding supplies of an exact substitute, or significant imports. Since demand and supply are expected to remain unbalanced, a substantial long-term price increase is a strong possibility.[16]

A good measure of future production potentialities is an evaluation of rates of new discoveries and developments relative to the production of natural gas. Table 47 indicates that from 1945 through 1951 new reserves

TABLE 47.   Estimated New Discoveries and Developments
of Natural Gas, United States
(billions of cubic feet)

Period	Estimated New Discoveries and Developments[a]	Production[b]	Ratio of New Discoveries and Developments to Production
1918 and earlier	23,296	8,296	2.8
1919–34	68,062	21,062	3.2
1935–44	105,013	33,513	3.1
1945–51	99,531	42,588	2.3

[a] The sum of accumulated production and estimated reserves at the end of the period minus the corresponding sum at the beginning of the period. Reserve estimates at beginning and end of the periods before 1945–51 were of very poor comparability.
[b] Marketed production prior to 1934; net production for 1935 and later.
SOURCE: *World Oil*, Feb. 15, 1952, pp. 181, 186; *Resources for Freedom*, Vol. III.

proved were over twice as large as net production. These past ratios were highly satisfactory. The Materials Policy Commission felt that when new discoveries and developments run closer to annual production it might be taken as a warning of an imminent slowdown of production. The figures previously presented for 1955 indicated a production of 10 trillion cubic feet and new additions to reserves of 22 trillion cubic feet. Thus the ratio of 2.2 was only slightly less than that for the 1945–51

[16] *Resources for Freedom*, Summary of Vol. I, p. 42.

period, and in addition some production was going into underground storage.

Natural gas discoveries and production are related directly to petroleum operations. The study of the Materials Policy Commission concluded that new discoveries of recoverable gas would be about 6 M cubic feet a year per barrel of recoverable oil and that in the long run this relationship could be expected to hold in production. If the oil industry produces from 2 to 4 billion barrels of crude oil a year, there should be an annual rate of net gas production of 12 to 24 trillion cubic feet. When oil discoveries taper off and decline, a roughly concurrent slowdown of natural gas production can be expected. The decline of natural gas production might come sooner if, as is possible, production for a time should outrun discoveries.

A May 6, 1955, study of *U.S. News and World Report* had this to say about the problem: "Supply good for years. The danger of shortage is not imminent however, even the producers concede. Pipelines, when first approved by the F. P. C. (Federal Power Commission), must have 20-year contracts for gas supplies. Thus, consumers who turned to natural gas in recent years are assured against a shortage for the better part of two decades. Any pinch would show up first in refusal to take on new customers. . . . Thus a shortage could develop only gradually—if at all."

The pinch to look for is not the refusal of pipelines to take on new customers, but the basic one of the ratio of addition to reserves and production. This is doubly so in the case of natural gas since the only limit to consumption is available production.

The conclusion can be drawn that policies encouraging the discovery, development, and production of petroleum will have a direct effect on natural gas reserves, production, and consumption. In addition, policies should be adopted that will encourage the discovery and development of natural gas independent of its relationship with petroleum.

B. Conservation at the Field

One of the most wasteful features of the natural gas industry is the venting to the air and flaring of casing-head gas and gas stripped of its liquids in conjunction with the production of petroleum. It is estimated that one cubic foot of gas out of every ten is wasted in this manner. As dramatic as this figure is, the present status is a vast improvement over the conditions of the early thirties. Principally responsible for this improvement have been the state oil and gas conservation and regulatory agencies, which have been facilitated in their efforts by the Interstate

Oil Compact Commission, and the development of a natural gas industry which made possible adequate price incentives.

Most significant progress has been made in Texas, which, as has been seen, produced 50 percent of the natural gas in 1954. This progress was achieved by conservation measures of repressuring of gas in the production of crude petroleum and unit pool operations. Much of it was brought about initially by conservation and regulatory measures which, when put into practice, proved economically advantageous. This, as is the case with petroleum, is an ideal solution to a difficult problem.

Some of the present waste is uneconomic to avoid, but future developments in technology and increase in price may overcome these difficulties. In the interim, the Interstate Oil Compact Commission should continue its fine efforts to encourage the states to pass and enforce proper conservation practices. In the leasing of federal gas properties every effort should be made to use the same standards as recommended by the Interstate Oil Compact.

C. Encouraging the Highest Economic Uses

There are many uses in which natural gas has such a considerable advantage over competitive fuels that it would be chosen even if its price were higher than the prices of other fuels. These uses can be estimated to include residential and commercial and specialized industrial applications such as heat treating and organic chemical production. Thus a large share of the industrial consumption is not put to its most advantageous purpose. The argument is sometimes advanced that direct end-use control is necessary to prevent gas from being utilized now for low-value general applications in order that it may be saved for higher-value special advantage uses later. The counterargument is that the proper method of allocation is through the price system. In pursuing this argument the fact must be kept in mind that in a great many instances administrative decisions by the Federal Power Commission, granting transmission facilities, and by state public utility commissions have long-term effects on use patterns.

One industry practice that led to inefficient natural gas end-use was off-season sale of natural gas for boiler fuel to electric generating utilities in the East. This practice is being rapidly corrected by the underground storage of gas during the summer period in abandoned Pennsylvania gas fields, or similar geological structures. Thus rather than being sold for boiler fuel, the stored gas can be used in the winter for such special high-value uses as house heating. At the beginning of 1954 there were

167 underground storage fields located in seventeen states, with an ultimate capacity of 1735 billion cubic feet of natural gas. The gas industry spent about $50 million on underground storage facilities in 1954, and estimates were for similar expenditures in 1955 and 1956. The President's Advisory Committee on Energy Supplies and Resources Policy recommended on February 26, 1955, that "The power of eminent domain for the acquisition of surface and mineral rights for the development of underground storage reservoirs [for natural gas] should be granted subject to appropriate safeguards to protect the public safety, including the mining industry."

One of the most inefficient uses of natural gas is in the burning of the gas in order to catch carbon black from the smoke. Carbon black producers made long-term contracts at low prices to buy the gas near the fields at steady rates when other customers were lacking. Since there are now opportunities to sell the gas at high prices for more efficient uses, there has been some argument to prohibit the burning of gas for carbon black. Some states already prohibit this practice or restrict it to types of gas that are not suitable for other purposes.

Carbon black is required for the manufacture of rubber tires and, if other sources were not available, the carbon black manufacturers would pay higher prices for gas. As new contracts are made, higher prices have been causing carbon black producers to change to nonmarketable residual heavy fuel petroleum products and to look for substitutes. This method of price allocation when it works is always preferable to allocation by legislative and administrative action. The decrease in use of natural gas in the production of carbon black from 1945 to 1955 (Table 46) indicates that this problem of waste is being solved.

The conclusion can be drawn that the price system is the best basis of allocating natural gas to its most efficient use. However, since the pipeline companies make long-term contracts for the supply of natural gas, and since they make tremendous capital investments in their facilities, there is ample justification for the Federal Power Commission to consider the type of consumption to be served in the granting of pipeline certification. This would be in the interest of consumers, the country as a whole, and the three parts of the natural gas industry—producers and gatherers, pipelines, and distributors.

D. Eventual Substitution for Natural Gas

This problem is so directly related to the problem of reserves, production, and demand that there is reason for considering it as a conclusion and recommendation in the solution of the first problem. Therefore the following conclusions and policy recommendations of the President's Materials Policy Commission are given:

Over the next 25 years or so, such substitutions as will be required of other fuels for natural gas need not cause serious problems. Some industrial users, such as electrical generating stations, who have been getting natural gas at bargain prices, largely in off-peak seasons, will probably have to shift to full-time use of coal or fuel oil, a process that has already begun on the East Coast. There will be some modest increase of their costs on this account but no serious further problems can be expected.

At some point beyond 1975, however, more serious problems are likely to arise when natural gas supplies will eventually have shrunk to the point that the general uses in gas producing areas and special uses in all areas are forced to shift to substitute fuels. Costly dislocations may result in the economy of the Southwest, heavy capital costs of conversion will be forced upon nearby and distant customers, and the extensive transportation, distribution, and utilization systems may be rendered useless. The impact could be reduced if it becomes economic to manufacture gas for at least some of these gas customers, presumably from coal, which could then be distributed through portions of existing transmission and distribution lines, though large segments of such lines would probably no longer be used. The present and currently prospective costs of deriving gas from coal, either by underground gasification or above-ground manufacture, are so high that the processes do not promise to be economic for any but those very high-grade special uses, such as household cooking, that can afford to pay very high prices. Improved methods of obtaining gas from coal are being sought, however, and the prospects may be considerably improved by 1975.

Meanwhile, in guiding the rapid development of the natural gas industry, it is important for regulatory authorities to bear in mind the ultimate exhaustion of natural gas supplies, with the aim of avoiding costly over-expansion. The Federal Power Commission has customarily required, as a condition for authorizing construction of a pipeline, that a certain number of years' supplies be reserved for the particular pipeline, usually 20 years, although shorter periods have sometimes been countenanced. As the natural gas industry matures, an even longer horizon may be appropriate.

It will become increasingly important for the Federal Power Commission, in considering "dedicated reserves" for a proposed pipeline, to take into account the eventual impact of new dedications upon the useful life of existing pipelines, upon the consumers they serve, and upon the long-range supply position of communities in the producing area. Excessive building of pipelines and over-commitment of limited reserves could lead, when reserves are gone, to premature obsolescence of costly capital equipment, for operators and consumers alike. The owners of the pipelines and those who extend them credit can generally be expected effectively to safeguard continued supplies for their transportation and distributing systems. However, the regulatory authorities must also have a strong responsibility in this direction.

E. Federal Government Control of Prices

The four preceding problems are really all part of one issue that might have been considered under the first problem—"Reserves, Production, and Demand"—which could have been followed by "Federal Government Control of Prices" as a second major problem of the natural gas industry. Interesting is the fact that this problem was not even presented by the President's Materials Policy Commission, although it was one of the major issues reported on by the President's Advisory Committee on Energy Supplies and Resources Policy in 1955.

Probably the simplest statement of the problem would be: Should the federal government (the Federal Power Commission) control the prices received by producers of natural gas? Congress was worrying over this problem in 1955 and 1956. It and related issues have a long and controversial background.

The three parts of the natural gas industry are all regulated:

Producers perform the functions of looking for, developing, producing, and gathering the gas. The latter operation consists of taking the gas as it emerges from the wellhead and releasing it into a pipeline which is one of a number forming a "gathering system." The networks of local pipelines come together at a central point, from which the gas is delivered to the second part of the industry, pipeline companies, which transmit the gas to distant points where it is purchased by the third part of the industry, local utilities, which sell it to the consuming public. Producers (production and gathering) are regulated by state agencies. Mr. Justice Clark explains: "The states have been for over 35 years and are now enforcing regulatory laws covering production and gathering, including *pricing*, proration of gas, retable taking, unitization of fields, processing of casinghead gas including priority over other gases, well spacing, repressuring, abandonment of wells, marginal area development, and other devices. Everyone is fully aware of the direct relationship of price and conservation. And the power of the states to regulate producers' and gatherers' prices has been upheld in this Court [the United States Supreme Court]."

Pipeline companies are granted franchises by the Federal Power Commission for the interstate transportation and resale of natural gas. They operate as public utilities and their transmission rates are regulated by the FPC.

Local distributing companies operate as public utilities. They are granted franchises and their rates are regulated by local and state commissions.

The Natural Gas Act was passed in 1938. According to the Supreme Court as stated in the Phillips case, 374 U.S. 672: "Protection of consumers against exploitation at the hands of natural gas companies was the primary aim of the Natural Gas Act." Section 1 (b) of the act made the regulatory provisions applicable "to the sale in interstate commerce of natural gas for resale for ultimate public consumption," but it also made them inapplicable "to the production or gathering of natural gas." The Natural Gas Act was a direct result of a Supreme Court decision (Missouri v. Kansas Natural Gas Company, 265 U.S. 298) which held that the state of Missouri was not empowered to prevent an increase in the price of gas sold to Missouri distributors because the gas had moved in interstate commerce. Edward F. Arn, Governor of Kansas, stated in September, 1954, that "Congress recognized this area wherein there was no control and so enacted the Natural Gas Act in 1938. During the extensive Congressional hearings held, many noted authorities made it explicit that the proposed legislation was not intended to regulate the field rates or the ultimate price which would be charged by the independent producers and other gatherers of gas."

In 1940 the Federal Power Commission ruled in Columbian Fuel Corp., 2 F.P.C. 200, that a company whose only sales of natural gas in interstate commerce were as an incident to production was exempted from the jurisdiction of the Commission.

In 1947 the Federal Power Commission stated in Order No. 139 of August 7: "The Commission gives its assurances to independent producers and gatherers of natural gas that they can sell at arm's length and deliver such gas to interstate pipelines and can enter into contracts for such sale without apprehension that in so doing they may become subject to assertions of jurisdiction by the Commission under the Natural Gas Act."

But in 1947, while the Federal Power Commission was denying any jurisdiction over independent producers, the Supreme Court in Interstate Natural Gas Co. v. F.P.C., 331 U.S. 682, held that the Commission had jurisdiction of the Interstate Company's sales and that the company was a natural gas company. However, the Court had this to say: "Thus, where sales, though technically consummated in Interstate Commerce, are made during the course of production and gathering and are so closely connected with the local incidents of that process . . . the jurisdiction of the F.P.C. does not attach."

This Supreme Court ruling created a feeling of uncertainty in the natural gas industry that resulted in the passage by Congress in 1950 of the Kerr bill, clearly stating that sales of natural gas to interstate pipelines by independent producers would be a part of production and gathering, and exempting the latter from FPC control. The Kerr bill was vetoed by President Truman.

The basis of this controversy is that, in order to protect natural gas consumers, price regulation must be in effect at the local public utility level, in transportation, and all the way back to the wellhead through the production and gathering system, or at least as far back as through the sale of natural gas by producers and gatherers to the interstate pipelines. The Supreme Court on June 7, 1954, in the famous Phillips case (347 U.S. 672) held that the interstate sales by producers and gatherers are subject to regulation under the Natural Gas Act, and thus established a clear legal basis for regulation by the FPC in direct conflict with previous FPC rulings.

Mr. Justice Douglas in dissenting in the Phillips case contended: "There is much to be said from the national point of view for regulating sales at both ends of these interstate pipelines. The power of Congress to do so is unquestioned. Whether it did so by the Natural Gas Act of 1938 is a political and legal controversy that has raged in the Commission and the Courts for some years. The question is not free from some doubts. For while P 1 (b) of the Act makes the regulatory provisions applicable 'to the sale in interstate commerce of natural gas for resale for ultimate public consumption,' it also makes them inapplicable 'to the production or gathering of natural gas.' "

The Phillips decision arose from a dual investigation of the activities of Phillips as an independent producer of natural gas by the FPC. First the Commission was to determine if these activities were within the jurisdiction of the Natural Gas Act. Second, it was to decide whether the rates for natural gas were unfair. The second point was not considered, as after hearings in April and May, 1951, the Commission made a specific finding of fact that Phillips was exempt from the jurisdiction of the act because Phillips transportation and sales constituted a part of or were connected with its gathering process.

The finding of the Commission was appealed to the United States Court of Appeals for the District of Columbia by the consuming states and on May 22, 1953, the Court reversed the decision by finding that Phillips was a "natural gas company" and that the Commission should fix the rates for its sales. This decision was carried to the United States Supreme Court by Phillips.

The Supreme Court held, with Douglas, Clark, and Burton dissenting, that an independent natural gas producer, which sold gas to interstate pipeline companies for interstate transportation and resale, was a "natural gas company" within the Natural Gas Act, and its sales were not within the section of the act exempting "production or gathering of natural gas."

In delivering the opinion of the Court, Mr. Justice Minton stated: "We are of the opinion . . . that production and gathering in the sense that those terms are used in P 1 (b) end before the sales by Phillips occur." Justice Minton cited directly to the point of the Supreme Court's decision in Interstate Natural Gas Co. v. Federal Power Commission: "We have held that these sales are in interstate commerce. It cannot be doubted that their regulation is predominately a matter of national contrasted to local concern. . . . Unreasonable charges exacted at this stage of the interstate movement become perpetuated in large part in fixed items of costs which must be covered by rates charged subsequent purchasers of gas including the ultimate consumer. It was to avoid such situations that the Natural Gas Act was passed." Justice Minton further stated, "Thus we are satisfied that Congress sought to regulate *wholesales* of natural gas occurring at both ends of the interstate transmission."

Mr. Justice Clark, with whom Mr. Burton concurs in dissenting, argued:

That Congress aimed at abuses resulting in the "gap" at the end of the transmission process by integrated and unintegrated pipelines and not at abuses prior to the transmission, is clear from the final report of the Federal Trade Commission to the Senate on malpractices of the natural gas industry. (S. Doc. No. 92, 70th Cong., 1st Sess., 1935) This report was the stimulus for federal intervention in the industry. The Federal Trade Commission outlined the abuses in the industry which the "gap" made the states powerless to prevent; the abuses were by monopolistically situated pipelines which gouged the consumer by charging local distribution companies unreasonable rates. The Federal Trade Commission did not find abusive pricing by independent producers and gatherers; if anything, the independents at the producing end of the pipelines were likewise the victims of monopolistic practices by the pipelines.

Mr. Justice Clark argued further to the impact of the decision on state regulation:

By today's decision, the Court restricts the phrase "production and gathering" to "the physical activities, facilities, and properties" used in production and gathering. Such a gloss strips the words of their substance. If the Congress so intended, then it left for state regulation only a mass of empty pipe, vacant processing plants and thousands of hollow wells with scarecrow derricks, monuments to this new extension of federal power. It was not so understood. . . .

There can be no doubt, as the Commission has found, that federal regulation of production and gathering will collide and substantially interfere with and hinder the enforcement of these state regulatory measures. We cannot square this result with the House Report on this Act which states that the subsequently enacted bill is so drawn as to complement and in no manner usurp State regulatory authority.

If we look to Interstate for guidance, we would do better to focus on the following words of the late Chief Justice:

"Clearly, among the powers thus reserved to the States is the power to regulate the physical production and gathering of natural gas in the interests of conservation or of any other consideration of legitimate local concern. It was the intention of Congress to give the States full freedom in these matters. Thus, where sales, though technically consummated in interstate commerce, are made during the course of production and gathering and are so closely connected with the local incidence of that process as to render rate regulation by the Federal Power Commission inconsistent or a substantial interference with the exercise by the State of its regulatory functions, the jurisdiction of the Federal Power Commission does not attach."

Mr. Justice Douglas, dissenting, presented the most important question as to the impact of the decision on the discovery, development, and production of natural gas:

The fastening of rate regulation on this *independent producer* brings "the production or gathering of natural gas" under effective federal control, in spite of the fact that Congress has made that phase of the natural gas business exempt from regulation. The effect is certain to be profound. The price at which the *independent producer* can sell his gas determines the price he is able or willing to pay for it (if he buys from other wells). The sales price determines his profits. And his profits and the profits of all the other gatherers, whose gas moves into the interstate pipelines, have profound effects on the rate of production, the methods of production, the old wells that are continued in production, and new ones explored, etc. Regulating the price at which the independent producer can sell his gas regulates his business in the most vital way any business can be regulated.

Thus we have in the words of the Supreme Court of the United States some of the principal arguments for and against federal regulation of the price of natural gas charged by the producers and gatherers.

The session of Congress meeting in 1955 offered the first opportunity to modify the Natural Gas Act in light of the Supreme Court decision so as to make it clear that federal control should be limited as it was before the Phillips decision, or to strengthen the act as interpreted by the courts. The arguments for and against less federal regulation have been presented in great detail. The principal advocates for less government control were the producers and gatherers, the interstate pipelines, and the state regulatory agencies. The opposed were representatives of the consumer interests. A summary of the arguments for and against modification of the Supreme Court's ruling follows:

For:

(1) The ABC's of free competition versus regulation and controls in the nation's sixth largest industry are:

a. One gas distributor. Because the local gas company has an exclusive franchise for gas in its area, it operates as a *public utility,* and its rates are regulated.

b. One gas transporter. Because the long-distance pipeline which brings gas to the local distributor is a sole supplier, it operates as a *public utility,* and its rates are regulated.

c. Thousands of competing gas producers. Because there are more than 8000 producers competing to find natural gas and sell it, controls are unnecessary. These freely competing producers have tripled supplies in sixteen years, and the average price of gas to residential users has risen only one-eleventh as much as the cost of living.

(2) Such price increases to the consumer as occur should be studied in the light of where the shares of each dollar of the consumer's gas bill goes: 9 cents is received by the gas producer; 21 cents is received by the pipeline transporter; and 70 cents is received by the local gas company distributor.

(3) Federal controls are unfair because they single out one competitive industry for such controls. "It is a step without peacetime precedent to price-fix a commodity at its source."

(4) Controls are dangerous because they could easily be the first step toward federal price-fixing of coal or oil—or lumber or grain or any business.

(5) Price controls are short sighted "because they will stifle the bold and risky exploring that is needed to assure adequate supplies of natural gas for the future."

(6) Less natural gas as a result of federal control will lead to increased prices to the consumer.

(7) Federal control of gas prices received by the producers of gas will drastically interfere with the functions performed and rightfully delegated to the state regulatory and conservation agencies.

(8) The Federal Power Commission by a vote of 4 to 1 is opposed to controlling gas prices of producers and gatherers. The administrative problem would be difficult. "Reasonable" rates for thousands of producers would have to be calculated and costs vary widely between producing

wells. In addition, gas and oil are joint products of many wells and cost allocations would be almost impossible. The Commission also feels that controls will lead to a diminution of gas supplies.

Against:

(1) Consumer prices of natural gas cannot be controlled unless control is exercised over prices received by producers and gatherers.

(2) Consumer prices will rise rapidly because of the anticipated short supplies of natural gas.

(3) Consumer prices will rise because cost of production of natural gas is rising. Although interstate pipelines make long-term twenty-year contracts with producers, these contracts include "escalator clauses" incorporating the "most favored nation principle" so that all producers of natural gas in an area selling gas to a pipeline must be given the benefits of price increases granted under new contracts.

(4) Owing to the "most favored nation clauses" prices will rise even though costs of production of natural gas at all wells or from all suppliers do not rise.

Many more arguments and details can be spelled out on each side of the issue. Fundamental to the solution of the problem is the extent to which price should be determined in a free market. Obviously it is not true that federal price regulations are not in effect in other areas of the economy. In most instances—e.g., agricultural—these controls have been to benefit the producer, not the consumer. There is no question about the fact that, faced with conditions of an increasing demand for natural gas, consumer prices will rise unless production of natural gas is increased. The solution to this problem must be on the basis of the maximum efficient production and utilization of a scarce natural resource. This is *the fundamental economic problem.* The solution should be sought first in the maximum use of the free market. This will facilitate shifts in the most efficient use of alternative energy sources and the maximum efficient production. Where regulation of production is necessary for conservation purposes, it can best be achieved, as already concluded, by state conservation and regulatory agencies.

Those forces advocating Congressional legislation to change the Supreme Court's ruling in the Phillips case by either a new law or modification of the Natural Gas Act received strong support from the President's Advisory Committee on Energy Supplies and Resources Policy which on February 26, 1955, recommended:

We believe the problem of natural gas regulation should be approached from the viewpoint of assuring adequate supplies and the discovery and development of additional reserves to support such supplies, in the interests of national defense, an expanding domestic economy, and reasonable prices to consumers.

To secure these objectives, it is essential to give due consideration to (1) the operations known as the production of natural gas, (2) the transportation of gas in interstate transmission lines, and (3) the distribution of gas in municipalities. Individual companies may engage in more than one of these activities. Each operation of such companies should be treated by like criteria according to its appropriate industry function.

In the production of natural gas it is important that sound conservation practices be continued. This area of conservation management is under the jurisdiction of State conservation commissions. In the interest of a sound fuels policy and the protection of the national defense and consumer interests by assuring such a continued exploration for and development of adequate reserves as to provide an adequate supply of natural gas, we believe the Federal Government should not control the production, gathering, processing or sale of natural gas prior to its entry into an interstate transmission line.

The interstate transmission of natural gas by the interstate transmission lines and the subsequent sale of such gas for resale is a public utility function and should be under the regulation of the Federal Power Commission. In considering the certification of new lines and applications for increased rates based on new or renegotiated purchase contracts, the Commission should consider, in order to provide protection for the consumer, not only the assurance of supply but also whether the contract prices of the natural gas which the applicant has contracted to buy are competitively arrived at and represent the reasonable market field price, giving due consideration, in the interest of competition, to the reasonableness and appropriateness of contract provisions as they relate to existing or future market field prices.

The several states or their political sub-divisions should continue to provide the public utility regulation of distributing companies in accordance with usual utility practices.

Thus the complete cycle of natural gas production, transmission and utilization will be appropriately regulated: The production and conservation of natural gas by the state conservation commissions; the interstate transmission of natural gas by the Federal Power Commission; and the distribution by the local public utility commissions.

After much debate the House passed a natural gas bill by a narrow margin in the closing days of first session of the 84th Congress during the summer of 1955. This bill moved through under the guidance of Speaker Sam Rayburn. Its purpose was to strip the Federal Power Commission of direct regulatory power over the prices charged for natural gas by producers. The FPC was to continue to have strict regulatory powers over interstate pipeline operators. These powers included the right to veto a pipeline company's contract with a gas producer if the FPC found the contract price was unreasonable. Key words in the bill were "reasonable market price," which the bill sought to guarantee producers for their natural gas.

If Senate Majority Leader Lyndon B. Johnson had not had a heart attack, he probably would have been able to force this bill through the Senate during the last day the Senate was in session during the summer of 1955. If this had been done the bill would have been signed and would have become public law.

Senator Johnson was back on the job by January, 1956, and he made the bill (H.R. 6645) the first subject for debate for the second session of the 84th Congress. During the fall of 1955 the regulation of natural gas was one of the major topics of public discussion, and this debate was carried to the Senate floor. Lobbying by both pro-producer and pro-distributor interests was intense. The latter claimed to be representing the interests of consumers of natural gas. H.R. 6645 was passed by the Senate. Just before the bill was to be voted on, Senator Francis Case of South Dakota announced that he had been offered a $2500 campaign donation in what a Senate resolution called an "alleged improper attempt" to influence his vote.

Business Week reported on February 11, 1956: "The Senate this week dumped one of the most controversial—and least understood—measures it will have to deal with this session on Pres. Eisenhower's desk. The measure: the so-called natural gas bill. Eisenhower is expected to sign it, even though he has not publicly committed himself on the bill. . . . He is understood to have given ranking Republican Congressional leaders private assurance that he will not veto the bill."

On February 17, 1956, President Eisenhower announced:

I am unable to approve H.R. 6645 "to amend the Natural Gas Act as amended." This I regret because I am in accord with its basic objectives. Since the passage of this bill a body of evidence has accumulated indicating that private persons, apparently representing only a very small segment of a great and vital industry, have been seeking to further their own interests by highly questionable activities. These include efforts I deem to be so arrogant and so much in defiance of acceptable standards of propriety as to risk creating doubt among the American people concerning the integrity of governmental processes.

At the same time, I must make quite clear that legislation conforming to the basic objectives of H.R. 6645 is needed. It is needed because the type of regulation of producers of natural gas which is required under present law will discourage individual initiative and incentive to explore for and develop new sources of supply.

In the long run this will limit supplies of gas, which is contrary not only to the national interest but especially to the interest of consumers.

I feel that any new legislation, in addition to furthering the long-term interest of consumers in plentiful supplies of gas, should include specific language protecting consumers in their right to fair prices.

President Eisenhower's veto was called: (1) "evidence of his integrity"; (2) "an outright political gesture indicative of his intention to announce for a second term." However, one thing was certain: President Eisenhower would not get his "needed legislation conforming to the basic objectives of H.R. 6645" during the election year 1956, and he did not.

In his address to Congress in January, 1957, the President stated:

In returning the Harris-Fulbright Natural Gas Bill to the 84th Congress without my approval, I stated that legislation conforming to the basic objectives of that bill was needed. I am still of that opinion. It is essential that the consumers of natural gas be protected. We must endeavor to make sure that there will be continued exploration and development of adequate field supplies of gas and that producers' sales prices are arrived at fairly and competitively. In this way, and with the authority vested in the Federal Power Commission to regulate interstate pipelines as to the price at which gas may be charged as an item of cost in fixing their rates, the cost to the public will be fair.

Legislation freeing gas producers from public utility-type regulation is essential if the incentives to find and develop new supplies of gas are to be preserved and sales of gas to interstate markets are not to be discouraged to the detriment of both consumers and producers, as well as the national interest.

5. Conclusion

The conclusion can be drawn that natural gas is truly a growth industry, the ultimate expansion of which is limited in terms of available supplies. The principal problems of the industry arise out of the basic economic problem of the allocation of scarce economic resources. Their solution should be sought in the maximum use of free market forces in a complicated three-part industry that is regulated by state agencies at two ends and the federal government in the middle. Extension of federal government regulation should be checked, and, where necessary and possible, regulation should be administered by state agencies. Problems and policy are almost entirely domestic in character and their international aspects are strictly limited.

CHAPTER 7

Atomic Energy

In the introductory section on energy resources the point was made that almost all of the energy man uses is of atomic origin. In the past the nuclear (atomic) energy has been stellar, chiefly solar, in origin and has been derived from current receipts (flow) and stored-up supplies (funds). The most significant advance in economic productivity was achieved when the shift was made from the exclusive reliance on flows of energy to the utilization of the funds of fossil fuels—coal, petroleum, and natural gas. This shift, accompanied by the harnessing of these fuels by the heavy metals, we have called the Industrial Revolution. Students of energy and material have told us before World War II that this phase of history was rapidly drawing to a close, and that we were entering upon a stage which would be characterized by continuous energy sources—water power converted into electricity as a carrier and direct solar radiation—harnessed by the light metals. Electricity has indeed been developed as a carrier of water power—both from falling flows of water power (hydro) and expanding water power (steam) produced from funds of fossil fuels. Direct solar radiation is now in its developmental stage. Light metals have become harnessers. Yet even as this stage was dawning a new era has exploded.

Current energy historians tell us that the "Atomic Age" began with the destruction of Hiroshima in 1945. This is a dramatic oversimplification of a complex development of a new energy source—a new source of fuel— which requires new metals and methods for harnessing. This era was thrust upon us with the remarkable discovery that matter turns into energy and energy into matter. The evolutionary origin of the new age is beyond the scope of this study; its development is still dawning; its revolutionary effects will be beyond the scope of imagination.

The atom is not new. In the fifth century B.C. one Greek philosopher concluded that all matter was composed of only four elements—fire, earth, water, and air. A contemporary Democritus developed the concept of the "atom"—the smallest, the indivisible particle of matter. Atomic theory stood still until 1774, when air was shown to be not a single substance but at least a mixture of two gases, oxygen and nitrogen. Today ninety-two natural elements are known, and eight others have been created, e.g., plutonium.

In 1896 the French physicist Antoine Henri Becquerel demonstrated that the atom is not an indivisible substance when he discovered that a piece of uranium ore had exposed a photographic plate. This phenomenon is called radioactivity. Following Becquerel, Marie and Pierre Curie discovered the radioactivity of radium.

About seventeen years after Becquerel's discovery Lord Rutherford in England and Niels Bohr in Denmark pictured the atom as a miniature solar system composed of (1) a central core or nucleus containing particles held together by strong forces and (2) rings of other particles circling about the nucleus. The particles rotating about the nucleus were identified as electrons. The particles in the nucleus were later identified as protons and neutrons. The stage was set for modern atomic science.

The atom is the smallest particle in which any element may exist and yet retain its peculiar chemical characteristics. The atom of one element is differentiated from the atoms of every other element by the number of protons contained in its nucleus. Uranium is the heaviest natural element and contains 92 protons. Hydrogen, the lightest element, contains 1 proton.

There are also differences between the atoms of any given element depending upon the number of neutrons contained in the nucleus. These atoms differ in weight and are called isotopes. The two uranium isotopes found in nature that are most often referred to are U-238, which contains 92 protons plus 146 neutrons, and U-235, which contains 92 protons plus 143 neutrons. More than 99 percent of all the uranium found in nature is U-238; slightly less than 1 percent is U-235.

In January, 1939, a German scientist, Lise Meitner, and her nephew, Otto Frisch, concluded that the Italian Enrico Fermi and two Germans Otto Hahn and Fritz Strassmann, in earlier work, had succeeded in splitting the uranium atom by bombarding it with neutrons. Meitner and Frisch called this process "fission."

When U-235 is "fissioned," the isotope absorbs a neutron, then splits approximately in half. Two new atoms are produced and two or three neutrons are released. The weight of the new isotopes and the neutrons is less than that of the original U-235 atom. The loss in weight appears as energy—the same energy which had formerly bound the protons and neutrons together in the atom's nucleus. This was the new source of atomic or nuclear energy.

By 1940 many scientists had split the atom—one at a time by bombarding it with neutrons. At that time, however, no way was known of bringing about a self-sustaining process, or chain reaction, that would release more energy than it consumed. By 1954 it was generally known that only three kinds of atoms—uranium 235, plutonium 239, and uranium 233 when split—could throw out enough energy and neutrons to strike and "fission" similar atoms and thus cause a chain reaction. This process occurs trillions of times in a fraction of a second and can produce an explosion (the atomic bomb); or the chain reaction can be controlled and directed to yield nuclear energy at a desired rate, in two forms: as heat, which can be harnessed to raise steam and drive a turbine, and as radiation.

The problem in the case of U-235 is that uranium as found in nature contains only one part of U-235, the fissionable isotope, as compared with 139 parts of nonfissionable U-238. Thus U-235 must be separated out on a large scale. This is done by a method of gaseous diffusion. Plutonium is not a natural element but must be produced as a by-product of a nuclear reactor in which the more abundant nonfissionable U-238 is bombarded with neutrons and transformed into fissionable plutonium. U-233 must be produced from thorium, a metallic element, in the same manner as plutonium. Atoms of thorium are put into a reactor, where they are transmuted by bombardment into U-233. U-235 and plutonium were used as the fissionable materials in 1957. At the same time thorium, which is much more abundant in nature than uranium, had not been used extensively but was considered to have future potentialities.

The second new source of nuclear energy is through the fusion reaction which is the basis of the hydrogen bomb. In this instance, instead of splitting very heavy atoms, very light atoms, such as hydrogen atoms, are heated to a temperature of millions of degrees and fuse together into atoms of helium, giving off tremendous quantities of energy as they do. Super-heavy hydrogen (tritium) is required. In order to obtain tritium, lithium must be split in a nuclear reactor in the same manner in which plutonium is produced.

RAW MATERIALS

Uranium as a source of energy is by far the most important raw material of the new energy era. Thorium may increase in importance in the future. Lithium is of tremendous significance in the fusion process. However, in 1957 plans for the development of nuclear power depended primarily upon the use of uranium. The Raw Materials Division of the United States Atomic Energy Commission is responsible for the procurement and processing of these supplies.

1. Uranium

Uranium is found in almost every kind of rock and natural water, but concentrated deposits are rare. In addition, the mining of uranium is a problem because it occurs in scattered pockets rather than in long veins.

Pitchblende is the richest uranium ore, ranging from 50 to 80 percent uranium oxide. Pitchblende deposits are found in the Belgian Congo, Canada, and Czechoslovakia. Uranium deposits in the United States are mostly found in flat-lying sedimentary beds, in which the uranium content ranges from 0.1 to 0.5 percent. Uranium can also be produced from domestic phosphate and shale deposits, which constitute a large low-grade uranium reserve. The Scandinavian peninsula and the Baltic territory of Russia contain shale deposits at least equal in extent and grade to our domestic deposits. South Africa has extensive uranium deposits which occur with gold. Australia, Portugal, and France are producing uranium. Uranium is known to occur in Mexico and many South American countries, but there has been little exploration and practically no development.

Prior to 1942 there was little interest in uranium. Partial operation of the Shinkolobwe Mine in the Belgian Congo supplied all that was needed for the production of radium. In 1942 uranium became a strategic material, but between 1942 and 1948 not one new source of uranium was brought into production. The Shinkolobwe mine became the mainstay of the United States energy program and the world's most important producer of uranium. In 1948 the Belgian Congo was almost the sole supplier of uranium to the United States. Canada had a very small production. The United States had almost none. South Africa, Portugal, and Australia were only possibilities.

In 1955 the Belgian Congo and South Africa were leading producers of uranium. Australia, Portugal, and France were also producing countries with important potential resources. South African reserves were safely estimated in large figures because of the extent and the uniformity of the deposits. Considering only moderate-cost uranium ($12 a pound or less for high-grade concentrate), the AEC estimated that reserves of these five countries should be well in excess of 500,000 tons. Additional reserves of greater tonnage would be available at intermediate ($12 to $20 a pound) and high cost ($30 to $50 a pound).

In January, 1957, the AEC reported as follows for the Belgian Congo, South Africa, Australia, and Portugal. In the Belgian Congo production from the Shinkolobwe mine continued at the normal rate. Production from South Africa increased with the completion of two new processing plants. Sixteen of the authorized seventeen uranium-processing plants now are in operation. It is expected that full production will be reached by the end of 1957. In Australia the Port Pirie chemical plant continued to treat at a normal rate low-grade mechanical concentrates produced at Radium Hill in South Australia, and production of uranium concentrates from the Rum Jungle operations in the Northern Territory was also as expected. Portuguese operations continued at a normal rate during the last six months of 1956. Some significance of these not very revealing comments can be gained through the realization that more than half of the AEC's 1955 and first-quarter 1956 supplies were being acquired from the Belgian Congo, South Africa, Australia, and Canada.

Canada in 1955 was making a strong bid for first place in world uranium production under the direction of the Canadian Atomic Energy Commission. Canada had been a producer of uranium for about twenty years. In 1952 *Mineral Resources of the World* reported that "The largest known uranium reserves are near Elisabeth, Belgian Congo, and Port Radium, Northwest Territories, Canada. . . . Canadian milling ore averaged 0.1 per cent uranium oxide (U_3O_8) in 1937." *Mineral Facts and Problems*, published in 1957 but apparently using information as of 1954, listed the following deposits in Canada with the first and last areas as being "actively mined":

Northwest Territory	Eldorado mine, Great Bear Lake area
Ontario	Blind River District
Saskatchewan	Beaverlodge area

In 1955 the AEC felt that the most important deposits from the standpoint of future production would be the then most recent discoveries in the Beaverlodge area of Saskatchewan and the Blind River District, Ontario. At that time the AEC felt that these developments were too recent for full appraisal of future potential but that the deposits were extensive and should be able to sustain production for many years. On the basis of information and geological evidence available in 1955, the AEC estimated that Canada had several hundred thousand tons of uranium in the moderate-cost class.

In January, 1957, the AEC reported for Canada that important developments continued in the three principal producing areas.

In the Blind River district of Ontario, Rio Tinto Mining Co. of Canada (a subsidiary of the British owned Rio Tinto Co.), through a merger with the Joseph Hirshhorn interests, acquired control of six major mining properties, including Pronto and Algom, which are in production. Five other companies in the district are constructing ore treatment plants of large capacity.

Production of concentrates from the Bicroft mill in the Bancroft area of eastern Ontario began in October. Mill construction in the area by Faraday Uranium Mines, Ltd., was well advanced.

In the Beaverlodge area of Saskatchewan the substantial mill expansion program undertaken by Eldorado Mining and Refining, Ltd., proceeded on schedule. Gunner Mines, Ltd. prepared for underground mining operations to supplement and ultimately supplant ore production from the open pit. It also completed installation of additional equipment to increase mill capacity. Lorado Mines, Ltd. began building a custom mill to treat ores from a number of small mines in the district.

A reader of this report might conclude that not only had the Blind River District and the Beaverlodge area increased in importance but in addition the Bancroft area had replaced the older Great Bear Lake Northwest Territory as one of the "three principal producing areas." The latter was hardly the case. However, the reference to the Blind River District's growth was a mild statement of the fabulous activity in that area, which was described by *Time* in February, 1957:

In the snow-covered wilderness north of Lake Huron, Canada's uranium industry came of age last week. The occasion was the official opening of two big mines, Algom-Quirke and Algom Nordic, in the world's richest uranium field, the Blind River camp. The mines were opened by Rio Tinto Mining Co. of Canada Ltd., a subsidiary of the 84-year-old British mining firm Rio Tinto Co., Ltd. of London, which acquired them along with other Blind River properties from Brooklyn-born Joe Hirshhorn for $60 million in cash and securities. At peak the mines will soon be turning out $110,000 worth of uranium concentrates daily to fill the guaranteed Canadian government purchases of $206.9 million.

Big as the Algom operation is (the two mines and mills have a daily ore-processing capacity of 6,000 tons, double the largest U.S. operation), their output will be only a fraction of Rio Tinto's eventual production. The company's three Northspan mines ($275 million in government contracts) are set to start producing before the end of 1957; its Milliken Lake mine ($94 million in contracts) by March 1958. Rio Tinto's smaller Pronto mine (1,250 tons of ore daily) was opened in 1955 but ran into production troubles, now being taken care of in an enlargement of capacity to 1,500 tons.

Not all of the Blind River field is Rio Tinto's. The mine which many geologists say has probably the biggest (136 million tons) reserve of uranium ore in the Western world is Consolidated Denison Mines Ltd., under the control of Latecomer Steve Roman. He expects to begin production next month, holds $201.2 million in government contracts.

Other Blind River production prospects:

Can-Met Explorations ($79.4 million in contracts), scheduled to begin production in June 1957.

Stanleigh Uranium ($90.5 million), to begin by the fall of 1957.

Stanrock Uranium ($95.2 million), to begin by October 1957.

By 1958 Canada expects to be producing uranium at an annual rate of $300 million, the bulk of it in the Blind River area, where all the mines are located within a ten-mile radius of the town of Elliot Lake. Two years ago Elliot Lake was only some lines on a chart.

The United States Atomic Energy Commission's program to develop domestic sources of uranium was launched in 1947. At that time there were two mills producing uranium from Colorado Plateau ores. These mineral reserves have been explored and exploited since about 1910—first for radium, later for vanadium, and now for uranium, formerly considered an almost worthless by-product. The ores mined in 1947 came from a small area known as the "mineral belt" in southeastern Utah and southwestern Colorado.

By 1951 uranium discoveries had been beyond the narrow limits of the "mineral belt" in other areas of the Colorado Plateau, which is the high land on both sides of the Colorado River (up to 200 miles) in Utah, Colorado, Arizona, and New Mexico. *Business Week* reported in March, 1951, that each time a new uranium deposit was discovered it was loudly touted as "fabulous" or "enough to free us from dependence on foreign sources." This was considered to be not true and not possible unless sizable quantities of pitchblende were discovered.

All the 1950 discoveries, and just about all previous uranium finds in the U.S. are hardly more than enriched rock or dirt. It's classed as rich ore if it contains as much as 1 percent uranium oxide (20 lbs. to the ton). In contrast, pure pitchblende from Canada or Belgian Congo contains up to 60 percent uranium, and, since the ore is rich in pitchblende, uranium content or a ton of raw ore may run up to 20 percent of more.

So domestic discoveries can never free us completely from dependence on foreign ore. By intensive exploration and major expansion of high-cost milling facilities, we could, if we had to, support a bare minimum war program on our own ores. If the Russians should ever overrun the Belgian Congo mines—where we get about 70 percent of our pitchblende—there would be feverish development of the plateau resources. But we'd still lean strongly on Canadian pitchblende.

Business Week should have known better than to underestimate the temperature set off by the bite of the uranium bug. One source described the 1953 activity in the Colorado Plateau as follows:

The feverish search for uranium ores both on the Colorado Plateau and in Canada has within the last year reached such a pitch as to be comparable to the famed Gold Rush of a hundred years ago. All over Colorado, Utah, Arizona and New Mexico—and in Wyoming and Montana, too—the number one subject of conversation is uranium. One cannot eat breakfast in Grand Junction, Colorado, site of the AEC's main Western office, without hearing about it, nor can one walk through any hotel lobby in Salt Lake City without overhearing a discussion of a claim or a new strike.

This uranium fever has drawn every able-bodied man and woman into the mountains and deserts of the West in search of the yellowish carnotite or its richer relative, pitchblende. Along with the traditional pick and shovel of the prospector goes the Geiger counter which discloses the characteristic radioactivity emitted by uranium ores. In fact, the pick and shovel these days are often left at home.

The only customer for uranium oxide (uranium never occurs as the pure metal) is the Atomic Energy Commission, and the prices, which vary with the concentration, are fixed until 1962. There are now more than 550 mines producing on the Colorado Plateau. The owners and operators of these mines vary from an individual to some of the largest mining firms in the world.

On April 5, 1955, Jesse C. Johnson, director, Division of Raw Materials, AEC, described the United States uranium reserves as follows:

In the United States, most of the uranium is coming from the Colorado Plateau. New production is being developed in Wyoming, North and South Dakota and other western states. Recent discoveries in Texas also may prove important. With few exceptions, these deposits are found in flat-lying sedimentary beds. The uranium content generally ranges from 0.1% to 0.5% U_3O_8 and many of the deposits are small. Early in the present program the bulk of our production came from deposits containing only a few thousand tons. A ten or twenty thousand-ton ore body was considered large. During the last three years numbers of deposits have been found which contain in excess of 100,-000 tons and at least one contains several million tons. Probably 80% of our present known ore reserves are in deposits larger than 50,000 tons. These are deposits that can supply uranium at moderate cost.

In spite of the great improvement in ore supply, which has made the United States one of the leading uranium producers, most of the deposits now developed may be mined out in less than ten years. However, if exploration continues as actively as at present, after ten years of full production developed ore reserves may be even greater than today.

There are vast areas throughout our western states that may contain uranium deposits similar to those being mined—but the problem is to find them. Deposits exposed on the surface will be found by surface and airborne surveys using Geiger and scintillation counters which are now standard equipment for every prospector. At present, the buried deposits can be found only by drilling.

Private exploration is now active in all parts of the country where some evidence of uranium has been found. New discoveries are adding uranium reserves faster than they are being mined. This activity will continue, however, only as long as there is a market for the production. At present, there is only a government market which is guaranteed through March 31, 1962 [now 1966]. Beyond that it still could be a factor until the commercial market can sustain a production rate of some importance.[1]

In February, 1956, Mr. Johnson brought the public up to date in remarks indicating that approximately 80 percent of the United States known ore reserves had been developed in the last three years. Most of them were discovered during this period. Over 70 percent of our known ore reserves were in three districts: the Big Indian Wash-Lisbon Valley area of Utah, the Laguna Indian Reservation, New Mexico, and the Ambrosia Lake area, New Mexico. Ore reserves in each of these districts were then measured in terms of millions of tons. The Ambrosia Lake deposits were discovered in the summer of 1955. In the history of the oil and mining industries there are a number of instances of several major discoveries within a short time followed by a considerable period with no outstanding new finds. This is an indication of the difficulty of forecasting long-range uranium production possibilities. The timing of important discoveries is unpredictable. Northern Michigan and Wisconsin, for example, may contain a Blind River field. The geology is similar to that of the Canadian Blind River district and numerous occurrences of uranium have been found, though none of commercial value.

On December 5, 1956, the AEC removed from classified categories of information data on reserves and production subsequent to June 30, 1955. The AEC reported in January, 1957:

The major sources of ore supply have shifted from areas containing many small- to medium-size ore bodies to new areas, such as Ambrosia Lake and Laguna, near Grants, N. Mex., which contain multimillion ton reserves. Large-scale integrated mining and milling enterprises in these areas give assurance of a long-term uranium supply.

Today, there are 33 ore deposits with known reserves of more than 100,000 tons each and at least 8 deposits with reserves in the million-ton class, in contrast to the end of 1954, when there were 15 deposits with reserves over 100,000 tons and one deposit with reserves of more than 1 million tons. Ten percent of presently known deposits now contain 93 percent of estimated reserves.

[1] *Commodity Year Book*, 1955, pp. 350–351.

Domestic ore reserves, by areas, were estimated as of November 1, 1956, as shown in Table 48.

Uranium ore production in the United States totaled 1,600,000 dry tons during the last six months of 1956 as compared to 840,000 dry tons during the second half of 1955, according to the AEC. The increase in domestic production of uranium ore and concentrates maintained the

TABLE 48.   United States Measured, Indicated, and Inferred Uranium Ores

Area	Tons	Percent of Total Reserves	Grade of Ore in Terms of Percent U_3O_8
New Mexico	41,000,000	68.4	.24
Utah	7,500,000	12.5	.34
Colorado	4,100,000	6.8	.33
Arizona	2,600,000	4.3	.30
Wyoming	2,300,000	3.8	.22
Washington	1,500,000	2.5	.18
Others	1,000,000	1.7	.24
Total	60,000,000	100.0	

United States' position as one of the world's leading uranium producers. Completion of new mills under construction, and construction of other mills under contracts will further increase production.

2. Thorium

Thorium, like uranium, is widely distributed. The thorium content of the earth's crust is believed to be three to four times that of uranium but high-grade deposits of thorium are rarer. Up until mid-1957 most thorium was derived as a by-product from processing monazite, an ore of rare-earth phosphate which occurs commercially with titanium and zirconium minerals, principally in beach sands, but also in dunes and stream gravels. India and Brazil had the world's largest known deposits of monazite, but they embargoed its export. The United States was depending principally on monazite reserves in Idaho, North Carolina, South Carolina, Florida, and South Africa.

In May, 1957, David F. Shaw, assistant general manager of the AEC reported that the most important thorium source—at least in North America—was uranium ore in the Blind River area of Ontario. This ore appeared to contain about one part thorium to two of uranium. Based on the target production of an annual 10,000 tons of uranium oxide from this area by 1959, thorium output might run 4,000 to 5,000 tons a year— probably ten times the 1957 world rate. Mr. Shaw expressed "little doubt that economic extraction of it could be achieved when and if there is sufficient demand."

The Atomic Industrial Forum, a nonprofit organization of top-flight businessmen, produced a study in May, 1955, which was made with the close collaboration of the AEC. The AIF discounted reports that thorium would replace uranium as the leading commercial nuclear fuel. The survey concluded: "Thorium requirements are apt to be quite small—only a few tons per year by 1961—increasing to perhaps as much as 300 tons per year by 1965." Mr. Shaw reported for the AEC in 1957 that as long as uranium is cheap and plentiful "the market for thorium will be very slow to develop."

PROCESSING ORE

Uranium ore mined in the United States must be concentrated at processing plants.

1. Colorado Plateau

Uranium ore mined in the Colorado Plateau may be sold at the government guaranteed price scale either to the AEC through its agent, the American Smelting and Refining Company, or to any one of the ore-processing plants located on the Plateau. At the beginning of 1957 there were twelve such concentration plants in operation, all privately owned and financed except for the one at Monticello, Utah, owned by the AEC. The mills were:

Operator	Location	Capacity, Tons Ore per Day
The Anaconda Co.	Bluewater, N. Mex.	3,000
Atomic Energy Commission	Monticello, Utah	600
Climax Uranium Co.	Grand Junction, Colo.	350
Kerr-McGee Oil Industries, Inc.	Shiprock, N. Mex.	500
Mines Development, Inc.	Edgemont. S. Dak.	300
Rare Metals Corp.	Tuba City, Ariz.	250
Union Carbide Nuclear Co.	Uravan, Colo.	850
Union Carbide Nuclear Co.	Rifle, Colo.	280
Uranium Reduction Co.	Moab, Utah	1,500
Vanadium Corp. of America	Durango, Colo.	430
Vanadium Corp. of America	Naturita, Colo.	350
Vitro Uranium Co.	Salt Lake City, Utah	550
Total		8,960

During the last six months of 1956 the AEC negotiated concentrate purchase contracts for production from the following mills to be built:

Operator	Location	Capacity, Tons Ore per Day
Atomic Fuel Extraction Corp.	Bedrock, Colo.	200
Dawn Mining Co.	Ford, Wash.	400
Gunnison Mining Co.	Gunnison, Colo.	200
Homestake-New Mexico Partners	Grants, N. Mex.	750
Lost Creek Oil & Uranium Corp.	Split Rock, Wyo.	400
Lucky Mc Uranium Corp.	Fremont County, Wyo.	750
Texas Zinc Minerals Corp.	Mexican Hat, Utah	775
Trace Elements Corp.	Maybell, Colo.	300

Contracts were signed which provided for increased production from the Salt Lake City mill of Vitro Uranium Corporation and a new mill of larger capacity at Rifle, Colorado, to be constructed by Union Carbide Nuclear Company. Union Carbide Nuclear Company also was to install upgrading plants at Slick Rock, Colorado, and Green River, Utah, to ship concentrates to the Rifle mill. The estimated investment in the privately owned mills in operation in January, 1957, aggregated $50 million, with an additional private investment of about $35 million in mills under construction or for which purchase contracts were signed. Continued expansion was necessary to concentrate the additional quantities of uranium produced. During the last half of 1956 the production of uranium oxide (U_3O_8) concentrate totaled 3400 tons, more than double the 1600 tons produced during the last half of 1955.

2. Phosphate Rock Recovery Plants

The uranium found in the phosphate rock formations in Florida and a number of Western states, which are a greater potential source of uranium than the Colorado Plateau, must undergo tremendous processing and concentration because uranium represents only 0.01 to 0.02 percent of the rocks. In 1955 there were four plants attempting economic recovery of uranium as a by-product of fertilizer production. These four plants, all of which used Florida rock, were located and operated as follows:

Joliet, Ill.	Blockson Chemical
Nichols, Fla.	Virginia Carolina Chemical
Bartow, Fla.	International Minerals and Chemical
Texas City, Texas	Texas City Chemicals

The extraction of uranium from phosphates offers important implications for the fertilizer industry. Its potential rests upon the development of less expensive extraction methods. Production of small tonnages of by-product uranium from Florida phosphate rock continued in 1957.

FEED MATERIAL PLANTS

The uranium ore processed in the United States and the concentrated ore obtained from foreign sources is manufactured into refined uranium metal and uranium compounds before it is "fed" to plants for the manufacture of fissionable materials. At the beginning of 1957 the AEC owned privately operated feed materials facilities located at Fernald, Ohio, St. Louis, Missouri, and Paducah, Kentucky; and progress on a new feed materials center at Weldon Spring, Missouri, was reported as satisfactory.

A new step was taken in the AEC's attempt to broaden private industrial participation in the atomic energy program when on October 27, 1955, the Commission invited private industry to finance and supply feed materials. The request was for private industry to supply up to 5000 tons per year of uranium oxide (U_3O_8) equivalent as uranium trioxide (UO_3), uranium tetrafluoride (UF_4), or uranium hexafluoride (UF_6) over a five-year period beginning April 1, 1959. Seven proposals were received by the October 1, 1956, deadline. On December 5, 1956, the AEC signed a letter of contract with the General Chemical Division of the Allied Chemical and Dye Corporation, New York, N.Y., whose proposal provided the lowest cost to the government. Utilizing uranium concentrates furnished by the Commission, the company proposes to supply 5000 tons uranium oxide (U_3O_8) equivalent of uranium hexafluoride a year. The company was to employ a new process which permitted by-passing a refining step used in Commission plants, and will accomplish purification by distilling the uranium hexafluoride. The company expects its new plant to be in operation by April 1, 1959.

MANUFACTURE OF FISSIONABLE MATERIALS

The refined uranium metal and uranium compounds produced at the feed materials plants are shipped to AEC plants for the manufacture of fissionable materials. The uranium metal is required for the production of plutonium, and uranium hexafluoride is required for the gaseous diffusion process in the production of U-235.

In 1957 there were three gaseous diffusion plants for the production of U-235 in the United States. The first two plants were located at Oak Ridge, Tennessee, and Paducah, Kentucky. Both were operated by the Union Carbide and Chemical Company. The third and newest gaseous diffusion plant was at Portsmouth, Ohio, operated by the Goodyear Tire and Rubber Company. Plutonium was produced at Hanford, Washington, and Savannah River, South Carolina. The Hanford plant was built and operated for the AEC by the duPont Chemical Company until 1946; since that time it has been operated by the General Electric Company. The Savannah River plant was built in 1951 as a part of the H-bomb project. It was designed so that either tritium can be produced from lithium or plutonium can be produced from U-238. The Savannah River plant is operated for the AEC by duPont.

One of the initial problems of the Manhattan project of 1942 was to produce enough fissionable material to build an atomic bomb. Two types of large-scale production were developed: (1) the separation of the fissionable U-235 isotope from the much larger quantity of nonfissionable U-238, and (2) the conversion of nonfissionable U-238 through neutron bombardment into fissionable plutonium.

Isotope separation of U-235 from U-238 was the function of the Oak Ridge plant. This was accomplished by gaseous diffusion and by an electromagnetic plant. From the beginning in 1945 the gaseous diffusion process was "unbelievably successful," and by 1947 the more expensive and inefficient electromagnetic plant was shut down.

Plutonium production by bombardment of U-238 was the function of the Hanford plant, on which construction was begun in the summer of 1943. This was accomplished in three reactors.

By the summer of 1945 shipments of highly concentrated fissionable materials were being made from Oak Ridge and Hanford.

For about two and one-half years after the destruction of Hiroshima on August 6, 1945, the atomic energy program stagnated while Congress arrived at a policy, the AEC was created, and the Manhattan District organization was rebuilt. However, in 1947 expansion was begun. At that time manufacture of plutonium in nuclear reactors appeared to be more promising, and the AEC concentrated its expansion plans on plutonium. The General Electric Company took over the Hanford plant, rehabilitated and restored the three reactors to wartime capacity, and began the construction of two new reactors and a chemical plant to extract the plutonium.

In 1948 the test of a more powerful A-bomb at the Eniwetok proving ground seemed to have demonstrated a continuing need for U-235 as well as for plutonium. A few months after the test the AEC announced a $60 million expansion at Oak Ridge. In 1949, after the Russians exploded a bomb, AEC began an additional $160 million expansion at Oak Ridge. This appeared to be about double the Oak Ridge capacity.

In 1950, with Korea and President Truman's decision to develop the H-bomb, AEC (1) began the construction of the second gaseous diffusion plant at Paducah, with the same capacity as Oak Ridge and (2) started work on three dual-purpose reactors at Savannah River, South Carolina: (a) to manufacture tritium from lithium for the super (H) bomb and (b) to produce plutonium from U-238.

In 1955 the above plants were in operation and the third gaseous diffusion plant was under construction at Portsmouth, Ohio. These five plants are gigantic installations, each of which cost in excess of $1 billion. Through the fiscal year 1954 total government expenditure for atomic energy was more than $10.3 billion. Thus these plants cost more than one-half of the expenditures. Total gross government investment in atomic plants was $6.2 billion. This is an amount greater than the total plant investments of duPont, Union Carbide, General Electric, and Westinghouse Electric. Therefore it is quite clear that only the government could have financed and constructed these plants for the manufacture of fissionable materials.

APPLICATION OF NUCLEAR DEVELOPMENTS

Nuclear research and development before World War II probably can be attributed more to the investigating urge of scientists than to an end-use application. The great urgency to beat Germany in the development of an A-bomb caused the United States to undertake the tremendous research and development program, greatly accelerated research, made possible the development through government expenditure, focused attention on the military aspects of the program, and caused the general public to lose sight of the fact that the applications of nuclear developments are twofold: for (a) military and (b) peace.

1. Military Applications

Major military applications include explosives, motive power, and radiological use. Obviously many peacetime applications are jointly shared with military use.

A. Explosives

To achieve an explosion was the purpose of the World War II atomic energy program. A chain reaction will not occur until there is present a minimum amount (a critical mass) of some atomic explosive. When the critical mass is brought together an explosion is spontaneous. Stated simply, an atomic bomb is a device containing at least two pieces of U-235 or plutonium, each slightly smaller than a critical mass, which slaps these pieces together at the moment an explosion is desired. The H-bomb differs in that very light atoms such as hydrogen and deuterium are combined or fused, releasing perhaps a thousand times more energy than splitting U-235 or plutonium in an A-bomb. The problem is that to bring about the fusion a temperature reaching millions of degrees is required. To produce this extremely high temperature, an A-bomb is required as a "kicker."

An appraisal of the problems and progress of developments of explosives is of course not a matter of public knowledge. Evidence indicates, however, that the 1945 A-bomb was a "rather clumsy and inefficient piece of mechanism." One of the major tasks of the AEC was to improve the bomb. This was the task of the AEC's Los Alamos Scientific Laboratory in New Mexico and the Western Electric Laboratory at Sandia.

The first job was to increase the efficiency of the A-bomb, and it appeared that substantial success had been achieved with the bomb tested at Eniwetok in the summer of 1948, which reportedly developed about 50 percent efficiency and released energy equivalent to about 100,-000 tons of TNT. The establishment of the Nevada proving ground and frequent additional tests have indicated further improvements in efficiency.

An additional improvement was made in the weight of the firing mechanism. A B-29 superfortress was required to carry the Hiroshima bomb. There were hints as early as 1951 that fast fighter bombers could carry the bomb, which made enemy interception harder. Other developments which perhaps resulted from improvements in the firing mechanism include the application of the bomb so that it could be fired from oversized mortars at targets twenty or thirty miles away.

Of tremendous significance was the use of an atomic warhead in a V-2 type of rocket, which in 1951 had ranges of around 200 miles. These rockets could be launched by land or sea. The possibility of intercontinental guided missiles with atomic warheads was approaching reality at the beginning of 1958.

The H-superbomb and nuclear explosives were so well perfected in 1954 that a Congressional committee concluded that nuclear energy could "ravage this planet beyond recognition."

B. Motive Power

The main obstacles to the use of nuclear fuel in transportation for military or peace have been (a) the extremely high cost of a nuclear reactor,

(b) the difficulty of safeguarding its operation—for example, in an aircraft—so that if the reactor and its shielding were accidentally damaged it would not be a source of dangerous radiation, and (c) the immense weight of shielding required to contain the radiation from even a small reactor.

The most intriguing thing about nuclear fuel is the packing of 10 million KWH into a pound of practically weightless fuel. This makes it possible for the first time for moving vehicles to cruise almost indefinitely without regard to refueling bases.

For the above reasons, naval craft were the first to use nuclear fuel. The nuclear-powered submarines, the *Nautilus* of 1954 and the *Sea Wolf*, were the first of the navy ships. A reactor is an ideal power source for a submarine not only because it will operate for months without refueling but also because it requires no oxygen and will propel the submarine with unmatched speed. Nuclear-fueled vessels are here—economics is the limiting factor.

Nuclear-powered aircraft have been a government project since the end of World War II. Not much progress was made while it was an Air Force—Fairchild—project, but by 1951 it was on the development schedule after being approved by the AEC, the Navy, and the Joint Chiefs of Staff. Although the project is a top secret, it is known that substantial progress has been made. The AEC in 1955 was spending more than $5 million on the aircraft program at the National Reactor Testing Station in Idaho. General Electric and United Aircraft were working on the power cycle for the aircraft and, at the same time, other companies were concerned with airframe design. The problems are difficult.

C. Radiological Warfare

The deliberate use of radioactive materials as weapons is possible. They could be used effectively to keep troops from entering a contaminated area or workmen from entering a contaminated plant. The length of period of contamination could be controlled by selecting isotopes with the right rates of decay. Waste materials are available from the Hanford and Savannah plants and other radioactive materials could be manufactured to required specifications.

2. Peacetime Applications

The same Congressional committee that reported that nuclear energy could "ravage this planet beyond recognition" went on to say "or make it fair beyond the wildest dreams of our fathers." Two of these amazing developments which were already in application in 1955 were (a) nu-clear power and (b) isotopes.

A. Nuclear Power

The reactor is the "key" machine of peacetime nuclear power. One ap-proach toward the understanding of the role of the reactor is to state that at Hanford the end-product is plutonium, and, as a by-product, heat is produced unavoidably. In 1951, for example, heat produced at Hanford was probably in excess of 1,000,000 KW. The heat is generated in the piles of the reactor. Water is flushed through the piles (or core) of the reactor in order to keep them cool and in sufficient quantity to carry away all the heat without raising the water to the boiling point. This hot water is then dumped into the Columbia River. As a result the Columbia is warmed and heat is lost. Obviously this intense heat could be used in the form of boiling water to make steam which would spin turbine-gen-erators to produce electric power—that is, of course, if there were a high-temperature reactor rather than a low-temperature reactor. Since the Hanford reactors are of the low-temperature type, they must be kept cool and the water comes out below the boiling point.

When the Savannah River reactors were designed the AEC gave seri-ous thought to installing reactors with a temperature high enough to make their energy output usable. Successful experience with the low-temperature reactors and the time element were the decisive factors. The AEC thus has these two huge reactor installations which are throwing away several million kilowatts of energy at the same time they are drain-ing several million kilowatts of electricity from the country's power facili-ties for the purpose of operating the plants.

The availability of high-temperature metals such as titanium and zir-conium, together with sufficient time for research and development of high-temperature reactors, will probably make it possible for future AEC reactor installations to produce utilizable heat converted into electric power at the same time that plutonium or tritium is being produced. This would put the government farther into the power business and would lessen the cost per KWH as most of the capital investment would be made to turn out end-products for military applications. Nuclear power for peacetime use is thus technically possible and would be eco-nomically advantageous, the latter in three ways: electric power is not used from existing facilities, energy in the form of heat is not thrown away, and the cost per KWH is reduced.

Private industry looks at the reactor as a machine to produce an end-product of heat to drive a turbine to make electricity. The by-product would be plutonium. Actually plutonium would be an end-product along with other isotopes which are of great importance because of their radio-active properties.

Private industry looks at a reactor as an instrument to receive a nuclear fuel, e.g., uranium. The reactor "burns" the U-235 that makes up 1 part of the 140 parts of natural uranium and produces heat for conversion into electric power. At the same time the burning of the U-235 transmutes the U-238 into fissionable plutonium. A chemical plant cleans the fission product "ash" out of the fuel and returns it to the reactor. The pluto-nium burns, producing energy and more plutonium.

What nuclear power scientists had as their objective was to develop a "breeder" reactor—a reactor in which more than one atom of plutonium was produced for every atom of U-235 burned in the process. The achievement of this objective made it possible for a reactor to produce more fuel than it burns and at the same time to produce power and other by-products. The feasibility of producing electric power by using a reactor to replace the boiler in a conventional steam power plant (or to replace a hydro plant) (see Figure 7.1) was proved by the AEC in 1951 with its Experimental Breeder Reactor, which developed 100 kilowatts of electricity. A year later the Homogeneous Reactor Experiment at Oak Ridge produced 150 kilowatts of electric power. Thus a reactor that pro-duces more fuel than it burns is a breeder; one that can make about the same amount it burns is a converter.

In 1955, *Business Week,* in its June 18 issue, reported that there were four types of reactors that looked good then. These are briefly described in Figure 7.1. In addition *Business Week* explained that designers of re-actors had a wide choice of fuels:

To begin with, there is uranium-235, the only natural material that can fission by itself. Uranium-233 and plutonium-239 also fission, but are man-made. They can be made, it happens, in the same sort of reactor that is used for power production. So a reactor operator can pad out his fuel with uranium-238 or thorium which are called fertile fuels because they are the raw material from which plutonium and U-233 are produced. . . . The reactor that is being built by Babcock and Wilcox for Consolidated Edison Co. of N.Y. is a converter that will use uranium and thorium together. The fission of U-235 also will convert the thorium to another fissionable element—U-233. General Electric is using straight uranium dioxide in its dual-cycle boiling reactor.

Thus nuclear power is technically feasible, but private enterprise is motivated by economics. One estimate in 1954 was that a sizable nuclear

1. Today's sources of power for generating electricity are these:

COAL
OIL
TURBINE
TURBINE
GENERATOR
HYDRO
ELECTRIC POWER

2. Nuclear power source changes part of this set-up.

GENERATOR
TURBINE
STEAM
WATER
CONDENSER
HEAT EXCHANGER
HOT FLUID
COOL FLUID
PILE
ATOMIC FUEL
ELECTRIC POWER

3. Tomorrow's nuclear power plant basically will operate like this:

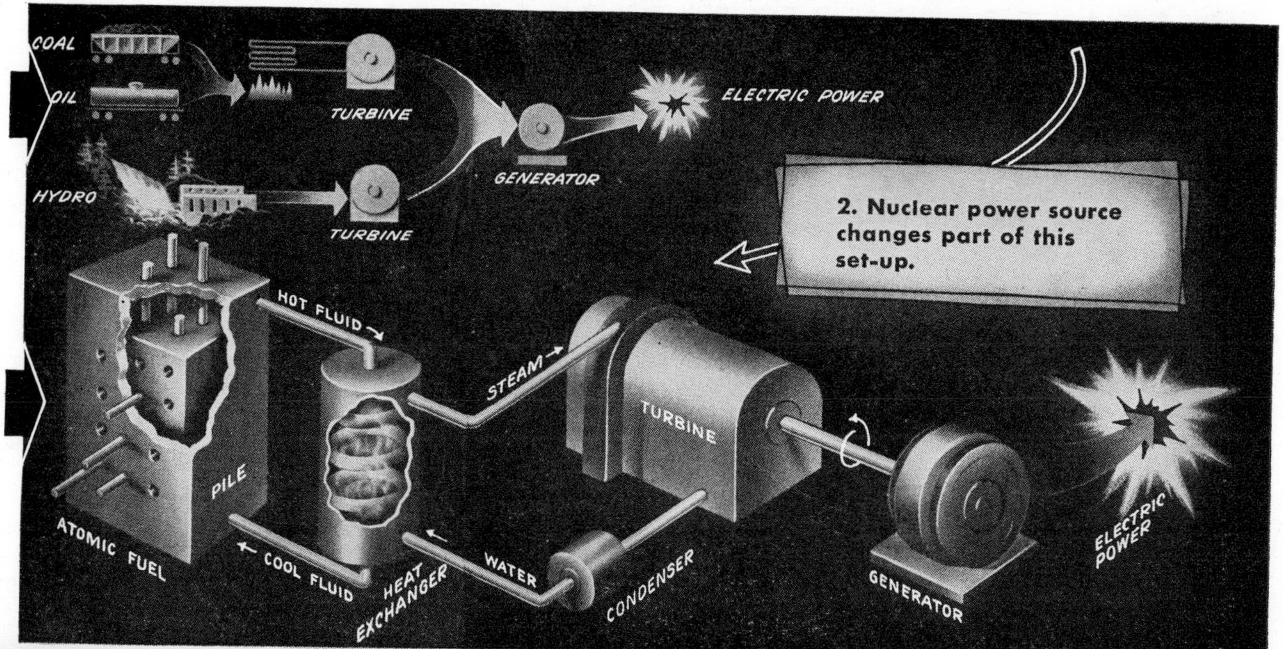

Here are four types of reactors that look good now.

1. Pressurized water flows through the reactor, picks up heat from the fission of fuels. High pressure keeps that water from boiling. The heat passes through an exchanger, makes steam from other water. The steam drives a turbine-generator.

2. A homogeneous reactor has a continuous fuel system, instead of one arranged in lumps in the reactor. A solution of a fuel and a liquid also carries heat to steam generators, much like the pressurized water method.

3. Liquid metal can replace pressurized fluid or solutions of fuel as a heat carrier. It has a very high boiling point, doesn't need high pressures. But sometimes it is difficult to handle.

4. Direct boiling is simple. Steam forms in the heart of the reactor, goes directly to a turbine. So it eliminates in-between heat exchangers, which have heat losses. But direct boiling hampers reactor chain reaction. One improved system of G.E. smooths that out.

Figure 7.1. Development of Power by Reactors. (By permission from *Business Week*, June 18, 1955)

power plant would cost $600 per installed kilowatt, as compared with $160 to $180 per kilowatt for a conventional coal-fired plant. For most corporations this would put the cost of a nuclear power station at a prohibitively high figure—from $50 million to $100 million. Thus *Time* concluded that even "groups of companies, working together, may need Government aid not only in financing the reactor but in the form of a purchase contract for all the plutonium produced."

Charles A. Thomas, president of Monsanto Chemical Company, estimated in 1954 that it would cost $60 million to build a 125,000 KW atomic power plant (about one-tenth the power used by greater Boston). Of this sum, $44 million would be the cost of the reactor for plutonium production and could come from government; the remaining $16 million would be for the heat-transfer units, turbines, etc., for the power plant and might come from private industry. By basing the price of power on the $16 million capitalization, Thomas estimated that power could be produced for as low as .003 cents per KWH as compared to .008 cents per KWH for coal. Other industrialists differed sharply with Thomas' estimates and proposals for government help and indicated that private enterprise should finance and develop nuclear power facilities.

Most power experts agreed in 1955 that for "years to come" conventional power would be more economical than nuclear systems, but that commercial nuclear power was "just around the corner" instead of several decades away as had been only recently predicted. This more optimistic estimate was based upon the rapid reduction in the cost of nuclear power. The hope was that a most significant contributing factor to lower costs would be the AEC's five-year Reactor Development Program, given below:

Reactor Type	Builder	Total Estimated Cost	Scheduled Completion
Pressurized Water	Westinghouse Electric Duquesne Light (Operator)	$85,000,000	1957
Sodium-graphite	North American Aviation	10,000,000	1955
Boiling water	Argonne National Lab.	17,000,000	1956
Fast breeder	Argonne National Lab.	40,000,000	1958
Homogeneous	Oak Ridge National Lab.	47,000,000	1959

With the exception of the pressurized-water reactor, which is a prototype plant, these projects were all reactor experiments. The Pressurized Water Reactor at Shippingport, Pennsylvania, was scheduled to be the nation's first large-scale (at least 60,000 kilowatts) civilian nuclear power plant (see Figure 7.2). The Sodium Reactor experiment ran into construction difficulties which postponed the date of completion until 1957. First of the reactors to begin operation was the Experimental Boiling Water (EBWR, see Figure 7.3), which began producing power early in 1957. It was designed to produce 20 megawatts of heat and 5000 kilowatts of electricity, which was considered to be the minimum capacity to provide the experimental data desired. The first core of the Fast Breeder

Figure 7.2. The United States' First Central Station Atomic Power Plant, Shippingport, Pa. (Westinghouse Atomic Power Division)

Reactor at Argonne National Laboratory was damaged, a new core was designed, and construction was scheduled to start in June, 1957. The Homogeneous Reactor at Oak Ridge National Laboratory, scheduled for completion in 1959, was undergoing testing difficulties in 1957. Additional experimental reactors were a part of the AEC's program and were under way in 1957. Information on these and other reactor programs is available through AEC reports.

Dr. Lawrence R. Hafstad, chief of AEC's reactor development, predicted that, at the conclusion of the Reactor Development Program, nuclear power plants could be built that would be competitive with conventional steam power generating stations.

Further reduction of costs was expected to result from the tremendous amount of research and development initiative released with the Atomic

Figure 7.3.   Experimental Boiling Water Reactor.

"The EBWR is the Atomic Energy Commission's Experimental Boiling Water Reactor at Argonne National Laboratory 25 miles southwest of Chicago.

"Argonne's new reactor will produce only a trickle of power (5000 kw.), but it is not intended as a commercial source of electricity. The first completed of the AEC's power reactors, it was designed specifically to evaluate one of the many approaches to the problem of cheap nuclear power.

"The reactor is housed in a dome-roofed steel building whose purpose is to keep radioactive matter from escaping into the air in the unlikely event of an explosion. Its nuclear core, enclosed in a thick lead and concrete shield, contains fuel elements whose active material is natural uranium and uranium slightly enriched with fissionable U-235. Among the fuel elements circulates ordinary water, which acts both as moderator (to slow neutrons down) and as a heat-absorbing agent.

"When the chain reaction starts, the water boils, forming high-pressure steam as in an ordinary coal-fired boiler. The steam, which is slightly radioactive, goes directly to a turbogenerator which turns its energy into electricity. Lack of an intermediate heat-exchanger to generate nonradioactive steam is the characteristic feature of the EBWR, and one of its advantages as an economical power producer. Chief disadvantage: because of the radioactivity of the steam, the turbine, condenser, and related equipment are also radioactive and must be operated by remote control." (Photo courtesy of International News Photos; data from *Time*, February, 1957)

Energy Act of 1954, which opened the door to private industrial development of nuclear energy. Private firms which want to build nuclear power
plants or other atomic facilities may apply to the AEC for a license. The
license permits them to build, own, and operate atomic power plants.
The companies can lease, but not buy, atomic fuel (U-235, U-233, plutonium) from the AEC at a fee, and they can produce and use additional
fuel or, if they wish, sell it to the AEC at a "fair price."

In February, 1955, Consolidated Edison of New York announced that
it intended to apply to the AEC for a license to build and operate an
atomic power plant near Peekskill, New York, which would generate
from 100,000 to 200,000 KW. This was to be done entirely without
government assistance. Commonwealth Edison Company followed with

the announcement of a nuclear plant which it expected to be in operation
in the Chicago area within five years. The Yankee Atomic Electric Company released plans for a plant in western Massachusetts. By mid-1956
forty-four private utility companies were participating in nine nuclear
power projects which had a total planned generating capacity of 1,112,-
500 kilowatts (see Figure 7.4). These included the AEC-financed Du-
quesne Light-operated plant at Shippingport, Pennsylvania, shown with
an ultimate capacity of 100,000 kilowatts. During 1956 Consolidated Edi-

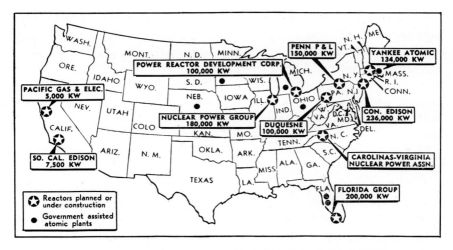

Figure 7.4.   Tomorrow's Power Sites. (*The New York Times*, July 8, 1956)

son of New York firmed up its plan and received a construction permit
for a 236,000-kilowatt plant in which 140,000 kilowatts will be supplied
by a nuclear reactor and 96,000 by an oil-fired superheater. Commonwealth Edison received a construction permit for the 180,000-kilowatt
nuclear power plant to be built at Dresden, Illinois, near Chicago.

By the end of 1956, plans had been announced for a total of seventeen
United States nuclear reactor power plants not owned by the government. The total investment was estimated to range between $400 million
and $500 million for an aggregate generating capacity of 1,400,000 kilo-
watts of electricity. This did not include the government-owned, privately operated plant at Shippingport, Pennsylvania. Thus a dream was
becoming a reality. General Electric Company's estimate was that the
total United States generating capacity in 1975 would be 375 million kilowatts which would include: nuclear, 40 million KW; thermal, 300 million
KW; hydro, 35 million KW. The Panel on the Impact of Peaceful Uses

of Atomic Energy gave a range of installed nuclear capability in 1975 from 20 million to 45 million KW, and for 1980, 52 million to 135 million KW. General Electric Company's estimate was 120 million kilowatts of nuclear power by 1980 out of a total United States generating capacity of 514 million kilowatts.

B. Isotopes

One of the most significant applications of nuclear developments has been with radioactive isotopes. The principal source of radioactive isotopes is the Oak Ridge National Laboratory. In 1946 the AEC initiated a policy of distributing isotopes at cost, and by 1955 almost 60,000 shipments to more than 2000 authorized users in the United States and 46 foreign countries had been made. This vast growth and interest in isotopes may be attributed in part to the facts that they can be used or studied without access to classified information, their cost has rendered their use economically possible, and they have numerous applications. These uses may be thought of as falling into three general types: industrial, agricultural, and medical. In reality, their uses may be thought of as innumerable and unpredictable.

Industrial users of isotopes were estimated in 1955 as in excess of 1000. Of these about 300 were using isotopes as thickness gauges. A radioactive source is placed on one side of a material and a radiation detection instrument on the other side; changes in the thickness alter the degree of radiation passing through. The changes are registered by the instruments and thus make possible continuous-process control as compared with old methods where the flow of material had to be stopped and a sample taken. Isotopes are being used to determine the point of separation of two products in petroleum pipelines. Oil companies are also measuring friction wear in pistons. They use an irradiated piston ring, and wear is calculated by the amount of radioactivity in the oil. In addition, radiations can promote chemical reactions; e.g., one use is the irradiation of polyethylene plastics, which improves their mechanical properties and greatly increases their heat resistance. Estimates were that by 1955 about $100 million had been saved each year by the industrial use of isotopes. The AEC forecast that in the next ten years these savings would be multiplied to a billion dollars annually.

Agricultural application of isotopes is of growing importance. Radioactive materials have been used to induce genetic changes. A rust-free variety of oats and a strain of peanuts with a 30 percent greater yield have been developed. Experiments have also shown that irradiated food can be preserved for longer periods without refrigeration. Forecasts of the effect of nuclear application on agriculture appear to have unlimited potentials.

Medical applications of radioactive isotopes and materials may revolutionize medical science. The value of radium in the treatment of cancer has been known for some time. The increased availability and lower price of radioactive materials have been factors that have placed medical uses of isotopes in the forefront of peacetime applications of nuclear developments. Radioactive materials have been used to determine the location of tumors. In addition, isotopes have been used in the treatment of leukemia, hypertension, and the heart disease polycythemia vera. Every day new discoveries are being made and applied. Medical research, using these new radioactive isotopes and materials made from them, is being carried out along three main lines: (1) to obtain a better knowledge of biological processes, (2) for diagnosis of diseases, and (3) for treatment of diseases. One leading authority in the field has stated that the use of radioactive isotopes had by 1955 advanced the state of medical knowledge to what it would otherwise have been in 1980. This was just the beginning.

Peacetime applications of nuclear developments will multiply as a result of private and government research. Christopher P. Keim, director of stable isotope research and production at Oak Ridge, stated in July, 1955, that 99 percent of the research in atomic energy at the Oak Ridge National Laboratory was constructive compared to 1 percent for destructive weapons. Dr. Keim predicted that "the constructive peacetime uses of atomic energy will increase in emphasis" and indicated that vast new developments in the fields of industry and medicine will soon be ready for public usage. Most significantly Dr. Keim concluded: "Controlled climate is also a distinct possibility of the future."

Technology is the indispensable finder, developer, and multiplier of natural resources. Nuclear developments have indeed made the "horizon unlimited."

THE UNITED STATES' NUCLEAR POSITION

An analysis of the comparative position of the United States and the rest of the world would be desirable in terms of, first, military and, second, peacetime applications. Unfortunately, this is not possible.

The basic raw material position of the United States and our dependence on outside sources of supplies were presented in the section on

"Raw Materials." Commenting on the Russian position in July, 1951, which is a long time ago in the "Atomic Age," *Business Week* concluded that an adequate uranium supply was a serious obstacle to expanding Russian production of bombs.

"The Russians are working their Bohemian mines with an urgency (ores are transported by air) that suggests that this field is their chief reliance. They are not known to have any other source of uranium except a little in Russian Turkestan.

"If this is the case, it's good news. For not only are the Bohemian mines strategically vulnerable; they produce ores of a quality the AEC wouldn't be bothered with."

Resources are dynamic. Harris, Upham and Company's *Atomic Energy Review* for November, 1956, reported: "The Soviet appears to have enough uranium to support her own [nuclear power] program and those of her [satellite] neighbors."

Another basic fact, which is often forgotten and which should be known with certainty, is that scientific discovery is not the monopoly of one country; and further, once a development is known to be possible, its realization is more rapidly achieved. One primary reason for the presentation of the development of nuclear science before World War II was to show how dependent the United States was on the contributions of European nuclear scientists. Our tremendous speeding up of nuclear development under war and "crash" programs has proved what was possible. With this knowledge, facilitated to some extent by "intelligence," scientists throughout the world have been able to achieve what we have accomplished in a far shorter period of time.

The basic comparative physical nuclear facilities by location are given in Figure 7.5, "An Atomic Map of the World."

Military nuclear comparative positions cannot be made because information from outside the United States is almost totally unavailable especially with respect to Russia. What is known about the United States is limited, but the previous discussion on military application was an attempt to develop some of the evidence of our strength. The best evidence on Russian nuclear bombs still seems to be obtained by monitoring radioactivity in the atmosphere. We know that the Russians made and detonated their first bomb in the summer of 1949 and that this bomb was probably as good as and possibly better than our first model since they had access through Fuchs and others to the work on this model. We know that they exploded no bomb between 1949 and the summer of 1951. We know of the subsequent tests they have made. Each new test

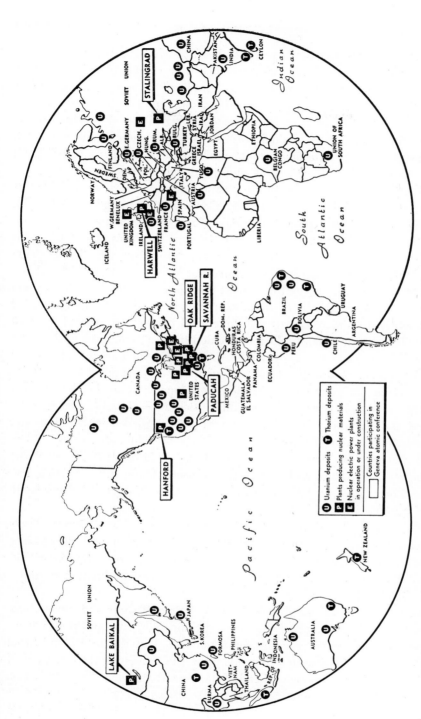

Figure 7.5. An Atomic Map of the World—Nuclear Fuel Deposits, Production Centers, and Power Plants. (The New York Times, August 14, 1955)

seemed to have come many months ahead of what the United States intelligence had anticipated. What we should have learned by now is that we cannot win an armaments race by standing still when it is known for certain that Russia is running as fast as she can. The only way to win is to run as fast as we can in nuclear technological developments. At the same time, we can build dual-purpose facilities, such as the Savannah River plant, so that military applications may be on an "and/or" basis with peacetime applications of nuclear developments.

Peacetime nuclear comparative positions are made easier each day as more information becomes available. Comparative strengths can best be measured in terms of power potentials of reactor developments. The rate of reactor development will be determined on the basis of (1) the need and/or demand for energy and (2) the supply of reactors that is made available by those countries that have the know-how to produce them.

The demand for energy throughout the world may be divided into two general areas: (1) where inanimate energy is now in full use and (2) where inanimate energy is meager and people are in need for lack of it. The first area can be further divided into (a) countries such as the United States and Germany where the demand for energy is high and increasing but the supply position is good, and (b) countries such as Britain, France, Belgium, Italy, Sweden, and Japan where the demand for energy is high but where supply difficulties have already been encountered and costs are rising. Russia might also be placed with this group. The second major group where the supply of inanimate energy is low and the need is great would include India, Pakistan, China, Southeast Asia, most of Africa, and large areas of South America. Greenland, Iceland, Puerto Rico, and Alaska would come under this list of "power have-not countries."

The supply of nuclear reactors for power appeared in 1956 most likely to come initially from the United States, Great Britain, and Russia. The first and most rapid developments will thus probably occur in Great Britain followed by Russia. These two countries have the know-how and a pressing need.

Great Britain, as has already been seen, is fuel short and power hungry. Coal is becoming more scarce and the cost of coal and power is increasing. The British government announced that the future industrial development of the nation depends upon the successful development of nuclear power. Britain was ahead of the United States in the construction of the first nuclear power plant.

A most dramatic nuclear development took place in Great Britain in

October, 1956, when Queen Elizabeth officially dedicated the first large-scale nuclear power station in the world, the 75,000-kilowatt plant at Calder Hall, in northern England. As the Queen pulled the switch, 10,-000 kilowatts of electricity were delivered into the lines of the Central Electricity Authority. The reactor producing this power—the first of two in the Calder Hall station—was designed to generate 40,000 kilowatts. Calder Hall B, identical to the first station, was under construction in 1956, as was a four-reactor plant at Chapel Cross in southwest Scotland. Also under construction in 1956 at Dounreay, Scotland, was a station using a fast breeder reactor. The Central Electric Authority had plans for three 100,000-kilowatt stations in 1957. Total British plans called for a nuclear-generating capacity of 4 million kilowatts to be completed before 1965 at a cost of more than $1 billion. British industry, which was participating in the construction of all these power plants, was actively seeking reactor business abroad. By January, 1957, British firms had already sold several research reactors to be used outside the country.

Only those in the know in Russia know how she stands nuclear-power-wise. In 1954 she had been operating plutonium reactors for five years and she must have devoted considerable effort to the development of power-producing reactors. Information available in January, 1957, indicated very rapid progress in the nuclear power field. The Russians were the first to build and operate a small nuclear power plant, a 5000-kilowatt pressurized water unit which they began to operate in June, 1954. Russia planned to build ten different types of power reactors by 1960 plus a nuclear propulsion system for an icebreaker vessel. These nuclear power units were part of a five-year program with a target of 2,500,000 kilowatts by 1960. Russia was coöperating very closely in 1956 with all of its satellite nations and had agreed to provide both reactors and "atom smashers" for nuclear research. Czechoslovakia was building a 2000-kilowatt reactor with Russia's help and was planning a 150,000-kilowatt power reactor to be supplied by the Soviet. Poland had a Central Atomic Research Center under construction which would use a Russian research reactor. East Germany planned to begin construction of a 100,000-kilowatt nuclear power plant designed by Russia. The Soviet offered a research reactor and other equipment to Yugoslavia in 1956, but the United States AEC reported in January, 1957, that discussions were under way with Yugoslavia.

In free Europe many nuclear activities had taken place prior to 1957, but the atomic achievement of that year was Euratom. Prior to 1957, the peak year of interest was 1955 with the United Nations Atomic Energy Conference in Geneva, which unfolded secrets and possibilities for the peacetime use of the atom. The Swiss purchased the swimming pool research reactor built by the United States and exhibited to the public during the Conference. The Swiss government and 100 industrial concerns followed this by building another research reactor near Zurich. In Italy, which had pioneered in nuclear research before World War II, the Fiat Company announced in 1955 its intention to buy a 10,000-kilowatt nuclear plant; the Italian government was negotiating a bilateral agreement with the United States government to implement the transaction. Belgium's interest in atomic energy began with her role as a major supplier of uranium from the Belgian Congo to the United States during World War II. The Belgian government had in 1956 a laboratory equipped with one research reactor and was planning a 100,000-kilowatt nuclear plant. France began a five-year program of nuclear development in 1952 and placed in operation in 1956 a reactor which produced 40,000 kilowatts of heat plus plutonium. A successor to this reactor was scheduled for the production of 50,000 kilowatts plus plutonium in 1957. A 60,000-kilowatt nuclear station was being built southwest of Paris, and construction on a second plant was started in 1957. The French cabinet had approved two additional nuclear power stations. France was supplying her own uranium, which was estimated to last until 1975, but in addition she had large thorium deposits in Madagascar. West Germany was prohibited from engaging in nuclear activity until May, 1955. In the eighteen months that followed Germany bought three research reactors in the United States and a fourth from Great Britain. In addition, German companies had designed and built three uranium-processing plants abroad. This was the free Europe picture prior to 1957.

Euratom (the six-nation European Atomic Community) brought together the nuclear power interests of the member countries of the European Coal and Steel Community in 1957. Thus the fissioned atom was organized and administered like coal and steel as an additional step toward the fusion of Europe. The six member countries pooled their nuclear resources and plans and set Euratom's 1963 reactor objective at 3,000,000 KW. Euratom's plans called for a nuclear power capacity in 1967 of 15,000,000 KW. This should be compared with the United States' definite plans for 1,500,000 KW, Great Britain's 4,000,000 KW 1965 objective and Russia's announced goal of 2,500,000 KW by 1960. Euratom's plans could make western Europe the leading atomic power center in the world by 1967. Euratom was spurred on by the fuel crisis caused by the blockage of the Suez Canal. Euratom's nuclear capacity of 15,000,000

KW was estimated to cost $2 billion more than conventional power, but the conclusion in 1957 was that European atomic power should be competitive with the high cost of conventional power there by the early 1960's.

In the rest of the world, interest in nuclear energy was keen among the "power have-not countries." Australia and the Union of South Africa, as free world sources of uranium, were in good bargaining positions to achieve the benefits of the Atomic Age. India was an exception to an almost-no-progress report in 1956. India had one research reactor nearing completion, and another powerful one was being obtained from Canada. India was developing its deposits of thorium, which are among the largest and highest grade in the world.

Canada, one of the wartime three which developed the atomic bomb, has long been a leader in peacetime nuclear research. Her Chalk River project has contributed much to reactor development and to other areas of nuclear research. The first Canadian nuclear power station with a capacity of 20,000 kilowatts was scheduled for completion in 1958.

Whether the other countries outside the United States and Canada in both areas of need and/or demand for inanimate energy are to have the benefits of nuclear power will be determined by the policies adopted by the United States, Great Britain, and Russia in making available reactors to these power-hungry countries. Euratom may become a power to be considered.

Great Britain as early as 1954 wanted to be the first nation in a position to export both power reactors and trained personnel to the many underdeveloped and other power-deficient countries. The possible economic power development would be of tremendous benefit both to these countries and to Great Britain. The latter promised to have a display equal to that of the United States at the Conference on Peaceful Uses of Atomic Energy in Geneva in 1955.

The Russians of course well know the advantage they could gain by perfecting and exporting nuclear power plants. The General Electric Company reported in July, 1955: " 'Have-not' Asia and Africa, and large, undeveloped areas of Latin America need it [abundant electric power that the atom promises] for their industry and their people. And so nuclear energy, for Russia, has become a long-range instrument for economic and political dominance. Communism *plus* atomic power might convert the world where Communism *alone* has failed."

The required United States policy was clear: "swift, broad progress in developing peacetime atomic energy for the world . . . with the prom-

ise of atomic fuels and technical knowledge sooner than anyone estimated."

U.S. News and World Report of July 1, 1955, headlined the problem
this way:

A RACE FOR ATOM MARKETS

There's a conference at Geneva soon that may prove more important than
the Big Four talks. It's about "atoms for peace." There the nations of the world
will show their atomic wares for industry, make their bids for a potential huge
market.

Favorites, so far, in the peacetime atomic race are U.S. and Britain. But
tipsters are warning: "Look out for the Soviets."

What are the basic problems that the United States faces? How have
we organized to arrive at the solutions? What policy decisions have been
made? These are questions that must be answered before clear recommendations for the future can be made.

UNITED STATES PROBLEMS AND POLICIES

After the announcement in 1939 that the uranium atom had been split,
a civilian Uranium Committee was established in Washington in 1940 as
a part of the national defense program. On December 6, 1941, the day
before Pearl Harbor, a new organization was set up, under the direction
of Vannevar Bush, to determine the practicality of nuclear fission; and a
planning board, headed by E. V. Murphree (now president of Standard
Oil Development Company and a member of the General Advisory Committee to the Atomic Energy Commission), was made responsible for the
vast amount of technical and engineering work, the procurement of materials, the building of pilot plants and full-scale production plants, which
were necessary before any serious consideration could be given to making an atomic bomb. During 1942 sufficient progress had been made to
justify an all-out effort to build the bomb, and all these activities were
turned over to the United States Army Corps of Engineers, which established the Manhattan District Project to administer the government's
atomic energy work.

The Manhattan District Project was in charge of this throughout World
War II until the passage of the Atomic Energy Act (the McMahon Act of
1946), when the atomic energy program of the United States was transferred from military to civilian administration. Chapter 1 of the Atomic
Energy Act of 1946 stated:

"It is hereby declared to be the policy of the people of the United States that, subject at all times to the paramount objective of assuring the common defense and security, the development and utilization of atomic energy shall, so far as is practicable, be directed toward improving the public welfare, increasing the standard of living, strengthening free competition and private enterprise, and promoting world peace."

This policy is carried over into the Atomic Energy Act (the Cole-Hickenlooper Act) of 1954 which replaced the 1946 act. The act is administered by the Atomic Energy Commission (AEC), which is composed of five civilians appointed by the President to serve five-year terms. The appointees are subject to confirmation by the Senate. The major divisions of the AEC are: Raw Materials, Production, Military Applications, Reactor Development, Research, Biology and Medicine.

Operating with the AEC are three committees set up by the 1946 and 1954 acts: the Joint Congressional Committee on Atomic Energy (nine members of each house), the Military Liaison Committee (two members of each branch of service plus a chairman), and the General Advisory Committee (nine civilians who advise the AEC on scientific and technical matters). The law requires the Joint Congressional Committee "to make continuing studies of the activities of the Atomic Energy Commission and of problems relating to the development, use and control of atomic energy." The Commission is required to keep the Joint Committee "fully and currently informed" concerning its program. In practice this administrative "watchdog" procedure has worked out most effectively.

Of the many problems that nuclear energy has created, three will be singled out for consideration: (a) the impact of nuclear energy on other energy sources, (b) the participation of private enterprise in nuclear development, and (c) the extension of the benefits of nuclear developments to other nations within the limits of security control.

1. Nuclear Energy and Other Energy Sources

The development of nuclear energy has brought the dawn of a new energy age. Does this have serious implications for other energy sources? The answer is "Yes," but in almost all instances the long-run effects appear to be favorable. This conclusion is drawn because energy needs are expanding so rapidly that the ultimate problem is not what fuel is going to be displaced but what new sources can be developed to meet the increasing demands of an expanding economy.

The major energy uses where nuclear fuel appears as a possible sub-

stitute or supplement for coal, petroleum, and natural gas are power generation, transportation, and space heating.

Electric power in 1955 was supplied about 50 percent by coal, 21 percent by hydro water power, and 29 percent by oil and gas. Estimates

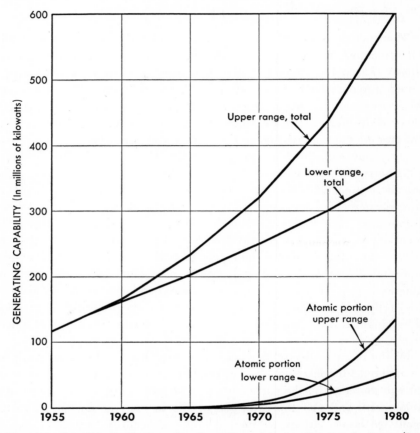

Figure 7.6.   Total U.S. Electric Generating Capability and Portion That May Be Atomic. (Data
from *Peaceful Uses of Atomic Energy*, report to 84th Congress, 1956)

have indicated that the United States requirements for electric energy
would increase 100 percent from 1954 to 1965 and that a three- or even
four-fold increase was possible by 1975. As fuel requirements for transportation and space heating increase, and as reserves of oil and gas are
used up and the best hydro sites are utilized, coal has been expected
to become the chief source of energy for the United States' rapidly expanding power demands. Since the first applications of nuclear energy
are likely to come in the generation of electric power, it appears that coal

will be the fuel most seriously affected. The cost of producing electricity by nuclear fuel, as has been shown, will for some time to come exceed the cost by coal, oil, gas, or water power because of the high capital cost of the reactor and its operation. In 1955 electric power utilities used 140.5 million tons of coal out of a total use of 423.3 million tons.

The Panel on the Impact of the Peaceful Uses of Atomic Energy in its 1956 report on *Peaceful Uses of Atomic Energy* to the Joint Committee on Atomic Energy made a detailed study of the impact on the coal industry. The panel prepared Figure 7.6 presenting United States electric generating capability and the portion that may be atomic. If atomic generating capacity grows as illustrated by the range forecast in the figure, the coal displaced by nuclear power and the net requirements for coal for power would be approximately as shown in Table 49.

TABLE 49. Coal Displaced by Nuclear Power and
Net Requirements for Coal for Power
(millions of tons)

Date	Pounds Coal Kilowatt-Hours	Coal Required		Coal Displaced by Nuclear		Net Coal Required		
		1 High	2 Low	3 High	4 Low	1–3	2–4	2–3
1960	0.95	175	159			175	159	159
1965	.90	240	183			240	183	183
1970	.85	350	220	23	13	327	207	197
1975	.80	600	364	86	38	514	326	278
1980	.75	845	459	232	90	613	369	227

SOURCE: *Mineral Facts and Problems*, Bureau of Mines, 1956.

Under the most favorable conditions for coal it is apparent that if the growth of atomic generating capacity reaches 135 million kilowatts by 1980 and if the total generating capacity approximates 600 million kilowatts by the same date, no disruption or dislocation in the coal industry can be expected. If this set of conditions prevails, a potential market for coal will be lost to the extent that atomic power displaces coal in the total generating capacity. The market for coal for generation of electricity will still be between four and five times the present power market for coal; hence this loss should not constitute a point of economic vulnerability or a focus of disruptive effects.

Under the most unfavorable conditions for coal, the Panel drew the following conclusion:

In this case, the total generating capacity of the United States follows the pattern of the lower values of the range given in [Figure 7.6], and reaches

358 million kilowatts in 1980. At the same time atomic generating capacity might follow the pattern of the higher values given in [Figure 7.6], reach 135 million kilowatts in 1980. The portion of the power generation market which would be open for coal is thus seen to be 223 million kilowatts or almost twice the present total electric power generated today. In terms of coal, reference to [Table 49] reveals that under these conditions 227 million tons will still be required for power purposes in 1980. Thus, in this case, the coal industry would have to supply over 60 percent more coal to the power industry than it is doing today.

The conclusion seems justified that the coal industry will have expanding demands for coal in electric power generation long before coal will feel the impact of nuclear fuel. When the impact does come it is likely to occur as costs reach a competitive level in regions like New England, where present power costs are relatively high because of the high transportation costs of coal.

Similarly the potentialities for the increased use of nuclear fuels for power purposes are great and may come earlier in underdeveloped areas where the need is great and the demand for electric power is growing and coal is unavailable or its cost is high. Thus the conclusion can be drawn that nuclear fuel will supplement coal in producing electric power in the United States and elsewhere, but the expanding demand for electric power will create a larger market for coal.

Transportation and space heating offer fewer opportunities for nuclear fuels than does the electric power industry. The Standard Oil Company (N.J.) sees three main obstacles to the widespread use of nuclear energy in transportation and space heating. "The first is the extremely high cost of the reactor. The second is the difficulty of safeguarding its operation—for example, in an aircraft—so that if the reactor and its shielding were accidentally damaged it would not be a source of dangerous radiation. The third obstacle is the immense weight of the shielding required to contain the radiation from even a small reactor."[2]

In transportation, petroleum is the fuel. Ships, locomotives, automobiles, and aircraft are the users.

Nuclear-fueled ships are already a technical reality and in operation for military purposes. The oil industry does not believe that nuclear-fueled commercial vessels will be an important factor by 1975. In 1954 about 20 percent residual fuel oil was used for ships. The petroleum industry does not appear to be worried about the impact of nuclear fuels for bunkers, however, for as one industry official stated: "If we should

[2] *Oil and the Atom,* Standard Oil Company (N.J.), 1955, p. 12.

lose the fuel-oil business of some of the larger ships after 20 years or so—what of it?"

In locomotive use, Robert E. Wilson, chairman of the board of the Standard Oil Company (Indiana), reported to the Atomic Energy Conference of the National Industrial Conference Board, New York, October 14, 1954: "But even if this should be both safe and economical in normal service (which I seriously doubt), can you imagine either the railroads or the regulatory authorities being willing to risk a possible wreck of an atomic engine in one of our large cities? I realize that a theoretically safe 'package' might be designed, but I think psychological factors would bar it for many, many years."

Nuclear-powered highway vehicles appear to the petroleum industry to be precluded by the shielding problem. There is of course the possibility of using electricity from nuclear power plants to charge some new kind of highly efficient storage batteries for electric automobiles (direct solar radiation also might be used). Here again the petroleum industry is not worried because it does not believe an electric car will give what the public demands—fast acceleration, agility in traffic, and other qualities that come under the general heading of "performance."

An atomic-powered aircraft is believed to be quite possible, but for commercial planes the shielding problems seem to constitute an almost insuperable bar.

In the field of space heating both oil and natural gas are affected. Coal is also affected, but coal's competition has and will come from the latter conventional fuels. The use of nuclear fuels appears to be ruled out by all of the three general obstacles. The consensus of industry was that the displacement of large numbers of oil- and gas-burning units appeared to be a remote possibility. There is of course the chance that in low-cost power areas the electric-driven heat pumps will become a substantial competitor for space heating. But as has already been noted, this electric power is likely to be coal generated for many years to come.

The conclusion that the long-run implication of the impact of nuclear energy on other energy sources would be favorable thus seems justifiable. The two following statements of Robert E. Wilson, while coming from the oil industry, may well be used to summarize the position of the conventional fuels:

"I believe that the impact on our industry will be negligible over the next 20 or 25 years. Beyond that, I believe we will welcome its aid in helping to take care of the country's rapidly growing needs for power."

"As a former chairman of the Atomic Energy Commission has pointed out, when we attempt to predict the future of atomic energy, we are in the same position as those who tried to predict the future of electricity ten years after Benjamin Franklin's experiment with the kite in the thunderstorm. In the period immediately ahead, however, it is clear that anything atomic energy does to promote industrialization and raise standards of living will create new needs for liquid energy."[3]

The Panel on Peaceful Uses of Atomic Energy concluded: "The realization of nuclear power as a practical source of energy should be welcomed by the American people including those related specifically to conventional fuel industries. While in particular instances nuclear power may displace power generated from conventional fuels, in most cases it will provide a necessary supplement to those fuels in meeting the Nation's rapidly expanding power requirements. But even where it does displace conventional fuels, those fuels may find uses that are more profitable to those who produce them and of greater value to the Nation's economy."

2. The Participation of Private Enterprise in Nuclear Development

Part of the declared policy of the United States in the Atomic Energy Act is to strengthen free competition and private enterprise "subject at all times to the paramount objective of assuring the common defense and security." So overwhelming was this "paramount objective" that the 1946 act made the entire atomic program a strict government monopoly.

Until 1954 private enterprise was given only a very limited look at AEC activities. Information was made available to five "study teams" from ten corporations so that they might consider the possibilities of commercial atomic power. These companies did not have a real incentive to act. Any of their discoveries and patentable processes had to be turned over to the United States. The net result was that the United States government had spent $8.6 billion and industry had spent only a few million dollars.

There was general agreement that at the start of the nuclear age the nation's security required that the government have absolute control over the atomic program. In 1952 and 1953 the argument began to be advanced that many of the secrets were no longer secrets. Russia already knew them. In fact, secrecy was retarding nuclear development by preventing the free exchange of ideas.

The recommendation was made that the Atomic Energy Act of 1946 should be amended so that:

[3] *Ibid.*, p. 13.

"Private companies should be permitted to own the fissionable materials needed to run their own reactors.

"Patents on nuclear discoveries made by companies with their own money should go to the private companies.

"Security restrictions should be relaxed to permit a freer flow of information between corporations to cut down duplications and wasted effort."

Those opposed to these recommendations argued that this would be a "giant giveaway" of the secrets of the atom. Those in favor said the recommendations "would merely give the corporations an opportunity to gamble hundreds of millions in a field where there is still no guarantee of any return."

Time magazine concluded: "With private industry in the field, atomic energy will stop being only an enormous drain; commercial projects will be taxable, and thus a source of revenue. And instead of being 'always ten years away,' industrial atomic power will be a reality."

The Atomic Energy Act of 1954 made possible the participation of private enterprise in the nuclear program. This act had its beginning in the summer of 1952 in the request for hearings on atomic power by Congressman Carl Durham, chairman of the Joint Congressional Committee. The point has been made that the final act of 1954 was not only committee-inspired but committee-written, as Commission Chairman Lewis Strauss said: ". . . This is not our bill. . . . We are . . . the beneficiaries, but not the authors."

The act of 1954 permits private enterprise, under license from the AEC, to build, own, and operate nuclear reactors and other facilities using nuclear fuels. Nuclear fuels (U-235, U-233, plutonium) can be leased but not bought from the AEC, and additional fuels can be produced and used, or, if desired, sold to the AEC at a "fair price." The act also permits patents for the normal seventeen-year period provided the inventions are not of value for atomic weapons and were not conceived under contract with or agreement, subcontract, or any other relationship with the AEC. Where patents are issued or applied for before September 1, 1959, the Commission retains the right to grant nonexclusive licenses to the use of any patent where it finds that the patent is of "primary importance" in the production or utilization of atomic energy and that the licensing of the inventions is of "primary importance" in carrying out the purpose of the act. Where licenses are granted, the patent owner is entitled to a "reasonable royalty fee."

Thus the government monopoly of nuclear energy was broken and the door to private industrial development was opened. The extent of this development through 1956 and plans for the future have been indicated. General Electric Company reported: "American free enterprise has made it possible for the U.S., with only 6% of the world's population, to produce almost 50% of the world's energy and industrial output. Working with the government, private companies have already begun to turn a major source of fear into a major source of fuel, and they are ready to risk their money and their time to do more. As we see it, this is progress in the American way."

The problem that was still unresolved in 1956 and 1957 was what the respective shares of government and private industry should be in the development of nuclear power. This, of course, was only part of the continuation of the public and private power ownership debate that had raged over the nation for more than twenty-five years and which will be considered in Chapter 8, "Electric Power."

The Panel on Peaceful Uses of Atomic Energy concluded that the impact from atomic power could come from exploring the field technologically, as well as from its commercial applications. "Thus two different determinations, as yet not clearly embodied in Government policy, must be made as to the urgency of getting on with atomic power. The first relates to the need for or desirability of technological development of atomic energy as a power resource; the second, related to the first, involves the rate at which this resource should be commercially developed."

The Panel was sharp and clear in its recommendations:

The prospect of an indefinitely expanding national economy which may require as much as 600 million kilowatts of installed electric-generating capacity or more by 1980 makes it clear that the Commission must explore this nuclear resource by a continuous program as promptly and efficiently as possible. In doing so it will be necessary not only to build pilot or experimental nuclear plants, but also full-scale "demonstration" atomic powerplants of each new and promising major reactor size and type. These are essential to permit development of the kind of engineering and operating data required for any intelligent decision as to how this particular resource can best serve the Nation.

Private enterprise should carry a substantial part of the burden of research and development, including construction and operation of full-scale "demonstration" plants. By "demonstration" we mean providing experimental and engineering data from which economic feasibility can be deduced reasonably. Where private enterprise does not assume the risk, we believe that the Commission should support expeditious development, if necessary, even up to and including construction of one "demonstration" plant of each major reactor size and type with public funds. In any event, we believe that continuing re-

sponsibility should rest with the Commission to encourage, and, where necessary, support basic research and development in this field.

. . . If progress is not expeditious and efficient, with private enterprise bearing its full share of the responsibility, it is clear that the Federal Government
has a fundamental obligation to carry it out. Although private participation
in this program is desirable, it should not be obtained at the cost of delay.

President Eisenhower was definite in his report to Congress of January,
1957: "Government policy places particular stress on private development of large-scale reactors that use the heat of atomic fission in the generation of electricity at competitive prices. . . . On the whole, there appears to be adequate incentive for participation by non-Federal interests
in the development and application of nuclear technology. But if there is

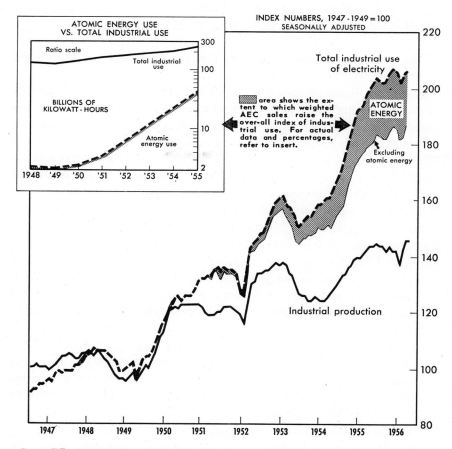

Figure 7.7. Industrial Use of Electricity, United States, 1947–56. (Data from Federal Reserve;
Electrical World)

a lag in the construction of large-scale commercial power reactors by these interests, it may be necessary to request funds at a later date for direct Federal construction."

However, the debate over public-private development of nuclear power was likely to reach such magnitude that a compromise might have to be reached. One possibility would be for the AEC to build some large-scale reactors adjoining AEC plants, which required about 20 percent of all the electricity used for industrial purposes in 1956. This large purchase of electrical power by the AEC as shown in Figure 7.7 was little known to many participants in the debate. Thus by generating its own power the AEC could release some of its purchased power for distribution to commercial users and, at the same time, avoid competing with private power if the AEC was required to build nuclear power plants which would be scattered throughout the United States.

3. The Extension of the Benefits of Nuclear Developments Within the Limits of Security Control

Part of the declared policy of the United States in the Atomic Energy Act is "promoting world peace, subject at all times to the paramount objective of assuring the common defense and security." In the discussion of peacetime applications of nuclear developments, the required United States policy was clear—"swift, broad progress in developing peacetime atomic energy for the world . . . with the promise of atomic fuels and technical knowledge sooner than anyone estimated." To this should have been added, "within the limits of security control."

Several proposals and counterproposals for release, control, and inspection of nuclear information have been made. It is well that some of the United States suggestions requiring international inspection were not accepted by Russia, for in July, 1955, President Eisenhower indicated that the United States was exploring a new arms control plan because it was no longer possible "through any type of inspection" to ferret out illegal production or storage of nuclear weapons.

On December 8, 1953, President Eisenhower proposed before the General Assembly of the United Nations that governments begin then and continue to make joint contributions from their stockpiles of fissionable materials to an international atomic agency. The Atomic Energy Act of 1954 authorized the President to exchange information on research reactors and to begin negotiations, under Congressional scrutiny, to carry out his proposal for a global atomic pool. In December, 1954, the United Nations adopted President Eisenhower's proposal of 1953 and recommended the formation of an international agency. On June 11, 1955, President Eisenhower stated that "The Soviet Union has indicated no willingness to share any part of its nuclear stockpile with such an agency. Our offer still stands."

In June, 1955, the United States took a bold new step in nuclear diplomacy. President Eisenhower announced two new programs as a part of the United States "Atoms for Peace" policy:

We have developed two new programs that I shall submit to the Congress in the conviction that they reflect the spirit and intent of law and of the American people.

First, we propose to offer research reactors to the people of free nations who can use them effectively for the acquisition of the skills and understanding essential to peaceful atomic progress. The United States, in the spirit of partnership that moves us, will contribute half the cost. We will also furnish the acquiring nation the nuclear material needed to fuel the reactor.

Second, within prudent security considerations, we propose to make available to the peoples of such friendly nations as are prepared to invest their own funds in power reactors, access to and training in the technological processes of construction and operation for peaceful purposes.

If the technical and material resources of a single nation should not appear adequate to make effective use of a research reactor, we would support a voluntary grouping of the resources of several nations within a single region to acquire and operate it together.

Our purpose is to spark the creative and inventive skills latent in the free world, to pool them and to put them to work for the betterment of the conditions under which men must live.

The research reactors acquired under this program will be fertile seeds for progress sown in the receptive soil of the free nations. The cost to the people of the United States will be small indeed when measured against the certain returns, tangible and intangible.

The second proposal will be of immediate interest mainly to the power-short areas of the world where atomic power may be economically feasible even today. Some of the countries, however, lack the knowledge and experience needed to construct and operate a commercial power reactor. This we can share for constructive purposes with friendly countries without real risk to our national security. Such sharing is expressly contemplated by the new Atomic Energy Act.

Together, these two provisions are designed, within the limits of prudence, to clear away some of the obstacles that have impeded progress in nuclear science to permit its peaceful application by all who propose to make it serve mankind.

Here is an invitation—to scientists and engineers, to industries and governments—to pool their energies and creative talents that this great achievement of the human mind may bear the fruit of its infinite promise.

The people of the United States instinctively reject any thought that their greatest scientific achievement can be used only as a weapon. Our increasing progress in its peaceful applications is evidence of that fact.

Congress moved quickly to back up President Eisenhower's program. The Joint Committee on Atomic Energy unanimously voted a $5 million authorization for research reactors for foreign countries. This was $2 million more than administration officials had requested.

These two new proposals were indeed a bold step which strengthened the hands of the United States at the "Atoms for Peace" conference in Geneva in 1955, which was designed "to find the way by which the inventiveness of man shall be consecrated to his life." However, there were some difficult security problems involved in the implementation of the agreements signed under the proposals. From a practical standpoint many of these difficulties were substantially overcome at the end of 1956 when almost all power-reactor technology was declassified.

The idea of "Atoms for Peace" presents man with one of the most challenging opportunities in converting technological feasibility into economic possibility.

Looked at from the fuel point of view, the economics appears simple. It costs about $35 to mine and purify a pound of uranium and sell it to the user. One pound of uranium can yield as much heat, and therefore as much power, as 1300 tons of coal burned in an efficient steam plant. This heat could generate about 3.5 million kilowatt-hours of electric power, which would require $10,000 worth of coal. This small bar of uranium could be transferred anywhere in the world by air and thus eliminate the coal transportation problem.

Looked at from the generation of electric power point of view, the cost of nuclear plants might not be prohibitive in some less-developed fuel-poor countries even though the cost is a multiple of conventional power. One recent study suggests that an atomic plant capable of producing 100,000 kilowatts of electricity might be regarded as costing $25 million. However, this study goes on to point out that, to put this much power to use, an expenditure of four to fifteen times as much is necessary—an additional $100 million to $400 million—for the industrial plants, the equipment and distribution systems, and the machines that utilize the power. Further, "the economics of transition of some less-developed areas of the world into the atomic age becomes puzzling indeed when it is realized that it can cost upward of one-third of a billion dollars to establish a 100,000-kilowatt atomic plant and make use of its power." Yet this plant is small when compared with the requirements of some of the larger industrial centers in the United States. This same study concludes: "Thus, a dream of world-wide plenty through the use of atomic power can be seen, but it is a distant vision. It might be noted that the investment in atomic power throughout the world, as so expectantly envisioned by many, rises to astronomical figures that are comparable only to the amounts of money that mankind spends on war. Can it be supposed that the human race now has come to the age at which it can think of making such investments in the tools of peace instead of the materials of war? The evidence for this position is scant indeed, but we may at least hope for such goals."[4]

The United States government is seeking to extend the uses of "Atoms for Peace" on the international front through bilateral agreements for coöperation, through encouraging regional nuclear organization, and by sponsoring and supporting the International Atomic Energy Agency.

Agreements for coöperation are for research purposes and/or power purposes signed on a bilateral basis with other nations. As of January 1, 1957, twenty-eight research agreements were in effect, negotiations were concluded with five other countries, and eight discussions were in progress.

Power reactor agreements were in effect with Belgium, Canada, the United Kingdom, and France. Negotiations were concluded by January 1, 1957, with Australia, the Netherlands, Norway, and Switzerland, and discussions were in progress with fifteen other countries.

Grants for reactors up to a maximum of $350,000 each were made from funds authorized under the Mutual Security Act of 1956. However, the real breakthrough in the United States' willingness to share came with two important steps taken by the government in 1956. (1) One hundred kilograms of uranium-235 were made available for use on research reactors; (2) President Eisenhower announced that 20,000 kilograms of uranium fuel would be made available for use in power reactors. Fuel shipped abroad for research use is leased to the foreign governments. As a big concession to foreign opinion, the United States sells the fuel used in power reactors.

The security rules, which are a part of the agreements, provide that when a country secures technical knowledge and fuel, and prepares to build a reactor and power plant, it must obtain United States approval

[4] W. Kenneth Davis, Shields Warren, and Walker L. Cisler, *Some Peaceful Uses of Atomic Energy,* Proceedings of the Atlanta Session of the National Academy of Economics and Political Science, December 29, 1955, p. 295.

of the plans. In addition, the country must account in detail for the nuclear fuel it uses and must give the United States the first option to buy the plutonium that is a by-product of the reactor.

Regional coöperation was being extended through Assistance to American States, the plan for an Asian Nuclear Center, and through backing and assisting Euratom.

The policy was to accelerate the application of peaceful uses of atomic energy in the American republics through existing components of the Organization of American States. The 1957 projects were: (1) inauguration of a program of special assistance to the University of Puerto Rico to enable that university to offer training and education in nuclear energy in the Spanish language; (2) the institution of a program of coöperation with the Inter-American Institute for Agricultural Sciences at Turrialba, Costa Rica, in use of radioisotopes in agricultural research; (3) an Inter-American Symposium on Nuclear Energy to be held at the AEC's Brookhaven National Laboratory, Upton, Long Island, N.Y. The symposium was for the purpose of discussing both scientific and economic aspects of atomic energy.

The Asian Nuclear Center is a United States proposal to establish a regional research and training center to be located in the Philippines. The United States offered to contribute approximately $20 million for capital expenditures and initial operating costs for the establishment of the Center, if mutually satisfactory arrangements could be worked out with other participating countries. There were many problems in the implementation of this proposal, most of which centered around the national interests of the countries concerned. To eliminate the United States tinge from the project, the proposal was made through the consultative assembly of the Colombo powers.

Euratom's strength as a regional nuclear agreement grows out of the participating countries' awareness of the need for economic unity in pooling and developing energy resources. However, political forces had more influence on the timing of Euratom's organization than economic considerations. In February, 1957, the United States adopted a policy of full support and promised to supply Euratom with technical assistance and nuclear fuel. The United States has a political, economic, and military interest in western Europe, and Euratom is another step in building up strength in all these areas. Euratom, like the European Coal and Steel Community and the Common Market, is a major step toward the unification of western Europe. In addition, however, Euratom could have an immediate effect on the United States' nuclear energy program. The shortage of fuel and power will make atomic power competitive with conventional electric power at an earlier date in Europe than in the United States. As a result, the United States reactor industry, by participating in Euratom, can test its equipment on an operational basis while nuclear power is developing in the United States. The United States, as has been noted, will be in competition with Great Britain in supplying reactors to Euratom. Our competitive position for the sale of reactors will be determined not only by their design but by the policies adopted by the United States for the supply of nuclear fuels as well as for the repurchase of plutonium. However, the latter may not be a conditioning factor in the initial stages, as the first United States reactors sold will probably be of the pressurized water type. On the other hand, in the long run Euratom may be competing with the United States in the sale of reactors.

The International Atomic Energy Agency statute was approved by seventy-two nations at the United Nations headquarters in New York on October 26, 1956. The Agency was first proposed by President Eisenhower in his "Atoms for Peace" address before the United Nations on December 8, 1953.

The Agency has been described as a banker and broker of atomic materials and skill for industrial development. It has tremendous advantages for the "atomic have-not" nations in making available some of the opportunities of nuclear development. Since the banker and broker is the United Nations, those countries which desired to remain neutral can share in the Atomic Age without having the choice of aligning themselves with an "atomic have" nation or falling behind in receiving the benefits of "Atoms for Peace."

The advantages of the Agency to the United States are at least twofold. First, since President Eisenhower proposed the Agency, the world knew that "Atoms for Peace" was the policy of the United States. Second, the Agency will bring into being part of the program of inspection and controls which the United States has insisted upon. Participating countries have agreed to permit inspectors to enter their territories, to examine plants using Agency materials or aid, and to make sure that none of such is used for military purposes. James J. Wadsworth, head of the United States delegation in establishing the Agency, was of the opinion that the article finally voted on inspection and controls seemed stronger than an original United States proposal. And this, it was claimed, augured well for an eventual agreement on a similar inspection system in an international disarmament agreement. This does not seem to be a point to become very excited about because, in so far as peaceful uses of the atom are concerned, Russia will not have to borrow anything from the Agency and thus will not be subject to inspection. Further, Russia was not in favor of the inspection and controls and has consistently opposed what the United States considers a workable system (if there is such) of inspection, so far as military atomic installations are concerned.

The United States agreed to make available to the International Atomic Energy Agency 5000 kilograms of uranium-235 from the 20,000 kilograms allocated in February, 1956, for distribution abroad. In addition, the United States will match allocations of special nuclear material made to the Agency by all other member nations, for a period ending June 30, 1960.

CONCLUSION

How can one draw conclusions at the dawn of a new energy age? The horizon is unlimited. However, we can share the best thoughts of President Eisenhower as he introduced his program in, appropriately, a commencement address at Pennsylvania State University on June 11, 1955.

Nuclear energy is too new for any man to chart its limits or predict its course with accuracy. But in ten short years the curtain has been pushed aside sufficiently to afford glimpses that have aroused atomic hopes commensurate with the awful dimension of atomic fears.

The extent of the economic and industrial changes that we can anticipate is indicated by estimates that world sources of uranium potentially available contain as high as twenty times the energy of the world's known reserves of coal, petroleum and natural gas combined. And power is only one of the results of nuclear fission. Many engineers and scientists believe that radiation and radioactive isotopes may provide even greater peacetime benefit. They are already opening new horizons in medicine, agriculture and industrial processes.

Our nation has no desire for a monopoly on the knowledge and practice of these possibilities. We want the world to share—as we always have.

Moreover, we know that the human talents essential to the advancement of science are not restricted to this country. Throughout the free countries there are men and women of great ability who, given the opportunity, can help further to advance the frontiers of knowledge and contribute to the peace and progress of the peoples of all nations.

Progress to date in nuclear science is not, of course, exclusively an American achievement. An international cooperative effort broke the barriers and made possible man's use of atomic energy. For maximum progress in the future, we must work for a continued partnership between the world's best minds—in science, engineering, education, business and in the professions.

CHAPTER 8

Electric Power

WATER RESOURCES AND ELECTRIC POWER

Electric power is not a natural resource. It is a carrier of energy developed from coal, petroleum, gas and nuclear fuels, and falling (hydro) water.

Water as a natural resource is of critical importance to a nation's productive capacity because of its multiple major uses—as water supply, for navigation, flood control, and irrigation, and as a source of energy. Because of the growing importance of water and its problems to the United States, a three-volume report—*A Water Policy for the American People* —was made by the President's Water Resources Policy Commission in December, 1950. More recently, in June, 1955, a further study with recommendations was made to the President and to Congress by the Commission on Organization of the Executive Branch of the Government, which was headed by former President Herbert Hoover.

The importance of water as compared with the total and other sources of energy in the United States was shown in Figure 6.6. Most noteworthy was the small (about 4 percent) and constant percentage of the total amount of energy expressed in BTU's which was derived from water power in the United States during the period 1914–56. For the early years the fuel equivalent was calculated from the reported horsepower of installed water wheels. After 1919 energy made available from water was arrived at by taking the kilowatt-hours of electricity produced by water power and estimating how much fuel was needed to generate the same amount of electricity.

Water power as a source of energy has had the tremendous advantage of being a "flow resource" while the other sources of energy have been "fund resources." The development of electricity as an energy carrier made it possible to transmit water power from its source and thus freed industry from the necessity of using falling water as energy at its source through the water wheel.

The true importance of water as a source of energy may now be measured by its contribution to electric power production. One measure is the percentage of the total electric power output developed by the fuels and by water (hydro) power. The general pattern in 1950 was 26 percent hydro power and 74 percent thermal. The latter was divided into oil, 11 percent; natural gas, 14 percent; coal 49 percent. The extent that this pattern is changing will be noted presently. To this one measure of importance of water to electric power must be added the fact that enormous quantities of water are required in the production of thermal electric power. Thus water as a natural resource is a requisite to electric power production.

THE IMPORTANCE OF ELECTRIC POWER

Electric power has truly revolutionized man's capacity to do work. In the United States over 90 percent of the power in industry is provided through electric motors. Expressed in another way, over 90 percent of industrial production depends on electricity, as does a large, but underestimated, portion of basic materials production. Residential consumers are so dependent on electricity that modern man can hardly function during a power failure. About 98 percent of all United States homes, both urban and rural, are served by electric power. A comparison of electric power generated in the United States with gross national product indicates that there was a very close relationship through the entire period of 1925–50. Thus electric power production is an excellent measure of productive strength. Expanding electric power capacity is requisite to continued increases in productive capacity.

PRODUCTION AND SALE OF ELECTRIC POWER

1. World Production

Electric power production in 1953 is given for the United States and selected countries in Figure 8.1. United States power production was 4 times that of Russia, which was in second place, and 6.7 times greater than that of the United Kingdom, which was in third place. A more indicative figure as a measure of productivity is per capita output.

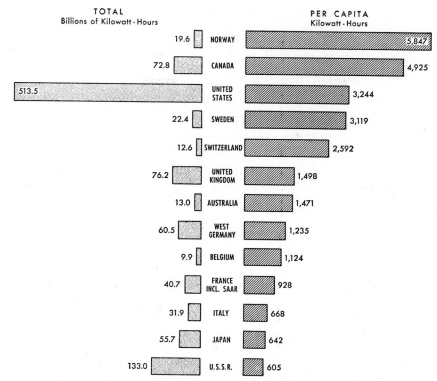

TOTAL Billions of Kilowatt-Hours		PER CAPITA Kilowatt-Hours
19.6	NORWAY	5,847
72.8	CANADA	4,925
513.5	UNITED STATES	3,244
22.4	SWEDEN	3,119
12.6	SWITZERLAND	2,592
76.2	UNITED KINGDOM	1,498
13.0	AUSTRALIA	1,471
60.5	WEST GERMANY	1,235
9.9	BELGIUM	1,124
40.7	FRANCE INCL. SAAR	928
31.9	ITALY	668
55.7	JAPAN	642
133.0	U.S.S.R.	605

Figure 8.1. Electric Power Production, U.S. and Selected Countries, 1953. Data include electric power produced by industrial plants, for own use or for resale to others, and by public utilities. (Data from Edison Electric Institute; United Nations)

When this measure is used, the United States was in third place behind Norway and Canada, and the U.S.S.R. was in last place of the countries shown in order of rank.

2. United States Production and Consumption by Types

Table 50 gives pertinent information on United States power production and sales.

A. Production

Production of electric power in 1945 was double what it was during the prewar period. By 1954 electric power production was more than double what it was nine years earlier, in 1945. This doubling in a decade was a dominant factor in the growth of the United States economy. This growth of electric power continued at an accelerated rate, and production in 1956 was up over 27 percent of the 1954 figure.

TABLE 50.　Electric Power Production and Sales

Year	Production (in millions of kilowatt-hours)			Sales to Ultimate Consumers (in millions of kilowatt-hours)				Revenue from sales (in millions of dollars)
	From Fuel	From Water Power	Total	Commercial and Industrial	Residential	Others[a]	Total	
1935–39 av.	70,120	41,857	111,977	66,112	17,594	9,644	93,350	2,119.1
1940–44 av.	125,784	61,926	187,710	115,621	27,053	16,495	160,432	2,863.1
1945	142,516	79,970	222,486	137,928	34,184	17,777	193,558	3,341.5
1946	144,733	78,397	223,130	131,901	38,571	20,313	190,785	3,459.6
1947	177,314	78,425	255,739	151,902	44,171	21,508	217,581	3,852.8
1948	200,228	82,470	282,698	167,281	50,978	22,481	240,740	4,313.0
1949	201,351	89,748	291,100	167,028	58,139	23,375	248,542	4,614.1
1950	233,203	95,938	329,141	189,511	67,030	23,998	280,539	5,086.5
1951	270,922	99,751	370,673	215,125	77,024	26,019	318,168	5,647.7
1952	294,122	105,102	399,224	229,438	86,780	26,306	342,524	6,137.3
1953	337,431	105,233	442,665	259,218	97,063	27,963	384,244	6,793.7
1954	364,617	105,069	471,686	273,528	108,465	28,911	410,904	7,277.3
1955	433,683	112,721	546,404	329,965	120,524	30,432	480,921	8,020.4
1956	478,579	122,013	600,592	363,476	133,851	31,886	529,213	8,690.7

[a] Including municipal street lighting, railways, etc.

SOURCE:　Edison Electric Institute; *Commodity Year Book*, 1956 and 1957.

Before World War II, 36 percent of the electric power was produced from water power. By 1945 this figure was only slightly lower at 35 percent, but in 1954 only 22.7 percent of United States power production was hydro. This is most significant as it is indicative of the increasing dependence on thermal-produced electric power.

Production of electric power by type of ownership is given in Figure 8.2 for the years 1920–53. Electric power production in the United States increased eleven times from less than 40 billion kilowatt-hours in 1920 to more than 440 billion kilowatt-hours in 1953. Of this latter total, more than 80 percent was produced by private facilities. Public power—state, local, and federal—which was only 4 percent of the total power produced in 1920, was almost 20 percent in 1953. The growth of public power production as a percentage of total production is shown in the small chart insert in Figure 8.2. The big increase in public power production came in the war years, 1939–44. In 1953, 65 percent of the public-produced power was federal owned and 35 percent was state and local. The extent of public ownership of power production is a much debated question which will be considered briefly in the section on "United States Problems and Policy."

B. Consumption

Consumption of electricity by sales to ultimate consumers in the United States is also given in Table 50. Here it can be seen that the growth in the production of electric power was a result of both commer-

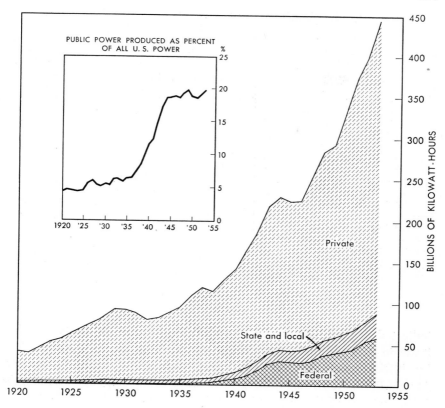

PUBLIC POWER PRODUCED AS PERCENT
OF ALL U. S. POWER

Figure 8.2. Electric Power Production, United States, 1920–53. (Data from Federal Power Commission)

cial and industrial, and residential uses. Residential use accounted for 25 percent of total power sales in 1956. More detailed information on consumption of electric power in the United States during 1925 and 1950 and estimates for 1975 are given in Table 51, which was prepared by the President's Materials Policy Commission. This study indicates an increase in total consumption of 353 percent between 1925 and 1950 and predicted a further increase of 260 percent between 1950 and 1975. The President's Commission noted that "in the 25-year span from 1925 to 1950, total national output of goods and services approximately doubled while consumption of electricity increased 3½ times. If total national output should double again from 1950 to 1975, demand for electricity may increase 2½ times." Thus, total generation of electric power required for 1975 was estimated at 1400 billion kilowatt-hours.

In 1954 an extensive survey made by the Edison Electric Institute

TABLE 51. Consumption of Electric Energy in the United States, Actual,
1925 and 1950; Projected, 1975
(billions of kilowatt-hours)

Class of Consumer	1925[a]	1950[a]	1975	Percent Change	
				1925 to 1950	1950 to 1975
Residential[b]	6.5	74.5	311	1,046	317
Commercial[c]	8.9	50.4	194	466	285
Industrial:[d]					
Major electro-process	4.1	37.5	207	815	452
Other	53.2	160.6	470	202	193
Miscellaneous	1.0	10.7	25	970	107
Total consumption	73.7	333.7	1,204	353	260
Losses[e]	11.0	55.1	196	400	256
Total generation	84.7	388.8	1,400	359	260

[a] Edison Electric Institute.
[b] Includes farm customers.
[c] Small light and power sales of electric utilities.
[d] Large light and power and railway sales of electric utilities, plus generation for industrial use in non-utility plants.
[e] Losses incurred in transmission and distribution.
SOURCE: *Resources for Freedom*, Vol. III.

indicated that by 1965 demand for electric power would be twice what it was in 1954 and that a threefold or even fourfold increase was possible by 1975. Francis K. McCune, vice-president and general manager, Atomic Products Division, General Electric Company, stated in March, 1955, that one of the economic realities was that the United States demand for "electrical energy will reach two trillion kilowatt-hours by 1975." Thus there is ample evidence of a sustained and continuing growth in the demand for electric power.

CAPACITY

1. Capacity, Production, Loads, and Reserve Margins

The capacity to produce electric energy is measured in kilowatts. The kilowatt is also a measure of demand for electric power at an instant of of time. Production and demand (or "load") over a period of time are measured in kilowatt-hours. One kilowatt of electric generating capacity operating for 1 hour will produce 1 kilowatt of electric energy; for one entire day, 24 kilowatt-hours of energy; and constantly for one year, 8760 kilowatt-hours of energy.

The demands for electric power fluctuate over each twenty-four-hour period and through the months and seasons of the year. The normal sustained demand or requirement on a particular generating capacity is referred to as the *base load*. The total of this base load and additional fluctuating demands (for example, evening home lighting and cooking requirements) is referred to as the *peak load*. Since electric power cannot be stored, there must be an installed capacity to produce the peak load. Since all generating plants must be taken out of service for repairs, electric generating systems must maintain as a part of their capacity a stand-by idle maintenance reserve. Stand-by reserve fuel capacity is often required to supplement fluctuating hydro capacity due to irregular stream flow. In addition, the electric power industry usually has a so-called *spinning reserve*, which is the excess capacity, over the load being furnished, of the operating units actually in use.

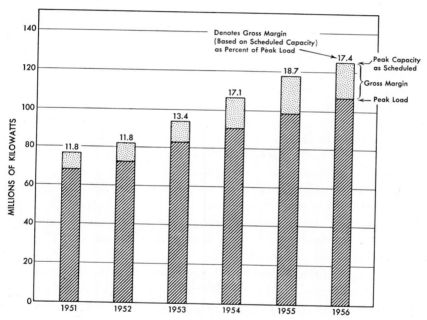

Figure 8.3.   Electric Power Peak Capabilities and Peak Loads. (Data from Armed Forces Industrial College)

Peak load, peak scheduled capacity and reserve (gross margin—capacity as a percentage of peak load), is given for the United States for the years 1951 through 1956 in Figure 8.3. A reserve margin of 15 percent is now considered a safe margin. During the Korean War the reserve capacity fell sharply below this minimum. Some regions had serious power shortages. Aluminum production was seriously affected. (The production of 1 pound of aluminum requires 10 KWH of electricity.)

Before 1938 the power industry never had less than 50 percent reserve requirements. The high pre-World War II reserve margins were the result of two factors: "(1) As a rule, each ownership unit operated on the principle of self-sufficiency, providing its full reserve requirements of generating capacity to carry peak loads and provide for shutdowns; (2) although there were some limited capacity interconnections between systems, no regions were tied together for large-scale transfers of power."[1]

2. Interconnection

Interconnection was a World War II development, facilitated both by government and by private industry. The Power Act of 1935 authorized the Federal Power Commission (FPC) to consider the availability of power for national defense production. In 1938 the FPC was authorized to order interconnections and interchange of power that might be required by war. During the summer of 1941 a serious power shortage developed in the southeastern United States. Following recommendations by the FPC, electric power systems operating in adjacent areas voluntarily coöperated to furnish power to the deficient areas. Experience gained from this project solved many operational problems which had previously been considered as limitations and led to the realization of the advantages of generating systems serving combined rather than separate system loads. Interconnection action taken from 1941 on was equivalent to a major expansion in power-generating capacity which was available for World War II. This was possible because of the more efficient utilization of generating capacity. Greater efficiency in the utilization of capacity through interconnection has had the permanent effect of reducing the reserve margin requirement to the point that 15 percent is now considered a safe minimum.

There are additional benefits of interconnection: Lower reserve requirements and capacity have made possible a higher load factor and lower fixed costs; greater diversity of demand has leveled out peak loads among systems; the effects of fluctuating water supply have been smoothed out in the case of hydro power; and continuity of power supply has been more effectively assured during peace and wartime emergencies.

3. Future Capacity Requirements

The President's Materials Policy Commission concluded in 1950 that, in order to meet the electric power needs, generating capacity would

[1] George A. Lincoln, *Economics of National Security*, Prentice-Hall, Inc., 1954, p. 224.

have to be increased from 83 million kilowatts in 1950 to close to 300 million in 1975. "Including a small amount for replacements, this would mean an average gross addition of close to 10 million kilowatts of capacity each year. By comparison, the gross additions in 1950 were about 7 million kilowatts and in 1951 about 8 million."

In 1954, the Edison Electric Institute concluded that in order to keep up with expanding electric demand from 7 to 12 million kilowatt-hours of new generating capacity would have to be added each year until 1965. After 1965 requirements for new generating capacity would be from 11 to 24 million kilowatts a year in order that by 1975 an expected total generating capacity from 301 million to 423 million would be available. Thus the estimated low total necessary generating capacity for 1975 was approximately the same as the total estimated by the Materials Policy Commission five years earlier.

4. Capacity by Type of Prime Mover and Class of Ownership

Total generating capacity for public use at the end of 1954 was 102.5 kilowatts. This total was made up of the following types of prime movers: hydro, 23.2 KW; steam, 77.0 KW; and internal combustion, 2.3 KW. This may be compared with a 1935–39 average total generating capacity of 36.3 KW, which included: hydro, 10.2 KW; steam, 25.4 KW; and internal combustion, 2.3 KW. Thus between 1935–39 and 1954, hydro capacity had more than doubled and steam capacity had more than trebled.

The class of ownership of total generating capacity at the end of 1954 was: privately owned utilities, 79.1 KW; publicly owned, 23.4 KW. The latter included: municipal, 7.2 KW; federal, 13.6 KW; and coöperatives, power districts, and state projects, 2.6 KW. Comparative figures for 1935–39 were: privately owned utilities, 32.5 KW; publicly owned, 3.8 KW. The latter included: municipal, 2.4 KW; federal, 0.95 KW; coöperatives, power districts, and state projects, 0.4 KW. Thus significant trends in class of ownership between 1935–39 and 1954 were that privately owned utility capacity increased only 2.4 times, while publicly owned capacity increased more than sixfold. Federal ownership of generating capacity grew over fourteen times.

The privately owned generating capacity operated as public utilities subject to public regulation at the state level. The rapid growth in federal ownership was due primarily to the large hydroelectric facilities, Grand Coulee, Bonneville, and the Tennessee Valley Authority (TVA), which were started in the depression as multiple-purpose water projects. These plants made possible unallocated quantities of electric power at the beginning of World War II for aluminum and electrochemical production and to provide power for the atomic energy program. Without these plants, the atomic energy time schedule might not have been possible because the time required to build hydroelectric plants is four or more years and that for steam plants is from one and one-half to two years.

Public power programs usually have been a part of multiple-purpose projects on entire river systems, joining construction of power facilities with flood control, navigation, irrigation, water supply, and recreation. In private hydro-power operations, the usual practice has been to develop sites primarily for the production of power, although in most instances other beneficial uses of water have been protected in these operations. The United States government entered the electric power business merely incidentally to a vast plan for watershed and regional valley resources development. The first step in this development was the realization that the proper way to regulate and control water is by managing entire river systems. The second step was the realization of the inseparability of the river system from its watershed environment. To accomplish integrated watershed control the multiple-purpose dam was required and power was a by-product.

TABLE 52.   Federal Multiple-Purpose Projects

	Invested in Projects Completed by Mid-1953	Total to Be Invested in Projects Completed, Under Construction, or Authorized
Tennessee Valley Authority	$ 924,513,490	$3,075,901,948
Columbia River Basin	590,578,249	3,245,725,166
Hoover and Parker-Davis	238,576,977	254,560,171
Central Valley, California	80,812,702	372,051,000
Missouri River Basin	106,587,440	1,308,945,655
Southwestern Power Administration	134,211,933	631,007,757
Southeastern Power Administration	212,426,000	720,147,400
All other federal projects	23,700,131	53,867,447
Total	$2,311,406,922	$9,662,206,544

The Tennessee Valley Authority was man's attempt to develop a river system and its watershed environment along with a comprehensive economic plan for a region. The results of this plan are briefly summarized in Figure 8.4. Other United States multiple-purpose projects are given in Table 52. The philosophy of valley and regional development led to a coördinated growth in hydro power capacity and public ownership.

TRANSMISSION

One great advantage of electric power is that it can be delivered from the energy source to the consumer with relative ease. This advantage is limited by the distance electricity can be efficiently transmitted. The usefulness of hydro power sites and interconnection is also in part determined by transmission distance. Most important is the effect on industry location.

An accepted rule has been that electrical energy can be transmitted efficiently about one mile for every 1000 volts of pressure. Commercial voltages have increased from 11,000 volts in 1890 to 287,000 in 1935 and to experimental uses of 500,000 volts. There is a line loss in transmission so that the generating company and the industrial user attempt to keep transmission distances to a minimum. In the early 1950's the average distance traveled by electricity in the United States was less than 25 miles and the longest transmission line was 285 miles from Hoover Dam to Los Angeles. Electricity can be transmitted greater distances by "displacement of power," transmitting power from one source into the area of another source, thus permitting the second source to transmit its power to the far end of its radius of transmission. Since the efficiency of this practice is low, "displacement of power" is limited to emergency use.

Electric power transmission distances have important economic effects in the location of industry. These involve problems of whether plants should move to the source of power or the power should be transmitted to the plant. In many instances in which a plant has more important locational factors there is no alternative except to move the power. Where the location is too far from hydro sites for efficient transmission of electric power, fuel plants are required. The same reasoning applies to the movement of fuel to thermal plants. In the discussion of coal two observations were made: (1) A short-run continuation of a long-term trend was seen in the move of industry to coal as a source of fuel and for multi-purpose use, and (2) the possibility of moving coal by pipeline to remote thermal generation stations seems near at hand. To these it should be added that the ease of shipment of nuclear fuel to the required source of power may help solve the electric power transmission problems.

The strategic military implications of electric power transmission were summarized as follows by the United States Military Academy Department of Social Sciences:

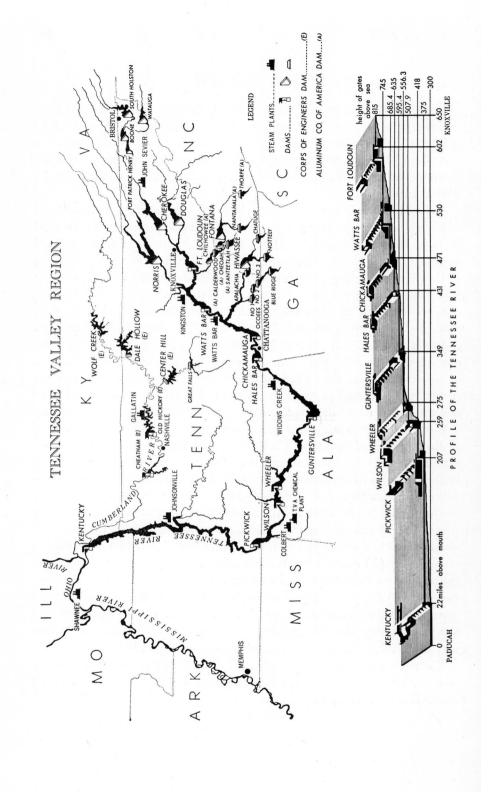

TENNESSEE VALLEY REGION

PROFILE OF THE TENNESSEE RIVER

LEGEND

STEAM PLANTS............
DAMS......................
CORPS OF ENGINEERS DAM......(E)
ALUMINUM CO. OF AMERICA DAM....(A)

Figure 8.4. The Tennessee Valley Authority.

The Tennessee River has its principal headwaters in the Appalachian Mountains of Virginia and North Carolina. Ranked by volume of stream flow, it is the fifth largest river system in the United States. The Mississippi, Columbia, Ohio, and Missouri outrank it. The main stem of the river forms at Knoxville, Tennessee, where two of its major tributaries join the Holston River from southwestern Virginia and the French Broad from western North Carolina. Its course goes southwest through eastern Tennessee, gathering the flow of important tributaries: the Clinch carrying water from southwestern Virginia, the Little Tennessee from North Carolina, and the Hiwassee and Ocoee rivers, whose headwaters are in North Carolina and Georgia.

Thus grown, the Tennessee flows into the northern part of Alabama, where it turns north and west, crosses that state, and swings north through western Tennessee and Kentucky. About 630 miles from Knoxville it joins the Ohio River to flow into the Mississippi River at Cairo, Illinois; the stream flow of the Tennessee accounts for about 25 percent of the Ohio's discharge into the Mississippi. The watershed of the Tennessee River is about 40,000 square miles.

This is the river system that 25 years ago wasted its great power in destruction of land, property, and human life. Now, the Tennessee River is the most completely controlled river system in the United States.

The Tennessee Valley Authority (TVA), a corporation owned by the Federal government, by Act of Congress, signed on May 18, 1933, was created as a new agency to supplement the efforts of a region to develop its total resources for the benefit of the area and the nation. A summary of the multiple-purposes of the project is found in Section 23 of the Act: "for the special purpose of bringing about in said Tennessee drainage basin and adjoining territory . . . (1) the maximum amount of flood control; (2) the maximum development . . . for navigation purposes; (3) the maximum generation of electric power consistent with flood control and navigation; (4) the proper use of marginal lands; (5) the proper method of reforestation . . . and (6) the economic and social well-being of the people living in said river basin."

In 1958, 31 major dams and 7 large steam plants were generating electric power which was sold to cities and rural coöperatives for distribution, and which was used by the Federal government in atomic energy projects and for other defense purposes. The TVA power system generated more than 45 billion kilowatt-hours of electricity a year. Over 50 percent of the power was used by atomic defense plants. More than one and one-third million consumers used TVA power, six times as many as had electricity in the same area in 1933. Ninety-three percent of the region's farms were electrified compared with 3.5 percent in 1933. Residential consumers paid less than half as much per kwh as did those in the nation as a whole and they used almost 100 percent more power.

TVA helps in the industrial development of the region. Its multi-purpose dams, its forestry and agricultural aids, and its service to industry had helped make it possible by 1958 for the people to increase their per capita income 539 percent since TVA began; in the nation the increase had been 364 percent. Since 1929, there had been a net increase of over 2000 manufacturing and processing plants in the Tennessee Valley region.

The dams have created a series of slack water lakes with a 9-foot navigable depth for 630 miles, from Paducah, Kentucky, to Knoxville, Tennessee. In 1958, river traffic ton-mileage was about 40 times as great as it was before TVA. An all-year navigation channel connects the great trans-Appalachian region with the inland waterway system directly connecting 20 states.

TVA operates chemical laboratories and plants for research and manufacture. Fertilizers are made in times of peace and munitions in times of war. The TVA made it possible during World War II to mobilize quickly the resources of a strategic region in the nation's scheme of defense to produce aluminum, chemicals, and the materials for atomic weapons.

TVA reservoirs have up to 12 million acre-feet of storage space reserved at the beginning of the flood season for flood control alone. This makes possible the reduction of floods in the Valley and aids in control of lower Ohio and Mississippi River floods. At times as much as 4 feet have been cut from the crest of a Mississippi River flood south of Cairo, Illinois.

Recreation, the bonus of river development, by 1958 had become a major industry in which states, counties, cities, and private individuals had invested $72 million. Many TVA achievements have been noted, but the full development of the Tennessee Valley is something more than the mobilization of economic assets for the achievement of greater material rewards. The Tennessee Valley's greatest asset is its people who prefer to live there because they like its hills and valleys, and its mountains and forests, its prevailing sense of community, and the depth of the region's cultural roots and traditions. These folk have now found productive and satisfying work and exercise their initiative freely. As a result, the freedom, security, and strength of these people and the nation have made significant gains which only one who has lived with this regional revolution can fully appreciate.

Transmission distance seems certain to increase. The meaning of 300-mile versus 500-mile transmission distances in the economics of power and in the development of emergency measures is indicated by a simple exercise in plane geometry. A circle with a 300-mile radius covers approximately ⅐ of the United States; a circle with a 500-mile radius covers more than ⅓ of the United States. As transmission distances increase, generators can be located near sources of cheap fuel rather than near load centers. Some hydro power sites may become more economically feasible. If power costs less and can be transmitted farther, the location of defense industries can be determined by strategic reasons rather than the proximity of sources of power. Finally, in case of atomic attack or similar disaster, emergency power can be transmitted to afflicted areas from more distant sources.[2]

UNITED STATES PROBLEMS AND POLICY

The basic power problem is to expand the generating capacity sufficiently to provide for the growing demands for electric power and adequate reserve requirements. One definite target established is a generating capacity of 375 million KW by 1975 and 514 million KW by 1980. This is approximately the average of the Edison Electric Institute upper and lower limit forecasts. The base at the beginning of 1955 was 102 million KW.

Two of the many subsidiary parts of the central electric problem that will be considered are (1) the type of generating capacity and (2) the class of ownership.

1. Type of Generating Capacity

Past trends of generating capacity have indicated a more rapid increase in fuel-generated electric power than in hydro-generating capacity. The President's Materials Policy Commission concluded that, except for coal, there were upward pressures in the real costs of production for hydro power and thermal-produced power by oil and natural gas. Atomic power cost estimates were not given. Nation-wide average cost of electricity from water power was seen to be less than for thermal generation, but the advantage of these lower costs is concentrated in special areas.

Hydro power is of course an ideal major source of electricity because the use of water power (a flow resource) does not cause a drain on the mineral fuel resources. The Federal Power Commission estimated that a total of 105 million KW capacity could perhaps be generated at known sites in the United States. As of January 1950, only 16 percent of this 105 million KW capacity potential had been developed and another 5

[2] *Ibid.*, p. 226.

percent was under construction. Federal water development agencies were well advanced in preconstruction planning for another 12 percent.

Opinions differed as to how much of the remaining 67 percent of the underdeveloped potential it would be economical to establish before 1975. The President's Materials Policy Commission concluded that by 1975 hydroelectric energy would be hard pressed to continue to supply one-quarter of the nation's total power requirements. After that date, if not before, thermal generation was expected to carry most of the burden of further expansion.

The Commission recommended "that the nation's hydroelectric potential be developed as fully and rapidly as is economically feasible. Priority should be given to projects that promise to contribute most economically to meeting the energy needs of particular regions, in the light of their present energy costs and supplies. Specifically, early action is important in the St. Lawrence, Niagara, and Columbia River areas where major projects already have been planned and which are among the Nation's most advantageous remaining hydropower opportunities."

Thermal power was expected by the President's Materials Policy Commission to carry a much heavier burden of the generating capacity after 1975 "unless solar or atomic sources can take over a sizable part of the burden."

The study of energy sources has indicated that, in so far as conventional fuels are concerned, coal will be expected to carry the burden of increased capacity and that there will be no problem about the availability of coal to do the job. To the contrary, increased demands for coal by the electric power industry are expected to help coal out of its sickbed. The problem with respect to thermal generation by coal is what the costs will be to mine and deliver the coal and how much of its energy can economically be utilized, transmitted, and delivered.

The Materials Policy Commission concluded:

The largest opportunity for cutting the costs of fuel transportation is provided by coal. . . . Great improvement has already been made in generating efficiency. Steam generating plants in 1950 averaged 1.2 pounds per kilowatt-hour, but the most efficient plants were down to 0.7 and 0.9 pounds. New types of gas turbines using coal might have not only the advantages of greater efficiency and lower capital investment, but also of not requiring large quantities of cooling water—a tightening commodity.

Increased economy of long-line transmission and local distribution provides another point for attack on costs. Experience to date with high voltage transmission is encouraging; for example, the Bonneville Power Administration contemplates a 600-mile transmission line. The combination of pit-head thermal generation and highly efficient transmission could eventually reduce costs in areas along the Atlantic Coast where distant fuel sources result in electric rates well above the national average.

As previously indicated, power costs from coal in 1955 were .008 per KWH. There appears to be ample opportunity to cut these costs. Thus coal as a fuel for thermal power should improve its competitive position with other fuels and at the same time produce power from increased capacity at lower costs.

Nuclear power has been discussed in detail. To achieve the goal of generating capacity of 375 million KW by 1975 and 514 million KW by

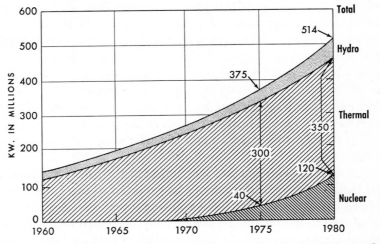

Figure 8.5. Total Generating Capability. (Data from *The Race for Atomic Power*, General Electric Company)

1980, Francis K. McCune has estimated that the 1975 capacity will include: nuclear, 40 million KW; thermal, 300 million KW; hydro, 35 million KW; the 1980 capacity will include: nuclear, 120 million KW; thermal, 350 million KW; hydro, 44 million KW (see Figure 8.5).[3] Beginning with an annual addition of 11 million KW to total generating capacity in 1955, the addition to total generating capacity was estimated to rise to 23 million KW per year in 1975 and to 31 million KW by 1980. Nuclear plants should account for 10 million KW of the increase in 1975 and 20 million KW by 1980 (see Figure 8.6).

This predicted size of the nuclear capacity is very impressive. It should

[3] Francis K. McCune, *The Race for Atomic Power*, General Electric Co., March 23, 1955.

be compared with the AEC's estimate that by 1965 the United States will have from 4 to 6 million KW of nuclear generating capacity in operation, and the coal industry's estimate that by 1975 nuclear fuel will account for 7.5 percent of electric power. The comparable latter figure for McCune's estimate is 10.6 percent. From looking at Figures 8.5 and 8.6 and from analysis, one can observe that McCune's study indicates a possible slower start and a more rapid build-up of nuclear generating capacity.

The effect of this expansion in nuclear generating capacity on the conventional hydro and thermal capacity moves in the same direction but at

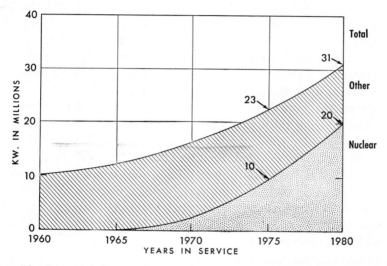

Figure 8.6. Generating Capacity Additions. (Data from *The Race for Atomic Power*, General Electric Company)

a different rate from that previously concluded. Hydro capacity would account for only 9 to 10 percent of total generating capacity in 1975. However, Mr. McCune does not feel that there is any need to be concerned lest nuclear fuels displace fossil fuels, for he concludes: "As of today there are about 80,000,000 kilowatts of capacity using conventional fuels. Even with the rapid rise in nuclear capacity which I have predicted, installed capacity in conventional plants will increase to 300,000,000 kilowatts by 1975 and 350,000,000 kilowatts by 1980. Thus if we look 25 years ahead, there is certainly ample opportunity for everyone if we assume, as we believe is sound to do, that the total power use by the country will continue to rise at some 6½ percent per year."[4]

[4] *Ibid.*, p. 7.

2. Class of Ownership

How the required addition to generating capacity is to be achieved is the fundamental issue of the basic power problem. Central to the solution of the issue are the much debated public and private ownership of generating facilities and the questions of initiative and incentive.

The electric power industry, partly because of the great depression of the 1930's, has been conservative in estimating future demand. The result was too slow expansion of capacity, which had a drastic effect of retarding industrial growth. As already noted, the growth in power capacity in the 1930's was due to public—federal—power projects. These were large multiple-purpose water installations which could not have been undertaken by private enterprise. There is no question about the contributions of the TVA to the economy of the Southeast or about the good fortune of having the electric power of these multiple-purpose facilities available at the beginning of World War II.

However, the growth of federal power facilities set up a yardstick method of gauging rates charged by private utilities. There have been at least two fundamental points at issue in the yardstick method that have been vigorously debated. First was the pricing policy advocated by the TVA—that low electric power rates would result in increased demand for electric power and increased total revenue with lower costs. Prior to the TVA, private power companies were reluctant to experiment with the effect of lower rates, knowing that once rates had been lowered it would be difficult to raise them if the experiment proved unsuccessful. Erich Zimmermann, who had a real sense of feeling for the TVA rate approach, argued the point: "Low rates for electricity attract industries, electrical machinery raises the productivity of labor, this in turn raises incomes and the standard of living, and this again calls for the use of more electricity. Similarly on the farm, the liberal use of electricity renders labor more productive and sets in motion a spiral of forces which raises the whole level of the economy." Private power companies will agree with this conclusion, but they want to know what the effect is on their cost-income-profit position. This led to the second and most heated part of the yardstick debate. What was the cost of multiple-purpose, by-product-produced power and did the rates cover the costs? The argument has been over whether low-rate policies made it possible for the public power facilities to pay their way or whether they were operating at a loss. Public power supporters advance the Zimmermann point of view and in addition claim that most of the projects show a return on the public's investment. The private power companies disagree with this view and contend that the cost allocations in the public power accounting and in the yardstick have not included interest charges and taxes, which private companies must use.

The effect of this whole argument was that private power utilities were uncertain as to the role of public power, and an additional element of conservatism was added to the private electric power industry. Power shortages and low reserve margins after World War II were results of this conservatism, results which only served to add fuel to the fire of the postwar debate over public and private power.

There seems to be some general agreement that federal power projects are justified when private capital is unable to undertake an investment. The points of disagreement arise in determining the circumstances under which this is true; in addition, where the federal facilities are established in an area, such as the TVA, should private power facilities be allowed to establish new fuel plants within the area to serve expanding demands? There are unlimited subsidiary issues which are a part of the debate.

Two recent reports on this controversial issue of public versus private power will point up and summarize many issues and policy problems involved. The first of these reports was from the President's (Truman) Water Resources Policy Commission in 1950. This Commission recommended as a part of *A Water Policy for the American People:*

Full development of the Nation's undeveloped water power resources, as an integral part of comprehensive basin programs, should be considered a major Federal responsibility, to be exercised in such a way as to assure ample supplies of hydroelectric energy well in advance of expanding regional and national needs.

Federal hydroelectric plants should be designed to produce ultimate capacity and energy which will best fit into the requirements of potential markets on the assumption of complete regional integration of power supply.

Future licenses for new non-Federal water power developments should be issued only with the joint consent of the Federal agencies responsible for power in basin programs. In exercising this responsibility, the Federal agencies should continue to recognize the preferential position accorded State and municipal applicants under the Federal Power Act.

The Federal power marketing policy heretofore adopted by Congress, authorizing Federal agencies to build transmission facilities, giving preferences in power sales to public and cooperative bodies and fostering low rates for residential and rural consumption, should be continued.

Federal power marketing policy should be carried out flexibly to assure sound adaptation of Federal power supply responsibility to regional power resources and the most effective cooperation of all power systems, public and private, in the task of assuring ample supplies of power at the lowest possible rates.

Since private power systems will probably continue to provide a large share of the new capacity required to meet future needs, Federal arrangements for marketing power should where possible take full advantage of private power facilities, provided the contracts preserve the preferential right of public bodies and cooperatives to a share of the power, or its equivalent, at the lowest possible rates.

Where the Federal Government assumes a major responsibility for the power supply to distribution systems, this should be recognized as a utility responsibility, requiring the construction of new generating capacity, whether hydroelectric or steam-electric, well in advance of expanding needs.

The second report was made in 1955 by the Commission on Organization of the Executive Branch of Government. This Water Resources and Power Report to Congress called for a revolution in federal power policy and in summary recommended an end to the expansion of federal power. Four of the twelve Commission members, including two top Republicans —Attorney General Herbert Brownell, Jr., and Defense Mobilization Director Arthur S. Flemming—dissented vigorously in the findings and recommendations, which included the following:

. . . A large number of the great multipurpose dams . . . were . . . beyond the financial and technical strength of private enterprise or the nongovernmental agencies. . . . But this situation does not prevail today.

The growth of savings in the hands of private citizens and institutions now enables both private companies and nonfederal public bodies to obtain enormous sums for the building of power plants. . . . Financially there is no present or prospective need for federal financing of power activities.

Federal power development might also be deemed necessary if privately owned electric utilities could not be regulated effectively in the public interest. The regulation of electric utilities . . . by both State and federal governments has become effective.

Federal power development might be deemed necessary if nonfederal sources could not supply whatever power was required for the current and prospective defense activities of the Federal Government. There is nothing to indicate any necessity of this sort.

It is clear that in the field of power the government is conducting functions and activities which are competitive with private enterprise. This competition "has taken on many aspects which are the negation of our fundamental economic system" of free competitive enterprise.

Rates charged for federal power are too low because "exemptions from tax charges and other economical rate making practices caused revenues from federal power sales in 1953 to fall about 40 percent below the value of the power."

Rate making authority over federal power should be given to the Federal

Power Commission and the FPC be directed to fix rates high enough to cover all costs—including amortization and interest on the federal investment, and amounts equal to federal, state and local taxes paid by private utilities.

All the federal multiple-purpose projects [see Table 52] should be self-supporting and made subject to the Government Corporation Control Act. These federal projects should be "required to secure their capital for future improvements when authorized by Congress, by issuing their own securities to the public. . . ."

In addition, the Commission on Organization insisted:

That private enterprise be offered the opportunity to provide the capital for the electric component of multiple purpose dams and dispose of the power through their own systems.

That Government cease the building of steam plants and connect federal power facilities with grids of neighboring systems.

That Government undertake no further building of transmission lines where such transmission services can be provided by nonfederal agencies.

That . . . private utilities be permitted to purchase a fair share of federal power.

The net effect of this second report was to recommend that all existing federal projects be made self-supporting and that no additional federal projects should be undertaken. Republican (!) Commissioners Brownell and Flemming believed that "the recommendations taken together would impede the Federal Government in exercising its proper role in the development of the nation's water resources."

The debate of public and private power has had many regional aspects which are clearly ascertained from Figure 8.7. The dominant role of public power in the East South Central states (TVA) and in the Pacific area (Columbia River Basin) has led to tremendous political backing from these two regions for public power. The sustained, rapid post-World War II development of public power in these two areas is clearly indicated by the chart at the lower part of the figure. Also shown is the tremendously accelerated increase in public power production in the West North Central region.

The debate over public and private power during the first Eisenhower administration, 1943–46, jumped from one political hot spot to another. Indeed, during this period of time and in the past, the volume of political energy expended seemed at times to be far out of proportion to the significance of the matter to the total energy economy of the United States. During 1957 there was evidence that the argument would center around some of the critical problems of the future in the nuclear power field. The big issue of 1957 was whether the United States government should

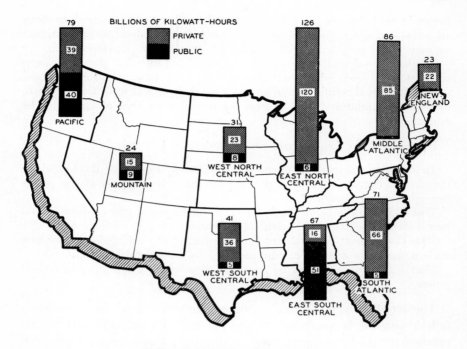

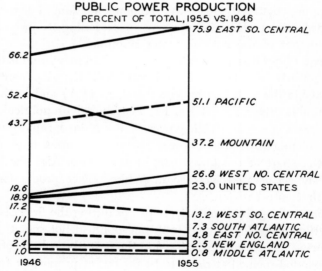

Figure 8.7. Private and Public Electric Power Production in the United States for 1955, by Geographical Regions. (Data from Federal Power Commission)

launch a large power reactor construction program, the principal justification for which was "to recapture world leadership in the peaceful development of atomic energy"—if in fact we had lost that leadership. All the evidence seemed to point to the contrary.

A reasonable position in the public-private power debate might be that the federal government enters the field of economic enterprise when multiple-purpose dams are built. The justification for this is that no other agency can command sufficient capital resources or provide the coördination necessary for the construction of such far-reaching programs. In addition, if there is inadequate incentive for the participation by non-federal interests in the development and application of nuclear technology which results in a lag in the construction of large-scale commercial power reactors, the United States government should undertake direct federal construction of these reactors in accordance with the recommendations in the section on atomic power. The government should not in any way supplant private enterprise; rather its position should be to strengthen the economy and to provide the opportunity for the further expansion and functioning of a free, competitive economy.

Of particular interest in 1957 in the solution of the United States basic power problem "to expand the generating capacity sufficiently to provide for the growing demands for electric power and adequate reserve requirements" were the St. Lawrence River and Niagara Falls projects. In this connection, the President's Materials Policy Commission's recommendations should be recalled: "Specifically early action is important in the St. Lawrence, Niagara and Columbia River areas where major projects already have been planned and which are among the Nation's most advantageous remaining hydropower opportunities."

The St. Lawrence and Niagara power projects have international implications and have involved disputes within the United States between the federal government, the New York State Power Authority, public power advocates, and private utility companies. The projects call for the completion in 1958 by the State Power Authority of a 735,000-KW power dam on Barnhart Island in the St. Lawrence, and the Authority was optimistic that Congress would permit it to build a 1,800,000-KW plant on the Niagara River near the falls. Plans called for the tying of the St. Lawrence and Niagara power systems together to increase the firm supply of kilowatts available at each by sharing reserve capacity to meet peak loads. Both plants would be integrated with the transmission systems of the private utilities in New York State (Figure 8.8).

The international aspects of these long-anticipated power developments are interesting. The St. Lawrence power project was tied up for years with the St. Lawrence Seaway proposal to make the St. Lawrence navigable for deep-draft ocean vessels. Canada finally forced the United States into making a decision by adopting the policy of building its own power and navigation facilities if the United States did not take action. At this point the power and navigation parts of the St. Lawrence projects were separated so as to disengage the opposition attending each. The United States agreed with Canada that the St. Lawrence power was to

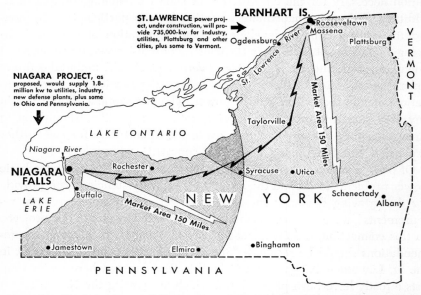

Figure 8.8. The St. Lawrence and Niagara Power Projects. (Adapted by permission from *Business Week*, February 23, 1957)

be developed separately by each country. The United States Federal Power Commission then issued the New York State Power Authority a license to build the Barnhart Island plant.

The United States Senate ratified a treaty with Canada in 1950 which provided for additional diversion of Niagara water for power generation. Canada went ahead and developed its own facilities. In ratifying the treaty the Senate stipulated that Congress should determine who would develop the power. This is normally a function of the Federal Power Commission. The project has been delayed by a three-way dispute among the New York State Power Authority, public power supporters, and New York private utilities which have been trying to push their respective bills through Congress. Public power supporters have insisted that preference be given to coöperative and municipal power systems in the distribution of Niagara power. Private utilities have been opposed to the development by the State Authority. A compromise bill was likely to be approved in 1957 that would give the State Authority the right to develop the power to be distributed as follows: The Niagara Mohawk Power Company would receive 445,000 KW to compensate for giving up its license to develop power at its 360,000 KW Schoellkopf hydro plant, which was destroyed by a rock slide in 1956; private power would receive an additional 730,000 KW for distribution through Niagara Mohawk and two other utilities. Also, 250,000 KW were set aside for expansion of existing industry in the Buffalo-Niagara Falls area, 300,000 KW for new defense plants, 125,000 KW for municipalities and coöperatives, and 150,000 KW for the states of Ohio and Pennsylvania. However, the public bodies would receive, if necessary, an additional 200,000 KW to be withdrawn from the allotment for the three private utilities.

The St. Lawrence power project once released from the Seaway Proposal was still complicated in 1957 by a three-way dispute that *Business Week* described as follows:

The all-out advocates of public power wanted a public agency—either federal or state—to generate the power and to grant preference in its sale to city-owned systems and cooperatives (through the controversial "preference clause" in power contracts).

The majority members of the State Power Authority, named by former Gov. Thomas E. Dewey, agreed that the state should generate the power, but didn't want to give special preference.

The private utilities wanted to develop the Niagara, although they didn't much care about the St. Lawrence—economically, not so attractive. Still, on principle, they were against the state's developing it.

In 1957 the issue over who should develop the power had been resolved and the State Authority had the plant under construction, but the controversy over who should get the power and how much remained was the public-private power dispute of the moment. The solution appeared at hand, however, because of changing elements on the demand side and on the cost side that tended to soften the controversy. First, a market area within a 150-mile radius from Barnhart was established. Second, a contract for sale of 239,000 KW was signed with the Aluminum Company for supply of its Massena, New York, plant, which had been in operation since 1903. Third, a firm user of power, Reynolds Metals Company, was given a contract for 239,000 KW to supply a new 100,000-ton aluminum reduction plant at Massena. The public interests were appeased when

General Motors announced that it would build a new castings foundry near the Reynolds plant. Thus employment opportunities were created. Fourth, when the municipal and coöperatives distributors complained about the share of power allocated to industrial concerns the State Authority pointed out that nonindustrial consumers and public bodies had already been guaranteed more than they need. Fifth, and most important in softening the public-private power conflict, was the changing cost pattern in New York State for hydro and steam power. *Business Week* explained this most important development:

> In New York State hydro plants no longer hold a decisive cost advantage over steam—which means also that they're not nearly so effective a "birch rod" as FDR once believed. This is because today's higher construction costs make the massive hydro plants more expensive. Steam plants also cost more to build than they used to, but the trend toward larger and more efficient generating units results in operating economies.
>
> Result: In 1933, the cost of generating and transmitting St. Lawrence power to Utica—largest city in the area—would have been 2.2 mills per kwh.; and it would have cost 10 mills per kwh. to produce the same juice at a steam plant in Utica.
>
> Today, it would cost 6 mills to generate and deliver the same St. Lawrence hydro power to Utica customers; a steam plant could do the job for 6.2 mills.

In August, 1957, Congress passed H.R. 8643 and Public Law 85–159 went into effect which gave the right to the New York State Power Authority to develop the Niagara power with the stipulation that in distributing the power, preference and priority for 50 percent of it should be given to public bodies and nonprofit coöperatives within economic transmission distances. Thus after decades of political bickering, there was a real possibility that a breakthrough had been made in the international, state, public-private power controversy, and that the mighty Niagara and St. Lawrence River systems surging down from the Great Lakes to the Atlantic might finally go to work to help solve the need for growing power capacity in the United States.

3. Conclusions

The expansion of the generating capacity sufficient to provide for the growing demands for electric power and adequate reserve requirements is in no way limited by the availability of energy sources. It is a matter of which sources are most economical. Present indications are that coal and nuclear fuels are most likely to bear the burden of the future. Private enterprise has a better knowledge of the growing demands for power and a greater availability of capital. Conditions favorable to the investment of these funds should be created. The public versus private power controversy, while hotly debated, seems to overlook the very fundamental fact that the federal government's position in the power development of the future will involve more far-reaching matters than those currently discussed because of the government's role in nuclear fuels and related security matters. These latter would include not only problems of making available nuclear fuels and reciprocal exchange of technical knowledge but also questions with respect to the location of future power facilities in order to accomplish industrial plant dispersal. In addition, there is a need for security purposes of an adequate power reserve.

All this leads to the summary conclusion that the electric power industry is in fact the key developer and distributor of energy to our industrial economy. The continued growth and strength of the United States economy depends on expanding availability of electric power. The federal government has a sustained responsibility for coördinating electric power development for security and regulatory purposes. Wherever possible these regulatory functions should be accomplished by state agencies. Most importantly, the federal government should create a favorable economic climate and provide the proper incentive where necessary for the expansion of electric power by private enterprise.

ENERGY RESOURCES AND POLICY

Our discussion of energy resources should be concluded as it was begun. Energy is the capacity to do work. Obviously, the availability of energy and the efficiency with which it is used is fundamental to productivity and economic progress. The conclusion is affirmed that: ". . . A supply of energy sufficient to meet the total demand of the United States can be achieved only if the Nation looks at its energy resources as a whole; . . . only if it takes the fullest economic and technical advantages of the flexibilities in end-use, in distribution, in drawing on each energy source for its best and most efficient contribution. Moreover, the energy position of this Nation must be judged and acted upon in the light of energy needs and resources of other free nations."

The individual energy sources and energy that have been studied are coal, petroleum, natural gas, atomic energy, and electric power. In each instance, policies have been recommended that would implement the qualifying requirements set forth in the above conclusions.

CHAPTER 9

Material Resources

This chapter deals with the materials for harnessing and applying energy. At the beginning of Part III the point was made that the natural resources of energy and materials were the basis of industrialization. The additional point was made that the discussion of natural resources required to harness and apply energy would be limited primarily to metals, which is one of the three parts of the Bureau of Mines classification of minerals—mineral fuels, metals, and nonmetals.

The plan of this chapter is first to discuss the general United States non-fuel minerals position and policy and then to discuss steel, copper, and aluminum as separate examples in which different problems exist that require policy decisions.

UNITED STATES NON-FUEL MINERALS POSITION

There are many non-fuel minerals problems but they are all a part of one central issue: How can the United States increase its supply of non-fuel minerals in order to meet the anticipated growth in demand and to provide for an adequate emergency reserve?

1. Consumption

One of the most spectacular features of our economy has been the rapid growth in the use of minerals. Figure 6.2, which was discussed in the introductory section to Chapter 6—"Mineral Characteristics"— shows this quite clearly for all minerals, and for mineral fuels, metals and nonmetals. The consumption of minerals has increased in two ways. First, the demand for each mineral has increased. For example, in 1950 as compared with 1900 the United States used three and one-half times more iron ore, three times more copper, and four times more zinc. These are the metals long known to man. Second, the number of minerals required continues to expand as technological developments call for special-purpose minerals. In 1900 few metals were used—iron, copper, lead, tin, zinc, gold, and silver. Aluminum has grown from a laboratory experiment just before 1900 to a position where in 1955 it was competing with copper for leadership in the nonferrous field. Technological developments have now made some 45 metallic elements and 8000 alloys of these metals essential to modern industry. Thus technology has made us more dependent on sources outside the United States rather than more self-sufficient.

This past growth in consumption seems Lilliputian when compared with estimated future requirements. Figure 9.1 presents estimated future United States consumption of selected major materials in 1975 as compared with 1950. This chart has the advantage of making possible a comparison of estimated rates of growth by classes and individual materials. Minerals are classified into mineral fuels, construction materials, and other nonmetallic minerals; and the metals are subdivided into: (1) iron and ferro-alloys; (2) nonferrous metals (except ferro-alloys). This latter sub-classification of the metallic minerals is particularly helpful. The anticipated expansion of iron will call for much greater expansion of the alloy metals for steel. The other nonferrous metals show a continued growing requirement for the older metals; gigantic increases in the consumption of the "light" metals, aluminum (bauxite) and magnesium; and anticipated spectacular gains for the "new metal," titanium. Titanium is an excellent example of a "new metal," the production of which was only three tons in 1948. So little was thought of titanium for years that great bodies of iron reserves lay idle for a long time because of the "contaminating" presence of titanium. Now many of these reserves are mined for titanium, with iron the "contaminator." One government agency predicted that by 1975 consumption of titanium would be 225 to 900 times the 1954 use of 5300 tons. Titanium is demanded for its excellent strength-weight ratio and its property to resist corrosion. Other defense and civilian uses for selected materials are given in Table 53.

Military requirements for certain metallic and nonmetallic minerals are such that the wartime demands far exceed peacetime consumption. This necessitates special preparation in the nature of a reserve to fill these requirements immediately. In addition, the military requirement for minerals is similar to the long-range peacetime trend. For example,

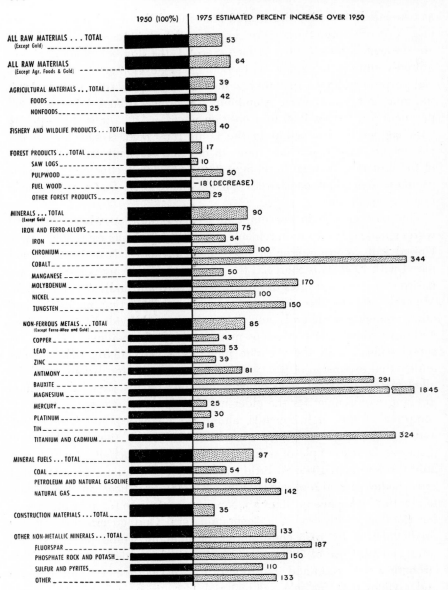

Figure 9.1. How United States Consumption of Materials Might Rise by 1975 (Assuming No Relative Change in Prices). (Data from *Resources for Freedom*)

the jet plane of the early 1950's used more than twice as much copper, steel, and aluminum as the plane of World War II; and artillery in Korea used ammunition more than five times as fast as in World War II.

TABLE 53. Defense and Civilian Uses of Some Vital Materials

Material	Defense Uses	Civilian Uses
STEEL	Production of guns, shells, tanks, ships, airplane engines; construction of defense plants, barbed wire, helmets.	Making of automobiles, washing machines, vacuum cleaners, refrigerators; building of hospitals, schools, roads, bridges.
ALUMINUM	Building of planes, electric power lines, pontoons for military bridges.	Pots and pans, furniture, parts for automobiles, washing machines, and refrigerators, screens, storm windows.
COPPER	Shell casings, electric wire, power generators, airplane instruments and wiring, communication systems on warships.	Copper and brass, which is the major alloy use of copper, are used in plumbing, roofing and siding, automotive parts, motors and generators, television parts.
MAGNESIUM	Aircraft castings, and as an alloy with aluminum for sheet metal for plane wings and bodies, used in incendiary bombs.	Light metallic objects, such as toys, baby carriages, ladders, wheelbarrows.
LEAD	Used in making bullets, batteries for military vehicles, paint and solder for maintenance of warships, atomic bombs and other atomic instruments.	Pipe, toys, automobile batteries, paperweights.
ZINC	Used with copper to make brass, which is used in airplane parts, gun parts, communication devices; also used as a coating to galvanize (rustproof) steel for naval use, roofing airplane hangars; for castings used in engines for military vehicles.	Used in galvanized steel for roofing, fencing, garbage pails; and used for parts for refrigerators, washing machines, toys, automobiles; also in paint and batteries.
TIN	Used to coat steel to make tinplate, which is used chiefly for metal containers to hold food, gasoline, and other supplies for troops in the field. Also an element used in bronze, out of which insignia, buttons, and parts for many military devices are made.	Tin cans used to preserve food, beverages, candy, tobacco, etc.; bronze used for electrical fixtures, ash trays, book ends; solder (of which tin is an ingredient) is used in plumbing repairs, fixing radio and television sets.
COLUMBIUM AND TANTALUM	Used in high temperature alloys to make steel for jet engines; vital to atomic-energy program in various forms.	Used as a stabilizer for chemical, oil and food industries where furnaces or other equipment call for steel alloys, highly resistant to corrosion.

(Continued on following page)

TABLE 53. Defense and Civilian Uses of Some Vital Materials (*Continued*)

Material	Defense Uses	Civilian Uses
COBALT	Used in jet engines; radar and electronics; weapons (gun-barrel liners); high-velocity, armor-piercing shot.	Used for tool steel; in permanent magnets for cast cobalt alloy tools and dyes; hard-facing electrodes; dental alloys; as catalyst for nylon and other chemical processes; vitamin B_{12} complex; live-stock feed; paint and ink dryers; ground coating for porcelain enamel in such items as appliances; magnets containing cobalt used in radio and TV sets, electric motors, telephones, toys, games, can openers, musical instruments.
NICKEL	As an alloying element in steel to make it hard and heat-resistant. Nickel-alloy steels are used to make gun and tank parts, aircraft engine parts, naval-gun-turret mechanisms, parts for antiaircraft guns.	Automobile trim and finishes for bumpers, toasters, waffle irons, faucets, office-building fixtures and railings, auto-engine parts.
MOLYBDENUM	"Moly" steels are used in tank and truck parts, machine tools, power-generating equipment, artillery undercarriages, etc.	Moly steels are used in automotive crankshafts, machinery, truck and auto axles, typewriter and office-equipment parts.
TUNGSTEN	Jet-aircraft-engine parts, gears and moving parts for machine tools, tank wheels, gun barrels, certain types of armor plate.	Cutting tools and fixtures used in machine tools, gears for all types of industrial machinery, parts of steel cranes, bits for oil-drilling equipment.
CHLORINE	Chemical warfare items, used in many defense industries as a cleansing agent.	Used in the home and in industry as a cleansing agent, also used in manufacture of certain types of plastics.
SULPHUR	Used in metallurgy to help achieve certain chemical actions, also used in making other vital chemicals.	Used by farmers for fertilizer, in the manufacture of petroleum products, and in producing many other chemicals.
INDUSTRIAL DIAMONDS	In industrial drilling, especially through the hard alloy steels used in munitions; also to drill through rock in petroleum drilling and drilling for certain nonferrous minerals.	Used in grinding wheels, and drill bits.
MICA	Used in communication equipment of all types, on land, at sea, and in the air.	Used in electrical devices, such as radios, television sets, electric phonographs, etc.

SOURCE: Defense Production Administration, *Expanding Our Industrial Might*.

2. Supply

The increased consumption and changing pattern of mineral use immediately raise the question of the availability of an adequate supply.

In 1947 the staffs of the Bureau of Mines and the Geological Survey prepared the most comprehensive appraisal of the mineral position of the United States which had been attempted up to that time. The report summarized:

Describing the mineral position of a nation in terms of its self-sufficiency or its ability to produce to meet its own needs is a well-established practice. Self-sufficiency is readily and effectively determined by comparing production and consumption during a chosen period, for such a comparison considers all the factors—resource, technologic, and economic—that influence the production that develops in response to a specific demand. For most commodities the basic factor is the quantity of the raw-material resource—the reserves—exploitable under prevailing conditions, particularly the spread between cost and price. Under special circumstances other factors, such as availability of labor and equipment and the limitations imposed by installed capacity, are equally important. Also, with the byproduct materials, output frequently is restricted more by the rate at which the associated metals or minerals are produced than by the size of the reserve or by other factors. However, the influence of factors other than reserves usually is relatively temporary, so that, for long periods, the degree of self-sufficiency provides a rough measure of the economic availability of resources.

Figure [9.2] compares the self-sufficiency of the United States in 39 important industrial minerals during the 5-year periods 1935 to 1939 and 1940 to 1944. Before the war, production equaled or exceeded consumption in 11 commodities. For 12 minerals, production ranged from 50 to less than 100 percent of consumption, for 6 commodities from 10 to less than 50 percent, and for 10 minerals less than 10 percent of requirements. During this period, there were few if any labor or equipment shortages or restraints imposed by production facilities. Thus, except for the byproduct minerals, the production record affords a fairly reliable index of the availability of domestic resources under the economic and technologic conditions prevailing at that time.

It will be noted that, from 1935 to 1939, the United States was fully or highly self-sufficient in coal and iron ore, the raw materials required to support an industrial economy based on steel. It was equally well situated with respect to supplies of other important minerals, such as petroleum, copper, sulfur, and phosphate rock. However, the record also reveals that this country depended on foreign sources for substantial proportions of its needs of other minerals that are indispensable in this machine age.

During the war there were notable increases in the ratio of production to consumption in some minerals and decreases in others. Significant improvement in self-sufficiency was obtained in iron ore, fluorspar, nitrates, mercury, potash, bauxite, vanadium, arsenic, tungsten, ilmenite, and flake graphite, whereas de-

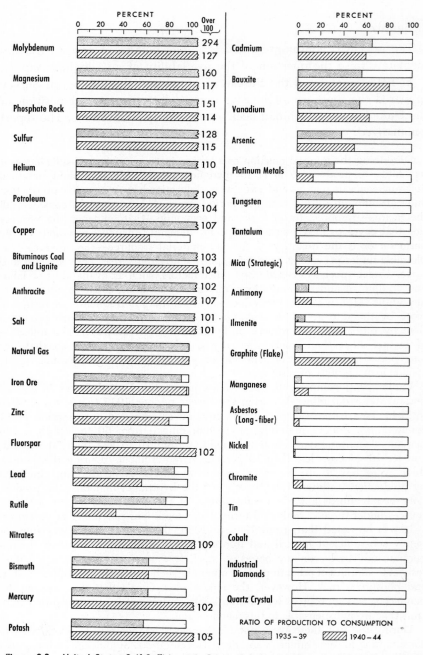

Figure 9.2. United States Self-Sufficiency in Principal Industrial Minerals, 1935–39 and 1940–44. Production is expressed in percentage of domestic consumption. (Data from U.S. Bureau of Mines and Geological Survey)

pendence on foreign sources of copper, zinc, lead, rutile, platinum metals, and tantalum increased substantially. It should be noted, however, that flake graphite produced during the war was substandard and unsuitable for some important uses.

On the whole, there was only a moderate improvement in American self-sufficiency during the war. In view of the tremendous need for minerals for the war program and the pressure for larger output, a more striking result might have been expected. Failure to achieve a larger measure of self-sufficiency under these conditions may be ascribed to many factors. Lack of reserves precluded significant production of many minerals, including chromite, nickel, tin, industrial diamonds, and quartz crystals. For some of the other metals and minerals, depletion of the reserves undoubtedly was an important but by no means solitary factor. During the war, shortages of manpower and equipment and the limitations of installed production capacity were real bottlenecks that prevented full realization of the reserve potential. Opinions differ as to the relative importance of these causes, but the fact remains that the war experience demonstrated weaknesses in the Nation's mineral position and emphasized the need for doing something about it.[1]

Also during 1947 the United States Military Academy published a comparative study of domestic self-sufficiency and that of other areas in *Raw Materials in War and Peace*. The results of this study, which was prepared by the Industrial College of the Armed Forces, are shown in Figure 9.3. The minerals and other materials included were those which were regarded as basic. The year 1938 was selected because it was the last peacetime year before World War II, and 1944 was selected because it was the last full year of a peak wartime demand.

These two 1947 reports have been presented because of their comprehensive and comparative scope, and because they were the outgrowth of the post-World War II realization of the need for an appraisal of the United States mineral position.

The sustained and accelerated demand for minerals after World War II gave rise to the comprehensive report of the President's Materials Policy Commission in 1950. In an attempt to answer the fundamental question of the availability of an adequate mineral supply the Commission prepared Table 54, which gives the domestic supply position of selected mineral materials, dividing them into three major measures of adequacy: known economic reserves adequate for well over twenty-five years; known economic reserves inadequate; and little or no known economic reserves, significant discoveries not expected.

[1] *Investigation of National Resources,* Hearings before a Subcommittee of the Committee on Public Lands, United States Senate, 80th Congress, 1st Session, on Investigation of the Factors Affecting Minerals, Fuels, Forestry, and Reclamation Projects, May 15, 16, and 20, 1947, Government Printing Office, 1947, pp. 177–178.

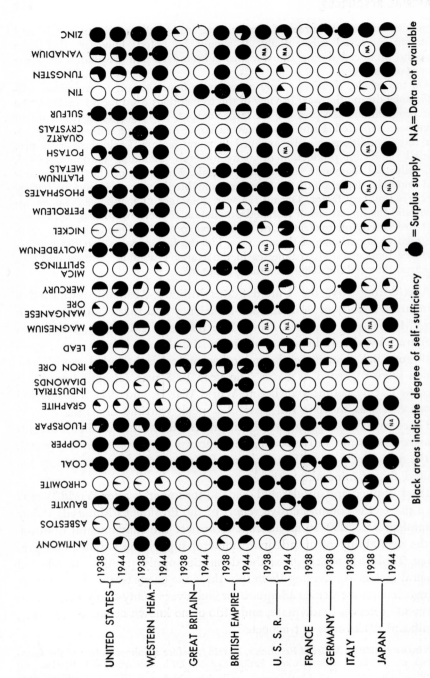

Black areas indicate degree of self-sufficiency ● = Surplus supply NA = Data not available

Figure 9.3. Self-Sufficiency in Mineral Raw Materials. (Data from *Raw Materials in War and Peace*, Department of Social Sciences, United States Military Academy)

TABLE 54. Domestic Supply Position of Selected Mineral Materials

Known Economic Reserves Adequate for Well Over 25 Years		
magnesium	lime	gypsum
molybdenum	salt	borax
coal	sand	barite
phosphate	clay	feldspar
potash		

Known Economic Reserves Inadequate		
Discoveries geologically likely—though not necessarily adequate:		
copper	vanadium	petroleum
lead	tungsten	natural gas
zinc	antimony	sulfur
uranium		
Beneficiation progress expected:		
iron	beryllium	fluorine
aluminum	thorium	graphite
titanium	oil from shale	
Synthesis progress expected:		
oil from coal	gas from coal	

Little or No Known Economic Reserves, Significant Discoveries Not Expected		
Beneficiation progress expected:		
manganese		
Synthesis progress expected:		
industrial diamonds	quartz crystals	
sheet mica	asbestos	
Significant beneficiation or synthesis not expected:		
chromium	tin	platinum
nickel	cobalt	mercury

SOURCE: *Resources for Freedom*, Vol. I, p. 26.

Another partial measure of adequacy is the degree to which United States mineral production is dependent on foreign sources. Figure 9.4 reveals this dependency in 1951 for thirty-eight minerals. Particular attention should be given to the extent to which the Eastern Hemisphere was a source of supply.

This is, of course, a static picture and should be considered in terms of trends of consumption and dependence. For example, the United States government list of Strategic and Critical Materials (Table 55) contains about seventy-five commodities, of which fifty are minerals. When classified by different grades, which often have to be obtained from widely scattered sources, more than sixty minerals are on the list. In 1940, there were only fifteen minerals on this list. Figure 9.5 gives another example by showing how the United States dependence on foreign sources for metals increased between 1936–38 and 1950–51. The United States shifted

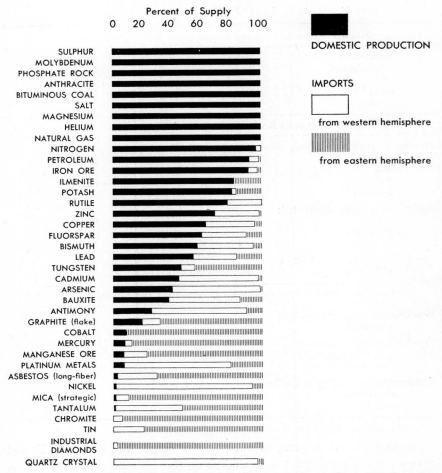

Figure 9.4. United States Dependency on Foreign Sources of Minerals. (Data from *Expanding Our Industrial Might*, Defense Production Administration)

from a net export to a large net import position in copper and lead. The net imports of other major metals increased many times. In 1953, of the mineral raw materials used, the United States imported: 10 percent of the iron ore, 27 percent of the zinc, 45 percent of the copper, 55 percent of the lead, 67 percent of the arsenic, 73 percent of the tungsten, 80 percent of the graphite, 82 percent of the bauxite, 84 percent of the cadmium, 86 percent of the antimony, 90 percent of the cobalt, 92 percent of the mercury, 93 percent of the manganese, 98 percent of the titanium and nickel, and 100 percent of the chromite and tin (see Figure 9.6). By 1954 the United States was a net importer of all metals except two—magnesium and molybdenum.

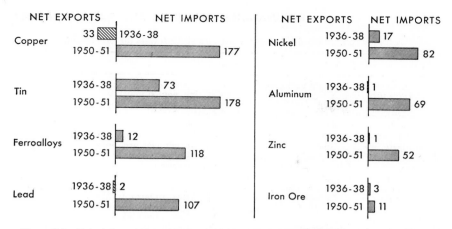

Figure 9.5. United States Exports and Imports of Major Metals (Annual Averages in Millions of Dollars). This chart shows the increase in our dependence on foreign sources. (Data from U.S. Government Printing Office)

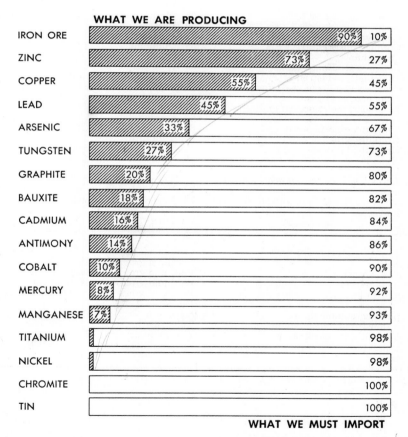

Figure 9.6. United States Ratio of Self-Sufficiency in Minerals. (Data from Armed Forces Industrial College)

TABLE 55.   List of Strategic and Critical Materials for Stockpiling

Group I

1. Abrasives, crude aluminum oxide	38. Jewel bearings, watch and time-keeping device jewels
2. Aluminum	
3. Antimony	39. Kyanite
4. Asbestos, amosite	40. Lead
5. Asbestos, chrysotile	41. Magnesium
6. Asbestos, crocidolite	42. Manganese ore, battery grade
7. Bauxite, metal grade	43. Manganese ore, chemical grade
8. Bauxite, refractory grade	44. Manganese ore, metallurgical grade
9. Beryl	45. Mercury
10. Bismuth	46. Mica, muscovite block, good stained and better
11. Bristles, hog	
12. Cadmium	47. Mica, muscovite film
13. Castor Oil	48. Mica, muscovite splittings
14. Celestite	49. Mica, phlogopite splittings
15. Chromite, chemical grade	50. Molybdenum
16. Chromite, metallurgical grade	51. Nickel
17. Chromite, refractory grade	52. Opium
18. Cobalt	53. Palm oil
19. Coconut oil	54. Platinum group metals, iridium
20. Columbite	55. Platinum group metals, platinum
21. Copper	56. Pyrethrum
22. Cordage fibers, abacá	57. Quartz crystals
23. Cordage fibers, sisal	58. Quinidine
24. Corundum	59. Quinine
25. Cotton, extra long staple	60. Rare earths
26. Diamonds, industrial	61. Rubber, crude natural
27. Feathers and down, waterfowl	62. Sapphire and ruby
28. Fluorspar, acid grade	63. Shellac
29. Fluorspar, metallurgical grade	64. Silk
30. Guayule seeds and seedlings	65. Sperm oil
31. Graphite, amorphous lump	66. Talc, steatite, block
32. Graphite, crucible grade	67. Tantalite
33. Graphite, lubricant and packing grade	68. Tin
34. Hyoscine	69. Tungsten
35. Iodine	70. Vanadium
36. Jewel bearings, instrument jewel except vee jewels	71. Vegetable tannin extract, chestnut
	72. Vegetable tannin extract, quebracho
37. Jewel bearings, sapphire and ruby vee jewels	73. Vegetable tannin extract, wattle
	74. Wool
	75. Zinc

Group II

Agar	Platinum group metals, osmium
Bauxite, abrasive	Platinum group metals, palladium
Cryolite, natural	Platinum group metals, rhodium
Diamond dies	Platinum group metals, ruthenium
Emetine	Rutile
Graphite crystalline fines	Selenium
Mica, muscovite block, stained and lower	Talc, steatite, ground
Mica, phlogopite block	Zirconium ore, baddeleyite
Optical glass	Zirconium ore, zircon
Pepper	

SOURCE: Munitions Board, *Stockpile Report to the Congress*, August 15, 1952.

3. Policy

Enough evidence has been presented to prove that there is a non-fuel minerals supply problem. It is not a problem about which the United States should be alarmed, but it calls for awareness and policies and actions designed to solve it. Although each specific mineral may require special study, certain measures are applicable to all non-fuel minerals. In addition, because of the time needed to develop, transport, and process minerals, policies required for peacetime are for the most part the same as those required for war.

There are several areas where appropriate policy and action will help solve the supply problem. Among these are exploration and development, stockpiling, imports, and the development of outside sources.

A. Exploration and Development

The Materials Policy Commission concluded that the critical problems of domestic mineral supply center in those minerals still produced in the United States but having reserves which no longer seem adequate. For these, e.g., copper, lead, zinc, uranium, vanadium, tungsten, etc., the job ahead is to find and develop new reserves. More difficulties stand in the way of discovery than of development. Two fields of action seem appropriate—factual knowledge and financial incentives.

Factual knowledge and analyses concerning reserves of the various minerals, costs and rates of exploration and development, and other pertinent factors were found to be seriously lacking. The Commission recommended:

> . . . that the Department of the Interior strengthen its programs for gathering and analyzing basic facts about minerals, that industry groups undertake an integrated complementary program, and that a complete census of mineral industries be taken in 1954 and every 5 years thereafter (see P.M.P.C. vol. I, p. 26).
> . . . that the U.S. Geological Survey accelerate the geologic mapping of the United States and Alaska, by 50 percent within five years and 100 percent as soon thereafter as possible, with priorities given to localities of most probable mineralization; that the Geological Survey and the Bureau of Mines, in cooperation with State mining agencies and the mining industry, develop a program for a coordinated national system of libraries of core samples and other geologic evidence; that an intensive program of basic scientific research and technical development be undertaken, led by a special committee under the National Science Foundation, on methods and instruments of exploration for minerals, enlisting experts in Government, private industries, and universities; and that direct exploration by Government—limited to situations in which private industry cannot be expected to undertake it—be part of the continuing activities of the Geological Survey and the Bureau of Mines (see P.M.P.C. vol. I, p. 29).

Financial incentives to exploration and development of several types have been used by the federal government.

Two provisions of the federal income tax which offer special incentives to the mineral industries—percentage depletion allowances and the privilege of "expensing" certain costs of exploration and development —have already been discussed in detail in the analysis of the petroleum industry. These were seen to be powerful incentives to investment in discovery and development.

The annual depletion allowances are deductions from taxable income permitted because of the gradual exhaustion of depletable property. The percentage depletion deduction allowed by the Internal Revenue Code is a stated percentage of gross annual income, ranging from 5 percent for certain common minerals like sand and gravel, through a 10 percent and 15 percent bracket, to 23 percent for sulfur and 27½ percent for gas and oil; but it may not exceed 50 percent of the net income from the property. Over the life of a property it is possible for tax-free recovery to reach a total far greater than the taxpayer's investment. This is justifiable because percentage depletion is used not only to permit recovery of investment in a wasting asset but also as an incentive for discovery and development in a risky business. There is a need, however, to adjust the percentage depletion among the minerals so that the rate will be higher where the risk is greater and/or the national need for the particular mineral is greater.

"Expensing" is the privilege of deducting as current expense certain outlays for exploration and development which would otherwise have to be treated as a capital outlay recoverable over a period of years. In oil and gas, all "intangible drilling and development costs" are expensible. These include most of the outlays for exploration and development. In the mining industries exploration costs may be treated as current expense only up to $75,000 a year, with a cumulative limit of $300,000. There is no limit on expensing the cost of developing a mine once a discovery has been made. Since expensing provides such a powerful direct incentive for discovery, it would appear logical that the present limitation on minerals other than oil and gas should be removed.

Another provision of the federal income tax which has been used to encourage development of minerals is the rapid tax-write-off program for new defense plants which was started in 1950 after the Communist invasion of South Korea. Under this program of accelerated tax amortization, applications are made to the Office of Defense Mobilization for a "certificate of necessity" for the construction or expansion of a facility "in the interest of national defense." The certificate holder is allowed to amortize over a period of five years that percentage of the cost of the new facility covered by the certificate, instead of the normal rate of twenty years as fixed by the Internal Revenue Code. This has presented a tremendous tax advantage to the applicant and resulted in an accelerated investment program. Certificates of necessity are granted mainly on the basis of the essentiality of the project to national defense.

The rapid tax-write-off program requires continuous review, and may result in inequities between firms. This review was under way in 1955, and in August, Mobilization Director Arthur S. Flemming issued an order ending the rapid write-off for nineteen industries including asbestos, lead, manganese ore, cement, tungsten, zinc, and various alloying minerals. In addition, thirty-eight others were indefinitely suspended —these included iron ore and oil among the minerals.

Under the fast tax-write-off plan many serious abuses occurred in the name of "defense." During 1956 the plan was thoroughly studied and the government was moving toward a policy in what *Fortune* described as a "commendable intention to overhaul and in so far as possible do away with the whole system." The last week in December, 1956, Director Arthur S. Flemming of the Office of Defense Mobilization rejected all pending applications for rapid amortizations. Of the original 228 items eligible, expansion goals and fast tax write-offs were still available for only twenty-two. These included chromite; research and development laboratories; manganese ore; medical supplies and equipment; mercury; nickel; oil and gas pipelines and petroleum storage facilities for specific defense programs; electric power facilities for military, Atomic Energy Commission, and defense-related needs; aircraft and other production facilities for military and AEC procurement; roll-on, roll-off ships; scientific instruments; selenium; steam boilers; steam turbines; steel castings; substitutes for strategic natural mica; ocean-going tankers; and titanium-processing facilities.

The announced fast tax amortization policy on January 1, 1957, after advice from the full Defense Mobilization Board, was that "The only consideration for new tax write-offs would be if a case could be clearly made that in a full mobilization—and only then—there would be a scarcity of materials for military, atomic energy, defense-supporting, or 'rock bottom' civilian requirements."

Another financial incentive authorized by the 1950 Defense Production Act as amended is the purchase of raw materials for government use to encourage the exploration, development, and mining of strategic materials. Long-term contracts and standing purchase offers between the United States government and domestic producers are desirable for use with certain minerals which either are chronically scarce or are expected to be so during the period of the contract or offer. These measures are very effective when substantial amounts of marginal production of minerals will be taken only if otherwise prohibitive market risks are eliminated by the assurance of sale at a price high enough to cover all costs. These contracts and offers are well adapted to preserving an active domestic production nucleus for certain minerals of which a quickly expansible domestic source is needed as a security measure. The Materials Policy Commission concluded: "The standing offer to purchase is administratively more practical than the long-term contract if the mineral is one produced by a large number of producers each operating on a small scale. Either device should be used with great caution and only where it promises a substantial amount of needed domestic production or productive capacity not otherwise obtainable at lower cost." Both types of these purchase agreements may prove politically difficult to terminate even when they may be deemed no longer justified.

The last financial incentive as an aid to discovery and development that will be considered is the premium price plan, also referred to as the "two price plan." During World War II the premium price plan was used to obtain additional quantities of copper, lead, and zinc, and oil from stripper wells. Premiums above ceiling prices were paid for output in excess of quotas based on "normal" production. The program was considered successful. During the program premiums were paid on 20 percent of the copper produced domestically, 40 percent of the lead, 70 percent of the zinc, and about 10 percent of the petroleum. Administrative expenses were under 1 percent of total payments. Costs in higher prices sufficient to induce this additional production would have been greater. The Materials Policy Commission concluded that in an emergency period when price controls are in effect the premium price plan can be a valuable device for stimulating production without undercutting a stabilization program or creating windfalls for low-cost producers. "Applied over long periods, however, it entails increasing administrative expenses, particularly in revising cost analyses and adjusting quotas. Moreover, since premium price plans primarily stimulate production from known reserves, their use might tend in the long run to divert energies from discovering and developing new sources of supply. In addition, they may set up a heavy drain on small reserves of scarce materials." Both of these latter conclusions would appear to be highly debatable, and equally applicable to other programs.

B. Stockpiling

Because of the critical importance of many minerals and other raw materials for military purposes and because of the time needed to develop, transport, and process these materials, reserve supplies must be accumulated and held in stockpiles during peacetime. In addition, the sharp rise in the demand for minerals during war periods require stockpiles as a cushion against the sudden increase in requirements.

Stockpiling should be against specific requirements. This necessitates a determination of (1) the total requirements of a major emergency, (2) the anticipated production during the emergency, and (3) the difference between (1) and (2) for each item in the stockpile. This difference is the quantity to be purchased and held in stockpile. The President's Cabinet Committee on Minerals Policy reported in November, 1954:

> To the degree that minerals are stockpiled within the United States prior to the start of a war, there will be less need, or no need at all for forced draft wartime expansion of raw materials production involving unreasonable increases in prices or substantial Government investment. Likewise, there will be less need for stringent wartime allocations, ceiling prices, and limitation orders on raw materials. In addition, stockpiling can greatly reduce the need for diversion of naval, air, and military efforts to the secondary task of protecting overseas sources of materials and supply lanes when they should be employed in the primary task of fighting the war.

The first Congressional stockpiling legislation was authorized by the Act of June 7, 1939. Inadequate funds were appropriated. Action was "too little too late." On July 26, 1946, the 79th Congress approved the Strategic and Critical Stockpiling Act (Public Law 520). At the end of World War II the government had a large unbalanced stock of materials on hand. These were not legally handled as a reserve for stockpile; instead, a large part was sold as war surplus. The act of 1946 made possible the transfer of the desirable remaining unbalanced and depleted war stocks to the stockpile. Once again Congress did not provide adequate stockpiling appropriations and they were not made available until after the beginning of the Korean War. Once again action was "too late."

The President's Cabinet Committee on Minerals Policy concluded in 1954: "Twice within the last 15 years, the United States has been drawn into international conflicts with almost no stockpile of strategic and critical materials. The absence of an adequate stockpile required the Nation in 1942–44 and again in 1950–52, to undertake costly and disruptive expansion programs to obtain materials which a stockpile, accumulated in advance, could have supplied. It was necessary at a most difficult time to divert scarce machinery and equipment, manpower, and military forces to obtain these materials."

Two of the costly and disruptive effects in 1950–52 were as follows: First, the demand for raw materials for mobilization plus the stockpile purchasing resulted in tremendous increases in prices and costs. Second, since our allies had to buy materials at these high prices, the effect was quite serious and disruptive for them as they were already critically short of foreign exchange. A third disruptive effect which came later was that while foreign sellers of raw materials benefited initially from higher prices, they suffered greatly from the drastic drop in prices when the United States stopped buying some commodities for stockpile purposes. These suppliers prefer a sustained purchase program. Where individual materials constitute a large part of the national income of producing countries, intermittent purchases on the part of the United States drastically upset the economies of the suppliers.

These errors of the past suggest the conclusion that building of a stockpile is a long-term and continuous matter and that major additions to the stockpile should be made so as to bring about the least possible disturbance to the mineral market.

There are other stockpile problems which require continuous attention. One such is the concern of producers that the stockpile is a surplus hanging over the market. There is reason for this concern because the stockpile was depleted during the peacetime boom after World War II. A most serious problem is the constant need for revision of the stockpile in terms of new military plans, new total requirements, new metals, and new supply sources.

The President's Cabinet Committee concluded that the objectives of the stockpile program were "minimum" in that they assumed substantial wartime imports, as well as stringent conservation measures. Therefore, the Committee recommended a complete review of all stockpile objectives for strategic and critical metals and minerals and the establishment in lieu of the "minimum" objective of new long-term objectives that would assure, over a period of time, the acquisition of adequate stocks of these materials and thereby reduce and where possible eliminate foreseeable wartime shortages. This recommendation was to be implemented as follows: (1) It is assumed that supplies from abroad will not be available to the United States in time of war except from a limited group of countries. (2) A supply sufficient to offset possible destruction of major metal- and mineral-producing facilities within the United States must be assured. (3) Materials will be upgraded and refined to the point at which they will be readily usable in an emergency. (4) Stockpile objectives were to be fulfilled from all sources as quickly as possible, but purchases of materials will be made to alleviate distressed conditions in domestic minerals industries that are an important element in the mobilization base of the nation. (5) Preference will be given to newly mined metals and minerals of domestic origin. (6) Acquisition will continue to be made by obtaining strategic and critical metals and minerals in exchange for surplus agricultural commodities which have already been paid for by the government. (7) In acquiring metals and minerals for the "long-term" stockpile objective, care should be exercised to avoid interfering with the normal relationships of regular trade in the United States and in friendly foreign countries.

These recommendations and their implementation were ordered into effect by President Eisenhower. In aggregate they would appear to put the stockpile on a much sounder basis. However, two interrelated points should be singled out for further comment because of their debatable character: (4) stabilization and (5) domestic priority.

The question has been raised: Is the strategic stockpile for security or subsidy? The answer is "Both" under the new program, because price and industry stabilization are clearly defined objectives: "Acquisitions should take place ordinarily at such times as the Government decides that purchases will help to reactivate productive capacity and in other ways to alleviate distressed conditions in connection with domestic mineral industries that are an important element of the Nation's mobilization base. . . ." "Upgrading of stockpile materials should normally be done only when it can be accomplished at favorable prices and in periods of lowered economic activity."

The military have expressed the opinion that "The stockpile should not be used as a stabilization device except in very extraordinary circumstances. This is not to say that we should flout incidental benefits of stockpiles to the stabilization of a peacetime economy. These can be reaped, since assured steady purchasing over a long period is a strong force for stabilization and for a high rate of production."[2] Putting it in proper context and perspective, the military have opposed the inclusion of stabilization as a stockpile objective because they have seen the stockpile depleted for this purpose, because they know that it confuses

[2] George A. Lincoln, *Economics of National Security*, Prentice-Hall, Inc., 1954, p. 19.

the primary issue of security, and because it increases the problems of political manipulation. The military would prefer to see other devices used to obtain stabilization.

One example of the use of the stockpile as stabilizer under the new program occurred early in 1955 when the United States producers of lead and zinc were in such serious trouble that they were, as in the past, asking for higher tariffs to protect themselves from cheaper foreign metals. President Eisenhower rejected the tariff increase, but instead almost doubled the rate of stockpile buying.

This example shows the interrelation of stabilization to the second point singled out for further comment—domestic priority. The first stockpiling legislation in 1939 contained a "Buy American" clause. "Buy American" legislation requires government agencies to buy only domestic goods, unless they are not available in sufficient commercial quantities or their cost is unreasonable or "otherwise inconsistent with the public interest." This clause was continued as a part of the 1946 legislation. Commenting on the 1946 act, the military concluded; "The Act provided a sound basis, with the exception of one aspect, for proceeding with stockpiling. The major weakness was the 'Buy American' clause. This is incongruous since one of the chief purposes is to get within the United States a larger supply of materials needed than would otherwise be available. If we merely move materials from United States ground to United States stockpile, we gain time and save labor and other resources in case of emergency, but we do not expand our total supply. Development of the available United States reserves should go forward, but other methods such as subsidies should be used to encourage domestic producers."[3]

This "Buy American" clause is clearly contained in the Committee on Minerals Policy recommendation: "Accordingly, in making purchases, preference should be given to newly-mined metals and minerals of domestic origin." The justification for such an approach is the subsidization and stabilization of the domestic industry plus what *Time* called a goal "that would make the U.S. virtually self-sufficient in strategic materials." *Time* made the following comment on this approach:

The program assumed that in wartime all sources of supply except Canada and Mexico would be cut off from the U.S., and that even some metal-processing plants in the U.S. might be blasted out of commission. But if the stockpile assumption is that the U.S. will be cut off from all supply, it is the only aspect of U.S. defense based on that idea. All the armed forces have planned

[3] *Ibid.*, pp. 193–194.

their strategy with the idea that the U.S. will have allies, and that it will be able to maintain supply lines back and forth across the oceans. Furthermore, if self-sufficiency is the goal, the U.S. should be spending its money only for those highly critical metals that cannot be found at home, instead of buying aluminum, nickel, molybdenum, etc., which are available in the U.S., Canada and Mexico.

Obviously, *Time* oversimplified the problem in stating only one goal out of a number of stockpile objectives. However, the President of the United States instructed his Committee by letter on October 26, 1953, to use as one of its guide lines: "3. To preserve the added economic strength represented by recent expansion of facilities by the domestic mining industry, through policies that would be consistent with our other national and international policies." It was also suggested: "That the prudent use and development of domestic mineral resources and assured access to necessary sources abroad are indispensable to the operation of an active economy and sound defense." The United States international policies have called for international trade. There is considerable evidence that the Cabinet Committee on Minerals Policy has in its stockpile policy overemphasized the domestic interests and deëmphasized the continued necessity of importing minerals from outside sources.

A final summary conclusion is that, while clearly stating that "overriding in importance in any consideration of policies relating to mineral production and utilization is the security of the Nation," the Committee may have partially deëmphasized the role of security of the stockpile program by stressing the use of stabilization in its implementations. The military have expressed the opinion that there is some danger that the possession of a large stockpile may develop a complacency which would be a brake on the necessary peacetime efforts of exploration, expansion, and technological improvement which need to be pressed because of our worsening raw materials situation. If the recommendations of the Cabinet Committee are carried out properly, this danger certainly should not materialize because the Committee's recommendations were in two parts: "I. The Problem of Security," and "II. The Development of Domestic Mineral Resources." The stockpile is one part of the first and an integrated part of the whole.

C. Import Policy

One of the most widely debated issues is the use of tariffs in the solution of the minerals supply problem. On the one hand the contention is that tariffs are essential as protective and development devices for the domestic industry. On the other hand, the argument is waged with equal force that these devices retard the importation of essential minerals and misdirect domestic productive efforts which could be put to a more effective use. These and other arguments already have been developed extensively in the discussion of petroleum.

IMPORTS. The increased dependence of the United States on imports of minerals already has been shown. In no commodity group has a greater change taken place in the trade of the United States than in metals and minerals.

Iron ore, the basic non-fuel mineral of industrialization, is expected to be imported in much greater quantities. Domestic reserves of high-grade iron ore are being depleted. Very large low-grade reserves are available in the United States, and the technology to develop these reserves is available. To supplement them high-grade ore is being developed and imported principally from Venezuela, Canada, and to a lesser extent from Chile and Brazil. Sweden is also a source of United States imports.

Nonferrous minerals have been seen to be available to the United States in varying percentages of self-sufficiency. The United States has shifted from exporter to importer of copper to the extent of 45 percent consumption in 1953. Imports of copper come primarily from Chile and Peru, where the production is for the most part United States-owned. There has also been a tremendous increase in imports of lead and zinc; in 1953 about 55 percent of the lead and 27 percent of the zinc consumed was imported. Imports of lead and zinc come primarily from Mexico and Canada. Imports of these three metals are expected to increase, even though new domestic reserves are being brought into production.

Aluminum, another major nonferrous metal, is produced from bauxite ore. About 60 percent of the bauxite ore used in the United States is imported, principally from Surinam. Domestic reserves of bauxite are being depleted and imports will grow with the rapid increase in the consumption of aluminum. New sources of supply are being developed in Jamaica. United States companies control most of the production in South America and the Caribbean area. Alumina, the first processed stage of aluminum, was not imported in 1954. But in mid-1955 estimates were that the United States would import about 225,000 tons of aluminum from Canada. This was about one-third of Canada's output for 1955. United States production was estimated to be 1,500,000 tons for 1955.

As has been seen, the United States produces a number of nonferrous minerals in very small quantities, if at all, and thus must depend on outside sources. Some of these minerals are available from nearby sources, like nickel from Canada. Others must be imported from distant, less assured sources—tin from Bolivia and the Far East, cobalt from the Belgian Congo, and tungsten from Bolivia and Peru. Mica, manganese, chrome, asbestos, and many other minerals of strategic importance are produced domestically in only small quantities.

POLICY. Import policy was stated in concise fashion in the report to the President by the Public Advisory Board for the Mutual Security— *A Trade and Tariff Policy in the National Interest;* therefore the resultant discussion, conclusions, and recommendations are repeated.

United States Needs and Foreign Sources—The United States would be following a dangerous policy if it were to close its eyes to its dependence on foreign sources for a substantial part of its supply of many of the most vital mineral commodities, or to disregard the importance of keeping down the materials costs of goods entering into the United States economy. When domestic production of some mineral is substantial, it is necessarily in competition with imports; but if this country depends on such imports, it must give the foreign producer access to the American market on a reasonable and fair basis and United States industry access to foreign supplies on as favorable terms as possible.

There can be only one valid policy on minerals: to assure adequate supplies for this country and the free world in the present and the future. Such a policy should encourage domestic and foreign production, and provide for the exploration and development of domestic and foreign deposits. The United States must give every encouragement to the expansion of production abroad and the participation of American companies in such development on equitable terms. Foreign countries will not offer such opportunities to American investors if the ores and metals cannot be exported to the United States on fair terms.

Nor can the United States expect to have assured sources of imports in the future, when its needs are greater, if it is unwilling to allow imports in the present, when its needs may be less acute. After foreign producers of minerals develop markets in other countries, they cannot cut off supplies to their usual customers to meet emergency needs of the United States. Finally, since a producing country abroad may be a source of various minerals, a policy of encouraging imports of some and restricting imports of others may be regarded as discriminatory by the supplier country. To participate in the development and use of the mineral production of other countries, the United States must permit imports to come in without serious restrictions and without penalizing the reduction and refining of ores abroad.

Tariffs on Metals and Minerals—With few exceptions, the duties on metals and minerals, including import excise taxes, are low, and many ores and unprocessed minerals are on the Free List. The duties are generally specific, and their ad valorem equivalent is seldom more than 15 percent and often below 10 percent on the basis of 1951 market prices. There has been a marked reduction in the impact of the specific duties because of the rise in prices. For many of these minerals and metals, moreover, duties have been reduced under the Trade Agreements, often by half and occasionally by more than half of the 1930 rate. Much of the reduction in duties has occurred since the war.

For most ores and unprocessed minerals, the relatively small duty has little restrictive effect on imports under ordinary conditions; it is a low hurdle over which imports pass easily, and does no more than give domestic producers a slight price advantage. For many imports, including the major nonferrous metals, such relatively low tariffs cannot possibly provide a significant inducement for expanding or maintaining the high cost segment of domestic output.

The specific duty on some metals provides a fixed differential between the price of domestic and imported metals. It thus becomes more protective when prices are high. As metals prices are subject to greater fluctuation than the prices of manufactured goods, the tariff does operate to keep prices in the domestic market from falling as low as they otherwise might when there is a sharp decline in demand. In fact, however, for most minerals and metals present duties are too low to have any significant effect on price stability.

A suggestion has been made to replace present duties with a sliding scale tariff. For example, in place of the present duty of $1\frac{1}{16}$ cents a pound on lead in metal, the duty would be placed at $4\frac{3}{4}$ cents a pound when the price of lead is 5 cents a pound and would be reduced by one-fourth cent a pound for each 1 cent a pound rise in the price of lead. Whenever lead is over 20 cents a pound, imports would be duty free. The proposal has several objectionable features, apart from the high rates which are recommended. Its stabilizing effect on the domestic price of lead would be great. But this stability would be achieved at the expense of very much greater instability in the price of lead abroad. Whatever contribution it would make to encourage domestic production would be more than offset by the serious blow it would give to production abroad. The United States cannot isolate itself from the world market and from the world supply of a commodity for which 50 percent of domestic requirements, and probably a larger proportion in the future, must be met by imports.

Tariffs and Domestic Needs—The effect of small duties in encouraging domestic exploration and development is very uncertain. Search for minerals is undertaken in response to the prospect for profit. Incentive is not provided by a tariff as such, but by an expanding market at profitable prices. Tax provisions covering exploration costs and depletion allowances offer far greater incentives for the metals and minerals industry than could be provided by tariffs. It would be dangerous to exclude imports which meet the needs of the American economy in order to encourage exploration and development of possible domestic sources of these minerals. If additional incentives are necessary to stimulate exploration and development in the United States, they can be better and more economically provided in other ways. The use of tariffs to encourage exploitation of low-grade ores now is particularly objectionable.

Tariffs on the minerals for which the United States produces all of its current needs and is a net exporter are unnecessary. Their effect in excluding imports is negligible, and their elimination would contribute to the simplification and rationalization of the tariff. Such minerals include molybdenum ore and concentrates, and magnesium metal. They should be transferred to the Free List.

The basic principle that a tariff is unjustified when imports are necessary to supply a large part of American consumption is as applicable to metals and minerals as to other commodities. At present, the excise tax of 2 cents a pound on imported copper is suspended. There is no reason to restore it at all. For lead and zinc, the present tariff is equivalent to about 6 percent ad valorem. The world market for these metals has not been as strong as that for copper; and high cost domestic producers have been more dependent on the tariff to maintain output. For this reason the tariff should perhaps be retained for the time being, but provision should be made to remove it when prices of these metals rise and conditions become favorable for eliminating the tariff.

A change in tariff policy is also desirable for the minerals of which domestic production supplies less than one-third of domestic needs. The principal reason for encouraging domestic production is to meet emergencies. In part this can be accomplished by stockpiling. If it is also necessary in the case of some minerals to foster a going domestic industry of moderate proportions in peace time, the Government purchase programs now in use for mica, chrome and manganese could be extended to other commodities and accomplish the same purpose as a tariff. Imports of such minerals, however, should be on the Free List.

The tariffs on metals and processed minerals should be no more than the equivalent of the tariffs on the ores and crude minerals from which they are derived. The existing differentials are undesirable. The reason for admitting an ore free of duty and placing a duty on the metal is to induce the establishment of smelting facilities in the United States instead of the country of origin. Continuation of such duties is prejudicial to the countries on which this country must depend for import supplies and places an unnecessary burden on domestic metals manufacturing industries. The assessment of an additional duty on the minor presence of a mineral in an imported ore, such as vanadium in iron ore, should also be eliminated.[4]

D. Development of Outside Sources

Ample proof has been given for the need of imports and of the dependence of the United States on foreign sources for non-fuel minerals. The question then is what policies, in addition to changes in import policies, might effectively help develop outside sources for non-fuel minerals and thus help alleviate the supply problem. The development of these sources is important because of the increasing requirements of both the United States and the rest of the free world. There is a need for

[4] *A Trade and Tariff Policy in the National Interest,* February, 1953, pp. 33–35.

policies and action which are advantageous to both the United States and the source countries.

The President's Materials Policy Commission concluded that the areas to which the United States must principally look for expansion of its minerals imports are Canada, Latin America, Africa, the Near East, and south and southeast Asia. The Commission found that in the high-tonnage materials, such as oil, iron ore, zinc, manganese, bauxite, and possibly copper, there is little doubt that the less-developed areas have high-grade reserves, which after satisfying their own expanding requirements can supply the rest of the free world beyond the 1975 terminal date of the study. The same was considered to be true for a wide range of other essential materials. "The real question, therefore, is whether capital, equipment, technology, and management skills will flow into the expansion of lowest cost sources of supply in the less developed countries at a rate sufficient to yield the necessary production."

To this real question should be added the question of the assured availability of this production to the United States as a part of a long-term peacetime program and during wartime.

The Commission saw need of action along four lines: "(1) to provide better inducements both abroad and at home for private investors in foreign materials production; (2) to assist resource countries in the progressive improvement of their productive capacity; (3) to relieve restrictions on trade in raw materials; and (4) to curb the violent fluctuations of materials markets."

All of these lines of action have much broader applications than to non-fuel minerals alone. Points (1) and (2) require extensive study as a part of capital resources. Point (3) was considered in detail in the previous discussions of imports and of the "Buy American" clause. Also point (4) has been referred to numerous times. However, a brief consideration of (1), (2), and (4) as they affect minerals will point up the required policy action to improve the non-fuel minerals supply position.

Private investment on the part of United States nationals is the best source of the development of minerals in raw material countries. Many of the primary resource countries in their desire to obtain the maximum benefits from their resources have been extending government control over their minerals and other raw materials.

At the end of 1950 United States private foreign investment in materials was about $6 billion out of a total of $13.5 billion of United States private foreign investment. Over 65 percent of this investment was in Canada and Latin America. Petroleum investment was $4 billion of the materials total; mining and smelting, $1.3 billion; and the balance was scattered. These investments are controlled by a few large corporations.

The President's Materials Policy Commission made a survey of fifty companies, together with underwriters, brokers, bankers, management engineers, and law firms active in materials enterprises abroad. It concluded that, in general, private investors recognize the legitimate interests of resource countries and are ready to work on equitable terms including, in cases, the sharing of investment, ownership, and management with local interests. However, the private investors want relief from threat of expropriation, foreign administrative restrictions on conversion of earnings into dollars, discriminatory taxations, and interference with operations. They also want relief from penalizing provisions of United States tax laws.

The results of this survey suggest that the United States government should extend its diplomatic efforts to create a more favorable basis for bargaining and the conclusion of agreements between investors and the governments of resource countries. The President's Materials Policy Commission believed that in achieving such ends there was considerable value in the investment treaties which the United States was negotiating with other nations. These treaties give the investor greater assurance of the right of appeal to the International Court of Justice in case of unresolved disputes over the interpretation of treaty terms, and against arbitrary and unfair treatment. In addition to investment treaties, the Commission recommended the negotiation of government-to-government special resource agreements when new investment in minerals would occur in a given place in a given country if legal and administrative deterrents were lifted. The suggestion is that these agreements would run from five to ten years, during which the private investor would have the pledge of the foreign government in specific terms concerning tax laws, ownership and management, exchange, restrictions, compensation in event of expropriation, and other familiar points of issue.

The Commission also concluded that the amount of private capital invested in the development of mineral resources abroad could be considerably spurred and new investors attracted by certain changes in the tax laws. The Commission recommended a series of actions: "Allowing taxpayers to elect annually between 'per country' and 'over-all limitations' in claiming credits on their United States tax bills for taxes paid abroad; permitting deferral of reporting income until actually received;

extending the privilege of filing consolidated returns with foreign subsidiaries; allowing stockholders in foreign corporations which have invested in exploration and development to treat part of their dividends as tax-free return of capital rather than as taxable income."

Assisting resource countries in the progressive improvement of their productive capacity is the task of private enterprise. However, in some countries the task may be too great for private capital, and public loans and technical assistance may be called for to aid in educational programs and the diversification of economic development.

To accomplish this task the United States should encourage a wider use of the United Nations technical assistance in geological surveying and minerals exploration in the underdeveloped countries. The United States might also expand its own technical assistance program in return for the assurance that the recipient countries will develop the new mineral resources discovered.

In addition, the expansion of minerals output is often impossible in some countries without public improvement in transportation and electric power. In such instances, public capital supplied by the United States Export-Import Bank and by the International Bank is called for. The Commission recommended that the International Bank should be the principal source of such public loans and that the Bank should consider the effect of the loans on materials output in reviewing requests from member countries.

Reducing market instability would aid tremendously in the development of outside sources for minerals. This problem has been discussed at length in the agriculture policy section and considered as a part of the minerals stockpile program. In the latter instance the recommendation was made that the United States as a buyer enter into long-term purchase contracts and buy in an orderly fashion rather than in the spasmodic economy-upsetting fashion that has been practiced in the past. There is a real need on the part of United States administrative officials to consider the impact of purchases on raw material suppliers. More orderly markets with more stable prices would aid greatly in encouraging and operating mineral production.

Intergovernmental Commodity Agreements have been used with varying degrees of success. In the past they have been dominated by producer interests and therefore have not been acceptable to the United States. In general, it has not been the policy of the United States to approve such agreements. However, the Materials Policy Commission thought that multilateral contracts, such as the International Wheat

Agreement, offered the most promising prospects and that such contracts might work for selected minerals.

International buffer stocks, as yet untried, have been suggested and discussed over the years as a means of stabilizing prices. When world prices for a mineral fell, the buffer stock would act as a residual buyer; when prices rose, the stock would act as a seller. "The object is to confine price fluctuations to a moderate range, but not to interfere with the market price mechanism." This stated objective makes absolutely no sense in so far as the "but not" clause is concerned. United States policy makers have never approved a buffer stock. The complications of its administration would be many, and it would inevitably result in international interference with the market mechanism.

The Commission concluded that it was aware of the extreme difficulties inherent in such international undertakings. But it believed "that the alternative to giving them a trial would be an open door to the evils of restrictions and the monopolistic practices of cartels, limiting production, consumption and trade."

4. Conclusions

The basic problem of the non-fuel minerals position is this: How can the United States increase its supply of non-fuel minerals in order to meet the anticipated growth in demand and to provide for an adequate emergency reserve? The solution to this problem has been seen to be possible in the development of policies and their implementation which will further domestic exploration and development; provide for an adequate stockpile integrated with a growing economy and a mobilization base; establish an import policy in the national interest; and aid in the development of outside sources of supply through encouraging private investment, assisting resource countries, and reducing market instability.

STEEL

Steel is the basis of industrialization. Since steel in one form or another enters into every part of the economy, the steel industry has always been considered an important barometer of general business conditions. More fundamentally, however, the capacity to produce steel, sustained production, and the availability of raw materials are excellent measures of the productive capacity and strength of a country.

How steel is made from its principal raw materials of iron ore, coal,

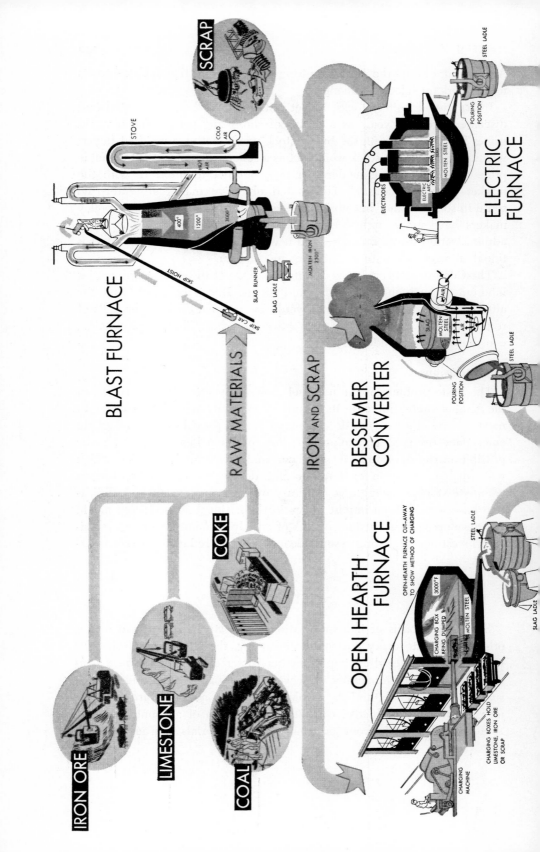

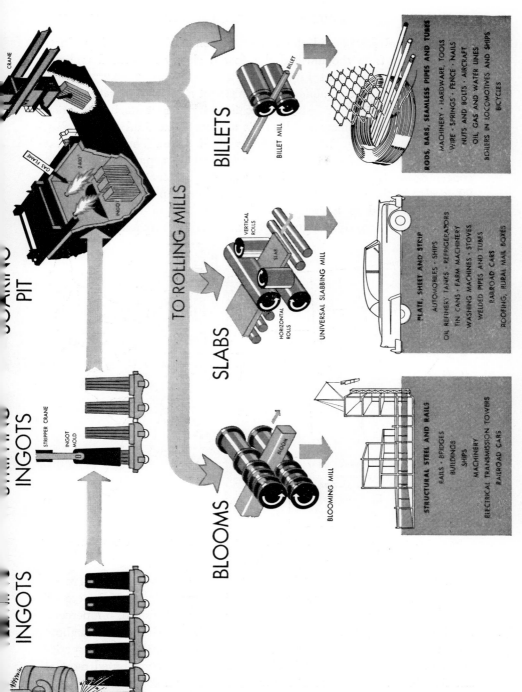

Figure 9.7. How Steel Is Made. (United States Steel Corporation)

limestone, and scrap, and the names of some of the chief products manufactured from the finished shapes are clearly illustrated and described in the flow chart Figure 9.7.

In 1957 about 84 companies produced ingot steel and operated plants in 118 communities in 27 states. The industry's ingot steel production was finished for ultimate markets by an estimated total of 255 companies with plants in 270 communities of 31 states. The three largest companies account for 54 percent of steelmaking capacity. Ownership concentration is also accompanied by geographic centralization. About 90 percent of the United States 1957 steelmaking capacity of 133,459,150 tons was located in a comparatively small area in the northeastern section of the country (Figure 9.8). Steelmaking capacity by district

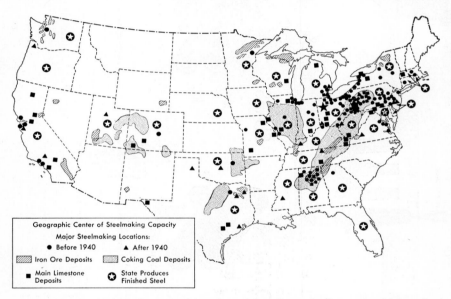

Figure 9.8. Steelmaking Centers and Locations of Raw Materials. (Data adapted from *Steel Facts*, February, 1957)

as a percentage of the total was as follows: Eastern, 21.1 percent; Pittsburgh-Youngstown, 35.4 percent; Cleveland-Detroit, 10.2 percent; Chicago, 21.9 percent; Southern, 5.7 percent; and Western, 5.7 percent. Additional evidence of concentration is that in the United States about 80 percent of past iron-ore production has come from the Lake Superior region; Alabama, New York, Utah, and Texas have contributed most of the remainder. The United States Steel Corporation controls over three-

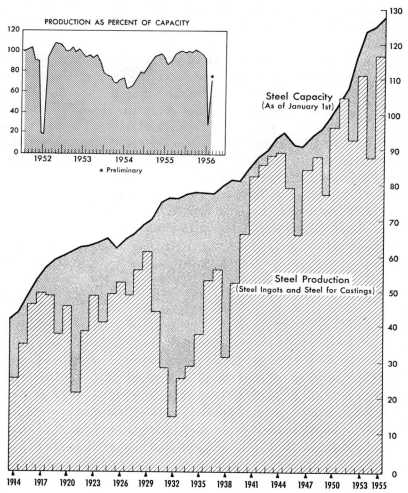

Figure 9.9. Steel Production and Capacity, United States, 1914–56. (Data adapted from American Iron and Steel Institute)

fourths of the listed reserves in the Mesabi range, which is the principal range of the Superior district.

1. Capacity and Production

The sustained growth of the United States steel capacity from 1914 to 1956 is shown in Figure 9.9. The long-run increase in steel production in the United States is also shown in this figure. Production in 1954 of 88.3 million tons was down from the peak production of 111.6 million tons in

1953, but this mild but ominous recession was followed by a remarkable production of about 118 million tons in 1955 and 128 million in 1956.

World steel capacity and production are given in Table 56. The estimate that there was in 1956 a world capacity to produce more than 327 million tons of steel annually was a combination of measured and calculated capacities. Few if any countries other than the United States and Canada and perhaps the United Kingdom measure and report publicly the total capacity of the operable steel furnaces located in each, thus these figures are at best an estimate by the United States Department of Commerce. By these data the United States had 39.2 percent of the world's steel capacity in 1956, the European Coal and Steel Community 19.3 percent, the United Kingdom 7.3 percent, and Russia 16.7 percent. Total free world countries had 76.7 percent of the capacity as compared with 23.3 percent for countries in the Soviet orbit.

Probable capacities for 1960 were even less assured than those for 1956. The announced goals or programs are subject to change, but in addition their attainment depends upon the successful accomplishment of many lesser goals including the financing of the projected expansion. Between 1956 and 1960, assuming all these programs are accomplished, world steel capacity will increase 81,139,000 tons or 24.8 percent. The free world plans to build 50,094,000 tons additional capacity, an increase of 19.9 percent, while the Soviet orbit countries intend to construct 31,045,000 tons, or an addition of 40.0 percent to 1956 capacity. Including the conservative 14,637,000-ton expansion shown for the United States, the steelmaking capacity of the Western Hemisphere will increase 18,514,000 tons. Western European capacity, including the United Kingdom, will rise 23,420,000 tons or 37.0 percent and of this total 15,000,000 tons will be in the European Coal and Steel Community.

2. Consumption

Most steel products are made to order for users who receive shipments directly from the mills, but about one-sixth of the steel industry's shipments of finished products goes to warehouses and other distributors, for resale in their areas. The shipments of finished steel by market classifications in the United States is presented in Figure 9.10. The three great markets for steel are the automotive and building industries and the manufacturers of machinery. These three industries took 45.5 percent of the steel mills' direct shipments in 1955, and when the steel that these industries use out of warehouses for local sale is included, the share is increased to considerably more than 50 percent.

TABLE 56. World Steel Production and Capacity—Ingots and Castings
(thousands of net tons)

Area and Country	Production[a]					Capacity[b]			
	1937	1940	1954	1955		1956		1960	
				Tons	Per-cent of World	Tons	Per-cent of World	Tons	Per-cent of World
Free World Countries									
North America (except Mexico):									
United States[c]	56,637	66,983	88,312	117,036	39.3	128,363	39.2	143,000	35.0
*Canada	1,571	2,254	3,195	4,529	1.5	5,525	1.7	6,000	1.5
Total North America	58,208	69,237	91,507	121,565	40.8	133,888	40.9	149,000	36.5
Latin America:									
*Argentina[d]	10	20	213	256	0.1	260	0.1	1,250	0.3
*Brazil	84	156	1,266	1,225	0.4	1,490	0.5	2,500	0.6
*Chile	15	20	354	341	0.1	440	0.1	440	0.1
Colombia	—	—	15	85	(#)	220	0.1	275	0.1
*Mexico	17	104	686	812	0.3	1,268	0.4	2,085	0.5
*Peru	—	—	10	10	(#)	10	(#)	65	(#)
*Uruguay	—	—	10	10	(#)	20	(#)	50	(#)
Venezuela	—	—	15	15	(#)	20	(#)	465	0.1
Total Latin America	126	300	2,569	2,754	0.9	3,728	1.2	7,130	1.7
Total Western Hemisphere	58,334	69,537	94,076	124,319	41.7	137,616	42.1	156,130	38.2
Free Europe:									
*European Coal and Steel Community:									
*Belgium	4,281	2,083	5,521	6,495	2.1	7,275	2.2	8,265	2.0
*France	8,730	4,865	11,714	13,880	4.6	15,430	4.7	18,740	4.6
Saar	2,578	1,242	3,092	3,490	1.2	3,640	1.1	4,410	1.1
*Germany, West	17,211	18,295	19,217	23,519	7.9	25,905	7.9	33,620	8.2
*Italy	2,300	2,485	4,637	5,947	2.0	6,280	1.9	7,715	1.9
*Luxembourg	2,767	1,148	3,117	3,555	1.2	3,640	1.1	3,855	0.9
*Netherlands	54	169	1,023	1,073	0.4	1,090	0.4	1,655	0.4
Total Community	37,921	30,287	48,321	57,959	19.4	63,260	19.3	78,260	19.2
*Austria	716	845	1,822	2,013	0.7	2,040	0.6	2,315	0.6
Denmark	22	25	219	265	0.1	265	0.1	265	0.1
Finland	53	85	195	206	0.1	210	0.1	210	0.1
Greece	11	10	46	44	(#)	50	(#)	50	(#)
Ireland	—	—	15	15	(#)	25	(#)	25	(#)
*Norway	77	76	133	183	0.1	330	0.1	770	0.2
*Portugal	—	—	—	—	—	—	—	165	(#)
*Spain	184	886	1,212	1,325	0.4	1,490	0.4	2,865	0.7
Sweden	1,237	1,262	2,052	2,369	0.8	2,480	0.7	3,085	0.7
Switzerland	11	44	165	183	0.1	195	0.1	220	0.1
*Turkey	—	41	188	217	0.1	220	0.1	440	0.1
*United Kingdom	14,542	14,538	20,742	22,165	7.4	23,810	7.3	28,660	7.0
*Yugoslavia	186	224	679	888	0.3	965	0.3	1,430	0.3
Total free Europe	54,960	48,323	75,789	87,832	29.5	95,340	29.1	118,760	29.1
Other Free World Countries:									
* Australia	1,221	1,474	2,486	2,458	0.8	2,535	0.8	2,865	0.7
Egypt	—	—	55	55	(#)	85	(#)	275	0.1
Federation of Rhodesia and Nyasaland	—	5	37	40	(#)	70	(#)	80	(#)
*India	1,002	1,447	1,887	1,910	0.7	1,985	0.6	6,720	1.7
*Japan	6,394	7,557	8,543	10,370	3.5	11,160	3.4	13,225	3.2
Union of South Africa	372	400	1,574	1,741	0.6	1,875	0.6	2,200	0.5
Other	—	—	e55	e55	(#)	f205	0.1	f710	0.2
Total other free world countries	8,989	10,883	14,637	16,629	5.6	17,915	5.5	26,075	6.4
Total free world countries	122,283	128,743	184,502	228,780	76.8	250,871	76.7	300,965	73.7

TABLE 56.   World Steel Production and Capacity—Ingots and Castings (*Continued*)
(thousands of net tons)

Area and Country	Production[a]					Capacity[b]			
	1937	1940	1954	1955		1956		1960	
				Tons	Per-cent of World	Tons	Per-cent of World	Tons	Per-cent of World
Soviet Orbit Countries									
U.S.S.R. (Russia)	19,510	20,172	45,525	49,824	16.7	54,565	16.7	75,290	18.5
Soviet Europe:									
Bulgaria	—	—	55	63	(#)	75	(#)	275	0.1
Czechoslovakia	2,537	2,497	4,883	5,236	1.8	5,620	1.7	6,950	1.7
Germany, East	1,469	1,567	2,584	2,756	0.9	3,415	1.0	3,860	0.9
Hungary	733	827	1,644	1,764	0.6	1,900	0.6	2,470	0.6
Poland	2,174	1,287	4,370	4,960	1.7	5,370	1.7	8,265	2.0
Rumania	261	287	693	772	0.2	850	0.3	1,765	0.4
Total Soviet Europe	7,174	6,465	14,229	15,551	5.2	17,230	5.3	23,585	5.7
China	493	728	2,447	3,307	1.1	3,750	1.1	7,715	1.9
Korea, North	112	115	660	660	0.2	700	0.2	700	0.2
Total Soviet orbit countries	27,289	27,480	62,861	69,342	23.2	76,245	23.3	107,290	26.3
World total	149,572	156,223	247,363	298,122	100.0	327,116	100.0	408,255	100.0

[a] Statistics of production in 1955 are preliminary and subject to revision. For most principal producers the figure shown repeats reported production for the complete calendar year. The "production" of the Soviet bloc countries repeats estimates developed by the Economic Commission for Europe, a subsidiary organization of the United Nations.

[b] Capacity data for 1956 in the case of the United States and Canada are carefully measured figures. However, for most other countries of the free world they are calculated figures based on the best information available on the capacity of existing steel furnaces. The data shown for Soviet orbit countries are based on estimates of the Economic Commission for Europe of the United Nations. The figures shown for 1960, except for the United States and Canada, are planned figures announced by the respective governments, and have varying possibility of realization.

[c] Excludes steel melted in independent foundries.

[d] Steel ingots only.

[e] Includes small tonnages of steel made in Algeria, Israel, Pakistan, the Philippines, Taiwan (Formosa), and Thailand.

[f] Includes steelmaking capacity for the following countries, in net tons:

	1956	1960
Algeria	10,000	15,000
Burma	30,000	30,000
Israel	45,000	65,000
Pakistan	15,000	385,000
Philippines	45,000	155,000
Taiwan (Formosa)	55,000	55,000
Thailand	5,000	5,000

* Steel and/or iron ore industries in these countries have been extended financial assistance by the United States government and/or the International Bank for Reconstruction and Development.

(#) Less than 0.1% of world production or capacity.

SOURCE: Dispatches of the Foreign Service of the United States, American Iron and Steel Institute, Monthly and Annual Statistical Bulletins of the British Iron & Steel Federation, and Monthly and Quarterly Bulletins and special studies developed by subsidiary organizations of the United Nations; *International Iron and Steel*, United States Department of Commerce, August, 1956.

Steel continues not only to be the basic capital goods metal but also to find its major markets in capital goods. However, in recent years there has been an ever-increasing volume of consumer products into which steel enters. The following are indications of this trend: (a) Between

DOMESTIC SHIPMENTS OF FINISHED STEEL BY MARKET CLASSIFICATIONS Percent of total domestic shipments		
MARKET	1954	1955
Automotive	19.5%	23.1%
Warehouses and Distributors	16.4%	16.7%
Construction and Contractors' Products	15.7%	13.8%
Machinery (including electrical) and Industrial Equipment	8.7%	8.6%
Containers	9.7%	8.3%
Converting and Processing Forgings, Bolts, Nuts, Etc.	7.0%	8.0%
Oil and Gas (including drilling)	7.8%	6.7%
Domestic and Commercial Equipment	5.3%	5.4%
Rail Transportation	4.1%	4.3%
Agricultural	1.9%	1.7%
Ordnance and other Direct Military	1.6%	1.1%
Shipbuilding, Marine Equipment, Aircraft	0.9%	0.9%
Mining, Quarrying, Lumbering	0.3%	0.3%
All other	1.1%	1.1%

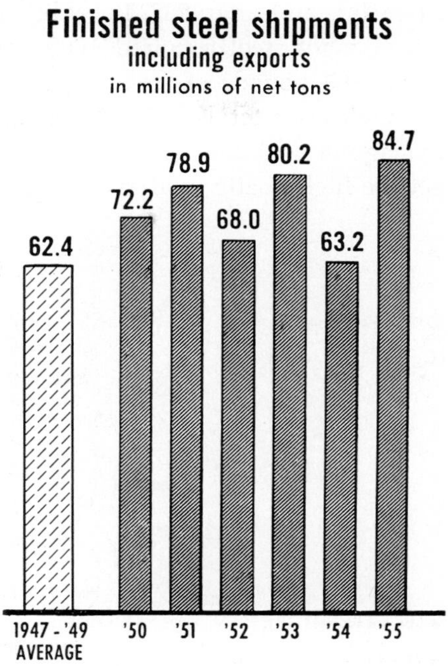

Finished steel shipments
including exports
in millions of net tons

Figure 9.10. Finished Steel Shipments by Market Classifications. (Data adapted from American Iron and Steel Institute)

1900 and 1905 steel rails accounted for about 20 percent of the industry's steel production. Today, tin cans and containers require more steel than rail transportation. (b) More than 20 percent of today's steel goes into automotive production. (c) Steel equipment has become a major item in building and furnishing every home. This increased volume of consumer goods has increased the stability in the demand for the products of the iron and steel industry.

The more stable capital-consumer-goods mix in the market for steel has been facilitated by the industry's march in the developing of new steels and by its promoting new applications of steel. This broadening of the market for steel has served to increase the fundamental importance of the steel industry to the United States economy.

3. Raw Materials

About two and one-half tons of iron ore, coke, limestone, scrap, and other materials are required to make a ton of ingot steel. In 1955, to make the 1175 pounds of pig iron that went into a ton of steel required

3652 pounds of raw materials as follows: iron ore 1953, coke 1026, limestone 441, and scrap 232. In addition to these 1175 pounds of pig iron, a ton of ingot steel required 1000 pounds of scrap, 145 pounds of limestone, 165 pounds of iron ore, 140 pounds of coal, and 28 pounds of ferro-alloys—a total of 5130 pounds. This does not include the substantial tonnage of coal and iron ore which must be washed and beneficiated to get the high-quality materials required for efficient iron production.

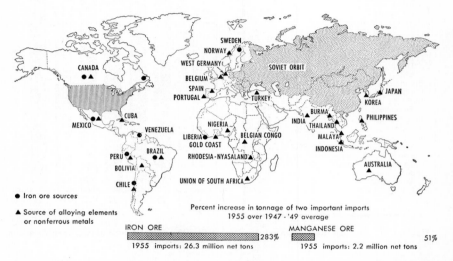

Figure 9.11. United States Dependence on Foreign Supplies of Iron and Steelmaking Raw Materials. Until recent times, Soviet Russia was one of our most important sources of manganese and chromium ores. China was a major source of tungsten. (Data from U.S. Department of Commerce)

The availability of coal, and problems of the industry have already been studied. In addition to coal, oil and gas are used as fuels. Limestone is used as a flux. The Bureau of Mines has reported: "There are adequate domestic supplies of coking coal, oil, gas to take care of the needs of the steel industry, as well as fluxes, except fluorspar, which is included in the National Stockpile. With a sound scrap program the supply of this important raw material should be sufficient to meet the needs of the industry." What about the ferro-alloys and iron ore? The United States' critical position with respect to the former has been studied in detail. However, in addition, Figure 9.11, supplemented by the data in Table 57, points up the dependence of the United States on foreign supplies of iron and steelmaking raw materials.

Total reserves of present commercial or usable iron ore in the United States, as estimated by the Bureau of Mines and the Geological Survey

TABLE 57. Imports of Nonferrous Commodities Used by the Iron and Steel Industry

United States Imports of Chromium Ore, 1951–55
(net tons of contained chromic oxide)

	1955	1954	1953	1952	1951
Metallurgical grade:					
Cuba	3,707	—	11,627	15,939	1,210
French Pacific Islands	15,270	15,568	48,737	29,779	33,813
Philippines	18,040	21,509	38,938	19,490	1,337
Rhodesia, Southern	150,703	113,899	151,090	82,514	89,645
Turkey	180,014	141,746	256,801	208,153	134,430
Union of South Africa	50,645	48,066	90,551	40,174	23,206
Yugoslavia	1,176	—	22,099	9,511	10,275
Other countries	20,542	6,206	18,914	16,704	8,132
Total imports, metallurgical grade ores	440,097	346,994	638,757	422,264	302,048
Total imports, refractory grade ores	218,093	175,595	207,913	206,629	158,517
Total imports, chemical grade ores	96,324	86,072	94,004	83,732	150,171
Total imports, all grades	754,514	608,661	940,674	712,625	610,736

United States Imports of Manganese Ore, 1951–55
(net tons of contained manganese)

	1955	1954	1953	1952	1951
Metallurgical grade (35% plus):					
Angola	18,943	22,978	30,537	28,504	15,603
Belgian Congo	66,951	79,854	70,198	28,032	5,402
Brazil	60,061	45,260	68,844	77,448	44,247
Cuba	113,985	110,871	169,170	110,854	63,446
Gold Coast	120,725	76,684	126,459	108,277	145,338
India	390,039	432,700	540,643	352,018	294,345
Mexico	49,236	52,808	55,312	39,254	43,305
Morocco, French	45,298	29,539	29,416	34,478	20,259
U.S.S.R. (Russia)	—	—	—	—	1,282
Union of South Africa	95,981	101,168	168,421	129,567	180,509
Other countries	55,033	46,742	87,177	60,866	31,163
Total imports, metallurgical grade (35% plus)	1,016,252	998,604	1,346,177	969,298	844,899
Total imports, battery and chemical grades (35% plus)	45,650	29,356	52,320	32,359	35,926
Total imports, other grades (10%–35%)	35,302	22,766	41,979	40,667	46,649
Total imports, all grades	1,097,204	1,050,726	1,440,476	1,042,324	927,474

United States Imports of Other Selected Commodities Used by the Iron and Steel Industry, 1951–55
(net tons)

	1955	1954	1953	1952	1951
Ammonium sulphate	173,118	305,012	523,858	238,063	21,6106
Naphthalene—solidifying under 79°C.	60,808	33,436	41,668	46,052	36,777
Fluorspar not over 97% CaF_2	158,248	87,545	151,779	224,521	128,284
Tin—pigs, blocks and bars	72,484	73,299	83,482	90,107	31,118
Palm oil	22,120	33,057	17,846	25,623	50,624
Tungsten ore[a]	10,303	12,066	13,863	8,714	3,194
Magnesite—brick and shapes	8,462	7,247	6,297	5,864	4,517
Nickel—pigs and ingots	109,800	97,707	85,585	79,875	77,471
Copper—pigs and ingots[a]	454,344	467,906	553,353	520,764	371,106
Lead—pigs and bars[a]	264,104	274,287	379,041	510,718	178,896
Zinc—pigs, blocks, and slabs	195,839	161,328	227,594	113,051	87,983
Aluminum-metals, crude	177,652	215,250	300,928	128,233	122,404

[a] Content weight.

SOURCE: *International Iron and Steel*, United States Department of Commerce, August, 1956.

as of January 1, 1950 (Table 58), were over 6000 million tons. The Bureau of Mines in commenting on this table stated: "Even after 100 years of iron mining in the Lake Superior district and numerous geologic and engineering studies by reputable scientists, no one can state factually the tonnage of remaining ore. Substantial agreement, however, is

TABLE 58. Estimates of Iron Ore Reserves of the United States, by Geographical Regions as of January 1, 1950;[a] Direct-Shipping Ore and Concentrates by Present Methods of Beneficiation
(million gross tons)

Region and State	1 Measured	2 Measured and Indicated (includes column 1)	3 Measured, Indicated, and Inferred (includes column 2)
Lake Superior region: Minnesota, Michigan, Wisconsin: Total	1,124	1,720	3,605
Northeastern region: New York, New Jersey, Pennsylvania: Total	—	300	380
Southeastern region:[b]			
Alabama and Georgia	—	968	968
Tennessee, Virginia, North Carolina, West Virginia, Kentucky	—	160[c]	659[c]
Total	—	1,128	1,627
Central and Gulf region:			
Missouri	—	2	4
Texas[d]	17	27	60
Total	17	29	64
Western region:			
Utah	—	100	350
Wyoming[e]	—	25	25
California	28	33	54
New Mexico[f]	—	19	39
Nevada[g]	—	11	16
Total	28	188	484
United States	1,169	3,365	6,160

[a] Compiled by Geological Survey and Bureau of Mines.
[b] Measured and indicated not differentiated.
[c] Possible commercial production from this material will require thorough appraisal as to availability and value of deposits.
[d] Geological Survey and Bureau of Mines, 1950; unpublished compilation.
[e] Measured and indicated not differentiated.
[f] Excludes manganiferous iron ore and other deposits of marginal grade or less than 10,000-ton reserve.
[g] Bureau of Mines, 1950; unpublished compilation.
SOURCE: *Mineral Facts and Problems*, Bureau of Mines, 1956.

apparent among the various groups that have estimated domestic reserves."

Estimates of world iron reserves have been subject to wide variations. The Department of Economic and Social Affairs of the United Nations completed in 1955 a comprehensive *Survey of World Iron Ore Resources —Occurrence, Appraisal and Use.* Table 59 presents a general summary

TABLE 59. Estimated World Iron Reserves, 1954
(Millions of Long Tons)

	Reserves	Iron Content
North America and the West Indies	14,100	6,600
South America	19,700	10,000
Europe	16,480	6,400
Africa	4,100	2,000
U.S.S.R.	3,200	1,900
Asia and the Middle East	26,000	14,300
Oceania	1,000	500
Total	84,580	41,700

SOURCE: United Nations, Department of Economic and Social Affairs.

of the detailed regional studies. The figures refer only to reserves— mineral masses—considered exploitable for usable material under existing economic and local conditions, leaving aside "potential ores," which required more favorable conditions than those which obtained at the time of the survey. In general, the lean siliceous bedded materials of the Lake Superior type were not estimated. The conclusion was as follows: These potential ores probably average over 25 percent in iron content, and in such countries as Brazil, the Union of South Africa, India, Australia, and Canada the total tonnage is undoubtedly many times that of the richer reserves that have been estimated. The "mineral reserves" reported in the table embrace the standard concepts of "proved," "probable," and "possible." These classifications conform closely to the United States Geological Survey and Bureau of Mines' "measured," "indicated," and "inferred."

The United States' share of world iron reserves of 84,580 million tons was reported as 6900 million tons. These reserves were considered according to five regional subdivisions, some of which contain several types of deposits. The subdivisions are in part geologic units and in part economic units. A summary of the measured, indicated, and inferred reserves in the five regions is as follows: Lake Superior (50 percent iron), 2300 million tons; concentrates from taconite (60 percent iron),

1700 million; Northeastern region (60 percent), 400 million; Southeastern region (35 percent), 1950 million (45 to 50 percent), 80 million; Central and Gulf region (45 to 50 percent), 70 million; Western region (45 to 50 percent), 400 million.

A thorough analysis of the United Nations' detailed report of world iron reserves is recommended. However, for present purposes the following is a concise summary of the iron ore reserves which was published just prior to the UN's comprehensive study.

The "place value" of these reserves is highly important. Iron ore is a desirable ballast material but its low unit value limits its economical radius of distribution. Available transport facilities thus assume great importance; for example, it costs as much to haul ore for 250 or 300 miles by rail as it does to carry it across the Atlantic by boat.

Swedish, Spanish, and North African ores have been shipped to the United States in widely varying quantities, and much smaller shipments of ores from the Western Hemisphere have been made to Europe. In general, however, the two hemispheres have been self-contained. Japan obtained ore from mines as much as 5,000 miles from the homeland. Its widely scattered sources were almost entirely in Asia or Oceania, chiefly British Malaya, China, the Philippine Islands, and Australia.

Asia has large reserves in India and the Philippine Republic, but China and Japan are deficient in this respect. Australia seems to have enough for local needs. The Union of South Africa has ample reserves for a budding iron and steel industry, but they are not well-situated for export. French and Spanish North Africa have a moderate reserve of good ore that is all exported. Further exploration in other parts of Africa may disclose additional large supplies in excess of the anticipated needs of that continent.

Western Europe as a whole is well-supplied with iron ore, but eastern Europe, excluding Russia, is not. England has large reserves, but they consist mainly of low-grade ores, whereas a substantial portion of the British iron and steel industry is based upon imports of high-grade ores.

Germany has long been an importer of iron ores because that part of Lorraine annexed by Germany after the war of 1870 included only a small part of the Minette Basin. After the restoration of Lorraine to France following World War I, Germany had to increase further imports of high-grade ores that could be delivered cheaply by water. The deficits of Germany and England in high-grade ores were largely met by shipments from Scandinavian, French, Spanish, and North African sources while the needs of other European countries were balanced chiefly by exports of low-grade ores from France. The Soviet Union is reported to possess abundant reserves in the Urals, in addition to the high-grade ores of the Krivoi Rog field, other deposits in the southern and central regions, and a few deposits in the Asiatic part of Russia. . . .

Western Hemisphere reserves available for shipment, if necessary, to the United States include the exceedingly large and rich deposits recently discovered in the Labrador Peninsula, extensive undersea deposits on Belle Isle in Newfoundland, Cuban lateritic ores and extremely high grade hematite ores in Venezuela and Brazil, and deposits in Chile. It is reasonable to suppose that estimates of ore reserves in the United States and Western Europe are more conservative than those of sparsely settled areas in Latin America, Africa, and Asia. As current sources of easily accessible high quality iron ores are depleted in the industrialized countries, Europe as well as the United States may be expected to draw more heavily on Latin America, which has high grade deposits in comparative proximity to tidewater. Increased deliveries of African ores to Europe are also anticipated.[5]

The adequacy of the iron ore reserves of the United States is a problem that must be studied in connection with the increased capacity and production of steel.

4. Problems and Policy

The sustained progress of the United States production strength depends on the capacity to produce steel and the available raw materials. We will consider first the capacity problem and then the iron ore problem.

A. Capacity

If steel capacity is not expanded the United States economy cannot expand. But every United States steelmaker vividly recalls 1932 when steel operated at 19.5 percent of capacity. For this reason the industry has been cautious in expanding capacity. Asked in 1954 what steel output would be in 1955, with remarkable unanimity steelmen predicted a 10 to 15 percent increase from the 91-million-ton output of 1954. Only one top steelman predicted a 25 percent increase, to 112 million tons, but still short of the 118 million tons of steel produced in 1955. This conservatism is influenced further by the increased cost of new capacity. For example, the original cost of one company over a long period averaged $77 per ingot ton compared with an estimated cost exceeding $200 in 1952. United States Steel's new Fairless plant at Morrisville, Pennsylvania, completed in 1953, cost $250 to $275 per ingot ton of capacity. This includes all finishing facilities for a fully integrated plant.

The industry agrees that new capacity is required. As of January 1, 1957, capacity was 133,459,150 tons, which represented an increase of

[5]Reprinted by permission from "Iron Ore" by Paul M. Tyler, in *Atlas of the World's Resources:* Vol. II: *The Mineral Resources of the World*, by William Van Royen and Oliver Bowles, pp. 63–65. Copyright, 1952, by Prentice-Hall, Inc., Englewood Cliffs, N.J., and published for the University of Maryland.

5,096,150 tons over the rated capacity of 128,363,000 tons on January 1, 1956. The indicated estimated capacity for 1960 was given in Table 56 as 143,000,000 tons. This we described as a conservative 14,637,000-ton expansion over 1956. Yet the Bureau of Mines in *Mineral Facts and Problems,* published in 1956, estimated required steel capacity at only 130,000,000 tons for 1960; 140,000,000 tons for 1965; 150,000,000 tons for 1970; and 160,000,000 tons for 1975 (see Table 60). Thus an average increase of only 1.9 million tons' capacity per year was estimated during the twenty-year interval 1956–75. However, the report did conclude: "Since the average annual increase during the preceding 20 years was 2.2 million tons, the estimate of 160 million tons capacity for 1975 may be too conservative." *Business Week* reported on November 26, 1955, that discussion of expansion up to 1970 by steelmen centered around whether 2 or 4 million tons per year are required.

President Truman gave some expression of national policy when he announced that if the steel industry did not increase steel capacity the government would. In the same issue of *Business Week* referred to above, the statement was made: "Steelmen admit that if they don't add capacity the Government will. That's the only thing they fear more than the cost of wholly new plants." This was not the policy of the Eisenhower administration. Further, as just noted, in 1955 industry estimates of future steel capacity requirements showed much more growth than did government estimates. However, with a vivid memory of what overexpansion means and with the knowledge that future expansion may cost as much as $300 a ton, the industry has reason to plan carefully.

The problem as seen by the steel industry is that in the near future perhaps 50 million tons of new capacity must be built which the industry cannot afford to build at $300 a ton, but cannot afford not to build.

At the beginning of 1956 two factors combined, and were likely to continue to do so through 1958, which delayed the time when new capacity would have to be financed at $300 a ton. First, cash flow was heavy owing to the very high operating rate, and because the post-Korean War expansion investment was being charged off at a fast five-year write-off rate. Second, some relatively cheap expansion was still possible through the process of modernizing and enlarging existing plants. Between 1947 and 1956, 30 million tons of capacity were added by this method.

Actually it appeared that the steel industry would find it necessary to borrow, to do equity financing, and to retain more earnings. To increase earnings, prices were raised in 1956. The industry contended that steel

TABLE 60. United States Crude-Steel Capacity and Iron-Ore Requirements and Supply

United States Crude-Steel Capacity and Iron-Ore Requirements at Full Operation
(million gross tons)

	1950	1951	1953	1955	1960	1965	1970	1975
Steel capacity (ingots and steel for castings net tons Jan. 1)	99.4	104.2	118	126	130	140	150	160
Iron-ore requirements, gross tons:								
Domestic use[a]	106.6	117.7	132	140	146	157	168	179
Export	2.5	4.3	4	4	4	4	4	4
Total	109.1	122.0	136	144	150	161	172	183

United States Potential Iron-Ore Supply Apparent from Present Industry Plans
and Other Available Information
(million gross tons)

	1950	1951	1953	1955	1960	1965	1970	1975
Domestic—Lake Superior:								
Direct ores:								
Open-pit	42.8	53.6	52	50	30	10	5	5
Underground	17.5	18.2	18	20	20	20	20	20
Concentrates:								
Taconite	—	.2	26	2	15	20	25	30
Other	18.8	22.0		30	35	35	30	25
Total Lake Superior	79.1	94.0	96	102	100	85	80	80
Southeastern states:								
Direct ore	5.4	6.0	8	7	7	7	7	7
Concentrates:								
Red ore								
Brown ore	2.2	2.4		3	3	3	3	3
Northeastern states (virtually all concentrates)	4.6	5.1	5	6	6	6	6	6
Western states:								
Utah (direct ore)	3.1	4.7	9	6	7	10	12	12
Other:								
Direct ore	1.6	2.6		3	3	3	3	3
Concentrates	1.2	1.0		1	2	2	2	2
By-product ore	.6	.6	.6	1	1	2	2	2
Total domestic supply	97.8	116.4	118	129	129	118	115	115
Total concentrates included	27.4	31.3	38	43	62	68	68	68
Concentrates, percent	28	27	30	33	48	58	59	59
Foreign supply:								
Canada:								
Quebec-Labrador	—	—	—	5	15	20	30	30
Steep Rock				3	5	5	5	5
Michipicoten	1.9	2.0	2	1	2	5	5	5
Other				1	1	1	1	1
Latin America:								
Brazil	.7	1.0	—	1	2	2	2	2
Chile	2.5	2.8	6	—	—	—	—	—
Venezuela	—	.6		6	13	15	20	20
Other	.2	.2	—	1	1	1	1	1
Africa:								
Algeria and Tunisia	.7	.6	1	1	1	1	1	1
Liberia and British West Africa	.2	.4	1	2	3	4	4	4
Europe:								
Sweden and Norway	2.0	2.5	2	2	2	2	2	2
Total foreign supply	8.2	10.1	12	23	45	53	68	68
Total iron-ore supply	106.0	126.5	130	152	174	171	183	183
Foreign ore, percent of total supply	8	8	9	15	26	31	37	37
Total foreign supply other than Canada	6.3	8.1	9	13	22	25	30	30
Foreign supply other than Canada, percent of total	6	6	6	9	13	15	16	16

[a] Assumes that adequate supplies of scrap will be available.
SOURCE: *Mineral Facts and Problems*, Bureau of Mines, 1956.

users would be better off with price increases because more products would be forthcoming in 1960.

However, before taking the steps to build wholly new plants at $300 a ton the possibilities of applying technology to existing facilities needed to be explored fully. For example, if steel operating engineers could raise average open-hearth performance to the level of the best, the result would be a 35 percent increase in capacity. Engineers were not optimistic for a major breakthrough on open-hearth technology, but considerable attention was being given to the oxygen converter and to the "H-Iron" process as a means of making steel.

In the oxygen converter high-purity oxygen is blown down on a molten iron bath in a small (about forty tons) batch type converter which burns out excess carbon, silicon, phosphorus, and manganese. But most important, the oxygen lowers the nitrogen content of the steel and thus improves its quality. The oxygen converter costs about half as much to install, per annual ton, as new open-hearth capacity and takes up less space. Space is important in existing plants. The oxygen converter process can produce steel at a rate of more than fifty tons an hour compared with twenty to twenty-five tons hourly for the open hearth. One of its defects is that it uses much less scrap than an open hearth and requires more hot iron from the blast furnace. This is an obvious disadvantage when ore is short. There were also arguments about the quality of steel produced. Indications were that only low-carbon steels could be produced. *Steelways* reported that by June, 1956, two million tons of oxygen steel had been produced with excellent results and that it seemed especially suitable for making cold-rolled sheets, a tonnage product widely used in many mass-produced consumer products, such as automobiles and household appliances. Thus it appeared that, in order to lower costs, oxygen converters would be installed gradually at first to complement existing steelmaking furnaces, and then if operating experience remained favorable, they would be added where they could be most efficiently employed.

The "H-Iron" process has been described as "one of the boldest new ideas." Iron oxide is reduced to metallic iron in a single step, using hydrogen. The significant advantage of this process is that it by-passes the blast furnace. Thus charging the blast furnace with limestone, coke, and ore in successive layers is eliminated. Under the "H-Iron" process hydrogen gas is passed under pressure through a mass of fine ore and the product is sponge iron free of the carbon and sulfur that pig iron picks up from the coke in the blast furnace. On the other hand, this process has the disadvantage that it will not remove any contaminant of the original ore except oxygen. Thus if the ore is high in silica and phosphorus, the end product will be. Hence, depending on the quality of the original ore and the amount of beneficiation before or after reduction, "H-Iron" could require more refining in the steelmaking processes than standard blast-furnace iron. But by chance many of the newest ores available from Venezuela, Brazil, and Liberia contain fewer impurities than the Mesabi's best, and in addition are already powdered.

Sponge iron could provide the steelmakers with an additional and low-cost "iron unit" to supplement scrap and blast-furnace pig iron. Sponge iron was being produced experimentally at the beginning of 1957 by two "H-Iron" methods. A high-pressure, low-temperature (900° F.) method was being used by Hydrocarbon Research, Inc., and Bethlehem Steel, and a low-pressure, high-temperature (1100–1700° F.) method was being developed by U.S. Steel. The essential raw materials for these two "H-Iron" methods were low-cost hydrogen and high-grade iron ore. A third process for producing four parts sponge iron and one part ore was being developed by Standard Oil (N.J.) which instead of hydrogen used natural gas as the reducing agent. These direct-reduction processes of producing "iron units" offered the ultimate possibility of freeing the iron and steel industry from its dependence on coke, but most important was the possibility of fitting these reducers into existing integrated steel plants and thus adding to capacity at lower costs.

The above and many other technological improvements require thorough investigation. The chapter on steel in the Bureau of Mines' *Mineral Facts and Problems* points out that "Research by American iron and steel companies is relatively small compared with that of some foreign companies or with that of other American industries." The pressure of rising costs certainly requires that the steel industry intensify research to develop technical solutions to its capacity problems.

At the beginning of 1956 the industry accepted the challenge of the future as Benjamin F. Fairless, president of the American Iron and Steel Institute, announced on January 18 that the steel industry would spend $1.2 billion annually for the next three years to increase steel-producing capacity by 15 million tons, or nearly 12 percent. Over 5 million tons were added in 1956.

B. Iron Ore

The December, 1945, issue of *Fortune* in a feature article, "Iron Ore Dilemma," concluded that unless the United States is to turn increasingly to foreign sources for its ore it must give new life to the wasting Mesabi. *Fortune* summarized the problem in the following fashion:

One diagram of the U.S. economy might show it as an immense inverted pyramid, its needle base resting on a single strip of gently rolling land, 110 miles long by one to four miles wide, in northern Minnesota. Such a diagram would be oversimplified but far from fantastic. For out of this tiny strip the steel-age economy has sucked, like milk from the earth mother's breast, by far the largest portion of the principal food out of which its bones and muscles have been built: its machines and tools, its buildings and bridges, its railroads and automobiles and generating plants. Blasted and gouged from the strip's awesome open pits and scattered underground mines came a full two-thirds of the iron ore for the 400-odd million tons of steel out of which the U.S. fashioned the war plants, ships, planes, tanks, guns, bombs, and shells of World War II.

This fabulous strip, which came within an ace of being included in Canada when the boundary lines were being argued after the Revolution, is the Mesabi iron range. With the neighboring lesser ranges in Minnesota, Wisconsin, and Michigan, which combine with it to form the Lake Superior iron-ore district, it produced no less than 85 per cent of the nation's wartime iron-ore supply. Small wonder that the Sault Ste. Marie (Soo) Canal between Lakes Superior and Huron, through which its ore boats must pass on their way to the steel mills of Chicago, Gary, Cleveland, Pittsburgh, and the rest, burgeoned with barrage balloons and anti-aircraft guns to become the most heavily guarded inland spot in the U.S.

The Mesabi and its neighboring ranges have nourished the U.S. economy for half a century, through two world wars; even on their incomparably rich resources the drain, particularly of World War II, has been immense. Now some serious and farsighted men are saying that the Lake Superior District's day is almost done. In 1942 Director Edward Wilson Davis of the University of Minnesota's Mines Experiment Station reported to WPB that, at the anticipated rate of wartime consumption, the Mesabi's best ores would be gone between 1950 and 1954. Other investigators have given them up to twenty years more, at the outside. Meantime angry champions of the district insist that it can and will continue to supply the major portion of U.S. iron ore for at least a century.

One simple and reassuring observation concerning this complex controversy can be made at once: the U.S. is in no foreseeable danger of a peacetime iron-ore famine. Iron is the earth's fourth most plentiful element (the first three: oxygen, silicon, aluminum). Iron ore is now mined in twenty states, and there are abundant deposits in Russia, South America, North Africa, Australia, Newfoundland, Labrador, many another foreign land. Minnesota alone has enough known iron deposits to supply the U.S. for perhaps a thousand years.

But the fact of iron's abundance makes its economics dependent not on mere supply but on two other factors: (1) how cheaply the ore can be mined and prepared for the steel mills; (2) how cheaply the ore can be transported to the mills. Even the easily mined, high-grade ore of the Mesabi might never have been tapped if the Great Lakes did not provide cheap transportation to the coal-rich region around the lower lakes. The abundant ores of Alabama, on the other hand, are low grade and expensive to mine. They are mined—and the Birmingham steel industry therefore exists—only because Alabama happens also to be rich in the other two items of blast-furnace diet, coal and limestone.

Thus the real issues in the current controversy are two. One is how long Lake Superior ores can continue to compete with those from eastern states and foreign countries. The other is whether the U.S. can risk the prospect of another war without a large and quickly available stockpile of iron ore or pig iron. The first involves either a Bunyanesque industrial transformation of the Superior District or a conceivable major dislocation of U.S. industry through removal of midland steel mills to the Atlantic coast. The second involves the national existence.[6]

In considering this problem in 1946 the writer concluded that the steel industry would work out the solution by (1) the utilization of Class II iron ore and Class III iron reserves of Minnesota, Wisconsin, and Michigan; (2) a partial shift in new capacity location to the east coast and increased dependence on foreign ores following the pattern of Bethlehem Steel at Sparrows Point; (3) increased imports of ore to existing facilities (in this connection, the development of the St. Lawrence Seaway project for ocean-going vessel navigation was recommended); and (4) further decentralization of the industry on a limited scale by increased facilities in the Birmingham area and in the Western region based on the local iron reserves.

The opinion of the writer was that the industry would follow past trends in solving future problems and that it was fully cognizant of these problems and to protect its own interest would work actively toward their solution. It appeared that the principal area of national policy decision was the development of the St. Lawrence Seaway project. At the state level policy decisions were required for favorable tax legislation to facilitate the utilization of Class III, principally taconite, reserves.

Experience from 1946 to 1957 indicated that the above predictions have been borne out.

How much ore will be required and the sources of supply to meet the planned and future steel capacity expansion must be continuously reviewed. Table 60 presents this information for the conservative predictions (outdated before published) of the Bureau of Mines. However, these estimates are indicative of the trends of the future.

[6] "Iron Ore Dilemma," *Fortune*, December, 1945, p. 129. Copyright 1945 by Time Inc.

United States iron ore requirements in 1975 were estimated at 183 million tons. The total domestic supply in 1975 was estimated at 115 million tons, with required imports of 68 million tons. Since domestic supply of 115 million tons in 1975 is almost equal to the 118 million tons produced in 1953, imports will have to be about equal to increased requirements. Summarizing the iron ore supply outlook, the Bureau of Mines concluded:

(1) The indicated potential iron-ore supply is adequate to support United States iron and steel production at projected rates until 1975.
(2) The proportion of iron ore from foreign sources increases to 37 per cent by 1970. Two paramount problems require attention:
    (a) National security as related to the increasing dependence upon foreign supplies.
    (b) Adequate supply after 1975.[7]

A summary of the *domestic iron* resources and those of selected *foreign* countries that the United States has used or is likely to use as import sources is given in Table 61.

Domestic iron supply will continue to come from the Lake Superior region, with an estimated annual output of 100 million tons through 1960; during this period it is expected that the United States will have lost one of its important strategic assets—"the ability to expand and contract production in quick response to demand."[8]

Imports of ore produced in Canada and Venezuela will relieve the pressure for further expansion of domestic output. The indications are that the sustained high level of domestic production in the Lake Superior region may lead to a rapid subsequent decline. If for any reason imports of iron ore should be interrupted, the open-pit ores of the Superior region will respond again but with increasing difficulty and in decreasing quantities as the reserves decline.[9]

The Bureau of Mines expects concentrates from Class II, lean ores, to make up the greater part of the Lake Superior production after the decline of open-pit ores and before concentrates from Class III, taconite, reserves expand beyond the 25-million-ton level. The reserve picture on ores is not accurate, but the Bureau concluded: "It is expected that output cannot be maintained high for a long period of time."

The taconite story is different. Probably one of the most optimistic reports is a special study entitled "One More Scarcity Ends for U.S.

[7] R. W. Holliday, "Iron," a chapter from *Mineral Facts and Problems*, Preprint from Bulletin 556, Bureau of Mines, Government Printing Office, 1955, p. 23.
[8] *Ibid.*, p. 25.
[9] *Ibid.*

TABLE 61. Summary of Iron-Ore Resources of the United States
and Selected Foreign Countries[a]
(million gross tons)

Country	Grade of Ore (Percent Fe)		
	Over 50	35–50	25–35
United States:			
Lake Superior	3,605	—	60,000[b]
Northeastern	—	1,000[c]	—
Southeastern	105[d]	1,127	1,033
Central and Gulf	—	63	—
Western	460	25	—
Total	4,170	2,215	61,033
Canada:			
Labrador-Quebec	1,000	1,000	—
Newfoundland	3,500	—	—
Ontario	70	—	100
Total	4,570	1,000	100
Venezuela	1,060	—	—
Brazil	1,500	3,500	—
Chile	20	—	—
Cuba	—	3,000	—
Algeria and Tunisia	125	—	—
Liberia	20	100	—
Sweden	2,300	150	—

[a] Measured, indicated, and inferred.
[b] Taconite.
[c] 25–45 percent ore will probably yield 380 million tons of concentrates.
[d] Concentrates.
SOURCE: *Mineral Facts and Problems*, Bureau of Mines, 1956.

Industry" in the June 17, 1955, issue of *U.S. News and World Report*. The results of this study are shown in Figure 9.12 which shows what taconite is, where it is found, how it is used, how it is growing, and how it is to compare with major sources of iron ore in 1972. This report was summarized in the following fashion: "U.S. blast furnaces will not grow cold for lack of iron for many years to come. That's the promise seen in Minnesota's new industry that extracts iron from hard taconite rock. Costs are a problem, but mining engineers are bringing them down all along the line. And there's plenty of taconite to work on—at least 5 billion tons in the Mesabi Range alone."

Southeastern states, principally Alabama, are not expected by the Bureau of Mines to increase their output beyond 10 million tons a year, because imported ore is counted upon to supply additional requirements. However, it was felt that good possibilities exist for developing economic

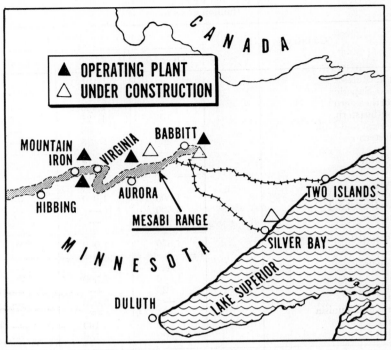

Fig. 9.12.   New Source for U.S. Iron: Taconite.

What it is: a hard rock which yields iron

Where it is found: chief known deposits are in Minnesota and Michigan

How it is used: in the form of iron-rich pellets, put into furnaces for making iron
                             and steel

How taconite is growing as an industry—

Plants now can produce	1,000,000 tons a year
Plants being built will be able to produce	11,250,000 tons a year
Plants planned for the future could produce	9,250,000 tons a year
Total now in prospect	21,500,000 tons a year

How taconite is to compare with major sources of iron ore in 1972—

Imports of iron ore from Labrador and Venezuela	50,000,000 tons
Output of iron ore from Lake Superior mines	35,000,000 tons
Taconite	40,000,000 tons

(Data from Federal Reserve Bank of Minneapolis)

means to beneficiate the important reserves of low-grade materials and for discovering additional large tonnages of self-fluxing or partly self-fluxing ores similar to those now being used.

Northeastern states, producing premium-grade iron-ore concentrates, are expected to maintain an output of approximately 6 million tons a year. The anticipated sustained demand will bring a few additional small mines into production, but output in quantity from the many small deposits of siderite and brown ore will come only after considerable increase in the price of ore.

West of the Mississippi River the principal output has come from Texas, California, Utah, and Wyoming. Distances, freight costs, and increasing population tend to encourage the growth of an iron-producing industry; however, the Bureau of Mines concludes that evaluation of possibilities west of the Mississippi is difficult.

Foreign iron ore as a source of supply became of critical importance to the United States after World War II. On February 11, 1950, *Business Week* announced: "A Basic Industry Solves a Basic Problem."

> One of industry's great postwar problems has been partly solved. . . . The country came out of the war with a problem: It was using steel as never before—and it had hardly more than 10 years' ready supply of ore to count on firmly.
>
> Solution—Last week, the big final piece was fitted into a three-way program for future ore supply. It came in a surprise announcement—U.S. Steel had struck it rich in Venezuela.
>
> Steelmen this week can relax for the first time in years. The ore they need to keep them going will come from the new Venezuelan field; from the Quebec-Labrador field, proved out in 1948; and from beneficiation of Mesabi's limitless low-grade ore, which began to look really practical last year.

The United States Steel Cerro Bolivar Venezuelan deposit is believed to contain some 500 million tons of ore, with a higher iron content than in the Mesabi—better than 60 percent. Bethlehem Steel was in Venezuela in advance of United States Steel, but Bethlehem's leased property at El Pao is not of the order of magnitude of Cerro Bolivar.

The other big foreign ore source is in Labrador. This reserve was reported by *Business Week* on September 11, 1948. The iron deposit is 350 miles north of the St. Lawrence River. Potential tonnage estimates range from 500 million to 1 billion tons.

The St. Lawrence Seaway is vitally connected with the availability of these two new sources of iron ore. When this project is completed the river and the Great Lakes it drains will be transformed into a man-made

Mediterranean, on which seagoing ships can move 2300 miles into North America's industrial heartland. More than 8000 miles of new coastline will be added to the United States and Canada. The lake-front cities, such as Chicago, Cleveland, Duluth, Buffalo, Toronto, and Hamilton, will become genuine deep-water ports, 500 miles closer to Europe by seaway than at present.

As early as 1895 the United States and Canadian governments began discussing the great inland seaway. The Canadian government favored the project from the beginning, but in the United States it became what *Time* magazine described in the June 6, 1955, issue as "one of the longest, most stubbornly fought issues ever introduced in Congress." *Time* briefly summarized the history of the project:

U.S. railroads, East Coast ports and industries, fearing heavy losses if traffic were diverted to the St. Lawrence, formed a powerful lobby that managed to block the project for half a century. Every U.S. President from Wilson to Eisenhower came out in favor of it. But Congress after Congress turned it down; eight seaway measures were pigeonholed or defeated outright between 1934 and 1952. . . .

After World War II, new factors tipped the scales in the seaway's favor. Mesabi's iron ore dwindled, and a rich, new field was developed in Canada's Quebec-Labrador area. The inland water route was the shortest way—and the safest in wartime—to bring the vital Quebec-Labrador ore to Midwestern U.S. steel mills.

Finally, in 1951, the Canadian government applied the maximum pressure, passing legislation to go it alone and build an all-Canadian seaway if the U.S. delayed any longer. The challenge cracked the opposition, and Congress passed the seaway bill last May [1954].

The flow of "tomorrow's ore" from Venezuela and Labrador directly to the United States and through the St. Lawrence Seaway is illustrated in Figure 9.13.

The Bureau of Mines summarized the United States' estimated dependence on foreign sources for iron ore as shown in Table 60:

Inasmuch as it appears necessary for United States industry to go abroad for supplemental supplies of iron ore, it is fortunate that a good part of these supplies may be obtained from nearby deposits. Canada may be supplying nearly 40 million tons annually by 1975.

The Great Lakes–St. Lawrence Seaway is an important factor in the possible tonnage available from the Quebec-Labrador deposits. A target date of Spring 1959 has been set for opening the seaway to shipping.

Nearby, yet subject to open-sea transportation, are the rich iron-ore deposits in Venezuela. In magnitude they appear to be comparable to those of Quebec-Labrador. Security considerations favor the Canadian deposits, but year-round operation and premium grade favor Venezuela. The first shipment from Cerro Bolivar arrived at Morrisville, Pa., on January 20, 1954.

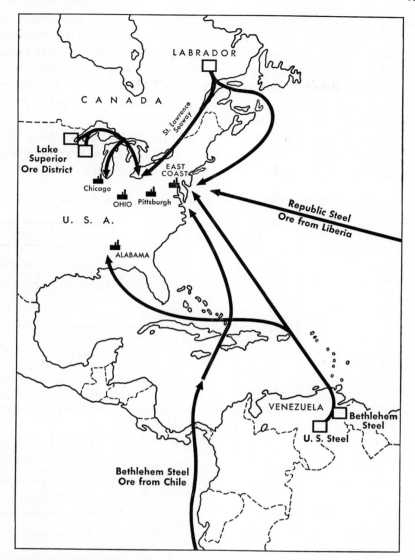

Figure 9.13. Tomorrow's Ore. (Data from *Business Week*, February 11, 1950, by special permission)

Chile, Peru, Brazil, and Cuba will provide additional supplies, but ores from Europe and Africa (with the possible exception of Liberia) will more probably find markets in Europe.[10]

The United States Steel Corporation concluded a report on *Cerro Bolivar—Saga of an Iron Ore Crisis Averted:* "For 60 years the steel

[10] *Ibid.*, p. 26.

industry has viewed its ore problem with all the bland indifference of the heavily endowed. But with the endowment about gone, it is apparent from all the foregoing that the challenge has unleashed a great dynamic drive from Hibbing to Venezuela, from Labrador to Liberia, from Trenton, to Pittsburgh, to Birmingham. It all involves enough imagination, ingenuity and romance to quicken the most sluggish pulse. Steelmen are long going to remember the 1950's."[11]

The increasing imports of iron ore into the United States from 1951 through 1955 and the growing importance of Canada and Venezuela as sources of supply can be observed clearly in Table 62.

TABLE 62. United States Foreign Trade in Iron Ore, 1951–55
(net tons)

	1955	1954	1953	1952	1951
Imports from—					
Canada[a]	11,293,425	3,961,458	2,075,400	2,053,170	2,214,398
Brazil	1,120,544	667,416	513,276	1,132,229	1,162,367
Chile	1,196,769	1,864,015	2,647,009	2,084,964	3,099,272
Cuba	45,021	35,689	220,277	98,040	5,042
Mexico	197,449	157,767	270,632	128,026	189,911
Peru	1,740,593	2,152,164	945,819	—	—
Venezuela	7,991,188	5,834,989	2,183,572	2,067,269	711,666
Sweden	1,367,894	1,729,005	2,349,225	2,364,432	2,823,512
Algeria	22,686	32,592	23,688	73,929	499,826
British West Africa	154,223	280,919	259,392	243,891	286,515
Liberia	1,039,345	856,593	806,893	641,183	123,338
Tunisia	—	—	22,064	21,504	150,948
Other countries	116,494	103,827	110,540	35,414	105,786
Total imports[a]	26,285,631	17,676,434	12,427,787	10,944,051	11,372,581
Exports to—					
Canada	4,717,249	3,105,076	4,316,010	4,245,084	3,740,991
Japan	318,755	372,099	445,518	1,490,695	1,069,423
Other countries	5,650	4,649	1	13	1,037
Total exports	5,041,654	3,481,824	4,761,529	5,735,792	4,811,451
Net imports	21,243,977	14,194,610	7,666,258	5,208,259	6,561,130

[a] Includes dross from burnt pyrites imported from Canada only.
SOURCE: *International Iron and Steel*, United States Department of Commerce, August, 1956.

Iron ore problems are summarized in *Mineral Facts and Problems* as follows:

Chief among the problems of the industry are those stemming from the approaching depletion of readily accessible, high-grade domestic ores. The factors involved include:

(1) The problem of determining the safe minimum level of domestic production. This requires consideration of domestic and foreign ore reserves, eco-

[11] T. W. Lippert, *Cerro Bolivar—Saga of an Iron Ore Crisis Averted,* United States Steel Corporation, 1950, p. 16.

nomic, political, and technical data regarding foreign sources, and transportation to the United States during both peace and war.

(2) The problem of maintaining domestic production at or above the safe minimum.

Secondary problems include adjustments in transportation and furnace practice.

Development of furnace techniques to accommodate beneficiated, imported and blended ores is hampered by the great cost of experimenting with large units.

Upgrading of ore and ore preparation, such as sintering, by adding another operation, lead to an additional cost, which must be defrayed at least in part by increased efficiency.

Expanding utilization of taconites introduces new problems to every phase of the industry. Greater tonnages of ore are required, and the ore is harder and must be finely ground, concentrated, and reagglomerated.

Beneficiation of various ores other than taconites, such as the laterites of Cuba, the brown ores of Texas, the ferruginous sandstones of Alabama, and the lean ores of Minnesota, presents many problems.

Other raw materials—particularly fuels—must be supplied in proportion to the demand for iron ore. The problems of cost, quality, and transportation of these raw materials are increasingly difficult.

Development of economic methods of producing iron on a small scale would permit some decentralization of the industry and foster utilization of smaller deposits.[12]

C. Problems and Policy Summary

The conclusion can be drawn that the iron and steel industry has taken the initiative to solve the problems of capacity and iron ore. The United States is committed to a policy of an expanding economy, and basic to such is the expansion of the steel industry. Increased steel capacity will require increased iron ore. Revision in tax policies may be required to facilitate use of low-grade domestic reserves. Imports of ores from foreign sources will become of increasing importance. The opening of the St. Lawrence Seaway will increase the availability of Venezuelan and Labrador ores to existing plants. The increased dependence on imports of iron ore to supply the vital basic steel industry is a matter of serious policy concern to the United States and of critical importance in relation to our strategy for security. We are fortunate that these sources of supply are in the Western Hemisphere.

COPPER

Copper has been described as "the most important nonferrous metal, both in quantity and the value of world output; among all metals it is

[12] Holliday, *op. cit.*, p. 26.

surpassed only by iron." Copper has held this position for a long time. Bronze, a combination of copper and a tenth part of tin, was the first alloy in wide use by man. Bronze was used to such an extent to replace stone in making weapons, tools, and utensils that this era of importance became known as the Bronze Age. The use of copper in electrification was an important contributing factor in the "electrical age." Today, copper faces new metals of competition.

The copper industry consists of the functions of mining, smelting, refining, and fabrication.

Copper is mined by both underground and open-pit methods; in Michigan it is produced by dredging old tailings from a lake for retreatment. Copper ore deposits may be grouped into two classes: disseminated "porphyry" and all others. The low copper content, and the size and physical character of disseminated ore necessitate large-scale, low-cost mining and metallurgical methods. In 1953 the average copper content of ores mined in the United States was 0.85 percent. Thus these ores must be milled into a copper concentrate in operations closely associated with mining. The typical flow sheet is made up of crushing, grinding, flotation, thickening, and filtering. Concentrates of United States copper contain about 25 to 30 percent copper and significant quantities of gold, silver, and minor metals like selenium. Flotation has been the principal method of treatment for twenty-five years. There are many exceptions—leaching, for example, is used for oxide ores. However, leaching is not competitive with flotation for sulfide ores.

Smelting of copper ores and concentrates in reverberatory furnaces is used to produce copper matte, or "blister copper," as it is called. Although blister copper contains approximately 99 percent copper, it is still too impure to be used for electrical purposes.

Refined copper is produced from the blister copper matte, which serves as an anode. Electrolysis is used to dissolve the anode and to build up pure copper on the cathode. Some cathodes are cut to specified sizes and sold to consumers, but most of the electrolytic copper is fabricated (the fourth function) into semifinished forms—wire, rods, extruded and rolled shapes, etc.—which are the raw materials for many other industries.

The size, nature, and capital requirements of the copper industry have led to concentration of ownership in the United States. The Kennecott Copper Corporation, Phelps Dodge Corporation, and Anaconda Company usually mine over 75 percent of the total United States output and with the American Smelting and Refining Company smelt and refine a substantial part of the primary materials in the United States. Some of the largest fabricators are affiliated with these four companies. Thus the industry is characterized by vertical integration of the functions of mining, smelting, refining, and fabrication. United States smelting, refining, and fabricating facilities have excess capacity, which is used to treat foreign materials.

1. Reserves

About 90 percent of the unmined copper in the world is in five regions: south central Africa, Chile, the western United States, eastern Ontario and southern Quebec in Canada, and Kazakhstan, U.S.S.R. Table 63

TABLE 63. World's Copper Resources, 1950; Twelve Districts Containing 85 Percent of the World's Copper Resources, 1950[a]

Deposits	Country	Major Ownership	Nationality
"Mine series"	Northern Rhodesia	Selection Trust, Ltd.	British
		Anglo-American Corp., Ltd.	British
Chuquicamata	Chile	Anaconda Copper Mining Co.	United States
"Mine series"	Belgian Congo	Union Miniére du Haut Katanga	Belgian
Butte, Mont.	United States	Anaconda Copper Mining Co.	United States
Braden (El Teniente)	Chile	Kennecott Copper Corp.	United States
Bingham, Utah	United States	Kennecott Copper Corp.	United States
Keweenaw, Mich.[b]	United States	Copper Range Co. and Calumet & Hecla, Inc.	United States
Morenci, Ariz.	United States	Phelps Dodge Corp.	United States
Sudbury, Canada[c]	Canada	International Nickel Co. of Canada, Ltd.	Canadian
	Canada	Falconbridge Nickel Mines, Ltd.	Canadian
San Manuel, Ariz.[b]	United States	Magma Copper Co. (Newmont Mining Co.)	United States
Kazakhstan	U.S.S.R.	State-owned	U.S.S.R.
Urals region	U.S.S.R.	State-owned	U.S.S.R.

[a] Bureau of Mines and Geological Survey, Copper: NSRB Materials Survey, 1952.
[b] Large reserves are considered marginal awaiting production tests. (NOTE: Subsequently it has been decided to bring the deposit into production—anticipated in 1956.) The San Manuel mine was one of the most significant new producers in 1956.
[c] Copper is a by-product of nickel production.
SOURCE: *Mineral Facts and Problems*, Bureau of Mines, 1956.

presents twelve districts or mines which contain 85 percent of the world copper resources. This list includes both developed reserves that are economic under present conditions and partly explored semi-economic deposits that are so large they will be important in the future. World copper reserves are estimated in excess of 100 million short tons of recoverable metal, with the prospect that, when conditions for production improve in foreign countries, reserves may be double the quantity. Adequate power, transportation, and other facilities must be supplied and political, labor, and other problems solved to achieve this figure.

The United States is estimated to have about 25 million tons of recoverable copper. The present major producing mines have about twenty to thirty years of life at the 1940–50 production rates. The Bureau of Mines reports that "exploration campaigns of the past decade around old mines and in new areas indicate an additional 10 to 15 years supply. If intensive exploration is continued, it is expected that this favorable position will be maintained."

The United States ranks first among the three major copper regions of the world in current economically profitable reserves, or resources, but

TABLE 64.   United States Copper Reserves, 1950; Twelve Mining Districts Containing 95 Percent of the United States Copper Reserves, 1950

District	Principal Ownership
Butte, Mont.	Anaconda Copper Mining Co.
Bingham, Utah	Kennecott Copper Corp.
Keweenaw, Mich.	Copper Range Co. & Calumet & Hecla, Inc.
Morenci, Ariz.	Phelps Dodge Corp.
San Manuel, Ariz.	Magma Copper Co. (Newmont Mining Co.)
Ely-Kimberly, Nev.	Kennecott Copper Corp. and Consolidated Copper-mines Corp.
Central, N. Mex.	Kennecott Copper Corp.
Ray, Ariz.	Do.
Ajo, Ariz.	Phelps Dodge Corp.
Yerington, Nev.	Anaconda Copper Mining Co.
Miami, Ariz.ᵃ	Miami Copper Co. and Inspiration Consolidated Copper Co.
Bisbee, Ariz.	Phelps Dodge Corp.

ᵃ Includes Castle Dome, Copper Cities (Sleeping Beauty), Inspiration, Miami, and Globe.
SOURCE: *Mineral Facts and Problems*, Bureau of Mines, 1956.

may ultimately rank third because of the relatively lean quality of domestic ore. The African deposits are very large reserves of 3 to 6 percent copper content, in contrast to the United States average of less than 1 percent. The Chilean deposits have "huge tonnages averaging 2 percent copper." Russian grades are about the same as those of the United States.

Three-fourths of the United States production comes from large-scale, low-cost, open-pit deposits, in contrast to South American and African mines, which are predominantly underground mines. However, United States open-pit operations face termination within ten to twenty years, with thirty years the exception, because of increasingly adverse ratios of waste rock that must be removed to uncover copper ore.

About 95 percent of the United States reserves occurs in a dozen mining areas. These deposits including both economic and semi-economic reserves are given in Table 64. Addition of the following mines and districts brings the total to 98 percent: Magma, Arizona; Silver Bell, Arizona; Cornwall, Pennsylvania; Bagdad, Arizona; Tryone, New Mexico; and Glacier Peak, Washington. The remaining 2 percent of reserves is widely distributed.

Thus in ownership and geographic location the copper reserves are highly concentrated.

2. Production

Mine production, refinery production by source of materials, production from scrap, and other salient copper statistics for the United States copper industry are given in Table 65 together with world smelter copper production from 1919 to 1953.

Most of the mine production of copper in the United States comes from the Western states. For many years after 1815, Michigan was by far the leading producer. Montana took over first place just before 1890 but was displaced in 1907 by Arizona, which, except for 1909, has ranked first since that date.

World mine production of copper, by principal countries, 1949–53, is given in Table 66; and world smelter production of copper by countries is given in Table 67. In 1953 the United States mined 30 percent of the world's copper but smelted over 40 percent. This points up the increased use of copper scrap and the dependence on foreign materials as shown in Table 65.

Data on smelter and refinery production are not available by states, but over half of the United States electrolytic refining capacity is on the Atlantic seaboard in metropolitan New York and New Jersey and Baltimore, Maryland. This concentration has been brought about by a combination of large nearby markets, together with ocean transportation.

3. Consumption

Fabrication of copper, the fourth part of the copper industry, takes place in the consuming countries. The major consuming countries are the United States, Russia, the United Kingdom, France, and Germany. Of these only the United States and Russia are important producers of copper. Canada is growing in importance as a consuming country.

During the fifty-year period 1900–1950 United States copper consumption increased almost ten times as shown by Table 68. As closely as can be estimated the actual consumption of copper in 1950 was 1,730,000 tons. This growth was due to the exceptional qualities of copper: as a conductor of electricity (only silver is better) and heat; its ductility,

TABLE 65. Salient Statistics of the Copper Industry, 1919-53
(all figures in short tons, except price and tenor of ore)

Year	Mine Production	Average Tenor of Copper Ores (percent)	Refinery Production (Primary) From— Domestic Materials	Refinery Production (Primary) From— Foreign Materials	Refinery Production (Primary) From— Total	Imports (Refined)[a]	Exports (Refined)[a]	Apparent Consumption of New Copper[b]	Quoted Price at New York[c] (Cents per Pound)	World Production (Smelter)	Production from Scrap as Metal and in Alloys Old Scrap	Production from Scrap as Metal and in Alloys New Scrap	Production from Scrap as Metal and in Alloys Total
1919	606,167	1.65	716,743	168,341	885,084	17,569	219,080	457,236	18.90	1,095,696	152,600	134,590	287,190
1920	612,275	1.63	591,212	171,871	763,083	54,372	275,613	526,919	17.50	1,057,200	168,960	143,500	312,460
1921	233,095	1.70	304,707	170,682	475,389	34,625	298,059	305,494	12.65	614,600	131,990	85,310	217,300
1922	482,292	1.74	452,335	175,423	627,758	51,572	326,333	448,317	13.56	952,400	202,800	133,100	335,900
1923	738,870	1.58	732,083	257,835	989,918	80,356	364,690	650,237	14.61	1,341,500	270,900	140,000	410,900
1924	803,083	1.59	837,107	292,931	1,130,038	72,955	504,812	677,371	13.16	1,493,600	266,200	122,100	388,300
1925	839,059	1.54	841,448	260,839	1,102,287	49,887	484,033	700,506	14.16	1,546,500	291,010	129,200	420,210
1926	862,638	1.46	865,649	295,594	1,161,243	85,283	428,062	785,068	13.93	1,608,300	337,300	142,500	479,800
1927	824,980	1.41	859,476	303,406	1,162,882	51,640	461,233	711,480	13.05	1,673,300	339,400	150,800	490,200
1928	904,898	1.41	895,899	347,905	1,243,804	42,365	474,737	804,269	14.68	1,880,500	365,500	170,900	536,400
1929	997,555	1.41	991,366	378,690	1,370,056	67,007	411,227	889,293	18.23	2,098,800	404,350	222,200	626,550
1930	705,074	1.43	695,612	382,918	1,078,530	43,105	297,057	632,509	13.11	1,760,000	342,200	125,000	467,200
1931	528,875	1.50	537,303	213,418	750,721	87,225	202,698	451,032	8.24	1,536,000	261,300	85,700	347,000
1932	238,111	1.83	222,539	117,895	340,434	83,897	110,977	259,602	5.67	1,027,000	180,980	67,200	248,180
1933	190,643	2.11	240,669	130,120	370,789	5,432	124,382	339,350	7.15	1,143,000	260,300	77,800	338,100
1934	237,401	1.92	233,029	212,331	445,360	27,417	262,366	322,638	8.53	1,448,000	310,900	66,500	377,400
1935	386,491	1.89	338,321	250,484	588,805	18,071	260,735	441,371	8.76	1,681,000	361,700	87,200	448,900
1936	614,516	1.54	645,462	177,027	822,489	4,782	220,390	656,179	9.58	1,895,000	382,700	101,900	484,900
1937	841,998	1.29	822,253	244,561	1,066,814	7,487	295,064	694,906	13.27	2,585,000	408,900	123,200	532,100
1938	557,763	1.34	552,574	239,842	792,416	1,802	370,545	406,994	10.10	2,254,000	267,300	92,500	359,800
1939	728,320	1.25	704,873	304,642	1,009,515	16,264	372,777	714,873	11.07	2,396,000	286,900	212,800	499,700
1940	878,086	1.20	927,239	386,317	1,313,556	68,337	356,431	1,008,785	11.40	2,734,000	333,890	198,156	532,046
1941	958,149	1.15	975,408	419,901	1,395,309	346,994	103,602	1,641,550	11.87	2,905,000	412,699	313,697	726,396
1942	1,080,061	1.09	1,064,792	349,769	1,414,561	401,436	131,406	1,608,000	11.87	3,076,000	427,122	500,633	927,755
1943	1,090,818	1.04	1,082,079	297,184	1,379,263	402,762	175,859	1,502,000	11.87	3,038,000	427,521	658,526	1,086,047
1944	972,549	.99	973,852	247,335	1,221,187	492,395	68,373	1,504,000	11.87	2,847,000	456,710	494,232	950,942
1945	772,894	.93	775,738	332,861	1,108,599	531,367	48,563	1,415,000	11.87	2,436,000	497,095	509,421	1,006,516
1946	608,737	.91	578,429	300,233	878,662	154,371	52,629	1,391,000	13.92	2,067,000	406,453	397,093	803,546
1947	847,563	.90	909,213	250,757	1,159,970	149,478	147,642	1,286,000	21.15	2,513,000	503,376	458,365	961,741
1948	834,813	.92	860,022	247,424	1,107,446	249,124	142,598	1,214,000	22.20	2,580,000	505,464	467,324	972,788
1949	752,750	.91	695,015	232,912	927,927	275,811	137,827	1,072,000	19.36	2,600,000	383,548	329,595	713,143
1950	909,343	.89	920,748	319,086	1,239,834	317,363	144,561	1,447,000	21.46	2,915,000	485,211	492,028	977,239
1951	928,330	.90	951,559	255,429	1,206,988	238,972	133,305	1,304,000	24.37	3,095,000	458,124	474,158	932,282
1952	925,359	.85	923,192	254,504	1,177,696	346,960	174,135	1,360,000	24.37	3,115,000	414,635	488,542	903,197
1953	926,448	.85	932,232	360,885	1,293,117	274,777	109,510	1,435,000	28.92	3,275,000	429,388	529,076	958,464

[a] Imports and exports may include some refined copper produced from scrap. Categories not wholly comparable from year to year. Copper is also imported in crude form and shows up as refinery production from foreign ore. Exports, on the other hand, take place also in forms beyond the refined stage.

[b] Adjusted for changes in stocks.

[c] American Metal Market price for electrolytic copper in New York: f.o.b. refinery through August, 1927, New York refinery equivalent thereafter.

SOURCE: Mineral Facts and Problems, Bureau of Mines, 1956.

TABLE 66. World Mine Production of Copper, by Principal Countries, 1949–53
(short tons)
(Taken from tables compiled by staff of Division of Foreign Activities, Bureau of Mines)

	1949	1950	1951	1952	1953
North America:					
Canada	263,000	264,000	270,000	258,000	252,000
Cuba	19,000	23,000	22,000	20,000	18,000
Mexico	63,000	68,000	74,000	65,000	66,000
United States	753,000	909,000	928,000	925,000	926,000
Total	1,098,000	1,264,000	1,294,000	1,268,000	1,262,000
South America:					
Chile	409,000	400,000	418,000	446,000	400,000
Peru	30,000	33,000	36,000	34,000	38,000
Other	6,000	6,000	5,000	5,000	5,000
Total	445,000	439,000	459,000	485,000	443,000
Europe:					
U.S.S.R.[a][b][c]	223,000	249,000	283,000	330,000	334,000
Yugoslavia[c]	38,000	44,000	35,000	36,000	34,000
Other	76,000	75,000	78,000	90,000	81,000
Total[a][b]	337,000	368,000	396,000	456,000	449,000
Asia:					
Japan	36,000	44,000	47,000	59,000	64,000
Other	59,000	65,000	69,000	75,000	70,000
Total[a][b]	95,000	109,000	116,000	134,000	134,000
Africa:					
Belgian Congo[c]	157,000	194,000	212,000	226,000	236,000
Northern Rhodesia	286,000	328,000	352,000	363,000	411,000
Union of South Africa	34,000	37,000	37,000	39,000	39,000
Other	13,000	14,000	15,000	18,000	16,000
Total	490,000	573,000	616,000	646,000	702,000
Australia	15,000	17,000	19,000	21,000	40,000
World total[a]	2,480,000	2,770,000	2,900,000	3,010,000	3,030,000

[a] Approximate production.
[b] Output from U.S.S.R. in Asia included with U.S.S.R. in Europe.
[c] Smelter production.
SOURCE: *Mineral Facts and Problems*, Bureau of Mines, 1956.

machinability, and strength; and its resistance to corrosion when alloyed with other metals to form brass or bronze. This versatility of copper properties has led to the many uses of copper shown in Table 69.

These manifold uses of copper spell out its importance to the productive strength of our peacetime economy but perhaps do not emphasize

TABLE 67. World Smelter Production of Copper, by Countries, 1949–53
(short tons)
(Taken from tables compiled by staff of Division of Foreign Activities, Bureau of Mines)

Country	1949	1950	1951	1952	1953
North America:					
Canada	226,000	238,000	245,000	196,000	236,000
Mexico	54,000	53,000	65,000	56,000	57,000
United States[a]	860,000	1,009,000	1,037,000	1,025,000	1,048,000
Total	1,140,000	1,300,000	1,347,000	1,277,000	1,341,000
South America:					
Chile	386,000	381,000	397,000	422,000	372,000
Peru	23,000	26,000	27,000	23,000	26,000
Total	409,000	407,000	424,000	445,000	398,000
Europe:					
Germany, West[b]	160,000	223,000	235,000	215,000	241,000
U.S.S.R.[c d]	223,000	249,000	283,000	330,000	334,000
Yugoslavia	38,000	44,000	35,000	36,000	34,000
Other	72,000	65,000	75,000	80,000	92,000
Total[c d e]	493,000	581,000	628,000	661,000	701,000
Asia:					
Japan	42,000	41,000	48,000	54,000	70,000
Other	25,000	28,000	36,000	40,000	43,000
Total[c d]	67,000	69,000	84,000	94,000	113,000
Africa:					
Belgian Congo	157,000	194,000	212,000	226,000	236,000
Northern Rhodesia	290,000	308,000	346,000	350,000	406,000
Union of South Africa	33,000	37,000	36,000	38,000	39,000
Other	—	2,000	1,000	2,000	1,000
Total	480,000	541,000	595,000	616,000	682,000
Australia	11,000	17,000	17,000	22,000	40,000
World total[c]	2,600,000	2,915,000	3,095,000	3,115,000	3,275,000

[a] Smelter output from domestic and foreign ores, exclusive of scrap. Production from domestic ores only, exclusive of scrap, was as follows: 1949, 758,000; 1950, 911,000; 1951, 931,000; 1952, 927,000; and 1953, 943,000.
[b] Includes scrap.
[c] Approximate production.
[d] Output from U.S.S.R. in Asia included with U.S.S.R. in Europe.
[e] Belgium reports a large output of refined copper which is believed to be produced principally from crude copper from Belgian Congo and is not given here, as that would duplicate output reported under the latter country.
SOURCE: *Mineral Facts and Problems*, Bureau of Mines, 1956.

the strategic importance for military purposes for use in munitions, in vehicle production, in airplane manufacture, in naval and other ship construction, and in signal equipment and ordnance manufacture. A new

TABLE 68. Supply and Consumption of Copper in the United
States, Selected Years, 1900–50
(thousand short tons)

Year	Mine Production	Production from Old Scrap	Net Imports[a] (+) or Exports (−)	Apparent Consumption (Total Production Plus Imports Minus Exports)
1900	303[b]	Not available	−117	186
1910	544	65	−182	427
1916	1,003	175	−166	1,012
1920	612	169	−70	711
1925	839	291	−198	932
1929	998	404	−13	1,389
1940	878	334	+1	1,213
1943	1,091	428	+559	2,078
1950	907	475	+448	1,830[c]

[a] Figures for 1940, 1943, and 1950 are on the basis of imports for consumption, all other years on the basis of general imports.
[b] Smelter output from domestic ores.
[c] Actual consumption 1,730.
SOURCE: U.S. Bureau of Mines, except actual consumption; *Resources for Freedom*, Vol. II.

Sabre Jet requires over 500 pounds of copper, a medium tank 800 pounds, and a cruiser 1000 tons. A 37mm. antiaircraft gun in action uses a ton of copper every twenty minutes and a fighter-bomber squadron of fifty planes expels seven tons of copper every sixty seconds in combat.

TABLE 69. Use of Copper in the United States

Industry Division	Percent
Electric lines (light, power, and communications)	19
Electrical equipment (including communications equipment)	18
Construction including building materials, pipe and tube for plumbing, and sheet metal	14
Motor vehicles	8
General components	6
Consumer durable goods	3
Miscellaneous industries	3
Electronics	2
General industrial equipment	2
Railroad equipment	2
Scientific and technical equipment	2
Engines and turbines	1
Metalworking equipment	1
Military (conjectural)	17
Undistributed	2
Total	100

SOURCE: Copper & Brass Research Association. Computed from Business Reports of the Copper Division, Business Defense Services Administration,. Department of Commerce, supplemented by CABRA regroupings and estimates; *Mining Congress Journal*, Annual Review, 1957.

The future consumption of copper will be vitally affected by the availability of substitutes. The price of copper rose from a stabilized level of 11.87 cents a pound during World War II to 21.46 cents in 1950, to a fixed level of 24.37 cents during 1951–52, to 28.92 cents in 1953, to 30 cents in 1954. During 1955 the price of copper was advanced to 33 cents in January, to 36 cents in March, and to 43 cents in August. While copper went up 13 cents a pound, aluminum went up only 2 cents, from 23 cents to 25 cents a pound. The net effect was aluminum's already considerable price advantage increase to 18 cents. Since 1946 the price of copper had gone up 258 percent, aluminum only 63 percent. *Forbes* reported that a typically annoyed reaction to this state of affairs was that of a Westinghouse Electric executive, a big buyer of copper. "A dollar," said he, "will go farther in aluminum these days than it will in copper, so we're studying means of switching over." However, price is only one of several factors which have contributed to substitution for copper. The sudden increase and sustained growth in the demand for copper after the outbreak of the Korean War in 1950 brought about a condition in which production of copper could not be expanded rapidly enough and many major consumers were forced to search for substitutes.

A widespread substitution is practical because of the basic similarity between the properties of aluminum and copper (or brass). Aluminum wire with a steel core has almost completely displaced copper in high-tension power transmission and is making inroads on urban distribution systems. Other examples of substitution of aluminum for copper in the electric industry are fractional horsepower motor windings and light-bulb bases. Aluminum and stainless steels have also reduced the use of copper in the building industry. The introduction of copper-clad metals requires less metal than would solid copper. Printed electric circuits have also been substituted for copper wire. Even the military have changed some specifications and design. An example is the increased use of steel for brass in shell cases. These proved satisfactory during the Korean fighting for howitzers but not for heavier guns, which often jammed.

A study of the use of copper and aluminum in the first quarter of 1953 compared with an average quarter of 1947 showed conclusively that copper was not keeping pace with aluminum as the demand increased for nonferrous metals. During this period the following changes took place: Electrical equipment for internal-combustion engines—copper rose 39 percent and aluminum 205 percent; radio and radio products —copper rose 133 percent and aluminum 246; motor vehicles and parts

—copper rose 18 percent and aluminum 82; metal stampings—copper dropped 42 percent while aluminum rose 57; telephone and telegraph equipment—copper rose 61 percent and aluminum 97; and the total for all groups in the study—copper rose 11 percent and aluminum 95 percent.

The net effect of the substitutions for copper in the future will be to cause a shift in the overall consumption pattern and to make more copper available for those uses for which it is peculiarly fitted and for which no substitute is available. The largest increase in the consumption of copper during the period 1950 to 1975 is expected to take place in the rapidly growing electrical industry, but the increase of copper use in that industry is expected to be much less than it would have been in the absence of an appreciable substitution for copper. Many other substitutions are expected including alloy steels and plastics in a variety of uses.

Taking into account all these possibilities of substitution, the President's Materials Policy Commission concluded that between 1950 and 1975 the consumption of copper would increase 45 percent, from 1,730,-000 tons in 1950 to 2,500,000 tons in 1975. The source of the United States supply of copper in 1950 and the projected position for 1975 are given in Table 70.

TABLE 70. United States Copper Position 1950 and Projected 1975
(thousand short tons)

	1950[a]	1975
Consumption (actual)	1,730	2,500[b]
Production:		
Mine	907	800
Secondary	475	700
	1,382	1,500
Imports (net)	448	1,000[c]

[a] 1950 consumption derived from data from American Bureau of Metal Statistics and U.S. Bureau of Mines; 1950 production and imports, Bureau of Mines.
[b] Projected.
[c] Required.
SOURCE: *Resources for Freedom*, Vol. II.

4. Problems and Policy

Two long-standing copper problems have been price instability and international interdependence. These two problems are directly related.

A. Price Instability

The year 1955 was noteworthy in that the price of copper advanced 13 cents to a new high of 43 cents a pound. It then rose to 46 cents in

February, 1956, and held through July, 1956, when it fell to 40 cents, the first downward move since March 31, 1953. Prior to 1955, prices had often varied six or seven cents a year. Since 1927, the price of copper had fluctuated between 5 and 46 cents a pound. Many attempts have been made to stabilize the price, but except during wartime no cartel or government has been successful in its attempt for a period of more than two or three years.

During World War I copper production was greatly stimulated and at the end of the war huge supplies accumulated for which there was no market at prices the industry was willing to accept. In 1918, immediately after the passage of the Webb-Pomerene Export Act, the United States Copper Export Association was organized under the law to reduce competition in the export business. The last copper was sold by the pool in 1933. The Association failed in its attempt to stabilize world prices partly because higher prices stimulated production from new mines discovered in the 1920's in Northern Rhodesia and Canada. In 1926 Copper Exporters, Inc., was formed on an international basis. This organization included foreign as well as United States companies and fixed prices and quotas, which the individual firms sold. This cartel controlled 86 percent of world copper. Prices were raised and maintained after the 1929 crash. But with the depression, United States firms could not sell their copper at the high prices, and this, together with scrap that was thrown on the market, broke the domestic price level. In the meantime foreign producers continued to benefit for a short period from increased production and higher prices. Of particular importance were the accelerated deliveries from the discovery of an immense copper-bearing district in Northern Rhodesia in 1927 and the development at about the same time of the Noranda, Frood (International Nickel) and Hudson Bay mines in Canada. For nearly eighty years prior to this time the United States had dominated the world copper industry, but these new mines radically changed the position of the United States and the world copper industry. Not only are these mines large but they are also low-cost producers because of their relatively high-grade ores. In the case of the three Canadian mines, which have complex ores, the development of the selective flotation process made possible the recovery of important quantities of other metals. The aggregate capacity of these mines exceeds 600,000 tons of copper a year.

In 1936 foreign producers entered into an International Copper Cartel in order to restrict their supplies, which were in excess of what could be sold outside of the United States market. Foreign subsidiaries of

Anaconda, Phelps Dodge, and Kennecott participated. Once again the higher prices stimulated greater production and ultimate collapse from 13.27 cents in 1937 to 10.10 cents in 1939. Prices were stabilized under wartime government controls at 11.87 cents from 1941 to 1945. The post-World War II demand rose rapidly, and quoted f.o.b. refinery prices rose from 11.87 cents when price controls were removed on November 10, 1946, to 19.37 cents by the end of the year.

The outbreak of the Korean War in mid-1950 caused a sudden increase in the demand for copper and an increase in copper prices. The manner in which controls were administered during the Korean emergency is described as follows by the Bureau of Mines.

Ceiling prices for copper were established by the General Ceiling Price Regulation issued by the Economic Stabilization Agency and effective January 26, 1951. This order set maximum prices at not to exceed the highest prices received by individual producers between December 19, 1950, and January 25, 1951, inclusive. Most primary producers were selling electrolytic copper, delivered Connecticut Valley, at 24½ cents a pound, and that price became the ceiling for those producers. Some other companies, representing a relatively small aggregate tonnage, sold for substantially higher prices during the period selected, and these higher prices became their ceilings.

Foreign countries, like the United States, had mobilization plans calling for increased quantities of copper, and world consumption in 1951 was rising. Efforts of all countries to obtain supplies of metal led to increasing world prices and to speculation, causing further price increases. Rumors had it that prices up to 60 cents a pound were paid for copper on the European continent, while United States prices were frozen substantially at 24½ cents.

The situation led to an agreement between the United States and the Chilean Government in May 1951 providing for payment of an additional 3 cents over the United States ceiling for Chilean copper sold in the United States. A little later the Office of Price Stabilization permitted all copper refined in the United States from imported materials to be paid for on basis of 27½ cents a pound.

Another factor that tended to confuse the price situation was action of the Defense Materials Production Agency to avoid loss of production from mines that faced closing because of rising costs. Maintenance-of-production contracts based on production costs of the mines involved were entered into with these companies; thus additional sets of prices were established.

Prices in foreign countries continued above those for foreign copper sold in the United States (27½ cents), and Chile became dissatisfied with the foregoing arrangement. The outcome was abrogation, in May 1952, of its agreement with the United States.

On May 21, 1952, the Office of Defense Mobilization authorized importers to pay higher prices for imported copper and to pass 80 percent of increased costs on to users. Early in June it was decided that the increases were to be calculated using 24½ instead of 27½ cents as a base. In an effort to distribute the effects of these price ceilings fairly among consumers, the National Production Administration began to allocate domestic copper production and foreign entitlements to all users on an approximate 60–40 percent basis instead of just allocating copper. As a result of this move, some domestic consumers whose domestic copper-producing affiliates usually supplied ample copper had to sell some of their production to competing companies and to buy some foreign metal or to decrease consumption. Domestic fabricating affiliates of American mining companies producing in Chile, on the other hand, since May 1951 had been absorbing the 3-cent differential in costs between 24½ and 27½ cents but during that time were not receiving the higher prices permitted for their Chilean-produced metal. They continued to receive only 24½ cents for their output until July 1952 when they, with all other fabricators, were permitted to pass on to consumers 80 percent of increased costs over 24½ cents.

The improved supply-requirements relationship resulted in abandonment of price controls on copper and copper products in February 1953; and by the end of April domestic and foreign prices, except Chilean, were close together at about 30 cents a pound; the price for the Chilean outputs of the three large American mines was held, under Chilean Government direction, at 35½ cents a pound in Chile (about 36½ cents in the United States) until December 1953.[13]

In addition and supplementary to these price controls in 1951, the Defense Production Administration reinstituted the Controlled Materials Plan, used effectively in World War II, for distributing fabricated products made from copper, steel, and aluminum. Copper raw materials were placed under complete allocation control, effective August 1, 1951. Copper was placed under international allocation. And quotas for the free world were established by the International Materials Conference, beginning with the fourth quarter of 1951. The member countries voluntarily accepted restrictions upon quantities to be consumed and agreed not to dispose of copper to countries in the Soviet bloc.

There are many contributing factors to the instability of copper prices. In the first instance copper wire, ingot bars, billets, or cathodes are too expensive to be held in inventory for a considerable period of time in anticipation of orders. However, copper can be stored in the ground. When orders for copper slow down, the policy is to restrict operations or close the mine. Reopening the mine is expensive and will be done only when market conditions justify it. In the interim there is a time lag of 15 to 20 weeks between starting operation of the mine and delivery of finished copper to the purchaser. In the meantime a shortage may develop; to overcome it the mine is run at capacity operations and inven-

[13] H. M. Meyer, "Copper," a chapter from *Mineral Facts and Problems*, p. 24.

tories may build up and prices weaken. Then the cycle may begin to repeat itself.

Another contributing factor is the custom smelter which processes virgin and scrap copper. The nature of the smelting operation is that continuous operations are required twenty-four hours a day and seven days a week. Thus to insure a constant supply of copper to feed its furnaces the smelting company buys at the prevailing price for resale after three months, the time required to run a batch through. As a hedge the smelter balances inflow with outflow by selling each day as much copper as it buys. At the first sign of a decline in sales, the smelter cuts the selling price to attract buyers. This is looked upon as evidence of a decline in the level of copper prices; so the buyers withhold orders, accelerating the downward spiral.

These domestic problems are compounded with international problems, brought about in part, as we have already seen, by the international interdependence for copper. Governmental policies in foreign producing areas as noted have been a causative factor. More recently, in 1955 and 1956, labor policy resulting in strikes and the closing of mines in Chile have caused prices to advance.

On the domestic government policy front the United States movement in and out of the copper market can be a factor contributing to both instability and stability.

Once again it would appear that in so far as the United States government engages in the purchase and sale of copper it should do so, whenever possible, within the limits of military security, with the objective of stabilizing the copper price.

B. International Interdependence

Copper was not on the original list of scarce metals which was prepared as a result of the passage of the Strategic Materials Act of 1939, because at that time the United States was a copper exporter. By 1940 it became apparent that the United States would be unable to fill all of its expanded requirements by a substantial margin. The study of the United States Nonfuel Minerals Position showed how the United States changed from a pre-World War II self-sufficiency position in copper to a wartime and postwar dependence on outside sources. From Figure 9.6 it may be seen that the United States imported 45 percent of the copper used in 1953. Figure 9.4 gave the percentage of United States total supply of copper which came from the United States and from the Western and Eastern Hemisphere. In addition, Table 55 indicated that copper was in Group I of the most recent list of Strategic and Critical Materials for Stockpiling.

Table 68 shows the extent to which the United States has shifted from a pre-World War II exporter to a post-World War II importer of copper. Table 71 indicates the sources of imports of copper into the

TABLE 71.   Copper (Unmanufactured) Imported into the United States,
1949–53, by Countries
(short tons)
(General imports: U.S. Department of Commerce)

Country	1949	1950	1951	1952	1953
Australia	941	1,307	1,143	684	13,041
Belgian Congo	—	103	—	(a)	5,799
Belgium-Luxembourg	273	474b	—	646	5,615
Bolivia	4,671	5,220	4,449	3,097	3,972
Canada (including Newfoundland and Labrador)	82,821	82,365	54,554	81,932b	107,447
Chile	285,386	292,215	268,359	362,303	281,176
Cuba	15,849	22,891	22,302	19,934	18,206
Ecuador	812	640	—	—	—
France	158b	3,801	1,587	1,806	2,160
Germany	—	44	—	8,932c	3,570c
Japan	1,167	54,400	1,908	223	—
Malta, Gozo, and Cyprus	6,888	6,530	5,556	5,441	3,680
Mexico	64,706	62,748	47,878	50,997	65,818
Netherlands	234	352	47	41	175
Northern Rhodesia	27,244d	87,300d	43,717	28,225	88,042
Norway	37b	4,098	—	1	4,427
Peru	22,316	28,502	10,054	11,317	26,523
Philippines	7,969	10,129	12,608	14,787	13,815
Sweden	—	57	—	—	2,217
Turkey	4,572	3,266	—	3,779	11,894
Union of South Africa	8,919	9,859	7,353	8,588	8,244
United Kingdom	1,925	940	6	37	2,194
Yugoslavia	14,727	10,998	6,223	14,833	7,775
Other countries	1,094b	2,150b	1,391b	1,277	1,279
Total	552,709	690,389	489,135	618,880b	677,069

a Less than 1 ton.
b Revised figure.
c West Germany.
d Tonnages credited to Southern Rhodesia by the U.S. Department of Commerce have been added to Northern Rhodesia, inasmuch as copper of the grades reported does not originate currently in Southern Rhodesia.
SOURCE: *Mineral Facts and Problems*, Bureau of Mines, 1956.

United States from 1949 to 1953. A predominant dependence on Chile, Canada, Northern Rhodesia, Mexico, and to a lesser extent Peru is clearly seen.

Thus the foremost United States copper problem is the shift from being a pre-World War II exporter of copper to being a World War II and post-World War II importer of copper. As indicated by Table 70, net imports in 1950 were 448,000 tons, or 26 percent of consumption. Estimated import requirements for 1975 are projected at 1,000,000 tons, or 40 percent of the estimated consumption of 2,500,000 tons.

The Bureau of Mines in the chapter on copper in *Mineral Facts and Problems* lists eight "anxieties of the industry" and then concludes: "Of all these and many others that may be named, *the most serious long-term problem relates to the United States increasing dependence on foreign sources of supply.*"

The President's Materials Policy Commission drew the conclusion: "*It is clear that the principal future problem in copper will be maintaining production in the United States and increasing production abroad.*"

An examination of Tables 70 and 72 will show the interrelation of these

TABLE 72. New Copper Position of the Rest of the
Free World 1950 and Projected 1975
(thousand short tons)

	1950	1975
Consumption (new copper)	1,343	2,050[a]
Net exports to United States	448	1,000[b]
Mine production	1,608	3,050[b]

[a] Projected.
[b] Required.
SOURCE: 1950 consumption and production based on International Materials Conference data; 1950 exports from U.S. import statistics, U.S. Bureau of Mines; *Resources for Freedom*, Vol. II.

two statements. In 1950 the rest of the free world produced 1,608,000 tons of copper and consumed 1,343,000 of new copper and exported 448,000 tons to the United States—total 1,791,000 tons. The export thus was made possible by drawing down stocks. The United States consumption of 1,730,000 tons was made possible by domestic mine production of 907,000 plus 475,000 of scrap for a total of 1,382,000 from domestic sources, and the 448,000 of imports.

With the estimated increase in domestic consumption of copper it is clear that not only is "maintaining production in the United States" a problem but production should be increased if possible. The Materials Policy Commission estimated that domestic production in 1975 will be 1,500,000 tons—800,000 mine and 700,000 scrap. Thus the Commission saw declining domestic mine production and a greater use of scrap.

From 1940 through 1955 domestic mining capacity ranged around 1,000,000 tons a year (Table 65). Production was maintained during World War II by government price subsidies and, after price decontrol in November, 1945, through high open-market prices. Open-pit mining of low-grade ores has been the trend in the United States. On an ore basis about 76 percent of the output came from pits in the early 1950's as compared with less than 40 percent in 1939. The average ore grade of all domestic ore mined was 0.90 percent in the early 1950's and 0.85 percent in 1953 as contrasted with 5.35 percent in 1889. Open-pit mining and mechanization are the contributing factors that make it economically possible to mine such low-grade ore.

The United States government recognized the need for expanded domestic mining capacity and under the impact of defense needs after the Korean War underwrote the output of certain mines through government contracts at 22 to 25½ cents a pound, plus escalation for certain increases in costs. The effect of this policy, together with fast tax write-offs on expanded copper capacity after 1955, is shown in Table 73 in summary and in detailed enumeration of the mines. Owing to the length of the development period of the mines, the result of the domestic expansion of capacity was not felt until 1956.

The indicated domestic annual full copper mine capacity of 1,244,000 tons in 1960 should be compared with the United States Bureau of Mines' 1956 estimate that by 1960 the annual consumption of new copper in the United States might average 1,600,000 tons. This estimate was made on the assumptions that "international tension, with attendant semimobilization, continues for several years, if there is a continued high level of industrial activity, and if the population increases as anticipated . . . . This figure makes no provision for Government stockpiling, but includes consumption of manufactured goods for export."[14] Production of new copper at full capacity would require 240,000 tons net imports. The United States Bureau of Mines based its estimates of domestic production at a lower figure and arrived at this conclusion: "United States production may be 1,000,000 to 1,100,000 tons at that time (1960), which means, of course, that net imports of copper must average one-half million tons annually."[15] United States net imports of copper in 1955 were 334,913 tons.

There are obviously a great many factors which will affect these estimates. Although there is not much factual evidence on the cost of production of copper, it is believed that about 90 percent of the world's production can be produced at 30 cents a pound. This figure does not give the true picture for the United States, where two-thirds of the out-

[14] Bureau of Mines, *Mineral Facts and Problems*, Government Printing Office, 1956, p. 243.
[15] *Ibid.*, p. 213.

TABLE 73. Estimated Free World Copper Capacity, 1955 to 1962
(thousands of short tons)

	U.S.A.		Outside U.S.A.		Total	
	Tons	Increase Over 1955	Tons	Increase Over 1955	Tons	Increase Over 1955
1955	1,014	—	1,997	—	3,011	—
1956	1,130	116	2,183	186	3,313	302
1957	1,190	176	2,315	318	3,505	494
1958	1,226	212	2,391	394	3,617	606
1959	1,237	223	2,444	447	3,681	670
1960	1,244	230	2,578	581	3,822	811
1961	1,278	264	2,652	655	3,930	919
1962	1,278	264	2,666	669	3,944	933

Copper Mine Expansion
(thousands of short tons)

	Expansion	Annual full capacity
United States:		
1955		1,014
1956		1,130
1957	60	1,190
San Manuel (pre-1957 equaled 50)	20	
Berkeley	17	
Pima (pre-1957–3)	15	
White Pine	5	
Inspiration	3	
1958	36	1,226
Berkeley (1958–29)	4	
White Pine	5	
Ray	20	
Inspiration	7	
1959	11	1,237
Inspiration	8	
Anaconda (Mont.)	3	
1960 Anaconda (Mont.)	7	1,244
1961 Anaconda (Mont.)	34	1,278
1962		1,278
Outside United States:		
1955		1,968
1956		2,183
1957	132	2,315
Canada:		
Gaspe (pre-1957–30)	6	
Geco (start)	10	
Heath Steele	3	

	Expansion	Annual full capacity
Tilt Cove (start)	7	
Chile:		
Chuquicamata (pre-1957–25)	25	
La Africana	4	
Ireland: Avoco (start)	4	
Israel: King Solomon	7	
Nicaragua: Rosita (start)	1	
Philippines:		
Atlas (pre-1957–18)	12	
Sipalay	9	
Cobapa	1	
No. Rhodesia:		
Chibuluma (pre-1957–12)	6	
Bancroft (start)	24	
Kansanshi	5	
Kenya: Macalder, Nyanza	2	
Uganda: Kilembe (pre-1957–4)	6	
1958	76	2,391
Canada:		
Geco	8	
Tilt Cove	10	
Others	10	
Ireland: Avoca (completed at 13)	9	
Nicaragua: Rosita (completed, 5)	4	
No. Rhodesia: Bancroft	24	

	Expansion	Annual full capacity
Fr. W. Africa:		
Mauritania (start)	11	
1959	53	2,444
Canada:		
Gullbridge	6	
Brunswick	3	
No. Rhodesia:		
Bancroft	24	
Fr. W. Africa:		
Mauritania (completed, 22)	11	
So. Rhodesia:		
Molly	9	
1960	134	2,578
Chile:		
El Salvador (completed, 100)	100	
Potrerillos (minus)	−50	
Peru: Toquepala (start)	60	
No. Rhodesia: Bancroft (completed, 96)	24	
1961	74	2,652
Peru: Toquepala (completed, 120)	60	
Yugoslavia: Majdenpek	14	
1962	14	2,666
Yugoslavia: Majdenpek (completed, 28)	14	

Note: Cuajone and Quellaveco are schedules to come into production after 1962.

SOURCES: American Bureau of Metal Statistics; Copper & Brass Research Association estimates, based on first 10 months ABMS reports; *Mining Congress Journal*, Annual Review, 1957; *Engineering and Mining Journal*, February, 1957.

put is high cost. The consensus is that a 30-cent price level would bring about a voluntary curtailment of domestic production and would offer very little, if any, incentive to high-cost producers to look for and develop new sources of supply. The consensus in 1957 was that a price of about 35 cents a pound would result in a high level of demand in the United States and that domestic mine output would be near capacity levels. The net effect of future consumption and production of copper in the United States on the problem of international interdependence would be an increasing need for copper imports. A factor which further supports this conclusion is that the planned and indicated expansion of domestic mine capacity was government supported and the Office of Defense Mobilization "closed" the copper expansion goal in September, 1956, because it considered that national defense was no longer an acceptable reason.

The problem as to "increasing production abroad" is even more obvious. If the free nations could not supply us with our import requirements in 1950, how are they going to supply us more than twice those imports in 1975? But to make the solution more difficult, it is estimated that the demand for new copper in the rest of the free world in 1975 will increase by more than 50 percent of the 1950 total. It is quite clear then that increased copper production abroad is absolutely essential to meet the consumption requirement of the rest of the free world and the United States import requirements.

There are adequate reserves in the rest of the free world to meet these productive requirements. Indeed, the President's Materials Policy Commission concluded that Western Hemisphere sources alone, plus withdrawal from the national stockpile, would assure an ample supply for expanded wartime requirements. This conclusion was drawn on the assumption that productive capacity in the Western Hemisphere outside the United States will expand commensurately with the growth of free world demand.

Copper mine capacity in the free world outside the United States in 1956 was 2,183,000 tons. Planned expansion shown in Table 73 will increase this total to 2,578,000 tons in 1960 and to 2,666,000 tons in 1962. Per capita use of copper outside the United States has been far below that in this country. Per capita consumption in the United States in 1956 was about 15 pounds as compared with 1.8 pounds for foreign countries. United States and foreign consumption trends of copper are given in Figure 9.14. Foreign consumption is increasing and will continue to increase at a greater rate than United States consumption. However, the conclusion seems warranted that planned copper mine capacity in the free world outside the United States is expanding at a rate commensurate with the growth in free world demand.

Since foreign copper production costs are lower than domestic, and foreign mine capacity seems more than adequate to meet foreign demand and United States import requirements, there are those who contend that to encourage more foreign production "is utterly fantastic." This overlooks the fundamental points that the United States must have assured foreign sources of copper imports to supplement domestic pro-

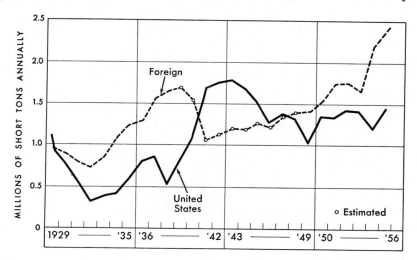

Figure 9.14.   United States vs. Foreign Consumption of Copper. (Data from American Bureau of Metal Statistics)

duction and that there are major obstacles in the way of the development and production of copper. These are seen to fall into two categories. First, there are man-made obstacles such as governmental taxes, exchange rates, foreign investment, capital transfers, labor, and expropriation. Second, there are physical obstacles such as shortages of fuel, power, transportation, and labor.

The United States national policy should be designed to help overcome these man-made policies. As a minimum the following three are recommended: Price stabilization, investment protection, and the removal of the United States tariff on copper. Full discussion has already been presented of all three of these recommendations.

Any copper price stabilization arrangement would certainly help both foreign and domestic producers. There are dangers inherent in such arrangements, but there are definite advantages. However, there is no danger in repetition of the recommendation that the United States government should give greater attention to long-term price stabilization whenever it enters into a copper transaction.

Problems of investment protection and the development of a more favorable framework for expansion abroad, and policy recommendations were covered in detail under "United States Non-Fuel Minerals Position."

The tariff on copper is one of those that makes no sense. A 4-cents-a-pound excise tax on imported copper was imposed in 1932 when the United States was an exporter of copper and the domestic price had fallen to an average price of 5.67 cents a pound. The tariff rate was reduced from 4 cents to 2 cents a pound in 1948 in connection with the General Agreement on Tariffs and Trade. It was temporarily suspended in 1947 and the suspension was subsequently extended until February 15, 1953, or until the end of the national emergency, whichever was earlier, so long as the price did not fall below 24 cents a pound. The suspension was extended again to continue to June 30, 1955, and again to continue for a three-year period to June 30, 1958. In view of our sustained and future import needs for copper this tariff should be abolished and the domestic industry should be protected when necessary by more direct methods. Our national policies should be directed to facilitate the importation of copper and to assure sources of production in the free world outside the United States.

5. Conclusions

Copper is the most important nonferrous metal. The reserves are highly concentrated in geographic location and ownership. Increased United States consumption of copper has been brought about because of its use for electrical purposes and in recent years has been made possible by the increased use of copper scrap and imported copper. The consumption patterns for the future are that copper will be put to those uses for which it is best suited and aluminum and other substitutes will continue to take over many markets formerly supplied by copper. The United States will become increasingly dependent on domestic scrap and imported copper. Recommended policy measures are those which will assure foreign sources of production and facilitate imports of copper. Copper is a vital necessity for peacetime strength and military security. Security measures in line with those previously recommended for strategic and critical materials are absolutely essential as a part of our national policy.

ALUMINUM

Students of energy and material predicted that the phase of history of the harnessing of fossil fuels by heavy metals was rapidly drawing to a close, and was being replaced by a new stage which would be characterized by continuous energy sources harnessed by light metals. As this stage was dawning a new energy era exploded. The forecast was correct for the light metals. The shining star is aluminum. By 1955 the United States was producing aluminum at a rate of more than 1,500,000 tons a year. This was almost ten times the level of prewar 1939 and about double the actual output either at the World War II peak or as recently as 1950.

The aluminum industry consists of five basic stages: mining the bauxite ore, separating alumina from the bauxite, reducing alumina to aluminum pig and ingot, fabricating pig and ingot into semifinished and finished aluminum, and manufacturing end products.

Aluminum is the most abundant metallic element in the crust of the earth. Nevertheless it is relatively scarce because of its affinity for oxygen and the silica content of the reserves. For these reasons the principal raw material is bauxite. High-grade bauxite ore has an alumina (aluminum oxide) content of 55 percent or more and contains less than 7 percent silica. About 85 percent of the bauxite produced in the United States and imported is used for aluminum and the balance goes into the chemical, abrasive, and refractory industries. Most bauxite is mined in open pits, although some is mined by underground methods, in which variations of the room-and-pillar technique are employed. Open-pit mining may require stripping an overburden several times the thickness of the ore body; but mining recovery is greater than from underground mines. The ore as mined is called crude, green, wet, or undried bauxite. Only the alumina plants located at Hurricane Creek and Bauxite, Arkansas, use crude bauxite. Most of the treated bauxite is dried in cylindrical kilns at 200° to 250° F. to drive off free moisture and reduce the shipping weight. The percentage by weight of free moisture in undried bauxite varies from 5 percent to 25 percent and averages 15 percent for domestic ores. Thus the removal of this excess weight is absolutely necessary where bauxite is to be shipped to an alumina plant.

Alumina must be clearly distinguished from the metal, aluminum. Alumina is the name for aluminum oxide, a fine white powder extracted from bauxite by a chemical refining operation. The Bayer process, which is usually employed, requires 8 to 10 million BTU of heat to process 2.2 tons of dried bauxite into one ton of alumina. This heat requirement is equivalent to about 10 MCF of natural gas or three-fourths of a ton of coal. Other raw materials needed include 150 to 200 pounds of soda ash and about the same quantity of quicklime per ton of alumina, while the labor factor is five to six man-hours. A low silica content in bauxite is desirable because silica, when heated, combines with alumina and soda ash, reducing the amount of recoverable aluminum. It is estimated that for each pound of silica content in bauxite, 1.1 pounds of alumina and 1.2 pounds of soda ash are lost in the Bayer process. In order to separate alumina from low-grade bauxite, the lime-soda-sinter process is used, which recovers alumina from the "red mud," a waste product of the Bayer process.

Aluminum is obtained from alumina by an electrolytic "reduction" process which separates the metal from oxygen. The reduction takes place in a "pot" and a series of such pots is referred to as a "potline." Electricity requirements are very large with about 20,000 KWH needed to produce one ton of metal (about 10 KWH per pound). Raw materials used, per ton of aluminum pig, include 2 tons of alumina, about 1200 pounds of carbon paste for electrodes, and smaller quantities of cryolite and aluminum fluoride. The labor factor is about thirty man-hours. The product at this stage is aluminum pig with a purity of 99 percent or greater. When pig is remelted to remove further impurities, it becomes ingot. During this process other metals may be added to form various aluminum alloys. Aluminum reduction must be a continuous operation; otherwise the mixture in the pot will freeze, and the initial expense of starting up the process is considerable.

Fabrication converts aluminum ingot into (1) wrought products and (2) castings. The most important wrought product classifications are: (a) sheet, plate, and strip; (b) rolled structural shapes; (c) extruded shapes; and (d) powder, flake, and paste. Castings, which range from sand and mold castings to die castings, account for approximately 15 to 20 percent of the shipments of aluminum wrought and cast products, while wrought products make up the remainder. Although in 1950 there were three producers of pig and ingot aluminum in the United States, there were some thirty to fifty independent fabricators of wrought products, accounting for 10 to 30 percent of industry output depending on the product classification. A much larger number of independents made castings, accounting for about 80 percent of the output. A third major use of aluminum, in addition to wrought and cast products, is in

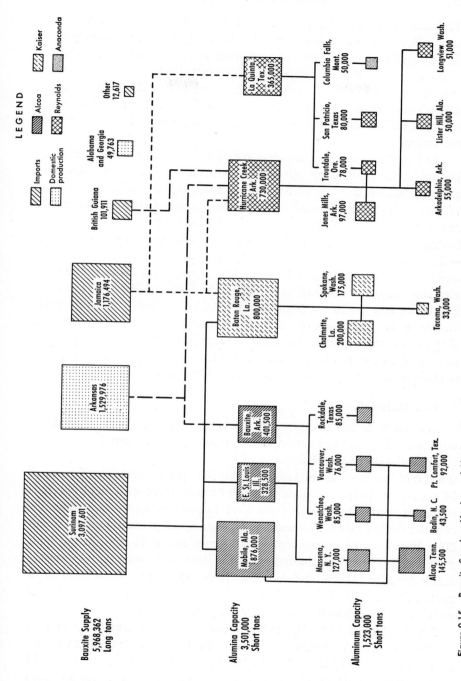

Figure 9.15. Bauxite Supply—Alumina and Aluminum Plant Capacities in the United States in 1953. Capacities include facilities under construction but not in operation. (Data from *Mineral Facts and Problems*)

dissipative or destructive uses in which the metal loses its identity, such as an alloying element in other metal base alloys, as a metallurgical reducing agent, or as a source of aluminum for aluminum chemicals.

The manufacturing of end products converts sheet, forgings, extrusions, and castings into finished products such as foil, pots and pans, automobile parts, Venetian blinds, window frames, and approximately 4000 other end uses. Only a small portion of manufacturing is done by the integrated producers.

The bauxite supply and alumina and aluminum plant capacities in the United States in 1953 are given in Figure 9.15. This figure shows the extent to which the United States relied on imports of bauxite (about 74 percent); the high concentration of the sources of bauxite; the limited number of alumina plants (6) and aluminum plants (17) in the United States; and the control of the production of alumina by three companies —the Aluminum Company of America, the Reynolds Metals Company, and the Kaiser Aluminum and Chemical Corporation. These companies also controlled the production of aluminum, although Anaconda Copper had under construction a 50,000-ton plant in 1953 and began producing aluminum in 1955. However, this high degree of concentration of ownership of primary aluminum production seems almost like decentralization compared to the pre-World War II control of primary aluminum production by one company—the Aluminum Company of America.

1. Raw Materials

The raw materials necessary for the production of aluminum and the outline of the processes employed are presented in Figure 9.16.

The estimate of world reserves of bauxite in 1950 shown in Table 74 was 1.6 billion tons, about 115 times the 1953 production. The Bureau of Mines reports that a comparison of this reserve figure with eight previous estimates made at intervals from 1941 to 1953 indicates that new discoveries during that period were made at an average annual rate of about 50 million tons or approximately 3.6 times the 1953 production. This relationship, when considered with the fact that great areas exist in South America, Africa, and Asia that have never been thoroughly prospected for bauxite, led the Bureau to conclude that the possibility of world bauxite exhaustion was very remote.

The President's Materials Policy Commission estimated that if production of primary aluminum should grow to 3.5 million short tons by 1975, and if combined United States and Canadian production should reach 5 million tons a year, the 1950 bauxite ore reserves would be about two-thirds consumed by 1975. But this did not worry the Commission because of the possibilities of development of reserves in Brazil, Venezuela, Colombia, and Ecuador. The Commission emphasized the fact that only twelve years before 1950 the large Jamaican reserves were unknown.

However, the fact remains that only 2.5 percent of the world reserves of bauxite are in the United States. The only bauxite deposits known on the North American continent occur in two districts in the United States: (1) central Arkansas and (2) the southeastern part of the country in two areas: (a) the coastal plain in Georgia, Alabama, and Mississippi and

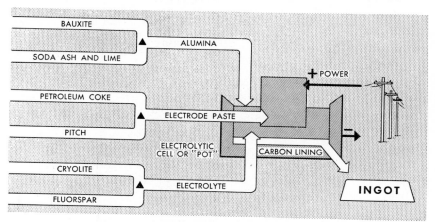

Figure 9.16. Basic Raw Materials and Diagrammatic Process for Aluminum Production.

(b) the Appalachian Valley in Georgia, Alabama, Tennessee, and Virginia. The deposits in Arkansas are by far the largest in the United States. They are in about 275 square miles in Saline and Pulaski counties extending about twenty-five miles southwestward from Little Rock. Although the reserves of low-silica, low-iron bauxite in the district have been largely depleted, there is a large tonnage of lower-grade material suitable for the production of alumina. This district also has large reserves of bauxitic and kaolinitic clays associated with the bauxite.

The President's Materials Policy Commission considered as a most favorable factor the presence in the United States of huge deposits of lower-grade bauxitic ores and non-bauxitic materials such as clays and anorthosite containing about 30 percent or more of alumina. The estimate was made that the use of the best of such materials might possibly yield aluminum at roughly 3 cents a pound above present actual costs.

A final most favorable factor is the continuation of the trend of expanding bauxite resources as a result of technological improvements. For

TABLE 74. Estimate of World Bauxite Reserves as of October, 1950

Country	Million Metric Tons	Percent of World Reserves
British Commonwealth of Nations:		
Jamaica	320.0	19.9
Gold Coast	229.4	14.3
British Guiana	65.0	4.1
India and Pakistan	25.4	1.6
Australia	21.0	1.3
Federation of Malaya	9.6	.6
Subtotal	670.4	41.8
U.S.S.R. and satellites:		
U.S.S.R.	30.0	1.9
Hungary	250.2	15.6
Rumania	20.0	1.2
Subtotal	300.2	18.7
Brazil	192.0	12.0
Yugoslavia	105.0	6.6
France	60.0	3.7
Greece	60.0	3.7
Surinam	50.0	3.1
China	50.0	3.1
United States	40.5[a]	2.5
Indonesia	25.8	1.6
Haiti	23.4	1.5
Other	28.0	1.7
Total—world	1,605.3	100.0

[a] Dry basis, 8 feet or more thick.
SOURCE: *Mineral Facts and Problems.*

example, the technological improvement, accompanied during World War II by the construction of capacity to handle the high-silica ore, effectively increased economic domestic reserves (resources) from about 7 million metric tons in 1945 to about 40 million tons of higher-silica ore in 1951.

However, in spite of these favorable factors, the fact must be borne in mind that, had it not been for these 40 million tons of higher-silica ore, the United States reserves of bauxite would have been close to exhaustion as early as 1950. In addition, these reserves, containing approximately 10 million tons of aluminum, would be able to support the requirements of the United States for only a few years in an emergency. As reserves are gradually used up, they will become increasingly deficient in their ability to support aluminum production if overseas supplies should be cut off. This suggested to the President's Commission the possibility of setting aside a portion of the remaining domestic bauxite deposits as an insurance against war needs. It also means that further development of the processes for using lower grades of bauxite and aluminum-bearing clays must be vigorously pursued.

In addition to bauxite, soda ash and lime, and fuel oil or coal are required for alumina production. Unlimited supplies of lime and soda ash and plentiful supplies of coal or petroleum will be available for alumina production.

The auxiliary raw materials in aluminum production are petroleum coke and pitch to manufacture electrode paste, and cryolite and fluorspar used for the electrolyte flux.

Petroleum coke is a by-product from the production of heavy fuel oils, and pitch is a by-product of the coal-coke industry. There is no problem about present shortages of these two materials. But the carbon electrode made from these two raw materials constitutes a significant cost item in aluminum production. Therefore costs must be held down.

Natural cryolite is found only in Greenland, and in a very few years the aluminum industry will probably depend almost entirely upon synthetic cryolite produced in part from fluorspar. Fluorspar is in very short domestic supply and is in Group I of the list of Strategic and Critical Materials for Stockpiling. The Materials Policy Commission in a special report on fluorspar concluded that the supply of fluorine from natural fluorspar probably could be substantially supplemented by fluorine recovered from phosphate rock.

The conclusion can be drawn that sustained technological effort will be necessary to improve the supply of raw materials required in the production of aluminum. Of critical importance is the United States dependence on outside sources for bauxite.

2. Production and Capacity

The following is a concise summary from *Mineral Facts and Problems,* the facts of the growth of production and capacity of the aluminum industry.

Throughout most of the years of the aluminum industry's phenomenal growth, which has been taking place since 1886, the United States has been the world's major aluminum producer. Germany held the leadership for a few years during its military buildup before World War II, but in 1941 the United States again became the world's largest producer. In 1942 Canada became the second largest producer, and the two North American countries held these relative positions through 1953. Primary aluminum production of the major producing countries and the total world production for 1949 to 1953

TABLE 75.   World Production of Aluminum by Countries, 1949–53
(thousand short tons)

Country	1949	1950	1951	1952	1953	Percent of 1953 Total
United States	603	719	837	937	1,252	46
Canada	369	397	447	500	546	20
U.S.S.R.[a]	182	209	220	276	331	12
France	59	67	100	117	125	5
Germany, West	32	31	82	111	118	5
Italy	29	41	55	58	61	2
Norway	39	52	55	56	59	2
Japan	23	27	41	47	50	2
Austria	16	20	29	40	48	2
United Kingdom	34	33	31	31	35	1
Hungary	15	18	24	26	33	1
Switzerland	24	21	30	33	31	1
Other	17	16	24	27	28	1
Total	1,442	1,651	1,975	2,259	2,717	100

[a] Estimate.
SOURCE: *Mineral Facts and Problems.*

are shown in [Table 75]. The principal bauxite producers have been United States, Surinam, British Guiana, France, Hungary, U.S.S.R., Italy, Indonesia, Yugoslavia, and, since 1952, Jamaica. Large undeveloped reserves also exist in French West Africa and Gold Coast. World production of bauxite, by countries, is shown in [Table 76].

TABLE 76.   World Production of Bauxite by Countries, 1949–53
(thousand long tons)

Country	1949	1950	1951	1952	1953	Percent of 1953 Total
Surinam	2,093	2,048	2,629	3,104	3,221	23
British Guiana	1,758	1,583	2,003	2,388	2,115	15
United States	1,149	1,335	1,849	1,667	1,580	12
Jamaica	—	—	—	376	1,434	11
Hungary	551	563	722	1,153	1,378	10
France	773	795	1,107	1,097	1,146	8
U.S.S.R.[a]	640	738	837	886	984	7
Other	1,132	979	1,464	1,869	1,965	14
Total	8,096	8,041	10,611	12,540	13,823	100

[a] Estimate.
SOURCE: *Mineral Facts and Problems.*

United States production of bauxite began in Georgia in 1889. A decade later the relatively large deposits of central Arkansas were opened up, and these soon became the chief source of domestic ore. Alabama and Georgia have consistently produced small quantities, and for several years bauxite was mined in Tennessee and Virginia. However, over 85 percent of the domestic production has come from Arkansas every year since 1914. Until the early twenties, domestic production far exceeded imports—in fact, in many of those years United States was a net exporter. In 1923 this pattern began to change significantly as imports from the large Surinam and British Guiana deposits began to flow into the United States.

In 1940–41 it became apparent that the aluminum and bauxite industries required a large expansion to meet wartime needs. At that time the Federal Bureau of Mines and the Federal Geological Survey launched an extensive exploration program that resulted in a substantial increase in the known reserves of ore in Arkansas. In addition, the Government began to stockpile Arkansas bauxite. These activities resulted in expansion of mining operations, and Arkansas production increased to over 6 million tons in 1943.

At the beginning of World War II the Government also embarked on a program that resulted in greatly increased imports of aluminum from Canada and in the construction of 2 commercial and 4 experimental alumina plants and 9 commercial-size aluminum plants. Both large alumina plants and all of the aluminum plants except one at Tacoma, Wash., operated by Olin Corp., were built and operated by the Aluminum Co. of America. This company was the only domestic aluminum producer until the Reynolds Metals Co. began production in 1941. During the war Reynolds owned and operated two aluminum plants, which were constructed with Government financial aid. The designed capacity of the Government-owned reduction plants at the end of World War II approximately equaled the total capacity of the plants owned by Alcoa and Reynolds. Government-owned alumina and aluminum facilities were disposed of under the Surplus Property Act of 1944. The plants capable of competitive operation were purchased by Reynolds and the Permanente Metals Corp., later renamed the Kaiser Aluminum & Chemical Corp. Over half of the Government-owned capacity, which was constructed for war emergency use only, was considered uneconomical for peacetime operation because of the lack of low-cost electrical power; these plants were dismantled and converted to other uses.

Military requirements for aluminum were reduced toward the end of the war, and primary production dropped from 920,000 tons in 1943 to a low of 410,000 tons in 1946. Between 1946 and 1950 aluminum production and civilian consumption grew steadily. Domestic production of bauxite declined to 1.0 to 1.5 million tons during this period, but imports increased to over 2.5 million tons, or about twice as much as domestic production. The aluminum industry used approximately 85 percent of the total bauxite consumed, while most of the remainder was used in producing artificial abrasives and chemicals. Metal and refractory-grade bauxite was also added to the National Stockpile after World War II.

The outbreak of the Korean War in June 1950 and the decision of the Government to establish a defense economy resulted in passage of the Defense Production Act of 1950. The need for large expansion of the United States aluminum industry and increased supplies of bauxite became evident. An expansion program was planned to create enough new processing capacity to meet essential civilian requirements and military requirements and to leave a surplus for stockpiling. At the start of the program, the capacity of new facilities required to meet these demands was variously estimated at 500,000 to 1,000,000 tons of primary aluminum a year. A number of industrial concerns, consisting principally of established metal fabricators and secondary aluminum producers, investigated the possibilities of producing primary aluminum. Most of these companies did not participate in the program because of the large capital investment required for constructing production facilities with capacities great enough for economical production. The costly integration of producing bauxite, alumina, and aluminum was a practical necessity to achieve a competitive position in the industry. The Harvey Machine Co., Torrance, Calif., a fabricating firm, negotiated with the Government to begin aluminum production but encountered difficulties in obtaining a Government loan. Harvey later joined in a minor capacity with the Anaconda Copper Mining Co. in constructing a reduction plant with 50,000 tons annual capacity at Columbia Falls, Mont. An alumina supply was contracted for with the Reynolds Metals Co. The remainder of the expansion was carried out by the three established producers, Alcoa, Kaiser, and Reynolds.

All new facilities built under the expansion program were financed with private funds. Government aid was furnished in the form of accelerated amortization for tax purposes, guarantees for private loans, market guarantees, and priorities for equipment and construction materials. Unlike some of the facilities constructed during World War II, all new plants were designed and located for continued operation in the postemergency period. The location and estimated annual capacity of United States alumina plants and reduction plants before and after expansion are listed in [Tables 77 and 78].

As a result of this program, the alumina capacity of the United States was nearly doubled, and United States dependency on foreign bauxite increased.

TABLE 77. Estimated Annual Alumina Capacity of the United States
(short tons)

	End of 1950	Increase, 1951–53	Total
Aluminum Co. of America:			
Mobile, Ala.	602,250	273,750	876,000
East St. Louis, Ill.	182,500	146,000	328,500
Bauxite, Ark.	—	401,500	401,500
Total Alcoa	784,750	821,250	1,606,000
Reynolds Metals Co.:			
Hurricane Creek, Ark.	521,000	209,000	730,000
La Quinta, Tex.	—	365,000	365,000
Total Reynolds	521,000	574,000	1,095,000
Kaiser Aluminum & Chemical Corp.: Baton Rouge, La.	440,000	360,000	800,000
Total	1,745,750	1,755,250	3,501,000

SOURCE: *Mineral Facts and Problems.*

TABLE 78. Estimated Annual Primary Aluminum Capacity of the United States
(short tons)

	End of 1949[a]	End of 1950[b]	Expansion Planned in 1950–51[c]	Total
Aluminum Co. of America:				
Alcoa, Tenn.	145,300	145,500	—	145,500
Badin, N.C.	33,850	43,500	—	43,500
Massena, N.Y.	57,500⎱	127,000	—	127,000
St. Lawrence, N.Y.	—⎰			
Vancouver, Wash.	76,100	76,000	—	76,000
Point Comfort, Tex.	57,000	57,000	35,000	92,000
Wenatchee, Wash.	—	—	85,000	85,000
Rockdale, Tex.	—	—	85,000	85,000
Total Alcoa	369,750	449,000	205,000	654,000
Reynolds Metals Co.:				
Jones Mills, Ark.	73,850	74,000[d]	23,000	97,000
Troutdale, Oreg.	72,000	76,000[d]	2,000	78,000
Listerhill, Ala.	48,600	50,000	—	50,000
Longview, Wash.	30,500	31,000	20,000	51,000
San Patricio, Tex.	—	—	80,000	80,000
Arkadelphia, Ark.	—	—	55,000	55,000
Total Reynolds	224,950	231,000	180,000	411,000
Kaiser Aluminum & Chemical Co.:				
Spokane, Wash.	108,125	155,000	20,000	175,000
Tacoma, Wash.	24,250	25,000	8,000	33,000
Chalmette, La.	—	—	200,000	200,000
Total Kaiser	132,375	180,000	228,000	408,000
Anaconda Aluminum Co.: Columbia Falls, Mont.	—	—	50,000	50,000
Total	727,075	860,000	663,000	1,523,000

[a] Represents economic capacity, having reference to the availability and price of electrical energy.
[b] Economic capacity plus capacity requiring high-cost power.
[c] Data represent capacities as "scheduled" in the expansion program and may differ from "actual" capacities as determined by production. All of this new capacity was installed between 1951 and 1955.
[d] Does not include capacity available from programmed expansion.
SOURCE: *Mineral Facts and Problems.*

Both Kaiser and Reynolds planned to meet most of their increased bauxite requirements with Jamaican ore. Part of the funds to develop this great reserve of ore was supplied to Reynolds by the Government before enactment of the Defense Production Act. Alcoa planned to increase shipments from Surinam to meet its expanding needs. In addition to bauxite for alumina, requirements for abrasives and other uses have increased. The Aluminium Co. of Canada installed new facilities in British Guiana to provide the United States refractory industry with calcined bauxite to replace the dwindling supply of domestic diaspore. In July 1951 the Government agreed to contribute funds for approved bauxite-exploration projects. Probably as a result of the thorough search for bauxite during World War II, requests for such assistance were few.[16]

3. Consumption

Aluminum's tremendous growth in production and capacity has been a result of ever-widening markets and increased consumption. These have stemmed from the metal's own virtues—lightness, resistance to corrosion, high heat and electricity conduction, together with a continuing favorable price relationship to competitive nonferrous metals.

Apparent consumption of aluminum increased over tenfold from 1920 to 1950 and almost fourfold from 1940 to 1950 (Table 79). Table 80,

TABLE 79. Supply and Consumption of Aluminum in the United States,
Selected Years, 1900–50
(thousand short tons)

Year	Domestic Primary Production	Production from Old Scrap	Approximate Net Imports[a]	Apparent Consumption (Production Plus Imports)
1900	3	n.a.	n.a.	n.a.
1910	18	n.a.	n.a.	n.a.
1920	69	6	16	91
1930	115	15	12	142
1940	206	46	5	257
1943	920	33	79	1,032
1946	410	91	55	556
1950	719	63	186	968[b]

n.a. = not available.
[a] Computed from data on imports for consumption of crude and semicrude, and exports of ingots and scrap.
[b] Actual consumption, 983,000 short tons.
SOURCE: Based on U.S. Bureau of Mines data; *Resources for Freedom*, Vol. II.

TABLE 80. Apparent Consumption of Primary Aluminum and Ingot Equivalent
of Secondary Aluminum in the United States, 1949–53
(thousand short tons)

	1949	1950	1951	1952	1953
Primary: Apparent consumption[a]	634	896	974	1,072	1,542
Secondary recovery:					
From old scrap	45	76	77	71	79
From new scrap	136	167	216	233	290
Imports (net)[b]	36	60	17	5	20
Total	851	1,199	1,284	1,381	1,931

[a] Production and producers' stock changes of crude and net imports of crude and semifabricated products. Net imports may include small quantities of secondary.
[b] Ingot equivalent of net imports (weight × 0.90). Imports are largely scrap pig. Some duplication of secondary aluminum occurs because of the small amount of loose scrap imported, which also is included as secondary from old scrap.
SOURCE: *Mineral Facts and Problems.*

[16] H. F. Kurtz and D. D. Blue, "Aluminum and Bauxite," a chapter from *Mineral Facts and Problems*, p. 4–5.

which is tabulated on a slightly different basis, indicates that by 1953 consumption was up over 60 percent from 1950. United States per capita consumption of aluminum increased to 18.2 pounds in 1954 from 9.6 pounds in 1950, while copper use was down to 15.2 pounds from 19, lead 9.2 pounds from 11.7, and zinc to 10.8 pounds from 12.7. In addition, aluminum's lightness makes one pound go two to four times as far as other metals. The competitive position of aluminum and copper has already been discussed.

As indicated by Table 81, military uses including those of the Atomic Energy Commission accounted for approximately 30 percent of the 1952

TABLE 81. Shipments of Aluminum by Consuming Industries in 1952[a]

Industry	Thousand Short Tons	Percent
Direct military uses	396.4	29.8
Building materials	170.5	12.8
Consumer durable goods	132.8	10.0
Transportation	126.3	9.5
(Motor vehicles)	(110.1)	(8.3)
Machinery and equipment, excluding electrical	122.8	9.2
Construction	122.5	9.2
(Electric power construction)	(92.0)	(6.9)
Destructive uses	68.6	5.2
Electrical and communications equipment	66.6	5.0
Containers and packaging	45.6	3.4
Exports, chemicals, photography, and others	78.7	5.9
Total	1,330.8	100.0

[a] Bureau of the Census and Business and Defense Services Administration, Facts for Industry: Ser. BDSAF–122–03, May 5, 1954.
SOURCE: *Mineral Facts and Problems.*

shipments of aluminum. As a strategic metal, aluminum's principal use has been in the construction of aircraft. It is also required in many other military items including air-borne equipment, ships, bridges, radar and fire-control towers, rockets, portable shelters, and fuel pipes.

The principal civilian use of aluminum is in building materials and accounted for almost 13 percent in 1953. These applications, which have expanded tremendously since the end of World War II, include hardware, windows, blinds, awnings, roofing, siding, wall panels, and insulation. Consumer durables, such as refrigerators and dehumidifiers and the like, took 10 percent of the aluminum in 1953. Another significant and growing market is the automotive industry, which is a part of, but shown separately from, the transportation industry. Weight saving is of great importance to the transportation industry in automobiles, trucks, buses, tractors, trailers, ships, and rail cars, and complete train units. The automotive industry is using increasing quantities of aluminum for pistons, bearings, door handles, panels, body trim. Tremendous potentials are seen for automobile radiators, cylinder heads, and engine blocks. Average use of aluminum rose from 10 pounds a car in 1945 to 35 pounds in 1956. One 1956 model contained 192 pounds, including a gold-anodized grille. Every automobile manufacturer used some aluminum trim on 1957 cars.

Aluminum will continue to replace other materials in both military and civilian uses and many new appliances will be developed. The President's Materials Policy Commission concluded that:

Although it is clearly impossible to project the 1975 level of demand for aluminum with any degree of assurance, it is probable that it will continue to grow vigorously over the foreseeable future. A demand in the neighborhood of 4.5 million short tons by 1975, or nearly 5 times the level of consumption of 1950, is considered plausible. Old scrap can be expected to constitute an increasing proportion of supply so that by 1975 it may be furnishing 20 percent of total consumption as contrasted with 10 percent in recent years. Accordingly, the projected United States demand for primary aluminum in 1975 might be about 3.6 million short tons or about 4 times consumption of primary aluminum in 1950. Domestic capacity is scheduled to rise to about 1.5 million tons by 1954. Consequently, the projected level of demand for 1975 would require a further increase in capacity of 2 million tons, or an addition 1⅓ times the scheduled 1954 level.

The manner in which this scheduled increase in aluminum capacity was implemented in a realized 1,523,000 tons by 1954 is clearly indicated in Figure 9.15.

4. Problems and Policy

Three related aluminum problems, for which we have presented many of the facts and policies, will be discussed—the growth of the industry, the availability of electric power, and security.

A. Growth

In 1940 the writer was present at a conference of the National Defense Advisory Commission when a question was put to industry officials: Do we have enough aluminum to provide for wartime requirements? The answer was "Yes!" How wrong it was. Even though at that time the figure of 50,000 required military aircraft per year was being tossed about, no one took the time before that quick answer of "Yes" to multiply an estimated number of pounds of aluminum by 50,000 and then to compare this result with aluminum capacity. Even with that one requirement the answer would have been "No." Aluminum's accelerated growth began with World War II, and national policies related to growth have been closely associated with military requirements.

Before World War II United States national policy in aluminum was directed unsuccessfully toward breaking up the monopolistic position of the Aluminum Company of America. In 1940–41 it became apparent that the aluminum and bauxite industries required a large expansion to meet wartime needs. The United States government incorporated decentralization of ownership as a part of its policy to increase aluminum capacity. The manner in which this was accomplished and the government's part in expanding bauxite production has been described in section 2, "Production and Capacity."

In 1945, the Circuit Court of Appeals for the Second Circuit, sitting as a court of last resort in an antitrust action started by the government in 1937, held that Alcoa had monopolized the aluminum ingot market in violation of the Sherman Act. The Court ordered that remedial action be deferred until plans were developed for the disposal of government-owned plants built during the war.

The successful threefold expansion of aluminum economic production capacity during World War II and an overestimation of aluminum requirements for military aircraft during 1945 created a problem during the early postwar years of disposal of surplus plants and enlarging the aluminum market. Once again the government followed a policy of decentralization of ownership in the disposal of the government-owned surplus plants to Reynolds and the Permanente Metals Corporation, later renamed the Kaiser Aluminum and Chemical Corporation. Actually the haunting fear of an inadequate postwar demand, due to expanded capacity and the loss of the military aircraft market, probably turned out to the advantage of the industry. During 1945 and 1946 other nonferrous metals were in short supply so that aluminum at that time began to capture old markets for copper and to develop new markets and consumer acceptance. Thus, what appeared to be a disadvantage for the industry probably resulted in stimulating the postwar growth. The peak production of 920,000 tons in 1943 was down to 410,000 tons in 1945, but by 1948 the growth was under way, with a production of 622,000 tons.

In 1950 the Federal District Court, passing on the remedial action appropriate under the 1945 judgment, refused to declare, as petitioned by Alcoa, that "effective competitive conditions now prevail" in the aluminum ingot market. This decision was made despite the intervening development of two other important producers. In order to promote competitive conditions the Court ordered owners of shares of both Alcoa and Aluminium Limited, the sole Canadian producer, to sell their holdings of one or the other. The Court denied at that time the government's request for an order requiring Alcoa to divest itself of an integrated group of plants.

As we have seen in section 2, "Production and Capacity," with the outbreak of the Korean War in June, 1950, the government passed the Defense Production Act of 1950 and was active throughout the emergency period in promoting the growth of the aluminum industry. A brief review of these activities is in order.

The Office of Defense Mobilization (ODM) started in 1950 what has been designated as round one of the expansion program. In 1950, production was about 800,000 tons of aluminum, and the expansion goal for the first round, in 1951, was 446,000 tons; for the second round, in 1952, the goal was 231,000 tons. To achieve this expansion the government offered the following incentives: (1) "certificates of necessity" that allowed fast tax write-offs for depreciation; (2) government-guaranteed loans to insure and speed the companies' expansions; and (3) guaranteed markets, under which all aluminum that the companies could not sell would be bought by the government for the strategic stockpile. Again in attempt to break up Alcoa's position, these incentives were given to Kaiser and Reynolds.

In 1952 the ODM promoted a third round. In this round ODM wanted to bring smaller firms into the industry. *Business Week* of August 13, 1955, described the progress of round three as follows:

This time it wanted to bring smaller outfits into the industry. But this time there were complications; some of the smaller companies lost interest, were caught up in squabbles, or were stricken by financing troubles.

Week after week through this summer [1955], ODM has been trying to decide whether to offer more incentives. It's likely to make up its mind soon.

WIDE MOVES—Meanwhile, the whole face of the industry is changing. The big three are finding that other companies are getting deeper and deeper into aluminum.

Anaconda has moved in. Next week it dedicates its $65-million primary aluminum plant at Columbia Falls, Mont., adding 60,000 tons of new capacity. This expansion is part of the government-sponsored second round.

And Aluminium Co. of Canada, which must be figured as a big factor in the U.S. market, has 91,000 tons of new capacity coming in between now and the end of 1956 from its Kitimat plant. (By the end of 1959, Alcan reckons to have Kitimat's capacity stepped up to 331,000 tons.)

DELAYS—So it's clear that the market is there for the expansion that's now under way. The question that's holding up ODM's decision probably is: How far should government incentives for expansion go?

It's a question that has produced explosive arguments with ODM. One side —backed by Treasury Secy. George M. Humphrey—argues that the government has done enough, that most companies applying for fast tax write-off are big enough to handle expansion on their own. The other side argues that aluminum must be urged to expand because of the great demand for it.

Beyond this row there's the noisy bitter tussle between the independent fabricators and the big producers. The independents' cry is that the big producers have been giving them short shrift on supplies.

But out of all the strong words shot back and forth only one thing has come clear: There just isn't enough aluminum this year for everybody.

Secretary Humphrey won his argument, and new "certificates" were halted in September, 1955, for rapid amortization.

At the beginning of 1956 a continuing shortage of aluminum, due to the growth of demand, set off the third round of expansion which promised to add 850,000 tons to United States capacity and 380,000 tons in Canada within five years. This would mean a 53 percent rise in United States capacity and physically more tonnage than was added in 1951–55.

The predictions were for the following additions by the big three:

Alcoa	240,000 tons—up 34 percent
Reynolds	145,000 tons—up 34 percent
Kaiser	226,000 tons—up 52 percent
Total	611,000 tons

This round would include four new companies:

Olin-Mathieson	60,000 tons
Harvey Machine	54,000 tons
Revere Copper and Brass	60,000 tons
St. Joseph Lead and Pittsburgh Consolidation	66,000 tons [abandoned]
Total	240,000 tons

Olin-Mathieson and Harvey Machine had holdover "certificates," but only Olin-Mathieson of the new companies had made arrangements for raw materials. In late 1956 Olin-Mathieson and Revere Copper and Brass formed Olin-Revere Metals after they found that, by pooling, the same investment capacity could be increased by 50 percent from 120,000 to 180,000 tons. Olin was to get 120,000 tons and Revere 60,000 tons of this production.

Thus the aluminum industry accepted the challenge of growth. Without rapid amortization and government purchase contracts it was quite possible that the industry would need larger profit margins to meet higher capital costs, including costs for raw materials and in some cases their own power sources. However, there is no question that the United

States government aluminum policy was thoroughly committed to aiding the growth of the industry if the industry could not "go it alone." In the past the United States had incorporated as a part of this policy the implementation of its policy to increase competition within the aluminum industry.

B. Electric Power

The alumina, as we have seen, is reduced to aluminum metal through an electrolytic process that, under present technology, requires about 9 to 10 kilowatt-hours of electric energy for each pound of metal produced. The power is thus an important cost factor, amounting to between 1.7 and 2.3 cents per pound of metal, or approximately 10 to 13 percent of the market price of aluminum.

The President's Materials Policy Commission concluded that if all the 3,600,000 tons of new aluminum capacity projected for 1975 were to be supplied from domestic primary production, and if no significant change were to occur in the ratio of power consumption to output, the demand for electric power to produce aluminum would increase from about 13 billion kilowatt-hours in 1950 to approximately 65 billion kilowatt-hours by 1975. By comparison, total power generated in 1950 was 389 billion kilowatt-hours, and of that total, hydroelectric production was 101 billion kilowatt-hours. Under ideal operating conditions (i.e., 100 percent load factor) the electric generating capacity needed to supply this quantity of power would be 7.4 million kilowatts as compared to 1.5 million kilowatts in 1950. Our previous study of the electric power industry indicated that total power requirements would reach close to 300 million kilowatts in 1975 as compared with 83 million in 1950. This would be an increase from 1.8 percent to 2.4 percent of aluminum's share of the total power requirements.

Aluminum's power problem has been stated in two ways, the first by the President's Materials Policy Commission and the second by the Bureau of Mines: (1) "The principal question then is whether an adequate supply of power will be available for aluminum production in the next 25 years at a real price that will not impede the industry's growth." (2) "Assurance of adequate, steady, low cost electrical power has become one of the greatest problems in the reduction phase of the domestic aluminum industry." Both of these statements emphasize the cost factor.

The Bureau of Mines comments: "Power generated from natural gas, coal, and lignite char [has] been used in place of water power, usually at greater cost per kilowatt-hour. Construction of production facilities in foreign countries whose hydro-electric potentials are undeveloped may also be considered by United States companies."

The President's Materials Policy Commission concludes: "It appears likely that ample quantities of electric power can be made available to meet any possible future expansion of the aluminum industry without significantly increasing the total real cost of production." This conclusion was based on the power potential of the Columbia River system and the large amounts of electric power that could be produced from steam generating plants using gas, coal, or lignite. A key factor in this conclusion is the marked increase in efficiency with which power can be produced from steam generating units.

Probably the most significant effect power availability will have on the aluminum industry will be on its location. Prior to World War II the practice of the industry was to locate the alumina extraction plants as close to the source of bauxite as possible and to establish reduction plants where low-cost hydroelectric power was available. The fabricating plants were located in the market areas for fabricated products. The resulting high total transportation costs were more than offset by the economic advantage of using low-cost hydroelectric power in preference to steam power.

As for the effect of power on the aluminum industry location in the future, the President's Materials Policy Commission concluded:

When total production and marketing costs are taken into account, including the relationship of transportation costs to the location of bauxite, electric power, fabricating facilities, and markets, it appears that no significant increase in the real cost of producing and marketing aluminum would result from using power derived from well-located deposits of coal or lignite, compared to new hydroelectric power in the Pacific Northwest. The trend away from dependence upon hydroelectric power can be expected to continue in the future, and aluminum producers will increasingly have alternative choices in the location of primary reduction capacity, depending upon their own particular cost situations. During the next 25 years, domestic primary aluminum capacity may expand in a number of areas, including the Pacific Northwest, the lignite regions of Texas, and the western Mountain States, and near the low-cost coal deposits of Tennessee and the Ohio Valley.

Thus the conclusion can be drawn that the aluminum industry's specific power problem is not one of overall availability but one of sustained low-cost power. The manner in which it was to be solved for the three large new aluminum developments projected on the Ohio River was fully covered in the section on coal. These plants were Kaiser at Ravenswood, West Virginia, and Olin-Mathieson, and Revere at Hannibal, Ohio. This is a move of industry to coal. Similarly, expansion of capacity of the Aluminum Company at Massena, New York, and the new plant of Reynolds Metals Company at Massena, as firm users of power, were seen to be contributing factors to the solution of the St. Lawrence hydro-power controversy. Plant location in the future will be determined by power costs, but these will be analyzed in terms of total costs of production and marketing. It is possible that the result may be more integrated plants. The fact still remains that electric power is of critical importance to the aluminum industry and its power requirements must be integrated with the total power requirements of the electric power industry. Finally, the United States government's concern in this matter is the relation of the aluminum industry's power problem to the total power problem. The solution of the industry's power problems must be achieved in harmony with the electric power policies recommended for the entire industry. Current developments in 1957 in achieving this objective were encouraging.

C. Security

Aluminum's vital importance for military purposes, coupled with the fact that known economic reserves are inadequate, places both aluminum and bauxite in Group I of the list of Strategic and Critical Materials for Stockpiling. In addition we have seen that United States government policy has been directed toward promoting the growth of the industry by: (1) a bauxite exploration program of the Bureau of Mines and the Federal Geological Survey; (2) erection of government-owned industry-operated facilities; and (3) fast tax write-offs, government-guaranteed loans, and guaranteed markets.

Table 82 shows the extent to which the United States relied on foreign sources of bauxite from 1940 through 1953. Reserves compared with requirements for the growing aluminum industry led the Bureau of Mines

TABLE 82.   United States Self-Sufficiency in Bauxite for Selected Years
(thousand long tons)

Years	Domestic Production (Long Tons, Dry Basis)	Imports (Crude and Dried, Long Tons as Imported)			Percent Self-Sufficiency $\left(\dfrac{\text{Domestic production}}{\text{Imports} + \text{domestic production}} \times 100\right)$
		Ja-maica	South America	Total	
1940	439	—	616	630	41
1943	6,233	—	1,548	1,548	80
1946	1,104	—	851	852	56
1949	1,149	—	2,113	2,688	30
1952	1,667	265	3,214	3,498	32
1953	1,580	1,176	3,202	4,389	26

SOURCE: *Mineral Facts and Problems.*

to this conclusion: If the United States had to be entirely self-sufficient with respect to raw materials for over five years, grades of reserves would have to be used that have never been employed commercially; however, low-grade domestic reserves can be used by known processes if cost is no consideration. Further, if another wartime emergency should cut off imports from South America, but not Jamaica, the United States could import enough bauxite to maintain its aluminum production without large increases in production costs.

Table 83 indicates that aluminum imports have been much smaller than

TABLE 83. United States Imports and Exports Compared to Production
of Primary and Secondary Aluminum[a]
(thousand short tons)

	1940	1943	1946	1949	1952	1953
Production: Primary and secondary	287	1,234	688	784	1,242	1,621
Imports:						
Crude (pig, ingot)	17	136	41	77	128	301
Semifabricated	—	—	1	8	16	32
Scrap	1	—	15	40	7	27
Total	18	136	57	125	151	360
Exports:						
Crude (pig, ingot)	12	57	1	8	1	2
Semifabricated	15	61	15	29	8	8
Scrap	1	—	1	—	1	5
Total	28	118	17	37	10	15
Net imports:						
Crude (pig, ingot)	5	79	40	69	127	299
Semifabricated	−15	−61	−14	−21	8	24
Scrap	—	—	14	40	6	22
Total	−10	18	40	88	141	345

[a] Compiled from records of the U.S. Department of Commerce.
SOURCE: *Mineral Facts and Problems.*

domestic production. Semifabricated aluminum products showed a net import balance for the first time in 1951. Except for 1939 and 1944, crude aluminum has shown a net import balance, and most of this metal has come from Canada. Total United States aluminum supply in 1956 was 2,348,000 tons. The sources were: domestic primary production, 1,683,000 tons; primary imports, 244,000 tons; scrap, 421,000 tons.

The stockpiles of bauxite and aluminum are an excellent means of providing for emergency needs. National policy in implementing the stockpiling program should take into account that an aluminum stockpile has many advantages; it represents a stockpile of electric power, ocean transportation, labor, and time. The latter is of critical importance to the military.

Import policy must be directed toward aluminum and bauxite. The new Canadian aluminum plant at Kitimat, British Columbia, was designed for an expansion to a capacity of 550,000 tons. Most of this production was expected to be exported. There are several factors that would favor increased imports from Canada. Before these are considered it should be pointed out, that although for military planning Canada is strategically well situated as a supplier to the United States, Canadian production depends entirely on imports of ore. For 1955, estimates were that the United States would import about 225,000 tons of aluminum from Canada; this was about one-third of Canada's output for 1955 and should be compared with United States production of 1,500,000 tons in 1955.

Security considerations permitting, it is possible that in the future the United States could secure an increasing part of its aluminum supply from Canada and possibly from overseas sources where abundant low-cost power is potentially available near large bauxite deposits. The President's Materials Policy Commission recommended that, to the extent cost of producing aluminum may be higher in the United States than elsewhere, the United States should encourage expansion of primary output abroad in so far as cost savings are passed on and within the limits of security. "If the lower costs of the Canadian production were to be passed on to the United States consumers, there would be a strong argument for greater dependence on Canadian production with appropriate adjustments of stockpile policy to conform with military estimates of the security of Canadian installations as compared with those in the United States." On the other hand, the argument is advanced that increased imports and/or lower prices for aluminum might act to the detriment of the United States policy of furthering the domestic expansion of aluminum production and encouraging new concerns to participate in the industry.

The tariff policy recommended by the President's Materials Policy Commission was that the tariff should be neither so high as to prevent recourse to low-cost sources outside the United States nor so low that it leads to an unbalanced dependence on foreign plants. The Commission concluded that there was no justification for the United States bauxite tariff of 50 cents a long ton, in view of the dependence on foreign bauxite and the desirability of slowing down the rate of withdrawal of domestic bauxite reserves. It would appear that a tariff on bauxite is unjustified;

and even more significantly the suspended tariff of 1.5 cents per pound on aluminum scrap should not be reimposed. United States tariff on aluminum pig and ingot is 1.5 cents a pound. The President's Commission concluded that the tariff of 3 cents per pound on fabricated aluminum in the form of coil, sheet, plate, and bars was unnecessary because of the higher costs of fabrication abroad; it recommended that this tariff be adjusted to correspond with the level of tariff on pig and ingot, allowing for the fact that to produce a pound of fabricated aluminum requires more than a pound of aluminum.

All the above suggests that, as far as security considerations permit, lower-cost aluminum production facilities in Canada and possibly those along the northern coast of South America should be included in the pattern of future development of United States supplies, with appropriate adjustments in tariff and stockpiling policies.

Further, in so far as the domestic industry is concerned, government policy should be directed toward a sustained interest in the growth of the industry.

5. Conclusion

The aluminum industry is representative of the light metal age. Its principal problems are those associated with growth—past, present, and future. Most significant have been the problems of making the industry more competitive and providing adequate growth of productive capacity for security purposes. Sustained government-industry coöperation will be required to achieve this latter objective. Government policies will be directed toward the task of insuring requirements for military purposes. United States government policy will continue to strive for greater competition in the industry and to see that adequate electric power is available. One very delicate problem will be the reconciliation of the security needs of the United States with low-cost producing possibilities elsewhere in the Western Hemisphere. Government policy in the future requires a sustained surveillance of the industry and, when necessary, will be implemented by fast tax write-offs, long-term purchase contracts, the stockpile program, and possible tariff adjustments.

CHAPTER 10

Energy and Material Resources

Problems and Policy

This is the concluding chapter of the three parts on natural resources in this Unit Two on Strength and Production Potentials. The plan of Part III—Energy and Material Resources—was to discuss briefly certain general characteristics of mineral resources and minerals that give rise to special problems; then to study separately and in detail energy and materials; and finally, in this chapter, to summarize briefly and collectively some of the United States' problems and policy in the area.

The basic problem of this entire study is: How can we raise our plane of living by making economic progress and at the same time attain a maximum degree of security and a maximum amount of individual and national freedom in a political democracy? The objective of economic progress places an ever-increasing burden upon our energy and material resources. Requirements for security add to this burden.

World War II proved emphatically the productive strength of the United States economy and showed the possibility of channeling this strength to achieve economic progress; but at the same time, the drains of the war on the resource base gave rise to the question this nation had never before considered seriously: Have we the resources for freedom?

To answer this question the President appointed the Materials Policy Commission on January 22, 1951. The Commission saw "as its central task an examination of the adequacy of materials to meet the needs of the free world in the years ahead." The report was made in June, 1952. The problem was found to be larger and more pervasive than a "shortage" problem, local and transient, which in the past has found its solution in price changes that have brought supply and demand back into balance.

Powerful historical streams have converged to make the problem uniquely intense today. First, there has been a profound shift in the basic materials position of the United States—a worsening relationship between our requirements and our means of satisfying them. Second, other high-consuming nations, primarily in Western Europe, are in difficulties which stem from the serious depletion of their own domestic resources coupled with the weakening or severing of their former colonial ties. Third, many resource-rich but less-developed nations, especially of former colonial status, now focus on industrialization rather than materials export. Fourth, there lingers from the Great Depression a worldwide fear of the possible collapse of markets, which dampens the willingness of private investors and resource-rich countries to develop new free world resources. Finally, a great schism divides the world between the totalitarian and democratic nations, disrupting normal trade patterns and making necessary costly measures of armed preparedness.

The fundamental concepts upon which the report was based were clearly stated:

First, we share the belief of the American people in the principle of Growth. Granting that we cannot find any absolute reason for this belief we admit that to our Western minds it seems preferable to any opposite, which to us implies stagnation and decay. Whether there may be any unbreakable upper limits to the continuing growth of our economy we do not pretend to know, but it must be part of our task to examine such apparent limits as present themselves.

Second, we believe in private enterprise as the most efficacious way of performing industrial tasks in the United States. With this belief, a belief in the spur of the profit motive and what is called "the price system" obviously go hand in hand. This method, motive, and system have served uniquely well in America. We believe in a minimum of interference with these patterns of private enterprise. But to believe this is not to believe that this minimum must be set at zero. Private enterprise itself has from time to time asked for helps, or restraints, or counterpoises from Government to keep the system working at its best; for this reason, among others, we have experienced for a long time a mixture of private and public influences on our economy. The Commission sees no reason either to blink this fact or to decry it; as we see the future, the co-existence of great private and public strength is not only desirable but essential to our preservation.

Third, we believe that the destinies of the United States and the rest of the free non-Communist world are inextricably bound together. This belief implies, for example, that if the United States is to increase its imports of raw materials —as we believe it must—it must return in other forms strength for strength to match what it receives. It is this Commission's belief that if we fail to work for a rise in the standard of living of the rest of the free world, we thereby hamper and impede the further rise of our own, and equally lessen the chances of democracy to prosper and peace to reign the world over.

Security and economic growth for the United States and the rest of the free world must be the essential aim of any policy worth the name. Materials strength is a prime ingredient of general economic strength and growth. This Commission is convinced that if the United States and other free nations are to have such strength they must coordinate their resources to the ends of common growth, common safety, and common welfare. In turn, this means that the United States must reject self-sufficiency as a policy and instead adopt the policy of the lowest cost acquisition of materials wherever secure supplies may be found: self-sufficiency, when closely viewed, amounts to a self-imposed blockade and nothing more.

The major premise upon which all the report was based was as follows: "The over-all objective of a national Materials Policy for the United States should be to insure an adequate and dependable flow of materials at the lowest cost consistent with national security and with the welfare of friendly nations."

The Commission found in brief that "In area after area we encounter soaring demands, shrinking resources, the consequent pressure toward rising real costs, the risk of wartime shortages, the strong possibility of an arrest or decline in the standard of living we cherish and hope to share." "The Materials Problem now demands that we give new and deep consideration to the fundamental upon which all employment, all daily activity, eventually rests: the contents of the earth and its physical environment."

The dynamic nature of changing demands, technology, resource availability, political, economic, and military factors continuously create new problems and call for sustained study and policy recommendations and action. There is plenty of evidence that the United States government and private industry have been alerted to the dynamic nature of the energy and material problems and have taken action.

The United States government followed the President's Materials Policy Commission Report with: *A Trade and Tariff Policy in the National Interest*, a report to the President, February, 1953; *Commission on Foreign Economic Policy*, a report to the President and the Congress, January, 1954; *The Report of the President's Cabinet Committee on Minerals Policy*, November, 1954; and *The Report on Energy Supplies and Resources Policy* by the President's Advisory Committee, February, 1955. In 1956 the Bureau of Mines published *Mineral Facts and Problems*. These major reports were augmented by hundreds of significant separate studies which led to the establishment of policy and its implementation.

Private industry became acutely aware of the post-World War II energy and materials problems and has progressively solved many of them and thus contributed to the sustained growth and strength of the United States economy.

But what of the future? In summary, sustained action is required in the domestic and in the international area, and in the integration of the two to provide for an adequate mobilization base and its expansion for security purposes. The coördination and implementation of these three inseparable parts must be accomplished by government-industry coöperation.

In the domestic area more energy and materials can be obtained by working on the supply and use problems. On the supply side more resources can be made available by exploration and discovery, more efficient extraction, using lower-grade reserves, employing flow resources, using presently unemployable reserves, synthesizing new material, and developing technologies to accomplish unknown tasks. On the use side "phantom resources" can be created by shifting from the scarce to the abundant, using energy and materials more efficiently, and using more scrap.

In the international area these same recommendations will increase the available supplies of resources. The United States' role is to make available its technology and its capital, and to adopt a trade policy which will lead to the most efficient use of the world's energy and material resources.

Mobilization and security plans must be continually revised, while we remain ever mindful of the fact that energy and materials are one of the basic requisites of productivity; "only the productive can be strong and only the strong can be free."

Government-industry coöperation is required to study the ever-changing problems, to formulate policy, and to initiate and execute the required action in the above three inseparable areas. To this end, the President's Cabinet Committee on Minerals Policy recommended "that the Secretary of Interior develop ways and means of establishing and maintaining through some workable body the contacts between the mining industry and Government necessary to give force and effect to policies recommended herein." This is not enough. Workable bodies must be developed to aid in the development and implementation of energy and material policies present and future. This is a required, sustaining, and reciprocal task.

The United States can develop the energy and material resources for economic progress, security, and freedom if this nation remains alert and follows the principles of action recommended.

CHAPTER 11

Man-Made Facilities

The basic problem of this study is: How can we raise our plane of living by making economic progress and at the same time attain a maximum degree of security and a maximum amount of individual and national freedom in a political democracy? By economic progress we mean rising planes of living, i.e., increased want satisfaction through increased consumption. How much effective demand a consumer has is a function of his income which is derived through his creation of utilities in the production process. The objective of the production process is the creation of utilities, and production is accomplished through the use of land (natural resources), man-made facilities (capital resources), and manpower (human resources). The primary purpose of this analysis is to study the United States' national resource production potential and policies related thereto.

Natural resources (spatial, agricultural, and energy and material) have been studied in detail. The purpose of Part IV is to discuss capital resources as a contributing factor to production potential, and some United States policies. The topics to be considered are the nature of capital; the function of capital; and problems and policy in the areas of capital facilities and security, investment and growth, and international investment and underdeveloped areas.

THE NATURE OF CAPITAL

Capital is customarily defined as produced goods used in future production. These are sometimes called producer goods, investment goods, or capital goods. One type of investment goods will be emphasized in this chapter: man-made capital facilities. These include buildings, plants, machinery and equipment, electrical and transportation facilities, etc. In addition to capital facilities, capital includes a tremendous amount of raw materials and semifinished and finished materials which fill the industrial "pipelines."

The building of capital facilities is known as "investment." Investment is capital accumulation. In order to accumulate capital (investment) a portion of the national income from current production must be saved. About the only way an agricultural civilization can save is to tighten the belt so that something will be left over for investment. On the other hand a nation which, in addition to "flow" agricultural natural resources, has "fund" natural resources of energy and materials is able to build up net products from its past accumulations. As a result, capital accumulation can be accomplished at a much greater rate. And production potential is increased. It is in this respect that the United States has been and continues to be in a most advantageous position.

THE FUNCTION OF CAPITAL

1. Capital as an Equalizing Agent

The capital which the United States has been able to accumulate because of the advantageous natural resources has been put to its most effective use to overcome the shortage of labor. Capital labor-saving machines have increased the output per worker and have thus increased total income and per capita income.

In western Europe, where labor has been the long factor, or agent, of production and natural resources the short factor, capital has been used to improve the productivity of the land. A particular case in point is the strategy of invention which led to the development of the basic process that made possible the use of the iron reserves of Lorraine. However, with poorer natural resources, the western European countries have had less opportunity to accumulate capital than has the United States.

In many Asiatic countries (e.g., India) labor is so abundant and so cheap that it is not profitable to use capital to the extent that it is used in the United States. There is no incentive to use a harvester for food crops. Some capital accumulation does occur, but only at a slow rate because production barely covers consumption. Thus both the incentive and the capacity to accumulate capital are lacking.

Therefore, in countries rich in natural resources but deficient in manpower, capital made with the aid of natural resources, especially inanimate energy, replaces or supplements manpower. In countries poor in natural resources but rich in manpower, capital made by man through hard work and abstention is used to increase productivity. Capital thus should be used as an equalizing agent which replaces and supplements the short factor of production in order to increase productivity. The important point is that capital varies in its origin and should be so used as to take into account the relationship existing between natural resources and human resources in each area.

2. Investment, Gross National Product, and Income

To maintain the nation's stock of capital facilities there must be enough investment each year to cover the depreciation of the existing facilities. When investment is greater than the rate of depreciation the nation's capital facilities are expanded. Thus the most significant function of investment is that it maintains and expands productive capacity.

Investment is also a component of aggregate expenditure along with personal expenditure and government expenditure. Savings out of current national income are put to work by channeling them into investment. Investment expenditure, like the other components of aggregate demand, is a demand for goods. It creates output, employment, and income. Thus investment increases total income and individual income.

One of the most widely accepted measures of economic development or growth (or rising planes of living) is the extent to which people or regions come to utilize the resources available to bring about a sustained increase in per capita production of goods and services. Over the last several decades output per man-hour has risen about 3 percent a year in the United States. This increase is the joint product of investment, invention, and improvement in skills.

Thus capital has functioned in the United States to facilitate the most effective use of resources and has created a rising plane of living by contributing to the growth of the economy and output per worker and resulting higher incomes. A further conclusion can be drawn that these factors working together have set up a reciprocal relationship between an expanding resource base and greater want satisfaction interacting upon one another to generate an ever-increasing productivity and higher plane of living.

PROBLEMS AND POLICY

The three major capital resource problems and related policies to be studied are: first, capital facilities and security; second, and most important, investment and growth; and third, international investment and underdeveloped areas.

1. Capital Facilities and Security

"Only the productive can be strong and only the strong can be free" (Wendell Willkie). "Without American production, victory would not have been possible" (Stalin).

A. Mobilization of Facilities

Mobilizing capital facilities for security requires:

1. Computation of requirements based upon strategic plans.
2. Determination of what to produce.
3. Determination of which firms produce what items and arrangements therewith for production.
4. Arrangement for current and future facilities, materials, tools, manpower, and other components of the productive process.
5. A system for scheduling and controlling production to include items for the civilian population as well as for the security effort.

Mobilization for production before World War II was started from an economy operating at less than full capacity, and on the basis of completely inadequate mobilization plans. There are possible advantages in the former, but none in the latter.

The obvious advantages of mobilizing an economy that is operating at less than full capacity are that facilities are immediately available for expansion purposes, and thus some time may be gained for the construction of additional facilities which will be required. Nevertheless, there are greater advantages of mobilizing from an expanding economy in which facilities are newer, and research and development are active. In addition, the United States is more likely to institute and maintain industrial preparedness during periods of growth than during recessionary or depressed conditions. During periods of growth, required expenditures for security represent a smaller percentage of aggregate national expenditure.

The United States has had time and resources to afford inadequate mobilization plans in the past; national security will not permit this today. The United States Military Academy has given us a summary of our past production preparedness:

The history of production preparedness prior to 1950 is one of plans and piecemeal arrangements with little tangible effort to maintain ready production capacity for military-type items. The United States entered the World War II emergency with an industrial mobilization plan which had attempted to arrange munitions manufacture with producers on the basis of assumptions as to the military requirements of a war effort. The estimates of requirements proved to be grossly inadequate. The program for teamwork with industry was scrapped, to a considerable extent, with the scrapping of the IMP. But perhaps the salient point is that the United States had no munitions industry worthy of the name, and no effective steps were taken to ready munitions production facilities. There was an attempt in the late 1930's to give industry experience in making munitions through the placing of "educational orders," but the funds appropriated were inadequate. Also, American industry was reluctant to engage in such a program because of the propaganda against "the munitions makers" who had been portrayed as "merchants of death." We were fortunate in making some progress on production preparedness through the impetus given by war orders from the Western allies prior to our own mobilization.

Following World War II the production preparedness program continued. Government agencies and private industry planned which firms would produce specific military-type items in an emergency. Also, 444 plants built by the government, at a construction cost of about $8 billion during World War II, were retained. Some of these plants were in use for their wartime purpose—Navy shipyards and Army arsenals—some were leased to private industries or to other government agencies for civilian-type production, and some stood idle. Government plants leased, sold, or transferred were operated under the so-called "national security clause" which required that they be available on call of the Secretary of Defense for conversion to specified wartime production within 120 days. This reserve included airplane plants costing about $1 billion, explosive and ammunition loading plants costing about $2.5 billion, shipyards worth about $1.75 billion, and about $2.75 billion worth of metal processing, chemicals, and other types of plants. Very few plants in this reserve were complete facilities. The majority of the plants were cannibalized of their productive capacity. In some instances, the plants were not properly maintained, and production equipment was allowed to deteriorate. The reserve was not balanced or nearly sufficient for production of needed military-type items in an all-out mobilization. By the end of the first two years of the Korean emergency, 408 of these plants were in operation and about $6 billion had been appropriated by Congress for expansion of production capacity and for machine tools. . . .

Thinking men had long recognized that the need for ready military production capacity is as pressing as the need for trained reserves. General Eisenhower in 1949 commented that the fundamental defect of past industrial mobilizations had been "the lack during peacetime years of coordinated preparation by the industrial and military establishments for the future effort that would be demanded jointly of them." Prior to 1950 we had no experience forcing us to heed these warnings. During both World Wars, the giant United States industry was given time to prepare for battle. Our allies fought as a covering force for United States industrial mobilization. The meaning of the changed situation since World War II has been accepted reluctantly. Time must now be bought in peacetime through industrial preparedness measures. The experience of the first two years of the Korean war showed the inadequacy of those preparedness measures. Lacking a ready munitions capacity, at least two years was required before supplies of long leadtime military-type items began to flow in volume from production. We had again the warning of experience. In the Korean remobilization, we had to develop an industrial preparedness program containing not only plans and arrangements, but also ready munitions production capacity.[1]

The Office of Defense Mobilization of the Executive Office of the President is charged with the responsibility of coördinating all aspects of the nation's defense mobilization program. In a report to the Director of Defense Mobilization entitled *Production Capacity, A Military Reserve,* the Advisory Committee on Production Equipment stated in January, 1953, that it was "convinced that capacity to produce is, in fact, a military reserve of the highest order." The Committee proposed that the policy of the government, in preparing for a mobilization period, be to substitute, to the greatest extent practicable, production capacity for the stockpiling of military end items. The Committee felt that the suggested policy and the recommendations in support of it were in some respects a new approach to the task of maintaining a strong national defense over an extended period of time, and that the substitution of production capacity for stockpiles of military end items must be recognized by the military departments, the civilian planning agencies, and the Congress. The Committee concluded: "Only when this policy is fully accepted and applied to our mobilization efforts shall we obtain the highest practicable degree of preparedness that defense appropriations can provide."

The development of an industrial mobilization base requires the expansion and maintenance of (1) the basic economic capacity of capital facilities and (2) the capacity for producing military supplies. The first point has the effect of strengthening the basic industries that support

[1] Reprinted by permission from *Economics of National Security*, 2nd ed., by George A. Lincoln and Associates, pp. 332–334. Copyright, 1954, by Prentice-Hall, Inc., Englewood Cliffs, N.J.

munitions production. In addition, this expansion of basic industry permits sustaining a high level of preparedness without materially interfering with the flow of durable consumer goods. The second point means the development of a ready munitions industry and, by implication, a departure from the United States' traditional dependence during war on time-consuming conversion of civilian-type industry and new construction.[2]

The ODM adopted the recommended policy that productive capacity should be the basis of our mobilization program. By the end of 1953 expansion goals had been set for over two hundred industries and products. An expansion goal is a determination of the amount of expansion which should be undertaken to meet defense needs. Many of the goals were determined on the basis of requirements for a partial mobilization program. Others were determined on the basis of preliminary data for full mobilization. The goals indicate the kind and amount of expansion needed for which the government is willing to use rapid tax amortization of investments authorized by amendments to the Internal Revenue Code; and government loans, loan guarantees, and purchase programs authorized by the Defense Production Act. These expansion goals should be continuously reviewed by the ODM in order: (1) to take into account new full mobilization military requirements and overall measures of total mobilization requirements and capacity as they become available, and (2) to make sure that existing goals have an important relation to national security—either for the present defense program or for future mobilization needs.

The ODM adopted as "a prime objective of the defense mobilization program" the maintenance of a mobilization base. "It is our policy to maintain a mobilization base adequate to meet war-time requirements. But maintenance of the base must be carefully defined if we are to avoid costly and ill-advised sustaining and storage programs."

Maintenance of the mobilization base [means] having in readiness that combination of facilities, production equipment, and skilled workers whose production, together with withdrawals from military reserves of weapons, can meet rapidly accelerating war-time requirements. It is a dynamic concept. For any individual item the relative weight of the elements required for an adequate base may change from time to time. As reserves go up, it may be possible to reduce the number of operating production lines. As techniques and arrangements are developed for getting plants back into production quickly, the period over which a sustaining rate of production is continued may be shortened.

[2] *Ibid.*, p. 334.

Conversely, when reserves are low, facilities may have to be maintained in a higher state of readiness.

The program for maintenance of the mobilization base is as follows:

A. *Current production*—Emphasis on current production will diminish as those facilities remaining in production, plus capacity of stand-by facilities and reserves of end items, approach the point at which full mobilization requirements can be met.

B. *Government-owned plants*—When no longer needed for current production, these plants will be placed in stand-by status. The Department of Defense has submitted to ODM a list of such plants which, when no longer needed, will compose the reserve of the military departments and the national industrial reserve. Contractual arrangements are already in existence to insure their maintenance.

C. *Selected privately-owned plants utilizing Department of Defense, Government-owned production equipment*—The Department of Defense has prepared a tentative list of key plants for which it wishes to assume responsibility for developing plans to insure continued availability. The Department is at present consulting with the owners of these plants, some 800 to 900 in number, regarding plans for maintenance.

D. *Government-owned equipment*—In the past, central storage has been used to house Government-owned equipment not required by defense contractors. The experience since 1945 has shown that this does not provide a fully satisfactory solution, although it may continue to be necessary to resort to that method in the case of private plants where the number of Government-owned tools involved is small. Central storage can prevent deterioration of tools but, once tools from a number of plants have been placed in a common warehouse, their plant identity may be lost. Delay is likely to occur in distributing them for effective use in a new emergency. There is also the added cost of transportation and handling, and the possibility of shipping bottlenecks when they are needed again.

For these reasons, whenever possible, arrangements will be made to keep Government-owned equipment in or near the plant in which it may again be required. Where there is room on the owner's premises for the storage of the tools, negotiations will be initiated to work out satisfactory arrangements for maintenance. Where the owner has no space in or near the plant, the use of adjacent sheds or warehouses may be necessary.

E. *Private defense plants not containing Government equipment*—For many private plants, peace-time use is sufficient to insure adequate maintenance. In some instances peace-time demand, after the completion of current defense production programs, will be insufficient to supply the incentive for continued maintenance. In this event a positive determination must be made of the essentiality of such plants for meeting national defense needs in the future. Then the types of arrangements and incentives that the Government should offer to insure necessary maintenance must be developed by the Executive Branch and presented to Congress.[3]

[3] *Defense Mobilization,* Report to the President by the Director of the Office of Defense Mobilization, October 1, 1953, pp. 15–16.

An interagency Defense Facilities Maintenance Board was created to develop additional concrete recommendations for dealing with the problem of maintenance of the mobilization base.

B. Decentralization of Facilities

Prior to World War II Russia decentralized her heavy industry behind the Urals. This measure of economic-military planning enabled her to trade time for space when Germany occupied or destroyed her other major industrial areas. When the United States began to award defense contracts prior to World War II the War Department Planning Branch issued a statement of factors which were required to be given consideration in selecting locations for new munition plants. The first three of these factors were as follows: (a) The location should be such as would assure the earliest possible production of powder or shells. (b) The area selected should be reasonably secure from long-range bombing operations, preferably located between the Allegheny and Rocky Mountains and strategically placed with reference to the North and South borders. (c) The new plants should be distributed so as to avoid adding any more than necessary to the existing concentration of defense industry in limited areas. In addition, the War Department expressed a desire to decentralize all defense contracts and established as a requirement that all new defense plants should be located at least 250 miles inland.

Defense Commissioner of Agriculture Chester Davis established a Division of Rural Labor and Plant Location in an attempt to carry out the War Department's desire to decentralize. A study made by the writer in 1941 led to the conclusion that these early attempts were a failure. "What happened was that the centripetal pull of established industrial centers was once again too great to be offset by a mere desire to decentralize. Orders went to plants already established. And when expansion of plant capacity was necessary, industrialists were anxious to expand at or near their existing location. When they proved that such a move would mean going into production sixty to ninety days earlier, they won their case. . . . Thus the net result of the first phase of the defense program was to further concentrate production facilities in limited areas."[4]

A study of *The Geographic Distribution of Manufacturing Facilities Expansion* made by the War Production Board near the end of World War II and published in June, 1945, drew this general conclusion:

[4] Olin T. Mouzon, *The Industrial Role of North Carolina and the South in National Defense*, Chapel Hill, North Carolina, 1941, p. 3.

"*Concentration of expansion.* Military and economic considerations resulted in a heavy concentration of these war expansions in the same states and areas where specific industries had chiefly operated before the war. This conclusion runs counter to impressions that a widespread relocation of industrial plants has occurred. Actually, effective dispersion has been the exception rather than the rule. Certain exceptions are important, however; new facilities now exist in areas previously not devoted to such industries."

During the Korean War the Joint Committee on the Economic Report published a study in 1951 by the Committee staff: *The Need for Industrial Dispersal*. The Committee calls attention to the fact that the National Security Resources Board issued Executive Order 10172 for the administration of the accelerated amortization program. The order emphasized the need for considering, among other criteria, the necessity for and adequacy of facilities or materials or services for a particular region, the location of the facility with due regard to military security, and the availability of manpower, housing, community facilities, transportation, and other elements of production. The Committee on the Economic Report pointed out:

Despite these objectives and instructions, the House Committee on Expenditures in the Executive Department was led to observe, after extensive hearings on all phases of the program, that—

"One of the crucial questions which has arisen in the administration of the certificate-of-necessity program concerns the dispersal of industry. Under the present policy no effort is being made by the government to control the location of new facilities through certificates; the selection of the site is left entirely to the applicant. Quite naturally, this policy results in further concentration of industry in areas favored by economic factors wholly without regard to considerations of military security or the avoidance of knock-out blows in the event of a sudden enemy attack. Moreover, not only has the Government taken no initiative in this direction but has refused to aid, through a higher percentage certificate, an applicant who proposed to construct a facility in a location chosen primarily for reasons of military security. (Fifth Intermediate Report, May 28, 1951.)"

Plant location has become a science of evaluating economic factors. The United States experience to date has shown that decentralization for security purposes has had very little weight in the building of new facilities. In a program of mobilization this past policy, or lack of one, makes no sense.

The advent of atomic explosives, the long-range airplane and submarine, and the guided missile make the location of industry a matter of national security.

Active defense measures can be only partially effective, as General Vandenberg explained in the following terms: "Should war come, we can be expected to destroy not more than 30 percent of the planes making an attack on the United States before their bombing missions are completed. And our preparations today are not yet beefed up to achieve even that figure. Even if we had many more interceptor planes and antiaircraft guns and a radar screen that blanketed all approaches to our boundaries, a predictable 70 percent of the enemy's planes would penetrate our defenses despite the extraordinary valor and skill of our pilots." Actual defense against other types of carriers of atomic warheads will continue to be very difficult.

Active defense measures therefore must be combined with passive measures, which include cover, concealment, and dispersion. Cover is the most effective, but the following statement indicates why it is not practical on a large scale:

"Any solution must reflect a judicious balance between economic possibility and reasonable strategic security. Underground installations, although probably providing maximum protection, are not thought practical for application on a large scale. Among other things, they generally entail higher construction costs. This is also true of special construction of above ground facilities employing fire, blast, or radiation resistant materials. Resort to this type of security will probably be economically justifiable only in connection with such highly strategic facilities as may be determined by the Armed Forces."[5]

Successful concealment, according to the United States Military Academy, requires that an installation be hidden from observation of eyes and instruments. It is a useful supplement to other measures of defense and includes the use of camouflage, dummy plants, and smoke screens but cannot be expected to be effective when used alone.

Dispersion is the most effective passive measure for guarding against atomic attack. Dispersion for defense purposes does not necessarily mean the relocation or new development of industry far from its former site. The National Security Resources Board bulletin recommends that, wherever possible, areas of industry concentration be held to less than five square miles, or located in urban concentrations of less than 50,000 separated by about ten miles of relatively open country. The purpose of this recommendation is to restrict urban concentrations below some size which makes them attractive as a target of attack and to disperse the concentrations so that no two are close enough to form one target.

[5] *National Security Factors in Industrial Location,* National Security Resources Board, September, 1948.

This type of recommended dispersion of facilities would mean (a) that many industries which need to be integrated with established facilities could be dispersed in existing production and marketing areas, and (b) that other plants that do not need to be closely integrated with related industry could be located in the many underdeveloped industrial areas of the United States.

Thus mobilization and decentralization of facilities might be accomplished in accordance with the conclusions and recommendations of the Joint Committee on the Economic Report.

The requirements of a defense economy operating at peak capacity and the need for strategic location against possible atomic attack make essential the increasing dispersion of industrial facilities in the United States. Present Government programs providing for accelerated tax amortization, direct guaranteed loans, and direct construction have tended to add to rather than relieve existing industrial concentration. There are a number of criteria which if used in guiding the direction of future expansion could do much to insure maximum military and economic security but no adequate machinery now exists for insuring that these considerations get into the procurement, amortization, or loan process.

It is recommended that the Defense Production Act be amended to the end that adequate steps be taken by all departments of Government concerned with the expansion of industrial facilities to insure a pattern of industrial development which would:

1. Consider the advantages of the present distribution of communities and production facilities and employ their present and potential productivity to a maximum.
2. In accordance with this aim, minimize the occasion for needless migration of labor, with the attendant dislocation of State, local, and family institutions.
3. Establish new or expanded facilities in areas which have greater geographic security from enemy attack.
4. Establish new or expanded plants in areas which have the potential transport, labor, and other requirements so as to economize, by avoiding undue or overconcentration in already-congested areas.
5. Develop, as natural results of plant, corporate, industrial, and geographic decentralization, the opportunities for smaller, medium-sized local businesses and industries to undertake more direct participation in the defense effort, and by opportunity for normal growth to add to the productive capacities of the economy.[6]

There are two very obvious advantages to decentralization or dispersal of facilities. The first is that dispersal is a requirement for defense

[6] *The Need for Industrial Dispersal*, Senate Joint Committee on the Economic Report, Government Printing Office, 1951, pp. 6–7.

purposes. The second is that dispersal can be used to add capital facilities in underdeveloped areas. The accomplishment of these two ends with an expanding mobilization base will increase the total strength and security of the United States.

2. Investment and Growth

Investment is necessary for growth and leads to rising planes of living by increasing output and income per worker. Thus the principal problem with respect to capital resources is sustained growth of investment. Herein lies the strength of productive capacity.

An editorial by McGraw-Hill Publishing Company, "Business Investment Holds Key to Both Growth and Stability," points up the necessity and advantages of investment for growth and argues that overinvestment, which has been considered to contribute to instability, is no longer a problem.

There is general agreement that *the key to economic growth is investment in new plant and equipment.* Growth depends decisively on new facilities to increase production, and also to produce new and better products in new and better ways. At the same time, new plant investment provides employment for the important, and well-paid, one-fourth of our industrial workers who manufacture and build new production facilities. So if the process of business investment is kept on an even keel, the result is not only growth but also stability in a substantial sector of our economy.

But authorities disagree on the possibility of maintaining a high level of business investment for any great length of time. Some fear that it will lead to an excess of producing capacity and the glutting of markets, with recession or depression not far behind.

The history of our country offers some basis for the fear that it is dangerous to maintain a very high level of business investment. There have been times when the economy has suffered under the weight of excess producing capacity. *This fear, however, has been made obsolete by the recent course of our economic history which, in its earlier phases, nourished the fear.*

Here are some of the major considerations, cited at the Joint [Economic Committee of Congress] hearings, which support the conclusion that we not only *can have* a high level of business investment and economic stability but that we actually *need* a high level of such investment to assure stability.

(1) Over the next 20 years our population is expected to increase by about one-third. But most of the population increase will come in age groups younger or older than normal working ages, and people will probably work fewer hours per week. Thus hours worked are not expected to increase more than 15%. Consequently, we must have a relatively large increase in the amount of production equipment per worker if our standard of living is not to suffer. This means a high level of new investment.

(2) About half of our present business investment goes to replace worn-out

equipment, rather than to expand capacity as was true during the early stages of our industrial development.

(3) Thanks largely to the impact of organized research—for which we as a nation now spend about $4 billion a year—a large share of capital investment now goes to provide new products and new processes, rather than to expand existing capacity.

These developments make it unlikely that we shall develop the burden of excess capacity that plagued the economy in earlier periods. *Moreover, most capital investment plans are now made on a long-range basis. Companies are building facilities to anticipate their needs for several years ahead.* This increase in long-range planning has reduced the disturbing effects of temporary shortages and excesses in producing capacity.

What then are the prospects for growth and investment? The key factor in projecting economic growth is productivity, which strictly defined means the amount of national product resulting from one man-hour of labor. Based on the assumption that the labor force would increase to 82 million by 1970 (a dependable forecast, since the people who will increase that force are already born) and that there would be an increase in output per man-hour of 2.5 percent per year, the estimation by McGraw-Hill was that gross national product would grow from $367 billion in 1953 to $415 billion in 1960 and $560 billion by 1970 in 1953 prices. These estimates allow for a drop in the average work week from forty-one hours in 1953 to thirty-eight hours in 1960 and only thirty-five hours by 1970. To keep pace with the growth of population to 200 million and gross national product, the estimate indicated that 65 percent increase in manufacturing capacity would be needed by 1970. Electric power companies were seen to need three times their generating capacity. Railroads and truck operators would require equipment to handle 80 percent more freight. All these needs for new capacity and needs for modernization indicated a requirement of as much as $32 billion per year of business capital expenditure in 1960 and over $40 billion by 1970.[7] Figure 11.1 gives business capital spending and capacity in manufacturing from 1930 to 1950 and estimates for 1960 and 1970.

During 1956 the indicated required investment for growth based on the above estimate appeared to be no longer a problem. Capital spending was $29.2 billion in 1953, $27.9 billion in 1954, and $30.0 billion in 1955. McGraw-Hill's May 19 survey for 1956 indicated that businessmen were planning to spend $39.0 billion for new plants and equipment. This was up 30 percent from 1955, and above the $32 billion that

[7] *The American Economy—Prospects for Growth 1950 · 1960 · 1970*, McGraw-Hill Publishing Company, Inc., 1954, p. 9.

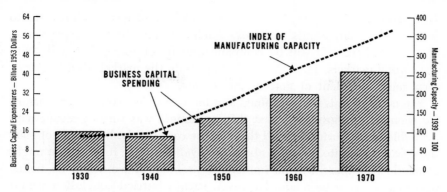

Figure 11.1.   Business Capital Spending and Capacity in Manufacturing. (Data from U.S. Department of Commerce; McGraw-Hill Department of Economics)

McGraw-Hill had previously estimated would be required by 1960. In addition, the survey showed that industry was making preliminary plans as far ahead as 1959, as indicated in Figure 11.2. A previous McGraw-Hill study also showed that three out of four companies intended to maintain or raise their capital expenditures in 1957. The conclusion was drawn that since, in the past, companies have usually added to their advance estimates as time went on, "the capital goods boom promises to hold its great momentum through the next two years."

One question that had to be answered before the above conclusion was reached was: "Can all this be financed?" The answer that McGraw-

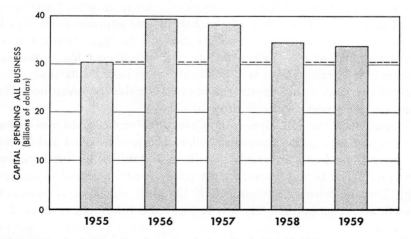

Figure 11.2.   Capital Spending. (Data from *Business Week*, May 19, 1956, by special permission)

Hill gave was "Yes." Yes, because the great bulk of new facilities was to be paid for from profits and from funds accumulating in depreciation reserves. "There will still be companies, many of them, that will go to the capital markets. Their demands may strain the market—but businessmen seem confident of getting the money."

The conclusion is that sustained and increasing investment is necessary for economic progress and that this investment was surging ahead with available funds during 1956. If this was the case (at the beginning of 1957 there was a definite question about the availability of funds), one might conclude that there was no immediate problem at hand and no policy decisions were to be made. However, such a hurried conclusion would ignore the fact that established policy had brought about these favorable results. What was this policy?

The Employment Act of 1946 charged the federal government with the responsibility "to use all practical means . . . to promote maximum employment production, and purchasing power." Both major political parties have accepted the obligation imposed by the Employment Act that the federal government work to maintain high and stable employment. However, the policy of the Eisenhower administration was to encourage long-term growth through investment under conditions favorable to free enterprise. These conditions were spelled out in detail in the Economic Report of the President of January, 1955, and in Chapter 3—"Program for Sustained Economic Progress"—in particular.

The level of investment depends on many factors—the degree of business confidence, the strength of consumer markets, the attitude of organized labor toward the use of more efficient machinery, government fiscal policy, etc. The policy of the Eisenhower administration was to create a favorable climate for business and thus the "Eisenhower Factor" was an important contributing factor to business confidence. But the Eisenhower administration was particularly emphatic in its stress upon tax policies that would create conditions favorable to investment "for fostering long-term economic growth."

During 1955 the Joint Economic Committee of Congress was asking a "crucially important question in public hearings": "What federal tax policy will best promote both growth and stability in the American economy?" The thought was that tax policy must be geared to foster a high level of business investment, if the dual objective of economic growth and economic stability was to be attained. Limited revisions had been made to achieve these objectives—e.g., the allowance of the $50 dividend exemption and dividend credit on personal income tax—but corporation taxes were maintained at the 52 percent rate. One could argue that since investment was continuing at such a high level no tax revisions were necessary. However, the important factor to businessmen was the recognition of the need of tax and other fiscal policies that would facilitate investment.

The conclusion can be drawn that government policies were directed toward conditions favorable for investment and growth and economic progress. The Economic Report of the President to Congress of January, 1956, again "urged concentration of governmental policy on facilitating long-term growth, rather than on measures for imparting an immediate upward thrust to the economy."

Finally, let President Eisenhower speak for himself on two topics in his letter to the Congress of the United States, January 24, 1956:

Recent Economic Achievements

Full employment, rising incomes, and a stable dollar have been cherished goals of our society. The practical attainment of these ideals during 1955 was the year's great economic achievement.

The past year has brought fresh witness to the basic strength and resiliency of our economy. We have broken through to new and higher ground, and have reached the threshold of a 400 billion dollar economy.

[The statistical extent of this breakthrough and the growth of investment expenditure are shown in Table 84. The detailed growth of business investment expenditure for new plant and equipment, 1939 and 1945–56, is given in Table 85.]

Building for Future Prosperity

Lasting prosperity of the Nation depends far more on what individuals do for themselves than on what the Federal Government does or can do for them. The rate of our economic advance in the years ahead will depend largely on our ability as a people to preserve an environment that rewards individual initiative and encourages enterprise, innovation, and *investment*.

Government can contribute to the strengthening of competitive enterprise through monetary, fiscal, and housekeeping policies that promote high and rising levels of economic activity. . . .

3. International Investment and Underdeveloped Areas

The third and final capital resources problem we will study is that of international investment and underdeveloped areas. As we have just been looking at our domestic policy of growth and investment, the following from the January, 1956, Economic Report of the President summarizes in part the United States policy in "Promoting the International Flow of Goods and Capital."

TABLE 84. National Income or Expenditure, 1929–55
(billions of dollars)

Period	Total Gross National Product	Personal Consumption Expenditures	Gross Private Domestic Investment						Net Foreign Investment	Government Purchases of Goods and Services					
			Total	New Construction			Producers' durable equipment	Net change in business inventories		Total	Federal				State and local
				Total	Residential (nonfarm)	Other					Total	National security	Other	Less: Government sales	
1929	104.4	79.0	16.2	8.7	3.6	5.1	5.8	1.7	0.8	8.5	1.3				7.2
1930	91.1	71.0	10.3	6.2	2.1	4.1	4.5	−.4	.7	9.2	1.4				7.8
1931	76.3	61.3	5.5	4.0	1.6	2.4	2.8	−1.3	.2	9.2	1.5				7.7
1932	58.5	49.3	.9	1.9	.6	1.2	1.6	−2.6	.2	8.1	1.5				6.6
1933	56.0	46.4	1.4	1.4	.5	1.0	1.6	−1.6	.2	8.0	2.0				6.0
1934	65.0	51.9	2.9	1.7	.6	1.1	2.3	−1.1	.4	9.8	3.0				6.8
1935	72.5	56.3	6.3	2.3	1.0	1.3	3.1	.9	−.1	10.0	2.9				7.1
1936	82.7	62.6	8.4	3.3	1.6	1.7	4.2	1.0	−.1	11.8	4.8				7.0
1937	90.8	67.3	11.7	4.4	1.9	2.5	5.1	2.2	.1	11.7	4.6				7.2
1938	85.2	64.6	6.7	4.0	2.0	2.0	3.6	−.9	1.1	12.8	5.3				7.5
1939	91.1	67.6	9.3	4.8	2.7	2.1	4.2	.4	.9	13.3	5.2	1.3	3.9		8.2
1940	100.6	71.9	13.2	5.5	3.0	2.5	5.5	2.2	1.5	14.1	6.2	2.2	4.0		7.9
1941	125.8	81.9	18.1	6.6	3.5	3.1	6.9	4.5	1.1	24.8	16.9	13.8	3.2		7.8
1942	159.1	89.7	9.9	3.7	1.7	2.0	4.3	1.8	−.2	59.7	52.0	49.6	2.7	0.2	7.7
1943	192.5	100.5	5.6	2.3	.9	1.4	4.0	−.8	−2.2	88.6	81.2	80.4	1.5	.6	7.4
1944	211.4	109.8	7.1	2.7	.8	1.9	5.4	−1.0	−2.1	96.5	89.0	88.6	1.6	1.2	7.5
1945	213.6	121.7	10.4	3.8	1.1	2.7	7.7	−1.1	−1.4	82.9	74.8	75.9	1.0	2.2	8.1
1946	209.2	146.6	27.1	10.3	4.0	6.3	10.7	6.1	4.6	30.9	20.9	21.2	2.5	2.7	10.0
1947	232.2	165.0	29.7	14.0	6.3	7.7	16.7	−1.0	8.9	28.6	15.8	13.3	3.8	1.3	12.8
1948	257.3	177.6	41.2	17.9	8.6	9.3	19.1	4.2	2.0	36.6	21.0	16.0	5.6	.5	15.6
1949	257.3	180.6	32.5	17.5	8.3	9.2	17.8	−2.7	.5	43.6	25.4	19.3	6.6	.4	18.2
1950	285.1	194.0	51.2	22.7	12.6	10.1	21.1	7.4	−2.2	42.0	22.1	18.5	3.9	.3	19.9
1951	328.2	208.3	56.9	23.3	11.0	12.4	23.2	10.4	.2	62.8	41.0	37.3	4.2	.4	21.8
1952	345.2	218.3	49.6	23.7	11.1	12.6	23.1	2.8	−.2	77.5	54.3	48.8	5.8	.4	23.2
1953	364.5	230.6	51.4	25.8	11.9	13.8	24.4	1.2	−2.0	84.5	59.5	51.4	8.5	.4	25.0
1954	360.5	236.5	47.2	27.8	13.5	14.3	22.3	−2.9	−.3	77.0	49.2	43.2	6.3	.4	27.8
1955	387.4	252.4	59.4	32.4	16.6	15.8	23.8	3.3	−.3	75.9	45.8	40.8	5.3	.3	30.1

SOURCE: *Economic Report of the President to Congress, 1956.*

The orderly growth of our economy exerts a strongly favorable influence throughout the world. In turn, economic developments abroad are of profound importance to us. Recent experience illustrates this interdependence. By 1953 the nations of the Free World had achieved sufficient economic strength to be able to absorb the adverse reactions from the mild contraction that got under way in the United States that year. Not only that, but they continued buying from us on a scale that helped to check our economic decline and to speed renewed expansion. In turn, the resumed rise of our imports toward the end of 1954, reinforced by a heavy outflow of private capital, helped to sustain economic expansion in other parts of the Free World and thereby stimulated further expansion in our own exports during the past year.

It is clear that our long-term interests are well served by expansion of the international flow of goods, capital, enterprise, and technology. Sound policies

TABLE 85. Business Expenditures for New Plant and Equipment, 1939 and 1945–56
(billions of dollars)

Period	Total[a]	Manufacturing			Mining	Transportation		Public Utilities	Commercial and Other[b]
		Total	Durable Goods	Non-durable Goods		Railroad	Other		
1939	5.51	1.94	0.76	1.19	0.33	0.28	0.36	0.52	2.08
1945	8.69	3.98	1.59	2.39	.38	.55	.57	.50	2.70
1946	14.85	6.79	3.11	3.68	.43	.58	.92	.79	5.33
1947	20.61	8.70	3.41	5.30	.69	.89	1.30	1.54	7.49
1948	22.06	9.13	3.48	5.65	.88	1.32	1.28	2.54	6.90
1949	19.28	7.15	2.59	4.56	.79	1.35	.89	3.12	5.98
1950	20.60	7.49	3.14	4.36	.71	1.11	1.21	3.31	6.78
1951	25.64	10.85	5.17	5.68	.93	1.47	1.49	3.66	7.24
1952	26.49	11.63	5.61	6.02	.98	1.40	1.50	3.89	7.09
1953	28.32	11.91	5.65	6.26	.99	1.31	1.56	4.55	8.00
1954	26.83	11.04	5.09	5.95	.98	.85	1.51	4.22	8.23
1955[c d]	28.27	11.32	5.42	5.90	.93	.93	1.60	4.38	9.11
Seasonally Adjusted Annual Rates									
1953: First quarter	27.84	11.99	5.80	6.19	0.94	1.34	1.47	4.40	7.70
Second quarter	28.10	11.90	5.69	6.21	.91	1.34	1.51	4.52	7.92
Third quarter	28.82	11.94	5.60	6.33	1.03	1.30	1.65	4.81	8.08
Fourth quarter	28.53	11.83	5.53	6.30	1.05	1.26	1.62	4.48	8.28
1954: First quarter	27.46	11.62	5.40	6.22	.94	1.04	1.57	4.33	7.97
Second quarter	26.92	11.09	5.18	5.90	1.04	.91	1.44	4.37	8.07
Third quarter	26.84	10.98	5.06	5.93	1.00	.80	1.51	4.12	8.42
Fourth quarter	26.18	10.58	4.80	5.79	.91	.68	1.53	4.01	8.46
1955: First quarter	25.65	10.17	4.78	5.39	.80	.74	1.46	4.01	8.46
Second quarter	27.19	10.84	5.06	5.78	.94	.80	1.62	4.09	8.90
Third quarter	29.65	11.97	5.77	6.20	.99	.96	1.60	4.43	9.70
Fourth quarter[d]	30.86	12.64	6.23	6.41	.97	1.15	1.66	4.70	9.74
1956: First quarter[d]	31.60	13.44	6.80	6.64	.95	1.41	1.64	4.52	9.64

[a] Excludes agriculture.

[b] Commercial and Other includes trade, service, finance, communications, and construction.

[c] Annual total is sum of seasonally unadjusted quarterly expenditures; it does not necessarily coincide with average of seasonally adjusted figures, which include adjustments, when necessary, for systematic tendencies in anticipatory data.

[d] Estimates for fourth quarter 1955 and first quarter 1956 based on anticipated capital expenditures reported by business in late October and November, 1955.

NOTE.—These figures do not agree precisely with the plant and equipment expenditures included in the gross national product estimates of the Department of Commerce. The main difference lies in the inclusion in the gross national product of investment by farmers, professionals, and institutions, and of certain outlays charged to current account.

This series is not available for years prior to 1939 and for 1940 to 1944.

Detail will not necessarily add to totals because of rounding.

SOURCE: Securities and Exchange Commission and Department of Commerce.

to promote these ends will powerfully advance our national security and economic welfare, and help to build a stronger and more unified community of free nations.

. . . The field of foreign investment also offers opportunities to encourage economic activity and trade on a world scale. A larger outflow of American capital would benefit both ourselves and other economies. By helping to develop the resources of friendly countries, it would enlarge and diversify the supply of materials on which we can draw. At the same time, it would enable less developed countries to achieve higher rates of economic growth and to become more active partners in the trade of the Free World. To the greatest extent possible, the funds for foreign investment should come from private sources. When private capital moves abroad, it is often accompanied by the export of technical, managerial, and financial skills.

It is highly desirable, as stressed in last year's Economic Report, that we "encourage investment in all countries whose desire to speed their economic development has led them to create a hospitable climate for business investment."

President Truman in his Inaugural Address of 1949 outlined four courses of action which he believed the United States should emphasize in its international relations. He assured the world of steadfast adherence to our then current policies; he said we would continue to give unfaltering support to the United Nations and related agencies; we would continue our programs of world recovery; and we would strengthen freedom-loving nations against the dangers of aggression. Then he added a fourth point: "We must embark on a bold new program for making the benefits of our scientific advances and industrial progress available for the improvement and growth of underdeveloped areas. . . . We should make available to peaceloving peoples the benefits of our store of technical knowledge in order to help them realize their aspirations for a better life. And, in cooperation with other nations, we should foster capital investment in areas needing development. Our aim should be to help the free people of the world, through their own efforts, to produce more food, more clothing, more materials for housing, and more mechanical power to lighten their burdens."

The proposed program envisaged two major methods by which international coöperative effort could aid and accelerate economic development. These were (a) the sharing of technical knowledge and skills and (b) the fostering of international investment facilities and equipment.

The Congress of the United States authorized the proposed program in June, 1950, with the passage of the Act for International Development. In that act it was declared to be "the policy of the United States to aid the efforts of the people of economically underdeveloped areas to develop their resources and to improve their working and living conditions by encouraging the exchange of technical knowledge and skills and flow of investment capital to countries which provide conditions which such technical assistance and capital can effectively and constructively contribute to raising standards of living, creating new sources of wealth, increasing productivity and expanding purchasing power."

A. Need

"The traditional model of underdeveloped economies presents the problem of capital formation as a scarcity of total output and income. Given the low level of per capita real income characterizing underdeveloped economies, the model assumes that average and marginal consumption propensities are high, that savings are low, and that the formation of new productive capital is therefore restricted. The low level of capital formation, in turn, sharply restricts the rate of growth in real output, and, allowing for population growth, a tendency toward static equilibrium results, with no growth in per capita real output and no tendency toward such growth. In brief, too much tends to be consumed and too little left over for investment; and this situation in turn perpetuates the initially low level of income."[8]

We have seen that one of the most widely accepted measures of economic development or growth (or rising planes of living) is the extent to which the people of a nation come to utilize the resources available to bring about a sustained increase in per capita production of goods and services. Thus a proper measurement of the degree of development of a nation would be per capita production. However, per capita income is the measure most often used.

The Department of State in its presentation of the great need of the underdeveloped areas expressed the opinion that "the annual income of the people of a country is probably the most representative single indicator of their standard of living. It also provides the most logical criterion for dividing the countries of the world into general groups of well-developed, intermediate and underdeveloped areas." In the State Department's official publication *Point Four,* issued in 1950, the Department stated: "The years just before the war are the last which are generally representative of the relative standards of living of the world's peoples as a whole. They also form the period for which the broadest and most representative figures exist."

The State Department presented, as given in Table 86, the national per capita income in the last prewar year, 1939, of fifty-three countries with 85 percent of the world's population. Ranked in order of highest income, as measured by equivalent value in United States dollars, these countries fell into three definite, clearly distinguishable groups. Group I contains fifteen countries with annual per capita income valued at over

[8] Charles Wolf, Jr., and Sidney C. Sufrin, *Capital Formation and Foreign Investment in Underdeveloped Areas,* Syracuse University Press, 1955, p. 11.

TABLE 86. Per Capita Income, Population, and Population Groups of 53 Countries, 1939

Country	Per Capita Income[a] (U.S. dollars per annum)	Rank	Population (in thousands)[b]	Population Types[c]
Upper income group (over $200):				
United States	$554	1	131,416	1
Germany	520	2	69,317	1
United Kingdom	468	3	47,778	1
Switzerland	445	4	4,206	1
Sweden	436	5	6,341	1
Australia	403	6	6,997	1
New Zealand	396	7	1,642	1
Canada	389	8	11,368	1
Netherlands	338	9	8,834	1
Denmark	338	10	3,825	1
France	283	11	41,950	1
Norway	279	12	2,937	1
Belgium	261	13	8,396	1
Eire	248	14	2,946	1
Argentina	218	15	13,132	2
Middle income group ($101–$200):				
Union of S. Africa	188	16	10,251	2[f]
Finland	184	17	3,684	1
Chile	174	18	4,940	2
Austria	166	19	6,650	1
U.S.S.R.	158[d]	20	196,500[e]	2
Italy	140	21	43,864	1
Greece	136	22	7,200	2
Czechoslovakia	134	23	15,239	1
Hungary	125	24	9,129	1
Bulgaria	109	25	6,308	2
Lower income group ($100 and below):				
Cuba	98	26	4,253	3
Yugoslavia	96	27	15,703	2
Poland	95	28	35,090	2
Japan	93	29	72,520	2
Venezuela	92	30	3,650	3
Egypt	85	31	16,650	3
Palestine	81	32	1,502	3
Costa Rica	76	33	639	3
Colombia	76	34	8,986	3
Peru	72	35	7,000	3
Panama	71	36	620	3
Ceylon	63	37	5,922	3
Mexico	61	38	19,380	3
Uruguay	56	39	2,147	3
Dominican Republic	51	40	1,650	3
Haiti	50	41	2,600	3
Nicaragua	50	42	883	3
Guatemala	48	43	3,260	3
Bolivia	47	44	3,400	3
Honduras	45	45	1,090	3
El Salvador	45	46	1,745	3
Brazil	46	47	40,900	3
Ecuador	44	48	3,000	3
Paraguay	39	49	970	3
India	34	50	382,000	3
Philippines	32	51	16,300	3
China	29	52	450,000	3
Indonesia	22	53	69,435	3
Total			1,836,145	

[a] Source: Per Capita National Income, *Foreign Assets and Liabilities of the United States and Its Balance of International Transactions*. A Report to the Senate Committee on Finance by the National Advisory Council on International Monetary and Financial Problems, Dec. 18, 1947.

[b] Source: *Statistical Yearbook of the League of Nations*, 1941–42.

[c] Countries are grouped by population types as follows:

Type 1. *Low growth potential*. Birth rates below 25 per thousand population. Low death rates. Small natural increase with prospect of relatively stationary populations in the future.

Type 2. *Transitional growth*. Birth rates 25–35. Both birth and death rates generally falling. Rapid population growth.

Type 3. *High growth potential*. Birth rates over 35. Death rates (but not birth rates) generally declining. Rapid growth in absence of civil disturbance, famine, and epidemic.

The birth rates refer to average annual figures for the period 1931–40. Official vital statistics were used where available, though for a number of countries these were corrected to take account of apparent under-reporting of births. Birth rates were estimated from other demographic information for countries lacking official vital statistics.

[d] Source: P. A. Baran, "National Income and Product of the USSR, 1940," *Review of Economic Statistics*, November, 1947. This applies to enlarged area after the annexations in 1939 and 1940.

[e] Source: OIR, Department of State. Population after annexations in 1939 and 1940. Prior population 174,000,000.

[f] White population only.

SOURCE: *Point Four*, United States Department of State, 1950.

$200. In Group I, which includes one-fifth of the world's population, the people of the United States had the highest per capita annual income: $554. The United States raised the mean average per capita income of the people of Group I to $461, although the median of the countries in the group was $389. Group II contains ten countries the average income of whose people ranged from $100 to $200. The people of these countries, comprising one-sixth of the earth's population, had a mean average annual income of $154. Finally, there were twenty-eight countries in Group III whose people received on the average less than $100 per year income. In sharp contrast to the countries of Group I and even of Group II, the incomes of the two-thirds of the world's people in Group III averaged only $41.

The details of Point Four were spelled out for the first time in March, 1951, in the report of the International Development Advisory Board, headed by Nelson Rockefeller. This report divided the world into the seven underdeveloped areas outside of Communist Areas shown in Figure 11.3: (1) Latin America, (2) Africa, (3) Greece-Turkey, (4) Middle East, (5) South Asia, (6) Southeast Asia, and (7) Oceania. These areas comprise 51 percent of the world's area and contain 46 percent of the world's people. They were described as being plagued by hunger, poverty, illiteracy, and disease. Once again the overall measure of *need* used in this report was per capita income, based on postwar data. Figure 11.4 shows, as compared with annual income per person of $1453 in the United States and $473 in western Europe, the per capita income for: Latin America, $152; Africa, $118; the Middle East, $89; South Asia, $55; and Southeast Asia, $30. The average per capita income for these five underdeveloped areas was $80.

Specifically to help meet these needs these areas require (a) technical assistance and (b) capital of two types—private investment and social investment. The latter is not suitable for private investment, and capital for it must be supplied by government lending, national or international.

B. The Importance of Underdeveloped Areas to the United States

In the past, some portion of the people in the United States has had a humanitarian interest in the underdeveloped areas of the world and another segment of our people has had direct economic interests in these areas. Today, there is an increasing realization that the economic, political, and security interests of the United States, as well as of the underdeveloped countries, will be served if the planes of living of these areas are raised. Within the last decade countless studies and a great

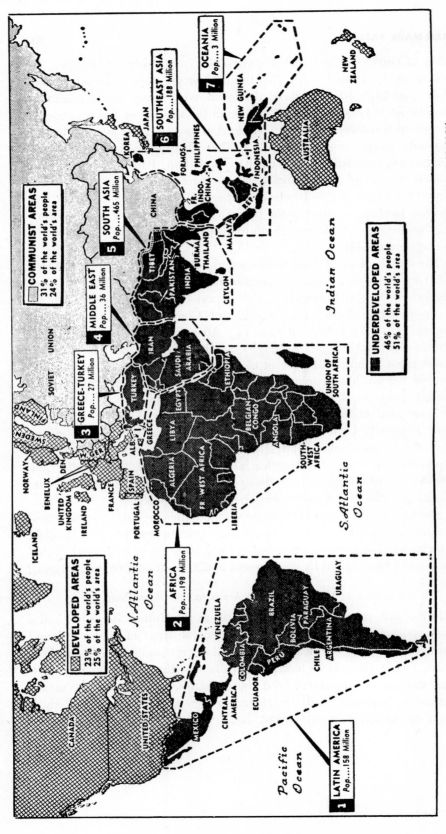

Figure 11.3. The World's Seven Underdeveloped Areas—Major Factors as U.S. Studies a New Aid Plan. (*The New York Times*, March 18, 1951)

body of literature have been produced. One of the most definitive reports was made in February, 1956, by the Research and Policy Committee of the Committee for Economic Development: *Economic Development Abroad and the Role of American Foreign Investment.* The CED concluded that the United States had in the *short run* and the *long run* "a big stake in the future of the independent underdeveloped countries of the world."

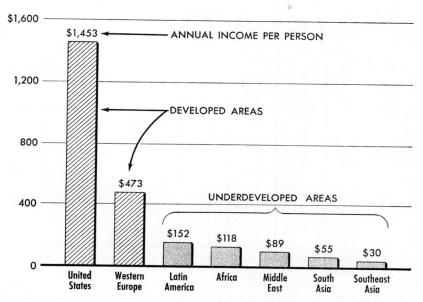

Figure 11.4. Per Capita Income in Developed and Underdeveloped Areas. The annual income per person averages only about $80 in underdeveloped areas, as compared with an average of $1,453 in the U.S.

In the *short run* the security of the United States is involved in preventing Communism from subverting these countries. If Communism is able to organize the resources of any large number of the now independent countries, the effect on Western security will be serious. In addition, our principal allies, Britain, Canada, the industrial nations of western Europe, and Japan are heavily dependent for their economic growth on expanding trade with the underdeveloped world. It is possible that political instability and economic nationalism in underdeveloped countries may well contract trade channels at a time when it is important for the strength of the Western community that they expand.

Both in the *short run* and in the *long run* these underdeveloped areas are of critical importance to the United States as sources of raw materials. This point has already been developed fully with special reference to petroleum and iron ore and strategic and critical materials. The report of the International Development Advisory Board presented Figure 11.5 to show how important the underdeveloped areas are to us. This chart shows our imports from these areas as a percentage of consumption: rubber, 100 percent; chromium, 83 percent; tin, 74 percent; manganese, 77 percent; bauxite, 70 percent; lead, 19 percent; and cop-

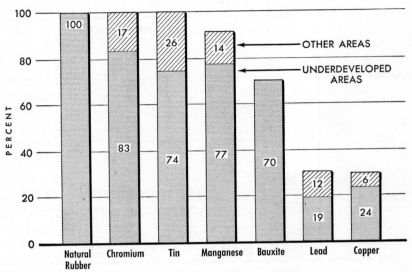

Figure 11.5.   Underdeveloped Areas as Sources of United States Raw Materials. The chart shows our imports as a percent of consumption (U.S. production accounts for the difference between total imports and 100%). (Data from *The New York Times*, 1951)

per 24 percent. We know from our previous study that these percentages have grown and will continue to grow.

In the *long run*, the CED study concluded, the profound internal transformation now going on in the underdeveloped countries could determine the political shape of the world. "The underdeveloped countries may in time evolve free and democratic institutions which express the spirit of freedom and toleration at home and a willingness to cooperate abroad with other countries in the maintenance of world peace. Or, in an attempt to solve their growing problems, some of them may turn to totalitarian rule at home and aggression abroad. At the very least the climate in which western democracy will have to live and grow will be greatly affected by the kinds of societies that finally emerge in the underdeveloped world."

The conclusion can be drawn that these areas are of tremendous importance to the United States, and thus their accelerated economic development is in our interest.

C. Obstacles to Economic Development

If accelerated economic growth of the underdeveloped areas is of advantage to the United States, it is important that a study of the obstacles to development be made before plans and policy are recommended. The CED concluded that there were three obstacles to economic development which should be of prime concern in United States policy: (a) the shortage of capital, (b) the shortage of entrepreneurial and managerial talent, and (c) the need for balance in economic development.

THE SHORTAGE OF CAPITAL. The shortage of capital is the central problem of the underdeveloped areas. The CED study showed that the over-all rate of investment in a number of important underdeveloped countries is low in comparison with Western countries and with Communist China and Soviet Russia. In India and Pakistan the rate was found to be only just sufficient, and in Indonesia to be probably insufficient, to keep national income growing a little faster than population. The rate of investment was found to be higher in Latin America than in southeast Asia, but so was the growth of population. As a result, in much of Latin America per capita income is not growing rapidly enough.

One way to meet this problem is to increase the supply of foreign capital. The underdeveloped countries, excluding colonial territories, were receiving in a representative period just prior to 1956 long-term capital investment funds from the United States and other industrial countries at a rate of approximately $1.1 billion (net) a year as follows:

From	*$1,000,000 a Year*
United States	
Mutual Security Program	415
Export-Import Bank (net)	72
Private long-term investment (net)	500
World Bank (net)	98
Western Europe, public and private (net)	50
TOTAL	$1,135

The CED estimated conservatively that the underdeveloped countries might use effectively as much as $500 million to $1500 million more a year.

THE SHORTAGE OF ENTREPRENEURIAL AND MANAGERIAL TALENT. A problem of human resources related to investment is the shortage of businessmen who know how to build and operate new capital facilities. The business class of underdeveloped areas is typically a class of traders and merchants. In most underdeveloped countries the government has had to assume a major responsibility in the promotion, financing, and managing of industrial enterprises. Governments, too, lack trained personnel.

The CED believed that supplying technical assistance to foreign governments was one of the most important ways in which the United States and other Western powers could help accelerate economic development in the underdeveloped world. Most important, however, the United States through its foreign investment policy could help develop a responsible business class in the underdeveloped areas. This might lead to less government direction and control of capital facilities in these areas.

THE NEED FOR BALANCE IN ECONOMIC DEVELOPMENT. We have seen that a proper function of capital is that of an equalizing agent. Care must be taken in the underdeveloped countries to achieve a balanced growth of agriculture and industry and to achieve the most efficient use of human and natural resources.

The tendency in many underdeveloped countries has been to expand industrialization programs—particularly heavy industry—at the expense of agriculture, with a resulting waste of economic resources, inflation, and foreign exchange difficulties.

Similarly, technical aid and investment have been advanced to improve health and sanitary conditions which have resulted in increased population. This would seem to be a desirable objective. However, a real danger lies in population growth at such a rate that per capita income and food supply may be reduced.

The two dangers cited above can be avoided by greater emphasis on agricultural development.

OTHER SPECIFIC OBSTACLES. The three obstacles to economic development which the CED concluded should be of prime concern in United States policy need to be supplemented by a study of definite obstacles encountered in making foreign investments. Such a study was published by the National Industrial Conference Board in 1951 under the title *Obstacles to Direct Foreign Investment*. The summary of the Board's findings is presented in Table 87. It can be seen from this table that the most troublesome burdens in the underdeveloped areas of Africa, Asia, and Latin America were export and import quotas; limitation on remittance of profits; control of capital movements; lack of trained native personnel; and lack of adequate roads, railroads, harbors, and storage facilities.

TABLE 87. Ranking of Problems Encountered in Making Foreign Investments

	All Countries		Africa		Asia		Latin America		Europe	
	Rank	% of Total	Rank	% of Total	Rank	% of Total	Rank	% of Total	Rank	% of Total
Export or import quotas	1	51.4	1	55.4	1	57.7	1	43.5	1	57.5
Limitation on remittance of profits	2	36.7	3	35.7	2	36.2	2	32.2	2	43.5
Control of capital movements	3	27.6	7	17.0	3	30.7	4	24.5	3	34.1
Burden of social security legislation	4	18.7	8	13.4	10	11.0	3	28.2	4	11.4
Lack of trained native personnel	5	18.1	2	42.0	6	20.2	6	21.4	10	3.6
Lack of adequate roads, railroads, harbors, or storage facilities	6	14.6	4	20.5	4	24.5	7	19.1	17	1.0
Multiple exchange rates	7	13.8	12	4.5	12	8.0	5	21.9	5	9.1
Inadequacy of housing, recreational, and shopping facilities for employees	8	9.9	5	18.7	5	20.9	11	7.5	9	4.2
Inadequate power facilities	9	9.6	11	5.4	7	17.2	9	12.5	11	3.2
Foreign restriction on importation of personnel from home country	10	8.8	9	9.8	16	4.3	8	12.9	6	5.2
Instability of government	11	8.0	17	1.8	9	13.5	10	9.6	6	5.2
Lack of health and sanitary facilities	12	7.6	5	18.7	8	16.6	13	6.1	17	1.0
Nationalization and expropriation	13	4.7	19	0.9	14	5.5	14	5.4	8	4.5
Special taxation of foreign enterprises	14	4.6	17	1.8	15	4.9	11	7.5	16	1.3
Undeveloped banking system or other credit facilities	15	4.1	15	2.7	12	8.0	15	5.2	17	1.0
Inability to recruit personnel in the United States	16	3.5	15	2.7	11	8.6	17	3.1	14	1.6
Restriction of foreign investment to certain fields	17	3.0	14	3.6	16	4.3	17	3.1	13	1.9
Inability to deal with responsible government officials	18	2.6	19	0.9	16	4.3	17	3.1	14	1.6
Required local participation	19	2.4	12	4.5	19	3.7	21	1.2	12	2.6
Discriminatory enforcement of tax laws	20	2.1	—	—	22	0.6	16	4.0	17	1.0
Unequal treatment before the law with respect to property holding and conveying, contract enforcement, right to use local courts for redress, etc.	21	2.0	10	8.0	20	1.8	20	1.6	22	0.3
Requirement for reinvestment of earnings	22	0.9	—	—	21	1.2	22	0.9	17	1.0
No problems	—	21.0	—	12.5	—	17.2	—	22.8	—	23.7

NOTE: This table is taken from "Technical Papers Number Two" published by The Conference Board in 1951 under the title: "Obstacles to Direct Foreign Investment." The problems are ranked according to the frequency with which they were listed in replies to questionnaires circulated by The Conference Board. No attempt was made to learn how these cooperators would rank them with respect to their importance as deterrents to direct foreign investments. The rankings were determined from replies coming from firms with investment ventures currently active.

SOURCE: The Conference Board.

D. The Role of United States Investment in Underdeveloped Areas

The United States has used three direct methods to accelerate economic development in underdeveloped areas: (a) technical assistance to the governments, (b) measures to stimulate foreign investment by

United States firms and individuals, and (c) programs of public investment, using both intergovernmental loans and grants, and government loans to private firms.

TECHNICAL ASSISTANCE. As we have already seen, there is a critical shortage of skilled personnel in the underdeveloped countries, in government, in private industry, and in agriculture. Technical assistance provides the governments of underdeveloped areas with expert assistance in many fields. The United States government participates in technical assistance through the United States Point Four Program, the United Nations Technical Assistance Program, and the Colombo Plan for Southeast Asia. These have been effective in promoting economic development, and since they are primarily concerned with supplying trained manpower, they will not be discussed in detail. However, they are mentioned in this study of capital because they are necessary and supplementary to the most efficient use of investment in the underdeveloped areas.

PRIVATE INVESTMENT. The Point Four Program was initiated on the premise that the major part of the capital invested in underdeveloped countries must come from sources within the countries themselves. An integral part of the technical coöperation program was to provide advice and assistance in techniques to encourage, mobilize, and channel domestic savings into productive investment. From the very nature of our problem we have seen that domestic savings, even though effectively mobilized, will be inadequate, just as they were in the United States, to support a satisfactory rate of development. Particular emphasis has been placed from the very beginning of the Point Four Program on the stimulation of a greatly expanded flow of United States private investment into the underdeveloped areas. It was felt that the importance of United States private investment rested not only on the fact that it was potentially the major source of foreign funds for development purposes but also on the fact that it would contribute to the development process, enterprise, managerial experience, and technical knowledge as well. We have seen that this was the same emphasis and policy advocated by President Eisenhower.

However, the volume of United States private long-term investment in the underdeveloped areas has been small. In the three years 1952–54, only about $500 million a year (net) in private long-term capital was invested in independent underdeveloped countries, and 60 percent of it was in Latin America. According to the CED more than 90 percent of this investment was direct investment by United States corporations, most of which were pursuing one of two specific objectives: to open up new sources of raw materials (e.g., petroleum, copper, and iron ore) mainly for export; and to establish branch plants abroad in order to gain or hold local markets. Except in Israel, there has been very little portfolio investment by United States citizens in underdeveloped countries since World War II.

The type of capital needed in the underdeveloped countries is for basic economic facilities such as railroads, telecommunications, electric power, roads, and harbors. These fields lend themselves to public investment rather than private investment and are not now attractive to private foreign investors. We have already seen that there are many other obstacles to private investment in the underdeveloped areas. Many of the obstacles and risks are beyond the reach of United States policy as they are the result of the present stage of economic development and political evolution. Some of the most troublesome points which United States policy is being directed toward are the barring of foreign companies from mining or use of natural resources; the restriction of foreign investors to minority stock ownership; and security risks such as political instability, foreign exchange difficulties, the danger of expropriation, and the nationalistic hostility to foreign investment. Four specific policies are singled out to show what the United States is doing to attempt to alleviate these troublesome points and to stimulate a gradual increase in private investment in the underdeveloped areas: investment treaties, investment guarantees, tax incentives, and public-private partnership investments.

The United States government had in 1956 signed *investment treaties* with Colombia, Ethiopia, Haiti, Israel, and Uruguay. Under these treaties the United States government attempts to get underdeveloped countries to change laws and regulations which discriminate against foreign investors. The treaties seem to be desirable instruments since they show the underdeveloped countries some of the obstacles which must be overcome to attract capital.

Since 1948 the United States government, through *investment guarantees*, has attempted to reduce the risks of investors abroad by insuring new investments against losses from expropriation and against the inability of foreign governments to convert local currency profits into dollars. Guarantees are available only in countries which coöperate under the program. In 1955 fifteen underdeveloped countries were covered but only five investment projects, totaling $7.3 million, had been guaranteed. Apparently even guarantees were not enough to overcome the obstacles where private enterprise thought the risk was great enough to ask for insurance.

Tax incentives may also stimulate foreign investment. Corporations which can qualify as "Western Hemisphere trading corporations" under Sections 921 and 922 of the Internal Revenue Act of 1944 are entitled to a 14 percentage-point reduction on the federal corporate income tax. A proposal has been made to extend this same tax reduction to all domestic corporations with respect to that part of their income which comes from the active conduct of trade or business abroad. President Eisenhower recommended in his Economic Report to Congress in January, 1954, that our tax laws might well offer some encouragement to investment abroad. "This can be accomplished by taxing the business income after January 1, 1954, of foreign subsidiaries, or of segregated branches of American corporations which operate and elect to be taxed as subsidiaries, at a rate somewhat lower than the current relatively high corporate rate."

In President Eisenhower's Economic Report to Congress in January, 1955, he made several recommendations for fostering foreign investment, among them the following:

As recommended by the Commission on Foreign Economic Policy, the tax rate on corporate income from all foreign sources should be reduced by 14 percentage points, making it equal to the rate already applicable to Western Hemisphere trade corporations. Our law now requires that income from foreign sources be taxed in the United States to the extent that it is not taxed abroad. This has two consequences. First, American firms doing business in a foreign country with low tax rates operate at a tax disadvantage in comparison both with domestic firms of that country and with firms of other nations that levy low taxes on foreign income. Second, countries desiring to attract American capital cannot very well use favorable tax rates as an incentive. Indeed, our present tax policy might even encourage a country in which American capital has been invested to increase its taxes on business income. The proposed rate reduction would tend to improve the competitive position of our firms doing business in other countries; it would reduce a barrier to further investment abroad; and it may stimulate foreign countries to use favorable tax rates as a means of attracting American capital.

In President Eisenhower's Economic Report to Congress in January, 1956, he called attention to the fact that recommendations in the 1955 report, "with respect to the taxation of corporation income from foreign sources, have not yet been acted on by Congress. Legislation on these proposals, which can have a significant influence on foreign investment, is again requested."

It is quite possible that the legislation had not been forthcoming because there was a doubt that a fourteen-point reduction would be enough to stimulate much foreign investment, coupled with a certainty that oil corporations with existing investments would benefit. Nevertheless, tax incentives to investment abroad are potentially an effective way to stimulate private foreign investment, and they should be a fundamental part of United States policy.

Public-private partnership investment is the fourth suggested way of stimulating private investment in underdeveloped areas. The International Bank for Reconstruction and Development (the World Bank) and the United States Export-Import Bank, by participating with private American and foreign investors in development projects, can greatly reduce the risks and difficulties of the private investor. They make loans principally for basic economic facilities which would usually be financed by public funds or regulated by government.

In 1955 the International Finance Corporation was established as an affiliate of the World Bank. Unlike the World Bank, the IFC can invest without any government guarantee in new private enterprises needing capital. In addition, it is permitted by its charter to provide venture capital (investments yielding income only if earned). The IFC invests exclusively in private undertakings in underdeveloped areas in association with private investors and in cases where sufficient private capital is not available on reasonable terms. The IFC is not allowed to acquire voting stock or to share in the management of the enterprises in which it invests; but it may help find experienced management and it may sell its investments to private investors in the form of voting stock. On the one hand, the IFC has been endorsed as a practical and useful means of stimulating private foreign investment. On the other hand, the objection was made that the IFC should not provide equity or venture capital for manufacturing, mining, and commercial enterprise, "because fear of competition by government supported enterprises is a serious deterrent to the flow of private capital into similar ventures."

The United States policy was directed toward the creation of the IFC. President Eisenhower commented: "The new institution is expected to expand investment abroad by its own lending and also be helping to create an investment climate in foreign countries that will be more attractive to their own citizens and to those of other nations."

In conclusion: Private capital has been flowing into underdeveloped areas at a slow rate although United States policy has been directed toward an accelerated rate. Perhaps one fundamental reason for this lack of investment rests not so much in the obstacles abroad as in the opportunities at home for expanding capital needs. The CED concluded that "Even after all practical measures are taken to increase private foreign investment from the United States and other industrial countries, it seems probable that most of this shortage of capital is in basic facilities which are not attractive to private investment." The growth of mining, manufacturing, and trade, which offer opportunity for private investment, depends on investment in these basic facilities.

PUBLIC INVESTMENT.   The third major method used by the United States to accelerate investment in underdeveloped areas has been by public investment. The Export-Import Bank has done most of the United States public investment in Latin America. The Economic Cooperation Administration and its successor agencies, Mutual Security Administration, Foreign Operations Administration, and International Cooperation Administration, have been responsible for the major part of our public investment in the rest of the world. In addition, a very large part of United States capital flowing into underdeveloped countries is administered by the World Bank. The annual investment rates previously presented were from the United States Export-Import Bank (net), $72 million; from the Mutual Security Program, $415 million (includes technical assistance); from the World Bank (net), $98 million.

The fundamental questions about United States public investment in underdeveloped areas are: Why? How should it be administered (by United States or United Nations agencies)? and What period of time (short or long run)?

The why of public investment has been covered adequately in showing the need of capital and the importance of the underdeveloped countries to the United States. However, during 1955 Russia began to recognize the success of our program and launched a counteroffensive of technical and capital aid. This is an additional reason for increasing our public investment in many critical areas because of our success and the sustained need. A selective program for the building of basic economic facilities is urgent.

The how by United States or United Nations agencies is not an easy point. The most obvious advantage of investment by United States agencies is that we retain selection and control. On the other hand, investment through an international agency has the advantage of support of vigorous economic programs without the real or imagined attachment to them of political or economic strings. There has been some fear that in granting loans for specific political purposes the United States might lose friends.

The CED pointed out that Americans should not forget that our foreign investment policy also has humanitarian aims, as well as the long-term objective of building community between the West and the peoples of Asia, Africa, and Latin America. These wider and longer aims are often served better by an agency like the World Bank than by public investment programs closely identified with the United States.

Further, on the practical side, the World Bank should be able to obtain additional funds from sources other than the United States such as western Europe and Japan as their ability to export capital increases.

A final reason for the use of an international lending agency is that some countries with their growing spirit of nationalism might be unwilling to borrow from the United States but would do so from an international agency, and at the same time accept some direction in the appropriate use of the capital for development purposes.

There is no question about the fact that there have been strong voices of criticism of the United States from many areas to which we are making grants and loans. Even in Canada the charge was made in the election of 1956 that United States private investment was making Canada an economic appendage of the United States and that Canada was "in danger of losing its economic, if not its political independence." Thus, United States capital was cast as a villain.

In spite of all these arguments in favor of international lending agencies the conclusion seems justified that so long as the United States is supplying the bulk of the funds control should be exercised by the United States. There is problem enough in selling to the taxpayer the necessity of loans and grants to underdeveloped areas without going a step further and turning these funds over to an international agency for administration.

It is possible that steps may be taken to eliminate some of the criticisms of United States administration of loans and grants. One recommendation might be that we pay more attention to the recipient countries' ideas. For example, the members of the Baghdad Pact, meeting at Teheran, Iran, in April, 1956, were not asking for a great new program of gifts and loans. What they wanted was a different approach to funds already available. The Baghdad Pact countries wanted coöperation in studying their development problems with the area considered as a whole whenever interests of different countries interlocked. Specifically they asked the United States to allot available funds for projects that covered two or more countries, instead of insisting on treating each country as a separate unit. This appears to be a reasonable request asking for greater flexibility and placing greater autonomy in a regional group. Through acceptance of such a proposal the United States would develop friends and probably obtain more efficient use of the funds supplied.

The what period of time (short run or long) question has arisen in several different connections. Two time policy issues will be presented.

The first time policy question arose in 1950–51 during the Korean War and may recur. It was concerned with whether economic assistance should be limited to projects in underdeveloped countries that would yield relatively quick results in the production of strategic and other materials contributing directly to the rearmament effort, or whether the interests of the United States would be served better by a program of longer-run objectives of economic development. The fact was recognized that these two objectives were not necessarily conflicting; nevertheless it was felt that they were likely to come into conflict at some points. Therefore a choice between the two types of programs could not be avoided.

The Brookings Institution argued the question this way in its *Major Problems of United States Foreign Policy, 1951–1952:*

The first alternative is to devise a program of assistance on the assumption that the long-range general economic development of underdeveloped countries is fundamental to the defense of the free world. The other alternative is to restrict assistance mainly to projects for increasing the supply of critical materials on the assumption that first things must come first. Since the arguments for and against these alternatives are interrelated they are discussed together.

Two general considerations are important in choosing between the alternatives. A large-scale program, such as that suggested by the report of the International Development Advisory Board, involving an annual capital export from the United States of the order of 2 billion dollars a year, would impose a severe drain on the available supplies of capital goods and other resources that are urgently needed for the defense efforts of Western Europe and of the United States. On the other hand, a program that emphasizes immediate results in the production of critical materials will almost inevitably direct the course of development of the countries concerned into channels different from those that would be chosen if much less priority were given to defense needs. Both the priority to be given to production for defense and the magnitude of a feasible program are therefore involved.

The question of priority was debated at the Inter-American Conference of Foreign Ministers held in Washington in March and April, 1951. The United States advocated a development program that would give unequivocal priority to the urgent requirements of defense; the Latin American countries continued to advocate extensive developmental programs that would contribute to their general economic strength and well-being. In the final resolutions adopted, the priority given to defense was much less than was desired by the United States. Interpretation of these resolutions will be necessary in the light of the claims of defense and of other underdeveloped areas for assistance.

It is argued in favor of the first alternative that economic development programs are political as well as an economic instrument of policy. Long-term security requires the maintenance of free institutions in the underdeveloped countries, a political end to which an increase in their economic strength is said to be essential. It is argued in addition that the opening up of the vast economic frontier represented by the latent resources of these countries will stimulate an expanding world economy.

Those who oppose this view argue for the second alternative on the ground that first things must come first in an emergency, and that unless the immediate requirements of rearmament to redress the balance of military strength between the free world and the Communist world are met, all hope for the future may be lost. In the interests of the underdeveloped countries themselves, it is argued, the supply of critically short materials that can be provided by them should be expanded as rapidly as possible even if the attainment of long-run objectives is delayed and problems of over expansion are created. Special assistance in the future to deal with the problems so created is regarded as preferable to going without the badly needed raw materials.

The second time policy question arose in 1955–56. The time factor in this instance was the period over which the United States would give sustained aid to underdeveloped areas.

On March 19, 1956, President Eisenhower sent a message to Congress on foreign aid in which he made the following among several other requests:

We should be able to assure the nations of the free world that we will continue to participate in particular nonmilitary projects and enterprises which will take a number of years to complete. Such assurance from us will help these nations to mobilize their own funds for projects which will contribute to an important degree to their economic strength, to enlist public and private loans and investment, and to plan ahead intelligently. It will be difficult for these nations to organize such projects unless Mutual Security Program support can be relied on for more than a single year.

I request authority of the Congress to make commitments up to ten years in length to assist less-developed countries in long-term projects important to their development. Funds to fill such commitments would come from appropriations for nonmilitary security and would not exceed an aggregate of 100 million dollars in any year.

President Eisenhower's request immediately met strong opposition in the election year of 1956. Senate Leader Lyndon B. Johnson challenged the President's proposals on March 26, 1956. "The Administration will have to make a compelling case to convince Congress of the need of economic aid and long-term commitments. I doubt whether there is any substantial sentiment for committing our resources for an indefinite period in the future. The world situation is changing very rapidly. We do not know exactly what will be wise next year or the year after that . . . let alone 10 years from now."

Nevertheless, the President's idea made sense even in several areas which he did not mention. For example, the request might answer some of the criticisms of the United States program and make economic aid through United States agencies more readily acceptable as well as more effective. If strings were attached there would be a greater chance they could not be pulled at the end of a year. The United States would be expressing a vote of confidence in the underdeveloped areas over a period of years. Most importantly, the request for long-term development projects coupled with a request for greater flexibility in the use of funds was the administration's answer to Russia's new economic offensive in Asia.

E. Policy Recommendations in 1957

During January and February, 1957, five studies on United States "foreign aid" programs were completed and recommendations were made. Two of these were made for the executive office of the President: a report of the President's Citizen Advisers on the Mutual Security Program and a report of the International Development Advisory Board. The other three studies were made for the Senate's Special Committee to Study the Foreign Aid Program.

The President's Citizen Advisers on the Mutual Security Program, headed by Benjamin F. Fairless, former chairman of the United States Steel Program, showed that during the fiscal year which ended June 30, 1956, foreign countries received $28.6 billion from the following sources:

United States private trade and business	$20.4 billion
United States government spending for "collective security"	7.9 billion
$3.9 billion in military aid	
1.7 billion in economic aid	
2.3 billion in spending abroad by U.S. troops and government agencies	
Other sources: interest on public debt owed to foreigners; pensions and transfer payments; gold purchases by U.S.	0.3 billion
Total private and public spending abroad	$28.6 billion

The Advisers recommended: Aid from government funds need not exceed $8 billion a year; the cost of this "collective security" does not outweigh the results achieved; gifts of dollars for industrial purposes abroad should be limited severely and loans should replace gifts wherever possible; good management and technical ability, not capital, are the world's most critical shortages; Congress should make two-year appropriations for foreign aid instead of one-year allotments. The Advisers concluded that they could not foresee the time when the aid program can end, because in the conflict with Communism "the United States must resolve to stay the course, and must abandon the false hope that collective-security costs are temporary."

The International Development Advisory Board under the chairmanship of Eric Johnston, president of the Motion Picture Association of America, Inc., recommended to the President that the United States establish an International Development Fund to promote long-term projects in underdeveloped areas; the Fund should be given enough money to operate for a minimum of three years without new appropriations; the first appropriation should provide for a "substantial increase" in capital investment, technical assistance; emphasis should be on loans rather than grants; and finally, a "clear distinction" should be made between the military and the economic aspects of our total foreign aid program.

The three reports for the Senate's Special Committee to Study the Foreign Aid Program were made by the Center for International Studies at Massachusetts Institute of Technology, the Research Center in Economic Development and Cultural Change at the University of Chicago, and the American Enterprise Association.

The MIT study recommended: Backward areas should be developed to the point at which they can grow through their own efforts; economic aid alone should be for five to ten years at a rate of $3.5 billion a year as compared with the then current $1.7 billion and should continue for a long time because, "as an instrument of short-term policy, development assistance is wasteful and ineffective"; economic development programs should be stressed in Asia, Africa, and the Middle East; no strings— military or political—should be attached to the programs of aid.

The University of Chicago study recommended: Economic aid alone should be for ten to twenty years at a rate of $3 billion to $5 billion a year; economic aid should go to all underdeveloped areas outside the Soviet sphere; aid should be given regardless of whether receiving countries are military allies of the United States, and without attaching military or political strings; the objective of all projects should be to achieve "balanced development" of backward countries.

The American Enterprise Association report to the Senate Committee took a different approach to show that private investment and private industry are more reliable and effective than a program of government aid for underdeveloped areas "to improve their levels of living." To achieve this goal the Association suggested that the United States government stress loans to private firms, both at home and abroad, rather than to other governments; that public projects be limited to such things as roads and schools that could contribute to private developments; and, finally, that treaties and other government measures be used to promote a favorable climate for outside investment in the less-developed areas.

From these five 1957 studies these conclusions can be drawn: (a) All of the studies emphasize that underdeveloped countries need assistance from the United States and that the interest of the United States requires some measure of aid. (b) One of the studies concluded that the 1956 spending rate was not too high, three recommended increases in economic aid, and the fifth called for a smaller government program with increased private investment. (c) All of the studies agree that the need for aid will be sustained for a long-term period. (d) Appropriations should be provided by Congress on a longer-term basis than year-by-year.

F. Conclusion

In discussing the major problem of international investment and underdeveloped areas we have considered an old economic problem that since 1950 has been singled out for study as if it were something new. It is new to the United States as a major policy problem in capital resources. We have seen the need for capital in underdeveloped areas, the importance of these areas to the United States, the obstacles to economic development in the underdeveloped areas, and the role of United States investment in these areas. We may conclude that the United States has been making an effective partial approach to some of the problems, the solutions to which will require sustained effort over a long period of time. President Eisenhower in his message to Congress on March 19, 1956, put the extent of the success of our policy in very positive terms:

Because our people and the peoples of other nations in the free world have been willing to make the necessary sacrifices, the past mutual-security programs have achieved a real measure of success. By combined effort the free world has advanced toward stability and toward economic strength. It has achieved the power and the will to resist aggression. Collective-security arrangements have brought into existence free-world defense forces and facilities far greater than those which we, by our unaided efforts, could have raised and maintained from our own resources without a crushing burden of taxation on our people. In their economic aspects our programs have made significant advances toward the solution of many problems of the free world. Without this assistance many other nations, beyond doubt, if existing at all, would exist today only in the grip of chaos. Moreover, we ourselves are more secure, more prosperous, better fitted to go forward in the common enterprise of freedom than ever before.

GENERAL CONCLUSIONS

The United States has been uniquely blest with the opportunity to accumulate capital. The efficient use of this capital has enabled us to make enormous gains in productivity which have raised our plane of living, our strength, our security, and have facilitated the achievement of individual and national freedom within a free economy in a political democracy. Capital facilities are a significant part of our mobilization plans for security. There is tangible evidence that this sustained growth of capital will continue in the future. The importance of investment has been recognized by the United States government, and policies especially under the Eisenhower administration have been directed toward achieving sustained growth of investment. Further, the United States has recognized the need of investment in underdeveloped areas and has adopted as a cardinal principle of international policy the supplying of capital to these areas in an attempt to raise their planes of living and their strength in the hope that they may be free and support us in common objectives and in supplying raw materials required for the growth of our domestic economy.

CHAPTER 12

Manpower

The evaluation of the production potential of our third, final, and most important national resource—manpower (human resources) is the purpose of this Part V. We are those human resources and are concerned with and a part of each phase of our basic problem. How can we raise our plane of living by making economic progress and at the same time attain a maximum degree of security and a maximum amount of individual and national freedom in a political democracy? It is our per capita income which must be increased if we are to raise our plane of living. To accomplish this, production must increase at a greater rate than population. As a recipient of the rewards of production and as a factor of production man has a dual interest in production potential. As a factor of production we must allocate our natural, capital, and human resources in order to achieve maximum output with a minimum of input.

The fact has already been established that the availability of fund natural resources has been an important factor in enabling the United States to increase its capital. This advantageous position could have been lost without proper managerial allocation of these resources together with our human resources. In addition, if United States population had expanded as fast as or faster than production, per capita output and income would not have increased.

Production potential is a function of quantitative and qualitative characteristics of the population. Quantitative dimensions of the population include (1) numbers of people, (2) composition by age and sex and labor force, and (3) rate of growth. Qualitative characteristics are a function of the economic resources available and man's ability to use them most efficiently. Furthermore, production potential and economic growth depend on those qualitative values which man derives from the moral-psychological and political environment in which he lives.

The plan of this chapter is to present a comparison of the quantitative characteristics of the United States population with those of other nations and of the Western powers and the Soviet bloc, and to analyze the trends within the United States population. Chapter 13 will study three major problems and related policies—man and resources, mobilizing manpower, and man and freedom. The total purpose is to show the production potential of the nation's human resources and its part in the solution of our basic problem.

WORLD POPULATION

Total world population is a result of two variables, the birth rate and the death rate. For some particular areas it is necessary to consider the variables of emigration and immigration. The latest United Nations estimates of world population by countries and continents are given in Table 88.

Warren S. Thompson has divided the different regions of the world into three classes from the standpoint of their present and probable future growth. The basis on which the different countries were assigned to the growth classes is the degree of control exercised over their death rates and birth rates.

Class I covers those countries in which there is a large measure of control over birth and death rates. In general, both the birth rate and the death rate are declining and the birth rate is declining faster than the death rate. The result is that most of these countries have a falling off in their rate of increase of population and may eventually have a decreasing population. Countries included in this class are the United Kingdom, France, Denmark, Norway, Sweden, Finland, the Netherlands, Germany, Belgium, Austria, Czechoslovakia, Hungary, Switzerland, Italy, Canada (although French Canadian Quebec still has a large increase),

TABLE 88.   Population and Population Densities, Mid-Year 1955

Area	Population (thousands)	Area 1000 Sq. Km.	Population per Sq. Km.
World	2,691,000[a]	135,085	20
Africa	223,000[a]	30,132	7
Algeria	9,620	2,191	4
Belgian Congo	12,600	2,344	5
Egypt	22,934	1,000	23
Ghana[b]	4,620	238	19
Morocco:			
Former French Zone	8,495	391	22
Former Spanish Zone	1,045	20	53
Tangier	183	0.3	524
Nigeria	31,254	878	35
Rhodesia and Nyasaland, Federation of:	7,069	1,263	6
Northern Rhodesia	(2,130)	(746)	(3)
Nyasaland	(2,640)	(127)	(20)
Southern Rhodesia	(2,399)	(389)	(6)
Tunisia	3,745	156	24
Union of South Africa	13,669	1,223	11
America, North and South	366,000[a]	41,985	9
Argentina	19,111	2,778	7
Bolivia	3,198	1,099	3
Brazil	58,456	8,514	7
Canada	15,601	9,961	2
Chile	6,761	742	9
Colombia	12,657	1,138	11
Costa Rica	951	51	19
Cuba[c]	5,829	115	51
Dominican Republic	2,404	49	49
Ecuador	3,675	271	14
El Salvador	2,193	20	110
Guatemala	3,258	109	30
Haiti	3,305	28	119
Honduras	1,660	112	15
Mexico	29,679	1,969	15
Nicaragua	1,245	148	8
Panama	910	74	12
Paraguay	1,565	407	4
Peru	9,396	1,249	8
United States	165,271	7,828	21
Uruguay	2,615	187	14
Venezuela	5,774	912	6
Asia (excluding U.S.S.R.)	1,481,000	27,078	55
Burma	19,434	678	29
China: Mainland[c]	582,603	9,700	60
Taiwan	8,907	36	248
India	381,690	3,288	116
Iran	21,146	1,630	13
Israel	1,748	21	85
Japan	89,100	370	241
Lebanon	1,425	10	137
Philippines	21,849	299	74

TABLE 88.   Population and Population Densities, Mid-Year 1955 (*Continued*)

Area	Population (thousands)	Area (1000 Sq. Km.)	Population per Sq. Km.
Asia (excluding U.S.S.R.) (*Continued*)			
Syria	4,145	181	23
Thailand	20,302	514	39
Turkey	24,122	777	31
Europe (excluding U.S.S.R.)	409,000	4,929	83
Belgium	8,868	31	291
Denmark	4,439	43	103
France	43,274	551	79
Germany, West	49,995	245	204
Saar	992	3	386
Greece	7,973	133	60
Italy	48,016	301	159
Luxembourg	309	3	119
Netherlands	10,751	32	331
Norway	3,425	324	11
Sweden	7,262	450	16
United Kingdom	51,215	244	210
Oceania	14,600	8,558	2
Australia	9,201	7,704	1
New Zealand	2,136	268	8
U.S.S.R.[d]	200,200	22,403	9

[a] Adjusted estimates of mid-year population.
[b] Former Gold Coast and British Togoland.
[c] 1953.
[d] April 1, 1956.
SOURCE: United Nations, 1957.

Australia, and New Zealand. The United States entered this group in the 1930's and was placed in this class by Thompson as late as 1948. However, post-World War II experience indicates that we probably had only a temporary slowing down in the rate of increase of our population. Thompson raised the question as to whether the countries included in Class I could "continue to play the part they have in world history as they become a smaller and smaller part of the world's population."

Class II includes those countries in which both birth and death rates are declining but the death rate has been declining more rapidly than the birth rate. These countries have a positive rate of increase of population. Included in Class II are Russia, Japan, Spain, Portugal, Greece, Yugoslavia, Bulgaria, Rumania, Brazil, Argentina, and Uruguay, and possibly French North Africa (Algeria, Tunis, and Morocco).

Class III countries are those in which both birth and death rates are high. Most of Asia, the Middle East, and Africa are in this group. In these countries the abundance or scarcity of means of subsistence and the lack of control of epidemic diseases are the chief determinants of population growth. The birth rate approaches the physiological maximum. If, through improved health and other measures, the death rate is lowered, there will be an explosive growth in population.

Thompson asks, "Why is this change in the source of population growth from West to East, from the more industrialized to the less industrialized countries, of economic and political importance?" He concludes: "The answer is that, assuming also a diminishing differential between West and East in the efficiency of their economic systems, the center of economic strength, and with it the center of political and military power, is certain to shift in the direction of the more rapidly expanding populations."[1]

COMPARISON OF THE WESTERN POWERS AND THE SOVIET BLOC

Questions such as the foregoing led the Joint Congressional Committee on the Economic Report, realizing the great importance of as accurate an assessment as possible of comparative economic trends, to direct its staff on February 26, 1954, to survey the problem of East-West economic trends. The report was published on January 3, 1955, and summarized the essential known facts bearing upon the comparative rates of economic growth of the United States and independent Europe, on the one hand, and of the Soviet Union and the captive states, or satellite countries, on the other. The latter states include Albania, Bulgaria, Czechoslovakia, Hungary, Poland, Rumania, and East Germany.[2]

1. Population and Manpower

Table 89 gives the summary tabulation of population and manpower prepared for the Committee. In summary the report found that although the population of the United States and western Europe is larger than that of the Soviet bloc and increased more rapidly than the latter in the period 1938–50, current and prospective changes in its age structure are less favorable. However, in recent years output per worker in manufacturing has been increasing more rapidly in the United States and west-

[1] Warren S. Thompson, *Plenty of People,* The Ronald Press Company, 1948, pp. 107–115.
[2] *Trends in Economic Growth, A Comparison of the Western Powers and the Soviet Bloc,* A Study Prepared for the Joint Committee on the Economic Report by the Legislative Reference Service of the Library of Congress, Government Printing Office, 1955.

TABLE 89. Population and Manpower of the Western Powers and the Soviet Bloc

	United States	Western Europe	Soviet Union	Captive Europe
Total population: Change (1938–52)	20 percent increase.	Western Europe: 9 percent increase. Independent Europe: 7 percent increase.	9 percent increase within postwar boundaries.	4 percent decrease, 12 percent decrease excluding East Germany.
Annual increase (1948–52)	1.76 percent.	0.9 percent (range f: −0.01 percent in Austria to 2.4 percent in Turkey).	1.5 to 1.7 percent.	1.1 percent (1950–52).
Size (end 1953)	161 million.	280 million (western Europe), 332 million (independent Europe).	212 million.	92 million.
Trends in age structure	Total growth has far exceeded increase of working-age groups in recent years.	War losses largely offset by natural increase, but trend toward "aging" is accelerating.	Prewar gains in survival rates now yielding large additions to working-age groups.	War losses and refugeeism depleted working-age groups.
Labor forces: Trends	67 million (1953), 56 million (1939).	125 million (1952–53), 10 percent increase, 1938–48.	105 to 110 million (1953), 95 million (1940).	Near complete labor mobilization.
Labor distribution	Agriculture: 11 percent of employed persons and declining. Manufacturing and mining: 40 percent of nonfarm employees.	Agriculture: Half the active males in southern countries; under 20 percent in northwestern countries. Industry: Number employed increased 20 percent or more over 1938 in 10 countries.	Agriculture: 50 to 55 percent of labor force. Industry: 60 to 65 percent of nonagricultural labor of which 70 percent in "heavy" branches.	Agriculture: Over half the active males in population. Industry: About 8.5 million.
Participation of women	Aged 14 and over: 32 percent (1953), 27 percent (1940).	Range: Under 20 percent (Italy, Netherlands, Belgium) to over 50 percent (Turkey, Yugoslavia) employed.	Over half those over 15 employed, higher seasonally. Important in Soviet bloc agriculture.	Pressed to enter urban employment.
Hours weekly in industry	41 (1953), 38 (1939).	Median: 45 (1952 to 1953) (range Italy, 39; Germany, 48).	48 minimum (1953), 40 average (1937).	46–48 minimum.
Unemployment	Near "frictional" level in recent years.	Postwar: High employment in northwestern countries, but chronic unemployment in southern countries.	None officially admitted but low concealed underemployment.	productivity reflects considerable
Output per man or man-hour in manufacturing	Man-hour output increases 2 to 3 percent per year. 30 percent above 1938.	Risen 18 percent since 1938; 25 percent since 1948. Present levels range from 15 to 50 percent of United States level (value added basis).	1953 man-hour output equaled 1937 (1937 level about 30 percent of United States). 1953 man-year output up 20 percent.	Very low and not advancing as planned.
Projections (to about 1970): Total population	204 million.	302 million, western Europe; 360 million, independent Europe.	260 to 280 million.	100 million.
Working-age groups	103 million, 15 to 54.	200 million, 15 to 64, western Europe; 240 million, 15 to 64, independent Europe.	146 million, 15 to 54.	62 million, 15 to 59.
Retirement-age groups	10 percent, 65 and over.	15 to 17 percent, 65 and over.	Generally shorter life expectancy.	

SOURCE: *Trends in Economic Growth, A Comparison of Western Powers and the Soviet Bloc*, Government Printing Office, 1955.

ern Europe than in the Soviet bloc. The report indicates that total population of the Soviet Union at the end of 1953 was approximately 212 million, compared with about 280 million in western Europe and 161 million in the United States. Captive Europe's 92 million made the Soviet bloc total 304 million as compared with 441 million in the West. However, in June, 1956, Russia released the first official estimate of population since 1939. Her population was announced as 200.2 million in April, 1956. This was about 20 million less than Western estimates. The U.S. Census Bureau estimated the population of the United States on July 1, 1956, at 168.174 million, and on July 1, 1957 to be 171.229 million.

A. Population Structure

The report found that one of the outstanding characteristics of European and other "Western" nations is the "aging" of their population owing to declining death rates. It was estimated that in western Europe the proportion of persons sixty-five years of age or over will increase during the next fifty years from 10 percent to between 15 and 17 percent.

In addition, since World War II, birth rates in the West have risen. This together with the increases in the upper age groups resulted in relative small gains in the working-age groups. This trend will continue until 1960 when the "war babies" start entering the working force.

The report also found that in the Soviet Union there was an upsurge in survival rates just before World War II. The age groups born then are now entering the labor force in large numbers. This, together with the smaller proportion of aged people than in the West, has resulted in a more favorable relationship between population in the productive age group and dependents than in the West.

B. Labor Forces

The World War II losses of the West were largely offset by natural increase, whereas in Russia war losses were about one-fourth of all males between twenty-five and forty-four. The Soviet losses together with those of eastern Europe led to labor conscription of young people and increased dependence on women workers.

The labor force in western Europe was estimated to be 125 million in 1952–53, a 10 percent increase over 1938–48. Captive Europe had nearly complete forced mobilization of its population of 92 million in 1953, but underemployment and low productivity are characteristic of this area. Estimates indicated that the employable labor force (persons fifteen years of age and older) in the Soviet Union was between 105 and 110 million persons in 1953 compared with 95 million in 1940. Between 75 and 80 percent of all males and females fifteen years of age and older were probably in the labor force. The comparable figure for the United States was 58 percent, or, in 1953, a labor force of about 67 million persons. The difference was accounted for principally by the higher employment rate of women in the Soviet Union (about 55 percent compared with 33 percent in the United States) and the smaller numbers attending school on a full-time basis in the Soviet Union than in the United States.

Longer work weeks are characteristic of the Soviet bloc as compared with the Western powers. A work week of 48 hours is compulsory in the Soviet Union. In captive Europe a six-day week is required, which indicates 46 to 48 hours as the minimum. In western Europe 45 hours is the median work week, and in the United States it is 40 hours in manufacturing.

However, numbers of workers and hours must be supplemented by what the workers are doing and how efficient they are. The report to the Joint Committee concluded that from 50 to 55 percent of the labor force of the Soviet Union is engaged in agriculture compared to 11 percent in the United States. Over half of the active males in the population of captive Europe and about half of those in the southern countries of western Europe are in agriculture as compared with under 20 percent in the northwestern countries.

Total output in the Soviet Union has been increasing only slightly more rapidly than the increase in the size of the labor force. The northern countries of western Europe have made impressive post–World War II gains in productivity, but in captive Europe wages and absence of rewards have apparently resulted in low output per man. Further, the report concluded that the United States "is far superior to both Western Europe and the Soviet bloc in labor productivity. . . . Even though the labor force of the United States is only 67 million compared with 105 to 110 million in the Soviet Union, the productivity of the average worker in the United States is so much greater, that total production is far greater. Total performance of the West is raised by American productivity more than Western superiority in numbers alone would provide."[3]

2. Projected Population Trends

Population projections for western Europe (the OEEC countries of Austria, Belgium, Denmark, France, Federal Germany, Greece, Iceland,

[3] *Ibid.*, p. 7.

Ireland, Italy, Luxembourg, Netherlands, Norway, Portugal, Saar, Sweden, Switzerland, Trieste, Turkey, and the United Kingdom) indicate the total population should reach 303 million in 1970. Projections for Spain, Finland, Yugoslavia, and West Berlin total about 60 million to give a total projected population for independent Europe of about 363 million in 1970. According to the Economic Commission for Europe there will be much greater possibilities for expansion of industrial output in western Europe, notwithstanding smaller increases in the working-age population, than in southern Europe, where population pressures make such expansion more urgent. However, if industrial production should lag in northwestern Europe, the situation in southern Europe will be even more serious since that area depends so heavily upon exports of raw materials and foodstuffs to the northern countries.

The population projection for captive Europe was that it would not reach its pre–World War II level before 1956 and that by 1970 the total should reach about 99 million. The forecast was for a continuation of the high birth rates in the eastern countries, which indicates a population containing a relatively high proportion of children in marked contrast to the "aging" of Western populations. The result will be a comparatively low proportion of population that will be included in the working ages, fifteen years and over—slightly over 62 percent in comparison with 66 and 67 percent for western Europe and the Soviet Union, repectively.

Estimates of the population of the Soviet Union in 1970 range from 244 million to 282 million. The report for the Joint Committee narrowed the range to 260 to 280 million. The June, 1956, Soviet official release suggests a possible downward revision in this range. The 1970 population of the United States was estimated at about 204 million.

The report concluded that the population of the West will grow about 15 percent by 1970 while that of the Soviet bloc will grow as much as 25 percent. The West will have a greater total population, but the Soviet bloc population will become equal to or larger than that of independent Europe. "As in other spheres, the dynamism of the United States provides the main element of growth in western trends while the Soviet Union provides the element in its orbit."

Some significant projections of manpower strength were included comparing the future population growth of the United States with that of the Soviet Union for the period ending 1970 on the basis of working ages 15–54 years and prime military ages for males, 20–34. Figure 12.1 shows the results of these projections.

The projections indicate that for the period 1950–70 the total number of persons in the 15–54 age group in the Soviet Union will increase 28

percent and in the United States will increase 22 percent. The margin
between the two countries will be greatest in 1970 with 146 million in the
Soviet Union compared with 103 million in the United States. The difference with regard to males is much greater—an increase of 40 percent
for the Soviet Union and 25 percent for the United States. This latter
gain for the Soviet Union is brought about by replacement of war losses.

Males of prime military age will remain constant from 1950 to 1960 at
17 million in the United States while they increase from 22 to 31 million

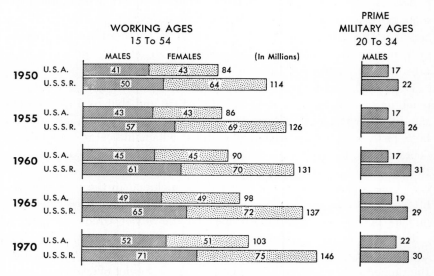

Figure 12.1.   Projected Population in Working and Military Ages, U.S.A. and U.S.S.R. (in Millions).
(Data from *Trends in Economic Growth*)

in Russia. The gap will begin to narrow thereafter with an increase in
the United States to 19 million in 1965 and 22 million in 1970, while a
decrease in Russia is indicated to 29 million in 1965 and 30 million in
1970. This is a result of the low birth rates in the United States in the
1930's—from 18 to 19 per 1000—and the increased post–World War II
birth rate in the United States to 25 per 1000 in 1954, while birth rates in
Russia slumped sharply from 37.7 per 1000 in 1940 to 24.9 in 1953.

The general conclusion of the study prepared for the Joint Committee
on the Economic Report was that the population of the Soviet bloc appears destined to surpass that of independent Europe in the foreseeable
future. The United States and independent Europe, together, will continue to outweigh the Soviet bloc over the next fifteen to twenty years,
but the gap will apparently narrow considerably. In addition, trends in

age structure seem more favorable to high economic activity in the Soviet bloc. Productivity advantages in the West and efforts to extend the working-age span seem the likeliest means by which these Soviet gains may be offset. "There is no apparent reason to expect that American output per man will not continue to offset the difference in numbers."

UNITED STATES POPULATION

1. Trends

After a period of very rapid growth prior to 1900 the rate of increase of United States population began to slow down. The indicated trend in the 1920's and the predicted trend in the 1930's and 1940's was that the population would reach a peak, then either level off or decline. The long-term decline in the birth rate became greater in the 1920's and 1930's. Total number of births actually declined between 1924 and 1936; immigration decreased after 1900 and stopped in the 1930's; and the crude death rate appeared to be reaching a minimum from which it could only rise. One of the accepted forecasts of 1938 was that peak population of less than 140 million would be reached by 1960, and another was for 154 million to be reached about 1980. Revisions of these forecasts were released by the United States Department of Commerce in 1943 and 1947, but as late as 1951 the official estimate of the peak population was 165 million and a decline before 2000 was indicated. The implications of these trends and their actual effects were a decreasing number of young people and an increasing number of old people. After World War II the drastic jump in the birth rate was thought of as a temporary phenomenon, so that no revision in the long-term trend of population growth was deemed necessary.

In an article, "Our Changed Population Outlook and Its Significance," which appeared in the June, 1952, issue of the *American Economic Review,* Joseph S. Davis stated emphatically in his introduction:

The population of the continental United States has radically changed in numbers, age composition, and marital composition since 1940. Numbers alone increased by about 25.1 million in the 12½ years from September 1, 1939, to March 1, 1952. The most striking increases were in young children under 5, 10, and 15 and in persons 65 and over. The number of married couples has greatly risen while the proportion of single persons 14 and over has impressively declined. More important accumulating data leave no room for doubt that our population outlook has undergone an outstanding if not revolutionary reversal in 1947–52.

American demographers, official and unofficial, are increasingly recognizing these facts, although they have been slow to acknowledge the upset of their best forecasts and their firmest convictions, and are naturally reluctant to go on record with revised ones. But the character and extent of these changes, and their profound economic and social significance, are not yet generally realized in academic and business circles.

Recognizing these changes the Bureau of the Census of the United States Department of Commerce released *Population Projections to 1975* on May 17, 1956. The key figures for "recent growth of the United States population" were given as follows:

1. In the decade between the Censuses of 1940 and 1950, total population increased by 19,000,000 as compared with an increase of 9,000,000 from 1930 to 1940; 17,000,000 from 1920 to 1930; 14,000,000 from 1910 to 1920; and 16,000,000 from 1900 to 1910.
2. On a percentage basis, the increase from 1940 to 1950 was 14.5%, about double the 1930 to 1940 increase, but about the same as the 1910 to 1920 rate of increase and less than the rate of increase in the other decades since the establishment of the United States.
3. Reliable statistics built up from births and deaths and net immigration, show that the increase in numbers 1950 to 1955 was 13,000,000, about 8½% of the 1950 population and that the gain in the 1940 to 1950 decade as compared with the previous decade was due mostly to a sharp increase in births in the second half of the decade.
4. In words, the declining trend in the rate of growth of the United States population which was noted in 1940 flattened out at or a little before that time and a rising trend was established before 1950.

The Bureau of the Census stated quite conservatively: "This important reversal of trend has aroused great interest and stimulated several lines of thought." The Bureau called attention to the following factors which had been suggested as responsible for the recent noteworthy rise in the birth rate and the large net annual gains in population: (a) change in the attitude of young people toward larger families; (b) improvement in relative earning power of young workers; (c) absence since World War II of depressions or severe recessions; (d) greater willingness of parents of young couples to help support their children; (e) reduction in mortality rates and in the extent of disabling sickness, with resulting betterment of the family financial background, and increase in the duration of married life.

By population projections the Census means a series of figures for the population in 1960, 1965, 1970, 1975, computed on the basis of (a) the population classified by age and sex as recent Census Bureau estimates show it to have been at a recent date, and (b) a defined set of assumptions as to birth rates, death rates, and net immigration up to 1975.

The Census release of 1956 used four projections which were pub-

lished in October, 1955, in *Current Population Report*, Series P-25, No.
123, as follows, as compared with the actual July 1, 1955, figure of 165,-
248,000:

Series AA	193.3M in 1965 and 228.5M in 1975
Series A	190.3M in 1965 and 221.5M in 1975
Series B	190.3M in 1965 and 214.6M in 1975
Series C	186.3M in 1965 and 206.9M in 1975

Figure 12.2 gives the United States population from 1900 to 1955 and
the four projections. The percentage increases in the total population
for the twenty-year period 1955 to 1975 would be 38, 34, 30, and 25 per-

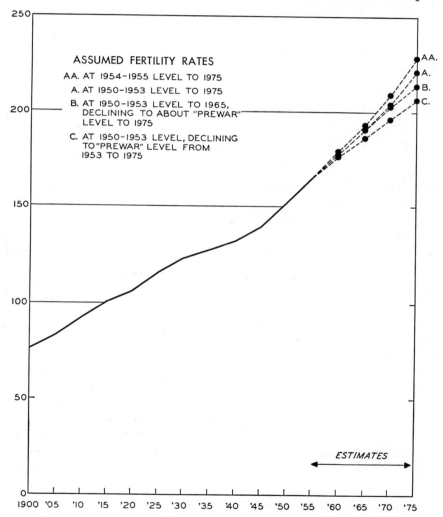

Figure 12.2.   U.S. Population. (*Population Projections to 1975,* Bureau of the Census)

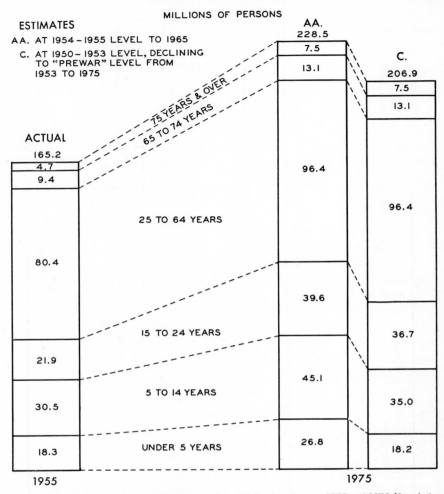

MILLIONS OF PERSONS

ESTIMATES

AA. AT 1954-1955 LEVEL TO 1965

C. AT 1950-1953 LEVEL, DECLINING
   TO "PREWAR" LEVEL FROM
   1953 TO 1975

AA.
228.5

C.
206.9

ACTUAL
165.2

75 YEARS & OVER
65 TO 74 YEARS

25 TO 64 YEARS

15 TO 24 YEARS

5 TO 14 YEARS

UNDER 5 YEARS

1955   1975

Figure 12.3.   Projections of Total Population of the U.S. by Age Groups, 1955 and 1975. (*Population Projections to 1975*, Bureau of the Census)

cent respectively. For each of the four projections the mortality rates used were a continuation until 1960 of the rate of decrease observed in the 1940's, but it was assumed they would remain constant after 1960 at the average 1955–60 levels. Net immigration was taken as 1,400,000 in the period 1955–60, approximately the same number of net arrivals during the previous five years 1950–55, and as 1,200,000 per five-year period 1960–75. The assumptions as to fertility rates are shown in Figure 12.2.

Figure 12.3 and Table 90 supplement the projections. Figure 12.3

TABLE 90. Estimated School Enrollment and the Labor Force

Elementary and High-School Enrollment		
	Elementary Grades	High-School Grades
Actual enrollment 10/1/52	22,000,000	7,058,000
Projected enrollment, basis A or B		
1955	25,699,000	7,594,000
1960	30,548,000	9,422,000
1965	31,868,000	12,145,000
Percentage of increase:		
1952 to 1965	45	72
1952 to 1955	17	8
1955 to 1960	19	24
1960 to 1965	4	29

Population of College Age—18–24 Inclusive		
	Number	Percent Increase over 1955
Actual 7/1/55	15,106,000	—
Projected 1965	20,043,000	33
Projected 1973	26,360,000	75

Labor Force, Age 14 Years Old and Over			
	Both Sexes	Male	Female
Actual April 1955 level	67,784,000	47,593,000	20,191,000
Revised estimates based on population projections A or B			
April 1960	71,905,000	50,078,000	21,827,000
April 1965	77,614,000	53,108,000	24,506,000
April 1970	84,530,000	56,997,000	27,533,000
April 1975	91,565,000	61,071,000	30,494,000
Percent increase			
1975 over 1955	35[a]	28	51

[a] Population increase, 1975 over 1955: Projection A, 34% — Projection B, 30%

SOURCES: U.S. Bureau of the Census Current Population Reports: (a) Projections of School Enrollment in the U.S. 1953 to 1965, Series P-25, No. 85, December 7, 1953; (b) Illustrative Projections of the College Age Population by States, 1958 to 1973, Series P-25, No. 132, February 20, 1956; (c) preliminary unpublished revision of "A Projected Growth of the Labor Force in the U.S. Under Conditions of High Employment, 1950–1975," Series P-50, No. 42, December 10, 1952.

gives the distribution by age groups for 1955 and for 1975 for the AA and C projections. Table 90 presents detailed information on the A or B basis for estimating school enrollment and the labor force.

The *U.S. News and World Report* used the AA projection as the basis of an article in the January 6, 1956, issue and dramatized the changes in the following fashion:

This country is heading for its greatest boom ever in population. Already the number of Americans has grown, since World War II, at a rate far exceeding the wildest forecast.

Ten years ago, when servicemen returned from the war, an explosion occurred in the birth rate. The baby crop, previously around 2.7 million a year, zoomed past 3 million, then past 4 million. Population growth of around 1.5 million a year soon became 2.8 million.

The nation still is trying to adjust itself to this great growth. Schools are inadequate. Highways can't handle the traffic. Communities are spreading out in every direction.

What's going to happen in the next 20 years, however, is going to make present growth seem small, by comparison.

About 10 years from now, all those children born in the bumper baby crops that followed World War II are going to start getting married and raising families.

Then a second explosion is going to occur in population from 1966 onward; for at least 10 years, the baby crop will grow by leaps and bounds, until nearly 6 million babies are being born every year.

Result: By 1975, experts forecast, this country will have a population around 228.5 million.

That means an increase of 63.3 million people, or 38 percent in 20 years.

2. Implications of Change in Growth

The change in population growth in the United States will have revolutionary effects and innumerable implications. Some of the more important will be suggested with the thought that each one requires much more intensive study and action.

A. Education

The educational system since shortly before 1950 has been struggling with the number of World War II and postwar babies as they enter elementary school and have required more school teachers and facilities. Table 90 gives the projected enrollment on the A or B basis for the elementary and high-school grades, and the projection of the college age population 18–24. For the elementary grades this projection would indicate a growth from the actual enrollment of 22,000,000 in 1952 of 17 percent to 1955 and 19 percent from 1955 to 1960, to be followed by only a 4 percent increase from 1960 to 1965, or an overall increase of 45 percent in enrollment by 1965. The high-school figures reflect the moving mass of children as enrollment peaks up in the latter years. Thus the actual enrollment of 7,058,000 in 1952 increased by only 8 percent by 1955, but will go up by 24 percent between 1955 and 1960 and 29 percent between 1960 and 1965, for a total increase of 72 percent between 1952 and 1965. Careful planning to meet these enrollments is required for facilities and in preparation of, and financial incentives for, teachers.

The projection for the 18–24 group is titled "Population of College

Age" as there is no certainty, as there is for the elementary and high-school grades, that most of the total population will attend college. For the college age the projection is given for an additional eight years to 1973 to take care of the mass of population moving up from the high-school ages. College population of 15,106,000 in 1955 was expected to increase 33 percent by 1965 and 75 percent over 1955 by 1973. In April, 1950, according to census reports, 18.6 percent of those aged 18–24 were "enrolled in school," as compared with 13.3 percent in 1940. There is evidence that this higher percentage of attendance will be maintained and possibly increase, as it was 31 percent in 1956.

United States policy at the local, state, and federal level has consistently recognized and supported public education. It is not the purpose here to present and discuss the various problems and policies involved. The basic need is an awareness of the trends of student population and avoidance of such stupid questions, heard in the past, as: "Where are all these students coming from?" They are on their way in large numbers. Facilities and faculties must be intelligently planned and adequately supported financially.

B. The Older Age Group—65 and Over

Demographers have been correct in forecasting a rapid growth of the population aged 65 and over. As we have seen, the growth has been due to improved mortality rates and has resulted in an "aging" population. Projections of the total population of the United States in Figure 12.3 show that the number of this age group was 14.1 million, or 8 percent of the total population, in 1955, as compared with 6.9 percent in 1940. Projections on the AA basis estimate 20.6 million aged 65 and over in 1975, or 9 percent of the total population. If the C basis is used the rate will increase to 10 percent.

This aging of the population presents many problems ranging from how the group will secure its support to the provision of recreation and avocation programs for the "retired." At the national level the need for social security has been recognized in the passage of the Social Security Act in 1935. Since that time coverage and benefits of Old Age and Survivors Insurance have been extended. In 1935 only one out of ten people was included under retirement systems; by 1955 nine out of ten people were under Social Security alone. In addition, increasing earned incomes are being achieved through pensions and personal investments. Perhaps even more important, occupational changes are placing higher premiums on mental skills than on physical powers, so that an increasing number of older persons are able to support themselves. The problem of support must also be studied in connection with the labor force.

C. The Labor Force

The casual reference in Table 90 to "Labor Force, Age 14 Years Old and Over" requires full and careful definition. "Labor force" as used in this table is total labor force and includes armed force and the civilian labor force. (The civilian labor force includes those of the civilian non-institutional population 14 years of age and over who are classified as employed or unemployed in accordance with the following definitions: Employed—those who in the survey week did any work for pay or profit or worked without pay for fifteen hours or more on a family farm or business, and those with a job but not at work. Unemployed—those who did not work during the survey period, and who were looking for work. Also included as unemployed are persons who would have been looking for work except that they were ill, they were temporarily laid off, or they believed no work was available in their line of work or in the community.) One of the most interesting facts about the United States labor force is that, except for the war years 1942–43–44–45 and 1951–52 when the labor force was 58.2, 61.6, 62.4, 61.2, and 58.2, 58.1 percent respectively of the total population, the labor force from 1929 through 1955 varied within the narrow range of 55.4 to 57.8 percent of the total population. During the first quarter of 1955 this percentage was 56.3. Thus there is considerable justification for predicting that the labor force will be maintained within this percentage order of magnitude and adjustments will be made to take into account the aging population and the number under 14 years of age. This assumption is reflected in the projection on basis A, which indicates an increase in the labor force of 35 percent in 1975 over 1955 compared with an increase of 34 percent in the population.

The questions have been raised about the increase of the labor force as to whether there will be a serious shortage of labor supply, on the one hand, or unemployment, on the other.

In the first instance this fear seems to arise from the increased burden on the labor force to support the old and the young. The pressure is real at present because of the dent in the United States population pyramid (see Figure 12.4) caused by the low birth rates of the 1930's. As this dent is removed by the moving up of the World War II and postwar babies, the problem will be partially solved. In addition, as already suggested, adjustments are being and can be made to bring an increasing number of the older age groups into the labor force. One other group, which also includes the older group, can be tapped: persons outside the labor force in the "labor pool." The "labor pool" includes those outside the "labor force" who could work: the young, handicapped, women, and other nonworkers, in addition to the aged, who are not part of the "labor force." The "labor pool" is also illustrated in Figure 12.4. Further, this first fear,

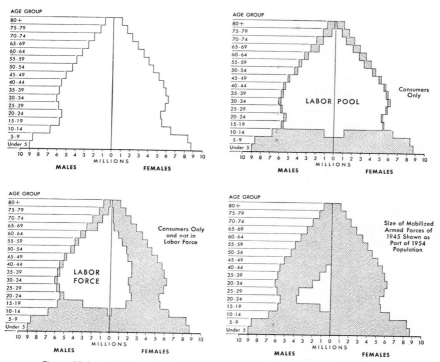

Figure 12.4.   U.S. Population—1954. (Data from Armed Forces Industrial College)

of an inadequate "labor force," does not take into account fully the possibilities of automation and increased per capita productivity.

On the other hand, those who fear that the increased labor force will lead to unemployment lack the vision of those who see an expanding economy and the increased labor force as a supporting factor of production. Some who express this concern are still acutely aware of what happened in the great depression of the 1930's, but others are worried that automation may lead to unemployment. It is in the area of unemployment that United States policy has been most specific. The paramount declaration of policy by Congress appeared in the Employment Act of 1946:

. . . The Congress hereby declares that it is the continuing policy and responsibility of the Federal Government to use all practicable means consistent with its needs and obligations and other essential considerations of national policy, with the assistance and cooperation of industry, agriculture, labor, and State and local governments, to coordinate and utilize all its plans, functions, and resources for the purpose of creating and maintaining in a manner calculated to foster and promote free competitive enterprise and the general welfare, conditions under which there will be afforded useful employment opportunities, including self-employment, for those able, willing, and seeking to work, and to promote maximum employment, production, and purchasing power.

The measures and detailed policies adopted to implement this broad policy to promote maximum employment have been many and varied. Section 3(a) of the Employment Act of 1946 requires that the President make an Economic Report to the Congress of the United States. It is prepared with the "assistance and advice of the Council of Economic Advisers" and is transmitted to the Congress each January under the title *Economic Report of the President.* This report contains a full statement of the efforts to maintain full employment. There is ample evidence that almost full employment was achieved from 1946 to 1956 and that this is a paramount national policy. The dispute is over the means to attain the end with ever-improving economic tools. Under the circumstances the specter of unemployment is alive as a problem but much less likely as a mass problem than in the past.

Another problem of the labor force is that out of a limited age group of the total force must come the armed force. This is also illustrated by the population pyramids shown in Figure 12.4. The problem has already been presented briefly in the comparison between the United States and Russia. The "military manpower pool" is generally considered to be those men in the age bracket from 18 to 45. This group is almost entirely determined by the birth rate in the period 18 to 45 years prior to the time of military need. We have seen that the size of the pool, which was a dynamic problem during the Korean War, will be increasing in the future. The major problem that must be solved is mobilizing manpower. This is of such importance to the strength and security of the United States that it requires separate analysis in Chapter 13, "Human Resources Problems and Policy."

D. Households

One of the most important implications of the changes in the rate of growth of the population is in the increased number of households formed. Expanding population means more marriages, and when a marriage occurs, a new household usually is formed. Figure 12.5 gives the actual number of new households formed per year from 1945 through 1955 and the projected number on the AA basis through 1975. In 1955 there were 47,788,000 households in the United States. The prospects are for 18,500,000 new households by 1975. The new households are a guide to future markets for basic durable goods such as homes, furniture, appliances, and automobiles, thousands of consumer nondurable goods, and countless services. Sustained employment of the breadwin-

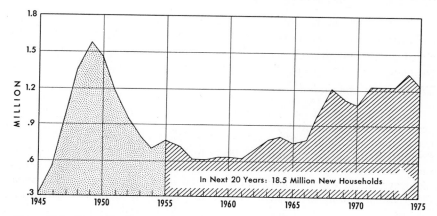

Figure 12.5. New Households: A Guide to Future Markets. (Data from Census Bureau and Department of Health, Education and Welfare through 1955; later years, estimates by Economic Unit of U.S. News and World Report)

ners of these new households will thus provide effective demand for the production potential of our economy.

United States policy has been to extend liberal credit for home financing through such agencies as the Federal Housing Administration. Business policy has also been to grant liberal credit for purchase of all types of consumer goods. These policies will doubtless be continued. The main problems involved will be those requiring credit controls through monetary and fiscal policies which will facilitate expansion without inflation. Inflation has been one of the most serious post–World War II problems in the United States. Increased population growth will increase the size of the problem, which can only be solved through sound policy and firm action.

E. Production

Increased growth of population offers a stimulus to production through demand, but this is only part of the story which might be told at great length in the expansion of both private and social production.

There will be numerous problems and policy decisions, but these will represent challenges and opportunities of a growing economy.

F. Resources

Finally, what effect will growth of population have on resources? Truly a major problem, which in part we have already answered but which requires separate and more detailed consideration in the next chapter.

3. Population Projection Policy

The recommendation of the Bureau of the Census is that sound policy calls for a check each year, or perhaps each quarter, for indications of a significant worsening of economic conditions. In presenting *Population Projections to 1975* for the Bureau of the Census on May 17, 1956, Robert W. Burgess concluded:

The financial strain on families which started in 1947 or which began to grow more rapidly in that year, will increase year by year unless family income increases along with the increasing needs of growing children. The financial strain on the community, likely to be reflected in rising taxes, is already becoming significant because of requirements for schools, roads and highways, better water supply, and similar facilities. As long as the Consumer Price Index continues to hold stable, the index of industrial production follows the usual seasonal pattern with only mild cyclical fluctuation, the level of personal income remains satisfactory in relation to individual needs, and employment expands in line with the growth of population of working ages, projection AA may well prove a good guide. After a period of weakness in several of these indicators, population growth may shift temporarily or permanently to one of the lower projections. It is desirable, therefore, sometimes to test a proposed plan against several other projections as well as the one accepted as the best forecast.

All factors considered, it is my judgment that if these projections are checked regularly against current economic indicators and reviewed carefully every two or three years, they will provide a helpful guide for general policy discussions and many governmental and business operation decisions.[4]

---

[4] Robert W. Burgess, *Population Projections to 1975*, Department of Commerce, Bureau of the Census, May 17, 1956.

CHAPTER 13

Human Resources Problems and Policy

Of the thousands of problems in the area of human resources only three will be singled out for a brief discussion—man and resources, manpower mobilization, and man and freedom.

MAN AND RESOURCES

Joseph J. Spengler has defined *the population problem* as follows: "The population problem of any collectivity (e.g., a nation) has its origin in imbalance between numbers, output, and desired level of consumption." He points out that it resembles in part the general economic problem, "for this problem also has its origin in imbalance—that between a collectivity's aggregate of conduct—determining material wants and its capacity to satisfy these wants." The capacity to satisfy these wants is limited by the resources available. Population growth is limited by the resources available, but, as we have already pointed out, population as a factor of production facilitates production and on the other hand is the source of effective demand which stimulates production. The argument can be made that the real population problem is: Are there enough resources available to support a sustained population growth and a rising plane of living?

If this were indeed "one world" this problem might be discussed on an international basis. We have already seen the limits and possibilities of agricultural, energy and material, and capital resources on an international basis as well as a national basis. We have, in general, reached the conclusion that even though there are serious limitations in many specific commodities we can, through proper policies and their implementation, solve our basic problem. We have seen in the chapters on agricultural resources that, while the United States was faced with a surplus of food, the unavailability of adequate food supplies to over half of the people of the world was considered to be "the fundamental agricultural problem." However, we postponed to this chapter the discussion of the relation of population growth to the food supply. This we will single out for study as *the problem* under our present topic "Man and Resources."

1. Malthus and Neo-Malthusianism

Thomas Robert Malthus, who died in 1834, predicted that the world's population would soon outgrow its food supply. He reached the conclusion that the growth of population was determined almost entirely by the *means of subsistence,* by which was meant chiefly the food supply, although clothing and shelter were also included. He believed that where subsistence was abundant population grew rapidly, because the death rate would be low. Where subsistence was scarce population could grow only slowly if at all. Malthus saw that disease and war, especially disease, by increasing the death rate also affected population growth, but he placed the major emphasis on subsistence, food, as the great controller of population growth. The result was that Malthus held out little hope for any permanent improvement in human living conditions (a rising plane of living), since he believed that population always had a tendency to grow faster than food supply.

Malthus believed that even in a new country such as America, where food supply could be expanded greatly, population growth would about keep pace with it. When new land was exhausted, America would be in the same position as older countries, where there was great need and poverty. This belief rested on the assumption that (1) the birth rate was approximately fixed at physiological capacity, and (2) subsistence was not often capable of being expanded rapidly and then not for a long period of time. However, Malthus did modify his reasoning by considering that postponement of marriage and abstinence from marital relations, as well as certain customs and taboos, reduced the birth rate slightly. Taking these possibilities into consideration, he did not see any way out of the dilemma created by a high birth rate and a limited amount of tillable land. He never saw the possibilities of birth control as a method of adjusting population to the means of subsistence, or of increasing the efficiency of agricultural production.

By the end of World War II, the world's population had more than doubled from the one billion of Malthus' time. New lands were cultivated and old lands produced more. Trade and transportation brought surplus foods to areas of deficiency. There were many who contended that the world never ran out of food, and that Malthus had underestimated both "nature's resources and man's resourcefulness"; in fact they claimed "Malthus was wrong." Others claimed that there was a good deal of truth in the relation of the growth of subsistence and population.

Following over a century of very little interest in Malthus' doctrines, two books were published in the United States in 1948—*Our Plundered Planet,* by Fairfield Osborn, and *Road to Survival* (a Book-of-the-Month Club selection), by William Vogt. *Time* reported that these books were "glowingly reviewed and selling like hot cakes" and in them the ghost of Malthus was "on the rampage" in the form of "Neo-Malthusian" predictions of world-wide overpopulation and hunger.

In analyzing these books, *Time* stated that the Neo-Malthusians admitted that Malthus was wrong but claimed that new and frightening threats had developed recently. In summary, the present-day world has almost no fresh land to cultivate. Its old lands, "plundered" by reckless exploitation, are losing fertility as their "irreplaceable topsoil" washes down the rivers. Farmlands cannot keep up their present production. The world's population is still increasing rapidly, and modern medicine, by cutting the death rate from infectious diseases, is sure to stimulate this increase. The falling food-production curve will soon cross the rising population curve. *Time* concluded that there was some merit in the Neo-Malthusian purpose of encouraging soil conservation but that the over-all effect was to give unintended comfort to political and social policies advocating: "Go out and grab more land, clearing it, if necessary, of its present population."

As opposed to the "Neo-Malthusians" soil scientists claimed that every main article of this creed "is either false or distorted or unprovable." Soil scientists are sure that the modern world has both the soil and the scientific knowledge to feed well twice as many people as were living in 1948. Further, by the time the population had increased that much, man would have discovered new ways of increasing his food supply.

There are two main parts of the Neo-Malthusian thesis: (a) that dealing with the soil and its productivity and (b) that dealing with population and its growth. Let us examine the thesis and the replies.

A. The Soil Thesis

The soil thesis has three central ideas.

The first idea is that "soil cannot be stretched," that each acre has a certain production capacity (Vogt calls it "biotic potential") which cannot be increased without dire consequences. Part of this idea is that the fertility of soil is limited, another part is that topsoil is "irreplaceable," and an overlooked part is that man can improve plants.

The notion that the fertility of the soil is limited (or land is static) is disputed by the soil scientists, who admit that virgin soils vary widely in fertility but assert that once the soil is in use man, by proper planting and fertilization, can adapt it to its best use. Man is the master of the soil, not its servant.

That topsoil is irreplaceable is also disputed by the soil scientists, who cite instances in which proper measures have been used to create topsoil. They do not produce evidence of cost, however.

Most emphatic, however, is the contention that "soil" *can* "be stretched" by man, who is the master of the plants that grow in it. A whole list of new hybrid varieties of crops can be given that have increased the "biotic potential." A favorite illustration in North Carolina is the "Dixie" hybrid corn, which, when highly fertilized and planted thicker than ordinary corn, made 125 bushels to the acre as compared with a previous yield of 22 bushels with ordinary varieties.

The second idea of the Neo-Malthusians is that productivity of the world's cultivated land is falling now and is sure to fall more because of erosion and exhaustion. The United States Soil Conservation Service has its very basis of existence in the fact of a serious erosion problem during the 1930's; however, the Service believes that United States soils are now getting better on the whole and that the downward trend has been reversed. The Service has little conclusive information about soil conservation in the rest of the world. There is no question about the fact, though, that once fertile areas throughout the world are badly depleted. The Food and Agricultural Organization and technical aid are means to help solve the problem. The obstacles to conservation are economic and social, not technical. *Time* reported: "For the Neo-Malthusian scare-dogma that the world's soil must inevitably lose its productiveness, the soil men have a one-word answer: bunkem!"

The third idea of the soil thesis is that the world has little new soil to cultivate. Soil men claim there is plenty of new soil. The chernozems and other temperate grassland soils are for the most part in use, but there are still large areas of unused forest soils (podzols) which can be made productive by up-to-date methods as soon as the market appears for their produce and transportation makes them accessible. In addition there are large areas of land available in the tropics.

Robert M. Salter, of the United States Agricultural Research Administration, calculated how much food the world could produce. He took the estimate of the Food and Agricultural Organization of how much food it would take to give every person in the world in 1960 an "adequate diet" (about that of the United States). A 1960 world population of 2250 million (FAO estimate) would require 21 percent more cereals than the 1936–39 average, 46 percent more meat, twice as much milk, etc. Dr. Salter calculated that if the world's croplands in cultivation in 1948 were cultivated at efficiency levels considered attainable in the United States by 1950, they would produce almost enough food to meet the FAO's generous requirements.

Looking for the new soil the Neo-Malthusians said did not exist, Dr. Salter eliminated 48 percent of the land area in ice, tundra, mountains, or deserts as hopeless for agriculture. In the remaining 52 percent he found an abundance of room for expansion since only 7 to 10 percent of the total was cultivated. He estimated that the world's total food production could be more than twice the 1960 FAO goal if, in addition to the world's efficiently cultivated croplands, 10 percent of the podzols (300 million acres) were cultivated by Finland methods and 20 percent of the tropical red soils (one billion acres) were cultivated by Philippine methods.

On the soil and productivity side of the Neo-Malthusian thesis *Time* drew the conclusion that "if the world wanted to make the great effort, it can, by applying present day techniques, provide food for more than twice its present population."

B. Population and Growth Thesis

The second part of the Neo-Malthusian thesis dealing with population and its growth is the conviction that people will multiply blindly (like fruit flies) as long as they get enough food.

The counterarguments which have been made are many:

First, human beings are not like fruit flies. Population increase, either among families or among nations, has no simple connection with food. High-income families, which get all the food they want, usually have fewer children. The same is often (but not always) true of nations.

Second, the most spectacular increases in population have come with industrialization. The "laws" which have been taught are that the early stages of industrialization, in any country, seem to be associated with a moderate rise in the birth rate, a sharp fall in the death rate, and a resultant steep rise in the population. After a period of years there is a decrease in the rate of increase and the population begins to level off or in some instances decline. This is brought about as the death rate keeps on declining but the birth rate falls faster. This was the case of all industrialized countries up to the end of World War II. We have seen, however, that recent United States experience has upset this leveling off. Could it be that we are in a new stage of industrialization?

Third, birth control practices and planned families are now common-place in the developed countries.

The foregoing three and many other arguments are used to refute the second part of the Neo-Malthusian thesis. One very questionable argument that *Time* concluded with was as follows: "When their populations rise, following the classic curve, they can probably raise enough food to keep their people supplied until the curve begins to flatten out normally." Think of the problems this happy conclusion ignores.

What are the elements of truth in the relation of population to the food supply? Let us not forget the previously quoted statement of Gove Hambidge which it was suggested might be entitled *We Are Two Worlds*.

What we can be sure of is this: The world has long been divided into two parts.

We have a half-world of plenty, inhabited by the people of countries like the United States, Canada, Australia, New Zealand, and most of Western Europe.

We have a half-world of hunger and want, inhabited by the people of most of Asia and the Middle East, practically all of Africa, and large parts of Latin America.

We know too that since the war world food production has increased by 9 percent, while the number of people has grown by 13 percent. So there is less food for each person than there was before the war; and there was not enough then, by quite a long way.

The lag since the war has been in the half-world of want, which makes a bad situation worse. The tide of hunger has been creeping up on tens of millions of human beings.

In the half-world of plenty, where you and I live, production has continued to keep ahead of population growth, so that on the average we are now even better off than we were before. And we did not do too badly then.

2. Population and the Means of Subsistence

We know then that there is a very real need for food in half of the world. It is quite possible that this is *the fundamental economic, social, and political problem* of the world. We know that the food supply and all resources are not fixed but are relative to and a function of man's wants and abilities. We know that man has the technical knowledge to expand the food supply and to control population. These measures have been used in half the world. Further, we can conclude that the Malthusian concept of the relationship of population to the *means of subsistence* makes a great deal of sense if we include not only Malthus' food and little-emphasized clothing and shelter but also the total means of subsistence or resource base as we now understand it. However, we must repeat that our understanding of the resource base is a dynamic one subject to man's wants and abilities and that there is a dynamic reciprocal relationship between man and his environment so that the two can grow together. Man is not a "fruit fly"; he has the ability to organize his scarce resources, increase their supply, use them and reuse them more efficiently, and/or rationally limit his numbers and thus raise his plane of living.

3. Conclusions

In concluding this discussion of man and resources let us look briefly at (a) United States population projections and resources and (b) some international policy implications.

A. United States Population Projections

Can we conclude that the United States population can or will go on expanding along with the resource base in this snowball fashion which we have described? Will the rate of population projections to 1975 be continued into the future with an expanding resource base? Let us pass this question to Robert W. Burgess, speaking for the Bureau of the Census:

As a test of the reasonableness of these projections 25 years beyond the 1950 Census, consider the effect of the repetition of the 1950 to 1975 rate of increase for the next three quarter-centuries after 1975. The rate of increase from 152,000,000 at July 1, 1950 to 228,000,000 at July 1, 1975 is exactly 50% of the 1950 figure. Applying the same percentage increase for the next three quarters would give year 2000, 342,000,000; 2025, 513,000,000; 2050, 770,000,000.

This mathematical computation of the population of the United States by the middle of the next century, at over five times the 1950 population, strikes me as ranging beyond the bounds of what the physical resources of this country would permit, assuming adherence to our present standard of living. I have no recent analysis in mind on which to base this speculation, and must admit that some people have rosy dreams of greatly increasing our supply of water and food and mineral resources and our ability to draw on other countries for items of which the domestic supply proves inadequate. The Paley Commission (Resources for Freedom) pointed out commodities for which the United States is already a net importer rather than an exporter. It seems more reasonable to assume that within a relatively few decades there must be reduction, largely due to increasing strain on the economic front, in the percentage rate of increase to a rate lower than the 50% every 25 years we are projecting for the period 1950 to 1975. It seems to me reasonable to expect a gradual reduction of the rates within the next 30 to 40 years and to allow for the possibility that some reduction may come before 1975, by using projections B and C as well as AA.

While the annual percentage increase in the population should not be assumed to continue to run indefinitely at present high levels, it is hard, on the other hand, to see signs of economic hardship and shortage of food or jobs of the sort that would be responsible for a sharp drop in the birth rate within the next five or ten years.

The Bureau of the Census has been wrong in the past and may well be in the future. Perhaps the one conclusion that we should agree upon is that change is the only thing normal in a dynamic economy such as ours. Joseph S. Davis in his 1952 article on "Our Changed Population Outlook and Its Significance" concludes: "We must unlearn much of what the demographers have too well taught us, realize the unsound bases for many past assumptions, and view their latest projections and assertions with highly skeptical eyes. We face an extremely different nation from the one they had led us to expect with assurance, and must make the best of its unpredictability where we had thought it most predictable."

Had we who held to a dynamic concept of resources accepted the predictions with assurance?

B. Some International Policy Implications

The Neo-Malthusians tend to advocate super-isolationism. Their argument is: "The world is already overpopulated. Some areas like the United States are more fortunate than others, but even the United States will soon run out of food. Therefore it should not help foreigners. Let them starve now, before they increase their numbers with our help and overwhelm us." According to *Time,* "Vogt suggests that the United States should help no country with food or anything else unless it first agrees to limit its birth rate. One method he favors; a bonus to males who allow themselves to be sterilized." A few epidemics or, better still, a nice war would be a fine solution to the population problem. Do not forget that Vogt's *Road to Survival* was a Book-of-the-Month Club selection in 1948. Certainly, this is no way for the United States to win friends and build up situations of strength throughout the world.

However, there are policy lessons to be learned from "scare books." One fundamental lesson is to remember that there is a relation between population growth and the means of subsistence. An increase in the population without a corresponding increase in the means of subsistence will lower per capita income and the plane of living. An increase in subsistence may lead to an increase in population. With an increase in population there may be a drive for more living space (*Lebensraum*). Thus new wars may be generated. Is such a simple act as spraying a little DDT around, or some other health measure, a truly humanitarian act? This and hundreds of other questions need be asked. In summary, *the fundamental* policy lesson to be learned is that our foreign aid programs of all types need to be thought through in advance and planned in an integrated manner.

Finally, as we think of "Man and Resources" and in particular of the specific topic "Man and Food," we might well recall a pre–World War II slogan "Food Will Win the War and Write the Peace." This writer never did think that food would win World War II, but United States food did start Europe on its road to recovery and has been a significant factor in other areas. Food may well "Win the Cold War and Help Maintain the Peace." With half the world hungry, unrest is assured. It is quite apparent that the United States is far ahead of Russia in agricultural knowledge and production. We must find a way to help other hungry people feed themselves, or their numbers will be absorbed in the Communist bloc. Hungry men have no time to think of politics or freedom. They do not even know the meaning of the latter when they are chained to the soil seeking their daily bread.

MANPOWER MOBILIZATION

Mobilizing capital facilities for security was discussed in Chapter 11. Our second major problem and policy area singled out for discussion in this chapter is mobilizing manpower. Although for organizational purposes these topics are treated separately, we must in fact consider them together, just as all phases of our economy must be studied together as a part of a whole contributing to our productive strength. The manpower problem thus is a part of the whole problem of balance in allocating the factors of production. The problem of mobilizing manpower for military security purposes is today a problem of military-industrial balance or, in its broadest application, a part of the problem of military-civilian balance.

1. Pre—World War II Experience

Neither the availability of manpower for the armed forces nor the issue of military-civilian balance became a serious United States problem until World War II.

In the Revolutionary War the American colonies used conscription to fill their quotas. In the Civil War the draft was employed by both the North and the South. During World War I selective service was used on the basis of an act passed on May 18, 1917.

Between World War I and World War II the small peacetime armed forces were composed of volunteers. However, a Joint Army and Navy Selective Service Committee kept in a state of readiness a proposed law together with regulations, forms, and an organizational plan. It also trained, through correspondence courses and regional conferences, a nucleus of reserve officers to administer Selective Service.

The following conclusions were drawn in a 1956 study of "Manpower Requirements of the Military Establishment":

Our military establishment was completely lacking in formulated ideas concerning its needs in manpower, raw or trained, at the beginnings of World War I and World War II. It was not prepared in 1917 for the war of position that was foreshadowed in 1914, nor was it prepared for the war of movement —blitzkrieg—in 1939–1940. The Eberstadt Report indicated that inadequate attention was given to the manpower aspects of mobilization and that realistic plans for effective over-all allocation and utilization of manpower did not exist.

The general neglect of manpower was also evident in the lack of plans for industrial mobilization. The Assistant Chief of Staff, G-1, was responsible for military manpower, and the Assistant Secretary of War was responsible for industrial mobilization. The responsibility to provide the manpower to make the weapons, munitions, and equipment needed by the Armed Forces was unassigned—and at a time when the Armed Forces were taking the younger workmen into service. The industrial mobilization plans even up to 1939 were devoid of adequate manpower provisions, although Enoch Crowder, in his report as provost marshal general in World War I, clearly indicated the need.[1]

2. World War II Experience

A. Military-Civilian Balance

World War II brought the United States economy face to face with the problem of maintaining the military-civilian balance. The Department of Social Sciences of the United States Military Academy de-

[1] Eli Ginzberg et al., *Human Resources and National Security*, National Academy of Economics and Political Science, Series No. 10, 1955, p. 125.

scribes the principle of the military-civilian balance in elementary terms: Every individual placed in uniform necessitates the provision of behind-the-lines facilities for his feeding, sheltering, transporting, arming, clothing, and recreation. The essential needs of his family must continue to be met, and the gap in production left by his departure from the civilian labor force must be closed either by reduction in civilian consumption or by expanded efforts on the part of those individuals remaining in civilian clothes. In addition to individuals actually in uniform there is a considerable drain by the military on the labor force for civilians to perform clerical and administrative jobs and to operate arsenals and other government installations. Civil defense may add to the drain in the future.

The maintenance of the military-civilian balance is seen to involve the following problems:

(1) The quantitative division of the labor force between the military and the home front. Hence, the amount of expansion of the labor force is a basic determinant of the size of the armed forces.

(2) The qualitative division of the labor force. Industrial conversion and expansion can be gravely handicapped by loss of skilled and professional people to the armed forces and government.

(3) The standard of living, which is the most important single factor in determining the balance between civilian and military requirements for production, and hence for manpower, in an emergency economy. The higher the peacetime standard, the greater the increment theoretically available for conversion to support of the emergency effort.

(4) Standards and conditions of work. Assuming a one-to-two ratio between men in the military forces and the workers supporting them, an increase of one hour in the United States workweek (assuming a 40-hour average) would provide for another 500,000 soldiers or over a dozen infantry divisions with all their supporting troops.[2]

B. Selective Service

A Selective Service and Training Act of 1940 was passed after a bitter debate and went into operation in November of that year approximately fourteen months after the beginning of World War II in Europe. The act provided for a maximum period of active training and service of twelve months unless Congress declared an emergency. As expiration of the required training period approached, President Roosevelt requested legislation to extend the service of selectees and to remove the restriction of 900,000 selectees to be inducted yearly. After an extremely bitter

[2] George A. Lincoln, *Economics of National Security*, Prentice-Hall, Inc., 1954, p. 132.

debate this request was granted and the act was extended by the House of Representatives on August 12, 1941, by the slim margin of *one* vote (203 to 202).

Under Selective Service, local boards were responsible for decisions concerning liability for induction, operating within the law and on the basis of regulations established by Selective Service headquarters in Washington. Inductions from November, 1940, to October, 1946, were slightly over 10.1 million men. This was approximately two-thirds of those who served in the armed forces during World War II. A large percentage of the remaining one-third was influenced to enlist or seek commissions because of their liability to be drafted. Voluntary enlistments were stopped in the middle of the war in order to eliminate recruiting competition between the services and also to keep essential workers from joining the armed forces.[3]

C. Evaluation of Selective Service

The Selective Service System was a popular success in World War II. A 1956 evaluation of selective service made the point that the fact that we "won the war" should not be taken as sufficient sanction that what was done was "best," but that one should recall the reference in the Eberstadt Report that achievement was gained at cost of much waste of material, manpower, and money.

The Selective Service System has been said to have had a twofold task: first, selecting the number and type of men desired for the armed forces; and second, leaving in the civilian economy the numbers of men essential to each critical occupation and activity. Another statement evaluating this function was as follows:

While the primary function of the Selective Service System was to secure men for the military service, the system was also responsible for attempting to maintain the military-industrial balance. Selective Service was obligated to see that the withdrawal of men for military service disturbed the civilian war effort to the least possible extent. As increased demands for men came from the Armed Forces, however, the balance could not be maintained. The absence of policy on the part of the War Department, the lack of an adequate survey of the industrial skills of the country, and the increased demand for manpower in the war industries made a full performance of the task impossible.

The great weakness of the Selective Service System was lack of a positive policy for industrial and civilian manpower. In World War II, when the balancing of the military and industrial manpower needs became critical, there gradually arose a number of problems that required additional administrative

[3] *Ibid.*, p. 137.

machinery. Among the administrative bodies set up to solve these problems were the War Manpower Commission and the Economic Stabilization Board. There was a very clear indication that the situation required the development of more definite machinery for the control and direction of civilian manpower. . . .

Although numerous agencies were created to handle this problem there was little actual coordination between them and the Selective Service System. The creation by Executive Order of the Office of Economic Stabilization (6 October 1942) and the Office of War Mobilization (May 1943) did not clarify or unify manpower policies.[4]

3. Experience from World War II to the Korean War

As we have seen, the United States permitted her position of military strength to deteriorate at a very rapid rate at the end of World War II. However, it is almost inconceivable that in March, 1947, the same month in which we announced the Truman Doctrine, the Selective Service and Training Act was permitted to expire. The rapidly deteriorating world situation and the failure of voluntary enlistments to meet manpower requirements brought about the enactment of the Selective Service Act of 1948.

The act of 1948 provided for the registration of all men between the ages of 18 and 26 and for the induction of enough men between the ages of 19 and 26 to maintain the armed forces at their then authorized strength of a little over 2 million. Voluntary enlistment, spurred by the jingle "if induction's near, volunteer," provided sufficient men to meet the requirements. By June, 1950, immediately prior to the Korean War, Selective Service had inducted only 30,000 men since 1948 and had become such a skeletonized organization that it was with difficulty that Congress was persuaded to extend the act to mid-1951.

At the start of the Korean War there was an insufficient backlog of nonveterans who had received training, and veterans had to be called back into service just as they had become reëstablished in civilian life. They were then retained in service until nonveterans could be trained as replacements and additions to the armed forces. This brought once again to the front the need for Selective Service as a permanent part of the United States mobilization program and the desirability of a permanent Universal Military Training Program. In addition, the Korean War, coming at a time of high employment, proved the need of a clearly formulated and administered national manpower mobilization policy integrated with a program of total mobilization.

[4] Eli Ginzberg et al., *op. cit.*, p. 128.

4. National Manpower Mobilization Policy

As a result of the realized need for a national manpower policy the President issued a basic document in the manpower field. Because of its importance it is given below in full and followed by comments as to its administration and implementation.

January 17, 1951

To the Heads of Executive Departments and Agencies

There is hereby promulgated, effective immediately, the attached National Manpower Mobilization Policy which I have approved on the recommendation of the National Security Council, the Secretary of the Treasury, the Secretary of Labor and the Director of the Office of Defense Mobilization.

This policy shall be adhered to by all departments and agencies with respect to programs under their control, subject to such amendments and supplements as may from time to time be issued by the Director of the Office of Defense Mobilization pursuant to authorities vested in him.

HARRY S TRUMAN

Aims of Manpower Mobilization:

1. The primary aim of manpower mobilization is to safeguard our national security through the maximum development and use of our human resources. In particular, this involves:

a. Providing manpower for the Armed Forces in sufficient numbers and with the mental, physical, and occupational qualifications necessary for national defense.

b. Providing manpower for producing the materials and services necessary to the Armed Forces, to meet commitments of aid to other nations and to support the civilian economy.

c. Constantly increasing our mobilization potential through training and educational programs to expand our supply of persons with highly developed skills essential to civilian and military activities. Providing manpower for protection of the civilian health and welfare.

2. The most efficient use of the Nation's manpower will be of vital importance in any prolonged effort to keep the strength of the United States at a high level and will be of the utmost importance in the event of full mobilization. Consequently, it is important that manpower measures taken now be consistent with and contribute to the most advantageous use of our manpower should full mobilization become necessary.

3. We must rely heavily on science and technology. The most effective use must be made of our supply of individuals having the special skills required to develop and produce the necessary equipment and to use and maintain it in the Armed Forces. Malutilization of such individuals represents a direct and unnecessary reduction of our defense potential.

4. While recognizing the very high priority of the Armed Forces' require-

ments for certain numbers and classes of manpower, the needs of mobilization also require a vigorous civilian economy. The manpower necessary to defense production, to civil defense, to agriculture, and to the production of essential civilian goods and services and to sustain our commitments of aid to other nations, must be considered as integral parts of a balanced mobilization program.

5. To assure the most effective use of our manpower to meet these needs, it is essential that we establish principles and adopt a series of policies which will lead to the most effective use of our manpower resources. Wherever statutory authorization is necessary to put these into effect, it will be sought from the Congress.

Principles of Manpower Mobilization:

6. In achieving these objectives, the national manpower mobilization program will be based upon the following principles:

a. Each individual will be expected to serve in the capacity in which he can contribute most to the total mobilization program.

b. Employers, both private and governmental, will assure full utilization of those abilities and skills of each individual which will contribute most to the total mobilization program through such measures as minimum manning, training, and assignment of duties in accordance with needs, skills, and potentialities.

c. The Government will develop and administer manpower programs designed to enlist to the fullest possible extent the support and resourcefulness of individuals in the achievement of the mobilization program.

Basic Manpower Mobilization Policies:

7. The following basic manpower mobilization policies are necessary to give effect to the principles stated above, but do not prejudice or limit extension of manpower policies as further needs of mobilization evolve.

a. The size of the Armed Forces will be determined by the President. He will be provided with the Department of Defense requirements to meet strategic plans; with full information on the prospective supplies of manpower, and on the manpower requirements for defense production, agriculture, civil defense, and other essential purposes.

b. The greatest care must be exercised to assure that the supply of persons possessing critical skills will be distributed among military and civilian activities in a manner which will contribute most to the mobilization program. When the total need for workers with critical skills for civilian and military assignments is expected to exceed the supply that can be made available, the requirements for persons with such skills will be reviewed and distribution of the supply will be measured by the relative urgency of the need for critical skills as between the Armed Forces and the civilian economy.

c. Policies in respect to recruitment of individuals from civilian life and call-up of members of the unorganized reserves will have as their objective the use of persons possessing irreplaceable skills where they can make their maximum contribution to the total mobilization program.

d. Policies governing occupational deferment of persons subject to induction under the Selective Service Act, will provide for: (1) The occupational deferment of persons possessing critical skills if they are currently using such skills in essential activities, except to the extent the military services require persons with those skills; (2) deferment of a sufficient number of individuals in educational and training institutions to provide an adequate continuing supply of professional and highly skilled manpower.

e. Recruitment, placement, distribution, training, and utilization of the civilian labor force (including Government employees) will be based primarily upon voluntary measures for manpower mobilization. This policy will be carried out through such measures as: (1) Providing appropriate employment information to guide workers to jobs in which they can make their maximum contribution; (2) developing recruitment and rehabilitation activities needed to expand the labor force; (3) training persons to meet civilian manpower requirements and providing appropriate placement services; (4) providing assistance to employers in promoting maximum utilization of the labor force including women, physically handicapped, older workers, and minority groups; (5) providing adequate housing and community services; and (6) assisting workers to arrange for their transfer to essential jobs in other areas.

f. Governmental manpower controls will be used when and to the extent needed to assure successful execution of the mobilization program. Such controls will apply to employers, to workers, or to both. They will include: (1) Restricting indiscriminate labor turn-over through control of separations; (2) giving effect to manpower allocations by placing employment ceilings on employers with respect to the total number of workers, the number of men or the number in particular skills; (3) controlling of employer hiring; and (4) enforcing adherence to utilization standards, including full use of women, handicapped workers, and minority groups.

g. All manpower programs will be geared to the needs and problems of specific geographical areas.

h. As mutually desirable to the United States and friendly nations, workers will be brought into the United States for, or their services utilized within the borders of their own country on, work of value to the mobilization program. Full use of domestic manpower resources will be made before bringing in foreign workers.

i. Production will be scheduled, materials allocated, and procurement distributed with careful consideration of available manpower. Whenever feasible from an economic and security standpoint, production facilities, contracts, and significant subcontracts will be located at the sources of labor supply in preference to moving the labor supply.

j. The full understanding and assistance of labor organizations, employer associations, professional societies, civic and community groups and State and local governments will be sought in carrying out these functions.

k. Each Department will, itself, implement the policy and be responsible for its supervision.[5]

[5] *Manpower for Defense*, Policies and Statements of the Office of Defense Mobilization, Government Printing Office, 1953, pp. 3–5.

As was pointed out in the previous chapter on capital, the Office of Defense Mobilization (ODM) is charged with the responsibility of coordinating all aspects of the nation's defense mobilization program. On January 15, 1953, the ODM issued a publication, *Manpower for Defense,* which indicated that one of ODM's objectives had been to make the best use of our human resources to accomplish the following: meet the manpower goals set for the armed forces and supply the manpower needed for the production of weapons for our armed forces and our allies while maintaining the civilian economy at a high level and constantly increasing our full mobilization program. The ODM printed in *Manpower for Defense* all the defense manpower policies that it had issued in implementation of the National Manpower Mobilization Policy.

The ODM reported that it had developed general policies under existing law, which assigned responsibilities to the various operating departments and agencies of government and made recommendations to labor, management, and other private groups, leading to the carrying out of the policies. All of these policies were developed with the active assistance and guidance of three advisory committees: the national Labor-Management Manpower Policy Committee, the Committee on Specialized Personnel, and the interagency Manpower Policy Committee.

The Labor-Management Manpower Policy Committee, which advises both the Director of Defense Mobilization and the Secretary of Labor, is composed of representatives of management and labor from various industrial fields as well as agriculture.

The Committee on Specialized Personnel is made up of scientific and technical representatives of industry, education, and government.

The Manpower Policy Committee is a governmental group comprising representatives of the Departments of Defense, Agriculture, and Labor, Selective Service System, Civil Service Commission, Defense Production Administration, Federal Security Agency, Housing and Home Finance Agency, Wage Stabilization Board, and Defense Transport Administration.

The Department of Labor is the operating agency for civilian manpower in the defense program, discharging its responsibilities through its bureaus and through the public employment service with its 1800 local employment offices.

The very listing of these groups included in the advisory committees is indication of the complexity of formulating and administering manpower policies. Presently we shall see that there are many other interested agencies.

5. Selective Service and Universal Military Training

The Korean War proved the need of a National Manpower Mobilization Policy and raised the question of the desirability of a permanent Selective Service System and/or Universal Military Training. Congress answered the question by passing the Universal Military Training and Service Act of 1951, which continued the Selective Service System indefinitely and provided the authority to induct men into the armed forces until July, 1955. In 1955 Public Law 118 extended this authority of the draft for four years, until July, 1959. Three important military manpower problems arose under Selective Service after Korea: First, the Air Force and the Navy were able to secure their manpower by enlistments, while the Army had to use Selective Service. Second, there were several problems arising from the deferment of students. Third was the broad question of standard for acceptance and service in military service.

The Universal Military Training and Service Act of 1951 established a National Security Training Commission, which was directed to draw up a UMT program for Congressional approval. The Social Science Department of the United States Military Academy describes and comments on this program as follows:

Training under the projected UMT program was to be very different from that following induction by Selective Service. Inductions are selective conscriptions to meet military manpower requirements for the active armed forces, whether in peace or war. UMT was designed to develop a large reservoir of partially trained citizens who, after their six-months' period of training would remain in a reserve status for the balance of their eight-year obligation. Their training would be under carefully prescribed conditions in the National Security Training Corps, not as members of the active armed forces. During their seven and one-half years of reserve duty they would be callable to active military service only in accordance with the regulations applying to the particular reserve component of which they were members.

Training under the UMT program would be designed to achieve several basic objectives:

1. To ensure the existence of an active training establishment
2. To provide the National Guard and reserves with a steady flow of basically trained personnel, thus reducing the time required for these components to achieve combat readiness
3. To provide a pool of basically trained men, ready for assignment to regular units with a minimum of refresher training and physical conditioning
4. By reason of the foregoing, to free the regular forces more immediately for combat missions in the event of war
5. To provide an opportunity for the development of records of individual qualifications and thus permit an orderly utilization of military personnel

6. To impress upon the youth of the country its obligation to defend the institutions which give to American life its distinctive qualities, and each individual's importance to the Nation in that supreme task.

The 1951 report of the National Service Training Commission points out:

. . . The action reflects a realization, even in the heat and tension of the present crisis, that the major problems we face in the world will be of long duration, that no tidy or decisive conclusion is to be expected soon; and that in consequence our basic and long-term military policies must provide for swift adjustment between periods of acute crisis which demand large standing forces, plus a large, trained, and ready reserve.

Congress did not authorize any action to implement UMT within the next three years, perhaps partly because a large proportion of the upcoming age classes were entering the armed services. Such implementation has a peculiar complication in its relationship to conscription. The authors know of no nation to look to for precedents in undertaking a conscription program for the armed forces and, at the same time, a universal military training program for those men coming to military age and not conscripted into the active forces. . . .

There appear to be three conditions for consideration in operating the two programs simultaneously:

1. The active forces manned by enlistment. Under this circumstance selective service is a standby program. All of the men coming to military age who do not choose to enlist, and who meet physical and mental standards, become UMT trainees for six months and then pass to the reserves for seven and one-half years.

2. Selective Service and enlistment bring substantially all physically and mentally fit men of new military age groups into active forces. This condition exists in wartime and may exist during a high level of preparedness. There would be few, if any, men available for UMT unless physical and mental standards were set below those for the active forces.

3. Selective Service needs only a portion of each new age class for the active forces, leaving a material portion of the class for UMT. This is obviously the most difficult of the three conditions to administer. Who goes where? Every able-bodied young man goes into uniform, the selectees for perhaps 24 months followed by 6 years in the reserve, and the trainees for 6 months followed by 7½ years in the reserve.[6]

The suggestion has been made that UMT might partially resolve the competition for manpower between military and civilian occupations.

[UMT] adherents claim that the logical break-point for military training in a young man's development is at the end of his high school years—before

[6] Reprinted by permission from *Economics of National Security*, 2nd ed., by George A. Lincoln and Associates, pp. 139–141. Copyright, 1954, by Prentice-Hall, Inc., Englewood Cliffs, N.J.

college for the one boy in five who goes to college, before their first permanent jobs for the four boys in five who go to work on completion of high school. The argument is that in a dangerous world, every eligible young man should have military training and that the training should be given as a prelude to, rather than an interruption of, his preparation for work.

Six months' training, UMT advocates hold, can provide the mental conditioning and discipline which neither home nor high school offers, teach men the elements of drill, how to handle small arms, and, most important, how to live as a soldier. A six-month training program can be combined with college—those who are going to college can either complete their training first or catch up lost time through summer work. Three men who have had UMT, its advocates estimate, and are in organized units of reserve components, offer as much national security as one man who has seen service.

The adequacy of the six-month training period, however, has been questioned by opponents of UMT. They doubt if in so short a time enough training can be given to be worth while in preparing young men for service in an army that requires pilots, tank operators, technicians of many sorts. Since further training in these specialties would be necessary once the boys were in service, those opposed to UMT prefer arrangements which would give all training in one period of military life.

Another objection to training at eighteen comes from those who think it unwise to remove youths from their home environment at a formative age and subject them to the influences of camp life. For boys who go to college, UMT is also a break in the normal course of education.

In any case, post-Korean military requirements have made active service, not merely training, necessary over a protracted period.[7]

With UMT and/or Selective Service there would be a need for policy and a mechanism to determine who shall serve. This and related issues are the military manpower policy questions in which the general public is most interested.

6. Manpower Policy

The National Planning Association in 1953 determined to study the problem of manpower policy and to call attention to manpower as an important area for careful public thought, understanding, and decision. An NPA Special Committee on Manpower Policy was formed and, since it could find no brief statement which put together the numerous segments of the problem in understandable form for the general reader, it prepared and published *Manpower: The Nation's First Resource.*

A. The Problem

The general manpower problem is, of course, the one we have already carefully defined. The NPA saw the problem, first as a part of the over-

[7] *Manpower: The Nation's First Resource,* Report of the National Planning Association Special Committee on Manpower Policy, Pamphlet No. 83, 1953, pp. 28–29.

all problem of allocation of scarce resources, second as a problem of allocation of scarce manpower, and third as a problem of understanding the myriad manpower issues and the necessity of formulating and implementing a coördinated manpower policy. These three phases of the problem as they relate to mobilization might be stated as follows.

First, in recent years the United States has become acutely aware of the shortages of certain natural resources. The growth of the economy, plus the addition of the defense program to the requirements of civilian production, forced the nation, which thought itself well supplied, to allocate a number of basic resources in order to supply its most essential uses.

Second, during the same time, shortages of manpower were felt—men for military services, specialists in science, medicine, engineering, teaching, and industrial production. These shortages cannot be overcome rapidly and, in a free society, they cannot be solved by government assignment of men to work.

Third, the manpower problem raises many and complex issues. The public is not aware of the problem as a whole, but only of those specific problems in which each member is directly involved and therefore interested in the applicable policy or lack of one. But if determinations of public policy are made piecemeal, with short-run ends alone in view, the United States will have far less balanced strength in the long run than if decisions are made with the various principal segments of the manpower problem "kept in proportion, comparably understood, and considered together."[8]

B. Interested Agencies

We have already seen the many agencies involved in the formulation, administration, and implementation of the National Manpower Mobilization Policy. In preparing its report the National Planning Association discovered and went to special effort to point out the variety of agencies which were giving intensive attention to the manpower problem in a number of specialized fields. Thus, military manpower is being studied by the Department of Defense, Selective Service, and the Department of Labor. Needs for scientific and professional manpower are being estimated by the National Research Council, the National Science Foundation, the Commission on Human Resources and Advanced Training, the Commission on Specialized Personnel of the Office of Defense Mobilization, and by engineering and scientific societies through the Engineering Manpower Commission of the Engineers Joint Council and

[8] *Ibid.,* p. iii.

the Scientific Manpower Commission. The Bureau of Labor Statistics is making elaborate studies of manpower resources and requirements. Many educational organizations are forecasting enrollments and required staff. Those government agencies previously mentioned in charge of mobilization are active in many phases of manpower. Finally, the NPA pointed out that only a few groups, particularly the National Manpower Council, are giving attention to research and policy formation in all phases of the manpower problem.

A rather straightforward and simple conclusion can be reached: that considerable coördination of all the studies of these agencies, the recommended policies and their implementation, is required.

C. The Questions

One purpose of the NPA study was to indicate the range of the problem and of policy needed if best use is to be made of the manpower in the United States. It was felt that along this range of the problem there was a series of points at which citizens should stop and seek specific answers to clearly discernible questions. The questions which follow are divided into three types: short-term policy, long-range policy, and policy for full mobilization. These questions are presented without indicating answers, but in the hope that they will stimulate our thinking with the clear knowledge that the answers that are found will determine both the immediate and the long-run strength of the United States.

Short-term manpower policy involves issues connected with civilian employment and military manpower which should be studied in terms of the following questions.

1. What programs should be actively advanced to make more complete and full use of existing capacities and skills of: a) the physically handicapped; b) women; c) racial and national minorities; d) older persons?
2. What short-term economic developments can upgrade the productivity of low-income regions and so provide a better economic base for general education, advanced training, and health in these areas?
3. If changes in the draft deferment rules are required over the next two years in order to maintain the necessary level of armed force, a) Should student deferment be continued? If so, should a scholarship system make college attendance possible by a larger number of able young men than are currently going to college? After completion of study, should further deferments be provided for students showing exceptional ability in science and engineering? Should deferment as fathers be allowed to students who have previously had a deferment for study? b) Should deferment of fathers generally be continued? c) What about occupational deferments in agriculture

and industry? Father deferments for young men who have already had an occupational deferment?

4. Should the ROTC program be revised so as to take in fewer men in accordance with realistic quotas and put more emphasis on subsequent military service by those who do join?

5. Should greater effort be made to see that more of the top group of high school graduates goes on to college?

6. Should more men who are educationally and physically handicapped be inducted, with programs instituted for training and for medical correction of minor defects after they are in service? Does more use of the less fit offer a major means of lessening the strain on manpower in both military and civilian occupations?

7. How much of the housekeeping, and storekeeping and other administrative and noncombat activity in the Defense establishment, now performed by men and women in uniform, could be equally well performed by civilians, thus lowering the over-all requirements for military personnel?[9]

Long-range manpower policy necessitates both remedial measures to decrease the numbers of less fit and positive measures for upgrading the population. This upgrading ranges from training to higher skills those who are employed in marginal production, or employed at levels below their actual capacities, to the more effective use of our most skilled. Major long-range policy questions are:

1. Should projects be started to raise the level of educational opportunity and of health in areas where the smallest percentage of young people now go on to higher education?

2. Should greater emphasis be put on apprenticeships and refresher courses for skilled workers?

3. Should continuing campaigns, like that for the employment of the physically handicapped, be maintained to upgrade the levels of skill of disadvantaged racial and national groups such as Negroes and Spanish-Americans, and hold them at the higher levels?

4. Should greater provision be made for the employment of womanpower under conditions that make practicable combination of work and home responsibilities, and use of trained womanpower at levels commensurate with training?

5. Should experiments be undertaken in the employment of older workers, who are not only living longer but have better health than did the members of their age group at the time present retirement practices became standard?

6. Are up-to-date rosters of specialists necessary in an increasing number of fields?

7. Should a Civilian Reserve, a reserve of competence composed of men and women with government experience, be set up to keep fresh the skills that have been demonstrated in past emergencies as a hard core available

[9] *Ibid.*, pp. 49–53.

against the call of new requirements. What legal changes must be made to give standing to such civilians?

8. How can a larger supply of people of greater ability be attracted to teaching?

9. Should more of the country's best brains be turned to basic research, on the ground that when too much attention is concentrated on applied knowledge the country runs out of intellectual capital to put into application?

10. What are practical means of locating the more able men and women in the population, and training them to the top of their ability?[10]

Policy for full mobilization must be given serious consideration. Because of the relatively large numbers of young and old in the population, the NPA concluded that the middle group would find difficulty in providing the manpower for the armed forces and civilian front if full mobilization came soon. The finding was that the limiting factor in such mobilization would not be natural resources or capital facilities but numbers of men and women available to work at required levels of skill; planning for all-out mobilization would do well to proceed from this assumption. Questions in the area of full mobilization to which answers are needed include:

1. Should policy regarding the military reserve be reconsidered in light of the fact that the same people who have had military experience in the past are the people who have industrial and agricultural skill in the present? In rostering a reserve, should account be taken in advance of the men who would have to stay in production if defense output were to be adequate to meet requirements?

2. What kind of government agency should be used to decide who goes into uniform and who stays on the production line; is that a decision which the services can carry out under pre-established rules, or is an agency preferable that would combine responsibility to meet military requirements and civilian judgment along lines comparable to the local draft boards of the Selective Service System?

3. What measures are needed to concentrate production and employment on first necessities: measures to channel materials to essential industry and so attract labor to priority jobs; measures to channel into taxes and savings the purchasing power that would otherwise induce less relevant production?

4. What kinds of advance planning for the use of manpower in post-attack rehabilitation should be readied now?[11]

The NPA drew the general conclusion that to the extent that citizens inform themselves about these issues, and work to get adequate action on them in time, "the nation will make better use of its first resource— its manpower."

[10] *Ibid.*
[11] *Ibid.*

7. Reserve Forces Act of 1955

Congressional effort to solve the Universal Military Training issue and other manpower policy problems resulted in the passage of the Reserve Forces Act of 1955. This legislation imposed an obligation on each person enlisted, appointed, or inducted into the armed forces to train in the Ready Reserve of the United States. Men from 18 to 26 years of age were under the draft rules. All men who entered the armed forces after the date of enactment (August 9, 1955) were required to serve on active duty for the period for which they were obligated (two, three, four, or five years) and in the Ready Reserve for a period of time which, when added to their period of active duty, totaled 5 years. An additional 1 year of duty was required in the Standby Reserve so that a total of 6 years of military duty was required. However, special provision was made so that young men 17 to $18\frac{1}{2}$ might enlist for a draft-deferred 8-year duty, 6 months of which was in full-time active army service and $7\frac{1}{2}$ years in the Ready Reserve part time. This latter provision was to enable students to complete their education. If a student was doing well in high school, the 6 months active service could be deferred until after graduation, but not after age 20.

Amendments in effect April 1, 1957, made it possible for a young man to enter the 6-month plan any time after he reached age 17 and before he was ordered for draft induction. If he entered the plan before he was $18\frac{1}{2}$ years old, he was obligated to drill in the Ready Reserve for only $4\frac{1}{2}$ years instead of $7\frac{1}{2}$ years. Then he would be transferred to the Standby Reserve, or in active status for 3 years. If a young man entered the Reserve plan after he was $18\frac{1}{2}$ years of age, he was required to drill in the Ready Reserve after 6 months' training, for $5\frac{1}{2}$ years, and then serve 2 years in the Standby Reserve. In each instance a total of 8 years' military duty was required. As soon as a young man became a Reservist, he was deferred from the draft.

Under the draft rules in effect at the beginning of 1957 registration was required at age 18, and all men from 18 to 26 were subject to draft for 2 years active service, 3 years in the Ready Reserve and 1 year in the Standby Reserve for a total of 6 years' military duty.

There were many alternatives to the draft, and the amendments to the Reserve Act of 1955, which became effective in 1957, increased the number. Some of the principal ways to meet military obligations by age groups were as follows.

From 17 to $18\frac{1}{2}$ years one could enlist in the Reserve for 8 years, serve

6 months on active duty, then be deferred from the draft. This was followed by 4½ years in the Ready Reserve with weekly drills and a 15-day annual training period, and by 3 years in the Standby Reserve subject to call to active duty through Selective Service only in an emergency declared by Congress. A Defense Department directive to become effective April 1, 1957, placed the National Guard on a similar training basis. Thus from 17 to 18½ the alternative was open to enlist in the National Guard, serve 6 months on active duty, then be deferred from the draft as long as one participated satisfactorily in the Guard for 4½ years with weekly drills and a 15-day annual training period followed by 3 years in the Standby Reserve. Beginning April 1, 1957, the Reserve obligation was changed to 3 years in the Ready Reserve and 4½ years in the Standby Reserve.

Prior to this equal-training directive, membership in the National Guard before age 18½ relieved one from draft liability and required weekly drills and two weeks of training each summer. All Guard members were subject to call into active service during periods of emergency. A person who joined the Guard after 18½ remained subject to the draft. The National Guard Association opposed the directive on the grounds that recruitment would be curtailed. The Defense Department felt that the Guard needed strengthening, that it was not the effective organization that it was before the Korean War, that only 17 percent of the Guard had prior training, and that there was no other choice but to strengthen the Regular Army. The controversy was so great that the effective date of the training directive was postponed. A compromise was worked out with the coöperation of Congress between the Regular Army and the National Guard Association to the effect that during the period ending October 1, 1957, young men aged 17 to 18½ could enlist in the National Guard for only 11 weeks of active-duty training. Those who selected the 11-week course, however, were required to remain in the National Guard on a ready basis until they reached the age of 28.

From 17 to 26 years one could enlist in the Reserve for 6 years, serve 6 months on active duty, then be deferred from the draft during 5½ years' participation in the Ready Reserve. Or one could volunteer for induction at the draft board and serve 2 years on active duty, 2 years in the Ready Reserve and 2 years in Standby. Or one could enlist in the Reserve for 6 years, including 2 years of active duty. Finally, one could enlist in the Army or Marine Corps for 3 or more years, or in the Navy, Coast Guard, or Air Force for 4 or more years, and serve the remaining portion of the 6 years of liability in Reserve.

From 18 to 28 years one could secure a commission by successfully completing a college officers' training program such as the ROTC, then after college enter on active duty as an officer for 2 or more years, and serve the balance of the 6-year obligation in the Reserve. If such a person was not needed on active duty, he could serve 6 months under active training and 7½ years of an 8-year obligation in the Reserve.

From 18½ to 26 years (or 35 if once deferred) one could enlist before age 26 in the Army for 2 years of active duty, 2 years in the Ready Reserve and 2 years in Standby. Or one could take his chances with the draft. Fathers were called after nonfathers so that fathers were practically exempt except in the case of a war. If one were inducted the requirement was 2 years on active duty followed by 2 years in the Ready Reserve and 2 years in Standby. Finally, one could enlist in the Reserve for 8 years if approved by Selective Service as critically skilled and employed in defense-supporting industry, then serve 6 months on active duty and 7½ years in Reserve, all of which could be served in the Standby Reserve.

This latter option was a very important feature of the Reserve Forces Act of 1955 which took cognizance of the ever-growing need for skilled and scientifically trained personnel. Another significant part of the act was the requirement that under regulations prescribed by the President each armed force of the United States shall provide a system of continuous screening of units and members of the Ready Reserve to insure that "members of the Reserve Forces possessing critical civilian skills will not be retained in numbers beyond the requirements for those skills except for persons who have military skills for which there is an overriding requirement."

The general rule in 1957 for students was that college could be completed before a young man was likely to be drafted because most inductions were being made at about age 22. Under the provision of the law, a college student could request deferment, which was guaranteed until completion of his degree so long as he maintained his academic standing. However, most students were not asking for deferment because usually if a student's number came up the draft board would let him complete college before induction. In addition, if the student asked and was granted deferment his draft liability was extended to age 35. Further, there was always the possibility that if he did not secure a deferment he might reach his twenty-sixth birthday before his number came up and thus be draft exempt. At the beginning of 1957 there were about 1,700,-000 boys in college, most of whom were over 18 and physically fit, but only 140,000 of them had student deferments. There was a decreasing number who took the college qualifying test leading to a deferment at the beginning of college.

Criticism of the Reserve Act of 1955, up to 1957 for the most part, centered around some limited possibilities of avoiding military service. This question was put to Arthur S. Flemming, director of ODM: Do you believe that the draft is working out in a fair manner? His answer was: "I don't think that there's any way of bringing about an absolutely fair and equitable handling of the manpower situation under present conditions. The demand isn't great enough to do it. In other words, as long as we keep our armed forces around 2.8 million, it's clear that many people in the manpower pool just aren't going to be used. And, if you don't need to use very many people out of the manpower pool, then there is a certain element of chance that is involved in it. I don't see how you can avoid that under present conditions."

Additional criticism was levied at the National Guard for the inequality of training and for its use as a means of avoiding active military service. This latter reached its peak in January, 1957, when Secretary of Defense Wilson charged that during the Korean War the National Guard was a "sort of scandal because of its alleged use by youths as a draft-dodging business." This was an unfortunate remark because of the valiant service and sacrifice of the Guard during the Korean War, although it was true that a large number of youths aged 17½ to 18½ were relieved of draft liability by joining the Guard and because their units were not called for federal service they were freed from an active part in the war.

The outlook in 1957 was that because of the growing number of youths entering military age and the limited size of the armed forces more men would not be called for military service. *U.S. News and World Report* spelled out the trends in four parts, as shown in Figure 13.1.

As these trends become effective, the same questions will be raised about the most equitable measures to achieve adequate manpower mobilization. This might reopen the whole question of a more Universal Military Training plan, which Congress had attempted to solve with the Reserve Forces Act of 1955.

8. Military Manpower—What Else?

In studying military manpower as one part of the total manpower problem a writer recently raised this question: Is a discussion of military manpower requirements entirely beside the point? He was well aware of

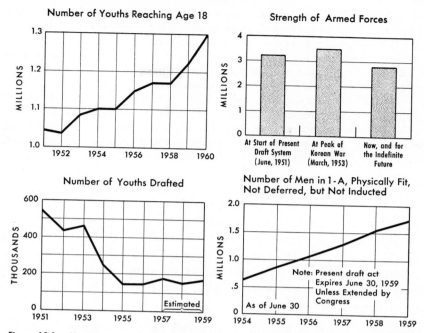

Figure 13.1. Manpower and Mobilization. (Data from Department of Commerce; Department of Defense; Selective Service System; Department of Defense Estimates)

the need for military-civilian balance and for maintaining a situation of strength. Why then did he raise this question and what conclusion did he reach? Let him answer the question.

The communists believe that everything can be achieved without a hot war. Armies are not needed when espionage agents, saboteurs, and fronts are successful. An error is often made in distinguishing between the U.S.S.R. as a nation and the Communist International as a world conspiracy and revolutionary movement. Communists use the national status of the U.S.S.R. to deal with other states and are accorded a position in the family of nations that the international conspiracy as such could not obtain. Cold war is communism's constant instrument in its clear, unmistakable, and unwavering purpose: the mastery of the world, the demise of capitalism, and the end of every religion not subsequent to its final purpose. In contrast to the drifting hopefulness and forgetful erring of the noncommunists, the communists never lose sight of their ultimate objective. No military campaign was ever worked out more painstakingly, with more attention to detail, with more careful timing, and with more patience than the seemingly irresistible day-by-day, hour-by-hour action of communists everywhere. They have devised the most subtle and cunning methods of making traitors in every country and of using idealists and the so-called intelligentsia, and their success has indicated no need for war. The threat of war has been a means of creating a state of unrest and insecurity for their enemy and a means of causing a waste of money, manpower, and materials in a mad armaments race for a mythical superiority.

In any case, the net result of a discussion of the military manpower problem should be that it is not a simple problem of numbers. It is not a problem of ratios of the mechanically minded or the compromises of a bureaucracy of budget makers. It goes to the basic characteristics of the people and the economy and to their international policies. It involves the highest type of imagination in procurement, training, and utilization. It builds most certainly on the efficiency of government and of military organization. And above all, the quality of manpower—in sufficient numbers and properly utilized in cold war or hot for the common defense—is the key to our national existence.[12]

9. Conclusions

No attempt will be made to draw together all the conclusions we have reached with respect to manpower mobilization. However, attention should be called to the fact that the ODM makes periodic reports to the Joint Committee on Defense Production. These cover all phases of mobilization and have one specific section on manpower measures giving a summary of manpower developments. Two 1955 and 1956 reports contained these conclusions.

Manpower programs have been developed for several assumed mobilizations levels in order to have in being manpower plans which would be reasonably adaptable to any type of national emergency. Manpower is readily available for the maintenance of the present level of mobilization for an indefinite period of years and for support of a high-level, expanding economy. Present policies, programs and organizational structures are adequate. At a stepped-up level of mobilization, short of all-out mobilization, manpower requirements could be met without causing significant shortages of nonspecialized personnel, but more serious problems would occur in relation to the supply of scientific, technological and skilled manpower. The third plan is based upon full mobilization of a conventional type but with the most accurate appraisal possible of the changes which would be required as a result of radically changed industrial and military technology since World War II.

Certain general measures have been developed which have important manpower implications in the event of an attack on the United States with thermonuclear weapons. In addition to the development of a plan to meet the manpower problems of an attack on the U.S., work has also progressed on a plan for full mobilization assuming no attack.

Organization for the wartime management of manpower has been basically determined and work is now progressing on the development of complete organizational requirements.

We can certainly conclude that proper organization and administration are needed to integrate all the various issues we have raised into a

[12] Eli Ginzberg et al., *op. cit.*, pp. 128–129.

positive policy for all levels of mobilization and all types of warfare, hot and cold. Perhaps the most subtle and difficult is cold.

MAN AND FREEDOM

Production potential is a function of quantitative and qualitative characteristics of the population. Qualitative characteristics are a function of the economic resources available and man's ability to use them most efficiently. However, in addition the production potential and economic growth depend on those qualitative values which man derives from the moral-psychological and political environment in which he lives.

Most of the data presented in this chapter have been measures of quantitative characteristics of our human resources. Similarly, our study, while not limited to quantitative characteristics, has not specifically called attention to the qualitative characteristics. These latter comprise tangible features which in part are measurable and intangible features that are not measurable. Tangible qualitative measures which might be presented would be those of health, education, and skill. Measures of these, while significant characteristics contributing to productivity, can often be misleading—first, because the averages and the data might cover up one unhealthy, uneducated, skilled genius who through one invention or discovery could create a new productivity revolution, and second, because they do not take into account the contribution of the immeasurable, intangible, qualitative characteristics which may be the most important factors facilitating the production, growth, and strength of our nation.

A case can be made, though perhaps not proved, that freedom is one such if not the most important qualitative characteristic which has contributed to growth. We are not saying that freedom is intangible. What we are saying is that we cannot measure freedom and its contribution to our production potential, although the overwhelming evidence of history is that freedom and the desire for freedom have been and are an incentive, a driving force, that has enabled individuals and nations to undertake superhuman efforts and to achieve increased productivity, economic progress, strength, and security.

In the section of Chapter 1 on "Objectives and Policies" we did not discuss the goal of freedom of other peoples prior to the course of formation of the United States because we are primarily concerned with United States objectives and policy and their significance. However, we did see that, along with security, freedom is one of two fundamental objectives of the United States which have been our principal accomplishment and enduring goal, and that freedom sets our economic system apart from alien philosophies. Indeed, our basic problem is: How can we raise our plane of living by making economic progress and at the same time attain a maximum degree of security and a maximum amount of *individual and national freedom* in a political democracy?

In Chapter 1 we showed and concluded: "Thus *freedom* rings as the major objective of the people of the United States, and we have taken the lead to advocate it as an international policy which we hope might be adopted as an objective and achieved by all men in all lands."

Further, one of our major problems is achieving the right balance between our dual objectives of freedom and security as individuals and nations as we maintain a position of strength and achieve rising planes of living. Some of the detailed problems of the military-civilian balance in mobilizing manpower have just been considered.

Freedom is central to the kaleidoscopic aspects of our life: First, in the moral-psychological area freedom to worship God each in his own way gives us faith and an underlying basis of moral strength of indomitable sustaining force. Freedom endows man with a psychological spirit to achieve greater goals (the paramount one of which is freedom) in the face of overwhelming odds. Or, where security is present and man is free from fear, his psychological spirit is so uplifted as to cause him to drive for greater goals of freedom.

Second, in the political area our democratic system is based on the right of the individual to cast his free vote for candidates of his own choice in the legislative, executive, and in many instances judicial branches of government. By exercising this right we enter into a process of self-determination of policies and their implementation which will lead to greater goals of economic progress, strength, and security.

Third, in the economic area freedom is central in that man votes his dollars for goods that he desires and thus is a determining force in production. Or as a factor of production acting in the capacity of labor and/or management he participates freely in the production of goods. Further, the right of ownership of property is an attribute of freedom, as is the right of proprietary investment in productive activities carried on by others. The economic driving force of our economy is the knowledge that man will receive the fruits of his own efforts and be able either to spend them on goods of his own choosing or to save his rewards for purpose of investment in his own or others' productive efforts. No other incentive has proved as successful in increasing production potential, economic progress, and strength.

Thus freedom is central to our way of life and is a contributing factor to economic progress and strength.

Do we believe that all men everywhere could achieve the same amount of progress that our nation has if they were free? Obviously not, for we would be imputing all our growth to freedom when we know that it is a function of many factors. However, a spokesman for our State Department, the executive arm of our government responsible for international policy, has certainly emphasized the role of freedom in presenting the United States views on *The Essentials of Economic Growth:*

There are certain essentials that must be present before any people, anywhere, can make rapid genuine progress toward the kind of economic development that will bring higher living standards widely diffused throughout the population.

With a full realization that one can hardly avoid oversimplification, may I suggest three essentials for the economic growth of a people which reflects itself in all segments of the life of a nation.

First, there must be freedom so that men and women willingly give their energies to the productive efforts of a nation.

By freedom, we mean both political and economic. It is impossible to separate the two. Freedom implies a regard for the human individual—his essential worth; his right to think for himself, to speak, to create, and to experiment; his right to improve his status by work and enterprise; his right to save and to risk his savings. In short, he must have the right to develop his individual capacities to the greatest extent possible.

Most Americans would consider individual freedom the most precious gift of all, not merely because it encourages economic growth but because in a larger sense—spiritually, morally, and intellectually—it gives meaning to human life itself.

It is of course possible to sacrifice the liberties and lives of whole generations of people, or whole classes of the population, in order to accelerate national economic development. Capital is thus formed through compulsory labor, forced savings, and even outright starvation of noncooperators. The Soviet Communist state has done this. Whatever sheerly physical gains in output may accrue to the state from this process, such gains are far less than those achieved in the free societies and they do not result in standards of living comparable to those attained by individuals in a free society. The judgment of history is that freedom is both the most potent generator of sustained economic growth and the only assurance that the benefits of that growth will be enjoyed by the individual man, regardless of race, religion, or political creed.

The second essential for the economic growth of a people is a climate conducive to the creation of capital—that is, the physical means to increase production and improve distribution. Whether a country calls itself capitalistic or not, it must have capital if it expects to grow economically.

The more capital a country creates through the productive efforts and savings of its people, acting as individuals for their own gain, the faster and healthier the economic development will be. . . .

The third essential for the economic growth of a people is that there must be integrity and intelligence in government. . . .

America is great because individual men have freedom and equality, because individual men have been given the incentive to create, to produce, and to save, because every man is rewarded for his labor with a generous share of the goods he helps to produce. America has taken its place among the great civilizations of history because the cornerstone upon which the Republic rests is the social, economic, and spiritual betterment of individual men.[13]

Hence, man and his freedom are reciprocal generating forces in the United States economic progress and strength. In conclusion, however, we must remember one of the four freedoms—freedom of speech and expression. So important is this that *the real strength of our nation may rest in the free voices of free men.*

GENERAL CONCLUSIONS

Thus we have seen the comparative importance of United States human resources with other areas in the world and studied the implications of changes in growth in our population and found them favorable to our sustained economic progress. We have examined in detail the problems and policies of man and resources, and manpower mobilization; and we have seen the importance of freedom to man as a contributing factor to economic growth and strength.

However, in Part V on human resources we have not emphasized the importance of man's mind. We are familiar with the quotation "Wars are born in the minds of men." But even more importantly *great productive efforts* are born in the minds of men. For some unaccountable reason the importance of man's mind has been deëmphasized in recent years in the United States. The intelligent thinking man has become the target of satire—"the egghead." As a part of this trend, our educational system in emphasizing the "whole child" has neglected his mind. We may not know the answer to the age-old riddle of which came first "the goose or the egg." This we do know, the gilt of intelligence of the "golden egg" must never be lost, for herein lies the genius of productivity.

[13] Herbert V. Prochnow, "The Essentials of Economic Growth," *Department of State Bulletin,* March 26, 1956, pp. 530–531.

"Johnny's inability to read" created a debate on the strength and weakness of our educational system which might prove to be one of controversy and creativity in a new look at objectives and methods.

We have pointed out that part of our manpower policies should be to further pure research, scientific and general education. For several years there has been growing concern on the part of many individuals and those in the responsible policy-making positions that the U.S.S.R. was emphasizing what the U.S.A. was deëmphasizing, and thus was catching up with us.[14] Russia's Sputniks I and II appeared to shock the United States public into a general awareness of this problem at the beginning of 1958. If this proved to be the case, we may have witnessed another Pearl Harbor that has given us time to revitalize in the goose that intangible qualitative substance which generates the gilt of the golden egg of productivity.

In addition, although a major purpose of this study is to measure production potential, we have not singled out for detailed discussion in this chapter a measure of productivity. In Chapter 11 on "Man-Made Facilities" we presented per capita income figures which showed that the United States ranked first among the nations, and in Chapter 12 comparative productivity data have been given. For reasons of emphasis Figure 13.2 has been reserved for this conclusion to show the tremendous gains that have been made in per capita productivity in the United States from 1850 with projections to 1960. The figure illustrates the study of the Twentieth Century Fund which calculated that the estimated rise in output per man-hour was from 33.7 cents in 1850 to $1.93 in 1950 (in constant 1950 prices).

Thus the productivity of labor was multiplied almost six times during the 100-year period. Although the average increase per decade was 18.4 percent, the changes from one decade to another varied greatly. Generally speaking, the gains from 1900 to 1950 were greater than those from 1850 to 1900. Between 1850 and 1900, productivity per man-hour little more than doubled; between 1900 and 1950 it increased almost three times. The Fund predicted that productivity would increase about 25 percent between 1950 and 1960, or approximately 2.3 percent per year.[15]

[14] See, for example, Brigadier General Carlton S. Dargusch, *The Russian-American Race for Technological Dominance*, talk by the Assistant Director for Manpower, Office of Defense Mobilization, before the Council on World Affairs, Cleveland, Ohio, April 6, 1956.

[15] J. Frederic Dewhurst and associates, *America's Needs and Resources*, The Twentieth Century Fund, 1955, p. 42.

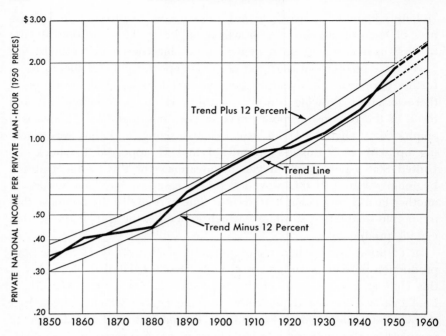

Figure 13.2. Estimated Productivity Trend, 1850–1960. (Data from J. Frederic Dewhurst and Associates, *America's Needs and Resources*, The Twentieth Century Fund, 1955)

To what can these tremendous gains in productivity be attributed? To the way in which we have allocated and used our natural resources, our capital resources, our human resources, including their manifold quantitative and qualitative characteristics; to the reciprocal aid of our international interdependence, and to all these factors working together.

Thus we have shown our production potential and economic progress. We know that only the productive can be strong and only the strong can be free. Finally we have seen how freedom contributes to strength. Now we will turn our attention in Unit Three of our study to seeing how these elements of strength can best be employed strategically to achieve security—the United States' second major objective.

Unit Three

Strategy of Security

CHAPTER 14

Geopolitics and Economics—
Geoecopolitics

How can the elements of strength of the United States best be employed strategically to achieve security? The object of this chapter is to study the meaning and development of geopolitics and its implication for United States national policy, to show the extent to which economic factors have been a part of geopolitical thinking, to indicate the major contributions of geopolitics, and to suggest the need of revision of geopolitics to include a greater emphasis on the study of the economics of resource appraisal in the development of a science of *geoecopolitics*. Finally, Soviet power policies will be briefly reviewed in order to show how these must be taken into consideration in the development of a United States *strategy of security*.

During World War II geopolitics was "discovered" in the United States and we learned of a new "science" which was being used by the German general staff under the direction of General Karl Haushofer. Since that time students of geography, political science, and military science have become interested in geopolitics; but few students of economics have more than a vague concept of the meaning of geopolitics, its development, and its significance as an instrument of national policy.

THE MEANING OF GEOPOLITICS

The term "geopolitics" was coined by Rudolf Kjellén (Shallen), a "Swedish professor of government" and a "geographer," in 1916. He believed that the history, present status, and potentialities of each state should be analyzed from several viewpoints. First, one should study the state as a spatial organism—this is *Geo-politik;* then the population—*Demo-politik;* and finally, the economic structure—*Eco-politik.* Thus we note that *Geo-politik* was only one section of the whole study of the state.

In 1904 Sir Halford J. Mackinder read a paper on "The Geographical Pivot of History" before the Royal Geographical Society in which he sketched the World-Island and the Heartland; and in 1905 he wrote in the *National Review* on the subject of "Man-power as a Measure of National and Imperial Strength." In 1919 he wrote on these subjects at greater length in his *Democratic Ideals and Reality—A Study in the Politics of Reconstruction.* Mackinder has been described as "the father of geopolitics," and we will examine his thesis in detail, but the writer has not discovered in these works a helpful definition of geopolitics.

General Karl Haushofer was the German leader of the Geopolitik. A commander of an artillery brigade during World War I, he became the leader of a pseudo-scientific group that turned to geography as an explanation of Germany's defeat and as a basis for another plan of conquest. This group was referred to as "Geopolitikers." Dorpalen reports that they were quite often in disagreement among themselves and sought to create an atmosphere of profundity through the deliberate confusion of the general reader. However, he concludes that they were in accord as to the definition of geopolitics: "Geopolitics is the science of the earth's relationships of political processes. It is based on the broad foundations of geography, especially on political geography, which is the science of the political organisms in space and their structure. Moreover, geopolitics sets out to furnish the tools for political action and the directives for political life as a whole. Thus, geopolitics becomes an art, namely the art of guiding practical politics. Geopolitics is the geographic science of the state."[1]

The Armed Forces Industrial College uses the two following dictionary definitions of geopolitics:

"Geopolitics is the making of national policy with due regard for physical and human geography." (*Webster's Dictionary*)

"Geopolitics is the application of political and economic geography to the external political problems of States." (*American College Dictionary*)

Professor Nicholas John Spykman of Yale University concluded that

---

[1] A. Dorpalen, *The World of General Haushofer*, Farrar and Rinehart, Inc., 1942, p. xii.

the confusion in the minds of most people about the nature of geopolitics was due largely to the fact that the term had been used to refer to at least three different categories of thought.

It has been adopted by some students, particularly those of the German school, as the framework for a whole philosophy of history. They make it into a theory about the nature of the state and use it as a doctrine supporting the need and desirability of territorial expansion. Secondly, it has been used as a synonym for political geography, in which case it becomes merely a branch of the general science of geography describing the structure of individual states, and the world in terms of its political subdivisions.

Finally, the term may be applied to the planning of security policy of a country in terms of its geographic factors. It then answers the question: Given a particular geographical situation, what is the best policy to follow to achieve security?[2]

Professor Spykman concluded that the specific field of geopolitics is foreign policy, and its particular type of analysis uses geographic factors to help in the formulation of adequate policies for the achievement of certain justifiable ends.

GEOPOLITICAL THEORIES

1. Admiral A. T. Mahan's Theory

Admiral Alfred Thayer Mahan, author of *The Influence of Sea Power upon History 1660–1783*, published in 1890, was a geopolitical thinker long before the expression was coined. He was the first person to recognize comprehensively and analyze the fact that the sea had become a great artery of communication and a basis of change in the organization of world power facilitated by overseas empires. In the past, the pattern was one of great land powers based on the control of continuous land masses such as the Roman, Chinese, and Russian empires. According to Admiral Mahan, the oceans of the world had become the inland seas of the British Empire, and the world's trade routes were its life lines. In the last resort, armed force guarded the Empire and its life lines, and Great Britain looked to her navy to furnish the ultimate, if not also the only, guarantee of her political and economic interests.

From British naval history Mahan discerned that the essence of British naval strategy was to gain command of the seas by the concentration of battleships capable of dealing the enemy's fleet a knockout blow.

Admiral Mahan held that a nation must expand or decline, and that no

[2] Nicholas John Spykman, *The Geography of Peace*, Harcourt, Brace and Company, 1944, pp. 5–6.

nation could hold its own by standing still. He saw the United States as the world power of the future and called for an extension of naval power in keeping with the United States' imperial destiny. A fleet capable of taking the offensive, he proclaimed, would secure for the United States indisputable supremacy in the Caribbean and the Pacific.

Mahan's doctrine of battle-fleet supremacy was hailed in many countries as a strategy which others could employ to gain empire and world domination. In his writings one finds a colorful blend of closely reasoned theories on naval strategy and an expansionist ideology which helped to extend his ideas far beyond the circle of international naval experts. His doctrine had a great influence on the later work of General Haushofer and his Geopolitikers.

Admiral Mahan's theory of the influence of sea power was widely accepted, but his qualifying remarks were often overlooked. He saw the pitfalls that were inherent in the overstatement of principles deduced from British naval history. He repeatedly emphasized the uniqueness of Great Britain's geographic position. The home bases of Britain's navy could not be attacked across land frontiers, so Britain could spend much more money on her navy while keeping her land forces to the minimum needed to defend her naval bastions. In Europe, no other power was geographically so favored. Also there was no other power in Europe capable of supporting a land force large enough to defend a continental position while maintaining a navy at the same time that was powerful enough to challenge Britain's command of the seas. Geography had also endowed Britain with the advantage of a commanding position over all the important sea passages in the world at that time.[3]

Thus Mahan, one of the world's first geopoliticians, saw the concentration of naval power into a battle line second to none as the key to world power. This battle line plus the geographic advantage of bases commanding the world's important seaways could enforce great power in the world, but only so long as all these conditions were met.

2. Sir Halford J. Mackinder's Theory

Mackinder was perhaps the greatest of our original geopolitical analysts. He was in 1904 the first person to study in detail the relations between land and sea power on a truly global basis in his paper on "The Geographical Pivot of History" read before the Royal Geographical Soci-

[3] A. T. Mahan, *Influence of Sea Power upon History 1660–1783*, Little, Brown and Company, 1890, p. 219.

ety. In his best known work, *Democratic Ideals and Reality,* published in 1919, Mackinder again asked for a global view of world politics; and geopoliticians have stressed the geographic nature of these realities, although, as we shall develop later, Mackinder also discussed certain other important realities.

First of Mackinder's geographic realities was an understanding of the unity of global relationships. There is one ocean covering nine-twelfths of the globe. There is one continent—Europe, Asia, and Africa—the

Figure 14.1. Mackinder's Map of World (1904). (Data from Armed Forces Industrial College)

World Island, covering two-twelfths of the globe. The remaining one-twelfth of the globe is made up of many small islands, "whereof North America and South America are for effective purposes two." Mackinder's map of the world (1904) is shown as Figure 14.1. In 1919 Mackinder wrote:

Leading Americans have for some time appreciated the fact that their country is no longer a world apart, and President Wilson had brought his whole people round to that view when they consented to throw themselves into the War. But North America is no longer even a continent; in this twentieth century it is shrinking to be an island. Americans used to think of their three millions of square miles as the equivalent of all Europe; some day, they said, there would be a United States of Europe as sister to the United States of America. Now, though they may not have realized it, they must no longer think of Europe apart from Asia and Africa. The Old World has become insular, or in other words, a unit, incomparably the largest geographical unit in our Globe.[4]

[4] H. J. Mackinder, *Democratic Ideals and Reality,* Constable and Company Ltd., 1919, pp. 85–87.

Second of Mackinder's geographical realities is the World Island. The World Island is divided into two parts geographically and strategically.

The first part of the World Island is the Heartland or Pivot Area. The Heartland, as the sociologists would say, is a naturally delineated region. This vast area of Siberia can be treated as a unit because three of the largest rivers in the world drain northward into the icy Arctic Ocean, and the other major rivers to the south drain into the inland Black and Caspian seas. Thus, the Heartland is the great inland plain in the "heart" of the World Island which is inaccessible to the sea. Strategically it may be extended to include the basins of the Black and Baltic seas, because the Black Sea can be closed by land power and the Baltic by sea power. In another sense, this area is the "geographical pivot of history" in that Mackinder develops the theory that the history of the world is a result of the pressure which the landlocked people of the Eurasian plain —the Heartland—have exerted throughout the ages on the surrounding peoples of the coastlands.

The second part of the World Island, the coastlands, Mackinder calls the Inner or Marginal Crescent, which with the exception of the sub-continent of Africa have been the maritime or sea-power countries.

About the World Island Mackinder asks the question: "What if the Great Continent, the whole World-Island or a large part of it, were at some future time to become a single united base of sea-power? Would not the other insular bases be outbuilt as regards ships and outmanned as regards seamen?"[5]

Third of Mackinder's geographical realities are these other insular bases, the remaining lands of the globe, which he calls the lands of the Outer or Insular Crescent. These, as we have seen, make up only one-twelfth of the globe and include North and South America.

Mackinder's geopolitical thesis was that the concentration of power in the World Island (or Eastern Hemisphere) was made possible by the land power of the Heartland and the sea power of Great Britain. The strategy of security for countries of the Outer Crescent isles and the Inner Crescent isles (Great Britain, for example) was to preserve a power equilibrium between the maritime and continental states of the World Island. Mackinder held that if either the continental or maritime states gained the ascendancy, the whole continent would be dominated and the Pivot Area controlled by a single power. He contended that with this tremendous land mass as a base, a sea power could be developed

[5] *Ibid.*, p. 91.

which could defeat Great Britain and thus gain complete mastery of the sea. This theory fits closely with that of Mahan.

Mackinder's thesis was derived from his conclusion that land power was replacing sea power. In the past, sea powers with seafaring people had more or less controlled the world because of their hold over the margins of the great land masses. The use of land power was due to "the realities which the Continent presents for strategical thought." One of these realities lies within the Heartland and its strategic position. The reality of the Heartland is only a part of the many geographic realities spelled out in great detail which lead to the unity of the World Island. But here the economist must point out that the real rise of land power of the World Island is due to the increased mobility of power made possible by the growth of transportation, and the growth of population. Both of these realities Mackinder clearly depicted: "Today armies have at their disposal not only the Trans-Continental Railroad but also the Motor-Car. They have, too, the Aero-plane, which is of a boomerang nature, a weapon of land-power as against sea-power. . . .

"Not until about a hundred years ago, however, was there available a base of man-power sufficient to begin to threaten the liberty of the world from within this citadel of the World-Island."[6]

Mackinder stated clearly the strategy of security at the end of World War I: "When our Statesmen are in conversation with the defeated enemy, some airy cherub should whisper to them from time to time this saying:

> *Who rules East Europe commands the Heartland;*
> *Who rules the Heartland commands the World-Island;*
> *Who rules the World-Island commands the World.*"[7]

We will have ample reason for analyzing this quotable quote, but one will find it difficult to challenge the prophetic wisdom of the following post-World War I statement: "No mere scraps of paper, even though they be the written constitution of a League of Nations, are under the conditions of to-day a sufficient guarantee that the Heartland will not again become the centre of a World-War."[8]

Further, *economists* will be pleased to note that Mackinder, in concluding his discussion on "The Landsman's Point of View," suggested: "Now is the time, when the Nations are fluid, to consider what guaran-

[6] *Ibid.*, p. 143.
[7] *Ibid.*, p. 194.
[8] *Ibid.*, p. 143.

tees, based on Geographical and *Economic* Realities, can be made available for the future security of Mankind."[9]

3. General Karl Haushofer's Theory

Major General Karl Haushofer was the ultimate creator of German geopolitics. In the process he was influenced by many environmental factors, and by Mackinder, Friedrich Ratzel, and Rudolf Kjellén. In 1908, when he was 39 and a captain in the German Army, Haushofer went to Japan as the first military observer sent by the Bavarian General Staff to the Far East. In Munich in 1911 he secured his Ph.D. with a dissertation on Japan. He was greatly impressed by the unity of mind and purpose of the Japanese people in political undertakings, particularly in their whole-hearted backing of their aggressive expansionist policies. He saw that this unity was brought about by the proper mass psychology that had been poured into them for years. They sincerely believed that expansion was their right and their mission. Haushofer carefully studied the manner in which the Japanese government propagandized the people and how the expansion programs were carried out so successfully. Later he based much of his work on these methods.

Two years after World War I, Haushofer became a professor at the University of Munich in 1919 lecturing on political geography and military history. It is very difficult for us to understand the spirit of the interwar period in Germany and the atmosphere of hopes and fears that made possible and encouraged the movements culminating in the preëminence of the Nazi party. We are told that "All over Germany the restless war and post-war generation of students began to talk about the General Professor Haushofer and his geopolitics—and they talked in the same vague but enthusiastic way that they spoke of Spengler. The name of a third man in Munich also appeared in their conversation: Adolf Hitler."[10]

At Munich Haushofer worked zealously to perfect his geopolitical ideas of Germany's role in the future of the world. He established an Institute of Geopolitics and a very prolific *Journal of Geopolitics*. As he was primarily a major general in the German Army and only secondarily a professional person, it was quite natural that his followers and strongest supporters were among his army associates. Later, under Hitler, his disciples were the young men who in more normal times would have

[9] *Ibid.*, pp. 143 and 146.
[10] Hans W. Weigert, *Generals and Geographers—The Twilight of Geopolitics*, Oxford University Press, 1942, p. 56.

studied at a university but under the circumstances had decided to become professional soldiers since the army was the only place still relatively secure from the supervision of Nazism. This rapport between Haushofer and the German Army cannot be underestimated. Haushofer's ambitions were for the German nation, as were those of the army. His strategy won the army's support, and it was with the army that he worked and through it that he attempted to influence Hitler, the head of the German state.

Haushofer's relation with Hitler was very complex. Both of them dreamed of a German world empire and a coming world revolution from which Germany would emerge triumphant. To Haushofer and the army, Hitler and the Nazi party elite were strangers even when the Himmlers and Ribbentrops wore beautiful uniforms decorated with the medals of international Fascism. Haushofer did not publicize his views of Hitler and National Socialism. No doubt Haushofer considered Hitler and the party a passing phase, an instrument to be worked through to achieve the army's and Germany's objectives.

This background is necessary to the understanding and implementation of Haushofer's geopolitical theories. Some of the psychological aspects of German geopolitics, though difficult to comprehend, are important and cannot be omitted; but, in addition, there are rational and valuable aspects which can be traced from those who influenced Haushofer and the Geopolitikers.

A. Mackinder's Influence

Haushofer was Mackinder's most eager pupil, although the two never met. He readily admitted that he owed to Mackinder his own "concept of the powers that rule the spaces." Actually, Haushofer always considered Mackinder a spokesman of the enemy and in reviewing Mackinder's *Democratic Ideals and Reality* said: "This book should not be translated into German unless the German people are willing to lose all their self-respect, confronted with such a hateful enemy."[11]

Mackinder in 1904 feared that if Germany allied herself with Russia the balance of power would be offset in favor of the land power of the continent. Haushofer was steeped in Mackinder's belief in the strength and destiny of the great land mass of Russia and he did not underestimate the power potential of that vast area. Haushofer's policy was consistent throughout in his belief in the necessity of Germany's avoiding combat with Russia. He wrote in his *Journal* in 1939 that: "It is of vital

[11] Quoted in *ibid.*, p. 116.

importance that Russia and Germany unite their forces." He was convinced that it was far better for Germany to ally herself with Russia and have on her side the might of the Heartland, stabilize her continental power, and, if possible, guide and control the economic system of Russia. Then Germany would be in an invulnerable position to turn westward to achieve *Lebensraum*. Thus the German-Russian Pact of August, 1939, was, without a doubt, a triumph for Haushofer and the German Army. But their triumph did not last long. Hitler returned to his policy as formulated in *Mein Kampf*, "the crusade against the world enemy, Bolshevism," and Germany attacked Russia in 1941.

Another fear Mackinder had was the combination of manpower of China or Japan and their ocean frontage with the control of the Heartland and resources of the great Euro-Asiatic continent. We faced this threat in World War II with the bringing of Japan into the Rome-Berlin Axis. Today this fear becomes a reality with China's inclusion in the Soviet bloc. In addition, Mackinder fully appreciated the importance of the Middle East, though not for the same reason—oil—that we do today. "It cannot be wholly a coincidence that in the self-same region should be the starting point of history and the crossing point of the most vital of modern highways."[12] Haushofer's master plan called for Japan to be brought into the Rome-Berlin Axis and to carry out her conquest in the Far East simultaneously with Germany's expansion in Europe. In addition, the plan was to control the Mediterranean Sea by capturing the Suez Canal by way of the North African coast and force traveling through Turkey, but Britain's neutrality with Turkey and the United States' North African invasion prevented this possibility. Germany then changed her plans, we are told, to send her forces down the Iranian peninsula and then across through India where they would meet with the Japanese forces to surround Russia and cut off all effective aid from her. Had the Russians not held at Stalingrad, "this plan would have succeeded and Allied chances for victory would have been greatly reduced." (The writer believes that Allied chances for victory would have been reduced for quite another reason. The Germans had already occupied or neutralized the great Russian industrial areas with the exception of those behind the Urals which were protected by Stalingrad.

Thus, Haushofer's plans were not carried through. First, Russia was attacked at Hitler's insistence before Great Britain was defeated, and

[12] Mackinder, *op. cit.*, p. 115.

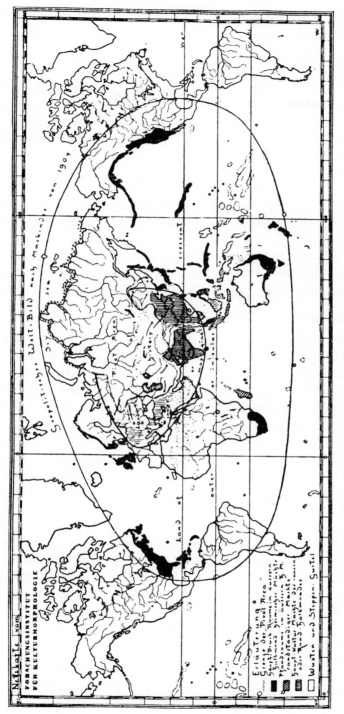

Figure 14.2. The World According to Haushofer. (Nickolas John Spykman, *The Geography of the Peace*)

most importantly, the aid and effective strength of the United States were discounted. The conclusion has been drawn that "The defeat of Haushofer was the defeat of Hitler and of Germany."

Finally, in commenting on Mackinder's influence on Haushofer, Spykman states that Haushofer took over Mackinder's interpretation of the constellation of power in the Eastern Hemisphere and adapted it to his own peculiar needs. Spykman suggests that a look at the map (Figure 14.2) which Haushofer drew to explain his theories will show that he added certain improvements. "He has indicated the flow of rivers, a detail from which one accustomed to interpret maps can make some estimate of the location of mountain ranges. He has also sketched in certain areas of 'political pressure' which illustrate the location of centers of power Mackinder discussed but failed to locate on his map. Nevertheless, this chart fails to afford a really adequate basis for discussion because it does not give the really important facts about topography which, in a geopolitical analysis, are indispensable."[13]

B. Friedrich Ratzel's Influence

Friedrich Ratzel, who died in 1904, was most significant in his influence on Haushofer in the development of a Law of Growing Spaces. He was a professor of geography at Leipzig who integrated his interests into a system of "bio-geo-politics" in which the state, a union of land and people, was seen as a spatial organism that grows like any other living organism: It requires room to live, to expand, to grow. "Space . . . thus becomes an inseparable part of the living organism of the state itself." Space becomes "living space"—the now well-known *Lebensraum*.[14]

Ratzel developed three main geographical categories of the state which were at the same time the fundamental criteria of state power: "*Raum*—size of territory; *Lage*—its geographic location; *Grenzen*—the nature of its boundaries."[15] He compiled "Seven Laws of Expansion" of which the seventh "law," in an awkward translation, reads: "The general trend toward amalgamation transmits the tendency of territorial growth from state to state and increases the tendency in the process of transmission."[16] It may be simply put: appetite comes while eating.

States in their efforts at growth are opposed by other states; this

[13] Spykman, *op. cit.*, p. 37.
[14] Weigert, *op. cit.*, p. 95.
[15] Jan O. M. Broek, "The German School of Political Geography," *Global Politics,* University of California Press, 1944, pp. 169–170.
[16] Robert Strausz-Hupé, *Geopolitics—the Struggle for Space and Power,* G. P. Putnam's Sons, 1942, pp. 30–31.

struggle is the essence of interstate relations, and the ability to conquer and hold space is the final test of national power.[17]

The whole space concept taken from Ratzel was a vital part of Haushofer's propaganda, and *Lebensraum* became under Hitler a battle cry, a powerful uniting slogan which has been described as the "core of Nazi ideology."[18]

C. Rudolf Kjellén's Influence

We have seen that Kjellén coined the term "geopolitics" in 1916. As a professor of government he revolted against the legalistic tradition of political science which considers only the constitutional organization of states and took the biological interpretation of the state of Ratzel, expanded it and exaggerated it. In his most important work, *The State as Living Form,* he made the following statements: "The state itself is 'earth'; it is, to a certain extent, 'organized soil.'. . . . The essence of the state as an organism is composed of elements of law as well as power; like every individual life on earth, it consists not only of morality but also of organic lusts. . . . The states, as we [can] follow their course in history and as we move among them in the world of realities, are material—rational beings exactly like human beings. . . ."[19]

These statements may seem unscientific and have been described as "irrational and even sinister" but they have a large enough element of truth to be considered carefully, especially when we remember Kjellén's suggestion that the state should be studied from the threefold aspect as a spatial organism: this is *Geo-politik;* then population: *Demo-politik;* and finally, the economic structure: *Eco-politik.*

One other part of Kjellén's ideas is worth noting in connection with Haushofer's geopolitics: "He believed that maritime, commercial empires with their far-flung, scattered possessions were a thing of the past and that their fate would be sealed by the rise of large but compact land empires, rooted in the soil by actual occupation. Eventually these land empires would also control the sea from their large land bases."[20]

D. Summary

In this brief review of General Karl Haushofer's theory of geopolitics we have seen that his emphasis was on the global aspects of space in which he emphasized the importance of the Heartland and space as an

[17] Broek, *op. cit.,* p. 170.
[18] Strausz-Hupé, *op. cit.,* p. 50.
[19] Quoted in Weigert, *op. cit.,* p. 106.
[20] Broek, *op. cit.,* p. 170.

organism. As his Geopolitik group interpreted the situation, Germany's *Lebensraum* had no boundaries and might someday extend over the world. His tactics were to sell this strategy to the army and to the people and to use Hitler and the National Socialist party as an instrument of implementation of political action. In addition to these spatial aspects of geopolitics, he also had definitive ideas on the use of space as an instrument of military strategy. His military doctrines undoubtedly contributed to the technique of encirclement and its corollary, the *Pinzer*. Because of his familiarity with Japan and the Asiatic region, he developed a whole doctrine of *Geopolitics of the Pacific*. His influence on Japan can perhaps be seen in the Japanese concept of a "greater Asia Co-prosperity Sphere" which was in part a result of Japan's study of the German "Great Space Economy."

4. Professor Nicholas John Spykman's Theory

The late Professor Spykman of Yale believed that the specific field of geopolitics is foreign policy, and its particular type of analysis uses geographic factors to help in the formulation of adequate policies for the achievement of certain justifiable ends.

The type of analysis Spykman endorsed was "something completely different from the geographical metaphysics which is so characteristic of the German school of 'Geopolitik.'"

Haushofer has managed to give to particular *types* of frontier a mystical, moral sanctity. Expansion up to such a frontier, whether expressed as a response to the compulsion of the magic concept "space" or in some other form, becomes an action in harmony with divine purposes. Such metaphysical nonsense has no place here. No particular geographic form is ethically better for a country than another form, and no mysterious good for the state, considered as a living organism which must expand and grow strong, can justify the unlimited use of power to achieve such ends. *Geographic position* and *physical power* are facts to be reckoned with in the international world and a technique is available for the more effective understanding of these facts. Wherever generalizations are drawn by the geopoliticians from them and applied to policy, standards of good and evil must condition their formulation. In any case, the objective of peace and security for a state and for the world as a whole must inspire the final choice of policy to the exclusion of such aims as expansion and aggrandizement of power.[21]

But Spykman recognized in the very opening sentence of his *Geography of Peace* that "We are confronted today with the spectacle of the great nations of the world engaging in a tremendous struggle for sheer

---

[21] Spykman, *op. cit.*, p. 7.

physical power." He had no tolerance for liberals and idealists who believed that the subject of power in the international world should not be spoken of except in moral disapproval, and who believed that studies concerned with the organization of peace and security should deal only with the ideals of our democratic civilizations and visions of a better world in which power would play no part. He demonstrated that "As a matter of fact, political ideals and visions unsupported by force have little survival value." Spykman was convinced that the security of states has a very close relationship to the organization of power, and that the final responsibility for the security of each state rests upon itself alone. He was therefore convinced that when "dealing with the problem of safety and independence, the nation has to act on the basis of strength it can mobilize, either within its own territory or through its allies and protectors."[22]

Spykman believed that geopolitics was an appropriate name for a type of analysis and a body of data which are indispensable to the process of reaching intelligent decisions on certain aspects of foreign policy. He began his analysis by using maps as a tool and he stressed the importance of using the correct type of map. In Chapter 2, "Spatial Resources," we referred to his clear discussion of the relative merits of different types of maps, and included as Figures 2.1–2.3 three of his maps. We also included in our study Spykman's initial proof that any country may be considered to be encircled if the center of the map projection is placed in the center of that country.

Spykman went on to say that: "On a globe, every point is surrounded by all other points. It is obvious therefore, that if such a conception as encirclement is to have any validity in a study of world relationships, it must be composed of more than mere land masses on a map. Other factors will have to be used to give it sufficient content to clarify the strategic and political position of a state."[23]

A. Spykman's Conditioning Factors of Foreign Policy

Spykman was very clear as to what these "other factors" should be in studying encirclement and world power relationships. "In other words, *geographic, economic* and *political* factors are all a part of the analysis and it is only when all three are examined that the real meaning of such a position can be grasped."[24]

[22] *Ibid.*, pp. 3–4.
[23] *Ibid.*, p. 19.
[24] *Ibid.*, p. 22.

GEOGRAPHIC FACTORS. Location, size, and topography are the geographic factors. Location is the prime consideration in a state's world power position. "It conditions and influences all other factors for the reason that world location determines the climatic zone and thereby the economic structure, and regional location defines potential enemies and allies and perhaps even the limits of a state's role as a participant in a system of collective security. Supplemented by a description of the topographical nature of the region in which the state is placed, a clear picture of geographical location will provide the framework for an understanding of security problems."

ECONOMIC FACTORS. The economic factors are the "power potentials" of states and include (1) agricultural resources, (2) industrial resources, (3) the people, and (4) industrial production.

Agricultural resources are conditioned by climate, and a "region which lacks these elements in any appreciable degree finds itself doomed to play a secondary role in the power relations of the world."

Industrial resources which a nation has and "the extent to which these materials can be used to produce the tools of modern Western civilization" are more directly important to the military and political strength of a nation." "It is, however, not so much the reserves which are important to the power of a state as the actual amount of the material produced."

Spykman considered the physical characteristics of the land and its natural resources as fairly permanent; it is only in times of exceptional technological development that these material conditions are rapidly modified. "The statesman who must determine the policies which his country is to follow, has thus to deal first with a group of factors of a clearly defined nature." Thus Spykman believed that power potentials could be readily shown by plotting reserves and production on maps. At this point we must remember our dynamic concept of resources as contrasted to this more static concept. However, we certainly have no argument with Spykman when he says that within the agricultural and industrial resources "lies the economic foundation of the role a state plays in world politics." We also agree with his further statement that the inanimate factors of agricultural and industrial production do not determine entirely the power of a nation.

The people who inhabit a country are also a basic element in its strength. Spykman saw that although it is impossible to measure the nature and spirit of a people and plot the results on a map "it is possible to get a certain picture of relative strength of nations by noting the distribution of population density in the world."

Industrial production is the fourth and final economic conditioning factor. This Spykman considered to be "most closely connected with the strength of a state." He noted that the world distribution of coal and iron production must inevitably form the basis of any industrial structure and then went on to point out the existence of a certain relationship between population density and industrial strength. He concluded:

In pre-industrial times, the number of human beings in a state had a direct bearing on its strength because it was their labor which produced most of the energy available. Today, we find the southern and eastern rimland regions of

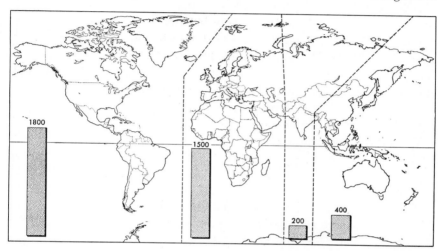

Figure 14.3. Daily Output of Work, Calculated in Millions of Horsepower Hours, 1929. (Data from Nicholas John Spykman, *The Geography of the Peace*)

Eurasia from Syria to Manchuria retaining a very direct relation between human energy and the output of work. In both Europe and America, however, machine energy accounts for the greatest proportion of the work done. It is possible, by reducing the amount of work done by both human and machine energy to a common unit, to compare the different parts of the earth in these terms. [Figure 14.3.] On this basis, it is clear that population density alone is inadequate to indicate the amount of energy produced by a group of people. The extraordinary investment in power machinery in the Western Hemisphere gives it great strength in comparison with the Eastern Hemisphere and particularly the Far East, in spite of its smaller total population.[25]

POLITICAL FACTORS.   Political factors comprise Spykman's third and final group of conditioning factors of foreign policy. His position was that the territorial encirclement of a state would have little meaning unless the state's own political integration and alliances were compared

[25] *Ibid.*, pp. 29 and 33.

with the nature and extent of alliances concluded between the states that, territorially, made up the encirclement. Thus *geographic, economic,* and *political* factors are all a part of the analysis of encirclement and strength.

B. The United States and the World

Spykman examined the United States' geopolitical position in a chapter on "The Position of the Western Hemisphere." He found that the United States is surrounded geographically by the Eurasian land mass plus the continents of Africa and Australia. "In terms of territory, this area is two and one half times the size of the New World; in terms of population, it is ten times the size; and, in terms of energy output, it is approximately equal." To the east of the United States is located western Europe, a center of power of both population density and mechanical energy. To the west of us there is another great power center expressing its force largely in terms of population density. Politically the United States has a big advantage because the surrounding states are not unified.

The most significant fact that confronted the United States was in 1942 when during the course of World War II German power reached its objective at North Cape and as far south as Dakar, while the Japanese Empire stretched its control from Manchuria along all-important coastal regions of China and south to New Guinea and the Solomon Islands. Even more significant, however, was the existence of a political alliance between Germany and Japan. "We were then confronted with the possibility of complete encirclement, in which case we might have had to face the unified power of the whole Eurasian land mass. The strength of the power centers of the Eastern Hemisphere would then have been overpowering. It would have been impossible for us to preserve our independence and security."[26]

Spykman concluded that if the United States is to avoid such an encirclement in the future, our constant concern must be to see that no nation or alliance of nations is allowed to emerge as a dominating power in either of the two regions of the Old World. Therefore it is obvious that the internal power relations between the states of the Eurasian continent will determine to a great extent the course of United States policies.

C. Eastern Hemisphere Geopolitics

Spykman, thus, saw that it was necessary to understand the geopolitical relationships in the Eastern Hemisphere in order to discover

[26] *Ibid.*, p. 34.

what effect they would have on the United States position. To do this he emphasized the fact that, largely as a result of fast-improving sea and air transportation and power, the total earth's surface has become a single field for the play of political forces; further, the conditions of power on one continent are inevitably reflected in the distribution of power on another.

THE EURASIAN MAP.   In Spykman's study of the United States, he divided the Eurasian continent into two regions, Europe and the Far East, but in order to see the relation of these two areas to each area, he returned to the Siberia-centered map of Mackinder. This, he found, needed to be revised and he substituted a map of his own (Figure 14.4) in which the regions and names were slightly changed. Spykman continued to call the central continental plain the Heartland but in effect it was equated with the political extent of the Union of Soviet Socialist Republics. Beyond the mountain barrier, the coastland region, "which is called by Mackinder the inner crescent, may more effectively be referred to as the rimland, a name which defines its character accurately." The surrounding string of marginal and mediterranean seas which separate the continent from the oceans were seen by Spykman to constitute a circumferential maritime highway which linked the rimland together in terms of sea power. Beyond the seas the offshore islands and continents of Great Britain, Japan, Africa, and Australia compose the Outer Crescent. The term "offshore" is used rather than Mackinder's "Inner Crescent" because it describes so well their essential relationship to the central land mass. "The oceanic belt and the transoceanic New World complete the picture in terms of purely geographical factors."

The Heartland region was first suggested to Mackinder by his conception of the value of a central position with interior lines of communication made powerful and unified by the development of land transportation to a point where it would begin to compete with sea communication. He also saw the transformation of the steppeland from an area of low economic potential to one of high economic potential. Spykman does not agree with this and shows that "The actual facts of the Russian economy and geography make it *not at all clear* that the heartland is or will be in the very near future a world center of communication, mobility or power potential."[27]

The rimland, the Inner Crescent of Mackinder, was in his conception the amphibian states surrounding the Heartland and consisting of three sections: the European coastland, the Arabian-Middle Eastern desert

[27] For proof, see *ibid.*, pp. 38–40.

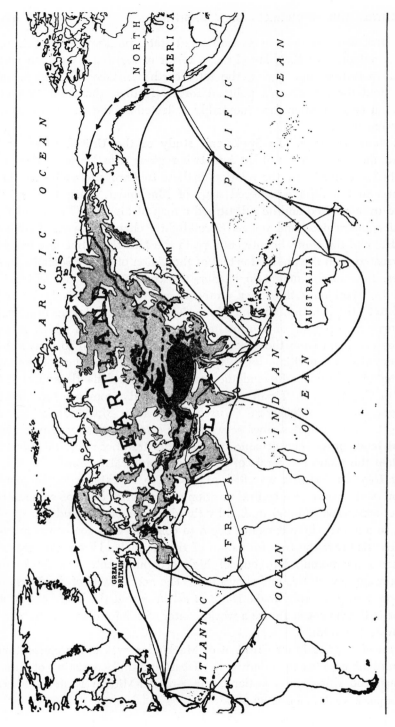

Figure 14.4. A Geopolitical Map of Eurasia. (Nicholas John Spykman, *The Geography of the Peace*)

land, and the Asiatic monsoon. Spykman saw the first two regions as clearly defined geographical areas, "but the third is a unit only from the special historical point of view represented by Great Britain." Spykman considered the rimland of the Eurasian land mass as an intermediate region situated between the heartland and the marginal seas. It serves as a vast *buffer zone* of conflict between sea power and land power. "Looking in both directions, it must function amphibiously and defend itself on land and sea. In the past, it has had to fight against the land power of the heartland and against the sea power of the off-shore islands of Great Britain and Japan." The rimland's amphibious nature lies at the basis of its security problems.

The offshore continents of the Eastern Hemisphere of Australia and Africa stretch beyond the two mediterranean seas which lie off the southeastern and southwestern shores of the Old World. Spykman concludes:

> The significance of both these off-shore continents in world politics is limited by climatic conditions which restrict their productive capacity and, consequently, their power potential. The greatest proportion of Africa lies in the tropical zone and is either extremely dry or extremely humid. In either case the continent does not contain, except at the extreme southern tip, the resources necessary for the building up of political units capable of exerting an important influence on the rest of the world. In the same way, the desert regions of Australia are so extensive that the remaining territory is left without the size and resources required for the formation of a power of the first rank.[28]

EURASIAN POLITICS. Mackinder defined the general pattern of political action on the Eurasian continent in terms of the pressure of nomadic peoples in the Heartland outward against the states of the rimland. Spykman says that there has never really been a simple land power-sea power opposition.[29] "The historical alignment has always been in terms of some members of the rimland with Great Britain against some members of the rimland with Russia, or Great Britain and Russia together against a dominating rimland power."

Spykman asserted that the Mackinder dictum "Who controls eastern Europe rules the Heartland; who rules the Heartland rules the World Island; and who rules the World Island rules the World" is false. If there is to be a slogan for the power politics of the Old World, it must be "Who controls the rimland rules Eurasia; who rules Eurasia controls the destinies of the world."

[28] *Ibid.*, p. 41.
[29] For proof, see *ibid.*, pp. 41–43.

The United States went to war twice within thirty years (World War I and World War II), and the threat to our security each time was the possibility that the rimland regions of the Eurasian land mass would be dominated by a single power.

Spykman points out that the most recent Heartland concept by Mackinder (H. J. Mackinder, "The Round World," *Foreign Affairs*, July, 1943) recognized the predominant importance of the rimland and the necessity of British–Russian–United States collaboration to prevent the growth of power in this area. We will remember that this was our policy during World War II.

D. Spykman's Strategy

The final chapter of *The Geography of the Peace* is a study of the "Strategy of Security." This consists of first presenting the concept of global war and global peace and the military aspects of World War II. Then Spykman turns his attention to the post-World War II problems of (a) Eurasian conflict zones, (b) access of the United States to Eurasia, and (c) a foreign policy for the United States.

EURASIAN CONFLICT ZONES. The power struggles of the Eastern Hemisphere have always been fought in reference to the relations between the Heartland and the rimland, the power constellation within the rimland itself, the influence of maritime pressure on the littoral, and finally "the participation in that pressure exerted by the Western Hemisphere."

The Heartland-rimland post-World War II period was seen by Spykman in 1944 as one which would "witness a continuation of the struggle of Russia and China for control and influence over Sinkiang Province and Outer Mongolia." "In fact, it may be that pressure of Russia toward the rimland will constitute one important aspect of the post-war settlement."

Within the rimland in Europe the distribution of power among France, Germany, and eastern Europe will be of extreme importance, and no one of the three regions can be allowed to gain complete control. India was seen as the dominant power on the Indian Ocean. In the Far East the dominant power was predicted to be China, providing she achieves real unification. "If the Western Powers are to retain any influence at all in the region, they will have to establish air bases for their power. In view of the limits which there undoubtedly are to the power resources of the Chinese state, such bases will probably be sufficient to counterbalance any future attempt of China to dominate the Far East completely."

The contact area between the littoral of Eurasia and the string of marginal seas which surrounds it is the region which has the most immediate concern for both Great Britain and the United States. Once the marginal seas were controlled by sea power, but now no geographical area in the world has been more profoundly affected by the development of air power. This does not mean, however, that it is inevitable that the whole littoral of the Eurasian land mass must fall into the hands of Eurasian air power because opposite coasts can support air power which could be used against a continental air force. This would be possible only if the power behind the air force on the continental side did not represent the unified strength of the European and Asiatic centers of power. Therefore, those nations which control the opposite coasts of the marginal seas must prevent the domination of the rimland by a single state.[30]

ACCESS OF THE UNITED STATES TO EURASIA. Since it is of interest to the United States that no overwhelming power be allowed to develop in Europe and the Far East, Spykman concluded that we must find some way of exerting our power in these regions during peacetime so as not to allow a situation to develop which will force us into a third war. In this discussion he is primarily concerned with military access by transportation.

Spykman concluded that the air power which the United States can exert across the Arctic Ocean would remain limited, as would peacetime transpolar traffic. Thus the United States will have to depend on her sea power communications across the Atlantic and Pacific to give her access to the Old World, and very close coöperation between Britain and the United States is absolutely essential.

Further, neither the United States nor Great Britain can exert her armed strength fully against the European continent without a continental ally that can provide a base from which land power can be exercised. Spykman did not think that the coöperation of France alone would be sufficient to assure the security of Europe. "Russia, on the other hand, will be the strongest land power on the continent and it will be to the advantage of both Britain and the United States to have her as an ally. Indeed, as long as she does not herself seek to establish a hegemony over the European rimland, the Soviet Union will be the most effective continental base for the enforcement of peace. At the same time, her own

[30] *Ibid.,* pp. 54–55.

strength, great as it is, would be insufficient to preserve her security against a unified rimland. The three super-powers together will, therefore, be the only effective guarantors of the European situation."[31]

However, Spykman saw clearly that a mere alliance with Great Britain and Russia would not be enough to insure the United States' ability to support her obligations to the security system, nor would it be enough to give her the strength necessary to make possible an equilibrium of power among the three states. The United States would be required to establish naval and air bases in the offshore waters of the Eurasian continent.

In the transpacific area the latter is doubly true.

A FOREIGN POLICY FOR THE UNITED STATES. As a final part of Spykman's strategy and in summarizing his *Geography of the Peace,* he concluded:

The distribution of power resources gives greater possibilities for the exertion of force to the Old World than to the New World.

The safety and independence of the United States can be preserved only by a foreign policy that will make it impossible for the Eurasian land mass to harbor an overwhelming dominant power in Europe and the Far East.

The United States must recognize once again, and permanently, that the power constellation is of everlasting concern to her both in time of war and in time of peace.

It is becoming more and more clear that there will be no superstate to guarantee to the members of the world community life, property, and the pursuit of happiness. Therefore, the United States must continue to depend primarily on her own national strength, for we know that the failure of a great state to consider power means its eventual destruction and conquest.

Balanced power on the Eurasian continent was one of the objectives the United States was fighting for during World War II and it should continue to be a peacetime objective. Therefore it is of interest to the United States to continue to collaborate with any powers seeking to prevent the consolidation of the rimland regions.

Finally: "The other two great powers in the world, Russia and Great Britain, will also find their security threatened by the establishment of any hegemony in Europe and Asia. These three states can, therefore, provide the foundation for an effective security system. Since neither of

[31] *Ibid.,* p. 57.

the three can afford to stand alone and isolated against the rest of the world, their co-operation will serve their own best interests."[32]

GEOPOLITICS REVIEWED

1. Summary

Geopolitics' specific field of study is foreign policy and in the solution of problems it uses an analysis which emphasizes principally geographic factors to help in the formulation of adequate policies for the achievement of certain justifiable ends. We have considered in detail the theories advanced by four of the best-known geopoliticians: Mahan, Mackinder, Haushofer, and Spykman. Mahan developed the role of sea power and "Insular Dominance." Mackinder stressed the importance of land power through his "Heartland and World Island Theory." Haushofer built upon this foundation, supplemented principally by Ratzel's "Law of Growing Spaces," a whole "power-mad scheme" of world supremacy, a theory which some tend to discount on the ground that "Haushofer and his group did not offer anything original to the idea of geopolitics." Who can discount the application of theories through policy and strategy that were a significant factor in World War II? Who can discount Haushofer's contribution to geopolitics when he brought geopolitics to the attention of the world? Spykman updated geopolitics, broadened its scope, stressed its useful purposes as a strategy for peace, and spelled out his theory by word and illustration in an articulate, understandable fashion. Significantly, though, Spykman's strategy for peace was narrowly confined to military-spatial relations without considering the strategic possibilities of economics.

2. The Role of Space

Central in the study of geopolitics is the role of *space and political action*. We have seen that the Geopolitikers agreed that geopolitics "is based on the broad foundations of geography, especially on political geography which is the science of the political organisms *in space* and their structure." Spykman has explained that the method of analysis of geopolitics may be compared to "the kind of thought which precedes the formulation and execution of policy in any field of action involving a choice of *location and* an awareness of the qualities of *space relations*."

Our analysis has shown spatial resources as one part of natural re-

[32] *Ibid.*, pp. 61–62.

sources, which also include agricultural resources, and energy and material resources. The fact was emphasized in Chapter 2 that spatial resources are a contributing element of strength and security and that the study of spatial resources should take into consideration: (a) the location of a country; (b) the size, shape, and depth of a country; (c) the topography of a country; (d) the locational relationships of a country's noncontiguous areas and commitments. We studied the significance of spatial resources in each of these respects and, in addition, emphasized the point that spatial resources are equally important with economic and military factors as contributing elements of strength and security. Thus the writer has no quarrel with the study of spatial resources, but he would like to stress at this time that spatial resources are but one part of natural resources and the latter are but one factor of production which together with capital resources and human resources constitute total production potential.

In addition, however, the fact should be noted that the geopoliticians' emphasis on space was limited to two dimensions in terms of area, and did not emphasize the three-dimensional aspects of space in terms of the availability of fund resources below the surface. This three-dimensional concept of the role of space will be stressed more and more in the future. Indeed, as we have already seen, Senator Lyndon Johnson expressed his recommended United States policy: "If out in space there is the ultimate position from which total control of the earth may be exercised, then our national goal and the goal of all free men must be to win and hold that position."

The President's Science Advisory Committee reported in March, 1958, that there were four reasons ("factors") for undertaking a national outer-space program:

The first of these factors is the compelling urge of man to explore and to discover, the thrust of curiosity that leads men to try to go where no one has gone before.

Second, there is the defense objective for the development of space technology. We wish to be sure that space is not used to endanger our security. If space is to be used for military purposes, we must be prepared to use space to defend ourselves.

Third, there is the factor of national prestige. To be strong and bold in space technology will enhance the prestige of the United States among the peoples of the world and create added confidence in our scientific, technological, industrial, and military strength.

Fourth, space technology affords new opportunities for scientific observation and experiment which will add to our knowledge and understanding of the earth, the solar system, and the universe.

The Science Advisory Committee concluded that an analysis of the reasons for undertaking the program and possible gains was necessary in reaching sound policy decisions for a United States space program and its management by the federal government.

3. Global Relations and Global Thinking

The means which students of geography have developed for the recording of spatial relationships and facts about the surface of the world are maps and globes. Maps, as we have seen, can give one a distorted point of view, and even Spykman, who tried so hard to prevent this, erred in his presentation of the relationship of the United States to Eurasia. The late S. Whittemore Boggs while Special Adviser on Geography to the Department of State in 1954 had this to say about maps: "A serious roadblock to understanding the new global relations of the United States is misconception of simple geographical relationships. This is in large part due to widespread use of Mercator and some of the other world maps in school textbooks, newspapers, and now even on television. It is disconcerting to discover how many people are quite oblivious to the characteristics of the maps they use. And among those whose job it is to prepare maps—seldom geographers or cartographers—few have an adequate knowledge of map projections and of the maps they make with which to convey basic information."[33]

One of the most significant contributions of geopolitics is the increased understanding of global relations in the process of studying *spatial relationships* on maps and globes. It is Mackinder who really gave us the impetus to global thinking. His fundamental "endeavor" was "to measure the relative significance of the great features of our globe as tested by the events of history, including the history of the last four years, and then to consider how we may best adjust our ideals of freedom to these lasting realities of our Earthly Home." With Mackinder's analysis of the Heartland and the World Island, the world takes on a unity of global aspects of which few individuals were aware. But what of the German Geopolitikers? We know of the importance of the study of geography in Germany, but Boggs has this to say: "If Haushofer and Hitler or the Japanese military strategists ever made intelligent use of globes, I have never been able to discover it. What they might have done or might have decided not to attempt, if they had visualized geographical relationships

---

[33] S. Whittemore Boggs, "Global Relations of the United States," reprint from *The Department of State Bulletin* of June 14, 1954, Department of State Publication 5536, General Policy Series 91, Government Printing Office, 1954, p. 903.

and situations more accurately, we can only guess."[34] Quite the opposite is true of Spykman. As we have seen, he worked diligently at the presentation of global spatial relations on maps. The latter he used because the globe was "an unwieldy piece of apparatus which is not adapted to the use of books and manuscripts." Spykman stated clearly: "The ideal tool for the study of geographic relationships is the globe."

However, the outstanding spokesman for globes and against flat maps and one who held out a hope for the future understanding of global relations of the United States was S. Whittemore Boggs. Let him speak for himself:

> But it is clear that misconceptions of global relations, concerning which many people speak very glibly—on the part of men in high places either in this or almost any other large country—can so distort, or in the past have so distorted, the facts of another nation's capabilities and intentions as to compromise peace or to start or lose wars. This is only one of the reasons why flat-map thinking about world relationships may be treacherously deceptive and politically and socially dangerous.
>
> We cannot really comprehend many of our own national problems except in their true relationships to the whole. As a corollary it is the writer's conviction that:
>
> > He who would solve world problems must understand them;
> > He who would understand world problems must visualize them; and
> > He who would visualize world problems should study them on the spherical surface of a globe.[35]

Boggs' hope for the future was that, as a result of new techniques in presenting geographical phenomena on the global surface and their study,

> A whole generation in all parts of the world should learn, soon, to think in truly "global" terms. Large as the earth may seem to us and complicated though its problems be, we dare not exclude any people or any region from our thinking. Perhaps if the earth were as large as Jupiter (with about 120 times the surface area of the earth) we could protest with some reason that it was too much for human beings to comprehend. But we need to introduce each generation at a relatively early age to concepts of the world as a whole, to its "wholeness-properties," and to the fact that the whole is more than the sum of all its parts, as the body is more than a mere aggregation of organs and parts. . . . When children begin early to see and think in world terms, realistically related to the roundness of the earth, the solution of world problems will become tractable.[36]

This is the hope of the future, but who started our thinking? Let us recall the words of Mackinder in his famous 1904 address: ". . . We shall

[34] *Ibid.*, p. 910.
[35] *Ibid.*, p. 908.
[36] *Ibid.*, pp. 911–912.

again have to deal with a closed political system, and nonetheless that it will be of worldwide scope. Every explosion of social forces, instead of being dissipated in a surrounding circuit of unknown space and barbaric chaos, will be sharply reechoed from the far side of the globe, and weak elements in the political and economic organism of the world will be shattered in the consequence."[37]

In this brief review of geopolitics we may conclude that its principal contribution has been understanding of global political relations. Its principal weakness has been an overemphasis of spatial relations to the neglect of other contributing factors to productivity, strength, and security. Finally, we should note that, while it is only within the last fifteen years that geopolitics has received the attention of a part of the United States general public, for a much longer period of time the United States Army has made geopolitics a subject of study. Similarly geopolitics has had the benefit of limited study by special groups in every country of military importance, mostly on the part of general staffs and advanced schools in the systems of military education. Colonel Herman Beukema, a long-time United States student, has drawn this conclusion: "Adopting the solid core of truth, restoring to their proper place the moral factors of international relations with their inherent demand that nations, like individuals, be held to a uniformly acceptable standard of conduct, statesmen will find in geopolitics the blueprints for peace as well as for war."

GEOPOLITICS REVISED

Today technological developments burst upon us so fast that the difficult problems are solved immediately; the impossible takes a little longer and we are not startled by the solution of the latter—we expect it. Why shouldn't we? Our education may be woefully lacking in certain respects, but space ships long ago became a reality to those of us smaller and larger fry who eagerly devour the so-called "comics." Spykman's "times of exceptional technological development" (the absence of which justified his "considering physical characteristics as fairly permanent") are now normal. On land, sea, and air, space has been annihilated. Transportation, communication, and energy availability have reduced the globe to the size of an orange.

Under these circumstances no one can dispute the fact that this is a global world where actions once isolated are now transmitted instantaneously to all parts of the world, producing results which may require

[37] *Geographical Journal*, April, 1904, p. 422, as cited by *ibid.*, p. 909.

simultaneous counteraction and thus a prior and ever-changing global policy. However, the argument is advanced that, since space has been destroyed, geopolitics and its political concern for space have no further purpose. This line of reasoning misses a fundamental point: that geopolitics is "the science of political organisms in space." The same physical territory (the total environment has, however, been expanded) is here to be occupied and/or used and requires political action. Indeed, the global action required has been tremendously enlarged.

The study of space as a factor of strength has tended to overemphasize the importance of two-dimensional space and has resulted in the overlooking and lack of stress of all the factors which contribute to production potential, strength, security, and power.

We know that both Mackinder and Spykman were aware of certain other factors of production strength potential. Mackinder wrote in the *National Review* in 1905 on the subject of "Man-power as a Measure of National and Imperial Strength," and he believed that he "first gave vogue to the term *Man-power*" and that in the term is implicit not only the idea of fighting strength but also that of productivity, rather than wealth, as a focus of economic reasoning. Further, in his chapters on "Social Momentum" and "The Freedom of Men" he elaborates on the role of free men, the function of capital, and space and fertility as elements of productive power. The latter he considered to be a most important "lasting reality of our Earthly Home." Yet with Mackinder's consideration of space and fertility (natural resources) he seems to have neglected or forgotten about the important role of the primary natural resources of industrial strength—inanimate energy and materials. Thus, the Heartland became more important than the western Eurasian rimland.

Spykman recognized the importance of the Rimland as a buffer zone but did not give sufficient emphasis to its real production potential. However, Spykman was fully aware, as we have seen, of the "conditioning factors of foreign policy": *geographic*—location, size, and topography; *economic*—agricultural and industrial resources, the people, and industrial production; and *political*. Yet Professor Spykman concluded: "The specific field of geopolitics is, however, the field of foreign policy, and its particular type of analysis uses geographic factors to help in the formulation of adequate policies for the achievement of certain justifiable ends."

It is certainly within the province of the geopoliticians, if they choose, to limit their analysis to the *geographic* factors of "location, size, and topography," although we know that they have not done so. But we would suggest (1) the minor revision of including (a) the other spatial

natural resources of shape and depth along with size and (b) the locational relationships of a country's noncontiguous areas and commitments where these have been omitted; and (2) the major revisions of
(a) including the three-dimensional aspects of space below and above
the ground and (b) continuously studying the dynamic impacts of these
normal "times of exceptional technological development."

What is needed is not just a revision of geopolitics but the development of a complete science of the study and application of those factors
which contribute to production potential, strength, and security. The
lack of such a science is not the fault of the geopoliticians because they
have been prophets, planners, and executers who have ranged far beyond
their narrow definition of geopolitics.

What shall we call this "new" science—*geoecopolitics?*

We have suggested that the contributing factors might be approached
from the study of: (1) *natural resources*—including (a) *spatial resources,* (b) *agricultural resources,* and (c) *energy and material resources;* (2) *capital resources;* and (3) *human resources.* This has been
the plan and part of the purpose of this book.

Even though there may be nothing "new" in the above recommendations, there is a real need in the United States for economics, and all
other interested disciplines which have a contribution to make, to join
in this interdisciplinary science in international relations which has as its
major aim the development of a strategy of security.

SOVIET POWER POLICIES

In order to develop a United States strategy of security and to conclude this study of geopolitics and revisions and supplements thereto,
we must give serious consideration, even though it will be brief, to the
international power policies of Soviet Russia. We dare not label them
with the narrow term "geopolitics," nor should we suggest that what
follows is more than an introduction.

First of all, "the fact of Soviet hostility was firmly established with the
sudden attack on the Republic of Korea on June 25, 1950, when the
tactics of Communist imperialism shifted from subversion and pressure
to open aggression." But who is the foe, why the delayed understanding
of hostility, and what are the plans and tactics?

1. Who Is the Foe?

The Russian nation is not the foe. The Russian people are not the foe.
They are for the present and may be in the future, but this is a result of

the political party in power—the Communist. International Communism is the foe and it achieves its power when it gains control of a nation. The amount of its power depends on the production potential of the nation. The United States might coexist with a Russian nation, even when organized along Soviet lines, but we could never do so in a peaceful world as long as the Communists were in control.

Even if Communist control of productive power were terminated, the free world must always understand that our enemy is a particular "Idea of Man." Man can be no more than a "material man," because only material is real. "He is not an individual, he is primarily 'social'—a biological unit of the dialectical process, whose welfare, happiness, and life purpose reside in the society in which he lives, who is wholly dependent upon the judgment of his leaders for his criteria of good and evil. . . ." "Thus the whole human struggle changes its meaning. The great ideals for which humanity has fought and suffered—the good, the beautiful, the true—the eightfold path of Buddha, the Christian vision of redemption, the Moslem communion with God—all these inspired revelations and ideals are just illusions on the surface of reality, eruptive phenomena thrown up from the depths of matter."[38]

2. Why the Delayed Understanding?

The delayed understanding of Soviet hostility was due to the fact that the United States failed to see clearly that the Communists were in power in Russia and we ignored or disbelieved what the Communists have set down as their basic objectives. Communism is committed to the communization of the world. Fundamental to Communism is that man exists for the state. Under Communism, the central government controls production and consumption through ownership and management. Man becomes slave not free. Free enterprise does not exist. Freedom must be suppressed not only within the area currently dominated by the Communists but everywhere, for it is a contagious and dynamic moral force which is a constant peril to them. Thus Communists are driven by their own doctrine and by their own fears to seek constantly to extend their control.

Why the delayed understanding? Russell W. Davenport makes the additional point that Communist ideology, derived from the philosophy pieced together by Karl Marx and Friedrich Engels, is abstruse, dogmatic, and apparently remote from the thinking of the average man. Thus we

[38] Russell W. Davenport, "The Real Power Behind Communism," *Fortune,* April, 1955, p. 154. (Derived from the book, *The Dignity of Man.*)

have refused to take Communist ideology seriously. "The truth is, however, that Dialectical Materialism—sometimes called 'Dimat'—has become one of the great intellectual moral forces of history. . . . Dimat is an intellectual organism, international in scope, clever, aggressive, and appalling in its implication."

Why the delayed understanding? Have we not already answered the question in Chapter 1? "The United States was confused with respect to Russian intentions. We did not distinguish between policy and objectives. The primary objective of Soviet Russia has been the communization of the world, the overthrow of democratic government with the resultant enslavement of all men everywhere—the very antithesis of the United States' primary objective of freedom." No, this is not all the answer. We now see that this was Soviet policy because the Soviet nation is controlled by the Communist party.

Who is our foe? The Communist party and the Idea of Man. Mr. Acheson said: "There can be no greater disagreement than when someone wants to eliminate your existence altogether."

3. What Are the Plans and Tactics?

Before World War I Russia was a badly governed country. When Russia was beaten by the Germans, she was ready for revolution. Men were planning that revolution according to the socialism of Karl Marx, who seventy years before had spelled out a plan to destroy capitalism and build a new world. In this he was helped by his friend, Friedrich Engels. Lenin and Trotsky, the planners, knew what to do.

Marx wanted to destroy capitalism, but he left the question open as to whether a political democracy could be maintained. "Workers of the world, unite!" he said; use force to break up the power of the owners and take charge of the nation. When workers are in power, and all the people own all the tools of production, "Communism" can finally be achieved. "Then every worker will do the best he can and every person will get all he needs from the common store of wealth." Marx's and Engels' plan was for the proletariat to acquire political supremacy, rise to be the leading class, and constitute itself the nation.

Marx and Engels were clear as to the objectives of getting control of a nation and the world; but Lenin and Trotsky were in disagreement as to the policies to follow once a nation was under control, and Trotsky was exiled from Russia. This was all according to plan. The "party line" is to throw out the members of the party who will not give up their ideas. This plan has been adhered to ruthlessly by Lenin, Stalin, and those who have followed. Disagree and you are thrown out of the "party" and executed, if possible, because of the fear you might have some influence later on. Execution is much easier if you are not in the party. Political power must be vested in one group.

Engels said that ultimately government would "wither away," and Marx said that the state was only an organization of force to protect the capitalist. One might ask: Why has not the state withered away? In November, 1938, the Russian leaders announced that the state could not begin to "wither away" until the whole world had gone Socialist.

Since the Communist party is out to destroy capitalism, Lenin reasoned that the capitalist countries would refuse to do business with Russia and therefore the best way to protect Russia was to send out propaganda for revolution in all other countries. This plan for world revolution was initiated by Lenin and it is still in force today. How do we know this? By observing the facts and by reading. For example, during the summer of 1956, *Pravda,* the official organ of the Russian Communist party, clearly stated the world-wide objective of the Communists while complaining about the United States counter policy. "The United States State Department, having abandoned diplomacy, has become the headquarters of a propaganda campaign launched by it around the personality cult. The aim of this campaign is to cast a shadow on the great ideas of Marxism-Leninism, to undermine the confidence of the working people in the first Socialist state in the world, the Soviet Union, and to introduce dissension and confusion within the ranks of the world's Communist and workers movement."

Force is fundamental to the Communist plan. Davenport explains: "In order to make good its claim to a scientific status, it must find positive proof in the actual events of history. The Communists, therefore, use force to *make* those events happen the way their theory tells them they ought to happen. To the Communists this is a logical—although unacknowledged—consequence of the theory. Force is the dialectical opposite of what the 'bourgeois' world knows as the search for truth. If force is used, therefore, to confound that search, the result will be a synthesis on a higher plane—namely, progress toward the social absolute. Because force is thus used by the Communists on behalf of the dialectical process, it has to be considered as an integral part of the whole proposition."[39]

The whole plan is that the Communists have as their objective world control. Their policies will change but their objective is clear.

[39] *Ibid.,* p. 156.

What are the Russian tactics? The United States Armed Forces Industrial College in a discussion of "Soviet Geopolitics" has given us this "Banse Formula":[40]

Select the weakest link in the social and economic structure—then concentrate propaganda against that weak link.

Discover or create a minority problem and emphasize it until it becomes a dominating issue in the political world.

Find a corrupt, or ambitious leader who could not obtain national power by himself and surround him with a group of agents, who, unknown to him, shape his policy and dictate his program.

Employ fanatics and hoodlums necessary to create social and political chaos.

If all these fail, then and only then, start a shooting war.

We know then that the Communists' planned objective is to dominate the world; we know that they achieve their power through the control of nations with production potentials; and we know that they pursue their objectives through use of force with an ever-changing set of policies and tactics that thrive in conditions of unrest, which the policies and tactics are designed to create when the latter do not exist. We know that the Communists have a *complete plan of international power.* Finally, we know that Communism is a ruthless enemy of the free world.

CONCLUSION

Against such an enemy what shall the United States do? We must always keep clearly in mind our objectives of freedom and security and the objectives of our enemies. We must develop dynamic global political policies backed by completely flexible economic and military power and policies in order to keep ahead of and counteract the changing policies and tactics of our enemies, whom we must learn to recognize clearly. Above all, we must not confuse policies, which are always changing, with objectives. To do these things we must intensify our study of *geoecopolitics* and the whole area of related international studies in order to develop a strategy of security.

[40] "Banse Formula" after Ewald Banse, who was appointed Professor of Military Science at Brunswick Technical College in February, 1933, by the Nazi government immediately on its accession to power. Two of his books, *Wehrwissenschaft* (*Military Science*) and *Germany Prepares for War*, established his position in the early 1930's as "the uncompromising advocate of barbaric methods of warfare." Actually in this latter book he called for a "new science of national defense," spelled out in detail in a "General Science of National Defense" which emphasized economics and psychology as new and particularly important branches. See Ewald Banse, *Germany Prepares for War*, Harcourt, Brace and Company, 1934, pp. 351–357.

CHAPTER 15

Strategy of Security

In the first two chapters we saw that the purpose of this study of resources was to evaluate them and determine how they could be used most strategically in the attainment of maximum freedom, security, strength, and economic progress. This we attempted to do in Unit Two— "Strength and Production Potentials." We also established in Chapter 1 that *freedom*, which sets our economic system apart from alien philosophies, rings as the major objective of the people of the United States, and that we have taken the lead to advocate it as an international policy which we hope might be adopted as an objective and achieved by all men in all lands. In addition, we showed that *security* stands out as a major objective and that it has a twofold, closely interrelated function: (1) the maintenance of peace through police and military action against internal and external forces and (2) the promotion of economic progress, by which is meant rising planes of living. In Chapter 2 we examined the United States locational relationships to noncontiguous areas and our commitments and policies related thereto through 1952. In the preceding chapter, we have analyzed in detail the science of this latter topic: geopolitics—geoecopolitics; the need for a strategy of security was stressed. The plan of this final chapter is to review the United States' additional commitments and foreign policies during the four-year period 1953–56 of the first Eisenhower administration and to suggest improvements in our policies to strengthen the strategy of security of the United States. This will be done under the closely interrelated functions of security—military and economic. Finally, we propose to discuss the moral aspects of the strategy of security.

MILITARY SECURITY

1. Collective Security

In 1956 the keystone to United States foreign policy was collective security, which was pursued through the United Nations, the North Atlantic Treaty Organization (NATO), the Rio Treaty, the Anzus Treaty, the Southeast Asia Treaty Organization (SEATO), and many bilateral arrangements with individual countries. These multilateral treaties and the bilateral treaties—Japanese, South Korean, Nationalist China, and Philippine—and the Spanish Agreement are shown in Figure 15.1. In addition, this figure shows the Balkan and Baghdad Regional Pacts with which the United States was concerned indirectly through allies. These undertakings assumed different forms and were designed to serve different purposes. Some have evolved elaborate joint defense programs, while others rely primarily for their deterrent effect upon pledges given and received. Despite their differences in form, the United States' "central purpose in all these arrangements is to insure that the human and material resources of the free world remain free and effectively serve the cause of freedom." The United States Department of State explains emphatically:

"Our collective security undertakings go far beyond mere pledges and commitments. They are working partnerships. We are not interested solely in keeping friendly nations out of Communist hands. We also want to make these nations as strong as possible so that they can more adequately protect themselves, can contribute to our protection, and can participate effectively in the worldwide struggle for peace and security."[1]

The first Eisenhower administration, 1952–56, added three treaties to the United States alliances for collective security—with the Republic of Korea (South Korean), 1953; the Republic of China (Nationalist China), 1954; and Southeast Asia (SEATO), 1954; and signed an agreement in 1953 with Spain which provided for economic and military assistance in exchange for the construction and use of military facilities. It also announced support of, without participating in, the Baghdad Pact of 1955, which was organized at the suggestion of the United States for defense against Russian aggression by Great Britain, Iraq, Iran, Pakistan, and Turkey. The world-wide system of military alliances that had grown up from World War II to March, 1956, is shown in Figure 15.2.

[1] Deputy Under Secretary Robert Murphy, "A Review of United States Foreign Policy," *The Department of State Bulletin,* September 26, 1955, p. 490.

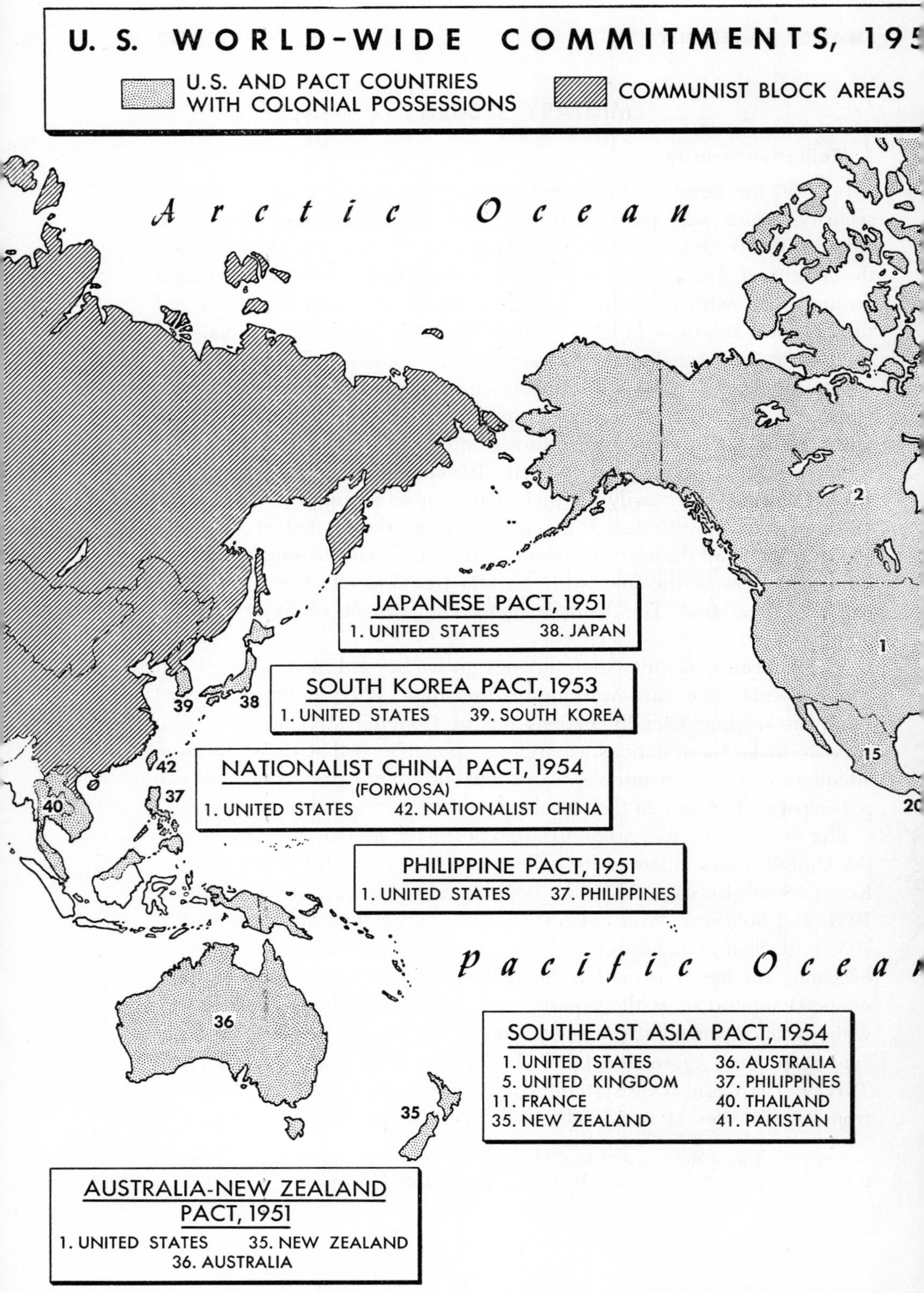
U. S. WORLD-WIDE COMMITMENTS, 195
U.S. AND PACT COUNTRIES WITH COLONIAL POSSESSIONS
COMMUNIST BLOCK AREAS
Arctic Ocean
Pacific Ocea
JAPANESE PACT, 1951
1. UNITED STATES 38. JAPAN
SOUTH KOREA PACT, 1953
1. UNITED STATES 39. SOUTH KOREA
NATIONALIST CHINA PACT, 1954
(FORMOSA)
1. UNITED STATES 42. NATIONALIST CHINA
PHILIPPINE PACT, 1951
1. UNITED STATES 37. PHILIPPINES
SOUTHEAST ASIA PACT, 1954
1. UNITED STATES 36. AUSTRALIA
5. UNITED KINGDOM 37. PHILIPPINES
11. FRANCE 40. THAILAND
35. NEW ZEALAND 41. PAKISTAN
AUSTRALIA-NEW ZEALAND PACT, 1951
1. UNITED STATES 35. NEW ZEALAND
36. AUSTRALIA
2
1
15
20
39
38
42
37
40
36
35

Figure 15.1. United States Collective Defense Arrangements. (James L. McCamy, *American Government*, Harper & Brothers, 1957)

NORTH ATLANTIC PACT, 1949-1955

1. UNITED STATES
2. CANADA
3. ICELAND
4. NORWAY
5. UNITED KINGDOM
6. NETHERLANDS
7. DENMARK
8. BELGIUM
9. LUXEMBOURG
10. PORTUGAL
11. FRANCE
12. ITALY
13. GREECE
14. TURKEY
43. WEST GERMANY

BALKAN PACT, 1953-1954

13. GREECE   14. TURKEY
47. YUGOSLAVIA

SPANISH PACT, 1953

DEFENSE AGREEMENT
1. UNITED STATES
46. SPAIN

Atlantic

Ocean

Indian

Ocean

RIO PACT, 1947

1. UNITED STATES
15. MEXICO
16. CUBA
17. HAITI
18. DOMINICAN REP.
19. HONDURAS
20. GUATEMALA
21. EL SALVADOR
22. NICARAGUA
23. COSTA RICA
24. PANAMA
25. COLOMBIA
26. VENEZUELA
27. ECUADOR
28. PERU
29. BRAZIL
30. BOLIVIA
31. PARAGUAY
32. CHILE
33. ARGENTINA
34. URUGUAY

BAGHDAD PACT, 1955

5. UNITED KINGDOM
14. TURKEY
41. PAKISTAN
44. IRAQ
45. IRAN

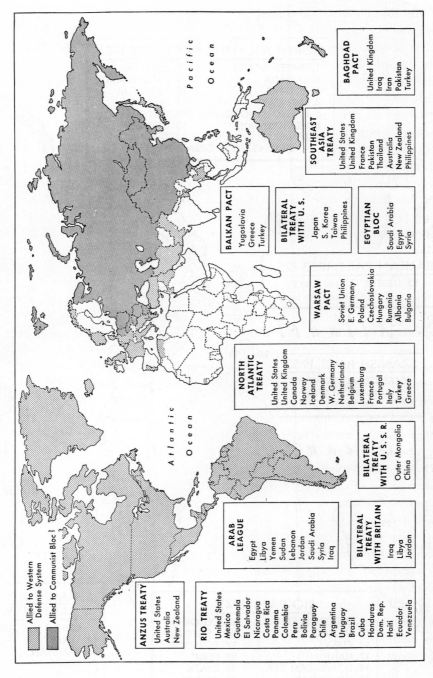

ANZUS TREATY

United States
Australia
New Zealand

RIO TREATY

United States
Mexico
Guatemala
El Salvador
Nicaragua
Costa Rica
Panama
Colombia
Peru
Bolivia
Paraguay
Chile
Argentina
Uruguay
Brazil
Cuba
Honduras
Dom. Rep.
Haiti
Ecuador
Venezuela

ARAB LEAGUE

Egypt
Libya
Yemen
Sudan
Lebanon
Jordan
Saudi Arabia
Syria
Iraq

BILATERAL TREATY WITH BRITAIN

Iraq
Libya
Jordan

BILATERAL TREATY WITH U. S. S. R.

Outer Mongolia
China

NORTH ATLANTIC TREATY

United States
United Kingdom
Canada
Norway
Iceland
Denmark
W. Germany
Netherlands
Belgium
Luxemburg
France
Portugal
Italy
Turkey
Greece

WARSAW PACT

Soviet Union
E. Germany
Poland
Czechoslovakia
Hungary
Rumania
Albania
Bulgaria

BALKAN PACT

Yugoslavia
Greece
Turkey

BILATERAL TREATY WITH U. S.

Japan
S. Korea
Taiwan
Philippines

EGYPTIAN BLOC

Saudi Arabia
Egypt
Syria

SOUTHEAST ASIA TREATY

United States
United Kingdom
France
Pakistan
Thailand
Australia
New Zealand
Philippines

BAGHDAD PACT

United Kingdom
Iraq
Iran
Pakistan
Turkey

Allied to Western Defense System
Allied to Communist Bloc !

Figure 15.2.   The World-Wide System of Military Alliances That Has Grown Since World War II.

The Eisenhower administration's foreign policy was described as "dynamic" in an attempt to offset the criticism that the United States policy of containment, at least by name alone, implied *status quo*. Charles J. V. Murphy in an article in the August, 1954, issue of *Fortune*, "America's New Strategic Situation," concluded that the "essential practical workings [of the Eisenhower-Dulles foreign policy] have so far differed little from those of the Truman containment policy, even to its failure to contain." Murphy argued that there is logic in trying to pursue a coalition policy whatever its label and that sound strategy must encompass something more than concentration upon positions of immediate military advantage. "It should also aim at denying valuable advantages—political and economic as well as military—to an enemy. And this is the underlying purpose of the regional alliances that Dulles, with extraordinary patience and resolution, is trying to complete around the Soviet periphery."

A. NATO

The North Atlantic Treaty Organization grew out of the North Atlantic Treaty, signed April 4, 1949, by which fourteen nations (see Figure 15.1 for nations included) agreed "that an armed attack against one or more of them in Europe or North America shall be considered an attack against them all; and . . . each of them . . . will assist the . . . attacked by taking forthwith, individually and in concert with other Parties, such action as it deems necessary including the use of armed force. . . ." NATO was thus a part of our military regional security program supplementing economic strength which had been developed under the European Recovery Program.

President Eisenhower, then General Eisenhower, was a strong personal factor in organizing NATO. Under his administration one of the critical issues was Germany's role in the West's strategy of security. The European Defense Community (EDC) was first proposed by and then rejected by France. This was a plan for a "European Army," in which German divisions would be intermingled with French, Dutch, etc., under a supranational authority, and thus presumably the German Army would never again be a threat to France. The restoration of German independence and the right to rearm were contractually linked to the general ratification of the EDC treaty. Thus by not ratifying EDC the French kept the German independence in suspense. Finally, the Federal Republic of Germany was included within the NATO defense system under a protocol to the North Atlantic Treaty signed at Paris on October 23, 1954.

This was considered by the United States as a severe diplomatic defeat for the Soviet Union because West Germany was then a part of the western arch of military defense.

In substitution for the EDC the Western European Union was formed, under protocols also signed at Paris on October 23, 1954, consisting of seven nations—Belgium, France, the Federal Republic of Germany, Italy, Luxembourg, the Netherlands, and the United Kingdom. The United States policy declaration on the Western European Union, indicating the purpose of the Union and the United States endorsement, is given in the following message, which was sent to the prime ministers of the signatory countries on March 10, 1955:

It is my belief that the proposed arrangements when effective:

Will promote progress toward unity in Western Europe and draw together those whose past differences have led to recurrent war and gravely depleted Europe's human, material and moral strength;

Will restore sovereignty to the Federal Republic of Germany, a sovereignty which has now been withheld for ten years, during which time the Government and people of that Republic have demonstrated that they are capable of worthily discharging their responsibilities as a self-governing member of the free and peaceful world community;

Will, by controlling armament levels through an appropriate Agency of the Western European Union, assure against militarism;

Will provide a core of unity at the heart of the North Atlantic Treaty Organization, thus permitting adoption of practical defensive measures which offer good hope that any enemy attack could be stopped at the threshold;

Will enable the Federal Republic of Germany to make its appropriately measured contribution to international peace and security, in keeping with the spirit of the North Atlantic Treaty Organization;

Will, through action of the North Atlantic Treaty Council, assure a closer integration of the armed forces in Europe of the member countries, thereby giving assurance that these forces cannot be used for nationalistic aggression or otherwise than for the security purposes envisaged by the North Atlantic Treaty.[2]

A second critical problem of NATO was the changing nature of its military function due to the development of nuclear warfare. Before Russia had the bomb, NATO's defense system could be organized along conventional lines. After Russia was able to employ nuclear warfare, the question was raised as to whether NATO's forces could be reduced to a sort of advanced warning radar screen. On the other hand, it was argued

[2] Report of President Eisenhower, "U.S. Policy Declaration on Western European Union," *The Department of State Bulletin,* March 21, 1955, p. 464.

that conventional forces would be required as nuclear weapons would not be used in western Europe because Great Britain and France held a veto power over United States retaliatory use. This veto power was part of the negotiations for United States strategic air bases.

This second argument subsequently evolved during the second Eisenhower administration into the necessity of conventional forces when missile bases were established. One answer to this latter question was that there should be no argument here at all because the employment of nuclear missiles would lead to annihilation and thus both missiles and conventional forces were required for the military shield of the West. One further and frightening discussion was provoked at about this same time early in 1958 when George F. Kennan, framer of the policy of containment, suggested that all western military forces be withdrawn from the European continent. This recommendation for "disengagement," which would create a vacuum in western Europe for Russia to fill in accordance with the Communist long-established settled objective, appeared to have been one that would not have been given serious consideration. Here indeed would have been "a one-hundred-and-eighty-degree turn in the wrong direction" in a policy for the West.

A third critical problem of NATO arose in 1956 out of the suggestion that NATO should be given more to do. The North Atlantic Council met in Paris in May, 1956, in an attempt to transform NATO from a purely military alliance directed against Soviet aggression into a permanent instrument of Western coöperation for the political, economic, and social advancement of its members and of the free world. The United States endorsed the point of view that the military defense of the West would have to remain the organization's principal function. However, the thought was expressed that owing to a combined expenditure of $312 billion on military preparations in seven years (with the United States alone contributing $252 billion) Western defenses, if still inadequate, were formidable enough to deter major Communist aggression and to force Russia to change its tactics. As a consequence, there developed a feeling that the time had come to supplement the military functions with a more positive and dynamic mission in other fields. Such a mission was considered essential not only to counter the Soviet "new look" policies of political and economic penetration but also to increase the unity of action among the fifteen member nations.

The United States opposed the idea that NATO should channel economic aid or plan it but favored expanding NATO's political, instead of economic, functions. Secretary of State Dulles proposed establishing a super-Atlantic political standing committee where "people of state" second only to the foreign ministers would meet regularly to thresh out such divisive issues as Cyprus, North Africa, and the Middle East. He proposed the appointment of "three wise men" to study the idea. The committee was appointed with instructions to report back by the fall of 1957.

In discussing NATO's third critical problem, the *New York Times* concluded: "There is room for the promotion of all those enterprises which aim at European unification as the first condition for the Continent's survival in freedom." Most important of these "enterprises" in "building a United Europe" is the European Community for Coal and Steel, which was discussed in detail in the section on coal. The importance of the Community in the world economy is vividly illustrated in Figure 15.3.

At the beginning of 1957, as an offsetting and related part to divisive Middle East developments, there was evidence that NATO was changing from a purely military defensive arrangement to an agency to weld the member nations closer together in a United Europe. NATO had failed to do this in its attempt to build through EDC a European army in a common uniform. Previously the post-World War II political idea of the Council of Europe had failed. In this third instance the approach was economic. The evidence of the possibility of a changing role for NATO was to be found in the fact that Paul-Henri Spaak, then Foreign Minister of Belgium and a convinced internationalist, had been chosen as Secretary General of NATO on his own terms. Mr. Spaak was the first president of the General Assembly of the United Nations, first president of the Consultative Council of Europe, and a strong supporter of the Marshall Plan and the twenty-seven-member Organization for European Economic Cooperation (OEEC) set up by the Plan; he backed the European Defense Command; he was one of the principal sponsors of the European Coal and Steel Community, comprised of Belgium, France, the Federal Republic of Germany, Italy, Luxembourg, and the Netherlands, and during 1956 he pushed for the formation of a European atomic energy plan—Euratom—for the same six nations. As one of the foreign ministers working on Euratom, Mr. Spaak was also the presiding officer of "the Six" who were drafting a Common Market (customs union) Treaty. The Common Market would be a major step toward a United Europe. Thus through the person of Paul-Henri Spaak there was evidence that NATO might be changing to an agency to weld the European member nations closer together in a United Europe.

Figure 15.3. (*Opposite page*). Building a United Europe—The European Community for Coal and Steel, 1955–56.

The Common Market plan called for an elimination of all tariffs and quotas and transportation barriers among nations, but members would retain a common tariff against the rest of the world. In addition, the Common Market plan included the elimination of barriers to the movement of labor and capital. This far-reaching integration would lead to common policies and political institutions. In October, 1956, before the British failure in the Suez venture, there was in Britain widespread enthusiasm backed by Chancellor of the Exchequer Harold Macmillan for joining the six Common Market members with an associated free-trade zone which in addition to Great Britain would include Austria, the Scandinavian countries, Greece, Iceland, Portugal, and Switzerland. These, together with "the Six," would be almost identical to the OEEC countries. The Free Trade Area would create a market of 260 million people, allow specific goods—principally manufactured items—to move between member nations free of tariff, and have no common tariff against outsiders, thus permitting Great Britain to continue to give imperial preference to the agricultural products which make up nearly 90 percent of Commonwealth exports to Britain. This writer considered the shift in British interest in part away from the Commonwealth and toward a United Europe through the Free Trade Zone and her drive to secure the Suez and oil of the Middle East as part of an integrated plan to establish a third force in Europe. One informed official of the International Monetary Fund agreed with this thesis in mid-November, 1956, but in view of the British-French failure in the Middle East concluded that the Common Market and Free Trade Area for Europe was dead.

"The Six" promoters of the Common Market were in favor of the idea of the Free Trade Area and were pleased by the British interest in October, 1956, but they chose, under Mr. Spaak's chairmanship, to hammer away at the solution of the Common Market problems. This they continued to do through November and December of 1956 in the hopes of obtaining approval early in 1957. After Mr. Eden's resignation as British Prime Minister, due to the failure of the Middle East venture, he was replaced by Mr. Macmillan to the surprise of a great many people. As a result, at the beginning of 1957 the Free Trade Area, far from being dead, was very much alive. There was an even greater realization that Europe must be strong. Great Britain was more actively interested because the Common Market might exclude many British goods and because economic and political domination of western Europe would ultimately shift to the Big Six. Great Britain expressed her opinion through Mr. Peter Thorneycroft, Prime Minister Macmillan's Chancellor of the Exchequer: "Make no doubt of it, we are behind the Free Trade Area."

The United States policy interest in the Common Market and the Free Trade Area is in their contribution to the strength of western Europe. There was a possibility in the short run that some of the European markets would be lost to United States exporters, but in the long run greater European productive efficiency should make Europe better able to afford dollar goods. In January, 1957, Mr. Thorneycroft stated for Great Britain: The Free Trade Area "will make us a better ally." The United States Department of State recognized the short-term problem mentioned above but was in favor of both the Common Market and the Free Trade Area because of their contribution to the strength of western Europe and thus to the United States.

On March 25, 1957, the six nations signed at Rome the two treaties for the European Economic Community (Euromarket)—previously referred to as the Common Market—and for the Atomic Energy Community (Euratom). The Free Trade Area was still in the discussion stage. On March 24, 1957, in a joint statement at the end of the Bermuda Conference, President Eisenhower and Prime Minister Macmillan said that benefits were likely to accrue from a European common market and a free-trade area if they did not lead to a high-tariff bloc. They also agreed on the importance of "close association of the United Kingdom with Europe." Figure 15.4 presents the Economic Community and its members as "European Union Advances."

Great Britain was not planning to join the European Economic Community or Euratom, but she was attempting to find a method under which other nations in the Organization for European Economic Cooperation could associate themselves in a free-trade area with Euromarket. In addition, and most important, she was taking the lead in planning for the establishment of a general parliamentary assembly that would coördinate the functions of many organizations in which western European nations were linked economically, militarily, and politically. Among these organizations were the Western European Union, the Council of Europe, the Organization for European Economic Cooperation, the European Payments Union, and the North Atlantic Treaty Organization.

Thus with the beginning of the second Eisenhower administration in 1957 there was a possibility that a combination of events and personalities might be moving toward a United Western Europe—a western arch of strength—a Third Force.

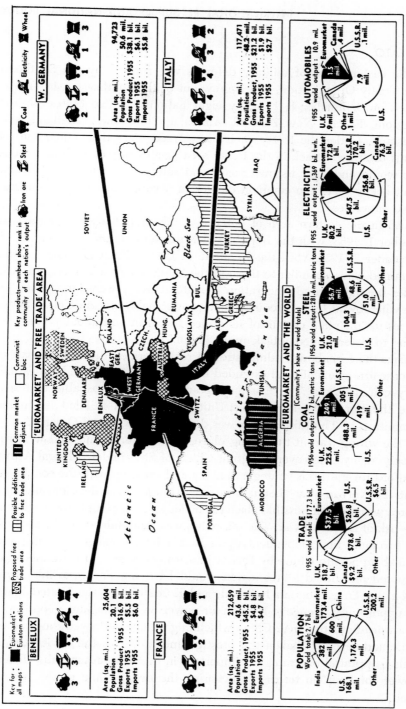

Figure 15.4. As European Union Advances—The Economic Community and Its Members. (*The New York Times*, March 31, 1957)

B. SEATO

The eastern arch of military defenses was formed by the Southeast Asia Treaty Organization, which grew out of the Southeast Asia Treaty, signed on September 8, 1954, by eight nations (United States, United Kingdom, France, New Zealand, Australia, Philippines, Thailand, and Pakistan). Under the treaty each party "recognizes that aggression by means of armed attack in the treaty area against any one of the Parties . . . would endanger its own peace and safety" and each will "in that event act to meet the common danger in accordance with its constitutional processes."

Also in the eastern arch of defense, a bilateral treaty was signed on October 1, 1953, with the Republic of Korea and another was signed on December 2, 1954, with the Republic of China. Each of these treaties contained clauses similar to those in the Southeast Asia Treaty. (In 1951 under the Truman administration a bilateral treaty was signed with Japan whereby, at Japan's request, on a provisional basis, the United States agrees to "maintain certain of its armed forces in and about Japan . . . so as to deter armed attack upon Japan.")

Thus the Eisenhower administration really formed the eastern arch of defense arrangements and extended tremendously the United States military commitments. The Eisenhower administration was able to terminate the Korean War after the United States had fulfilled its "moral commitment." The Korean War was described by General Omar Bradley as "the wrong war, at the wrong place, at the wrong time, and with the wrong enemy." However, the Joint Chiefs of Staff under Admiral Arthur Radford reversed this strategic thinking and came up with the conclusion that the Korean War should have been fought to a decision and that Korea was the best possible place to challenge Communist power without the risk of a general war. The reasoning was that China was, is, and will be for some time dependent upon Russia for its major weapons; sustained support to China by Russia in a war in which no restraints were imposed on United States action would have put an impossible strain upon the Trans-Siberian Railroad; and Korea offered the United States an opportunity to engage Russian air power on most advantageous terms in a war of attrition over China which might have destroyed the Mao regime and severely shaken the prestige and power of the Soviet Union. This reappraisal of strategy is important in that it represents the "Eisenhower thinking" in terms of anchoring the defense line of the eastern arch.

The military probably would have preferred to anchor the eastern line at Korea and run it down the island chain of Japan, Formosa, and the Philippines to Australia and New Zealand. But political considerations caused Thailand and Pakistan to be included in SEATO.

The eastern arch is complicated by many factors. The principal problem in the strategy of security is that, in contrast to the western arch, economic problems of underdevelopment are more difficult to solve and more fundamental than the military function which we are considering in this section. The once very strong interest of France and Great Britain has declined tremendously to where they have very little desire for military commitments even though they did join with us in SEATO. The Russian-Chinese strategy that will be employed in southeast Asia is likely to be infiltration and subversion rather than open aggression. If the latter should be used the United States could not afford to use ground forces, and the effectiveness of air power is doubtful unless it is employed without restraint as a tactical and strategic weapon against all possible targets. Thus the question might still be raised: Are the United States commitments too extensive?

Further, India under Nehru is becoming the dominant power in southeast Asia with a so-called policy of neutralism which is anti-Western in terms of commitments to defend the eastern arch in an attempt to contain the real enemy, Communism, and the production and military power behind it, Russia and China.

There was a running debate during the Korean War as to whether the forces of the Republic of China on Formosa under Chiang Kai-shek could have been more effectively employed. Actually Chiang had to be restrained from action. Under the revised strategic thinking, Formosa continued under SEATO to be an important link in the eastern arch by reason of the United States bilateral treaty; however, it is quite possible that a reappraisal was made for a more appropriate use of Chiang's forces.

Most importantly, the United States must recognize that Japan is the real factor of strength in the eastern arch of collective defense arrangements. It is in Japan that military bases are located and production potential could be made available. However, the post-World War II Japanese economy has been shored up only by means of United States grants of about $800 million a year to make up Japan's international trade deficit. If Japan is to become a strong anchor point in the eastern arch and defend herself against external aggression and internal subversion, her economy must be placed on a sound basis. We must face squarely the fundamental interdependence of the economic and military functions in the strategy of security. If Japan is to be strong, she must have markets for her goods and raw materials to utilize effectively her human resources and her capital. This means keeping open markets in southeast Asia and in the United States. The latter is the most difficult policy decision the United States must make because of the domestic interest group in textile and chinaware production. The alternative to United States imports is continued grants to Japan. The real question, then, that the United States must answer is: Do we want Japan as a factor of strength? If the answer is the same "Yes" that we have given in our current policy, then we must think hard. As it now stands, the United States consumer-taxpayer is paying double by giving to Japan and paying higher prices for textile goods.

C. SEESAW ("to move back and forth or up and down")

The southern arch of military defenses did not exist prior to 1957 in terms of United States collective defense arrangements. However, under a Tripartite Declaration with Britain and France, the United States in 1950 pledged aid to any Middle East victim of aggression. On April 9, 1956, President Eisenhower reaffirmed this commitment when he stated that it would be honored "within Constitutional means." While the 1950 Declaration covered both Israel and the Arabian states, it was widely interpreted before Israel invaded Egypt on October 28, 1956, as more of a pledge to aid Israel than to assist an Arab nation. On October 29, 1956, the day after the invasion, the White House issued a statement: "We shall honor our pledge" to "assist the victim of any aggression in the Middle East." On October 31, 1956, the day of the British and French armed attack on Egypt, President Eisenhower declared the use of force "was in error" and could "scarcely be reconciled with the principles and purposes of the United Nations"; but he went on to say: "There will be no United States involvement in these present hostilities." On November 29, 1956, the State Department declared that any threat to the "territorial integrity or political independence" of the Baghdad Pact nations of Iraq, Iran, Turkey, or Pakistan would be viewed by the United States with the "utmost gravity." It is also said the United States had revealed its readiness to "assist in measures to strengthen the security of those nations."

As we have noted, the suggestion was made that NATO might be extended to cover disputes within "Atlantic Territory" such as North Africa, Cyprus, or the Middle East. On this point the *New York Times* made this comment: "In such areas, every party to a dispute wants the United States to take its side, though such side taking might well aggravate the disputes and impair the chances for amicable settlements. This still leaves room, however, for mutual consultation to find 'liberal solutions' in keeping with the West's own principles. Such solutions would not only counter Communist anti-colonial propaganda but would also stimulate the urge for freedom in Soviet Russia's own colonies." There is no question but that anyone who wanted to "put NATO in business" could have assigned it some of the manifold Middle Eastern problems.

The problems of the southern arch have been since World War II so divisive that a regional collective defense arrangement appeared to be impossible to form. The appropriate agency was the United Nations, and the writer's conclusion in the summer of 1956 was that the United States might do well wherever possible to work within the framework of the U.N. This may present difficulties and we might remember that the Truman Doctrine and the new United States policy for the containment of Soviet Russia were launched in 1947 with individual aid programs to Greece and Turkey. These were two of our most successful post-World War II programs. There will be numerous instances in which the United States will have to maintain the freedom of independent action. This was the conclusion reached before Great Britain's and France's entry into Egypt; since that date it is even more warranted.

The United States policy for the Middle East has been described as "maintaining stability." The writer believes that in operation it might be more appropriately described "Seesaw."

There are those within the United States who clearly saw in World War II the critical importance of the oil of the Middle East to the strength and production potential of western Europe and the United States and to the Middle East. In fact, this was deemed so important during World War II that the United States government seriously considered becoming a partner with Ibn Saud in the development of oil in Saudia Arabia. Yet the United States actively supported the international Zionist movement in the partitioning of Palestine and in the establishment and recognition of Israel. Thus we helped implement and accelerate the Arabian-Israeli conflict.

Palestine became a mandate of Great Britain after World War I, but while other Arab countries moved toward independence, Palestine did not because of conflicts between Jews and Arabs. International Zionism, which holds that every Jew has the right to come to Palestine, had the beginnings of a political reality with the endorsement of the Balfour Declaration of the British government on November 2, 1917, and of President Wilson in 1918 and later the United States Congress. Jewish immigration into Palestine was accelerated, but by World War II the country remained predominantly Arab as it had been for 1300 years. In 1939 Great Britain issued a White Paper opposing the creation of Israel. At the end of World War II the British announced their intention of withdrawing from Palestine. Many people who were deeply aroused by the cruelty of Nazi persecution gave no thought to the consequences when public opinion gave the final push to the establishment of a Jewish state.

With full United States initiation and support the United Nations partitioned Palestine, the greater portion of which was to become the Jewish state of Israel and the other portion was to become a part of Jordan. When the United Nations decision was announced, the Jews accepted partition and the Arabs did not. On May 14, 1948, Israel proclaimed its independence and the new nation was given immediate recognition by the United States. At the same time open warfare broke out between Israel and Arab forces; a great many Arabs, whose families for generations had lived on land about to become the Jewish state, began to flee across the border and thousands more followed during the fighting. Fighting continued in one form or another until late October, 1956.

By 1955 the Arab refugees numbered 875,000 and they existed in adjoining Arab states in makeshift camps with few facilities for either health or work. Secretary of State Dulles described their plight: "Within these camps the inmates rot away, spiritually and physically. Even the Grim Reaper offers no solution, for as the older die, infants are born to inherit their parents' bitter fate."

By 1955 the state of Israel had a population of over 1,600,000, about 720,000 of whom had come from other lands in the preceding ten years. The population was deliberately built up under the Law of Return (July 5, 1950), which stated that every Jew had a right to come to Israel as a permanent settler. Israel is dependent on the outside world for both markets and materials to support her population, yet she is surrounded by unfriendly Arab states with whom there is no trade and no travel.

The United States Department of State reported in May, 1954: "The people of the Arab States have cried out against this action of the United States [in lending their support to the establishment of Israel]. The birth of the tragic Arab refugee problem out of the Palestine conflict has added to the real and deep-seated bitterness which replaced, to some extent at least, an earlier faith in the United States. The emotions which surround this problem in the Middle East are so tense that any immediate or dramatic solution of the problem is impossible. . . . There is today a blockade . . . between the Arab States and Israel. . . . It is a situation which, if not corrected, has in it the seeds of still more disastrous conflict in the Middle East"

King Saud of Saudia Arabia, a good friend of the United States, in one of his first published remarks after succeeding his father, King Ibn Saud, in 1953 asked his fellow Arabs, "Why don't we sacrifice 10 million of our number" to uproot Israel, which "to the Arab world is like a cancer to the human body?" King Saud is understood to have "vowed Israel's destruction."

President Eisenhower reported to the nation on October 13, 1956: "The United States—through all the years since the close of World War II—has labored tirelessly to bring peace and stability to this area." He chose to ignore the major exception of our part in the Israeli-Arab conflict. After this major misstep, the United States tried to remain neutral in dealings with the Jews and the Arabs and to promote peace. But both sides believed we were partial to the other and even if they thought we were neutral they tended to be guided by the Biblical statement: "He that is not with me is against me."

Between World War II and 1957 we "seesawed." Do we aid the Arabian states or do we aid Israel? Tanks for Saudia Arabia and/or arms for Israel? Arms and/or Aswan Dam for Egypt?

For years the critical economic and military importance of the Suez Canal has been drilled into every school student of geography. The oil from the Middle East and the Suez Canal are perhaps the two most important international factors contributing to the strength of the United Kingdom. The Suez has long been recognized as perhaps the most important of all man-made international seaways. Yet in August, 1956, right after President Nasser of Egypt seized the Suez Canal, United States Secretary of Defense Wilson described the Suez crisis as a "relatively small thing" and hoped "it would be a local friction and not something that would involve the East and West." This remark came after both Great Britain and France had partially mobilized their troops and President Eisenhower had pronounced himself "vastly disturbed."

Just the day before the Secretary of Defense of the United States had expressed such complete naïveté in security and world problems, the *New York Times* had developed the problems and issues in the following excellent fashion:

If the battle over Suez involved solely the control of a man-made, 105-mile ditch that links the Mediterranean with the Indian Ocean and expedites world trade, the outcome would be tremendously important. But the stakes are far bigger than the canal. What is involved, fundamentally, is the political destiny of a vast world of wind and burning sun, of deserts, green oases and wild, rocky hills—the world of the Middle East.

To Egypt's President Nasser, the Middle East is a theatre for Egyptian domination. His goal is to forge and lead a dynamic Arab bloc which would hold the balance of power between East and West. He has based his appeal for leadership on an emotional, nationalistic program of ridding the Mideast of "foreign domination"—a sure-fire appeal in view of the Arabs' hostility toward Israel and their resentment of a century of Western colonialism. His slogan: "From the Atlantic to the Persian Gulf there is but one Arab nation which no one will succeed in dividing again."

Nasser has already chalked up major victories; he forced concession after concession from the West; he won military, economic and diplomatic support from Russia and the Soviet bloc. But the Arab world is highly unstable and if Nasser once loses face, he is likely to lose power. Accordingly he must continue to hack away at the West's position in the Middle East.

The West's interests there are vital. *First,* there is oil. Britain and the United States have heavy investments in Mideastern oil fields; Britain, in fact, has almost no other sources. The Persian Gulf fields provide the oil that fuels and lubricates the British economy; the only short, relatively cheap route from the Persian Gulf to Britain is through the Suez Canal.

Second, there is the factor of British and French prestige. Both powers have been forced to relinquish large chunks of their once vast holdings to the Arab nationalists. The West has won no compensating gains—either in terms of Middle Eastern stability or Arab goodwill. On the contrary, after the British relinquished their Egyptian base, Nasser began his fight to drive them from Cyprus and Jordan as well; after France granted autonomy to her North African possessions, Nasser backed the extremists' demand for unconditional French evacuation. To London and Paris it looked as though their concessions served only to swell Nasser's appetite. They decided to give him no more.

Third, there is the factor of strategy. The West has built a network of air bases from French North Africa across the Eastern Mediterranean to British Cyprus and thence north to Iraq, Iran and Turkey. Washington and London believe these bases have a deterrent effect upon Moscow. In addition, London feels that so long as it has military power lodged in the Middle East, it can protect its oil in the Persian Gulf.

On July 27, 1954, Great Britain agreed to withdraw her troops stationed in the Suez Canal area as urged by Secretary of State Dulles. On June 13, 1956, the last British troops left the Canal zone. On July 19, 1956, the United States withdrew an offer to help Egypt build the Aswan High Dam because of growing lack of confidence in President Nasser of Egypt, who had begun to accept arms from Russia in September, 1955, in exchange for a large share of Egypt's exportable cotton. On July 26, 1956, President Nasser nationalized the Universal Suez Canal Company. Great Britain's immediate decision after Egypt's seizure of the Canal was to use force to recover it. The United States persuaded Great Britain and France not to use force and by mid-September Western policy played down the threat of Anglo-French military action and substituted economic sanctions; but Britain and France charged that the United States failed to take real economic action against Egypt. Secretary Dulles offered two plans: internationalization of the Canal and, after this was rejected by Egypt, a "users' association." After the British and French had agreed to the plan, the normally pro-American London *Times* reported, "Mr. Dulles weakened it out of all recognition." In addition, the *Times* stated: "The ham-handedness of the Americans landed us in the Suez mess and the reluctance of the Americans to face up to the consequent facts has delayed any safeguarding action."

During these negotiations of August, September, and October, 1956, plans for Anglo-French military action were continued and closely coördinated. France was further antagonized by President Nasser, who gave aid and guidance to Arab rebels in Algeria and thus increased trouble in that French colony. Nasser also moved against Israel with volunteer commandos in stepped-up raids, killing civilians, and in October he formed a joint command with Syria and Jordan, under an Egyptian general, to coordinate action against Israel. Thus by November, 1956, Great Britain, France, and Israel were convinced of the necessity to use military force to regain and increase their strength in the Middle East. Without prior consultation with or advising the United States, they launched their attack. Prime Minister Eden acted unilaterally in the national interest of Great Britain. He explained his action to Parliament in this fashion: "Now, it is, of course, an obvious truth that safety of transit through the Canal, though clearly of concern to the United States, is for them not a matter of survival as it is to us and, indeed, to all Europe and many other lands. . . . I do not think that we must in all circumstances secure agreement from our American ally before we can act ourselves in what we know to be our own vital interest."

One thing was certain: the Middle East crisis was brought suddenly to a head just at the end of the first Eisenhower administration. The United States was in the middle of the "seesaw." In this instance there was but one resort—to work through the United Nations, to control her own creature, Israel, to internationalize the Suez Canal, to try to stabilize the Arabian world, to restore the flow of oil, and to prevent Russia from extending her influence in the Middle East. If these things could be done the United States action in opposing aggression might strengthen her position in the Middle East. This break with our ally was viewed with great alarm, but it was certain to prove only temporary. The present writer tended to view the move by Britain and France as a part of a much larger pan-European move to become a Third Force along with the United States and Russia in this world which was dominated by two powers after the end of World War II.

Thus we see that the United States policy for the southern arch was to promote stability. In this the United States was tremendously unsuccessful and in the major instance of Israel injected into the Middle East one of the principal factors which created instability in the area. However, in numerous individual cases we offered our services and helped stabilize difficult problems—e.g., the Iranian oil crisis. There has been an awareness on the part of some people of the importance of the Middle East, but an appalling amount of ignorance on the part of the great mass of Americans. Secretary of Defense Wilson was one prime example. There was after World War II until 1957 an urgent need for thinking through clearly the problems of the southern arch, and for straightforward policy decision making and implementation.

We also can conclude that the military strategy for security in the southern arch consisted primarily in a string of air bases. Their purpose was not only to have a deterrent effect on Russia but also to be a part of the total United States defense structure including our radar screen and bases for "massive retaliation." These bases are shown in Figure 15.5.

During the Suez crisis the United States worked through the United Nations to secure the withdrawal of British, French, and Israeli forces and for the occupation of the Canal area by U.N. forces.

One clear result of the Suez crisis was the collapse of British and French influence in the Middle East and the emergence of the United States in a stronger position after having clearly demonstrated that it was opposed to the use of force by all nations, including its closest allies. During December, 1956, President Eisenhower concluded that, since the general consensus was that the United States had shifted its responsibility for "stability" in the Middle East to the United Nations, it was vital to dramatize United States determination to stabilize the area. Therefore, the decision was made to ask for a unilateral declaration of the United States' intent.

On January 5, 1957, President Eisenhower addressed a joint session of Congress and stated that "a high degree of instability in much of the Middle East," Russia's desire to dominate the area, and "the immense importance" of the Mideast to the free world had convinced him "that basic United States policy should now find expression in joint action by

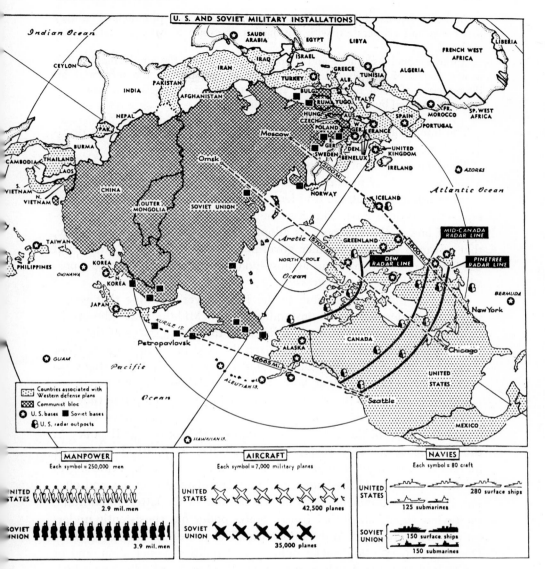

Figure 15.5.   How the Two Great Powers Line Up—Strategic Picture and Forces on Each Side.
(*The New York Times*, April 1, 1956)

the Congress and the Executive" which would have the following features:

Authorize the U.S. to cooperate with and assist any nation or group of
nations in the general area of the Middle East in the development of economic
strength dedicated to the maintenance of national independence.

Authorize the executive to undertake in the same region programs of military assistance and cooperation with any nation or group of nations which desire such aid.

Authorize such assistance and cooperation to include the employment of the armed forces of the United States to secure and protect the territorial independence of such nations . . . against overt armed aggression from any nation controlled by international communism.

The hope was that these three features would create conditions detrimental to covert aggression by international Communism.

Thus the purpose of the Eisenhower Doctrine was to establish in 1957 a southern arch of military and economic defenses. The United States was extending its strategic frontiers and commitments to a new and vital area—the Middle East. The Eisenhower Doctrine was a further statement of one of the first policies adopted by the administration, namely, that advance warning to other governments that the United States will use force to repel aggressions against independent nations is the best possible insurance against aggression.

However, there was nothing in the Eisenhower Doctrine that would solve the basic element of instability in the Middle East—the Arab-Israeli conflict—nor was there a solution to the future status of the Suez Canal. President Eisenhower recognized this and in his message to Congress indicated that in the United States view the United Nations remained the only competent body to work on these disputes.

Congress approved the Eisenhower Doctrine, but at the same time the Senate Foreign Relations and the Armed Services committees voted a complete review of the entire United States post-World War II policy in the Middle East. This review could fall flat in political rehash of SEESAW or it might recognize the United States role in contributing to the hard questions of the Suez Canal and Arab-Israeli relations and offer some positive recommendations for the solution of the latter. In addition, the review should show that United States policy has consistently underestimated the force of Arab nationalism. The success of the Eisenhower Doctrine in preventing Soviet military and political penetration, and of the United States in developing a total policy for the Middle East which recognized the force of Arab nationalism, might well be determined in large measure by the solution of the basic cause of instability in the area.

The dispatch of United States and British forces into Lebanon and Jordan following the unanticipated nationalist revolution in Iraq in July, 1958, was further evidence of the United States policy of vacillation. The hope was that this was the end of SEESAW and that United States policy would recognize the force of nationalism and would help develop situations of regional strength by unilateral action and through the United Nations.

D. RIO

The Treaty of Rio de Janeiro (1948) converted the oldest United States commitment, the Monroe Doctrine (1823), into a multilateral defense pact. This obviously was not one "of the regional alliances that Secretary Dulles, with extraordinary patience and resolution, is trying to complete around the Soviet." First, because it was a pre-Eisenhower Treaty; and second, because it was not part of the shield that made up the arch of military defenses around the Soviet. Thus an argument can be advanced for not including RIO in this section on Military Security.

We accept this argument for the point made, but the conclusion seems justified that the importance of Latin America is cardinal to the military security of the United States. In addition, we know that sound strategy must aim at denying valuable political and economic, as well as military, advantages to an enemy. There is ample evidence that while the United States policy has concentrated its attention on the arch around the Soviet during the post-World War II era, it has neglected its oldest commitment and basis of strength in the Western Hemisphere. This occurred at an accelerated rate during the first Eisenhower administration in spite of the fact that Secretary Dulles was vitally aware of the importance of RIO. In January, 1953, when the new Secretary of State was asked to comment on the gradual deterioration of the United States position vis-à-vis our Latin American neighbors, he replied: "We should attach the utmost importance to rebuilding and reinforcing the spirit of co-operation of the Americas, and we should never abandon the concept of the solidarity of the American republics, and we should not take it for granted that that solidarity is going to go on automatically."

Latin America is undergoing a violent process of growth—an economic and social revolution. The most powerful force in being has been nationalism—which could spill to the Right or Left. In the recent past the tendencies have been to the Right, but the Communism of the Left has been growing noticeably in some parts of the continent. The challenge to United States foreign policy is to deal with this growing spirit of nationalism so that it can be directed in channels useful to our neighbors and to an inter-American system of democracy. The basis of solution of such a problem is economic growth and stability to insure political and military strength.

Thus, when we include Canada, we can conclude that the United States is surrounded in this hemisphere by governments and peoples whose basic aims and aspirations of economic progress are the same as ours. We must so direct our policies to facilitate this growth that as it strengthens our RIO neighbors, it strengthens the United States.

In 1958, Vice-President Nixon made a "Good-Will Tour" of South America. During this visit he was met with riots on the part of Communist-inspired students. These riots were widely publicized throughout the United States and the world. It is the hope that these RIOTS would focus our attention on the neglect of RIO and, together with the first-hand knowledge that Mr. Nixon brought back of the economic and political problems of our neighbors to the South, would lead to the strengthening of the United States' oldest commitment.

2. Military Strategy

After World War II the United States sharply reduced her military strength. With the gradual realization of the Communist threat to the peace and security of the world, our strategic policy was drastically changed when President Truman drew the line against Communist guerrillas in Greece in 1947 and the United States containment policy was begun. Since the United States had a monopoly on the atomic bomb our military policy was to build up and maintain a strategic air force which could deliver the bomb as a defensive measure and thus could deter and contain Russia.

In 1948 China fell under Communist domination. In September, 1949, the Soviet Union exploded its first atomic bomb, and on June 25, 1950, the fact of Soviet hostility was firmly established in the minds of all United States citizens with the sudden attack on the Republic of Korea, when the tactics of Communist imperialism shifted from subversion to open aggression. The United States met its moral commitment with a military force that was totally inadequate to meet the ground warfare that followed. A rapid build-up of our ground forces followed and defense expenditures multiplied. This raised the fundamental problem of military strategy and economics. What should be the structure and strategy of the armed forces, and could they be accomplished with a stabilized military expenditure?

When the Eisenhower administration began in January, 1953, it was pledged to end the Korean War and to reduce military expenditures without reduction of military power. The Korean War was terminated with the signing of the armistice at Panmunjom in July, 1953; and, much to the surprise of the United States, by that time the Russians had broken our monopoly on the hydrogen bomb.

The military programs taken over by the Eisenhower administration from the Truman administration were described by *Fortune* in the following fashion: Secretary of the Treasury George Humphrey emerged from reviews of the programs with the dumfounding realization that the military were "trying to follow six strategies simultaneously—two for each service."

There were strategies for infantry wars and air-dominated wars; for ninety-day wars and four-to-five-year wars; for non-atomic "brush-fire" peripheral wars and atomic knockouts. The confusion of purpose sprang from indecision at the highest levels of government. Although the Truman Administration had fathered the so-called "containment" policy, it shrank from drawing any hard-and-fast containing lines except in front of the NATO allies and, almost too late, the Republic of Korea. Nor had it, for that matter, been able to make up its mind about using nuclear weapons in any war other than a general war with the U.S.S.R., and even here there was doubt whether such weapons would be employed unless the Russians used them first. With recourse to the principal weapon thus left in doubt, the budgetary demands of the Army and Navy were predicated upon the argument that an effective containment policy required a huge array of conventional land and sea forces—all this while the Air Force was being reorganized around and armed with decisive numbers of nuclear weapons.[3]

Eisenhower ordered that a study be made through the National Security Council of various military strategic courses open to the administration. Three general courses of strategy were considered. Course A was to continue the Truman containment doctrine. Course B was to draw a line around certain threatened areas—Formosa, southeast Asia, the Middle East—and make it known to Russia that a violation of these lines would invite general war. Course C was to pass over to the initiative and subject Russia to intense political and economic pressure. From the United States policy, it appears that the course finally decided upon was a compromise of A and B: more containment, but with the holes in southeast Asia and the Middle East to be plugged with new strategic alliances. Out of the entire study came also a strong recommendation that United States military policy be reshaped around nuclear weapons.[4]

President Eisenhower changed the entire Joint Chiefs of Staff and appointed Admiral Radford the new chairman. Before the JCS took office, they were directed by the President to make a study of military strategy and to come to an agreement on force levels, broad programs, and deployments to support the strategy. Recommendations were made in August, 1953. "The essence of the military judgment was that consistent

[3] Charles J. V. Murphy, "The Eisenhower Shift," *Fortune,* March, 1956, pp. 230 and 232.

[4] *Ibid.,* p. 234.

with our treaty commitments to allies, United States striking forces should be regrouped nearer the center of the strategic perimeter and that the ground and tactical air forces of our allies should thereafter take over as much of the perimeter as possible. It was further agreed that the U.S. could execute the new strategy with a total manpower of about 2,900,-000, compared with the Truman requirement of about 3,700,000."[5]

We are told by presidential advisers that President Eisenhower was determined to bring the army strength down sharply from its Korean strength of 1,500,000 men and that he insisted that United States strategy be reshaped around the assumption that nuclear weapons would be used in any situation where the military exigencies dictated.[6] We also know that the President was insistent on a program of stabilized military expenditures.

A. The First New Look

Out of these studies and recommendations there was developed in November, 1953, the military national policy decision that was called the New Look.

The New Look legitimized nuclear strategy and set in motion the strategic regroupment of United States forces. By ending the multiplication of strategies it made possible the economic concentration of forces behind a nuclear deterrent strategy—"massive retaliation." A slight revision of this program called for a flexible strategy—"measured retaliation"—for coping with small as well as large wars.

A fundamental part of the New Look was to establish Defense Department spending around $35 billion a year for a number of years ahead. This had the effect of stabilizing the program on an even level and thus ended drastic retrenchment during what appear as less urgent periods and expensive rapid build-up on a "crash" basis during emergency periods. Defense Department expenditures for the fiscal years 1953–57 were as follows:

1953	$43,700,000,000
1954	40,300,000,000
1955	35,500,000,000
1956	35,600,000,000
1957	36,100,000,000

These reduced expenditures covered higher service pay for an armed force of 588,151 fewer men; the tremendous intercontinental-ballistic-

---

[5] *Ibid.*, p. 237.
[6] *Ibid.*, p. 234.

missile project (ICBM); an elaborate radar early-warning system along the Arctic and ocean approaches; a more powerful air defense; and the Strategic Air Command.

Under the New Look the total armed forces strength was cut from 3,402,783 on December 13, 1953, to 2,814,632 on May 31, 1956. The comparative strengths by forces follow:

	1953	1956
Army	1,481,177	1,039,423
Navy	765,269	666,325
Marine Corps	243,800	198,309
Air Force	912,537	910,575
Total:	3,402,783	2,814,632

These drastic cuts in the armed forces strength, and especially in the army, caused profound interservices debates over military strategy. The most serious criticism leveled at the first New Look was that massive retaliation with air-borne nuclear weapons was unsound on moral and military grounds. The latter was especially true since parity in nuclear weapons between the United States and the Soviet Union left the free world vulnerable to attack by Russia's overwhelmingly larger conventional forces. These comparative forces as of April, 1956, are given in Figure 15.5.

B. The Second New Look

The arguments against smaller ground forces met with little success and in mid-1956 Admiral Radford, as chairman of the Joint Chiefs of Staff, proposed cutting the armed forces by about 800,000 men to a ceiling of about 2,000,000 men by 1960.

This proposal called for a continuation of the policy of reducing the army and also a major revision in policy which called for a gradual but large-scale withdrawal from foreign bases by 1960. Made at the end of the first Eisenhower administration, the proposal was certain to cause serious and prolonged debate especially because the Eisenhower military strategy had produced one major failure. The indigenous allied forces that were supposed to spring up along the outer defense perimeter had been slow to materialize, and NATO was described by some as a "shield that was more of a hope than a fact" because of French weakness and the delays in West Germany's rearmament.

As the discussion of the second New Look got under way, the arguments of the army for ground forces had little effect. To the contrary, the United States Senate was most interested in the status of our B-52 intercontinental jet bombers and the Strategic Air Command. When the Senate heard testimony in the summer of 1956 that Russia was surpassing the production of B-52's with her comparable Bison bomber, the senators voted for an extra $900 million after President Eisenhower had already made a concession and agreed to a $547 million increase for the Air Force in his defense budget.

A complicating factor in the discussion was Russia's announcement that she proposed to cut by May 1, 1957, 1,200,000 men from her armed forces, which then totaled 4,000,000 men. A simple comparison of United States and Russian strengths as given in Figure 15.5 is only part of the story. It is estimated that Russia's Asian allies had another 3,000,000 men under arms and that the European satellites had forces of about 2,000,000 men. The Russian Army was fully mechanized with about 200 divisions. The United States had a relatively small army of 18 divisions. Our NATO allies had about 3,000,000 men in the armed forces, with West Germany authorized to add another 500,000.

There were at least three explanations for the Soviets' announced reduction in armed forces:

First was the military-geopolitical reason that Russia occupies the Heartland surrounded by the satellites and sea. The satellites were sufficiently armed to hold their own territory in localized ground engagements and would be of tremendous help in a full-fledged war. Further, it was contended that in an all-out engagement nuclear weapons rather than conventional ground forces would be decisive.

Second was the economic reason. Russia's population was about 200 million as compared with 167 million in the United States. Russia's agriculture required almost 50 million people as compared with only 6.4 million in the United States. This left only about 49 million or 25 percent of the Soviets' total population for nonagricultural employment as compared with 57 million or over 33 percent in the United States. Russia was engaged in increasing her production of industrial and consumer goods for her domestic economy and had just launched a program of economic aid and exchange with foreign and underdeveloped areas. In addition, she was committed to an agricultural expansion program in Siberia. Thus it was contended that Russia faced a manpower crisis and that releasing 1,200,000 men from the unproductive armed forces for productive work in industry and on farms was a move to help solve a manpower problem.

Third, it was contended that the reduction in armed forces was a political-psychological propaganda move which would put pressure on the West and the United States in particular to make reductions. Few people realized that the proposed cuts in Russian forces were of about the same percentage as those already made by the United States. This propaganda was an astute move because it tapped the neutralist nations' sentiment for reduced armaments, the European and United States sentiment for reduced taxes, and the moralist sentiment everywhere that the way to peace was to disarm.

Thus the Russians announced proposed reduction of armed force was of vital importance in the second New Look. It gave added force to those who supported the reduction of the United States Army and to those who favored disarmament as a way to peace.

The fear on the part of many as the discussions of the second New Look took place was that implicit in the Radford plan, with its disengagement of United States forces from overseas, was a return to a modified isolationist attitude (of such persons as the late Senator Robert Taft), referred to as "Fortress America." The question arose as to whether this would undermine the whole system of collective security and whether the United States would return to a policy of making commitments without sufficient strength to back them up.

Another major fear was that the United States policy might again begin to be influenced by the pre-World War II dominant thought: that international law and disarmament were the way to peace. The writer is not one who wishes to argue against international law and disarmament. However, he does not believe that law and disarmament are the answer in developing a strategy of security.

The "skill and opportunity of the robber are prior facts to the Law of Robbery." We must face up to the *realities* and cannot operate "merely as lawyers defining rights and remedies."[7] The point is that we must be aware of the objective of our enemy—world communization and the destruction of freedom. He does not recognize law. Strength is necessary to prevent destruction. What is the enemy's strategic policy? War is his last resort, but we must plan to prevent it. We also must prevent the other strategic methods from succeeding. Other methods are least likely to succeed when economic strength is great. War is least likely to succeed where military strength is great. Thus both economic and military strength are required.

The argument can be made that disarmament on both sides reduces the amount that is required and necessary for military strength. If less is spent for the military, then more economic production can and must be spent to build up economic strength. If this is Russia's present strategy,

---

[7] Halford J. Mackinder, *Democratic Ideals and Reality*, Constable and Company, Ltd., 1919, p. 5.

does it follow that the United States policy should be to spend more on military strength and less on economic strength? Does it make sense that on almost the same day the Congress increased the President's request for military air power and reduced his request for international economic aid Russia was increasing her international economic aid?

There is a further complicating problem about disarmament: How do you know who is disarmed and in what fashion? So far Russia has refused to sign an agreement on international inspection, and even if she did, since she does not keep her agreements or abide by the law, what purpose would a signed agreement serve? A reduction in United States forces, then, can only be made in terms of what the United States can determine about the military strength of Communist forces, what our commitments are, and what we determine to be the most efficient strategic deployment of the United States forces while taking into account the military strength of our possible allies.

Thus the second New Look requires more than a study of military strategy. Like the first, it involves economic strategy. Like the first New Look and all the continuous Looks to come, it is a problem of *geoeconomics*. The outlook in 1957 was that military strategy would affirm its dedication to the United States commitments and to a "forward strategy" of defense against Communist imperialism, but with reduced United States forces overseas. The "forward strategy" would include the use of all types of nuclear and automatic weapons, which undoubtedly would reduce manpower requirements, especially in the ground forces, and probably would increase dollar costs.

President Eisenhower made it quite clear that some calculated risks would have to be taken. Obviously the United States policy was to continue to take many such risks in view of our extended commitments.

ECONOMIC SECURITY

A fundamental economic security objective of the United States, as we have seen, is the promotion of economic progress, by which is meant rising planes of living. We have also seen how the United States has adopted policies to achieve this objective in the national interest at home and abroad. We have presented plenty of evidence showing how we have achieved this objective within the United States and indicating the possibilities of continuing gains.

Outside the United States we have an economic interest in rising planes of living. In addition, as has been emphasized again and again, we have moral and political interests. Perhaps the easiest way to sell this policy today at home but not abroad is to bundle all these reasons up into the strategy of security and argue that regions of economic strength are infertile fields for Communism. Thus we have a real and sustained interest in helping create situations of strength outside the United States. Since freedom and strength are our co-objectives, we want to be sure that these situations of strength are areas of maximum freedom which will be associated with the United States in the pursuit of mutual objectives. It is our task to prove to all the world that situations of strength can best be developed where freedom exists. At the conclusion of this chapter we will want to look at the moral aspects of this problem, but at present we will consider only the economic aspects.

1. Trade Policy

Again and again we have demonstrated the economic interdependence of the United States and foreign areas. Pursuant to Public Law 215, 83rd Congress, the Commission on Foreign Economic Policy reëxamined the international relationships of the United States in the economic field and made a report to the President and the Congress in January, 1954 (the Randall Report). Prior to this, in February, 1953, President Eisenhower had had submitted to him by the Public Advisory Board for Mutual Security a Trade Policy Study—*A Trade and Tariff Policy in the National Interest.* President Truman had asked that a Trade Policy Study group be formed as a staff unit of the bipartisan Public Advisory Board and that the two be attached directly to the Executive Office of the President for the purpose of making a study and reporting findings and recommendations. The basic recommendation of this report was that what was needed at the beginning of the Eisenhower administration was a trade and tariff policy in the *national interest,* not one designed merely to protect small groups of domestic producers from competition from abroad.

In undertaking the Trade Policy Study for the Executive Office, the Public Advisory Board took into consideration certain major post-World War II developments. Since the end of the war the United States had exported far more and imported more than before the war. The rest of the free world had become more dependent on the United States for essential imports and for markets for its exports. United States exports constituted almost 20 percent and imports about 15 percent of the total trade of the free world. This trade was threatened by the inability of other countries to earn enough dollars to pay for their imports. The Public Advisory Board for Mutual Security reported to President Eisenhower that, unless the United States was prepared to increase its imports, the other nations of the free world would regard it as futile to take the measures they should to establish better balance in their payments and in their national economies, and that United States exports would decline and American industry and agriculture would be seriously affected.

The Advisory Board recommended that immediate action in formulating and carrying out a better United States trade policy was in the national interest and was vital to the strength and unity of the free world. The guiding aim of the policy was through national and international action, to increase production, trade, and consumption of goods and to eliminate unnecessary trade barriers and all forms of discriminatory treatment in international commerce, thus contributing to an expanding world economy, to the establishment and maintenance in all countries of rising levels of employment and real income, and to the creation of economic conditions conducive to world peace.

Further, the Board supplied President Eisenhower with a completed staff plan of action. The following are the summary recommendations:

1. That decisions on trade policy be based on national interest, rather than the interest of particular industries or groups; that in cases where choice must be made between injury to the national interest and hardship to an industry, the industry be helped to make adjustments by means other than excluding imports—such as through extension of unemployment insurance, assistance in retraining workers, diversification of production, and conversion to other lines.

2. That a new, simplified tariff act be adopted, providing for general reductions of duties and eliminating present uncertainties in the classification of goods by consolidating the many hundreds of present tariff rates into seven basic schedules: a Free List, 4 groupings of commodities bearing duties of 10, 20, 30, and 40 percent ad valorem, a Specific List for basic agricultural and mineral raw materials, and an Extraordinary List where commodities might be placed whose importation, for security or other reasons, should be limited by quotas or other restrictions, or by exceptionally high rates; that Congress establish appropriate standards for such an act and authorize the President to develop and carry out its details.

3. That the President be authorized to enter into reciprocal trade agreements without limit of time and with power to reduce tariffs, within specified limits, in return for reductions in tariffs or restrictions by other countries.

4. That, as an interim measure, customs procedures be simplified by prompt passage of a bill similar to that recommended by the Treasury and passed by the House of Representatives in 1951; that a commission be created to study and propose further measures of customs simplification.

5. That tariffs be reduced, and quotas on agricultural products be liberalized to allow the freer import of goods that are not produced in this country in sufficient quantity at world prices; that section 104 of the Defense Production Act, restricting the import of certain agricultural products, be repealed.

6. That tariffs be reduced and in some cases ultimately eliminated on metals and minerals of which imports are a major part of United States supplies; that, where necessary for defense reasons, domestic production be encouraged through special purchases or contracts rather than tariffs.

7. That import excise taxes now applying to petroleum be dropped; that, if imports reach a level where they impede domestic exploration and development, other measures be taken to assure a domestic industry adequate to defense needs.

8. That cargo preference, by which 50 percent of the cargo on aid and loan shipments is reserved to domestic carriers, not be applied to countries that let American shippers compete on a fair basis.

9. That the procurement policies of the Government which raise the cost of goods bought by the Government be reconsidered in the light of the principles and objectives of a foreign trade policy in the national interest.

10. That the Congress take the necessary steps to enable the United States to join in establishing an international organization to promote the objectives of the General Agreement on Tariffs and Trade (GATT); that active participation be continued in other international organizations to promote fair exchange and fair labor practices and the flow of investment capital.[8]

These recommendations and the entire report were unanimously agreed upon by the fourteen bipartisan members of the Public Advisory Board for Mutual Security, whose chairman was Daniel W. Bell, president of the American Security and Trust Company, Washington, D.C. The Board felt that the report would be of real value to the Eisenhower administration, and independent authorities considered the study to be outstanding. Further, the feeling was that the recommendations were in line with President Eisenhower's own economic foreign trade policies. On the other hand, it was quite clear that the recommendations were diametrically opposed to the trade philosophies held by the Old Guard members of the Republican party. Nevertheless, in view of the upsurge in interest in 1952 of United States businessmen in expanded international trade, there was a great ray of optimism that the Eisenhower administration would take the initiative in an expanding world trade.

Thus in contrast to the situation in military strategy, where President

[8] *A Trade and Tariff Policy in the National Interest,* The Public Advisory Board for Mutual Security, 1953, pp. 1–2.

Eisenhower was described as "angered" because he had a confusion of plans, in the area of international economic strategy he had a recommended trade policy, and in addition, as we have already seen and will refer to again presently, he had a recommended investment policy.

Just what was done with the Trade Policy Study of the Public Advisory Board for Mutual Security cannot be clearly stated. We do know that the Eisenhower administration chose to establish a Commission on Foreign Economic Policy, which in January, 1954, made the report previously mentioned. This report (the Randall Report, named after the chairman of the Commission, Clarence B. Randall of Inland Steel) covered not only trade policy but also the problems of foreign aid and technical assistance and foreign investment. The Commission included, in addition to the chairman, five presidential appointees, five senators, and five representatives. The idea behind the Commission was a good one in that the legislative branch of the government was included. However, as it turned out, Mr. Randall had to compromise his expanded foreign economic policy and that of his staff in the preparation of the report owing to the presence on the Commission of the ultraconservatives Senator Eugene D. Milliken and Representative Daniel A. Reed. Then when legislation was being prepared to implement some of the recommendations, it was stymied in legislative committees by these same gentlemen. The Commission's report was graciously described by President Eisenhower as "prepared in the American tradition of full debate and vigorous dissent." There was so much dissent that it is not possible to summarize the report as simply as the Bell Report was summarized.

However, using the Commission's report as a basis, President Eisenhower sent a message to Congress on March 30, 1954, entitled "Recommendations Concerning U.S. Foreign Economic Policy." The following are the principal *trade policy* recommendations:

A. Tariffs

The recommendation of the Commission on foreign economic policy was endorsed covering a three-year extension to the Trade Agreements Act with amendments to authorize: (1) reduction, pursuant to trade agreement negotiation, of existing tariff rates on commodities selected for such negotiations by not more than 5 percent of present rates in each of the three years of the new act; (2) reduction, by not more than one-half over a three-year period, of tariffs in effect on January 1, 1954, on products which are not being imported or which are being imported only in negligible volume; and (3) reduction, over a three-year period, pursuant to trade agreement negotiation, to 50 percent ad valorem, or its equivalent, of any rate in excess of 50 percent ad valorem, or its equivalent.

President Eisenhower stated that "These recommendations for renewal and amendment of the Trade Agreements Act are based on the plain truth that if we wish to sell abroad, we must buy abroad." In President Eisenhower's first year in office, 1953, he had tremendous difficulty in getting even a one-year extension of the nineteen-year-old Reciprocal Trade Agreements Act. In 1954 he got his recommended three-year extension. Actually, while the Republican Congress was in command from 1953–54, the administration was fortunate to stand still, in spite of the fact that the support for free trade was snowballing. During 1955 and 1956 some of the support for freer trade began to fall away, in the South especially, which began to feel the effects of Japanese textile imports. The fact remains that the Reciprocal Trade Agreements Program has been the most successful United States trade policy. But its uncertain duration and weakening amendments have impaired its effectiveness and made long-range planning difficult.

B. The General Agreement on Tariffs and Trade

Since 1948 almost all the trading nations of the world have become parties to a General Agreement on Tariffs and Trade (GATT). The contracting parties to GATT signed an agreement on March 7, 1955, for a proposed Organization for Trade Cooperation to administer the General Agreement on Tariffs and Trade and to serve as a forum for consultation on problems of international trade and commercial policy. This organization (OTC) was recommended by the Randall Commission and by President Eisenhower to Congress. Congress failed to act on the recommendation. A group of nongovernmental advisers representative of business, labor, and agriculture after first-hand observation of tariff negotiations at Geneva stated: "Failure on the part of the United States, the world's greatest trading nation, to join in setting up [OTC] would cause great dismay and disappointment throughout the free world at a time when the Soviet Union is stepping up its foreign economic efforts."

In the *Economic Report of the President* to the Congress of January, 1957, he concluded and again recommended the following: "Multilateral negotiations under the GATT have been more effective than bilateral negotiations in reducing trade barriers and discriminatory restrictions against our exports. To make the GATT an even more effective instrument for removing discrimination against our exports, an administrative agency—the Organization for Trade Cooperation—is required. In order to enhance the advantages that the GATT now provides, Congress is requested to enact legislation authorizing United States membership in the Organization for Trade Cooperation."

C. Customs Administration and Procedure

In many instances in the United States customs administration and procedures have been even more serious hindrances to trade than tariffs. Following the Bell Report, which vividly described these roadblocks, the Randall Commission made certain recommendations which were sent to the Congress by the President, as follows: (a) simplification of commodity definitions, classifications, and rate structure; (b) improvement in the methods of valuation of imports; and (c) establishment of more efficient procedures for customs administration.

Specific approval was asked in March, 1954, for the Treasury Department's customs valuation proposals which were embodied in H.R. 6584 and which had already been passed by the House of Representatives. One basic difficulty of the valuation system used by the United States was that, when an ad valorem tax was to apply, both "foreign" and "export" values had to be determined and the higher of the two used as a base. "Foreign value" represents the wholesale price at which an import is sold in the country of origin for export sale to the United States. "Foreign value" is very difficult to obtain and is usually higher than "export value," and the delays involved in knowing just what would be the price plus tariff paid by United States importers are considerable. The United States Treasury Department sought to simplify the problem by using "export value" as a base. The Senate refused to approve H.R. 6584 because it claimed that the use of a lower value was an indirect way of reducing tariffs.

Finally, in the summer of 1956, a compromise Customs Simplification Act was passed, to become effective in 1957. Space does not permit a description of its provisions, but the New York Times headlined an analysis "New Customs Act Refutes Its Title." However, the Times went on to conclude: "The new law, even in its compromise form, represents a major step toward liberalization of customs procedures. These already have been greatly improved with the elimination of excessive marking requirements and other hampering regulations. However, the basic objective of cutting down excessive paper work for the Customs Bureau is not likely to be obtained immediately." This latter is a prime problem. The Bell Report stated emphatically: "The most serious defect of customs administration is the time required for businessmen to learn their final customs liabilities after the goods have been imported into the United States. These delays frequently stretch out into years."

D. Instability of Prices

One of the strongest recommendations made in our discussion of agricultural problems and energy and material problems is that much greater emphasis must be placed on the stability of prices on goods imported into the United States. We have considered at length the impact that fluctuating prices have on exporting countries, particularly where the selling country exports only one or two commodities which thus constitute most of its foreign exchange and in most instances are a very large part of its national income. In addition, we have seen that stability of these prices is advantageous to United States importers.

In our discussion of international trade and agricultural policy we stressed the basic inconsistency between domestic and international trade policy and recommended that domestic agricultural policy must be modified to achieve more efficient utilization of resources, and international trade policy must place more emphasis on achieving stability of international prices. The Commission on Foreign Economic Policy stressed this inconsistency and made specific recommendations to facilitate production adjustments through the flexible price support scheme and greater stability of agricultural prices (see Chapter 5). President Eisenhower in his recommendation to Congress on United States foreign economic policy stated: "It is necessary to harmonize our agricultural and foreign economic policies without sacrificing the sound objectives of either. I am convinced such reconciliation is possible." President Eisenhower, against most vocal protests, consistently endorsed a domestic farm program of flexible price supports to facilitate production adjustments. Additional steps are required to solve the problem of greater stability of prices for agricultural imports. It would be a mistake to say that we have a United States agricultural trade policy. Indeed there seems to be a real need for an understanding of the problems. However, it is absolutely essential that our economic strategy of security for international trade in agricultural products must plan for more stable prices for export areas in order to increase their economic strength and security.

Similarly, in our discussion of international trade of minerals we pointed up time and time again the desirability of more stable import prices. The Commission on Foreign Economic Policy recommended that the United States government should make a constructive contribution toward greater stability of world prices of raw material by moderating or relaxing impediments to international trade, by encouraging diversification of foreign economies, by avoiding procurement practices which disturb world prices, by consultation with other nations, and by tempering the fluctuations in our own economy. In his message to Congress, President Eisenhower called attention to these recommendations and advised the Congress in March, 1954, that he had appointed a special Cabinet Committee which was then surveying the whole field of minerals policy and had drawn their attention to the Commission's recommendations. *The Report of the President's Cabinet Committee on Minerals Policy* issued in November, 1954, made no reference to these recommendations. However, in the discussion of the strategic stockpile under the general topic of the problem of security, the Committee recommended that minerals be stockpiled prior to the start of a war so that there would be less need or no need at all for forced-draft wartime expansion of raw materials production "involving unreasonable increases in prices or substantial Government investment." This certainly will be helpful especially as it is incorporated with the new military strategy of security of program planning on a long-range and stable basis.

Instability of mineral import prices and world prices cannot be corrected by United States stockpiling and long-term military planning alone. Indeed the problem was present for all foodstuffs and raw materials before military procurement was a factor. The Commission on Foreign Economic Policy emphatically opposed commodity agreements and buffer stock arrangements as means to solve the problems of price instability. Its conclusions are those of most economists, that past programs have proved too costly and that they impair the elasticity of economic adjustment and freedom of individual initiative, which are fundamental to economic progress. With this we can agree, but at the same time we may find that more and more exporting countries resort to such agreements in order to stabilize prices and we may have to compromise our international trade policy, especially so long as the United States continues to endorse domestic policies of the same type. However, the development of international study groups for each commodity with fuller exchange of complete market information may help reduce price instability.

2. Investment Policy

One of the fundamental elements of the United States strategy of security in promoting economic progress outside the United States, as well as inside, is increased investment. This is the means by which production and strength and power can be achieved. We have discussed in great detail in Chapter 11 the whole function of capital investment and the problems and policy of international investment in underdeveloped areas. This is indeed a part of our economic strategy of security and there is no need to review or even summarize the conclusions and recommendations made in Chapter 11. The first Eisenhower administration built upon the foundations laid by the previous post-World War II administration. The objective was to replace wherever possible direct economic aid by increased international trade and by investment—public and private. The United States has recognized the need of investment in underdeveloped areas and has adopted as a cardinal principle of international policy the supplying of capital to these areas in an attempt to raise their planes of living and their strength, in the hope that they may be free and support us in common objectives and act as sources of the raw materials required for the growth of our domestic economy.

There is no question about the success of the United States foreign economic aid program when it is evaluated in terms of its effectiveness in implementing European economic recovery and in strengthening selected situations of weakness in Asia. The measure of this success was described by President Eisenhower in his message to Congress on March 19, 1956, which was quoted in Chapter 11.

Despite opposition in the Republican party the Eisenhower administration, after first disavowing and threatening to abolish the foreign economic aid program, adopted it as an integral part of its strategy of security, and in his message to Congress on March 19, 1956, President Eisenhower made the unusual request for authority "to make commitments up to ten years in length to assist less-developed countries in long-term projects important to their development." The President not only did not get his long-term authority but experienced serious difficulty with his total (economic and military) foreign aid budget request for $4.9 billion. The House of Representatives cut the request by $1.1 billion and the Senate also would have done so had it not been for the support of the Democrats and Senator Walter George, who pleaded for the compromise $4.5 billion that his Senate Foreign Relations Committee had approved and the administration had agreed to accept. Senator George argued for a Republican administration in the *national interest*. "If we do not hold the torch of leadership and carry it forward, into whose hands will it fall? I cannot think that Divine Providence . . . has permitted us to become responsible leaders of the world . . . only to break that hope. . . . If the free people of this globe lose confidence in us, we shall disappoint the best hopes of mankind." A bill providing $4.3 billion for 1957 was finally passed after the administration brought extreme pressure on the recalcitrant Republican members of Congress.

Why the opposition to what had been a successful part of the United States strategy of security? Part of it of course came from what the *Washington Post* described as a substantial though minor go-it-alone element in Congress and in the country, the die-hards of the pre-aviation and pre-atomic ages who would be delighted to swing national policy back to what they conceive to be the good old days of isolationism. This opposition was supported in large part by relaxation of world tension during the first half of 1956 and by the uncoöperative attitude of those nations who had been supplied aid and others who believed that the time was ripe for an "agonizing reappraisal" of the foreign economic aid program.

Those of course who thought of relaxation of world tension were ignoring the real threat of Communism although there were many who attributed part of this relaxation to a public statement of President Eisenhower at the Big Four meeting in Geneva that he believed the Russians were as sincerely devoted to peace as anybody else. Maybe the Russians but certainly not the Communists and the Russian leaders.

Those who complained of the uncoöperative attitude of those nations who had been supplied aid were engaging in that practice for which the United States has been most severely criticized: We made economic grants to underdeveloped areas for the clear-cut and emphasized reason that it "is a painful necessity made inevitable only because they must be kept out of the Communist camp." Barbara Ward has described this process as follows:

> Nearly every program of assistance is finally rammed through the Legislature with the techniques of Dickens' Fat Boy—"I wants to make yer flesh creep." Refuse this appropriation and Bongaland will slip forever under the Communist yoke.
>
> But then, by a remarkable psychological somersault, the same legislators who have grimly consented in pure self-interest to provide perhaps half the necessary funds, denounce the recipient peoples as ungrateful scoundrels who show no due appreciation of the magnificent generosity shown them (in strict preservation of Western skins). Yet is it logical to expect gratitude for steps taken openly and crudely in self-defense?[9]

Those who believed that a reappraisal of foreign economic aid was necessary had their position conservatively stated by Democratic Senator

[9] Barbara Ward, "For a New Foreign Aid Concept," *New York Times Magazine,* March 11, 1956, p. 44.

Theodore France Green when he gave his reason, as quoted from *Time*, July 9, 1956, for supporting President Eisenhower's budget request:

" 'It has been my theory in the field of foreign policy,' he said, 'that, if in doubt, I should support the President. I shall do so this year [but] I cannot let the record rest there. . . . The coherence and rationality of the program are so open to question that I am close to the border of opposition. . . . I hope that the Administration by next year will be able to approach Congress asking authority for foreign aid in positive, rather than negative, terms. Our country will not be able to grasp the initiative until our energies are devoted to promoting freedom. . . .' "

It appeared that a reappraisal of the program was in order, and it was expected that a study would be made by both the Senate Foreign Relations Committee and the House Foreign Affairs Committee in 1956 and 1957. Five special reports made early in 1957 were summarized in Chapter 11. Three of these were made to the Senate Special Committee to Study the Foreign Aid Program, and two were made to President Eisenhower.

Basically it was certain that a positive program was in order, and even though many in the United States had felt that our economic aid, and especially our investment program, was a positive program to increase production in underdeveloped areas, it was quite apparent that we had failed to sell this point to the recipients. This latter was particularly true in Asia. United States foreign economic programs in the future will require at least the same and probably more careful planning and placement than domestic investment programs. They should be working examples of what had been accomplished in the United States, and thus illustrative salesmen of our political economy. They must be made with no political strings attached, if they are made. Communists have made political capital of our aid program in a negative approach of associating the United States with Great Britain and France as an example of imperialism by pointing to our aid program, and they cite as proof of the strings attached the wails of United States politicians. On the other hand, a small Russian loan with no strings attached is played up as an example of the achievements of Communism. We need have no fear of a contest with Russia in the foreign economic program because in investment and productive achievement lie the strength of the United States economy and the weakness of the Russian economy. What little productive strength the Russians may impart to an underdeveloped area may even prove to our advantage. But much more importantly we know that the Russians by their own admission cannot solve even their agricultural problem and in 1956 were having great difficulty with coal production in the Donetz Basin. Very carefully selected investment programs—public and private—to meet the requirements of individual regions could be working illustrations of the accomplishments of the United States economy. This should be the new positive look of our foreign investment program.

3. Coördinated Economic Policy

Mr. James Reston in a review in the *New York Times,* April 15, 1956, of foreign policy criticisms of the first Eisenhower administration had this to say:

CRITICISM NO. 2: The United States' foreign economic policy has not kept pace with its policy of military solidarity, and the United States, meanwhile, has been urging upon its allies trade and political-union policies it is not prepared to adopt itself.

On this one there is little difference in Washington between Government and non-Government opinion. The Eisenhower Administration is not happy about its policies on trade, ship subsidies or customs, or at least some members of it are not. The President, for example, favors a more liberal trade and aid policy.

One Cabinet member said to this reporter: "We don't have one foreign economic policy; we have forty-nine different foreign economic policies, some of them administered by one department and some by another. The whole thing needs to be pulled together."

In contrast to this position, *Business Week* reported on May 28, 1955: "This week Pres. Eisenhower is well on the way to becoming the first President of the U.S. to propose, and see through the Congress, an integrated foreign economic policy program." One thing is clear: during the closing months of 1954 President Eisenhower saw and attempted to correct a problem that was basic to the United States foreign economic policy program—there were perhaps as many as twelve different government agencies interested in this area. In addition he became convinced that foreign economic policy was a cardinal element in the United States strategy of security. To help work on this problem the President called back into public service Joseph Morrell Dodge, president of the Detroit Bank, who had previously served as United States Budget Director. Mr. Dodge proposed, and after it was formed was appointed chairman of, a Council on Foreign Economic Policy. The Council was composed of the Secretaries of State, Treasury, Agriculture, and Commerce, the Director of the Foreign Operations Administration (formerly the Mutual Security Agency—the FOA was transformed into a permanent semiautonomous International Cooperation Administration within the State Department), several members of the President's economic staff, and certain selected experts. The Council, although thought of as an advisory group, became an active working agency and Mr. Dodge acquired the power to overrule the members and thus became a coördinator of foreign economic policy. Mr. Dodge attended meetings of the National Security Council, and also cabinet sessions when he desired. It is generally conceded that through his own personal ability Mr. Dodge was able to help formulate an "integrated foreign economic policy." We see the results in the foreign economic programs that were presented to the Congress for approval. Lack of support and disintegration of these programs were often due to Congressional action. Poor government administration of the adopted programs is not easy to explain, difficult to correct, and in need of radical revision. Certainly the purpose of the programs needs to be made clear and those in charge of their administration and implementation need to be aware of and sympathetic to the purpose.

During July, 1956, Clarence Randall, who had served as chairman of the Commission on Foreign Economic Policy, was appointed to succeed Joseph Dodge as special assistant to the President and chairman of the Council on Foreign Economic Policy. Mr. Randall was eminently qualified for a most difficult job of developing, explaining, and administering the "New Look" of foreign economic policy.

As Mr. Randall took charge, he could recall the directive to him as chairman of the Commission on Foreign Economic Policy from President Eisenhower: "I commend to you an attitude both realistic and bold. Above all, I urge you to follow one guiding principle: What is best in the national interest." Then later the President explained: "The national interest in the field of foreign economic policy is clear. It is obtained in a manner that is consistent with our national security and profitable and equitable for all, the highest possible level of trade and the most efficient use of capital and resources." This was indeed a bold guiding principle that economists had been advocating for generations. Mr. Randall had a tremendous job cut out for him if the "New Look" of the United States foreign economic policy was to follow a highway in the "national interest." However, he was thoroughly familiar with the roadblocks.

Finally, part of Mr. Randall's job and that of the administration was to sell the fact that economic and military foreign aid were a permanent part of the United States strategy of security. As early as April, 1955, President Eisenhower had spelled out in no uncertain terms the permanency of his proposed "New Look": "I consider the program (foreign aid) an indispensable part of a realistic and enlightened national policy. . . . Apart from any obstacles created by the Communists, this is a long-term process."

MORAL STRATEGY OF SECURITY

Freedom, the fundamental objective of the United States, is the very antithesis of the primary objective of Communist Soviet Russia for the communization of the world, the overthrow of democratic government, and the resultant enslavement of all men everywhere. Why don't we make the most of our moral objective of freedom?

James Reston in his review summarizes:

CRITICISM NO. 4: The leaders of the free world coalition in Washington have no effective plan for waging the more subtle phase of the "cold war." They are inflexible and inexperienced moralizers who preach against the old pragmatic diplomacy of the past but have nothing practical to put in its place. . . .

It is true that after years of experimenting with planning boards at the State Department level, and at the Cabinet level, psychological warfare experts, "cold war" strategists in the White House, and the National Security Council, the United States still operates largely on a temporary basis, one crisis at a time.

On the other hand, Barbara Ward claims that the Russians in addition to the negative aspect of their strategy of associating United States aid with capitalist imperialism have a *positive* world political philosophy within which economic trade and token loans are offered as aid: "The Soviet Union, so the propaganda trumpet proclaims day after day, stands for a world in which all domination by one nation over another will cease, in which all will cooperate in creating a peaceful brotherly international order and in which socialist production already so brilliantly successful in Russia will raise living standards to undreamed-of heights. . . .

"Aid, in short, is simply part of a much wider sales talk on communism as a method and goal, a method of raising internal wealth and for sharing it in a cooperative world order."[10]

Miss Ward concludes that the political slant of Communist economic policies—whether of loans or technical assistance or barter or ordinary trade—is their great strength. *"Equally, the lack of any political or ideological framework is the greatest single source of weakness in the aid program undertaken by the West."*

We have already suggested one positive economic approach to the United States investment program. Now let us examine how we can

[10] *Ibid.,* p. 42.

tear down both the negative and positive aspects of the Communist program and then go on to establish a positive program of moral action.

1. The Communist Negative Approach

This approach is to associate United States aid action with a drive toward capitalist imperialism. Why not pull the facts of imperialism off the record and make them abundantly clear? During the period 1945–55 international Communism forcibly extended its dominion over more than 650 million alien people and destroyed or truncated the independence of some fifteen nations. During the same decade free nations were helping eighteen nations, totaling some 650 million—a quarter of the human race—gain independence. The record of Communist colonial imperialism is clear. Count some of the smaller nations that have fallen: Latvia, Estonia, Lithuania, East Germany, Poland, Czechoslovakia, Hungary, Rumania, Bulgaria, Albania, North Korea, and North Viet Nam. By contrast in freedom, security, and strength the Philippines can be used as an example. The Asiatic countries can and do understand this illustration. In recent history the really cruel colonialism has been the colonialism of the Communists, and Russia in particular. No more vivid illustration is required than the Russian slaughter of the Hungarians in the fall of 1956. The minds of all men can understand this cruelty, and the United States must take the initiative in facilitating this understanding.

2. The Communist Positive Approach

This approach as we have seen is to sell the benefits of Communism, which are proclaimed as (a) brilliantly successful socialist production which will raise living standards to undreamed-of heights, and (b) a peaceful brotherly international order.

A. Production

It is a simple matter to compare the Soviet's production success and lack of success by the Russians' own admission with United States success. The lack of Russian achievements in agriculture in particular should be emphasized. On the other hand, we must not dramatize United States success by statistical presentations; we must illustrate it by positive programs of action in the underdeveloped areas.

B. "Brotherhood and Freedom"

The Communists have been in control in Russia for some forty years. They have had ample opportunity to show some advancements toward their "brotherhood and freedom." Mr. Nikita Khrushchev, the head of the Soviet Communist party, in his speech before the twentieth party congress in early 1956 made what has been described as "the most damning indictment of despotism ever made by a despot." This attack, made on Communism under Stalin, showed not only that peaceful "brotherhood and freedom" have not existed under Communism but also that, by the Communists' own admission, they can never exist. The Communists have convicted themselves. Mr. Khrushchev exposed the inability of the Soviet Communist system to liquidate its own evil leadership, Stalin, because it was Stalin who had the supreme power to liquidate others. Mr. Khrushchev recounted the inhuman and extreme abuses that existed under Stalin and showed that the Soviet Communist systems had no checks and balances, no safeguards against even the horrible crimes he described. The system is, as Lenin said, one of "unlimited power, based on force and not on law." In short, it is one of no freedom, no brotherhood, no peace. The Communist parties throughout the world were forced to repudiate publicly the record of Stalin. But it is not just Stalin's record. It is inherent in the Communist system and follows of necessity from the principles of Marx and Lenin. Indeed, Mr. Khrushchev carried on according to that record in Hungary.

Thus, the United States had thrust into its hands a most powerful weapon to use to tear down the *positive* aspects of the Soviet political strategy, which Miss Ward described as "their great strength." In fact the Russians destroyed themselves, and we only have to repeat Mr. Khrushchev's own words. Secretary of State Dulles made a speech about this but what did he say? "Mr. Khrushchev's address . . . should be read and studied throughout the world." The State Department did release the text of the address in advance of its publication by Russia and this may have forced Russia to publish what had previously been a secret document. But the point is that the United States should use every conceivable means to make available in the simplest possible way to *all free people* and all persons under Communist domination the facts of Communist tyranny as related by the head of the Russian Communist party. What better instrument could the United States have to *tear down* the *positive aspects,* the political slant of the Communist policies—the so-called great strength?

3. A United States Positive Program of Moral Action

Barbara Ward tells us that *"the lack of any political or ideological framework is the greatest single source of weakness in the aid program undertaken by the West."*

In a special editorial entitled "Can U.S. Influence Match U.S. Strength?" *Fortune* drew a significant conclusion and raised a fundamental question: "U.S. power in the world has become greater than U.S. knowledge of the world, clearer than U.S. purposes in the world. What needs reappraising, at the bottom, is this: how do we bring American influence up to parity with American strength?"

Throughout our study we have made many suggestions toward the solution of this problem. In this final section we would like to recommend that the answer to Miss Ward's criticism and *Fortune's* question should be, in the United States, making the most of our moral objective of freedom.

At the Bandung Conference of Asian and African leaders in 1955 the attendants heard about freedom from one of their own chiefs of state, much to the surprise of a large number of delegates and United States observers, many of whom had come to hear a protest against the West.

One of the most important dates in freedom's progress occurred on April 19, 1775. On that date the shots at Concord, as Emerson wrote, were heard "round the world." Their echoes still stir men's minds round the world, for at Bandung almost two centuries after Concord and halfway around the globe, President Sukarno of Indonesia opened the Conference with an eloquent tribute to Paul Revere and to the spirit of the American Revolution.

President Eisenhower after reading President Sukarno's tribute to freedom had cause to ask the question: "Why do the musket shots of a few embattled farmers at Concord bridge still ring out in far-off lands?" Then he answered this question in a major address on United States foreign policy, April 21, 1956. Part of this address, which follows, is recommended as the United States positive moral policy in our strategy of security.

I

Why do the musket shots of a few embattled farmers at the Concord bridge still ring out in far-off lands?

The reason is clear.

Concord was far more than a local uprising to redress immediate grievances. The enduring meaning of Concord lies in the ideas that inspired the historic stand there. Concord is the symbol of certain basic convictions about the relationship of man to the state.

Those convictions were found in a firm belief in the spiritual worth of the individual. He must be free to think, to speak, and to worship according to his conscience. He must enjoy equality before the law. He must have a fair chance to develop and use his talents. The purpose of government is to serve its citizens in freedom.

Our forefathers did not claim to have discovered novel principles. They looked on their findings as universal values, the common property of all mankind.

These deep convictions have always guided us as a nation. They have taken deep root elsewhere in the Western world. In the nineteenth century they inspired a great surge of freedom throughout Western Europe and in our own hemisphere.

These ideas of freedom are still the truly revolutionary political principles abroad in the world. They appeal to the timeless aspirations of mankind. In some regions they flourish; in some they are officially outlawed. But everywhere, to some degree, they stir and inspire humanity.

The affairs of men do not stand still. The ideas of freedom will grow in vigor and influence—or they will gradually wither and die. If the area of freedom shrinks, the results for us will be tragic. Only if freedom continues to flourish will man realize the prosperity, the happiness, the enduring peace he seeks.

II

The appeal of the ideas of freedom has been shown dramatically during the past decade. In that time, eighteen nations, totaling some 650,000,000 people—a quarter of the human race—have gained independence.

In manifold ways these nations differ widely from each other and from us. They are the heirs of many ancient cultures and national traditions. All of the great religions of the world are found among them. Their peoples speak in a hundred tongues.

Yet they share in common with all free countries the basic and universal values that inspired our nation's founders.

They believe deeply in the right of self-government.

They believe deeply in the dignity of man.

They aspire to improve the welfare of the individual, as a basic aim of organized society.

The new nations have many of the sensitivities that marked our own early years as a free nation. They are proud of their independence and quick to resent any slight to their sovereignty. Some of them are concerned to avoid involvements with other nations, as we were for many years.

Certainly we Americans should understand and respect these points of view. We must accept the right of each nation to choose its own path to the future.

All of these countries are faced with immense obstacles and difficulties. Freedom and human dignity must rest upon a satisfactory economic base. Yet in many of these new nations, incomes average less than $100 per year. Abject poverty blinds men's eyes to the beauty of freedom's ideals. Hopelessness makes men prey to any promise of a better existence, even the most false and spurious.

Ofttimes the peoples of these countries expected independence itself to produce rapid material progress. Their political leaders are therefore under heavy pressure to find short cuts and quick answers to the problems facing them.

Under these conditions we cannot expect that the vision of a free society will go unchallenged. The Communists, aware of unsatisfied desires for better conditions of life, falsely pretend they can rapidly solve the problems of economic development and industrialization. They hold up the Soviet Union as a model and a guide. But the Communists conceal the terrible human costs that characterize their ruthless system of dictatorship and forced labor.

We have a vital interest in assuring that newly independent nations preserve and consolidate the free institutions of their choice.

The prospects for peace are brightest when enlightened self-governing peoples control the policy of nations. People do not want war. Rulers beyond the reach of popular control are more likely to engage in reckless adventures and to raise the grim threat of war. The spread of freedom enhances the prospect for durable peace.

That prospect would be dimmed or destroyed should freedom be forced into steady retreat. Then the remaining free societies, our own among them, would one day find themselves beleaguered and imperiled. We would face once again the dread prospect of paying in blood for our own survival.

In every corner of the globe it is far less costly to sustain freedom than to recover it when lost.

Moreover, our own well-being is bound up in the well-being of other free nations. We cannot prosper in peace if we are isolated from the rest of the world; if our economy is to continue to flourish and grow, our nation will need more trade, not less. The steady growth of other nations, especially the less developed countries, will create new and growing demands for goods and services. It will produce an environment which will benefit both them and us.

. . . .

III

The ideas of freedom are at work, even where they are officially rejected. As we know, Lenin and his successors, true to Communist doctrine, based the Soviet state on the denial of these ideas. Yet the new Soviet rulers who took over three years ago have had to reckon with the force of these ideas, both at home and abroad.

The situation the new regime inherited from the dead Stalin apparently caused it to reappraise many of his mistakes.

Having lived under his one-man rule, they have espoused the concept of "collective dictatorship." But dictatorship it still remains. They have denounced Stalin for some of the more flagrant excesses of his brutal rule. But the individual citizen still lacks the more elementary safeguards of a free society. The desire for a better life is still being sacrificed to the insatiable demands of the state.

In foreign affairs, the new regime has seemingly moderated the policy of violence and hostility which has caused the free nations to band together to defend their independence and liberties. [This was before the Hungarian slaughter in the fall of 1956.] For the present, at least, it relies more on political and economic means to spread its influence abroad. In the last year, it has embarked upon a campaign of lending and trade agreements directed especially toward the newly-developing countries.

It is still too early to assess in any final way whether the Soviet regime wishes to provide a real basis for stable and enduring relations.

Despite the changes so far, much of Stalin's foreign policy remains unchanged. The major international issues which have troubled the postwar world are still unsolved. More basic changes in Soviet policy will have to take place before the free nations can afford to relax their vigilance.

IV

At Concord, our forebears undertook the struggle for freedom in this country. History has now called us to special tasks for sustaining and advancing this great cause in the world.

As we take stock of our position and of the problems that lie ahead, we must chart our course by three main guide lines:

First: we must maintain a collective shield against aggression to allow the free peoples to seek their valued goals in safety.

. . . .

Our second guideline: within the free community we must be a helpful and considerate partner in creating conditions where freedom will flourish.

. . . .

Our third guideline is this: we must seek, by every peaceful means, to induce the Soviet bloc to correct existing injustices and genuinely to pursue peaceful purposes in its relations with other nations.

. . . .

V

We cannot doubt that the current of world history flows toward freedom. In the long run dictatorship and despotism must give way. We can take courage from that sure knowledge.

But as a wise American, Mr. Justice Holmes, once said: "The inevitable comes to pass through effort." We should take these words to heart in our quest for peace and freedom. These great aspirations of humanity will be brought about—but only be devoted human effort.

Concord is a symbol of the faith, courage and sacrifice on which the victory of freedom depends. We in our day must strive with the same dedication that brought the militia men to the Concord bridge. If we do so, freedom will surely prevail.

CONCLUSION

Thus we have the United States strategy of security: peace through strength—military, economic, and moral. And above all Let Freedom Ring.

This was the recommended United States strategy at the end of the first (1953–56) Eisenhower administration. The first year (1957) of the second Eisenhower administration has been described as one in which the basic problems of world leadership and the future shape of world society were, in the main, secondary in Western minds to local domestic issues. On the other hand, the Soviet's goal of world domination was patiently and consistently sustained. Before the end of 1957, Freedom's Ring was accompanied by the steady beep-beep-beep of Russia's first earth satellite, Sputnik I, and the harsh bark of Sputnik II, as they circled the globe.

What Russia had clearly demonstrated to the world was that she had made a major break-through in one area of most advanced technology. Charles J. V. Murphy noted that a distorted picture of the administration's own reaction to the Soviet feat was registered on the public memory, induced by such remarks as those of Clarence Randall, who called Sputnik "a silly bauble," and of the President himself, who called Sputnik I "one small ball." Perhaps President Eisenhower's reaction was due, in part, to the policy decision made in 1955 to separate the United States earth satellite program from the military missiles program and to put a low priority on the satellite project. President Eisenhower's position was stated to have been that "we" had underestimated the propaganda advantages that Russia would gain but that the United States had lost nothing of its military security. Top-ranking United States scientists were quick to point out to the President that one unexpected military factor was that the Russians, by launching Sputnik, had confirmed the fact that they had developed rocket engines of sufficient power and guidance systems of sufficient control for intercontinental missiles.

Another 1955 policy decision had been made to keep the United States missile program a secret. Thus an uninformed United States public and the free world were abruptly shaken with the Soviet's break-through. However, the President's Science Advisory Commission reported to the President that they were sure that the United States missile position was strong, possibly even stronger, when all the necessary resources were taken into account, than was the Soviet Union's, even though the Russians had manifestly benefited from a much earlier start. The scientists' real concern was that the United States would end up in a disadvantageous technical position five or ten years in the future.

The launching of Sputnik II gave President Eisenhower grave concern. This and subsequent events demonstrated clearly that Russia was ahead of the United States in space satellites and intercontinental ballistic missiles (ICBMs). However, because of the United States possession of the more accurate intermediate range ballistic missiles (IRBMs) and launching sites, and because of the magnitude of other military weapons and forces, the United States military appraisal at the beginning of 1958 was that the balance of power was still in United States hands. In addition, the conclusion was that enough effort could be made to deter a surprise attack by Russia and to keep the military balance from tilting. The President was quite candid in presenting the situation confronting the United States: "I must say to you, in all gravity, that in spite of both the present over-all strength and the forward momentum of our defense, it is entirely possible that in the years ahead we could fall behind. I repeat: we could fall behind—unless we now face up to certain pressing requirements and set out to meet them at once."

The hope was that the launching of the Sputniks and the cry of Mr. Khrushchev's "We shall bury you" would awaken the United States from its lethargy in developing an adequate strategy of security. If this was the result, a satellite circling overhead might prove to be of greatest advantage to the United States and the free world.

Russia had challenged the United States in the field of technology in which we were most able to respond. The recommended strategy at the end of the first Eisenhower administration would have been adequate, had it been employed, and the President's own advice was most appropriate: "When you have worked out a sound plan at a time you were able to be calm, the soundest policy is to stand by it." But one general thesis of this study has been that the dynamic environment of the twentieth century is not designed, as Barbara Ward has stated, "for the static, the stagnant, the complacent, or the smug. It is designed for men who dare greatly and dream greatly and let their work catch up with their dreams." What was needed, as in so many other moments of crisis, was "to make our vision adequate to the needs of our distracted planet and devote to its realization the unequaled energies of free men."

Positive containment, with the United States taking a strong military, economic, and moral initiative against the Soviet Union, should be the continuing strategy of security. This conclusion can be drawn: If positive containment means 20 years of economic strain and sacrifice before it is likely to bring real results, surely this is a short time in the history of a great nation. If it offers no absolute assurance of peace, neither does any alternative. What it does offer is the one chance we have for victory over communism without nuclear war—and the one chance we have to save the freedoms we have known.

There was limited evidence in August, 1958, that the United States was taking a stronger initiative against Communist aggression. After the show of military force by the United States in the Middle East in response to a call for help from the lawful and freely elected government of Lebanon, we formally committed ourselves to the four members of the Baghdad Pact—Great Britain, Iran, Pakistan, and Turkey—who were present at a London meeting, for the military defense of the southern arch of Turkey, Iran, and Pakistan. However, even more important than this additional commitment against "direct aggression" was the inclusion of a pledge against "indirect aggression." This latter was considered to be a new obligation which had not previously been a part of prior treaties and agreements. Yet President Eisenhower in a speech to the General Assembly of the United Nations in New York on August 13, 1958, in referring to the United States responses in the moments of clear danger we have faced since the end of World War II, stated: "A common principle guided the position of the United States on all these occasions. That principle was that aggression, direct or indirect, must be checked before it gathered sufficient momentum to destroy us all—aggressor and defender alike." Thus duly recorded before the United Nations this undefined commitment against "indirect aggression" would be extended to all treaties either by implication or signature.

This clear statement of the pledge against "indirect aggression" broadened the United States policy of containment to include military, economic, and moral. Still required was the development of more positive programs of action by the United States to implement our commitments through the necessary strength. There was justifiable reason to raise the question again as to whether the United States had the strength to defend our three-fold world-wide obligations. One thing was certain, the effort had to be made to develop the strength to cover our commitments, and if our strategy of security was successful, the burden on the United States would become less.

At this point in time one could paraphrase the eloquent declaration of Sir Winston Churchill and again conclude that never in the history of human conflict have so many nations depended for so much upon one.

Bibliography

Natural Resources—Agricultural Resources

"About the Wheat Agreement," *FAO Bulletin*, Food and Agriculture Organization of the United Nations, May–June, 1949, pp. 2–3.

Agricultural Outlook Charts (annual issues to indicate outlook for succeeding year), Agricultural Marketing Service, U.S. Department of Agriculture, Government Printing Office, issues 1952–56.

Agriculture in the World Economy, Food and Agriculture Organization of the United Nations, November, 1955.

Agriculture's Capacity to Produce, Agriculture Information Bulletin No. 88, Bureau of Agricultural Economics, U.S. Department of Agriculture, Government Printing Office, June, 1952.

"Base Book of Textile Statistics," *Textile Organon*, January, 1952, pp. 1–48.

"A Big Bank's Forecast—Boom Will Level Off Soon; More Trouble for Farmers," extracts from the monthly letter of the First City Bank of New York for May, 1955, *U.S. News and World Report*, May 20, 1955, pp. 104 ff.

Black, J. D., "Agriculture in the Nation's Economy," *The American Economic Review*, March, 1956, pp. 1–43.

Centrifugal Sugar World Trade, Foreign Agricultural Service, U.S. Department of Agriculture, August 9, 1956.

Collyer, John L., *The Rubber Outlook and a Study of Cartels and Their Consequences*, B. F. Goodrich Co., July, 1952.

Compilation of Statutes Relating to Soil Conservation, Marketing Quotas and Allotments, Soil Bank, Crop Insurance, Sugar Payments and Quotas, Price Support, Commodity Credit Corporation and Related Studies, Commodity Stabilization Service, U.S. Department of Agriculture, Agricultural Handbook No. 113, Government Printing Office, January 1, 1957.

Cotton Production and Distribution, Bulletin No. 188, U.S. Department of Commerce, Government Printing Office, 1952.

The Cotton Situation, Agricultural Marketing Service, U.S. Department of Agriculture, issues 1952–57.

Davis, John H., *Agricultural Problems and Policies—Particularly Those Relating to International Trade in Cotton*, statement before Thirteenth Plenary Meeting of the International Cotton Advisory Committee, São Paulo, Brazil, June 14, 1954, U.S. Department of Agriculture, 1954.

The Demand and Price Situation, Agricultural Marketing Service, U.S. Department of Agriculture, issues 1952–57.

Dodd, Norris E., *The Dangerous Gap,* address delivered by Director-General, Food and Agriculture Organization of the United Nations, to the Annual Meeting, Federal Reserve Banks, Dallas, Texas, December 8, 1949.

Dodd, Norris E., *The World Food Outlook,* address delivered by Director-General, Food and Agriculture Organization of the United Nations, before a Symposium on World Outlook for Food, Chemical Engineers Club, Washington, D.C., November 9, 1949.

Economic Policy for American Agriculture, statement on national policy by the Research and Policy Committee of the Committee for Economic Development, January, 1956.

Eisenhower, Dwight D., "President's Proposals to Congress for Farm Program," *The Washington Post,* January 12, 1954, p. 10.

"Export of Cotton Under Public Law 480," *Foreign Agriculture Circular,* U.S. Department of Agriculture, August 10, 1956, pp. 1–8.

The Farm Income Situation, Bureau of Agricultural Economics, U.S. Department of Agriculture, issues 1952–57.

Farm Output—Past Changes and Projected Needs, Agriculture Information Bulletin No. 162, U.S. Department of Agriculture, August, 1956.

Farm Products in Foreign Trade, U.S. Department of Agriculture, 1953.

The Fats and Oils Situation, Agricultural Marketing Service, U.S. Department of Agriculture, issues 1952–57.

Fibers—World Fiber Review 1949, FAO Commodity Series Bulletin No. 14, Food and Agriculture Organization of the United Nations, 1949.

"Food Supplies per Person 1947/48 Compared with Prewar (1934–38 = 100)," *FAO Bulletin,* 1948 Conference Issue, November, 1948, p. 12.

"For a Long-Run Answer: Fewer Farmers Instead of Higher Prices," *Business Week,* May 14, 1955, p. 29.

Foreign Agricultural Situation, Chart Books (annual issues to indicate outlook for succeeding year), Foreign Agricultural Service, U.S. Department of Agriculture, Government Printing Office, issues 1951–56.

Foreign Agricultural Trade, Foreign Agricultural Service, U.S. Department of Agriculture, issues 1952–57.

Foreign Agricultural and Trade-Statistical Handbook, Foreign Agricultural Service, U.S. Department of Agriculture, Statistical Bulletin No. 179, Government Printing Office, August, 1956.

Hainsworth, Reginald G., *A Graphic Summary of World Agriculture,* Miscellaneous Publication No. 705, Office of Foreign Agricultural Relations, U.S. Department of Agriculture, Government Printing Office, 1949.

Hines, Joseph W., "Trends in Flue-Cured Tobacco Export Trade," *The Southern Economic Journal,* January, 1952, pp. 384 ff.

Horne, M. K., Jr., *Economic Bases for Market Development Programs: The Case of United States Cotton,* statement before the American Farm Economic Association, Asilomar, California, August 28, 1956, National Cotton Council of America.

Horne, M. K., Jr., *A New Look at the U.S. Rayon Industry,* National Cotton Council of America, September 3, 1953.

Horne, M. K., Jr., *Problems and Opportunities for Cotton,* paper delivered before the Beltwide Cotton Production Conference, Memphis, Tennessee, December 15, 1955, National Cotton Council of America.

Horne, M. K., Jr., *A Realistic Look at the Future of Cotton,* paper delivered before the Seventh Annual Cotton Mechanization Conference, Gadsden, Alabama, October 28, 1953, National Cotton Council of America.

Horne, M. K., Jr., *What Kind of a Future for Cotton?* paper delivered before the Spring Meeting of the Farm Equipment Institute, Atlanta, Georgia, April 23, 1954, National Cotton Council of America.

Horne, M. K., Jr., McCord, Frank A., and Townsend, George, *Price and the Future of U.S. Cotton,* National Cotton Council of America, 1956.

How Is the Wheat Agreement Working? Agricultural Information Bulletin No. 74, U.S. Department of Agriculture, January, 1952.

"Ike's New Headache—$1 Wheat Coming Back?" *U.S. News and World Report,* May 13, 1955, p. 32.

"Imports of Cotton Textiles Spur Drive for Quotas on Japan," *Business Week,* September 22, 1956, pp. 118 ff.

"The International Wheat Agreement of 1949—First Year's Experience," *Foreign Agriculture Circular,* U.S. Department of Agriculture, October 4, 1950.

Johnson, D. Gale, "Competition in Agriculture: Fact or Fiction," *The American Economic Review,* May, 1954, p. 111.

Johnson, D. Gale, *Stabilization of International Commodity Prices,* University of Chicago, Office of Agricultural Economics Research, Paper No. 5911, April, 1954. (Preliminary: Not for publication or quotation.)

Johnson, D. Gale, *Trade and Agriculture,* John Wiley & Sons, Inc., 1950.

Jones, William O., "Current Farm Price-Support Proposals in the United States," Reprinted from *The Journal of Politics,* May, 1951.

Lowenstein, Frank, *The Outlook for Cotton,* statement presented at the 34th Annual Agricultural Outlook Conference, Washington, D.C., U.S. Department of Agriculture, November 29, 1956.

"Major Fibers, World Production and Trade," special feature, *Monthly Bulletin of Agricultural Economics and Statistics,* Food and Agriculture Organization of the United Nations, May, 1953.

Memo, North American edition, Food and Agriculture Organization of the United Nations, April, 1953.

The National Food Situation, Agricultural Marketing Service, U.S. Department of Agriculture, issues 1952–57.

"New 'Parity of Income' Formula to Be Sought," *The Washington Post and Times Herald,* December 25, 1956, p. B-8.

Per Caput Fiber Consumption Levels, FAO Commodity Series, Bulletin No. 21, Supplement No. 1, Food and Agriculture Organization of the United Nations, December, 1952.

Price Programs, U.S. Department of Agriculture, Government Printing Office, April, 1950, revised December, 1953, and January, 1955.

"Price Supports Cut on Unwanted Leaf Types—Demand for Filtered Cigarettes Slices Props," *Durham (N.C.) Morning Herald,* December 19, 1956, p. 1.

Published Information on Agriculture in Foreign Countries, U.S. Department of Agriculture, January, 1952.

"Record World Centrifugal Sugar Crop Estimated," *Foreign Agriculture Circular*, U.S. Department of Agriculture, November 30, 1956.

Report of the Rice Study Group, Food and Agriculture Organization of the United Nations, July, 1947.

Rhodesian Tobacco—What It Means to the American Farmer, Competition Study, Foreign Agriculture Report No. 94, U.S. Department of Agriculture, November, 1956.

The Rice Bulletin, Food and Agriculture Organization of the United Nations, March, 1949.

The Rice Situation, Agricultural Marketing Service, U.S. Department of Agriculture, issues 1952–56.

Rowe, J. Z., "Trends in Cotton Production," *Monthly Business Review*, Federal Reserve Bank of Dallas, February 1, 1956, pp. 17–23.

Rubber, annual reports by the Secretary of Commerce, U.S. Department of Commerce, issues 1949–55.

Second World Food Survey, Food and Agriculture Organization of the United Nations, 1952.

The State of Food and Agriculture, Food and Agriculture Organization of the United Nations, issues 1952–56.

Sugar, International Federation of Agricultural Producers, Commodity Memorandum, August, 1952.

Sugar Facts and Figures, United States Cuban Sugar Council, 1948.

The Sugar Situation, Agricultural Marketing Service, U.S. Department of Agriculture, annual issues 1952–57.

Swerling, B. C., *International Control of Sugar, 1918–1941*, Stanford University, Food Research Institute, Commodity Policy Studies No. 7, 1949.

Textile Organon, published by Textile Economics Bureau, Inc., monthly issues January, 1952, to date.

Thomas, George W., "Key to Bigger Tobacco Exports," reprinted from *Foreign Agriculture*, July, 1954, pp. 133–136.

The Tobacco Situation, Agricultural Marketing Service, U.S. Department of Agriculture, issues 1952–57.

Tolley, H. R., *Can We Use Our Full Productive Resources for Food?* address at National Farm Institute by Director of Economics and Statistics, Food and Agriculture Organization of the United Nations, Des Moines, Iowa, February 19, 1949.

"United States Cotton Exports—Review and Outlook," *Foreign Agriculture Circular*, U.S. Department of Agriculture, November 28, 1956, pp. 1–6.

"United States Import Quotas and Duties on Cotton and Cotton Waste and Imports Under Quotas," *Foreign Agriculture Circular*, U.S. Department of Agriculture, November 30, 1955, pp. 1–10.

The United States Sugar Program, Agriculture Information Bulletin No. 111, U.S. Department of Agriculture, July, 1953.

Van Royen, William, *The Agricultural Resources of the World*, Prentice-Hall, Inc., 1954.

"What Farmers Voted For" (wheat controls), *U.S. News and World Report,* July 8, 1955, p. 60.

Wheat, Food and Agriculture Commodity Series, Food and Agriculture Organization of the United Nations, issues 1947 and 1948.

The Wheat Situation, Agricultural Marketing Service, U.S. Department of Agriculture, issues 1952–57.

The Wool Situation, Agricultural Marketing Service, U.S. Department of Agriculture, issues 1952–57.

"A Workable Basis for Farm Policy," *Business Week,* May 6, 1950, p. 132.

"World Cotton Exports Holding Last Year's Level," *Foreign Agriculture Circular,* U.S. Department of Agriculture, January 26, 1956, pp. 1–22.

"World Cotton Exports Near Postwar Record Last Year," *Foreign Agriculture Circular,* U.S. Department of Agriculture, December 26, 1956, pp. 1–2.

"World Cotton Supply and Demand," *Foreign Agriculture Circular,* U.S. Department of Agriculture, November 29, 1956.

World Fiber Survey, Food and Agriculture Organization of the United Nations, 1947.

World Fibers Review 1948, FAO Commodity Series No. 9, Food and Agriculture Organization of the United Nations, 1948.

"World Food Situation," *Foreign Agriculture Circular,* U.S. Department of Agriculture, issues 1948–January 30, 1953.

World Food Survey, Food and Agriculture Organization of the United Nations, 1946.

World Producing More Food Over-All, but Average Diet in Deficit Countries Now Lower Than Before the War, FAO Reports, Food and Agriculture Organization of the United Nations, June 16, 1949.

"The World Sugar Balance," *Foreign Agriculture Circular,* U.S. Department of Agriculture, October 14, 1953.

"World Sugar Pact Is Set for Signing," *The New York Times,* August 23, 1953, p. 40.

"World Sugar Production—Prewar, World War II, and Postwar, by Areas," *The World Sugar Situation,* U.S. Department of Agriculture, December, 1950, p. 1.

World Tobacco Analysis, Foreign Agricultural Service, U.S. Department of Agriculture, issues for 1956.

Natural Resources—Energy and Material Resources

"ABC's of Middle-East Oil," *U.S. News and World Report,* October 12, 1956, pp. 62 ff.

"Allocating the World's Materials," *Illinois Business Review,* Bureau of Economic and Business Research, University of Illinois, January, 1952, pp. 2 and 6.

"Alloys: We Don't Have Enough," *Business Week,* March 22, 1952, pp. 56 ff.

"Aluminum Demand Up 100% by 1965 . . . Where All the Metal Is Going," *Business Week,* March 30, 1957, pp. 190 ff.

"Aluminum's Third Round Is On," *Business Week*, August 13, 1955, pp. 32 ff.

Arn, Edward F., "Effect on Independent Producer of Phillips Decision and FPC Orders 174 and 174-A," *The Interstate Oil Compact Quarterly Bulletin*, September, 1954, pp. 5–8.

Atomic Energy, National Industrial Conference Board, October 14, 1954.

"Atomic Energy, 1945–1951," *Business Week*, July 28, 1951, pp. 99 ff.

Atomic Energy Review, Harris, Upham and Co., issues for March and November, 1956, and March, 1957.

"Atoms and Automation," *Saturday Review*, Special Issue, January 22, 1955.

Atoms and Investors, Merrill Lynch, Pierce, Fenner and Beane, 1955.

"Atoms-for-Peace Conference Puts Its Main Emphasis on Power," *The New York Times*, August 14, 1955, sec. 4, p. 5.

"A Basic Industry Solves a Basic Problem," *Business Week*, February 11, 1950, pp. 19 ff.

Bituminous Coal and Lignite in 1952, Mineral Industry Surveys, Bureau of Mines, U.S. Department of the Interior, October 13, 1953.

Bituminous Coal Trends, National Coal Association, 1956. (Also prior editions from 1951, when publication was known as *Bituminous Coal Annual*.)

"Can America Meet Europe's Oil Needs?" *U.S. News and World Report*, November 16, 1956, pp. 76 ff.

"Canada Iron Ores Stage a Spurt," *Business Week*, March 30, 1957, pp. 68 ff.

"Canada's Arvida Works," *Esso Oilways*, Vol. III, No. 4, 1950, pp. 1–6, Esso Standard Oil Co. (a special issue on aluminum).

"Cerro Bolivar Ore Is Due in January," *The New York Times*, October 25, 1953, sec. 3, pp. 1 ff.

Charting Steel's Progress—A Graphic Facts Book on the Iron and Steel Industry, American Iron and Steel Institute, 1955 and 1956 editions.

"Coal for the Future," *Business Week*, April 2, 1949, pp. 41–46.

Coal Resources of the United States, Geological Survey Circular no. 293, U.S. Department of the Interior, October 1, 1953.

"Coal Turns the Corner—The Question Is: How Soon?" *Business Week*, July 9, 1955, pp. 81 ff.

Cowan, Donald R. G., *More Capital Equipment, Coal's Foremost Economic Need*, National Coal Association, July, 1948.

Critical Materials, Factors Affecting Self-Sufficiency Within Nations of the Western Hemisphere, Senate Document No. 83, 84th Congress, 1956.

Crude Petroleum and Petroleum Products, Mineral Industry Surveys Series, Bureau of Mines, U.S. Department of the Interior. (Last issue used December 27, 1956.)

Davis, Kenneth W., Warren, Shields, and Cisler, Walker L., *Some Peaceful Uses of Atomic Energy*, Proceedings of the Atlanta Session of the National Academy of Economics and Political Science, December 29, 1955.

"Disputes Hobble the Oil Lift," *Business Week*, February 2, 1957, p. 29.

Domestic Problems of Non-Fuel Minerals, Section IV, Mid-Century Conference on Resources for the Future, Washington, D.C., December 2–4, 1953, Resources for the Future, Inc.

Effects of Foreign Oil Imports on Independent Domestic Producers, Hearings before the Select Committee on Small Business, House of Representatives, 81st Congress, 1st Session, pursuant to H. Res. 22, Government Printing Office, Part I, 1949; Part II and Part III, 1950.

Effects of Foreign Oil Imports on Independent Domestic Producers, report of the Subcommittee on Oil Imports to the Select Committee on Small Business, House of Representatives, 81st Congress, 2nd Session, pursuant to H. Res. 22, Government Printing Office, 1950.

Energy Resource Problems, Section V, Mid-Century Conference on Resources for the Future, Washington, D.C., December 2–4, 1953, Resources for the Future, Inc.

Engineering and Mining Journal, Annual Survey and Outlook, February, 1957.

"Equipment Makers Vie for Atoms-for-Peace Customers," *Business Week,* July 9, 1955, pp. 86 ff.

Estes, B. E., "Steel: What Will Demand Output Be During 1955–1959?" technical paper from United States Steel Corporation, No. 23, reprinted from *The Iron Age,* April 8, 1954.

"Euratom Gets U.S. Blessing," *Business Week,* February 16, 1957, p. 148.

The European Coal and Steel Community, Studies in Business and Economics, Bureau of Business and Economic Research, University of Maryland, Part 1, December, 1955, and Part 2, June, 1956.

"Exploration Widens the U.S. Uranium Ore Belt," *Business Week,* March 3, 1951, pp. 102 ff.

Facts About Oil Imports, Standard Oil Co. (N.J.), April 15, 1953.

Facts on the Importation of Oil into the United States and the Policy of Standard Oil Company (New Jersey) on Oil Imports, Standard Oil Co. (N.J.), 1949.

A Factual Study of U.S. Foreign Trade in Petroleum, Independent Petroleum Association of America, 1953.

Fairless, Benjamin F., *Steel's Depreciation Problems,* presented at the 64th General Meeting of the American Iron and Steel Institute, New York City, May 24, 1956.

"15 Oil Companies to Form Pool Under U.S. Plan to Aid Europe," *The Washington Post and Times Herald,* December 1, 1956, p. A-4.

"Firms to Start Oil Lift, Get Antitrust Immunity," *The Washington Post and Times Herald,* December 12, 1956, p. A-4.

"For Gas, Freedom—With Strings," *Business Week,* February 11, 1956, p. 34.

Foreign Oil and Imports, American Petroleum Institute, 1953.

"Gas Frets over FPC," *Business Week,* March 23, 1957, pp. 48 ff.

Goormaghtigh, John, "European Coal and Steel Community," *International Conciliation,* Carnegie Endowment for International Peace, complete issue May, 1955.

Harris, Herbert, "Copper: Less Pinch in '56," *Nation's Business,* July, 1955, pp. 58–61.

Harris, James C. O., "Steel," a chapter from *Mineral Facts and Problems,* Preprint from Bulletin 556, Bureau of Mines, U.S. Department of the Interior, Government Printing Office, 1955.

Hedlund, C. J., *Energy Sources,* paper delivered at Joint Educational-In-

dustrial Conference, August 23–September 3, 1948, Standard Oil Co. (N.J.),
    August 24, 1948.

Holliday, R. W., "Iron," a chapter from *Mineral Facts and Problems*, Pre-
    print from Bulletin 556, Bureau of Mines, U.S. Department of the Interior,
    Government Printing Office, 1955.

Hoover, Herbert, Jr., "Petroleum Imports," *The Oil and Gas Compact Bul-
    letin*, June, 1956, p. 15.

"How Much Foreign Oil?—Another Oilman Goes East," *Business Week*, Feb-
    ruary 12, 1955, pp. 158 ff.

The Impact of Imports on Conservation, addresses presented at the 1953
    Spring Meeting, Interstate Oil Compact Commission, New Orleans, Louisi-
    ana, April 24–25, 1953.

The Independent Monthly, Petroleum Association of America, issues 1952–56.

"An Industry with a Boom and Problem—The Facts About Natural Gas,"
    U.S. News and World Report, May 6, 1955, pp. 94 ff.

International Iron and Steel, Quarterly Industry Report, Business and De-
    fense Services Administration, U.S. Department of Commerce, Vol. 1, No. 1,
    March, 1955, through Vol. 2, No. 3, March, 1957.

The International Petroleum Cartel, staff report to the Federal Trade Com-
    mission Submitted to the Subcommittee on Monopoly of the Select Com-
    mittee on Small Business, United States Senate, 82nd Congress, 2nd Ses-
    sion, Government Printing Office, 1952.

The Interstate Compact to Conserve Oil and Gas, A Summary of Its Or-
    ganization, Background, Purposes, and Functions, Interstate Oil Compact
    Commission, 1947.

Investigation of National Resources, Hearings before a Subcommittee of the
    Committee on Public Lands, United States Senate, 80th Congress, 1st Ses-
    sion, on Investigation of the Factors Affecting Minerals, Fuels, Forestry and
    Reclamation Projects, May 1, 16 and 20, 1947, Government Printing Of-
    fice, 1947, pp. 177–178.

Investment Patterns in the World Petroleum Industry, Chase Manhattan Bank,
    December, 1956.

"Iranian Oil Pact: A Two-Way Door," *Business Week*, August 7, 1954, pp.
    26–27.

"Iron Ore Dilemma," *Fortune*, December, 1945, pp. 129 ff.

Kayser, Paul, "Problems of Marketing Residue Gas as Complicated by the
    Phillips Decision," *The Interstate Oil Compact Quarterly Bulletin*, Septem-
    ber, 1954, pp. 13–17.

Kurtz, H. F., and Blue, D. D., "Aluminum and Bauxite," a chapter from
    Mineral Facts and Problems, Preprint from Bulletin 556, Bureau of Mines,
    U.S. Department of the Interior, Government Printing Office, 1955.

"Laying Steel to Bring Out Labrador's Ore," *Business Week*, July 18, 1953,
    pp. 82 ff.

Lippert, T. W., *Cerro Bolivar—Saga of an Iron Ore Crisis Averted*, United
    States Steel Corp., 1950.

McCune, Francis K., *The Race for Atomic Power*, General Electric Co., March
    23, 1955.

Metals of the Future, a series of articles describing the approaching revolution in the metals industry, Harris, Upham and Co., January, 1955.

"Metals for a New Kind of World," *Business Week,* March 1, 1952, pp. 19–20.

"Metals Non-Ferrous," *Standard and Poor's Industry Surveys,* August 23, 1956.

Meyer, Helena M., "Copper," a chapter from *Mineral Facts and Problems,* Preprint from Bulletin 556, Bureau of Mines, U.S. Department of the Interior, Government Printing Office, 1955.

"Mineral Position of the United States," by the staffs of the Bureau of Mines and Geological Survey, *Investigation of National Resources,* United States Senate, 80th Congress, 1st Session, Government Printing Office, 1947, pp. 165–310.

Mining Congress Journal, Annual Review, February, 1957.

"More Aluminum, More Steel Coming," *Business Week,* December 2, 1950, p. 25.

Mouzon, Olin T., *U.S. Petroleum Import Policy,* Trade Policy Study, a report for the Public Advisory Board for Mutual Security, Executive Office of the President, December 19, 1952.

Mouzon, Olin T., *The United States Petroleum Trade Policy,* a detailed study made for the Public Advisory Board for Mutual Security, Executive Office of the President, November, 1952.

A National Oil and Gas Policy, Independent Petroleum Association of America, 1947.

A National Oil Policy for the United States, National Petroleum Council, January, 1949.

"New Link in Europe" (Moselle Canal), *Business Week,* October 20, 1956, pp. 78 ff.

Oil and the Atom, Standard Oil Co. (N.J.), 1955.

"The Oil Shortage," *Time,* February 11, 1957, p. 84.

"One More 'Scarcity' Ends for U.S. Industry," *U.S. News and World Report,* June 17, 1955, pp. 90 ff. (special report).

"Ore Companies Look Ahead to Ample Supplies," *Business Week,* January 26, 1952, pp. 124–127.

Packard, William V., "New Iron in the Fire," *Steelways,* April, 1957, American Iron and Steel Institute. (A chapter in the story of taconite. Earlier chapters appeared in *Steelways* in the following issues: January, 1948; March, 1951; October, 1953; December, 1953; and December, 1956.)

Patterson, Ernest F., "Effects of Venezuelan Iron Ore on the United States Steel Industry and the Venezuelan Economy," *University of Alabama Business News,* January 15, 1952, pp. 1 ff.

Peaceful Uses of Atomic Energy, report of the Panel on the Impact of the Peaceful Uses of Atomic Energy to the Joint Committee on Atomic Energy, 84th Congress, 2nd Session, 1956.

Pehrson, Elmer W., "The Mineral Position of the United States and the Outlook for the Future," reprint from *Mining and Metallurgy,* April, 1945.

Petroleum Facts and Figures, American Petroleum Institute, 9th ed., 1950; 10th ed., 1952; 11th ed., 1954; 12th ed., 1956.

Petroleum Industry 1955, Annual Financial Analysis, Chase Manhattan Bank, July, 1956.

Petroleum Productive Capacity, a report of the National Petroleum Council, 1952.

"Petroleum Supply and Demand," reports of the Advisory Committee for Supply and Demand of the Independent Petroleum Association of America, *Oil and Gas Compact Bulletin*, 1952–56.

Petroleum in the Western Hemisphere, report of the Western Hemisphere Oil Study Committee, Independent Petroleum Association of America, October, 1952.

"Phillips Petroleum Co. v. State of Wisconsin *et al.;* State of Texas *et al.* v. State of Wisconsin *et al.;* Federal Power Commission v. State of Wisconsin *et al.*, Argued April 6, 7, 1954; Decided June 7, 1954, 347 U.S. 672," *Supreme Court Reporter*, West Publishing Co., 1954, Vol. 74, pp. 794–807.

Policy Declarations on Natural Resources 1955, Chamber of Commerce of the United States, 1955.

Position of National Coal Association with Respect to Proposed Trade Agreement Negotiations Between the United States and Venezeula, United States Tariff Commission, Committee for Reciprocity Information, 1951.

"Producers Await Gas Decision," *Business Week*, May 21, 1955, pp. 129–131.

Putting the Atom to Work, General Electric Co., 1955.

"Putting Hydrogen to Work in Steelmaking—Getting More Iron Out of Ore," *Business Week*, March 31, 1956, pp. 79 ff.

"Quebec—Labrador: Ore and a Frontier's Hopes," *Business Week*, July 31, 1954, pp. 78 ff.

"A Race for Atom Markets," *U.S. News and World Report*, July 1, 1955, pp. 53–54.

Radiation Safety and Major Activities in the Atomic Energy Programs, U.S. Atomic Energy Commission, January, 1957.

Reply to the Staff Report of the Federal Trade Commission on the International Petroleum Cartel, Interstate Oil and Gas Compact Commission, December 6, 1952.

Report, Atomic Industrial Forum, Inc., May, 1955.

A *Report of the Committee on Petroleum Imports*, National Petroleum Council, January 26, 1950.

"Report on Copper Industry by the Federal Trade Commission," Reprinted from *American Metal Market*, March 22, 1947, pp. 1–20.

Report on Energy Supplies and Resources Policy, Executive Office of the President, February 26, 1955.

Report to the President under Section 3 of the Trade Agreements Extension Act of 1951 (P.L. 50, 82nd Congress), with respect to certain petroleum products included in the President's List of August 29, 1951, United States Tariff Commission, 1952.

Report of the President's Cabinet Committee on Minerals Policy, Executive Office of the President, November 30, 1954.

Report on the Situation of the Community at the Beginning of 1954, The High Authority, European Coal and Steel Community, January 1, 1954.

"Rerouting World's Oil Flow," *Business Week*, September 15, 1956, p. 74.

"Resources for the Future," *Business Week*, December 12, 1953, p. 188.

"St. Lawrence Seaway," *Time*, June 6, 1956, pp. 40–45.

"The St. Lawrence Seaway and Power Project and National Security" (no publisher, no date), reproduced from typewritten copy, 10 pp. Personal library of Olin T. Mouzon, Chapel Hill, North Carolina.

The Schuman Plan Constituting a European Coal and Steel Community, Draft Treaty Constituting the European Coal and Steel Community and Draft Convention Containing the Transitional Provisions, U.S. Department of State, Government Printing Office, April, 1951.

"A Senate Probe for Lobbies" (gas), *Business Week*, February 25, 1956, pp. 30 ff.

Shuman, Allan, and Macmurphy, Allen B., *Facts About Coal*, Bureau of Mines, U.S. Department of the Interior, Government Printing Office, 1950.

Slater, J.E., *Oil and World Trade*, remarks made at the Virginia World Trade Conference, Creole Petroleum Corp., October 5, 1956.

"Spectacular Progress Makes Natural Gas Nation's Sixth Industry," *The New York Times*, July 17, 1955, sec. 3, pp. 1 and 7.

Steel Facts, American Iron and Steel Institute, No. 108, June, 1951, through No. 143, April, 1957.

"Steel Industry's Hope—Big New Source of Ore," *Business Week*, September 11, 1948, pp. 40 ff. (a *Business Week* Report.)

Stockpile Report to the Congress, July–December 1955, Executive Office of the President, Office of Defense Mobilization, March, 1956.

"Strategic Stockpile—Is It for Security or Subsidy?" *Time*, October 4, 1954, p. 90.

Survey of World Iron Ore Resources—Occurrence, Appraisal and Use, Department of Economic and Social Affairs of the United Nations, 1955.

"Tanker Shipping and Oil Supplies," *Index, Svenska Handelsbanken, Monthly Economic Review*, Stockholm, January, 1957.

"Three Reasons Why Germany Is Important to the Anti-Communist Nations of the West," *The New York Times*, February 3, 1952, sec. 5, p. 5.

To British Columbia for Aluminum—History's Largest Privately-Financed Aluminum Project, Aluminum Company of Canada (Alcan), J. Walter Thompson Co., 1954.

"Twice As Much Aluminum," *Business Week*, October 21, 1950, pp. 25–26.

"Two New Steelmaking Processes—How Steel May Invent a Way Out of Its Capacity Pinch," *Business Week*, November 26, 1955, pp. 58 ff.

U.S. Crude Petroleum Reserve Productive Capacity, National Petroleum Council, January 26, 1950.

"U.S. Iron Ore Reserves Low," *Business Week*, April 19, 1947, pp. 20 ff. (special report to executives).

"U.S. Oil Imports," Facts and Forecasts for the Independent Oil Producer by the Independent Petroleum Association of America, *The Independent Monthly*, August, 1956, p. 45.

"U.S. Running Short of Water—Enough for Power, but Growing Problems for Other Uses," *U.S. News and World Report*, July 8, 1955, pp. 38 ff.

"U.S. Steel's Fairless Works: Showcase of an Industry," *Business Week*, January 23, 1954, pp. 60 ff.

"U.S. Strategic Materials Stockpile," *International Financial News Survey*, International Monetary Fund, December 10, 1954, p. 189.

Van Royen, William, and Bowles, Oliver, *The Mineral Resources of the World*, Prentice-Hall, Inc., 1952.

A Water Policy for the American People, Summary of Recommendations, from the report of the President's Water Resources Policy Commission, Government Printing Office, 1950.

A Water Policy for the American People, The President's Water Resources Policy Commission, Vol. 1, *General Report;* Vol. 2, *Ten Rivers in America's Future;* Vol. 3, *Water Resources Law*, Government Printing Office, 1950.

Water Resources and Power Report to Congress, Commission on Organization of the Executive Branch of Government, Government Printing Office, June, 1955.

"Will Lack of Minerals Strangle U.S. in War?" extracts from the official text of the report on "Accessibility of Strategic and Critical Materials," issued by the Minerals Subcommittee of the Senate Committee on Interior and Insular Affairs, *U.S. News and World Report*, July 9, 1954, pp. 106–109.

Wilson, Robert E., "Atoms in Homes: How Soon?" *U.S. News and World Report*, December 17, 1954, pp. 116–118.

"The World Oil Picture—As the New Iranian Government Talks of Re-Entering the Market," *The New York Times*, September 13, 1953, sec. 5, p. 5.

"World Oil Picture—Trade, Supplies and the Impact of Suez," *The New York Times*, August 19, 1956, News of the Week section.

"World's Steel Makers Have Doubled Their Output . . . Plan to Add 100-Million Tons of Capacity by 1960," *Business Week*, September 15, 1956, pp. 30 ff.

Capital Resources—Man-Made Facilities

Allen, George V., "The President's Point Four Program," *The Department of State Bulletin*, July 4, 1949, pp. 862–868.

American Private Enterprise, Foreign Economic Development, and the Aid Program, a study prepared at the request of the Special Committee to Study the Foreign Aid Program by the American Enterprise Association, Inc., No. 7, Special Committee to Study the Foreign Aid Program, United States Senate, 1957.

"Developed and Undeveloped Countries in International Economics," *Studies in Business and Economics*, University of Maryland, June, 1953.

Economic Development Abroad and the Role of American Foreign Investment, Committee for Economic Development, February, 1956.

The Geographic Distribution of Manufacturing Facilities, War Production Board, June, 1945.

"Industrial Dispersal," *Time*, June 27, 1955, p. 80.

Mouzon, Olin T., "The Industrial Role of North Carolina and the South in National Defense," radio address, Chapel Hill, North Carolina, 1941.

National Resources and Foreign Aid, report of J. A. Krug, Secretary of the Interior, Government Printing Office, October 9, 1947.

National Security Factors in Industrial Location, National Security Resources Board, 1948.

The Need for Industrial Dispersal, materials prepared for the Joint Committee on the Economic Report, Senate Document No. 55, 82nd Congress, 1st Session, Government Printing Office, 1951.

A New Emphasis on Economic Development Abroad, a report to the President of the United States, International Development Advisory Board, 1957.

"Now It's Official—Foreign Aid Is Here to Stay," *U.S. News and World Report,* March 15, 1957, pp. 106 ff.

"Now—Permanent Foreign Aid," *Business Week,* April 30, 1955, p. 32.

"Now There's a New Kind of Foreign Aid," *U.S. News and World Report,* December 21, 1956, p. 83.

The Objectives of United States Economic Assistance Programs, a study prepared at the request of the Special Committee to Study the Foreign Aid Program by the Center for International Studies, Massachusetts Institute of Technology, No. 1, Special Committee to Study the Foreign Aid Program, United States Senate, 1957.

Obstacles to Direct Foreign Investment, National Industrial Conference Board, 1951.

"The Pace Grows Faster," *Business Week,* November 12, 1955, pp. 27–29.

Pacific Coast Conference on Private Investment in International Development, San Francisco, September 24–25, 1952, International Development Advisory Board, 1952.

Point Four, Cooperative Program for Aid in the Development of Economically Underdeveloped Areas, U.S. Department of State, 1950.

Production Capacity, A Military Reserve, a report to the Director of Defense Mobilization by the Advisory Committee on Production Equipment, January, 1953.

Report to the President by the President's Citizen Advisers on the Mutual Security Program, Government Printing Office, 1957.

The Role of Foreign Aid in the Development of Other Countries, a study prepared at the request of the Special Committee to Study the Foreign Aid Program by the Research Center in Economic Development and Cultural Change of the University of Chicago, No. 3, Special Committee to Study the Foreign Aid Program, United States Senate, 1957.

"U.S. Aid Reappraised in Congress," *The New York Times,* July 15, 1956, sec. 5, p. 5.

Wolf, Charles, Jr., and Sufrin, Sidney C., *Capital Formation and Foreign Investment in Underdeveloped Areas,* Syracuse University Press, 1955.

Human Resources—Manpower

"A Bonanza for Industry—Babies," *U.S. News and World Report,* January 4, 1957, pp. 32–34.

"A Boom in People Too," U.S. News and World Report, January 6, 1956, p. 48.

Burgess, Robert W., Population Projections to 1975, introductory remarks as a member of the Panel on Population Problems, 40th Anniversary Meetings of the National Industrial Conference Board, May 17, 1956, Bureau of the Census, U.S. Department of Commerce, 1956.

Current Population Report, Series P-25, No. 123, Bureau of the Census, U.S. Department of Commerce, October, 1955.

Dargusch, Carlton S., The Russian-American Race for Technological Dominance, talk before the Council on World Affairs, Cleveland, Ohio, April 6, 1956.

Davis, Joseph, "Our Changed Population Outlook and Its Significance," The American Economic Review, June, 1952, pp. 304–325.

Defense Mobilization, report to the President by the Director of the Office of Defense Mobilization, October 1, 1953.

"Eat Hearty" (Neo-Malthusians), Time, November 8, 1948, pp. 27–31.

Ginzberg, Eli, et al., Human Resources and National Security, National Academy of Economics and Political Science, Series No. 10, 1955.

Hyatt, Paul K., World Population and Future Resources, The American Book Company, 1952.

Manpower Curriculum, Unit II, Economic Mobilization Course, September–November, 1955, Industrial College of the Armed Forces, 1955–56.

Manpower for Defense, policies and statements of the Office of Defense Mobilization, Government Printing Office, 1953.

Manpower: The Nation's First Resource, report of the National Planning Association Special Committee on Manpower Policy, Pamphlet No. 83, 1953.

Osborn, Fairfield, Our Plundered Planet, Little, Brown and Company, 1948.

Prochnow, Herbert, "The Essentials of Economic Growth," The Department of State Bulletin, March 26, 1956, pp. 530–531.

Thompson, Warren S., Plenty of People, The Ronald Press Company, 1948.

Vogt, William, Road to Survival, W. Sloane Associates, 1948.

Policy and Strategy of Security

Acheson, Dean, The Strategy of Freedom, address to the National Council of Churches of Christ, Department of State Publication 4034, General Foreign Policy Series 39, December, 1950.

Acheson, Dean, "To Meet the Shifting Soviet Offensive," The New York Times Magazine, April 15, 1956, pp. 11 ff.

Adams, James Truslow, The March of Democracy from Civil War to World Power, Charles Scribner's Sons, 1933.

"America's New Strategic Situation," Fortune, August, 1954, p. 70.

Banse, Ewald, Germany Prepares for War, Harcourt, Brace and Company, 1934.

"Battle of Pentagon over Strategy of Future," The New York Times, May 27, 1956, sec. 4, p. 1.

Boggs, S. Whittemore, "Global Relations of the United States," reprint from

The Department of State Bulletin, June 14, 1954, Department of State Publication 5536, General Policy Series 911, Government Printing Office, 1954.

Broek, Jan O. M., "The German School of Political Geography," *Global Politics,* University of California Press, 1944.

"Can U.S. Influence Match U.S. Strength?" *Fortune,* August, 1954, p. 67.

Churchill, Winston, "Peace Rests upon Strength," *Vital Speeches,* November 1, 1948, pp. 44–46.

Churchill, Winston, "United We Stand," *Vital Speeches,* April 1, 1949, pp. 380–384.

"The Colombo Plan: New Promise for Asia," *The Department of State Bulletin,* September 22, 1952, pp. 441–448.

"Coming Changes in Arms Program," *U.S. News and World Report,* December 26, 1952, pp. 11–13.

The Council of Europe and the Schuman Plan, Council of Europe, Directorate of Information, Strasbourg, 1952.

"The Crisis in the Cold War," *Fortune,* June, 1955, p. 96.

Davenport, Russell W., "The Real Power Behind Communism," *Fortune,* April, 1955, pp. 154 ff. (Derived from the book, *The Dignity of Man.*)

Dorpalen, Andreas, *The World of General Haushofer,* Farrar and Rinehart, Inc., 1942.

Dulles, John Foster, *The Challenge to Freedom,* U.S. Department of State, Public Services Division S, No. 16, May 15, 1954.

Dulles, John Foster, "For a World in Crisis—This Is Basic U.S. Policy," unofficial summary of an address by Secretary of State John Foster Dulles to the North Atlantic Treaty Council in Paris on December 11, 1956, *U.S. News and World Report,* December 21, 1956, pp. 78 ff.

"Dulles Explains U.S. Foreign Policy," *U.S. News and World Report,* March 26, 1954, pp. 74 ff. Text of an article prepared by Secretary of State John Foster Dulles for the April issue of the magazine *Foreign Affairs.*

"Dulles Reveals Policy on World for U.S.," testimony of new Secretary of State at Senate hearing, *U.S. News and World Report,* January 23, 1953, pp. 100 ff.

The Economics of National Defense, Fifth Annual Report to the President by the Council of Economic Advisers, Government Printing Office, 1950.

"Egypt's Economy—Key Factor in High Dam Decision," *The New York Times,* July 29, 1956, News of the Week section.

Eisenhower, Dwight D., "Foreign Policy," major address to the American Society of Newspaper Editors, *The New York Times,* April 22, 1956, p. 28.

Eisenhower, Dwight D., "Recommendations Concerning U.S. Foreign Economic Policy," message to Congress on March 30, 1954, *The Department of State Bulletin,* April 19, 1954, pp. 602–607.

Eisenhower, Dwight D., "Report to the People of the Nation on Developments in Eastern Europe and the Middle East," text of President's speech, *The Washington Post and Times Herald,* November 1, 1956, p. A-18.

Eisenhower, Dwight D., "Text of Eisenhower's Address to Congress on Mideast Proposals," *The New York Times,* January 6, 1957, p. 34.

Eisenhower, Dwight D., "U.S. Policy Declaration on Western European Union," *The Department of State Bulletin*, March 21, 1955, p. 464.

"Eisenhower's Four Years—An Analysis of Defense Policies in a Changing Era of Nuclear Arms," eighth in a series of articles analyzing the record of the Eisenhower administration at the start of his second presidential campaign, *The New York Times*, July 29, 1956, pp. 1 and 53.

"Excerpts from Army Staff Paper Asking Basic Change in Military Set-Up," *The New York Times*, June 24, 1956, p. 46.

Expanding World Trade: United States Policy and Program, Department of State Publication 4032, Commercial Policy Series 133, January, 1951.

"Foreign Economic Policy: The Big Thaw," *Fortune*, April, 1955, p. 104.

In Quest of Peace and Security: Selected Documents on American Foreign Policy, 1941–1951, Department of State Publication 4245, General Foreign Policy Series 53, Government Printing Office, 1951.

"Is U.S. Spread Too Thin?" *U.S. News and World Report*, August 28, 1953, pp. 21 ff.

Israel, Department of State Publication 5674, Near and Middle Eastern Series 17, Government Printing Office, December, 1954.

Jordan, Department of State Publication 5907, Near and Middle Eastern Series 19, Government Printing Office, September, 1955.

" 'Keep Out' Sign in Middle East," *Business Week*, January 5, 1957, p. 31.

Kennan, George F., *American Diplomacy, 1900–1950*, The New American Library, 1952.

Lincoln, George A., *Economics of National Security*, Prentice-Hall, Inc., 1954.

Lippmann, Walter, *U.S. Foreign Policy*, Little, Brown and Company, 1943.

Mackinder, Halford J., *Democratic Ideals and Reality—A Study in the Politics of Reconstruction*, Constable and Co., Ltd., 1919.

Mackinder, Halford J., "The Geographical Pivot of History," *Geographical Journal*, April, 1904, pp. 422 ff.

Mackinder, Halford J., "Manpower as a Measure of National and Imperial Strength," *National Review*, March, 1905, pp. 136–143.

Mackinder, Halford J., "The Round World," *Foreign Affairs*, July, 1943, pp. 595–605.

Mahan, Alfred Thayer, *Influence of Sea Power upon History, 1660–1783*, Little, Brown and Company, 1890.

"Mid-East and North Africa—The Critical Area and Three Economic Factors Behind Current Unrest" (map and charts), *The New York Times*, August 30, 1953, sec. 5, p. 5.

"Milestone on the Road to Unity," *Business Week*, February 9, 1957, pp. 143–144.

"A Minimum Foreign Policy," *Fortune*, July, 1952, p. 65.

"A Moral Strategy," *Time*, April 16, 1956, p. 19.

Murphy, Charles John Vincent, "America's New Strategic Situation," *Fortune*, August, 1954, pp. 70 ff.

Murphy, Charles John Vincent, "The Eisenhower Shift," *Fortune*, March, 1956, pp. 110 ff.

Murphy, Robert, "A Review of United States Foreign Policy," *The Department of State Bulletin,* September 26, 1955, pp. 490–493.

Mutual Security for the Free World, U.S. Department of State, Office of Public Affairs, No. 4210, General Policy Series 49, May, 1951.

National Security and Our Individual Freedom, Committee for Economic Development, December, 1949.

"A New Strategy for NATO," *Fortune,* January, 1953, p. 80.

"New Tasks for NATO," *The New York Times* (editorial), April 29, 1956, sec. 5, p. 8.

North Atlantic Treaty Organization—Its Development and Significance, U.S. Department of State Publication 4630, Government Printing Office, August, 1952.

Objectives of U.S. Foreign Policy in Latin America, U.S. Department of State Publication 6131, Government Printing Office, November, 1955.

Organization for European Economic Co-operation—History and Structure, OEEC, Paris, April, 1953.

Our Foreign Policy, U.S. Department of State Publication, Office of Public Affairs, Government Printing Office, issues of September, 1950, and March, 1952.

"The Problem of Economic Assistance to Underdeveloped Areas," *Major Problems of United States Foreign Policy, 1951–1952,* The Brookings Institution, 1951.

"Reappraising U.S. Military Policy," *Business Week,* May 26, 1956, pp. 26–27.

Regional Organizations—Europe and the North Atlantic Area, U.S. Department of State Publication 4944, Government Printing Office, April, 1953.

"Report on the Middle East, A Vital Region in Upheaval," *The New York Times,* April 2, 1957, special section.

Report of the Office of Defense Mobilization to the Joint Committee on Defense Production for the Period July 1, 1954—January 28, 1955, Executive Office of the President, March 28, 1955.

Report of the Office of Defense Mobilization to the Joint Committee on Defense Production for the Period September 15, 1955—February 29, 1956, Executive Office of the President, March 12, 1956.

Report to the President and the Congress, Commission on Foreign Economic Policy (the Randall Report), Government Printing Office, 1954.

Reston, James, "Foreign Policy Criticisms Nettle Washington Officials," seventh and final report of a series on United States foreign policy, *The New York Times,* April 15, 1956, pp. 1 and 29.

"Saudi Arabia—The King Comes West," *Time,* January 28, 1957, pp. 27 ff.

Sherwood, Robert E., "There Is No Alternative to Peace," *Fortune,* July, 1955, pp. 84 ff.

Spykman, Nicholas John, *The Geography of the Peace,* Harcourt, Brace and Company, 1944.

Staff Papers Presented to the Commission on Foreign Economic Policy, Government Printing Office, February, 1954.

Strausz-Hupé, Robert, *Geopolitics—The Struggle for Space and Power,* G. P. Putnam's Sons, 1942.

"This Is the Middle East—Area U.S. Is to Defend," *U.S. News and World Report*, February 8, 1957, pp. 70–76.

A Trade and Tariff Policy in the National Interest, Public Advisory Board for Mutual Security, Government Printing Office, February, 1953.

Truman, Harry S, "Review of Post-War Foreign Policy," address to the National War College, *The New York Times*, December 20, 1952, p. 4.

"U.S. Foreign Economic Policy," *Fortune*, August, 1951, p. 71.

"U.S. Foreign Policy," *Fortune*, February, 1951, pp. 121 ff.

"U.S. Puts Another Part of World 'Off Limits' to Communists," *U.S. News and World Report*, April 5, 1957, pp. 71–72.

"U.S. Strategy Takes a New Turn," *Business Week*, August 18, 1956, pp. 149 ff.

"Vanishing Frontiers: A Common European Market Would Aid the Free World," *Barron's*, January 28, 1957, p. 1.

Ward, Barbara, "Containment Is Far from Enough," *The New York Times Magazine*, July 22, 1951, pp. 7 ff.

Ward, Barbara, "For a New Foreign Aid Concept," *The New York Times Magazine*, March 11, 1956, pp. 12 ff.

Ward, Barbara, "Is Our Reappraisal Agonizing Enough?" *The New York Times Magazine*, July 22, 1956, pp. 5 ff.

Ward, Barbara, "Our Foreign Policy Is 'Everyone's Destiny,'" *The New York Times Magazine*, September 16, 1956, pp. 15 ff.

Ward, Barbara, *Policy for the West*, W. W. Norton and Company, 1951.

Weigert, Hans W., *Generals and Geographers—The Twilight of Geopolitics*, Oxford University Press, 1942.

"Western Europe, Third Change," *Time*, January 28, 1957, pp. 24–25.

"What the Middle East Means to U.S.," *The Lamp*, Winter, 1956, pp. 2–5, Standard Oil Co. (N.J.).

General

The American Economy, Prospects for Growth, 1950–1960–1970, McGraw-Hill Book Company, 1954.

Annual Report, Resources for the Future, Inc., 1956.

Commodity Year Book 1956, Commodity Research Bureau, Inc., 1956.

Commodity Year Book 1957, Commodity Research Bureau, Inc., 1957.

Dewhurst, J. Frederic, et al., *America's Needs and Resources*, The Twentieth Century Fund, 1955.

The Economic Report of the President, Government Printing Office, issues 1951–57.

Expanding Our Industrial Might, Defense Production Administration, Government Printing Office, 1952.

Mid-Century Conference on Resources for the Future, rapporteurs' digests of Sections I through VII of the Mid-Century Conference, Washington, December, 1953, Resources for the Future, Inc.

A Mid-Century Look at Resources, a paper prepared as background for discussions at Mid-Century Conference on Resources for the Future, Washington, December, 1953, The Brookings Institution.

"The New World of Research," *Business Week*, May 28, 1955 (Special Report).

Policy Declarations on Natural Resources, Chamber of Commerce of the United States, 1955.

Raw Materials in War and Peace, Department of Social Sciences, United States Military Academy, 1947.

Renner, George T., Durand, Loyal, White, Langdon, and Gibson, Weldon B., *World Economic Geography*, Thomas Y. Crowell Company, 1951.

Resources for Defense, report of the Secretary of the Interior, Government Printing Office, 1952.

Resources for Freedom, a report to the President by the President's Materials Policy Commission, Government Printing Office, 1952. Vol. I, *Foundations for Growth and Security;* Vol. II, *The Outlook for Key Commodities;* Vol. III, *The Outlook for Energy Sources;* Vol. IV, *The Promise of Technology;* Vol. V, *Selected Reports to the Commission.*

Resources for Freedom, Summary of Volume I by a report to the President by the President's Materials Policy Commission, Government Printing Office, 1952.

Resources: From Abundance to Scarcity by 1975? a round-table discussion, National Industrial Conference Board, December, 1952.

Review of International Commodity Problems, Interim Co-ordinating Committee for International Commodity Arrangements, United Nations, issues 1947–56.

Smith, J. Russell, and Phillips, M. Ogden, *Industrial and Commercial Geography*, Henry Holt and Company, 1946.

Together We Are Strong, U.S. Department of State Publication 4614, Government Printing Office, 1952.

Trends in Economic Growth: A Comparison of the Western Powers and the Soviet Bloc, Joint Committee on the Economic Report by the Legislative Reference Service of the Library of Congress, 83rd Congress, 2nd Session, Government Printing Office, 1955.

"Twenty-five Years That Remade America," *Business Week*, September 4, 1954 (Special Report).

U.S. Concern with World Resources, Mid-Century Conference on Resources for the Future, Washington, December, 1953, Resources for the Future, Inc.

World Facts and Figures, United Nations Department of Public Information, October, 1955.

"The World in 25 Years: How the U.S. Economy Will Reach Around It," *Business Week*, October 31, 1953 (report to executives).

Woytinsky, W. S., and Woytinsky, E. S., *World Population and Production*, Twentieth Century Fund, 1953.

Zimmermann, Erich W., *World Resources and Industries*, Harper & Brothers, 1951.

Illustrations

Index

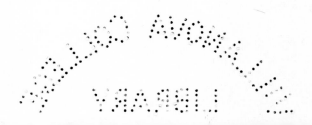